MORE SERMON SKETCHES

ON

OLD AND NEW TESTAMENT TEXTS

(Companion volume to Five Hundred Sketches and Skeletons
of Sermons and Cyclopedia of Sermons)

By

JABEZ BURNS, D.D.

Author "Five Hundred Sketches and Skeletons of Sermons"
and "Cyclopedia of Sermons"

KREGEL PUBLICATIONS

Grand Rapids 6, Michigan

1954

The Sermon Sketches appearing in this volume were formerly published in "The Pulpit Cyclopaedia and Christian Minister's Companion,"

CONTENTS.

ORIGINAL SKETCHES AND SKELETONS OF SERMONS.

CONTENTS.

CONTENTS

PULPIT CYCLOPÆDIA.

THE GOSPEL PREACHER.

"For though I preach the gospel, I have nothing to glory of; for necessity is laid upon me; yea, woe is unto me, if I preach not the gospel." —1 Cor. ix. 16.

WHAT an interesting and illustrious character ·was the writer of the text, the apostle Paul! Once an enemy of Christ, eager to destroy the Christian church; ravening as a wolf on his prey; arrested by divine power; humbled in the dust as a penitent sinner; glorying in the cross of Christ. Living to make Jesus known; counting all things but loss, &c.; encompassing sea and land to save souls. A disinterested, magnanimous preacher of the gospel. Toiling with his hands, &c. What a trophy of the Saviour's love! What a model for preachers! Hearken to the averment of the text; and let us notice how it should be a pattern for a Christian ministry. Observe what the Christian minister should preach, and the spirit in which his ministry should be discharged.

I. WHAT A CHRISTIAN MINISTER SHOULD PREACH. "The gospel." That is, the good news, the glad tidings, the message of mercy, the announcement of God's reconciliation to us, and his desire that the world should be reconciled to him. Now we do not assert that nothing but the gospel should be preached. We may refer to man's primitive state; to the entrance of sin; to the judgments of God on the ungodly; to the giving of the law; to the lives both of the wicked and the pious. But all is to be subordinate to the gospel. This is to be the first, and the chief, and the last. It is to be the theme; all else to be secondary.

1. *This is the subject commended to the the Christian minister.* "Go ye and preach the gospel," &c. We have nothing to do,

except as matters of divine history, with the ceremonials and institutions of the law; and the moral law is only to be preached that it may act as a schoolmaster to bring us to Christ.

2. *This subject alone meets the state of mankind.* Every thing else has been tried to elevate mind and morals, to make men happy and blessed. Philosophy, poetry, legislation, &c.; skepticism, polytheism, &c. The gospel declares man's real state; the gospel reveals his only hope; the gospel contains the only message of mercy: makes known present and eternal blessedness, peace with God through Christ Jesus, and eternal glory.

3. *This subject must be published in all its richness of blessing.* Pardon, acceptance, adoption, newness of heart, holiness, spiritual influences, &c. In all its aspects; for they are all lovely. In all its consolations and hope. In all its fulness and glory.

4. *This gospel must be urged upon sinners.* "Ho, every one," &c. Announce as the herald doth his master, "Prepare ye the way," &c. "Repent ye," &c. We are to entreat, persuade, yea, to compel them to come in, &c. Faithful, yet tender; solemn as the judge, yet meek as the mother; inflexible as truth, yet pitiful, and kind, and courteous.

5. *This gospel must be preached on all occasions and to all classes.* Like the tree of life, it yields many kinds of fruit; like the spring, its stream is ever fresh and cooling, &c.; like bread, it is ever precious to the hungry. It is the only subject to the aged and the young, to the rich and the poor, to the healthy and the sick.

II. WHY MUST THE CHRISTIAN MINISTER PREACH THE GOSPEL? "Necessity is laid on me."

1. *There is a necessity of duty, or a mor·*

al necessity. The Christian minister is called, and put into the ministry. This is his sphere, his work ; he is qualified for this express end. While God may give to another the talent and skill for painting, or for excelling in art or science, or muscular power for great physical exertion ; he gives the Christian minister spiritual knowledge, and utterance, and ability to show men the way of salvation. He says to them, "Follow me, and I will make you fishers of men." Now if such were not to preach, it would grieve God, and be sinning against his Holy Spirit. Therefore, there is a necessity that we preach the gospel. We are not to consult taste, or feeling, or convenience, or advantage, &c.

2. *There is a necessity of love, or a compassionate necessity.* "The love of Christ constraineth," &c. We are internally influenced. We see and feel for souls. Our benevolence urges and compels us. Bowels yearn ; eyes weep ; the soul intercedes ; and the mouth speaks :—

> "Oh that the world might taste and see
> The riches of his grace !" &c.

3. *There is a mighty responsibility.* As stewards we must give an account. Now the sower goes forth with the precious seed ; but he will come again, &c. The Lord will return and demand an exact account. So every one of us must give an account ; of what we have preached, how we have preached, for what end, with what spirit, &c. When we think of the great day, the white throne, all the congregations surrounding us, the book opened ; surely, surely, there is a necessity laid upon us, &c. Let us notice,

III. THE SPIRIT IN WHICH THE CHRISTIAN MINISTRY MUST BE DISCHARGED. That is, of self-abasement ; humiliation before God. "Nothing to glory of." We are as nothing, but the earthen vessels, &c. All the glory is the Lord's.

1. *Look at the subject of our preaching.* Not ours ; from God. Our wisdom did not devise ; our goodness, &c. Full of God ; Christ is its glory, the cross its attraction. "God forbid that we should glory," &c.

2. *Consider our qualifications.* These are physical, and mental, and moral. Ourselves not the source of any. Voice, and energy, and power of endurance ; all from God. Mind acute, imaginative, energetic ; all from God. A heart to feel

for the perishing, &c. All these are from God.

3. *Observe our opportunities for laboring.* We read of an effectual door being opened for preaching the word. Now God only can effect this. He fixes our sphere, disposeth persons to hear, gives us favor in their eyes, and removes obstacles, &c.

4. *All ministerial success is from God.* The apostles ever felt and confessed this. "Neither Paul nor Apollos, but God," &c. Who convinceth ? Who converteth ? Who preserves ? Who sanctifies ? Who keeps ? Who comforts ? Who glorifies ? No spiritual victory is achieved without the exertion of the divine power. "The weapons of our warfare," &c. "Not by might or by power," &c. How evident, that however faithful, or zealous, or successful, the Christian minister has nothing to glory of, &c.

APPLICATION.

1. *To you has the word of this salvation come.* Blessed are your eyes and ears, &c. Have you received it ? Have you given it a hearty, believing welcome ?

2. *If such be the responsibility of the Christian minister, how great should be the solicitous affection of the church for his comfort und well-being.* The apostle felt a necessity for this, "Brethren, pray for us," &c. Their hands require bearing up.

3. *With the preaching of the gospel there should be united the co-operation of every Christian.* The women labored with Paul, &c. Every Christian should be found accelerating the gospel, &c. All must do something in the gospel vineyard. Pray, &c.

4. *We urge this gospel upon all present.*

CONTENDING FOR THE ANCIENT FAITH.

"Ye should earnestly contend for the faith, which was once delivered to the saints."—JUDE iii.

IN the introduction of our discourse we cannot do better than define the terms of which the text is composed. By faith, it is clear, we are to understand the doctrines of the gospel, the great principles of Christian belief. By "contending" is meant a firm maintenance of those doctrines and principles against opposers and adulteration. By "saints" are meant the sincere and holy disciples of Jesus Christ. Now the duty specified is that of the church earnestly upholding and maintaining the great doctrines and principles of the gospel. This was necessary in Jude's time, see ver. 4; and it has been necessary in all ages of the world. The truth has never been long unassailed: it is the very design of Satan and crafty men to deceive, mislead, and then destroy. Let us then consider more fully,

I. The duty specified.
II. The manner of discharging it.
III. The reasons which oblige us to regard it.

I. The duty specified. This duty,

1. *Has respect to the faith.* That gospel system which is the object of every Christian's faith. Now the gospel system includes facts detailed by evangelists. These form the very basis of the Christian structure. The life, miracles, death, and resurrection of Jesus Christ. Doctrines which relate to the fall and depravity of mankind, their utter helplessness, their recovery by the mission and death of Christ. Salvation through grace by faith in the Lord Jesus Christ. The sanctification of the heart by the Spirit and blood of Christ. The doctrine of the supreme Godhead of the Saviour and of the Holy Ghost. Now each of these is essential to the very vitality of the Christian religion. The commandments of the gospel system are of two classes, moral and positive; the moral includes all our duties to God, to the church, and to the world. The practical obedience of faith. The positive includes attention to the ordinances of the gospel. Now these facts, doctrines, and ordinances, are evidently implied in the faith or gospel system. Observe,

2. *This faith has been committed to the saints.* Especially in two respects. Heb. i. 1, 2; 1 Cor. xv. 1. Also by the teaching and epistles of the apostles, who were inspired to teach and write infallibly, for the instruction, edification, and comfort of the first churches, and whose writings are contained in the New Testament scriptures. In being committed to the saints, is meant their being deposited to the vigilant care and guardianship of the first churches, and by them handed down to the generations following. We remark,

3. *That this faith is to be contended for by us.* The word contend, is literally to agonize for it; the same word is employed in reference to the Saviour's agony, or as the wrestlers and racers agonize for the prize. Now this signifies much more than extreme care to possess the faith, highly to esteem it; it is to be solicitous for its purity, to live and labor extensively for this; to employ all our powers, and influence, and energies, in its defence, and, if necessary, to suffer and die for it. Observe,

II. The manner of discharging this duty. We must take care,

1. *That it be the faith once delivered to the saints.* Not a faith professing to be it, but the identical faith. Not some learned man's definition or system of the faith, but the faith itself. Not our notions and opinions, but the faith. Not respecting this conjecture or that having to do with it, &c., and therefore we must have and hold, as sacred and essential to this, the very words of the faith as when delivered, the very scriptures which contain them. To these we must appeal, and for these we must contend always,—"to the law and to the testimony." Always, what saith the scripture.

2. *The contending for the faith must be in the spirit of faith.* Not in the spirit of proud and vaunting bigotry, but with enlightened candor. Not in the spirit of personal uncharitableness, but in the spirit of love to the mistaken,—compassion for them. Not in the spirit of wrathful denunciation, but in the spirit of affectionate prayer. Not in the employment of carnal weapons, as acts of parliament and the sword of state, but clad only in the armor of righteousness. Not in anger, calumny, and wrath, but in the spirit of tenderness and love. See an example presented in the 9th verse. Yet we notice,

3. *The contending for the faith must be firm and unyielding.* We must conflict for it, and not be indifferent, cold, and careless. We must be earnest and ardent, devoted and persevering. We must confess the faith, hold it fast, witness for it, buy it at any price, and never, never sell it. And this contending must respect the whole faith, there is nothing valueless or indifferent. Its author, its originator, bespeak its value and excellence. Indifference to minor parts has ever opened the flood-gate of error.

III. THE REASONS WHICH SHOULD OBLIGE US
TO THIS DUTY.

1. *For the faith's sake.* This is the mystery of heaven, the plan of salvation, the system of eternal benevolent truth. Who would not be anxious for pure light, pure air, pure water? This is the light of the soul, the atmosphere of the Spirit, the water of life.

2. *For our own sake.* There is an obligation, it is a duty, and therefore connected with conscience, with peace of conscience, with the smile of God, with the enjoyments of religion. We are to war for this, "fight the good fight of faith." "I have kept the faith."

3. *For the church's sake.* Purity and prosperity connected. Love, truth, and peace. "I have no greater joy," &c. Be valiant for the truth. Our forefathers did this for us. We are to do it for the present and the next generation. Remember too, the prosperity of the church and the salvation of the world are necessarily linked together. This is therefore united with the conquering car of the Saviour. "Ride on gloriously because of righteousness and truth."

APPLICATION.

1. Let every man test his faith; see that it is the ancient, divine faith, once committed to the saints; and let it be held fast; our times call loudly for it.

2. Let the faith be internal and influential in each of our souls. The main thing is the personal indwelling, &c., of this in the soul.

PURE RELIGION.

" Pure religion and undefiled before God and the Father is this, to visit the fatherless and widows in their affliction, and to keep himself unspotted from the world."—JAMES i. 27.

THE epistle of James has been very properly styled the practical epistle. It had to do chiefly with the duties of personal religion. It is not so much an exhibition of doctrines to be believed, as of the actions of piety which are to be performed. Two great errors exist, one which would represent religion as consisting in knowledge and belief only, and the other which sets forth a system of actions without reference to the principle and influence of faith.

Evangelical religion unites both, recognising faith in Christ as the basis of true personal piety, and good works as the superstructure to be reared upon it. Let us consider from the text,

I. THE RELIGION SPECIFIED.
II. THE EVIDENCE DEMANDED.
III. THE ADMONITION INVOLVED.

I. THE RELIGION SPECIFIED. Religion may be denominated the homage and obedience of man to his Maker. That course of belief and practice which God has revealed to his intelligent creatures. Now true and acceptable religion must,

1. *Be pure in its source.* This source is God's word. Here is the revelation of all doctrinal, personal, and relative piety. Every thing here has been written by the pure Spirit. All truths to be believed,—all precepts to be obeyed,—all ordinances to be observed. Just as the materials of revelation are interwoven with our religion, it is pure; and just as human opinions and ceremonies make a part of it, it is corrupt and adulterated. How important that our religious principles be drawn from the holy volume of the scriptures! Acceptable religion is,

2. *Pure in its principles.* Contrast Christianity with the dark systems of paganism, with the sensual allowances of Mohammedanism. Its principles are all lofty and ennobling. It has the broad stamp of divine holiness upon it. It is the transcript of the divine mind. Like God, it is light, and truth, and goodness. It demands sincerity of motive, and purity of aim, and uprightness of action. It allows nothing that is merely superficial, but demands truth in the inward parts, &c.

3. *It is pure in its influence.* Like water it cleanses. Like fire it refines. Like the wind it purifies. Like medicine it heals. It renews its possessor. Entirely transforms him. Imparts a pure motive, pure desires and purposes. Produces purity of speech and conduct. It changes the raven to a dove; the lion to a lamb. See this in the account the apostle gives of the Corinthian converts. 1 Cor. vi. 9, 10. Observe in reference to pure religion,

II. THE EVIDENCE DEMANDED. Pure religion, &c., before God, is this, " To visit," &c. Where pure religion exists, this goodness and mercifulness of spirit and practice will be exhibited. Especial reference is made to two cases which it will regard.

1. *The fatherless.* Those destitute of paternal solicitude,—support withdrawn,—thrown on the charity of strangers. This is a condition of extreme adversity. Without the kind of aid of others, they would often perish. God commends such to the merciful consideration of the humane and pious. Our school and orphan charities are eminently entitled to our patronage and support.

2. *Widows in their affliction.* And the afflictions of widowhood are often numerous and deep. Solitary, defenceless, unprovided for, sometimes health deeply affected, and many troubles endured. The weaker vessel tempest-tossed, how deserving of attention, goodness, and compassion! Now, pure religion will not overlook or despise these cases of suffering, but labor to assuage by counsel, comfort, and assistance. But observe in giving this evidence of pure religion,

III. THE ADMONITION WHICH THE TEXT INVOLVES. " And to keep himself unspotted from the world." As if the apostle had said, to maintain Christian mercy, we must avoid worldliness of spirit. This is the great evil which hardens the mind, and renders it callous when surrounded by misery and wretchedness. Worldliness is represented as defiling in its influence, it spots the garments, and spots the Christian character. By worldliness we mean an inordinate attachment to the things of the world. Now, this defiles, or produces spots,

1. *On the affections.* " Set your affections on things above," &c. It prostrates the soul, makes it carnal, and earthly, and grovelling. Such lovers of mammon cannot be lovers of God. It defiles, or produces spots,

2. *On the conscience.* When the conscience is enlightened and has been influenced by sanctifying grace, it cannot dwell with worldliness without being grieved, and ultimately becoming diseased. A hoarding worldling cannot have a good conscience towards God, who demands our chief affections, nor towards men, who stand in need of our pity and compassion. Worldliness,

3. *Defiles the conduct.* How meanly persons can act who are under its power. How it perverts the judgment,—darkens the mind,—freezes the emotions, &c. It produces overreaching, iniquitious fraud and imposition. Need we marvel that the claims of mercy are neglected, when persons are spotted with the world? Now, this admonition to keep ourselves unspotted from the world is of great importance, and may be sustained by many cogent reasons.

(1.) As Christians we profess not to be of the world. We have been redeemed out of it. Delivered from it, &c.

(2.) Worldliness and Christianity cannot exist in the same mind, the one will cast out the other, they are antagonist principles, a man cannot have his desires and delights in heaven and earth.

(3.) It has often been the source of apostacy. Some of the seed fell among thorns, and the thorns choked it, &c. " Demas has forsaken me," &c. How many have been thus ruined in their moral interests. "They that will be rich fall," &c.

(4.) Only that which is expended on works of goodness will survive the present life. Think you, immortal beings in the eternal world will ever meditate on the money they have hoarded or laid out on buildings, or fortunes left to their children? Oh no! but that which has been given in acts of beneficence will abide and follow us to heaven, be published to the universe, and be rewarded through all eternity. Oh think of this, and then let the admonition sink into your hearts, and keep yourselves unspotted, &c.

APPLICATION.

1. Do you possess pure religion? Is this your happy state? If so, cherish it and evidence it.

2. Let those who are strangers seek it. It is the one thing needful.

3. The practice of enlarged beneficence will greatly recommend religion. Of Jesus it was said, " He went about doing good." Are we Christians? then we must follow his steps, &c. "God is love," &c. Let us do good unto all men, &c.

THE KNOWLEDGE OF GOD.

" Then shall we know, if we follow on to know the Lord."—HOSEA vi. 3.

ONE of the most sublime sentiments in the world is one in the holy scriptures, which relates to the knowledge of Jehovah. " This is life eternal to know," &c. To communicate this knowledge, prophets and apostles were inspired with the influence

of heaven, and the Son of God became incarnate in human flesh. To diffuse this
knowledge, is the great end of the Christian
ministry. "Many shall run to and fro,"
&c. To attain this knowledge should be
the great and constant desire of every human being. "For the soul to be without
knowledge," &c. To increase in this
knowledge should be the constant aim of
the believer. "Grow in grace," &c. To
induce the people of God to aim at this, is
the passage which we have chosen as our
text. "Then shall ye know," &c. Consider,

I. The knowledge supposed to be possessed.

II. The means of increased attainment recommended.

III. The promissory declaration given.

I. The knowledge supposed to be possessed. The phraseology evidently involves the following, or supposes that some
attainments have been realized, &c. What
do Christians know of the Lord ?

1. *They know some things in common
with others.* His being—his dominion—his
providence—his revelation of himself—his
majesty, greatness, glory, goodness, &c.
But all who are not of skeptical mind may
know and understand these things.

2. *But they know some things specially.*
Things which others do not. Some men
have not the knowledge of God, &c. They
know him in,

(1.) His merciful and gracious character. "A God, forgiving iniquity, transgression," &c. "Ready to pardon, abundant in goodness," &c.

(2.) In his reconciled love. Accepting
them ; adopting them ; manifesting his love
to them ; receiving them into his bosom and
family, &c.

(3.) In his sanctifying power. Removing uncleanness ; cleansing, purifying, &c.
Taking away the heart of stone, &c. Putting his Spirit, &c.

(4.) In the elevation and peaceful influences of communion with him. It is
theirs to say, "We have fellowship," &c.
God dwells in his people, and they in him.
He walks with them, and they with him.
He is represented as suffering with them,
and they with him. This exalts to celestial dignity ; it gives true felicity ; it is the
antedate of heaven itself. But as to this
knowledge, observe,

II. The means of increased attainment. "If we follow on," &c. To follow on,

1. *Is to give diligent attention to the means
provided.* These are various. One is
contemplation of the divine works ; another,
diligent reading of the divine word ; a third,
regular attention to the public means of
grace,—hearing the word ; a fourth, meditation followed by prayer for the wisdom
that cometh, &c. "Following on," also
includes,

2. *The practical application of the knowledge we possess.* This leads to an increased experimental knowledge ; this is
the most certain and important part of
knowledge ; no way so effectual to our improvement as this ; it will apply to every
thing in art and science.

3. *The cherishing a deep internal desire
for more of this knowledge.* We must feel
its importance ; know its value, appreciate
it, and seek for it, &c. Thirst, &c. Seek
for the hidden treasure ; long for it, as the
tempest-tossed mariner for a haven, as the
sick man for the dawn of the morning, as
the exile for the freedom of his native air.

4. *Perseverance in adding to the amount
of this knowledge.* World of darkness ;
impediments ; an inaptitude to learn :
therefore we must be diligent scholars in
Christ's school, and persevering too. We
should often ascertain if our mental stature
is increasing ; if we are adding to the
stores of spiritual wisdom ; if we are increasing in divine knowledge and understanding.

III. The promissory declaration given.
"Then shall we know." Now this promise or declaration implies,

1. *That we shall increase in knowledge.*
Not labor for its attainment in vain.
Mind will expand, and be adorned. Path
become brighter and brighter, &c. Rise
from babes to young men, young men to
fathers.

2. *We shall know more clearly.* It is
not the first glance that always gives us
the whole of a subject ; we must sometimes read it again and again ; in various
lights, &c., become familiar with it. Thus
it is desirable on all religious subjects to be
clear ; to have lucid views both of doctrines and precepts ; now by drawing closely
to these subjects, we shall apprehend them
more lucidly.

3. *We shall know more satisfactorily.*

As we approach to certainty on any mental subject, we shall derive increased pleasure from it. With partial views, there is anxiety and restlessness; with certain and clear knowledge, satisfaction and delight. Think of the experimental peace of the apostle, "I know whom I have believed," &c. "We know if this the earthly house," &c.

4. *This will terminate in our perfection of knowledge in a future state.* "Now," says the apostle, "we see through a glass darkly," &c. Now we know in part, even at best, but then we shall know perfectly, no cloud, obscurity, or dimness. All subjects known directly; all transparent as light; not even a mistake left. All reflecting the infallible knowledge of the Most High. "What thou knowest not now," &c.

APPLICATION.

Now let me ask, do you,

1. Enjoy any portion of this knowledge of scripture? Of scriptural, personal, saving knowledge of the Lord.

2. Are you advancing in it? Try by the past.

3. How many motives press it upon our attention! We are formed for acquiring knowledge. It is the very light and atmosphere of the soul. It forms one part of the glorification of the happy in heaven. Shall we not feel the text as an incentive, &c. Let us all labor to diffuse, &c.

THE WORLD'S IGNORANCE OF GOD.

"The world by wisdom knew not God."—1 Cor. i. 21.

The value of the sacred scriptures may be illustrated in a variety of ways, but in no form more strikingly than by observing the darkness, sin, and misery, which have everywhere prevailed, where they have not been known. We often hear of the famous men of olden times. We hear of their legislators, philosophers, and poets; their sayings are handed down to us. Portions of their writings have been preserved from the wasting influences of time, and have survived the ravages of thousands of years. But did it ever strike you that with all their intellectual greatness, all their profound research, all their works of soaring imagination, they were ignorant of the one true and blessed God? Our text affirms this, "that the world by wisdom knew not God."

I. Let us briefly advert to some things which the wisdom of the worll did comprehend. Now the civilized nations of the earth for centuries before the text was spoken had great celebrity for their intellectual attainments. Their knowledge was extensive as to the principles of agriculture. They knew much of the laws of commerce and of political economy. They knew much of art and science. They knew much of figures, or the science of mathematics. They knew much of history and of the biography of the ancient heroes. They knew much of architecture, sculpture, painting, and poetry. They knew much of metaphysics and the laws of mind. I need only mention a few illustrious names to guarantee the intellectuality of the world referred to in the text. There was Thales the Milesian philosopher, Herodotus, Plato, Aristotle, Socrates, Democritus, Euclid, Hippocrates, Epicurus, Zeno, and a host of other philosophers. Then there were the celebrated orators, Cicero and Demosthenes; and of poets we may mention Homer, Virgil, and Ovid, and hundreds of others, who formed with these the mental galaxy of the ancient world. How mournful the conclusion of the text, that despite of their intellectual grandeur and profound study, they knew not God! Let us consider, then,

II. The affirmation of the text, that the world by wisdom knew not God. Now we must not conclude that they were without certain ideas of God. Neither that they did not employ their mind in the science of theology, or were indifferent to this matter. The text evidently means that they had not correct views of the supreme and blessed God.

1. *They had only confused views as to his existence.* Some of the philosophers taught that there was no God, and the great majority taught a plurality of gods. Hence they had their gods and goddesses for all events, and all places, and all circumstances. The winds, the waves, the air, the earth, the skies, the day and night, the flowers and fruits, all under their respective divinities. They had gods for adversity and prosperity, sickness and health

war and peace. Socrates obtained more extensive knowledge on this subject than his contemporaries. He taught that God " was one, immutable, and the creator of all things ;" yet he admitted that while he knew what God was not, he knew not what he was, and he thought they should worship the gods of the city where they resided.

2. *They were equally confused as to the Divine attributes.* Many gave to their gods the vilest passions of men ; the more enlightened knew nothing of his holiness and rectitude. The events of the world led some to believe that God was capricious, despotic, &c. . Plato, who it is supposed was acquainted with the writings of the Jews, seems to have had some idea of a Trinity, but all their researches ended in contradiction, uncertainty, and confusion.

3. *They had no correct views of the moral government of God.* I will give you a few of the ideas of their wise men. Seneca says, " Fortune scatters her gifts over the world, and rules without order the affairs of men." Others taught that the gods themselves were the subjects of an irresistible fate. The Stoics believed that providence only interfered on very great occasions. The Epicureans believed that all things were under the influence of an all-powerful fate.

4. *They knew not the will of God.* Some taught that pleasure was the end of life, that falsehood and even theft were only evil if discovered. They had no idea of personal purity, &c. Social order was utterly disregarded, they exposed children, and advocated suicide.

5. *They were ignorant of the true worship of God.* On some occasions they offered him human victims. Many of their rites were sensual, their temples were often scenes of infamy, and their whole services were those of anxiety, fear, and superstition.

6. *They knew not the way of reconciliation with God.* Many felt the wickedness and weakness of their nature, but they could not guess how the favor of Deity might be obtained. They wandered in the mazes of error, of darkness, tortured, fearing, and often overwhelmed with anguish and terror.

7. *They knew nothing of the enjoyment of God in a future state.* The opinion of most was the materiality of the mind with the body. Others had a vague notion of a world where the illustrious dead dwelt together, but in what that felicity would consist they knew not. Of a holy world, of immaculately pure spirits, and of the resurrection of the dead they were entirely ignorant. How true that the world by wisdom, &c.

LEARN,

1. The insufficiency of unassisted reason to the knowledge of the true God. They had the material universe, space, opportunities, talents, reason, yet they could not find out God.

2. The unspeakable value of the scriptures. This is the only guide to the knowledge of Jehovah. This is God's moral lever, it has raised our nation, it will lift up the world.

3. The obligations arising from our religious privileges. "Where much is given, much is required."

A RELIGIOUS SPIRIT HIGHLY RATIONAL.

" For God hath not given us the spirit of fear, but of power, and of love, and of a sound mind."— 2 Tim. i. 7.

TRUE religion has had to contend with difficulties and opposition in every age of the world. It has not only been violently opposed, but frequently misrepresented : it has been charged with the vices of hypocrites, and with all the infirmities of its friends. It has been disbelieved by many, ridiculed by some, and despised by others. I desire to establish in this discourse the following great truth, that the spirit of true religion is eminently one of rational and intellectual soundness ; that every disciple of Jesus is distinguished for the possession of a sound mind. Let me then define and illustrate this spirit; and then show that it is emphatically rational and intellectual in its character.

I. DEFINE AND ILLUSTRATE THE SPIRIT OF TRUE RELIGION. Now, by this spirit we do not mean that extravagance and fanaticism which some professors have exhibited, nor that bigotry and intolerance for which sects have been notorious ; nor that elevation of sentiment and opinion at the expense of the practical duties of life ; nor that deep-shaded melancholy which some seem to think is the essence of acceptable piety. But,

(1.) The spirit of knowledge, enlightened by the holy scriptures.

(2.) A spirit of devotion, holding communion with God.

(3.) A spirit of faith, relying on the sacrifice of the Lord Jesus Christ.

(4.) A spirit of obedience, walking in the ordinances and commandments of the Lord.

Now these are each and all necessary to form the religious character of man. And by piety we mean these in their united influence on the heart and life. Now I proceed to notice,

II. That this state of mind is pre-eminently rational and intellectual. Perhaps we shall perceive this most forcibly by contrast.

1. *Contrast it with disbelief or skepticism.* Such would persuade us they only are rational. Is it rational to conclude there is no God, no great first cause, no artificer? Or that he governs not the world—that chance reigns? Or that he is indifferent to his creatures, regardless of their conduct to himself, or to one another? That he will not judge or punish, that there is no heaven or hell, &c.; man a mere refined brute, &c. Now contrast this with the Christian system, and then I ask, does not religion evidently include a sound mind?

2. *Contrast it with a superstitious, credulous spirit.* To credit every statement, to accept every marvellous narrative, to hear and read, and never question, or inquire, or reason, this is unworthy of a thinking, reflecting being. And to be influenced by fears of the supernatural, forming hideous notions of what we know not—this is superstitious. Now contrast this with the belief of the Christian in the mysteries of revelation. There are doctrines beyond our comprehension, our bodies are so, our minds much more so, God still more so. But the belief of one supreme God, the belief of his love in sending Christ, the mystery of the incarnation, the doctrine of the Spirit's influence on the heart, do not pertain to superstition; they are truths revealed in a book that condemns weakness and superstition, and their reception rather argues soundness of mind.

3. *Contrast it with insensibility and irreligious indifference.* Thousands are utterly neglectful of religion; they never read the word, or pray, or meditate, or prepare for eternity; they neglect the subjects most momentous, death, eternity, &c. Now with the amount of evidence we have, is this wisdom? is this rational? Death is certain, an eternity is reasonable, yea, most probable. To trifle, to be careless is folly, the essence of folly. Now religion does not prohibit attention to the worldly duties of life; it enjoins these, urges diligence to them; but it enforces the care of the soul, preparation for death, and readiness for a future state. Now I ask if this is not the highest evidence of true rationality, in reality a sound mind?

4. *Contrast it with mere formality.* You say you are neither skeptical, superstitious, nor careless; you regard the external forms of religion, &c. But will these external observances do? are they sufficient? Religion must be of the heart, influencing the soul in all its powers and passions, having the pre-eminence, sought first and chiefly. Give all diligence. Now which is the most rational? What father would be satisfied with the form of filial obedience? what friend with the form of confidence and love? what scholar with the form of learning; or merchant with the form of business; or sick man with the mere form of advice and healing? Will the soul be satisfied with the form of future blessedness? with the name or sight of heaven?

5. *Contrast it with the spirit of procrastination.* Many admit all we have said, but defer these essential realities to some future indefinite period. They plead engagements, business, &c., &c. Is this an evidence of a sound mind? A man is crossing a pool from which the tide has receded; he says it may be seven or eight hours before it returns, therefore he loiters, although the tide may overtake him in as many minutes. Religion directs the soul to be the first and chief object of attention. It ever urges to-day, it knows nothing of to-morrow. "Boast not thyself of to-morrow," &c. Now I ask, which is wisdom, which is the evidence of a sound mind? Surely the Christian who prays, "So teach me to number my days, that I may apply my heart unto wisdom."

APPLICATION.

1. *We learn the difference between illiteracy and ignorance, between knowledge and wisdom.* All learning does not lead to

practical knowledge, nor all mere knowledge to sound wisdom, neither are illiteracy and ignorance synonymous. Look at that poor unlearned Christian, and then at that learned neglecter of religion. Who has the sound mind?

2. *The more eminently religious the more truly sound and intellectual the mind.* O yes, to grow in grace and in the knowledge of our Lord Jesus Christ, is the right wisdom and truest intelligence.

3. *Neglect of the soul and of God is the greatest evidence of folly.* Let the religion of the cross of Christ be yours. Seek it, enjoy it, profess it, &c. Then diffuse it, publish it to others, &c.

THE USE AND ABUSE OF REASON IN MATTERS OF RELIGION.

"I speak as to wise men, judge ye what I say."—1 Cor. x. 15.

It is desirable to avoid three evils in reading the word of God. The evil of inattention to the spirit and signification of what is written, which is to be avoided by care, reflection, and patient investigation. The evil of reading merely to inform the mind, and leaving out of sight the moral influence the word of God is destined to exert on the heart and character. The evil of neglecting or disbelieving the truths which are too lofty or too profound for our attaining, or clearly investigating them. Many subjects are too difficult for the grasp of reason, which are by no means in contradiction to it. Let us then endeavor to ascertain,

I. THE USE. And,
II. THE ABUSE OF REASON IN MATTERS OF RELIGION.

I. THE USE OF REASON IN MATTERS OF RELIGION. By reason, we mean that power of the mind, by which we judge and conclude as to the truth, or probability and importance of subjects presented to our observation. It is this power which distinguishes persons of sound mind from the idiot, or mentally deranged. This power, however, greatly depends on the possession of knowledge, the mental culture, the memory, and the testimony on which the subjects presented to us are based. Now enlightened reason in matters of religion seems to be fairly exercised,

1. *In judging of the principles of what is termed natural religion.* The existence, greatness, wisdom, and power of God, as deduced from the works of nature, and the government of the world. It is evidently a fit subject for reason to ascertain if there must not have been a first originating cause; that such a cause must have involved an exalted intelligence, an intelligence possessing a wondrous power, &c. Reason revolts at the notion of a world without a maker, a universe without a creator and ruler. The order, harmony, beauty, &c., of the visible creation address reason in a voice, which she must comprehend, and which she adores. What the poet says of the stars is equally applicable to all the works of creation,

> In reason's ear they all rejoice,
> And utter forth a glorious voice,
> Forever singing as they shine,
> The hand that made us is divine.

2. *Reason may examine the evidences of the truth of the Christian revelation.* As to the necessity, desirableness of such a revelation, reason cannot fail to decide; and of the variety of evidence as to the divine authenticity of the scriptures, it is the province of reason to judge and conclude. There cannot be any real contrariety in the volume of revelation, and in true unsophisticated reason, both of which have emanated from the one perfect source and author.

3. *Reason may fairly judge as to the subjects which revelation presents to us.* The divine character; the divine works; man's responsible state; the doctrines he is required to believe; the duties he is required to regard; the blessings which are offered for his reception, &c. Now all these must accord with sound, unbiased reason.

4. *As to the necessity and importance of a practical regard to the truths of revelation* In its bearings on personal conduct, domestic order, national morals, and the happiness of mankind at large. Now reason may judge whether the religion of the Bible is adapted to promote these or not; and here the past history of religion will supply ample facts and illustrations.

II. THE ABUSE OF REASON IN MATTERS OF RELIGION.

1. *When it is exalted to pronounce judgment on the subjects of revelation.* Reason should hearken and learn. She may compare and draw her deductions, but is not to

assume the place of God, who alone knows what is most right and excellent in itself, both in matters of faith and practice; hence unsanctified reason might quarrel with the mode of revelation, or with the medium of the mercy and love of God to man, in Christ Jesus, or on the grounds of human forgiveness and acceptance: reason is the subject not the legislator, the juryman not the judge.

2. *When it refuses to receive the doctrines which are too vast for its comprehension.* Allow reason this latitude, and the existence of one eternal, infinite, and unchangeable Deity is beyond all its power to grasp. Thus reason would stumble at the distinctions in the Godhead; at the divinity of Christ; at the doctrine of spiritual influences on the mind, &c., &c. If reason has pronounced the evidences in favor of revelation to be satisfactory, then the reception of its sublime mysteries should follow as a matter of course.

3. *Reason is abused when it is warped by prejudice and educational bias.* It requires a due balance of the powers of the mind to do justice to any subject, especially the great truths of religion. Skeptical training and influence will materially dim the candid light of reason, and induce it to reject what may be opposed to its own favorite peculiarities.

4. *Reason is especially abused when it is deemed sufficient for the guidance of the mind in matters of religion.* The most distinguished philosophers, in their contradictory systems, and inconclusive conjectures, have proved it insufficient; left to its own resources, it has allowed men to sink into the darkest depths of superstition and misery. It may be the eye of the mind, but it requires more light than nature imparts; it must have the rays of celestial truth irradiating and directing it. No one, by the most profound researches of reason, can discover even the first elements of Christian truth.

APPLICATION.

1. *Let reason be valued as its great dignity and importance demand.*

2. *Seek after its cultivation and improvement.* Educate it in the school of Christ. Give it the assistance, the essential assistance of revelation, and ever subordinate it to this highest authority.

3 *Reason spiritually directed, and faith in divine truth, constitute the intellectual and experimental Christian.*

THE NECESSITY OF A DIVINE REVELATION.

" O send out thy light and thy truth."—PSALM xliii. 3.

IT is quite evident that none of the works of God are in vain. He employs no unnecessary agency; all his ways and works are wise and perfect. Had reason or the works of nature been sufficient for man's moral instruction, no other means would have been provided. But man has ever found himself inadequate to the attainment of a clear and direct knowledge of the supreme Being, and in the midst of his ignorance and anxiety often has the spirit of the text been uttered, " O send out thy light and thy truth." The necessity of a divine revelation arises therefore from the insufficiency of all other sources to supply the mind with moral information.

I. MAN HAS NOT THIS KNOWLEDGE WITHIN HIMSELF. He has the capacity of understanding, the judgment, but these have no moral supplies of knowledge. Left to himself he grows up ignorant. The highest order of natural genius can do nothing without the communication of knowledge. However the mind may be exercised; whatever methods of thought, or mental effort may be put forth, still, without a revelation it can neither know truly of God, or his will concerning his intelligent creatures.

II. THIS KNOWLEDGE IS NOT SUPPLIED BY DILIGENT OBSERVATION OF THE DIVINE WORKS. Men may greatly expand their powers, and increase knowledge of a certain kind by a study of the divine works. They may form some estimate of the greatness and grandeur of the Deity. Some ideas of his power, wisdom, and goodness, but they can learn nothing as to his moral character, or his infinite counsels and will. They can learn nothing of law, of morals, of duty. Of disobedience, of rewards, of punishment. Nothing as to man's immortality and responsibility, &c.

III. THIS KNOWLEDGE IS NOT ATTAINABLE BY HUMAN LEARNING. The philosophers of old were learned, and yet morally benighted, or at best enveloped in fog or perplexing mist. The true character and mind of

God forms a part of no language, or system of metaphysics, or mathematics. It is to be met with in no system of human philosophy, in no scheme of jurisprudence, or legislation; in none of the ancient poets. The wisdom of the world, however profound and extensive, or sublime, does not involve in it the knowledge of God and his will.

IV. THIS KNOWLEDGE IS NOT ASSOCIATED WITH ART OR SCIENCE. These are legitimately connected with the mental elevation of man. But these have been found among all the absurd multifarious rites of polytheism. Athens was the seat of science, when her streets were crowded with false imaginary gods. And sculpture, architecture, and painting, have been most extensively patronized when the people were sunk in the very depths of moral ignorance and crime. We remark, further,

V. THAT THIS KNOWLEDGE IS UTTERLY BEYOND THE RANGE OF HUMAN DISCOVERY AND ATTAINMENT. Man by searching without divine assistance can never find out God, or attain to the knowledge of his will. This is corroborated by the experience of all countries, where a revelation has not been enjoyed. More than five thousand years has surely been sufficient to test the ability of the human mind to discover the supreme Being and a knowledge of his will concerning mankind. The wise metaphysicians of the East, the learned priests of China at this day, have not taken one step beyond the ancients as to moral knowledge: their views and systems are like those, puerile, gross, and superstitious. Then if man is to know aught of God clearly, fully, correctly, or if he is to know himself, his powers, his responsibility, and his destination, it must be revealed to him by God, the Father of light, and the Fountain of eternal truth and knowledge.

OBSERVATIONS.

1. Our subject does not teach men to neglect the works of nature, or of self-culture. Much may be thus known highly valuable in itself, and useful to the world. But the knowledge thus to be attained, does not meet our exigency, the necessities of our undying nature. With this, we must have more and more of that which neither the human mind, nor all the works of nature can supply.

2. With the necessities of our moral na-

ture, the supreme Being must be intimate. Such an intimacy with a benevolent Being must involve a desire to impart such a revelation.

3. The revelation man requires, God can supply. If one human mind can convey its ideas, and views, and desires, to another human being, surely God can do this, and much more perfectly.

4. The scriptures appear to contain such a revelation. A revelation worthy of their divine Author, and meeting all the moral exigencies of mankind.

5. In the absence of all other correct means of divine knowledge, surely this is worthy of our candid and careful consideration. On examination it will assuredly be found that God has " sent out his light and truth."

THE BIBLE A DIVINE REVLATION.

"Thy word is truth."—JOHN xvii. 17.

WE have already seen that man, without a divine revelation, is necessarily ignorant of God, and the way of holiness and peace: that he has no resources for obtaining this essential knowledge independently of a divine revelation. We now proceed to show that the Holy Scriptures evidently contain a revelation from God to man. The word of God professes to be such a revelation, and we have abundant evidence that the text is a glorious verity. " Thy word is truth." I shall not stay to prove that the scriptures were evidently written in the languages ascribed to them; nor is it necessary to show that their antiquity is beyond all disputation. That the Old Testament writings have been esteemed divine by the Jews for thousands of years needs no proof. That from the earliest centuries of the Christian era the gospels, epistles, &c., have been so esteemed is matter of historical certainty. Observe, then,

I. THE MATTER OF THE SCRIPTURES IS WORTHY OF A DIVINE REVELATION. The historical narrations in their antiquity, clearness, fulness, &c.—the sublime doctrines in their mysterious and resplendent grandeur, often vastly above, but never discordant with reason—its moral precepts, bearing upon all classes, conditions, circumstances, &c. of mankind, so comprehensive, yet so minute—so evidently in accordance with the internal convictions of right and wrong—its facts, so marvellous, interesting, and instructive—its counsels and directions so replete with judgment and wisdom—its threatenings so just, yet so awful and overwhelming. We observe,

(1.) It reveals to us the Divine Being in his nature, perfections, works, government, and glory.

(2.) It reveals to us man in his faculties, capabilities, endowments, and destination.

(3.) It reveals our true apostate state, with its cause and effects.

(4.) It reveals to us our accountability, and gives directions how wisely to be prepared for our final account.

(5.) It reveals all our duties, both towards God and men.

(6.) It reveals to us the soul's immortality, the judgment, and eternity.

(7.) It reveals heaven and hell, eternal life and endless death.

And as the glory of the whole,

(8.) It reveals to us the mercy of God in the redemption of the world by his own Son, Christ Jesus, and eternal salvation through his sacrifice, and in his name.

Now this is all matter of essential consequence to us ; all-essential to our present welfare and everlasting salvation. These are truths peculiar to the scriptures, and revealed nowhere else. The word of God is truth evidently,

II. FROM THE STYLE IN WHICH IT IS WRITTEN. There is great diversity of style evinced by the various persons who wrote as they were moved by the Holy Ghost. But each and the whole of the sacred writers have a style peculiar to themselves. No works extant which resemble them. There is a grandeur of thought and idea, presented with uniform gravity, seriousness, and simplicity. We cannot fail to discover here,

" Thoughts that breathe, and words that burn."

They fall upon the ear—they enter the mind—they affect the heart—unlike all other writings in the world. We refer,

III. TO THE UNVARYING FIDELITY AND IMPARTIALITY OF THE WORD OF GOD. The writers were exact in detailing their own imperfections and sins, as well as the sins of others who were the avowed servants of

God. Moses relates his own reluctance to undertake the divine mission—his killing the Egyptian—his rashness—his exclusion from the good land. The intemperance of Noah—the prevarication of Abraham—the incest of Lot—the idolatry of Aaron—the heinous sins of David—the weakness of the disciples—the fall of Peter, &c.—all are faithfully given. We refer,

IV. TO THE HARMONY OF THE SACRED SCRIPTURES. There may be occasionally apparent contradictions and discrepancies, but care and attention are only requisite to show that they are apparent only. The chronology and history of the events, &c. all agree, and many of these are amply attested by the concurring statements of profane authors. The same spirit and feeling pervade the entire sacred volume. The various dispensations and ceremonies also seem naturally to arise from one another. We refer,

V. TO THE PURITY OF THE SACRED SCRIPTURES. They teach and inculcate the highest degree of moral purity. They legislate not only for the life, but for the tongue and the inmost thoughts. They demand purity of principle, and motive, and aim. They pander to no vice ; they exempt no class of men. They allow of no evasion ; the highest model of excellency is exhibited before us for our imitation. The purest precepts are given, and the loftiest motives presented to our understandings, judgments, and hearts. How surprisingly different to the best schemes of the most celebrated moralists !

VI. THE SCRIPTURES DELINEATE MOST ACCURATELY THE STATE OF THE HUMAN HEART. No other book enters so deeply into the recesses of the soul. It presents the imaginings of the mind naked and loathsome before us. It directs us to the root, to the sources of moral evil. Who can read it, and not feel, that, like its divine Original, it searcheth the heart and tries the very inmost thoughts of the soul. Here we become intimate with the germs of vice ; and there is no character but may see, as in an infallible mirror, his true state here depicted. It is emphatically the book of the human heart, and could only be written by him who is conversant with all the thoughts and devices within us.

VII. IT PRESENTS TO MAN REAL AND ABIDING CONSOLATION. Severely faithful, yet it is inexpressibly tender. It denounces sin that we may be extricated from it. It reveals our remedy as well as our disease our refuge as well as our peril, our Saviour as well as our ruin. It offers to its sincere disciples present peace and joy through believing, and it opens before their hopeful anticipations, joys and pleasures of unfading immortality. It is the book for the promotion both of the felicity of this life, as well as of that which is to come.

THE BIBLE A DIVINE REVELATION.

" Thy word is truth."—John xvii. 17.

SECOND SKETCH.

In presenting additional evidence of the divine authenticity of the scriptures—We refer,

VIII. To the fulfilment of its prophecies. Passing by the prophecies which related to various events in the history of the Jews, we refer to the numerous prophecies regarding the Messiah,—prophecies running through nearly all the books of the Old Testament,—prophecies detailing the minutest circumstances in his life, character, sufferings, death, resurrection, &c. Now, it is evident these prophecies were in the possession of the Jews hundreds of years before the Saviour's incarnation. It is equally evident, not only from the New Testament, but from contemporary Jewish and Pagan writers, that such events did occur in the life and history of Jesus Christ. Observe, also, the prophecies of Christ regarding his own death, &c. Also respecting the doom of Jerusalem, which was fulfilled to the very letter. But this kind of evidence is sufficiently comprehensive for many volumes. Babylon, Tyre, Nineveh, Egypt, Judea, are all monumental attestations of the truth of scripture prophecy. We refer,

IX. To the evidence of the miracles of scripture. The miracles of the Old Testament were numerous, striking, well attested, and can never be legitimately overturned. But observe the miracles narrated in the New Testament scriptures—those of Christ and of the Apostles—wrought often not only in public, but in the presence of their bitterest enemies. If false or spurious, how is it that neither Jews nor Gen-

tiles demonstrated their fallacy ? By whom were they wrought ? By the most holy and self-denying. For what ? For the attestation of truths which were hated by the authorities and powers that then ruled, and which involved the workers of them in poverty, bonds, and death. These miracles were connected with moral instruction—with the mortifying doctrines of the cross of Christ, and were designed to corroborate and establish the holy truths of the Christian religion. We refer,

X. To the character of the penmen of revelation. They were, of necessity, wise or ignorant—sincere or hypocrites—the best or the very worst of mankind. Could ignorant men produce such a book ? Would hypocrites pen a volume so truly condemnatory of all pretence and deceit ? Would bad men, nay, I ask, *could* they write such truths of sacred, incomparable purity ? Were the writers deceived ; if so, by what, or where is the evidence of their mental imbecility ? What motives could urge them to write it ? Not worldly glory, for that it invariably condemns. Not avarice, for that it totally reprobates. Selfishness could not influence them. To do good, even by false methods, the virtuous would despise. Besides, we ask, is it not strange that the time when the scriptures were forged, or the country and language, or some at least of the confederates have never been discovered ? If written by the names annexed, then it is manifestly divine. To confute this is beyond the power and combination of skepticism to effect. We refer,

XI. To the singular preservation of the scriptures. Portions of the Bible were written more than three thousand years ago. Whole libraries of works have perished of much more modern date, yet no book has ever been more hated. What malevolent effort has been put forth for its annihilation ! Kings, and emperors, and generals, philosophers, statesmen, and legislators, have all aimed at its extirpation. With disciples and friends chiefly among the poor and uninfluential, yet it has survived. It has flourished, while its adversaries have been entombed one after another, and it never bade so fair as at present to be the Book of the whole family of mankind. Surely it is the Book of truth, and the Most High has been its conservator and defence. We advert,

XII. To its MIGHTY INFLUENCE ON THE CHARACTER AND MANNERS OF MANKIND. Its influence on nations is amazing. Our own a glorious proof. Its influence on the social circle. Its influence on personal conduct and manners. Its influence in convicting and converting men. Its influence in producing in its recipients the fruits of holiness. Its influence in imparting consolation in adversity, suffering, and death. Its influence in raising the mind and heart to spiritual and heavenly realities. Who can record its victories of moral power and beauty? Who can rehearse its mighty achievements—its delightful transformations? Its influence has not been impaired by the lapse of ages. Its power is not limited to any country, or clime, or color, or tongue. Everywhere it diffuses light, and liberty, and joy, and blessedness. Surely we may exclaim with holy rapture, " Thy word is truth."

APPLICATION.

1. *Be well established as to the truth of the evidence of the divinity of the Holy Scriptures.* This is a cardinal subject, and of the highest moment; the basis of the Christian superstructure.

2. *Let it be highly estimated.* If the book of divine truth, then how precious, how invaluable! Then, indeed, is it more to be prized than thousands of gold and silver.

3. *Let your regard be evinced by a constant and personal reference to it.* Read, study, meditate upon it. Let it dwell richly within you. Let it counsel and guide your steps. Live in the enjoyment of its consoling and sanctifying truths, and in the expectation of the glories it reveals.

THE INSPIRATION OF THE SCRIPTURES.

" All scripture is given by inspiration of God."
—2 TIMOTHY iii. 16.

BY scripture in the text is evidently meant the books of the Old Testament; but the evidence by which their inspiration is established will also clearly prove the inspiration of the writings of the New Testament. The subject is one of sublime interest to the Christian student, how, and in what manner God conveyed the know-

ledge of his will to mankind. Let us in considering this subject notice the various degrees of inspiration, and the diversity of modes by which that inspiration was given.

I. THE VARIOUS DEGREES OF INSPIRATION. It is clear that the truths of the scriptures would require a difference in the degree of divine assistance or communication to the writer. The lowest degree has been appropriately styled,

1. *General superintendence.* When the sacred writers reveal what they personally saw and knew. As in Moses, in reference to his own call, mission, and history of the Israelites to the period of his death. And as in the case of the evangelists, what they heard and witnessed in the life and history of the Redeemer. But here inspiration was required to bring to their remembrance in the exact order, and also to give a clear, full, and unprejudiced relation of the things which they wrote. In this department they were preserved from forgetfulness, prejudice, and mistake. The next degree of inspiration,

2. *Was that of spiritual elevation.* By which the writer was enabled to enter into the moral grandeur of his subject, and present such descriptions as were worthy of the theme, and also to convey the thoughts of Deity respecting such events or scenes. The comprehensive fulness in connection with the clear condensation peculiar to scripture, also seems to have rendered the inspiration of scripture indispensable. The next degree of inspiration,

3. *Is that of immediate revelation.* Where the subjects written were not within the range of the writer's knowledge, as in the account of the creation, &c., &c., more than two thousand years afterwards by Moses. So also all the predictions of the ancient seers, in some instances thousands of years before the realization. Now in this degree of inspiration God made known what had previously existed in his own mind, to those whom he inspired. It will be seen that each and all these degrees of inspiration secure the infallible accuracy of what was recorded. Observe then,

II. THE DIVERSITY OF MODE BY WHICH THE INSPIRATION OF THE SCRIPTURES WAS GIVEN. God revealed his will immediately and supernaturally to men,

1. *By the ministry of angels.* It would appear that one of these messengers is peculiarly distinguished above the rest by his

divine titles and superior nature. "The angel of the covenant"—the angel in whom is the name Jehovah, the redeeming angel, the angel of God's presence, &c., &c. Now these titles clearly have respect to the divine Son of God, Genesis xv. 1, 2, xlviii. 16. But God also employed the created intelligences to be the conveyancers of his mind to the prophets, Daniel ix. 20.

2. *By dreams and visions of the night.* Thus Abraham, Genesis xv. 1. Thus also Jacob, Genesis xxviii. 16. Thus Solomon, 1 Kings iii. 5–15. Thus Daniel, iv. 10. Thus Peter, Acts x. 10. Thus Paul, Acts xxvii. 24.

3. *By an audible voice from heaven.* Thus God revealed his mind to Adam, both before and after the fall. Thus to Noah, Genesis vi. 13. Thus also to Moses in the chief revelations which regarded the origin and history of the world, giving of the law, &c., &c.

4. *By resplendent visions and emblematical representations.* Thus the sublime vision of Isaiah, chap. vi. 1. Ezekiel, chap. i. 2, &c. And John, Rev. i. &c. And the emblematical representations of Jeremiah, Zechariah, &c.

5. *By direct communication of the truths to the mind.* In this way the light and signification of the things revealed were made vivid to the understanding and accurate to the judgment, and were deeply impressed on the heart, the tongue also acting as the amanuensis of the Spirit of God. See the inspiration of the seventy elders, Numbers xi. 25. Case also of Jeremiah, xx. 9 ; Micah iii. 8 ; 2 Peter i. 21. An extensive controversy has been waged as to the extent of inspiration, regarding the very words of scripture, whether the sacred writers were inspired as to the accuracy of thought and idea only, or were inspired with the phraseology of scripture. It would appear probable that neither rule would apply to all the sacred writings. It is obvious that the penmen of the divine word were extensively free to embody their thoughts according to their variety of talent and style ; but it is equally obvious that in all cases their expressions were in exact accordance with the mind of God, and the subject they revealed.

REMARKS.

1. *How transcendently precious and valuable must be the sacred writings!* The thoughts and mind of the blessed God. A revelation of the will of Jehovah to man. Well may it be styled the book of books. No veneration of it can be too high, no attachment to it too deep, no attention to it too extensive.

2. *No marvel that the Bible bears such extraordinary evidences of divine grandeur and majesty.* All God's works are thus distinguished from those of mankind. How visible is this in creation, in providence ! What heights we cannot reach, and depths we cannot fathom ! But how delightful that all its essential portions are clear and comprehensive to our finite and contracted minds !

3. *With what sacredness and awe we should consult its records.* Not to be perused lightly, or with inconsideration ; but with serious fear and reverence.

4. *How conclusive should be its laws and directions!* To this every mind should bow, every spirit submit, and every heart loyally obey.

5. *It is our great and holy privilege to have this precious book in our own tongue.* Thus it is given as an invaluable legacy to the poorest in our land.

———

THE SCRIPTURES NOT CUNNINGLY DEVISED FABLES.

"For we have not followed cunningly devised fables."—2 Pet. i. 16.

A FIRM persuasion of the truth of the Bible lies at the foundation of our religion ; doubts here render the whole uncertain and cheerless. To have the mind well established in this main principle, is of the very utmost importance to our satisfaction and happiness. The enemies of revelation have often asserted and reiterated the fallacy of the scriptures ; this is easily done ; any foolish, self-confident person can do this ; and the Bible itself predicts that it should experience this treatment from those who in the last days should rise up—scoffers, walking after their own lusts. It is for the Christian, therefore, to array himself with the armor of light, to be well furnished with the evidences that he is not following cunningly devised fables. That we may be edified by our subject, we shall,

I. MAKE SEVERAL GENERAL PRELIMINARY OBSERVATIONS.

II. SHOW HOW UNLIKE THE SCRIPTURES ARE TO CUNNINGLY DEVISED FABLES.

III. OFFER AN IMPROVEMENT OF THE WHOLE. We shall make,

I. SEVERAL GENERAL PRELIMINARY OBSERVATIONS.

1. *By the scriptures, we mean the whole of the books of the Old and New Testaments,* commencing with Genesis, and ending with the visions of the Apocalypse. In these books is embodied a period of more than four thousand years; from the creation of our world to sixty years after the ascension of our Saviour.

2. *In the matter of the scriptures we have endless variety.* A great portion of it is history—history of the world for two thousand years; history of the Jews for eleven hundred years; history of the origin and spread of Christianity for nearly thirty years. A great portion of it is narrative of the greatest and most wonderful events; the deluge; the dispersion of mankind; the destruction of Sodom; the emancipation of Israel; the overthrow of Babylon, &c., &c. There is much biography, both of good and bad men—of the most illustrious of the human race; the first of our race, Adam and Eve, Abel, Enoch, Noah, Abraham, Isaac, and Jacob, the twelve patriarchs, Moses, &c.; the judges, the kings, several of the prophets, especially the life of the holy Redeemer and his chosen apostles. Much of the Bible is doctrinal, containing the great truths of religion; the holy principles of God's mind and will. These doctrines include the character of God, and his holy principles of grace and mercy respecting our world; the sinner's ruin and redemption; the way of acceptance and eternal life. A great deal is preceptive or practical; the great duties men owe to God and to one another; duties of all classes, spheres, and circumstances. Much of the Bible is of a promissory kind; the word of God is full of great and precious promises, relating both to this life, and that which is to come; but this is the chief grand promise, eternal salvation through Christ Jesus. Another subject of the holy scriptures is prediction; referring to the various events which God has declared shall come to pass; many of these have been accomplished, many yet remain to be fulfilled.

3. *The word of God was written in divers manners and in various ages of the world.* The first five books were written by Moses; others by Ezra and the prophets, by the evangelists and the apostles. The writers were inspired, that is, enlightened and guided as to the subjects on which they wrote. "All scripture is given by inspiration of God," &c. "Holy men of old wrote," &c. Visions, dreams, voices from heaven, &c. What they saw and witnessed, &c.

4. *The word of God is a complete rule of faith and life.* We need know no more. It is full, copious, all-sufficient; a rule for every station, class, condition; from the king to the beggar, from the sire to the child. As adapted to the moral world as the sun to the natural.

5. *It comes to us in a translated form.* The Old was written in Hebrew, and the New chiefly in Greek; some difficulty in translating, as the idioms of languages are so different, yet the sense is easily transferred, and though there are different renderings of the scriptures, yet not one essential doctrine or duty is affected by it. Italics are words supplied by the translators to make the sense in our language good; it was divided into chapters by Hugo Caro, 1240, and into verses by Mordecai Nathan, 1445.

6. *These scriptures are God's gift to man.* They are for our information and use; not designed for any peculiar class, but for all men; not for the priesthood, but for all: they form the true guide from earth to heaven, and therefore are designed to be the treasure of every human soul. Several great reasons for grateful joy in reference to them.

(1.) That we have them in our own tongue.

(2.) They are now translated into nearly 200 different languages.

(3.) So accessible to the poor; an excellent copy of the New Testament, well bound, for one shilling; of the whole for two shillings. In 1429, a New Testament sold for £2 16s. 8d., more than £20 of our money. Observe,

II. How UNLIKE THE SCRIPTURES ARE TO CUNNINGLY DEVISED FABLES.

Several classes of fables. We do not understand the term here to refer to parabolical writings, where often good morals were taught; many of the ancient moralists conveyed their truths thus: but the text refers to the fabulous histories and doctrines which were inculcated by pagan priests, &c. Now every religion among the heathen, Hindooism, Budhooism, Mohammedanism, &c., had their fables; now these fables were,

1. *Without evidence.* No proof that the events ever took place; depended on the mere authority of the writer. But the Bible is fully supported by irrefragable evidence; pagan writers have established most of the events stated in the Old Testament. The facts and events of the New Testament can be proved to equal demonstration with the landing of Julius Cæsar on the shores of Britain. The fabulous events of paganism are without dates, or are said to be hundreds and thousands of years ago; but the year and often the very day of the occurrences of the Bible are given with the most scrupulous exactness. The ancient fables,

2. *Were full of absurdities*, gross, monstrous absurdities, opposed to reason and to common sense. Mohammedanism is one of the most intelligent, yet the scenes in that would be laughed at by the children of our sabbath schools. In the Koran the direct contradictions are endless; Mohammed, therefore, insisted the last revelation was the true. The Bible, intellectual and sublime, worthy of the great and wise Spirit of its Author.

3. *The fables were, many of them, grossly impure.* Not one which contains a sound elevated morality; many of them so gross that our missionaries would not dare to translate them. The Bible—holy, high, unrivalled in purity of speech, thought.

4. *The fables gave no clear views of the way of salvation or of a future state.* All dark, confused, contradictory; no certainty; no comfort; no good hope. The Bible is the chart of life; the revelation of God's salvation. "Life and immortality are brought to light," &c.

III. IMPROVE THE WHOLE.

1. *Be thankful for the scriptures*, every day, every hour, &c.

2. *Rightly use them.* By reading and meditation.

3. *Follow them.* Go where they lead; obey their mandate; then we shall be wise, holy, benevolent, happy. Thus be fitted for life, sickness, death, eternity.

4. *Follow them in their appropriate application to your souls.* In all your need, sorrows, &c.

THE CHARACTERISTICS OF DIVINE REVELATION.

"Thy word was unto me the joy and rejoicing of mine heart."—JER. xv. 16.

THERE are numerous reasons why the divine word should be hailed with joy, and be a constant source of delight to the pious soul. It is the book of our heavenly Father, in which is exhibited his amazing love to his dear children. It is the book of the Redeemer, in which his glories are resplendently manifested to his believing disciples. It is the book of the divine and blessed Spirit, in which he breathes upon us the saving words of grace and truth. It is the Christian's portion, and the heritage of his heart. Let us then ascertain some of those characteristics of revelation, by which it is so endeared to the joyous affections of the believer's soul. He rejoices in God's word on account,

I. OF ITS ADAPTATION TO ALL HIS CIRCUMSTANCES AND WANTS.—He is a *traveller*, and it is his map, both of the country in which he is a pilgrim, and the land to which he is journeying.—He is a *mariner*, and it is the chart by which he steers amid the rocks, and shoals, and perils of the ocean of time.—He is a *pilgrim*, and this is his staff. Here he leans and rests on his way of weariness and toil.—He is a *warrior*, and this is his armory, especially it is his sword; "the sword of the Spirit, which is the word of God."—He is a *subject* of the royal kingdom of heaven, and this is the code of divine laws, the statutes in which the path of obedience is revealed.—He is *frail*, and encompassed with infirmities, and here the consolations of God are abundantly provided.—He is a *student* of the heavenly mysteries, and here life and immortality are brought to light by the gospel.—It is adapted to the youthful Christian, and by this he cleanses his way.—To the mature Christian, and by this he overcomes the world.—To the aged believer, and by this he is mellowed for the celestial garner.—To the rich Christian, and here safety from the deteriorating power of affluence is provided.—To the poor Christian, and this is the charter of his spiritual wealth.—To the tempted Christian, and here the wiles of the enemy and the means of conquest are revealed.—To the suffering Christian, and here the solace of divine compassion and support are communicated

—To the dying Christian, and on this staff he reclines in the dreary valley and shadow of death, and fears no evil. Well may he exclaim, " Thy word was unto me the joy," &c. He rejoices in God's word,

II. On account of its clearness and perspicuity. We do not deny that it has its sublime mysteries, its lofty themes, its profound depths, its incomprehensible doctrines.

1. *But the doctrines essential to salvation are clear.* The depravity of the human heart, the redemption of the world by Christ Jesus, the way of salvation by repentance towards God and faith in the Lord Jesus. The Spirit's influence in the regeneration and sanctification of the soul, and practical obedience to the will of God.

2. *The duties of religion are clear.* Comprehended in two grand precepts ; supreme love to God, and unfeigned love to mankind.

3. *The counsels of the word of God are clear.* Adapted to every capacity ; a wayfaring man need not err.

4. *The promises of the word of God are clear.* Nothing here ambiguous or uncertain ; so clear that the weakest Christian may understand them and endorse them as his own. He rejoices in God's word,

III. On account of its fulness. In this respect the Bible is a most wonderful book. Its celestial treasures can never be fully explored, much less exhausted. Like the atmosphere, a world may inhale it, and yet it is ever fresh and invigorating. Like the light, its beams are sufficient for the family of man. Like the ocean, its channels are ever full and overflowing.

> " Enough for each, enough for all,
> Enough for evermore."

Here is no dearth, no famine of spiritual provision, no lack of the food of the soul ; the hungry and th'rsty find this a continual, an ever-flowing fountain.

IV. On account of its minuteness and particularity. It is a book for the great mass of men ; God's gift to the whole race of mankind. But it is equally a book of detail. It meets the particular circumstances and the diversified events of life ; circumstances of adversity and trial, Ps. ix. 18, cxlvi. 9. Of affliction and bereavement, Ps. xxxiv. 19, xlvi. 1. Of temptation and depression, 1 Cor. x. 13. Of sorrow and suffering, John i. 9 ; 2 Cor. i. 4.

Of slander and persecution, Matt. v. 11. Of perplexity and peril, Ps. liv. 7. O yes, the good man will find counsels, examples, and promises, to suit every condition in which he may be placed. He rejoices in God's word,.

V. On account of its truth and certainty. It cannot be falsified ; it cannot alter or fail, therefore the confidence. may be entire and unvarying ; the glory of God's truth and immutability render it essentially true and certain. " It abideth for ever."

APPLICATION.

1. Let this word be the choice of your heart.

2. Let it dwell in you richly.

3. Have recourse to it in all scenes of perplexity and trial.

4. Honor its divine Author by a constant study of its contents, and implicit faith in its great truths.

THE SUFFICIENCY OF REVELATION.

" They have Moses and the prophets."—Luke xvi. 29.

Our text is the reply of Abraham to the rich man in torments who desired an extraordinary messenger to be sent for the conversion of his brethren. He supposed that a messenger from the dead would arouse them from their state of lethargy and sin, and having heard him they would repent. To this Abraham replies, " They have Moses and the prophets," their writings are amply sufficient. In them are propounded the great truths of religion. They contain the revealed will of God, and are adapted to meet the condition of sinful men ; and if they fail to enlighten, convince, and save them, neither would a messenger from the dead succeed. If the law and the prophets were thus sufficient, how fully must that book be so, which in addition to these, contains also the discourses and life of Jesus, and the writings of the apostles ! We fairly then deduce this leading idea from the text, that the revelation given in the holy scriptures, is characterized by perfect sufficiency.

I. It is sufficient in the knowledge it communicates. It reveals to us the true knowledge of the nature, perfections, and will of God. It reveals to us the knowledge of man's original condition, his primeval state, his fall, and consequent misery and ruin. It reveals to us the way of our recovery by the intervention of the Lord Jesus Christ as the Saviour of the world. It reveals the character, offices, work, and doctrines of the Redeemer. It reveals clearly the way of salvation. It reveals to us the doctrines of the resurrection of the dead, and of an eternal state of future existence. It reveals the glories of the heavenly world as the dwelling-place of the righteous forever. It reveals a state of future wo as the punishment of the impenitent and ungodly.

II. It is sufficient in the duties it prescribes. A perfect rule of life. It prescribes the duties of all classes towards each other. Of monarch and subjects; of rulers and the people ; of masters and servants ; of parents and children ; of the rich and poor. It reveals the duties which are involved in self-government and self-cultivation. The duties which have direct respect to the blessed God. Fear, honor, trust, praise, worship, obedience, love, delight, &c. It gives rules for the regulation of the conduct, of the tongue, of the thoughts, of the desires, &c. It directs us as to the duties we owe to our families, our country, and the world. It shows us how we should treat our friends and our foes. It instructs us as to our food, and dress, and recreations, and business. In one word, it gives a direct response to the interrogatory, " Lord, what wouldest thou have me to do ?"

III. It is sufficient in the motives it presents. To enforce obedience to its requirements it refers us,—to the dignity of our nature—to the internal peace of a good conscience—to the enjoyment of the divine favor—to the abiding blessing of the Almighty—to the benign influence of a merciful providence—to the superintending care of our heavenly Father—to the ministrations of angels—to a hopeful and tranquil death—to an immortality of joy and blessedness—to the eternal beatific vision, and the crown of glory that fadeth not away. Motives richer, greater, higher, or more durable cannot be presented to the human mind.

IV. It is sufficient in the cautions and admonitions it furnishes. It reveals all the sources of evil and peril to which we are exposed,—the deceitfulness of sin,

the plague of the human heart ; the blandishments of the world ; and the wiles of the devil. It admonishes us as to the evil of self in all its varieties of form,—self-love, self-approbation, self-confidence, self-pleasing. It admonishes us as to the dangers of presumption. The evils of spiritual sloth, and the perils of procrastination. It admonishes us as to the brevity of life, the uncertainty of time, the probable nearness of death, and the realities of the judgment day.

V. It is sufficient in the promises and threatenings it proclaims. The promises of revelation are. precious, great, and innumerable. One vast chain of more than golden worth, composed of links adapted to every state and circumstance of life, death, and eternity. " The promise of the life that now is," &c. One great promise including the whole ; the enjoyment of God as the portion of the soul: " I am thy God." " Heirs of God." Threatenings of the most fearful and overwhelming description. Threatenings of the divine disapprobation in this life. His continued daily anger ; his wrath in the expulsion of the sinner at death ; his fiery indignation forever and ever. A hell enkindled with the breath of an incensed Deity.

OBSERVATIONS.

1. We ask, what more can responsible man require than a volume of such comprehensive fulness, such complete sufficiency ?

2. What could a messenger from the dead reveal that is not fully declared in the scriptures.

3. If the scriptures fail to enlighten men and to convince of sin, and lead men to repentance, equally so would the communications of one from the dead.

4. How inexpressibly precious is the Bible !

THE SCRIPTURES THE WORD OF CHRIST.

" Let the word of Christ dwell in you richly in all wisdom."—Col. iii. 16.

Christ is emphatically the light and glory of the sacred oracles. In the field of revelation Christ is the hidden pearl of peerless worth. In this system of divine truth Christ is the sun and centre. The Bible is a book of history, narratives, incidents, doctrines, laws, ordinances, precepts, and promises ; but in all these senses, Christ is vitally and essentially pervading, beautifying, and giving value and supreme excellency to the whole. Let us then consider the scriptures as the word of Christ, and then the counsel the text administers. Let us consider the scriptures,

I. As the word of christ.

They are so,

1. *As he is the Author of them.* Many of the revelations of the Old Testament were made expressly by him. Thus, in several instances to Abraham, and Jacob, and in an especial manner to Moses. The angel of Jehovah was none other than Christ, who appeared to Moses in the burning bush, and engaged to be with him, and said, " I will be thy mouth, and teach thee what to say ;" Exod. iii. 2 ; xii. 4–12. The spirit which dwelt in the prophets is also described as the spirit of Christ, 1 Pet. i. 11. Christ also promised to be with the disciples and apostles, and to bring all things to their remembrance. Paul received his gospel as a revelation from Jesus Christ. And John describes the visions of the Apocalypse as " The Revelation of Jesus Christ," Rev. i. 1.

The scriptures are the word of Christ,

2. *As they refer to his works, character, and glory.* They commence with the magnificent works of creation, and these were all the productions of the " Word," by whom all things were made, &c. They present to us the marvellous manifestations of his providential doings in the emancipation of Israel, in overruling the events of nations, and in the general government of the universe ; for " he upholdeth all things by the word of his power." He is " King of kings, and Lord of lords." Especially they reveal his stupendous achievements in the redemption of mankind. Hence he was predicted of, and promised as such, immediately on the entrance of sin into the world. He was also typified and shadowed forth in all the ceremonial institutions of the law. And as the burden of prophecy it is emphatically affirmed, " Unto him gave all the prophets witness." The New Testament scriptures open to us his advent, his life, his work, his miracles, his sufferings, his death, and his resurrection and ascension into heaven.

The scriptures are the word of Christ,

3. *As they reveal his dignity and offices.* His true and proper deity, Phil. ii. 6. His dignified and pure humanity, Heb. iv. 15. His office of prophet and teacher, Luke iv. 18. His office as priest and sacrifice, Heb. ix. 26. His office as king and ruler, Rev. i. 5.

4. *As they reveal to us the saving benefits of Christ.* Illumination, as he is the light of the world. Divine knowledge, as he is the great teacher, who " brought life and immortality to light by the gospel ;" who also revealed the Father. Pardon of sin, for he is exalted expressly to give repentance and remission of sin. Holiness— " His blood cleanseth from all sin." Acceptance with God— " For we are accepted in the Beloved." Grace to keep and sanctify— " His grace is sufficient," &c. He is the source of all strength and ability to his people. Eternal life— " The gift of God is eternal life through Christ Jesus our Lord." The resurrection of the body, and a glorious entrance into heaven, &c.— " Who is the resurrection and the life," and " who shall change our vile bodies," &c. Who shall say to those on his right hand, " Come, ye blessed of my Father," &c.

5. *As they reveal to us the true and the only way of receiving Christ.* By the knowledge of his word ; by the influences of his Spirit ; by the exercises of repentance towards God ; by a vital faith in his own name and word. How appropriately then is the Bible the word of Christ ! He is, indeed, the Alpha and the Omega, the sum and the substance, the all and in all of divine revelation. Withdraw Christ and the soul departs, and only the inanimate corpse remains. Withdraw Christ and the glory vanishes, and the scriptures would be as the original state of matter before the creation—dark, without form, and void. Notice, then,

II. The counsel the text administers. Let the word of Christ " dwell in you richly," &c.

1. *Let it be received into your hearts.* Not merely read or heard, but meet with a hearty reception. Not merely into the understanding or memory, but into the fervent affections of the soul. Received as good news, as good tidings, as the word of eternal life.

2. *Let it abide in your souls.* Have a residence, a permanent abode. Not visit

or tarry, as a guest, but dwell, be within us, as the soul is in the body. Be within us on all occasions and seasons, and for all spiritual purposes.

3. *It is to be abundantly within us.* Dwell in you " richly," or plenteously. In its rich variety ; in its rich fulness ; in its enriching plenitude ; making us rich in the knowledge of our Lord Jesus Christ, and in the experimental enjoyment of grace.

4. *It is to dwell within us in all wisdom.* In all the variety of wisdom which it imparts, and enabling us wisely to benefit by all the instruction it communicates. To become enriched with the wisdom that cometh from above, and finally made wise unto salvation.

APPLICATION.

1. *Learn the gracious character of the Christian revelation.* " Word of Christ." Full of the love of God to us, as evidenced in the gift of his beloved Son, Jesus Christ. A revelation of mercy and compassion to wretched, perishing sinners.

2. *The claims it has upon our sacred and grateful regards.* How it should be revered, and prized, and loved. How we should read, and study, and meditate on its blessed and all-glorious truths.

3. *The appropriate use of the scriptures.* To dwell in the heart ; to fill us with divine knowledge ; to influence the hidden springs of the soul ; to enlighten and sanctify the mind.

4. *The methods by which these great ends may be secured.* Receive the word of Christ with great humility ; in a docile, teachable frame of mind ; with a lowly spirit. To receive it in the exercise of unwavering faith : to obey its holy injunctions, and thus realize its saving benefits.

THE METAPHORICAL REPRESENTA-TIONS OF SCRIPTURE.

" His delight is in the law of the Lord."—PSALM i. 2.

A GREAT portion of the word of God is written in the language of metaphor and comparison. The sacred writers often clothed their thoughts in language borrowed from the rich oriental scenery by which they were surrounded. The great Teacher adopted this mode of instruction in an eminent degree. He scarcely ever spake but in the language of parable or simile. The word of God itself is often thus presented to our attention. And in this way the sanctified imagination enjoys peculiar pleasure and delight, in meditating on its rich and hallowed pages. Hence it is written, " His delight is in the law of the Lord." The metaphorical representations of the scriptures may be classified.

I. BY SIMILITUDES BORROWED FROM KINGS, LEGISLATORS, AND JUDGES. Hence it is a royal law. " The law of the Lord," containing the commandments of the supreme Jehovah, and clothed with divine authority and power. Hence it is also repeatedly represented as statutes, and testimonies, and judgments, forming a code of enactments for the regulation of the heart and life of man. It is also described as counsels, or wisdom, given by a teacher to the ignorant and unlearned, that they may know the will of the Most High. Observe,

II. THE SIMILITUDES BORROWED FROM EARTHLY TREASURES. Hence the word is called precious, and of more value than thousands of gold and silver. " I love thy commandments above gold, yea, above much fine gold." Here the purity, solidity, durability, and therefore preciousness of the scriptures are intended. It is also written, " Thy words are pure words, as silver tried in a furnace of earth," Psalm xii. 6. Here the pure unalloyed character of the word is intended, also its unfailing certainty and value. The psalmist also speaks of the word as imparting a joy equal to that of the man who findeth " great spoil," Psalm cxix. 162. In the scriptures are treasures of light, comfort, peace, joy, and glory. Treasures that never can be corrupted or stolen, or be a source of evil to the possessor. Treasures that enrich both for time and eternity.

III. THE SIMILITUDES BORROWED FROM THE WORKS OF NATURE. Heavenly, pure, radiant as light, and equally adapted to the mental and moral vision of mankind, Psalm cxix. 105. Warm, penetrating, and purifying as fire, Jer. xxiii. 29. Beautiful and plenteous as the dew ; sweet, and refreshing, and essential as the rain ; fertilizing as the stream, Isaiah lv. 10 ; Deut. xxxii. 2.

IV. THE SIMILITUDES BORROWED FROM THE NECESSARIES OF HUMAN LIFE. Divine truths are described as precious seed. The word of God is represented as bread, the staff of life, by which the soul lives. The prophet says, "Thy words were found, and I did eat them." Job says, "I have esteemed thy word more than my necessary food," Job xxiii. 12. The blessings of the gospel are likened by the prophet to waters and also to milk, which are freely offered without money and without price. "Desire the sincere milk of the word, that ye may grow thereby," 1 Pet. ii. 2. It is also said to be sweet as honey, yea, as the honey-comb, Psalm xix. 10.

V. Similitudes borrowed from weapons of war, and articles of important use. It is the Christian's sword, by which he both defends himself, and overcomes his enemies in the fight of faith. It is described as the quiver of the Saviour's arrows, by which he rides forth gloriously, his enemies falling under him, Psalm xlv. 4, 5. It is God's hammer, by which he breaks the rocky hearts of men, Jer. xxiii. 29. It is the Christian pilgrim's staff, and the rod of God's strength sent out of Zion, Psalm xxiii. 4, cx. 2. It is likened by the apostle to a glass in which is beheld the transforming glory of the Lord, 2 Cor. iii. 19 ; and also in which we may see our true character and condition, James i. 23.

OBSERVATIONS.

1. It is our duty to be intimately conversant with the word of God. This can only be the result of constant reading and meditation. Diligence is essential to an intimate and extensive acquaintance with the treasures of divine truth.

2. The meditating in God's law is associated with true delight to the spiritual mind. It is an exercise mentally elevating, as well as productive of moral profit to the soul. Here is abundant matter for mental research and spiritual investigation.

3. We should be careful to observe that there be a corresponding influence produced by a constant perusal of divine truth on our spirit and life. Do we make the scriptures the rule of our conduct? Do we obey the divine statutes? listen to the divine counsels? value these celestial treasures? live upon this spiritual food? Do we use the word of God as a part of the Christian armor? Do we lean upon this staff? Do we take it as our living heritage, and portion forever?

4. What pleasure, instruction, and profit those forego who live in the neglect of God's blessed word! Let us emulate the character, "Whose delight is in the law of the Lord."

PRACTICAL USE OF THE SCRIPTURES.

"Thy word have I hid in mine heart, that I might not sin against thee."—Psalm cxix. 11.

Various are the benevolent designs of God in favoring us with the holy scriptures. They are designed for our information, revealing what could not otherwise be known. They are designed for our instruction or tuition in the great principles of true religion ; for our correction, warning, counsel, and comfort. But they are designed, also, to exert a practical influence on our hearts and lives. And this use of the divine word is that to which David refers when he says, "Thy word have I hid," &c. Observe the course the psalmist piously adopted, and the holy design that course of action involved.

I. The course the psalmist piously adopted. "Thy word have I hid in mine heart." Now, the reception of the divine word, its perusal, meditation on it, love to it, and delight in it, are necessarily included. To hide the word of God in our heart,

1. *Implies diligent desire to understand it.* It can only benefit us as we ascertain its true signification. We must know the meaning of the word spoken to us. "Understandest thou what thou readest ?" was the necessary question to the devout Ethiopian, who was reading the prophet Isaiah. To understand the word of God often requires mental labor and diligent research. We shall be often assisted by ascertaining the occasion, design, and general scope of the writer, and especially by comparing scripture with scripture. The Bible is often its own expositor. See 1 Pet. i. 10, 11.

2. *It implies a storing up the word in our memories.* We read of some who "laid them up in their hearts," Luke i. 6. Mary also kept " his sayings in her heart." We are exhorted to give the more earnest heed to the things, &c. " lest at any time we let them slip." We should often have a remembrance of God's blessed word, laying it up richly in our souls.

3. *It implies an experimental acquaintance with the power of the word.* To know

the truth and sweetness of the word by our own experience of it—to have it incorporated with our feelings and enjoyments—to be illumined by it, controlled by it, comforted by it—to know its strengthening, sustaining, and sanctifying influence. In this way it must be hid in the heart. As seed in the ground—as leaven in the meal —as treasure in the cabinet—as the soul in the body.

4. *The highest esteem and value for the word.* We only lay up and conceal what is precious and of great worth. True attachment to the word involves a value for it more than we have to gold and silver, or even to our necessary food. It must be the joy and rejoicing of our heart, the soul's dearest treasure and most abiding heritage and portion. Notice,

II. THE HOLY DESIGN THAT COURSE OF ACTION INVOLVED. " That I might not sin against thee." Richly and deeply lodged in the heart, the word of God is our preservative from sin. By this the young man cleanseth his way ; by this the work of sanctification is carried on ; by this we are built up and made meet for the celestial inheritance, &c. But it keeps from sin,

1. *By the counsels it imparts.* It apprizes us of our peril, our enemies, our weakness, our defence, our only help. It shows us the way of peace and safety, and its directions are clear, direct, and infallible. God guides his people by his counsels.

2. *By the threatenings it denounces.* Against formality, hypocrisy, spiritual sloth, forsaking the good way, and drawing back to our first sinful state. Now these threatenings must be remembered, that in the day of temptation we may avoid the things which would be destructive to our peace.

3. *By the promises it makes.* These form a very extensive part of the divine word. They are various, precious, and numberless. What want or condition is not anticipated in these ? They are designed as so many rich clusters of the precious grapes of Canaan, for our refreshment on our way thither. How often faith would fail, hope decline, and joy cease, but for these ! These are the steps of the celestial ladder by which we ascend to the heavenly state. Oh ! let these promises be hidden in your hearts, that they may avail you in all the changing scenes of your earthly pilgrimage, &c. Now, these promises will preserve us from sinning against God by yielding to carnal doubts and unbelieving fears.

4. *By the practical duties it enjoins.* Religion enters into all the circumstances and concerns of life. Every state and condition has its practical duties. Now the word is the Christian's directory, not only showing the evils to be avoided, but the requirements God demands. Here God speaks, and says, " This is the way," &c. That we may not practically err or deviate, how necessary that this word of laws, and statutes, and ordinances, be hidden in the heart !

5. *By the strength it communicates.* The word of God gives spiritual power and might to the soul. This is the food of the soul. By this we appropriate Christ Jesus, in all his merits and benefits, and grow stronger and stronger in divine things. It commands and leads us to the source of obedient ability. It shows us what is to be done, and how we may do it. It directs in the Christian course, and gives power to run without wearying, &c.

APPLICATION.

1. Is the word of God hidden in the recesses of your hearts? Are you increasing this mental and moral store ?

2. A regular and methodical use of the word will greatly aid you in this work. Lay it up regularly, &c.

3. The despisers and neglecters of the word must perish.

———

THE SCRIPTURES THE TRUE AND LEGITIMATE SOURCE OF APPEAL

" To the law and to the testimony."—ISAIAH viii. 20.

OUR subject is connected with admonitory counsel, not to visit those who professed to have familiar spirits, &c.; but urges this great truth, that people should seek unto their God, and not the living seek instruction from the dead. Then follows the tex, " To the law and to the testimony." By the law is here meant the great law of God, that which he has clothed with his divine and absolute authority. By the testimony is intended the doctrines and counsels of God's blessed word. The scriptures contain both the law and the testimony, and are therefore the true and legitimate source of appeal in all matters of religion. Let us notice,

I. SOME OF THE STANDARDS TO WHICH MANY APPEAL IN RELIGIOUS CONCERNS.

1. *Some appeal to ancient traditions.* These are often obscure, easily corrupted, and frequently contradictory.

2. *To learned councils.* But these were but councils of fallible men, never perfectly agreed, one council anathematizing another.

3. *To systems of theological articles of faith.* All these are human productions, and partake of all the infirmities of our nature. There is not an absurd error or custom, which has not found a place in some theological system, or in the rites of some learned church. It is also evident, that all these are useless in preventing variety of opinion, or in effecting uniformity of religious sentiment.

4. *The avowed creeds of the sectarian denominations of the church of Christ.* All these stand arrayed in opposition to each other—the Romish, and Lutheran, and Greek church. The churches of England and Scotland, Calvinists and Arminians, Baptists and Pædo-Baptists, &c. These endless creeds would tend only to confuse the bewildered inquirer. Then let us consider.

II. THE DIVINE SOURCE OF APPEAL PRESENTED IN THE SCRIPTURES, " To the law and to the testimony." Now this is the source,

1. *Of infallible truth.* Every word of God is pure and true. Men's expositions may be erroneous; but the text itself is from God, the revelation of his mind to men.

2. *Of perfect and comprehensive truth.* Truth in glorious plenitude. Truth on all religious subjects. Truth for all men's moral exigencies.

3. *Of plain and lucid truth.* How striking the contrast between the divine simplicity of the scriptures in the main, and some of the explications and explanations of men who have labored to expound it ! All essential truths are within the reach of the unlearned, and adapted to the lowest capacities of mankind, " A wayfaring man, though a fool, need not err therein." Then observe,

III. THE USE WE SHOULD MAKE OF THIS DIVINE SOURCE OF APPEAL.

1. *Here we should test all doctrines.* No article of faith should be professed or maintained, unless we have brought it fully and fairly " to the law and to the testimony."

2. *Here we should test all ordinances.* Nothing can be binding, however apparently pleasing, instructive, or edifying, unless it is presented to us in the law or in the testimony. Customs, plausibility, should weigh nothing in these matters.

3. *Here we should test our experience.* Knowing and feeling as those did, or merely as persons whose diaries we have read, is valueless. Here are traits of character revealed in the word of God. Have we the experience of the holy persons exhibited in the divine word ? Do our joys, and hopes, and desires, respond to the requirements of the oracles of truth ? Have we the spirit and disposition recommended in the Bible ?

4. *Here we must test our practical character.* Have we the image of God's children ? the temper and conversation urged in the pages of the law and the testimony ? Are we the subjects of its benedictions, or the subjects condemned and threatened in the divine law ?

5. *Here we must test our joys and expectations.* Every holy grace and feeling has its counterfeit ; so that to guard against self-deception, our joys and hopes must be brought to the law and to the testimony. Do they take their rise as revealed in God's word. Have they features of purity as marked in the divine record ? Are our joys and hopes spiritual, self-abasing ? Do they tend to our furtherance in personal holiness ? Do they lead us to heavenly contemplations ? Is Christ the source of our unspeakable joy, and within us the hope of glory ?

OBSERVATIONS.

1. A neglect of the holy scriptures is one of the deplorable features of our times. Persons are often well acquainted with the creeds and catechisms, sermons and hymns, of their denomination, and know little comparatively of God's blessed word. How second-hand are such views of truth ! How easily shaken such professors ! How poor in spiritual consolations !

2. Honesty of heart, and candor of spirit, are essential to a right appeal to the law

and to the testimony. Without these we shall remain in the trammels of our sectarian peculiarities and assumptions.

3. A return to scripture appeals must precede the introduction of the Saviour's millennial kingdom and glory. How desirable that Christians of all denominations should lay aside their sectarian phraseology, and adopt the pure and unerring words of the Holy Spirit! Christians should not only mind the same thing, but follow the same rule, speaking always the truth in love.

ON READING THE SCRIPTURES.

" How readest thou ?"—LUKE x. 26.

HAPPY is that people who possess in their own tongue the oracles of eternal truth. This has been our eminent privilege for ages past ; but to avail ourselves of the advantages this privilege holds out, we must possess the ability of reading. In past times, education, even of an inferior order, was limited to the few; now, through the diffusion of knowledge and progress of truth, the first elements of instruction are open to the many ; but we may have the book, and the ability to read it, and yet the manner may be so defective and ill-adapted, that little benefit may be derived. Let us then contemplate the proper method of reading the holy scriptures, and enforce that method by several considerations.

I. NOTICE THE PROPER METHOD OF READING THE HOLY SCRIPTURES.

We should read the scriptures,

With profound veneration for their divine Author. This is the book of God ; the only book he has written ; full of his own mind and will ; sent in infinite condescension to our ignorance, weakness, and misery. A book that treats of the divine character, and works, and glory. How, then, ought it to be treated ? Lightly, flippantly, merely as a human composition ? Surely not ! The Jews in this may be held up as truly worthy of our imitation ; we say nothing as to slowness of manner, or posture of body, but at all events, there should be true reverence and veneration of mind.

2. *With a deep consciousness of our own unworthiness.* A self-righteous person cannot be instructed, delighted, or benefited by the perusal of God's word. The whole volume treats of human depravity and worthlessness ; it is designed to empty the mind of self, in all its variety of modifications. In this spirit only shall we value its humiliating truths, and gratefully receive its tidings of mercy and grace. We should read the scriptures,

3. *With exemplary diligence and constancy.* Much truth lies on the surface of the sacred page, but infinitely more in the deep mine of its profound resources. It cannot be accurately understood without mental labor—without study and reflection—without holy meditation. In this work especially, the diligent only can be enriched ; with this diligence there should be united untiring constancy ; the psalmist meditated therein, day and night. This must be our closet book, the family daily portion. It is profitable to have periods and seasons for the exercise of this delightful duty.

4. *With an earnest desire to learn by what we read.* Many read the word merely to be amused ; others as a matter of course or of mere duty ; some, again, read to establish more deeply their own theological opinions, or consult the Bible as a work of reference. The Christian reader should peruse its pages to know and learn what God has spoken—what the Spirit has revealed—what are the truths therein taught. Thus we cannot fail to grow and improve by our reading. Thus God's word is honored, and our own profit inevitably secured. We should read,

5. *With a holy purpose to exemplify our reading in our life and conversation.* Narratives of scripture will furnish both models for imitation, and beacons for warning. The doctrines of revelation will be believed—the precepts obeyed—the promises embraced—the privileges realized. Thus the word of God would be incorporated with our souls, as food is with our bodies, living, speaking, and acting in us, and by us. By this mode of reading the mind will be enlightened, the heart changed, and the life regulated.

6. *With fervent prayer for the Spirit to sanctify the word to our profit.* The Spirit must be sought to inspire with love to the word—to give us clearness and quickness of moral perception—to enable us to treasure it up in our hearts—to fill us with the spirit of humble faith in its blessed truths.

II. LET US URGE THIS METHOD OF READING BY SEVERAL CONSIDERATIONS.

1. *By the evils arising from a careless*

reading of the scriptures. These are numerous; God is dishonored—the mind is uninstructed, or more probably initiated in error. Thus one of God's especial blessings is abused and perverted, and our guilt greatly enhanced and aggravated.

2. *By the blessings we shall derive from such a perusal.* Increasing knowledge and understanding; a clear and harmonious apprehension of the divine mind; a certain and confidential acquaintance with the truth as it is in Jesus; an abiding sense of the divine approbation; a holy growth in the work of heart sanctification, John xvii. 17; an avoidance of the snares and fascinations of the present evil world; a holy meetness for the inheritance of eternal life.

3. *Thus only can we render a satisfactory account for the possession of the scriptures at the last day.* Of this book we are stewards, and as such, every one must give an account to God.

APPLICATION.

1. Address the neglecters of this book.
2. Admonish the careless reader.
3. Ask the question of each, " Understandest thou what thou readest ?"

THE EXISTENCE, &c. OF GOD.

" One God."—1 Cor. viii. 6.

THE first principle in theology is the existence of one supreme, independent, and blessed God. Against this first essential truth much has been spoken and written. In the days of the psalmist there were skeptical men who said in their hearts, " There is no God." In all ages and countries disciples of this school have lived, and reiterated the same dogmas of unbelief. These dogmas have been met by an almost endless variety of incontrovertible reasoning; and if unbelief has produced no other result, it has led the wise, and the great, and the good, to enter the arena of controversy, and to do great service to the interests of truth, by presenting this and other essential doctrines in a clear and convincing light to the world. Let us ask with reverence a few questions concerning the Being referred to, and then examine some evidences as to his existence.

I. LET US ASK WITH REVERENCE A FEW QUESTIONS CONCERNING THE BEING REFERRED TO. " God."

1. *What is meant by God ?* We mean the first great intellectual cause of all things ; the source of all existence; the originator of the world, and all that it contains.

2. *What ideas do we entertain of his essence ?* We cannot form any just ideas of his essence beyond what has been revealed to us. We judge, however, from the only source of correct knowledge, that he is a spiritual intelligence, and, therefore, incorporeal in his nature.

3. *What notions have we of his attributes and perfections ?* We conceive of God as possessing every perfection, and as infinite in all his attributes.

(1.) That as to his being, he is independent, self-existent, and eternal.

(2.) That as to space, his ubiquity filleth all things.

(3.) As to knowledge, he is acquainted with all creatures and events.

(4.) That as to power, he can do all things.

(5.) That he is holy, righteous, just, and true.

(6.) That he is good, bountiful, and gracious.

(7.) Merciful and compassionate. And that,

(8.) In all his natural and moral attributes, in all his will, and mind, and essence, and ways, he is immutable. But each of those must have a separate definition, proof, and illustration.

4. *What conclusions do we arrive at in reference to his greatness and perfections ?* That he is a being of unmixed good, the source of all excellency, of all light and blessedness. That he cannot be the author of darkness or moral evil ; but, as to the grandeur of his being and infinite glories, we cannot by any amount of research find out God, or know him to perfection. Finite cannot fully grasp or comprehend that which is infinite ; so that the immensity of God's glory and perfections must be ever above the reach of finite created beings, even of the brightest order of intellectual greatness. How admirably has the poet expressed the insufficiency of human reason to grasp this immense and overwhelming theme :

" But I lose myself in him,
   In light ineffable ; come, then,
   Expressive silence, muse his praise.

II. LET US EXAMINE SOME EVIDENCES AS TO HIS EXISTENCE.

1. *We refer to the works of nature.* The eternity of these is an absurdity; their self-organization a still greater absurdity; their accidental formation the greatest absurdity of all. Here obviously there must have been a creator; one having prior existence; power, knowledge, skill: for in creation there is vastness, beauty, harmony, design, adaptation. The heavens, the earth, the animal creatures, especially man, all display the exercised power, wisdom, and goodness of a first cause. All creation witnesseth as to God's being and glory.

2. *The preservation and government of the world.* The universe is sustained; all parts of it are under specific and absolute laws. The regularity of the seasons, the wants of all creatures, are met with bountiful supplies suited to their nature and uses. There is no confusion nor jarring in the universe. But all this involves the idea of superintendence and arrangement, power and skill. To account for these irrespective of God's existence is impossible.

3. *The deep impressions of this truth which have been evidenced by mankind in all ages of the world.* The mind, in the exercise of its emotions of veneration and awe, has generally recognised a superior, unknown, vast Intelligence. The fears of men, the hopes of men, the desires of men, all seem to recognise, though sometimes confusedly, the existence of God. Enlightened philosophers of all countries, the savage American Indians, &c., have equally had these impressions, convictions, and emotions. Hence the whole system of idol homage and worship. Hence the innumerable rites and ceremonies, &c.

4. *The opposite sentiment is so fraught with absurdity and inexplicable confusion.* Let a man contemplate a universe without a creator—an intellectual creature without an intellectual source of being, a world without a preserver, ruler, &c. Such a contemplation would tend to confound and overwhelm the reasoning powers, and would throw man into a condition of inextricable doubt and uncertainty.

5. *The influence of atheistical opinions on the minds and manners of mankind.* These opinions have led to national lawlessness, terror, and confusion; to domestic strife and wretchedness; to personal viciousness, pollution, and cruelty. With the establish-ment of these sentiments human responsibility evaporates, and man is left uncontrolled except by the feeble statutes of creatures like himself. The heavens, the earth, animate creation, the human mind, the convictions of all nations, all cry aloud, in a language consonant with reason itself, that there is "One God."

APPLICATION.

Learn,

1. *The folly of atheism.* Only the fool saith "There is no God," and this is consummate, egregious folly.

2. *The absurdity of acknowledging his being, and yet denying his providence and superintendence of human affairs and human responsibility.*

3. *The madness of acknowledging both his being and government, and yet living without him.* As though he saw us not; as though he were not holy and just; as though he would not judge us.

4. *The first essential principle of true religion.* To know God, in his nature, attributes, character, and will.

THE NATURAL PERFECTIONS OF GOD.

"Know that the Lord he is God, there is none else beside him."—DEUT. iv. 35.

THE unity of God is a subject much insisted on, both in the writings of the Old and New Testaments. The Jehovah of the universe is one, and there is none other beside him. It seems self-evident that there can only be one eternal, self-existent, independent, supreme Being. God is also described in his word, as a spirit; not a material or corporeal being. Inertness, extension, and divisibility, seem essentially to belong to matter, but none of these can be applied to Jehovah. As a spiritual being, God is invisible, whom no man hath seen or can see. God is self-existent and independent; there is none above him, none before him; none essential to his glory. Let us just glance at those perfections which are described as the natural perfections of Deity.

I. GOD IS ETERNAL. Not only prospectively, as angels, or the soul of man; but retrospectively, as one who never *began* to exist, but who ever was, and is, and is to come. "Even from everlasting to ever lasting," &c., Ps. xc. 2, cii. 27 ; 1 Tim. i. 17.

II. GOD IS IMMUTABLE. Whose essential nature is unchangeable ; " The same yesterday, to-day, and for ever." He is immutable in his own nature and perfections. Immutable in his counsels, and mind, and wisdom, and will. He is only said to repent in condescension to our feeble capacities, for he is " the Lord, and changeth not," Mal. iii. 6 ; James i. 17.

III. GOD IS OMNIPOTENT. Possessing all power to do whatsoever it pleaseth him. This power is especially manifested in the overwhelming wonders of creation. In the rule and dominion of the world. It was also put forth in our redemption by Christ Jesus. It is exerted in the sinner's conversion. Will be displayed in the resurrection of the dead, and in the inflictions of wrath on the impenitent forever, Psalm lxxvi. 10, lxii. 11.

IV. GOD IS OMNIPRESENT. That is, his immensity pervades the universe, and filleth all things. It appears that the presence of Deity should be as infinite as his works, and as infinite as his rule and dominion. The ancient doctrine of the unknown spirit being the life of the world, is an imperfect representation of the omnipresence revelation makes known. How sublimely this is presented to us by the psalmist, " Whither shall I go from thy Spirit," &c., Psalm cxxxix. 7. And God asks, " Do I not fill heaven and earth ?" Jer. xxiii. 24.

V. GOD IS OMNISCIENT, OR INFINITE IN KNOWLEDGE. He is everywhere present to know, and discern, and observe. His omniscience extends to all space, and to all creatures. It also embraces all that is past, all that is present, and all that is to come. With God nothing is doubtful, or perplexed, or contingent. He knows all clearly, precisely, and infallibly, Psalm cxxxix. 6 ; Acts xv. 18.

VI. GOD IS ALL-WISE. God is the truly wise Being, the source of all knowledge and intelligence. His wisdom is displayed in all his works. The heavens display the glory of this attribute in an especial degree. The grand and vast solar system, regulated by such simple yet sublime laws. The earth ; the animal creatures ; man in his complex character ; the whole of God's works are replete with the exercise of divine wisdom. Everywhere we see design, arrangement, method, adaptation. There is no deficiency—nothing superfluous—nothing redundant. How brilliantly it shines forth in the pages of revelation ! Well may we exclaim, " O Lord, how manifold are thy works, in wisdom hast thou made them all," Psalm civ. 24 ; see Rom. xi. 33.

OBSERVATIONS.

1. *How glorious a being is God !* How majestic his character ; how venerable his name ; how reverential should be our spirit and conduct towards him ! With what awe should we meditate on his perfections and works !

2. *What an object of confidence for the godly and devout !* The eternal, immutable God his refuge. Power of God his defence. Presence of God his security. Omniscience of God his conscious delight. The wisdom of God his support. With such a friend, how needless distressing fear and blighting care ! Who can be effectually against us if he be for us ? Who can subvert his counsels, frustrate his designs, or pluck us out of his hands ?

3. *The subject is full of terror to the incorrigible sinner.* How terrific an enemy is God ! His power to punish how awful ! His resources how infinite ! His presence how terrible ! His unchangeableness how appalling and overwhelming !

4. *How unlike the idols of the heathen is Jehovah !* Inanimate, senseless, and vain. Ignorant and powerless, and they who trust in them are like unto them.

5. *How precious the Bible !* For here only are these perfections of the Deity clearly revealed to us. The volume of nature is grand, and teaches us the magnificence and the power of the originator ; but in clearness of adaptation to the capacity of men in general is the volume of revelation. Revelation too is the best mirror for beholding the divine works.

HOLINESS OF GOD.

" Glorious in holiness."—EXOD. xv. 11.

By the holiness of God is meant the essential purity and perfection of his moral character. This attribute of Deity is often presented to our consideration in the scriptures. He often proclaimed his holiness to his ancient people, the Jews—" Ye shall be holy, for I the Lord your God am holy."

The seraphim and cherubim cry one to another, " Holy, holy, holy, is the Lord of hosts." He is said to be so holy that he cannot behold evil, nor look on iniquity. He says, by Isaiah the prophet, xliii. 15, " I am the Lord, your holy One." Now, we observe,

I. THAT GOD IS HOLY IN HIS NATURE AND ESSENCE. As a perfect being he is necessarily and infinitely removed from all evil. He is the centre of perfection. His will and mind are holy ; his purposes and counsels are holy. This is the supreme dignity of the divine nature, that it is perfectly holy. This constitutes the moral grandeur and beauty of God ; this, in the language of the text, is his essential glory— " Glorious in holiness." God cannot be otherwise than holy, for he is as necessarily holy as he is necessarily God. Nothing could affect his holiness—it is the immutable brightness of his character, " For in him is no darkness at all."

II. GOD IS HOLY IN ALL HIS WORKS. The first-born sons of glory were created in all the excellency of holiness ; they are called the holy angels. In the creation of man he displayed his holiness, creating him in his perfect and upright likeness. In all the works of nature he made every thing according to the counsels of his own purity and wisdom, and pronounced the whole very good. Whatever proceedeth from his hands must of necessity be holy.

III. GOD IS HOLY IN HIS DOMINION AND GOVERNMENT. All the laws which relate to intellectual and moral beings must be the emanations of his holy mind. Such was the law given to the first of our race ; such was the moral law, " holy, just, and good." So were all the ceremonial institutions, &c. designed to express the holy character of God, and the necessity of holiness in his creatures. However inexplicable to us the ways of God, however clouds and darkness may surround him, yet absolute purity and rectitude are the basis of his throne. He is righteous in all his ways, &c. The laws and principles of the government of God, whether affecting angels, or men, or devils, are all just and holy. There is no unrighteousness in him.

IV. GOD IS HOLY IN HIS WORD. Hence called " the Holy Scriptures." Every word of God is pure. His word must necessarily resemble himself, being the reve-lation of his holy mind. Here the holiness of God is made known to us. Without this we could not have seen it in the works of nature, &c. But the Bible is a mirror of the divine purity. Here he shines forth in all the resplendent rays of holiness. His word, also, is the perfect rule of holiness. Here are holy statutes— holy counsels—holy precepts—holy warnings—holy promises—and invitations to holiness. Here holiness is taught in all its principles, and features, and importance. It is also the instrument of holiness. It tends to the change of the character, and the sanctification of the heart. It cleanses like holy water—purifies and refines as holy fire—it renews as the pure and vital air.

V. GOD IS HOLY, ESPECIALLY IN HUMAN REDEMPTION. The great object of redemption was to exhibit the divine holiness to all creatures and all worlds. He embodied it in the obedience of his Son—he taught it in his doctrines—confirmed it by his miracles—wrote it in crimson characters with his precious blood. The end of man's redemption was his restoration to holiness— " To redeem him from iniquity." Hence the blood of the great sacrifice is represented as " cleansing from all unrighteousness."

VI. GOD IS HOLY IN THE DISPENSATION OF HIS GRACE. The revelation of that gracious dispensation is by the holy and glorious gospel of the blessed God. He calls with a holy calling ; he regenerates and makes men holy ; he imparts his Holy Spirit to dwell in the hearts of his people ; he adopts them into his holy family—he guides their feet in the way of holiness ; he beautifies them with holy virtues. Within them he infuses the holy graces of his Spirit—and they are enabled to have a holy conversation, and to grow in holiness of life, by increasing conformity to his holy likeness.

VII. GOD WILL BE HOLY IN THE DECISIONS OF JUDGMENT. He will then sit on the great white throne of his holiness. He will judge men by his holy law and word. His decisions, both as it regards saints and sinners, men and angels, will be in strict accordance with his holy nature.

OBSERVATIONS.

1. How greatly should God be feared by his saints ! With what awe, and lowli-

ness, and fear, should they draw near to worship him! How evil to use his name lightly, or to worship him with heedless levity!

2. How evil must sin be in his sight! It is the one and only thing that he abhors and hates.

3. We see why sinners must necessarily be excluded from heaven. It is God's holy place; there is his throne and attendants— it is his holy temple.

4. We see the moral grandeur of the gospel. To bring men back to holiness, and thus eventually to God, and to eternal life.

JUSTICE OF GOD.

"Just and right is He."—DEUT. xxxii. 4.

JUSTICE in God is that attribute, by which, according to the purity and rectitude of his nature, all his proceedings are based and regulated. It seems impossible to contemplate a perfect being, without ascribing to him the attribute of justice. The justice of God is repeatedly brought before us in the volume of revelation. He is termed "The Just One," the "Just Lord," "Most Just." He is said to be "without iniquity;" in him, it is said, "there is no unrighteousness; yea, surely God will not do wickedly, neither will the Almighty pervert judgment." Job xxxiv. 17. The more intelligent heathen conceived it necessary to speak of God as the Just One; hence, Plato says, "God is not in anywise unjust, but so far as possible most just." Now the justice of God may be viewed,

I. IN RELATION TO HIMSELF. In the revelation of himself to mankind he has made known the holiness of his nature, and the sovereign right he has to certain prerogatives,—to be glorified, and adored, and served by all his creatures. Now none of these claims will he forego. His glory he will not give to another. He has exhibited his eternal character and will, as absolutely unchangeable, the same yesterday, today, and forever.

II. HE IS JUST TO ALL HIS CREATURES. If pure unmixed justice be essential to God, then injustice cannot proceed from him, even as darkness cannot proceed from the orb of day. But let our thoughts be chiefly limited to his justice to mankind. Now it appears that justice requires that,

1. *He should give to mankind righteous laws.* Laws adapted to their natures, and suited to their powers and condition. The whole moral code may be evidently concentrated in these two;—supreme love to himself as the great and chief good,—and benevolent regard to our neighbor. Now these are so manifestly just and right as to need no proof. Righteous laws must,

2. *Be connected with equitable, that is, with suitable, rewards and punishments.* A good being may grant a reward superprotionate, but he cannot give less than a just equivalent. Thus the apostle says, "God is not unjust to forget your work and labor of love." Hence also, it is written, "he will reward every man according to his works." It does not now require us to show that the punishment of sin, as revealed in scripture, is not beyond the demerit of the transgression. This, at present, we assume. It is essential to justice, that righteous laws, with equitable sanctions,

3. *Be strictly and impartially executed.* That there be no favoritism—no conniving at any guilt, or overlooking iniquity in any transgression. As it regards punishment, God has said, that he will by no means "clear the guilty," and that every one shall reap as they have sown, whether of the flesh, corruption, or of the spirit, life everlasting. But in the exercise of impartial justice to all, the conduct of Deity must embrace both the present and future existence of his responsible creatures. He may justly reward or punish in this state or hereafter. The doctrine of the Saviour's sacrifice does not affect this view of the divine justice, as the atonement of Christ is as essentially a display of holiness and justice, as of goodness and mercy. In the remission of sin, God appears both as a just God and a Saviour. The just, and yet through Christ the justifier of the ungodly.

III. THE EVIDENCES OF THE DIVINE JUSTICE ARE MANY.

1. *They are exhibited in all the laws he has given in his word.* In every enactment of the decalogue shines forth the brightness of the divine justice. The scriptures are a mirror of righteous precepts and equitable laws.

2. *The evidences of divine justice have often been signally evinced in the history of our world.* Observe the tenure of man's primeval condition—his fall and exclusion from paradise. The destruction of the old

world,—overthrow of Sodom and Gomorrah,—the punishment of Pharaoh and his host,—the ruin of impenitent Jerusalem.

3. *There is the evidence of the human conscience.* That internal vicegerent which so powerfully acts upon our powers, and feelings, in responding to the divine claims; in condemning our disobedience, and in smiling upon the path of rectitude and obedience.

4. *The justice of God was most strikingly displayed in our redemption by Christ Jesus.* So just that he inexorably determined to punish sin, and did so in the sufferings of his own Son. So just that he demanded that his law should be exhibited to the universe in brightest characters, and it was so in the immaculate nature and perfect obedience of the Redeemer.

"Here the whole Deity is known,
  Nor dares the creature guess,
Which of the glories brightest shone,
  The justice or the grace."

5. *The justice of God will be displayed in the results of the judgment day,* when he will judge the world in righteousness by Jesus Christ.

APPLICATION.

1. A contemplation of the divine justice should produce reverential awe—holy fear—hatred to sin; and lead us to unfeigned repentance and faith in the Lord Jesus Christ.

2. Here the Christian should find reason for acquiescence in all the divine procedure.

3. The subject is fraught with indescribable terror to the impenitent sinner.

TRUTH AND FAITHFULNESS OF GOD.

"A God of truth."—DEUT. xxxii. 4.

By truth in Deity, we mean that veracity of character and faithfulness of conduct by which he is what his word represents, and never acts contrary to his own engagements. A pure and just God must also be faithful and true. Some of the ancients, with very imperfect notions of God's character and glory, yet supposed him to be clothed in the attribute of truth. Hence one said, "that truth is so great a perfection of God, that if he should render himself visible unto men, he would choose

light for his body and truth for his soul." And it was common for the most enlightened to describe their superior gods, as doing good to mankind and "speaking the truth." God has given a full revelation of this perfection in his holy word—to Moses he proclaimed himself abundant in goodness and truth—he is said to "keep truth for ever."—"Thy mercy is great unto the heavens, and thy truth unto the clouds." Now we observe,

I. GOD IS TRUE AND FAITHFUL IN THE REVELATION HE HAS GIVEN OF HIS OWN CHARACTER AND PERFECTIONS. In the spirituality of his essence—in the eternity of his self-existence—in the almightiness of his power—in the immensity of his knowledge—in the ubiquity of his person—and in all his holy, righteous, benevolent, merciful, and gracious moral perfections. We have no reason to doubt the testimony God hath given of himself.

II. GOD IS FAITHFUL AND TRUE AS IT REGARDS THE DESCRIPTION HE HATH FURNISHED OF HIS WORKS. In the records of scripture we have an account of our world's creation, Genesis i. Now there is nothing existing in the works of nature by which doubt is thrown upon that testimony—the state and the laws of our portion of the universe would tend rather to the establishment of the Mosaic account of the creation; the same remarks apply to the creation and original state of probation of our first parents, the entrance of sin, &c.

III. GOD IS TRUE AND FAITHFUL AS IT REGARDS HIS DIVINE PREDICTIONS. The revelation of future events is with God alone—a great portion of the word of God is formed of these predictions—our appeal must be to those of the past. Hence we might refer to the destruction of the old world, as revealed to Noah—the extensive posterity of Abraham—the future state, &c. of the various tribes—their possession of the land of Canaan—their captivities, sins, and final dispersion among the nations of the earth. So also those prophecies which regarded Egypt, Tyre, Nineveh, Babylon, &c. &c.—especially those prophecies which have gracious respect to the world's Redeemer—the time, the place, the manner of his advent—his ministry, offices, work, sufferings, death, resurrection, and glory. We may just add the predictions published in the visions of John. regarding the Asiatic churches, &c. &c.

IV. GOD IS FAITHFUL AND TRUE IN HIS DECLARATIONS AND PROMISES. How this was insisted upon by Moses, and Joshua, and Solomon, Deuteronomy vii. 9, Joshua xxiii. 4, 1 Kings viii. 56 ; see also Psalm cxlvi. 6. This subject is so rich in illustration as to render choice of incidents difficult. We see it in the promissory engagement with Abraham as it regarded his son—to Moses as it regarded the deliverance of his people, &c.—to Israel often as it regarded his protection and guardian care—to the world, as it regarded the appearance of his own Son—by Jesus too, as it respected the outpouring of the Spirit—also as it regards the progress of divine truth, and the continuance of his church in the world. So also how the experience of all Christians will amply corroborate the truth of God—in forgiving their sins, renewing their hearts, giving needful grace, delivering from evil, hearing their prayers, accepting their offerings, and in communicating rich and unspeakable consolation to their souls.

V. GOD IS FAITHFUL AND TRUE IN THE EXECUTION OF HIS THREATENINGS. In the spiritual death and in the ultimate bodily dissolution of our first parents—in the disastrous results of the flood—in the excision of the Jews as a nation from their position and favor, &c.—and often in the premonitory woes and misery of his incorrigible enemies, he has threatened to drive the wicked away in his wickedness, and how often has it been realized to the very letter ! Haman, Belshazzar, Herod, are a few of the many proofs of its confirmation. This will be awfully exhibited in the everlasting banishment of the wicked in the judgment of the last day.

OBSERVATIONS.

If God is clothed in faithfulness and truth,

1. *Then we ought implicitly to believe his word.* His word is the brightest reflection of his mind, and every saying, whether of comfort or terror, must come to pass. Then acceptable faith in God has respect to all he hath spoken.

2. *This subject is fraught with matter of greatest joy to the Christian.* All the declarations of mercy and goodness, and all the promises of grace and love, are yea and amen. Not one shall fail, and that because God is faithful and true :

" His truth shall firm, unshaken stay,
When heaven and earth have passed away."

3. *We see the spirit which will distinguish the true saint.* He will be the recipient and reflector of God's truth. He will speak only truth—love the truth—walk in the truth—diffuse the truth.

4. *By the truth of God we should urge sinners to flee from the wrath to come.* God is not a man that he should lie, or the son of man that he should repent. Heaven and hell will bear witness to his truth forever.

THE GOODNESS OF GOD.

" I will make all my goodness to pass before thee."—EXOD. xxxiii. 9.

By goodness we mean the benevolence of God—that disposition of Deity which causes him to delight in making his creatures happy. This is not so much an attribute of Deity as it is his essential nature, " For God is love ;" pure, unmixed, infinite love. Goodness, therefore, is rather the essential being and character of God. To this our attention is often invited in the pages of revelation—" O taste and see that the Lord is good." How great is his goodness—" Thy people delighted themselves in thy great goodness." " Thou preventest with the blessings of thy goodness." " My people shall be satisfied with my goodness, saith the Lord." And in the text, " I will make my goodness to pass before thee." Let us consider goodness,

I. IN REFERENCE TO THE DIVINE CHARACTER.

II. THE MANIFESTATION OF HIS GOODNESS TO HIS CREATURES.

I. LET US CONSIDER GOODNESS IN REFERENCE TO THE DIVINE CHARACTER. We remark,

1. *That God is originally and essentially good.* The goodness of God is not derived ; but is the very nature, essence, and habit of his blessed character. He is the fountain, the spring, and source of all goodness. He is essentially good as he is essentially God.

2. *God is absolutely good.* In him there is no mixture of evil—no dark shades of malevolence, or, in the words of inspiration, " No darkness at all." Just as he is

absolutely wise, and almighty, and independent, so he is perfectly and absolutely good.

3. *He is infinitely good.* Good in the most immense degree. His goodness cannot be measured or circumscribed. It is as vast and boundless as his essence. All the goodness existing in angels, and beatified saints, and the godly on earth, is but as a drop from the ocean, or as a ray of light to the beams of noonday splendor, compared with the richness and abundance of the goodness of God. Therefore, God is,

4. *Incomprehensibly good.* We cannot possibly conceive of that which is infinite, so that the goodness of God is higher than all our thoughts—"The breadth, and length, and depth, and height of the love of God passeth knowledge," Eph iii. 19.

5. *God is immutably good.* In him there is no variableness or shadow of turning. His goodness cannot be affected either by addition or diminution; and this immutability of goodness is from everlasting to everlasting; strictly and properly eternal, even as God is eternal. But consider,

II. The manifestation of his goodness to his creatures. He said to Moses, "I will make my goodness to pass before thee." The goodness of God may be considered,

1. *In its general manifestation.* In this sense the whole earth is full of it. He is good to all; he careth and provideth for every living thing; he openeth his beneficent hand, and all his creatures are supplied with needful good. Psalms xxxvi. 6; cxlv. 15, 16; civ. 21, &c. Now, of this general goodness man highly participates. The resources of creation are all for him; the numberless blessings with which this world is crowded are given to him. Every sense is met with corresponding enjoyment, every reasonable desire by the riches of God's bounty. His own frame, and the constitution of his own mind, are all adapted for enjoyment. Even his pains are monitors to warn him of his approaching peril; and for his maladies, both the surface and the interior of the earth are full of healing remedies. Now, this general goodness of God, like the atmosphere, extends to the whole earth, and to every living thing.

2. *God's special goodness is displayed to the objects of his divine complacency.* How it was manifest to our first parents in Eden! What dignity, felicity, and blessedness it conferred! How richly it is manifested to the glorified spirits and angels above! The bright effulgent beams of glory surround them—they drink of the rivers of his pleasure. At God's right hand, as the peculiar provision of his spiritual goodness, is fulness of joy, and pleasures forevermore.

3. *But the brightest displays of the divine goodness were manifested in the world's redemption.* This was the overflowing springtide of divine goodness, in which all the attributes of Deity were co-sharers in the wondrous work. "God so loved the world," &c. "He spared not his own Son," &c. Laid upon the Son of his highest delights the sin of the world. No previous development of goodness had startled angels, but this overpowered even their benevolent conceptions:—

> "The first archangel never saw
> So much of God before."

OBSERVATIONS.

1. *Goodness is that quality, or nature of God, in which he comes especially near to us.* His grandeur might overawe us, his power alarm, his holiness overwhelm; but in the habiliments of goodness he comes near to us as our Father. Here we may behold him as he passes by, and not be consumed.

2. *God in his goodness also draws man near to himself.* We now contemplate him with confidence. We may speak and commune. His goodness should attract us to him—bind our hearts to him—fill us with love to him—cause our hearts to overflow with grateful praise.

3. *God in his goodness should be the object of our imitation.* We should be followers of God as dear children—imbibe his spirit—evince the divine nature within us.

THE GOODNESS OF GOD TO HIS SAINTS

"Oh, how great is thy goodness, which thou hast laid up for them that fear thee!"—Psalm xxxi. 19.

God's goodness fills creation. It distinguishes all his works, and is the grand principle of his universal government. Only the obstinately rebellious deprive themselves of its rich blessings; and in this life even the unbelieving and wicked enjoy the tokens of his unlimited benevolence. But it is a most consolatory doctrine that he is especially good to his saints, to those who know his name, and put their trust in him. These partake of that goodness which includes the divine complacency and delight. Hence the appropriate language of the text, "How great is thy goodness which thou hast laid up," &c. God's especial and abundant goodness is laid up for his people,

I. IN THE COUNSELS OF HIS LOVE. God's affections and delights were with his people before the world was. He predetermined the privileges they should possess, and the blessings they should enjoy. Hence, in the prospective designs of Jehovah, his kindness, and mercy, and grace, were treasured up for all who should obey the truth, and believe in his name. It is laid up,

II. IN THE FULNESS OF HIS WORD. God's word is designed for the illumination and direction of mankind. It is for the benefit of the whole human race. But its precious promises, its rich consolations, its sweet assurances, its refreshing counsels, its hallowed instructions, are only efficiently enjoyed by them that fear him. Others may read, and admire, and be informed ; but the saint digests, meditates, and delights in it, even as one who rejoiceth in great spoil. And who can tell the goodness which is treasured up here :—

> "It sweetly cheers our drooping hearts
> In this dark vale of tears :
> Life, light, and joy, it still imparts,
> And quells our rising fears."

This goodness is laid up,

III. IN THE WELL-ORDERED COVENANT. That covenant of mercy and grace ratified by the inexpressibly precious blood of the cross ; that new and better covenant, of which Jesus is the adorable mediator. The blessings of this covenant include—the saint's high and celestial calling—his justification and remission of sins—his acceptance and peace with God—his adoption into the divine family—his perseverance and continuance in the knowledge and love of God—his triumphant death, bliss, final resurrection, and everlasting glory. Thus, exhaustless blessings are laid up in this covenant for them that fear him.

IV. IN THE FULNESS OF THE MEDIATOR. In Jesus all fulness dwells. He is full of grace and truth ; and this fulness, both of wisdom and love, is for the benefit of them that fear him. It is only believers who receive out of this fulness. They appropriate its riches by the exercise of continuous living faith. Now, this divine goodness, treasured up in Christ, comprehends all spiritual blessings ; grace sufficient for all the exigencies of his people ; that by which they have ability for every duty, comfort in every trouble, and deliverance from every peril. Christ Jesus is the grand depository of all needful good for them that fear him. God's goodness is also laid up,

V. IN THE ARRANGEMENTS OF A BENIGNANT PROVIDENCE. God's kindly regards are identified with all the dispensations of his moral government. His dominion is an especial source of joy and gladness to his people ; his providential goodness respects all that the godly man is, and has. It includes the exercise of the divine benignity to his family and dwelling—the divine care of his health and life—the divine blessing upon his basket and store—the divine direction of his steps. All the Lord's ways of providence are gracious and merciful to them that fear him. "The Lord is their shepherd," &c. I observe that the goodness of the Lord is laid up,

VI. IN THE ETERNAL RESOURCES OF GLORY. The treasures of grace are infinite and inexhaustible ; how, then, shall we describe the riches of everlasting life ! God has laid up dignified crowns—exalted thrones—princely sceptres—boundless inheritances—floods of meridian, celestial light—and oceans of unutterable felicity. A personal knowledge, an adequate power of contemplation, with a large, copious, and clear ability of expression, are wanting to speak rightly of the eternal goodness which God has laid up, &c.

APPLICATION.

Let the subject be a test,

1. *Of character.* Do we fear God with a holy, filial, affectionate feeling of reverence and delight in him ? Our subject is limited to this class, and to this only. Let the subject,

2. *Be a source of encouragement.* To the seeking sinner and penitent inquirer O yes ! to these we preach a God of infinite goodness, and one who ever waits to be gracious to the lowly and contrite, and such as tremble at his word. Let the subject fill with consolation,

3. *The hearts of the righteous.* How ex-

alted your state, how rich your privileges, how full, and sure, and exhaustless your enjoyments! Poor in yourselves, how rich in God's love! Pilgrims in the world, yet how enrapturing the hope of enjoying all that God has laid up for you in the land of bliss that is afar off!

EXCELLENCY OF GOD'S LOVING-KINDNESS.

"How excellent is thy loving-kindness, O God! therefore the children of men put their trust under the shadow of thy wings."—PSALM xxxvi. 7.

TRUE religion consists in knowing God —loving God—enjoying God—praising God. How all these traits are exhibited in the character of the psalmist—how adapted to guide, cheer, and strengthen the godly in all generations! Observe,

I. THE PIOUS EXCLAMATION.
II. THE INFERENCE DRAWN FROM IT.

I. THE PIOUS EXCLAMATION. "How excellent," &c. "Loving-kindness." God's kindness, flowing from love. One the source of the other—God is love. This is his essential nature, pure unmixed goodness. Thou art good and thou doest good. Now this is evidenced in the kindness of God towards us. It is seen in the world we inhabit. The earth is full of the kindness, &c. In the government of God, all is governed by the laws of righteous goodness. Especially in the world's redemption, Titus iii. 4. Also in the gracious dealings of God with his people in their conversion, regeneration, sanctification, comfort, &c. But the excellency of the loving-kindness of God is the subject of the psalmist's exclamation; "How excellent,"
(1.) In its infinitude—passeth knowledge.
(2.) In its freeness—pure grace.
(3.) In its superior and present sweetness.
(4.) In its unchangeableness.
(5.) In its perpetuity.
II. THE INFERENCE DRAWN FROM IT. "Therefore the children of men," &c. That is, the pious of mankind. Many are godless, careless, &c. "They that know thy name," &c.
1. Their peril is supposed. Danger from men, fallen spirits, storms and tempests.
2. God is their refuge. Shadow of thy wings—figure of the hen, or perhaps the wings of the cherubim, which covered the mercy-seat. How secure, &c.
3. Confidence and trust are expressed. Fly to God—dwell in God—the name of God, &c. In temptation, affliction, death, &c.

APPLICATION.

1. How God should be adored and loved!
2. Our happy privilege. Invites,
3. Sinners to come to it.

MERCY OF GOD.

"Unto thee, O Lord, belongeth mercy."—PSALM lxii. 12.

ONE of the most interesting characteristics of the Deity to fallen man is that of mercy. Angels may have noon-tide blessedness from the exercise of the divine goodness. But sinful dust and ashes overwhelmed with the misery of their state, require the interposition of mercy. Mercy in a certain sense may be considered a modification of the divine goodness, having for its objects, the guilty and the miserable. It differs from pity, as that may be called forth by the wretchedness of those who have had no share in procuring their adversities. But mercy regards its objects as miserable through their own personal guilt, and voluntary transgression. How delightful that the great and august Being we have been contemplating as holy, and just, and true, that unto him in an especial and infinite degree belongeth mercy! We might argue the divine mercifulness, from the benevolence of God, from the impress on the human conscience as to its excellency, and from the bounty which he is continually bestowing on the ungodly. But let us look at it, as it is resplendently exhibited in the volume of eternal truth. Notice,

I. THE DECLARATIONS AND DESCRIPTIONS OF THE DIVINE MERCY WITH WHICH THE HOLY SCRIPTURES ABOUND. He is the " Lord God merciful;" "Keeping mercy for thousands." His mercifulness is said to reach the heavens. He is "of great mercy;" "The Father of mercies;" "The God of all mercy." He is represented, as "rich in mercy;" that he "delighteth in mercy." We read of "his tender mercy." "The multitude of his mer cies." His mercies are said to be "over all his works," "and his mercy is from everlasting to everlasting." And it is reiterated in his word, that his "mercy endureth for ever."

II. NOTICE SOME OF THE EXERCISES OF THE DIVINE MERCY. It triumphed in the day of man's apostacy and ruin. It was exercised towards the most notorious sinners both in the Old and New Testament times. Manasseh, Nebuchadnezzar, the woman who was a sinner, the dying thief, Saul of Tarsus. To the inhabitants of Nineveh, and to the sinners at Jerusalem. These are but a few out of the many instances of the exercise of the divine mercy. Observe,

III. THE EMBODYMENT OF THE DIVINE MERCY IN THE PERSON OF THE REDEEMER. He is emphatically "the mercy promised to the fathers." His mission was one of pure mercy. His incarnation was the advent of mercy. His offices were all identified with the intentions of mercy. His doctrines were doctrines of mercy. His invitations, yea, and even his warnings, were the rich displays of his mercy. His work in all its variety of duties was one great work of mercy. His miracles were miracles of mercy. His sufferings and death were for the opening of a wide and deep channel of mercy. His resurrection, and ascension, and pleading in heaven, are all essential to the communication of the divine mercy.

IV. THE PUBLICATION OF MERCY IN THE GLAD TIDINGS OF THE GOSPEL. The gospel is the grand amnesty between God and a rebellious world; the revelation of his mercy in and through Jesus Christ. How merciful its provision—how merciful its addresses—how merciful its conditions—how free and universal is the mercy offered in the gospel! How vast the blessings of mercy which it publisheth! Mercy forgiving,—healing,—renewing,—sanctifying,—comforting,—preserving,—sustaining,—upholding,—restraining,—and finally bestowing the crown of eternal life. Salvation in its origin, progress, and consummation, is entirely of the divine mercy.

REMARKS.

1. The mercy of God is exercised in strict harmony with justice and holiness. It has been pertinently said, that justice seeks a fit object, mercy a fit occasion.

Justice looks to what is deserved, mercy to what is needed. Justice is never exercised unmercifully, nor mercy unjustly. God is infinitely just in punishing the incorrigible, and infinitely merciful in pardoning the penitent sinner. There is no clashing of interests in the exercise of the attributes of Deity.

2. We observe all men are the objects of the divine mercy. Equally needing it, and to whom it is equally announced. In a state of nature, guilt is the condition of every man, from the most moral to the most debased, and all must therefore have recourse to the fountain which mercy has opened for sin and uncleanness. As it is with sinners, so is it with saints. None are too holy to dispense with mercy. It must be by the exercise of divine mercy that their salvation must be carried on from the foundation-stone, to the completion of the superstructure.

3. Mercy flows to all men through the same channel. God is merciful to no man abstractedly and alone, but to all through the mediation of the better and merciful covenant. In Christ mercy rejoiceth against judgment. In him "mercy and truth met together, and righteousness and peace kissed each other."

4. The mercy of God is ever associated with believing penitence and prayer. A penitence which is the forsaking of all sin, and the lowly returning of the soul to God. "Let the wicked forsake his ways," &c. "Whosoever confesseth and forsaketh his sin shall find mercy." How appropriate then the prayer of the psalmist, "Have mercy upon me, O God." And of the publican, "God be merciful to me a sinner."

5. The divine mercy towards us must be the model of our mercy towards our fellow-men; see Matt. vi. 14, also xviii. 28, &c.

6. The divine mercy will be celebrated in the anthems of the redeemed forever and ever.

FORBEARANCE AND LONG-SUFFERING OF GOD.

"Forbearance and long-suffering."—ROM. ii. 4.

MERCY extended to guilty and impenitent sinners is long-suffering. Mercy restraining justly deserved wrath is forbearance.

Both of these are attributed to God in his holy word. Both forbearance and long-suffering are also inseparable from the patience of God, Rom. xv. 5. The text refers us to the riches of the forbearance and long-suffering of God. God abounds in these, is full of them, just as he abounds and overflows in mercy and goodness. Let us notice,

I. IN WHAT THE FORBEARANCE AND LONG-SUFFERING OF GOD CONSIST.

II. THE PRINCIPLES ON WHICH THEY ARE GROUNDED.

III. THE EXHIBITIONS WHICH HAVE BEEN GIVEN TO MANKIND. And,

IV. THE LESSONS WHICH THEY TEACH US. We ask then,

I. IN WHAT THE FORBEARANCE AND LONG-SUFFERING OF GOD CONSIST. Notice,

1. *The objects of forbearance and long-suffering.* These are sinful men. They are not necessary to holy, obedient beings. All sin deserves punishment, the punishment of death. But sinners live in the midst of their sins, often for years upon years of uninterrupted transgression. Wherefore do the wicked thus live? The answer is found in the forbearance and long-suffering of God. He is slow to anger, unwilling to punish, and delighteth in mercy. Not only unconverted men, but even the children of God are also the objects of the divine forbearance. Their manifold infirmities, their numerous back-slidings, their dulness and slothfulness in his service; their barrenness in the virtues and graces of holiness. All these require the extension of God's forbearance and long-suffering.

2. *In what way are forbearance and long-suffering exercised?* In the suspension of deserved punishment,—in their continuance in a state of probation,—in the supply of the divine bounties in the midst of their guiltiness,—in the invitations and means of grace which are employed for their restoration to God.

II. THE PRINCIPLES ON WHICH THEY ARE GROUNDED. They are not to be confounded with the indifference which some ascribe to Deity; nor to his disregard of the moral character and condition of his creatures. But,

1. *To the mercifulness of his nature.* He is rich in compassion, and he commiserates the woful condition of sinful men. He sincerely desires their well-being and salvation. He has demonstrated how he loves their souls, in the provisions of redemption, and thus he exercises long-suffering towards them.

2. *To the power which he ever possesses to punish.* By the exercise of forbearance, &c. the sinner does not thereby acquire a power to evade the threatened and justly deserved punishment. The sinner is every moment before him, always within his power; at any instant, therefore, he has only to will, and the probation of the sinner ends, and his everlasting misery commences.

3. *On his knowledge of the ultimate efficiency of the means he employs.* All the saints in heaven have been, both before and after their conversion, the subjects of the divine forbearance. How he had exercised his long-suffering to Manasseh, before the great and gracious end was accomplished! How to the dying malefactor, &c. How to the inhabitants of Jerusalem. How to the persecuting Saul, &c., &c.

4. *On the principle of displaying his justice before assembled worlds on the last day.* By this forbearance of God the sinner is left without excuse; thus every mouth will be stopped; like the man without the wedding garment, they must be speechless. Thus God will appear as the righteous governor of the world, and as the just judge of his accountable creatures.

5. *On the subserviency even of the wicked to the purposes of his providence.* The wicked are often God's sword. He sometimes employs pestilence, and earthquake, and storms, to fulfil his will in the infinitude of his righteous judgments. But he also often allows the wrath of man and the cruelty of man to be exercised in punishing one class of the guilty, and thus also to fill up their own iniquitous cup. By his forbearance also to the vilest of mankind, his people are tried and tested, their example and spirit also shine more resplendently, and an opportunity is given for the maturity of the divine image within them. In the world his people are to show forth the praises of him who has delivered them from its sinful influence and spirit.

III. OBSERVE THE EXHIBITIONS WHICH GOD HAS GIVEN TO MANKIND OF HIS FORBEARANCE AND LONG-SUFFERING. One hundred and twenty years after the total depravity of the old world, were its guilty inhabitants spared, 1 Pet. iii. 20. It was greatly displayed to the despotical Pharaoh. Wrath was restrained in the case of the Amorites, until their cup became full. For almost countless ages they have shone towards idolatrous lands, Hindoston, China, &c. They are exhibited daily to notorious and aged transgressors. Every living being is a monument of God's forbearance and long-suffering. Consider then,

IV. THE LESSONS WHICH THEY TEACH US.

1. *The benevolent character of God.* How truly is it manifest that God is love! How conspicuous does his goodness shine forth! How true that his tender mercy is over all his works!

2. *The grateful love which God justly claims.* Is it too much that the blessed God demands the grateful affections of the heart, the warmest emotions of the soul? If every feeling ascended to him in sacred, delightful thanksgiving, it could not be commensurate to his long-suffering and forbearance towards us.

3. *The improvement of our opportunities the subject suggests.* While he speaks in mercy let us hearken and obey, for

" While the lamp holds out to burn,
    The vilest sinner may return."

And ought he not? is it not his duty, interest, salvation, to return?

4. *The riches of the forbearance and long-suffering of God may be exhausted.* For,

" Mercy knows the appointed bounds,
    And turns to vengeance there."

When once the master of the feast has risen up and shut to the door, no penitency nor prayers, no agony or entreaty, will avail; and hell will be lit up with the fearful, unbearable reflection that the God whose wrath they endure, was rich in forbearance and long-suffering even towards them.

PRACTICAL APPLICATION OF THE DIVINE OMNIPOTENCE.

" I am the almighty God; walk before me, and be thou perfect."—GENESIS xvii. 1.

ABRAHAM was one of the most conspicuous and distinguished saints of the old dispensation. In all respects he was an extraordinarily godly man. His strong, self-denying faith; his prompt obedience; his family discipline; his power in prayer; his intimacy with Jehovah. Then if you look at him as the father of the faithful, as the root of the Jewish nation, and as one who stood out in bold and holy relief as a worshipper of the true God, in the midst of ignorance, superstition, and idolatry. Our text relates to the revelation God made to him when he was ninety years old. Observe,

I. THE ATTRIBUTE CLAIMED BY JEHOVAH. "I am the almighty God." This passage has been rendered God all-sufficient. Either representation will do. Both are true, and one is involved in the other. By almightiness in Deity we mean power to do whatsoever he desires to do. Whatever is fitting for a holy, wise, and good being. He cannot sin, nor love it; nor deny himself. He cannot change, &c. He can do nothing arguing inconsistency with his own blessed perfections.

1. *He is almighty in creation.* He could create an infinity of worlds. He can create without difficulty—he speaks, and it is done. The stupendous heavens are the works of his fingers. Had he pleased, he could have raised up children from the stones, &c. to Abraham. How sublime is the first chapter of Genesis, ver. 3–6, and he just *said it.* His word gave the command, and matter was modified and arranged, &c.

2. *He is almighty to govern and uphold.* "He upholdeth all things by the word," &c. It may be said, all the departments of the world have their respective laws. True, but they are *his.* Go from link to link, to the highest and last, and that is in God's hand. "He doeth according to his will among the armies," &c., Job xxvii. 7. But in the government of all things he has to provide for every existing creature. The intellectual hosts of glory,—mankind, every living thing. His kingdom ruleth over all. The eyes of all wait on him.

3. *He is almighty to redeem.* Redemption is represented as his great work. His own arm brought salvation. He made bare his holy arm. He displayed this in counteracting the powers of hell. In removing the mountains of opposition and difficulty, &c. In uniting interests which appeared at utter variance, and in opening a brilliant path-way from the gates of hell to the celestial paradise for the universal family of man.

"'Twas great to speak a world from naught,
  'Twas greater to redeem.''

I need not add to these observations, that he is therefore God all-sufficient. Sufficient as the protection of his saints; as their support, as their portion, as their everlasting all. Notice then,

II. THE COUNSEL GIVEN. "Walk before me," &c. Now this counsel implied,

1. *A constant recognition of God.* "Before me." Remember my eyes are upon thee. Thy bed and path. Remember I am ever near thee. Thou canst not evade, &c. Keep up a lively sense of this. It will produce holy, vigilant fear. It will produce diligent obedience. It will produce a constant desire to please me. It will also be a source of confidence. The counsel included,

2. *Progression in the divine life.* "Walk before me." Sometimes we must stand still, and see the glory of God. But experimental religion is truly progressive. "Speak unto the children of Israel," &c. "Go from strength to strength," &c. "This one thing I do," &c. "I press," &c. "Give all diligence," &c. "Be steadfast, &c. always abounding," &c.

3. *Maturity of holiness.* "Be thou perfect," or be sincere and upright. Now there was a reason for this. He had dissembled before Pharaoh. He had adopted unwarrantable means for the fulfilment of the divine promise as to a son, &c. Now God says, Be upright—sincere. Believe me entirely, always, for every thing. This integrity in some respects is the perfection of godliness, &c. But we may include in this, advancement in purity and excellency, and vigor of the graces of godliness. Also, setting the Lord always before us. Aiming at conformity to his likeness, resemblance to his image. "Be ye holy, for I am holy." Also, *as* I am holy. The entire sanctification for which the apostle prays, refers to this. "I pray God that he may sanctify you wholly, body, soul, and spirit." For this we should strive, labor, pray, believe.

APPLICATION.

1. *Learn the invincible defence, and foundation of the Christian.* "God almighty." Well may we exclaim, "Who can harm," &c. "If God be for us who can be against us?" This consideration should animate and encourage in difficulties, in oppression, in peril. "Walk before the Almighty God," &c.

2. *A recognition of God is ever desirable.* It tends to keep us in the way of duty. Besides, it will be well done. Especially it will preserve us from self, and from the vain applause of men.

3. *Never be satisfied with past attainments.* If any ought, it was Abraham, especially when ninety years old, after serving God for more than thirty years. God thus speaks to me, to each of you, to all, " Walk before me," &c.

4. *To the sinner he says,* "Turn ye, turn ye, why will ye die?" Oh hear, obey, and live.

THE GOOD AND COMPASSIONATE CHARACTER OF GOD.

"For thou, Lord, art good, and ready to forgive; and plenteous in mercy unto all them that call upon thee."—PSALM lxxxvi. 5.

To the possession of acceptable religion it is essential that we have a right knowledge of God, and of his will concerning us. Two views are extensively entertained of Jehovah, both of which are derogatory to his character, and which rob him of his glory. One of these is the exhibition of God as a being perfectly indifferent to human conduct, and who is regardless of the actions of mankind, and who will exercise indiscriminate mercy to all classes and grades of character. Well has the poet said,

"A God all mercy is a God unjust."

And the solemn declaration of God, that he will by no means spare the guilty, proves this to be one of the stratagems of the devil, and one of the deceitful fallacies of the human heart. The other view of Deity is that which clothes him in habiliments of wrath, and burning with hot displeasure towards the great mass of his creatures— whose anger it is difficult to appease, and whose mercy but few of the children of men can obtain. How different the character of God as given by the pen of inspiration—how glorious, and beautiful, and consolatory the truth of the text, " For thou, Lord," &c. Our text directs us,

I. TO TWO OF THE LEADING PERFECTIONS OF DEITY.

II. To HIS GRACIOUS DISPOSITION TO-WARDS THE GUILTY. And,

III. To THE CHARACTERISTICS OF THOSE WHO MAY FREELY BE FORGIVEN.

Our text leads us to notice,

I. TWO OF THE LEADING PERFECTIONS OF DEITY. " For thou, Lord, art good."

1. *The goodness of God.* By goodness we understand benevolence—a desire to diffuse happiness. Goodness is universally associated with kindness and beneficence, or liberality. God's goodness is the constant theme of divine revelation. He proclaimed this as a part of his blessed name, " abundant in goodness." This was the subject of the ancient songs of his people— " Oh, give thanks unto the Lord, for he is good." This goodness of God is great— the earth is said to be full of it—it endureth forever—it is said to follow the good man, and to satisfy all his desires. " We shall be satisfied with the goodness of thy house," &c. The evidences of the divine goodness are all around us. How can we avoid them, or fail to see them ? The glory of the divine goodness is seen in the outstretched heaven—the starry firmament. The beauty of the divine goodness is seen in all the rich and varied works of his hands—the beneficence of his goodness is seen in giving us rain from heaven, and fruitful seasons—the extent of the divine goodness is manifest, in that it is over all his works. Our formation—our faculties— our wonderful bodies—our temporal blessings—the air we inhale—the food, the raiment, all our comforts, &c. The marvellous patience of the divine goodness extends to the unworthy and vile, to the just and the unjust, &c. Oh yes, what a striking truth it is, " Thou, Lord, art good," &c. Our text refers,

2. *To the mercy of God.* Mercy is kindness to the unworthy—goodness to the undeserving. God is good to the holy angels in heaven, but not merciful. To our first parents in Eden, but not till after the fall, was he merciful. Merciful and gracious is the character Deity claims. Now, the great evidences of the divine mercy are seen in the redemption of the world by Christ Jesus. He spared the guilty, and devised the means of their restoration to holiness and salvation. The sacrifice he gave for this, is the most stupendous exhibition of mercy the world ever saw. It astonished angels—it surpasseth knowledge —and in the continued overtures of love and kindness to the wicked this mercy is still displayed. Long-suffering and forbearance is not the whole ; but expostulation, entreaty, continuance of means, &c. All the means of grace—all the kind providences—all the opportunities of repentance, are instances of the divine mercy. Of mercy God is said to be plenteous. In him it is an infinite fountain, a boundless ocean. As the light of the sun is plenteous—as the waters of the sea—as the air which surrounds the earth—so mercy is plenteous, infinite, exhaustless, and eternal. Notice,

II. HIS GRACIOUS DISPOSITION TOWARDS THE GUILTY. He will not only forgive sinners, but he is ready, quite willing, not backward ; he desires to do it—he delights to do it—he gave his Son, that, consistently with the claims of holiness and truth, sinners might be saved. He is ready to forgive the greatest of sinners—" Though your sins be as scarlet," &c. Though like the thick black cloud, &c.

1. *He is ready to forgive the most aggravated sinner.* Whose sins have been aggravated by many mercies, privileges, light, opportunities, &c. Jews, all sinners. Who shed his precious blood.

2. *He is ready to forgive the oldest sinners.* With all your infirmities—with all your train of years of ingratitude—with all your inability to do much for his cause and glory—at the eleventh hour, &c.

3. *He is ready to forgive all sinners.* No exception—no book of reprobation—no one will find himself excluded. Yet notice,

III. THE CHARACTERISTICS OF THOSE WHO MAY BE THUS FREELY FORGIVEN. " Unto all them who call upon him." This is just in accordance with his gracious declaration, " Whosoever shall call," &c. Application for mercy ensures it—ensures it to all. This calling is praying—asking for it—seeking it—knocking at the door. It must be the call of conscious need—a sense of our want of it—the plague of sin felt— the evil of sin deplored—spiritual healing desired.

1. *The call of earnest importunity.* The opposite of languor, indifference, or formality—as the drowning man calls for help— as the lost man calls for direction—as the starving man for food—as Jacob, " Lord, I

will not," &c.—as the Syrophenician woman, pressing and urging the suit.

2. *The call of faith in God's readiness.*
A belief of the truth—the test of the truth
of the gospel—a persuasion that God will
honor his word, fulfil his promise.

3. *Calling on the name of the Lord Jesus
Christ.* Christ must be our plea—our
foundation—to him we must refer, &c.
Christ is the meritorious Mediator. Through
him alone we can come to God, and for his
sake be forgiven. In his name is preached
remission of sins.

APPLICATION.

1. *Learn the great claims God has upon
every one of us.* Upon our love, and gratitude, and obedience.

2. *How cheering the revelation of divine
mercy.* Without it, despair would have
settled upon our world forever.

3. *How gracious the way of salvation.*
To call upon God for it.

4. *How desirable that each should experience, realize it.* And now we say to you,
as the mariners said to Jonah, " Awake,
thou sleeper, and call upon thy God."

THE NAME OF GOD THE CHRISTIAN'S
SECURITY.

" The name of the Lord is a strong tower: the
righteous runneth into it, and is safe."—Prov.
xviii. 10.

Our text is one of those very consolatory
declarations in which the word of God
abounds, and which all Christians so very
much require. The Christian is weak,
exposed to the malevolent attacks of fallen
spirits, and ever liable to sorrow, disap-
pointment, and trouble. The chief idea
implied, and which is not expressed in the
text, is the good man's peril. He is exposed to danger—a sheep among wolves—
a vessel exposed to the raging storms of the
mighty deep—a pilgrim, passing through
an enemy's country. The apostle has expressed this state in two sentences, " Fightings without and fears within." What is
ne to do? The text gives a comforting
reply. " The name of the Lord," &c.

I. The name of the Lord.

II. Its metaphorical representation.

III. The safety it affords.

These are the three topics of the text.
Let us consider,

I. The name of the Lord. God has

many names. Jehovah is one of the greatest, and signifies To Be, and expresses the
self-existence of the Deity. Oilion signifies the Most High, God's supremacy over
all beings and all worlds. Al-Shadi signifies All-sufficiency, usually translated
Almighty, God all-sufficient. Jehovah Sa-
baoth, Lord of Hosts. Adoni signifies Lord
or King, and refers to God's supreme authority and glory. But we shall consider
the text as referring chiefly to God's comprehensive name, as revealing his nature,
and perfections, and will, in his holy word,
Exod. xxxiii. 18, see also xxxiv. 5. Now
here is the revelation of God's name, as it
most concerns sinful man ; and is it not
just adapted to his fallen condition and
misery ? But the Messiah is also called
the name of God. Hear his voice and provoke him not, " For my name," &c. God's
merciful name is only so through Christ
Jesus. God's good, merciful, and gracious
name, especially as revealed in the redemption of the world, is a strong tower, &c.
Consider,

II. Its metaphorical representation.
" A strong tower." Often described as a
rock, high tower, fortress, refuge. A strong
tower must have,

1. *A deep and massive foundation.* On
this its security chiefly depends, especially
in case of siege, &c. The house which
stood upon the rock resisted the winds and
the rain. The church is built upon a rock,
therefore, &c. The immutability of Jehovah is the firm basis of this tower—he
changes not, he repents not, he is ever and
forever the same. A strong tower,

2. *Must have impregnable walls.* I need
not say next to the basis these are of essential importance. The almighty power of
God are the walls of defence. That arm
which marshalled the stars, that gave birth,
and form, and harmony, and stability to
the universe, see Eph. iii. 20, &c.

3. *A strong tower must have the means
of resisting an enemy.* Now these are the
infinite resources of Jehovah. All the machinery of his providence—all the irresistible energies of his mind—all the creatures
of his hands, he can convert into instruments of peril and death to his foes and the
foes of his people. Hail, lightning, darkness, flies, pestilence, mildew, angelic interference, all can be employed to execute
his will.

4. *Durability of material must be looked*

for in a strong tower. The hardest stone the rock could yield or the quarry present, was selected for this purpose, &c. Now, God is the enduring defence of his people. He abides through all ages—he is the everlasting God—inhabits eternity—he wearies not, fails not. Go back to the persecuted of the sixteenth and seventeenth centuries —to the early sufferings of the Christian church—to the martyrdom of prophets—to the early Jews—to the patriarchs. All his attributes endure forever. Observe,

III. THE SAFETY IT AFFORDS. "The righteous runneth," &c. Safety is the grand end proposed. Observe,

1. *The inquirer after righteousness runneth into it, and is safe from the guilt of sin.* Convinced of sin, condemned by the law, conscience alarmed, he seeks safety. God in the gospel opens his heart to him, "Return unto me," &c. "Turn ye, turn ye, why will ye die," &c. At length he obeys, and by faith makes God his habitation, his strong tower, obtains peace, and is saved. There is now no condemnation, he has hope and joy through believing.

2. *The tempted Christian runneth into it, and is safe from the assaults of the devil.* Who has subtlety, daring, or power sufficient to conflict with the fallen leader of the hosts of hell? In himself the Christian would necessarily be worsted, but he uses the weapon all-prayer, and by this runs into the high tower and is saved. We observe,

3. *The righteous in trouble run into this tower, and are kept or delivered.* The Christian is called to bear trouble, "they that will live godly," &c. It is through "much tribulation," &c. "Call upon me in the day," &c. And thus by prayer he runneth into this tower and he is delivered, and God glorified.

4. *The righteous in death runneth into it, and are saved from the power of the last enemy.* All human resources then fail. All refuges of lies, these are swept away. Society, scenes of pleasure, social circle, all, all fail. God is then the hope of the righteous. When flesh and heart fail, God is the strength of the heart, &c. Thus died Moses, thus David. Stephen amid the showers of stones. This is dying in the Lord—running into him, and committing the soul into his merciful hands.

APPLICATION.

1. *Is God your strong tower?* Can you say to God, thou art my God? This God is my God forever, &c.

2. *Are you righteous?* I mean evangelically so, by justifying grace, &c. Do you feel that you have chosen God for your portion, &c. How cheering is the text! You need a refuge, a defence. God is such for all seasons and circumstances. Rejoice, &c. "Happy art thou, O Israel," &c.

3. *Now choose the character and the portion of the righteous.* Now by penitence and faith return to him, &c.

CREATION.

"In the beginning God created the heavens and the earth."—GEN. i. 1.

IT does not follow from these words that the original matter of which our world was composed, was brought out of nothing at the period to which the Mosaic account of the creation refers. It has been conjectured by our first critics, that this verse states a truth antecedent to the events which follow in the chapter. It is clear too that the account of the creation must be confined to our earth, and that it was not designed to relate to the solar system, or starry worlds, (see Bush's admirable notes on Genesis, where the apparent difficulties are learnedly and satisfactorily removed.) Our present design is to refer to a few thoughts which the contemplation of the creation of our world is calculated to produce. Observe,

I. THE SUBLIME DESCRIPTION THE SCRIPTURES PRESENT. The supreme Being is introduced in all his self-existing and independent majesty and glory. He steps forth to give palpable form to the purposes of his infinitely wise and benevolent mind. He proclaims his authoritative mandate, and the elements of nature obey him. He says, "let it be," and "it is." He commands, and it stands fast. His voice possesses omnific energy. His volitions are fraught with almighty power. He says, "let there be light," and light instantly shines forth, the fairest, unconscious image of its creator. He says, let there be a firmament. &c., and it was so. Let there be earth and sea. Let there be herbs and grass. Let there be lights in the firmament, or let them now shine. Let there be animated creatures in the air, on the earth, and in the sea. And then with extraordinary marks of dignified attention it is written, " So God created man in his own image," &c.

II. THE ORDER AND ARRANGEMENT WHICH WERE DISPLAYED. Light was first formed to give visibility to the works of the divine hands. Then the different elements were separated. Light and darkness,—the waters above and those beneath,—the earth and the sea. The various orders of creatures were destined to their appropriate spheres of existence and action. And these various elements were prepared with sustenance before the creatures were formed. Then the power of reproduction was given both to the vegetable and animal kingdoms. When the palace was finished and the domain of earthly magnificence completed, then man the Lord of the whole was introduced into the Eden of the new and fair creation.

III. THE WISDOM AND POWER OF GOD WHICH WERE MANIFEST. The endless variety of indescribable beauty were evidences of God's wisdom and knowledge. The ease with which all was effected by the divine power. A word from the Omnipotent One was enough. " The works of the Lord are great, and sought out of all them who have pleasure therein." " O Lord, how manifold are thy works," &c. How striking these ideas are rendered when it is remembered that all nature is formed of only two or three original elements !

IV. OBSERVE THE PERFECTIONS OF THE CREATION. When contemplated as a whole, or examined with diligence and minuteness in its parts, how complete, how harmonious, how fully impressed with the skill of its great Artificer ! Nothing redundant, —nothing deficient,— nothing out of place. When infinite wisdom had surveyed the whole, it was pronounced very good. Answering all the intentions of its Maker, and adapted to all the purposes of its formation.

V. OBSERVE THE GOODNESS EVIDENCED IN CREATION. In the formation of all living creatures for enjoyment. In their circumstances being adapted to their variety of nature. In the provisions creation furnishes for their constant exigencies. But especially in the profusion of generous provision made for the happiness of man. The wonders of creation burst upon his vision in all its agreeable variety. The sounds of nature, from the gentle breeze to the roaring cataract, fall upon his ear. Its herbs, and plants, and flowers regale him with their fragrant and diversified perfumes. A thousand kinds of fruits, in endless and rich variety, gratify his taste ; while his frame is rendered delicately adapted to the influences and sympathies of feeling. And in all these, there is much to engage the mind, to furnish matter for contemplation, and grateful emotion and joy. The whole earth is full of the goodness of God. Its cheering light, its refreshing streams, its balmy air, its necessary and nightly darkness, all display the benevolence of the Creator.

APPLICATION.

1. The works of creation form a legitimate and interesting subject of pious contemplation, Psalm viii. 3, 4.

2. We should duly estimate the dignified scale we held among the creatures of God. Mid link and uniting chain between the angels and the inferior creatures.

3. Let creation lead our minds to the great Creator. To God—the Son of God, by whom all things were made, &c.

ANGELS.

" The chariots of God are twenty thousand, even thousands of angels."—PSALM lxviii. 17.

IT does not appear that angels are included in the Mosaic account of the creation, for they were present on that occasion as adoring spectators. For then, the morning stars sang together, and all the sons of God shouted for joy. The scriptures do not furnish us with an extended regular history of these blessed intelligences ; but a sufficiency of incidental reference is given to enable us to form a correct estimation of their holy and intellectual character, and the important position they occupy in the moral portion of God's universe. The name itself is indicative rather of their office than their nature, signifying messenger, or one sent. It is obvious from the scripture revelation,

I. THAT THE ANGELS ARE SPIRITUAL INTELLIGENCES. " Who maketh his angels spirits." It is not our present province to define what is meant by spirit. But, believing in the spirituality of the divine essence, and in the spiritual immateriality of the soul, we are not perplexed in conceiving of created beings, who are not formed of material substance, or clothed with corporeal bodies.

II. ANGELS ARE IMMORTAL, OR UNDYING INTELLIGENCES. This is clearly intimated in that passage, "Neither can they die any more, for they are equal to the angels," Luke xx. 36. This involves the idea, that by the very constitution of their nature they are immortal, and not liable to decay or dissolution.

III. ANGELS ARE HOLY INTELLIGENCES. "Sons of God." Often described as the holy angels. Of necessity, such in their creation. The offspring of a holy Deity. Their obedience to the divine will is referred to by the psalmist, who speaks of them as "his ministers, who do his pleasure." And the holy service of the angels is referred to by the Saviour, who has taught us, that the will of God should be done on earth, even as it is done in heaven. Their love of holiness is evident from their intense celebration of the divine purity. They rest not day nor night, but ever wait to know the divine pleasure; and, covering their faces with their wings, cry, "Holy, holy, holy, is the Lord of Hosts," &c. Isa. vi. 3. It is also clear, that the holy angels resisted the temptations of the leader of those who kept not their first estate, but by reason of their rebellion were cast down from their high habitations, &c.

IV. ANGELS ARE BENEVOLENT INTELLIGENCES. It is clear that they delight in the benevolent works of God, especially in the great scheme of redemption. Benevolence is one of the essential attributes of holiness; for they cannot love and delight in God without also loving his creatures, especially those who resemble him in purity. How they exulted in the advent of the Saviour—"Glory to God in the highest," &c. How gladly they revealed his resurrection; how deeply they study the mysteries of the cross, 1 Pet. i. 12.

V. THEY ARE ACTIVE AND POWERFUL INTELLIGENCES. Hence they fly to do God's bidding. See an extraordinary instance in the history of Daniel, ix. 20. See also Matt. xiii. 21. They also "excel in strength," and are called the "mighty angels." Hence some of their stupendous doings are related in the scriptures, when employed as the agents of God, and the instruments of his providence.

VI. ANGELS ARE INTELLIGENCES HIGHLY ENDOWED WITH KNOWLEDGE AND WISDOM. Their purely spiritual nature, their high rank, their exalted place of abode, their opportunities of observation, must all lead to their intellectual greatness. Doubtless they possess clearness of understanding, perfect soundness of judgment, and an expanded vigor of comprehension, belonging only to themselves.

VII. ANGELS ARE DISTINGUISHED INTO VARIOUS CLASSES, RANKS, AND ORDERS. Hence their diversity of appellations, as seraphim and cherubim, thrones and dominions, principalities and powers, and in number they are thousands of thousands.

VIII. ANGELS ARE THE SERVANTS OF GOD TO EXECUTE HIS PLEASURE.

1. *In ministering to the children of God.* Hence they *counselled* and instructed—Hagar, Gen. xvi. 7; Abraham, Gen. xviii. 2; Joshua, Gideon, Elijah, 2 Kings iii. 10–16; David, Daniel, Zacharias, Luke i. 11; Joseph, Matt. i. 20; Philip, Acts viii. 16; Peter, Acts x. 3. They *comforted*—Jacob, Gen. xxxii. 1; Daniel, x. 19; Paul, Acts xxvii. 24. They delivered—Lot from Sodom; Daniel from the lion's den; and Peter and the apostles from prison. They were the *attendants* of the Saviour at his birth—baptism—temptation—transfiguration—agony—death—resurrection—and ascension into heaven. They *rejoice* in the conversion of sinners, and bear the souls of the saints to the mansions of glory. They are *destined* also to attend Christ at his second coming, and witness the judgment of the world at the great day.

2. *In being the instruments of the divine vengeance.* As in the instances of the destruction of the Assyrian army, and in the death of the persecuting Herod, Acts xii.

APPLICATION.

1. The pious have the distinguished privilege of angelic ministration, Heb. i. 14.

2. They are worthy of our study and imitation.

3. They will be the companions of the redeemed in glory forever.

THE IMMORTALITY OF THE SOUL.

"And man became a living soul."—GEN. ii. 7.

MAN is not only distinguished above the inferior creatures by the possession of reason, but by the essential constitution of his nature. The difference, both in the mode and description of man's creation, over the animal creatures, is peculiarly striking and instructive—see Gen. i. 22–25, compared with ver. 26, 27. Now, this distinction consists in man having a compound nature, a material body, and an incorporeal mind; in other words, that man is distinguished as having a living soul. Let us attempt some account of the soul, and then endeavor to establish its immortality. We offer,

I. SOME REMARKS ON THE SOUL. The soul, or spiritual part of man, is characterized by its consciousness, its volitions, its desires, &c. There is,

1. *The understanding.* By which the soul perceives, observes, and attains knowledge. The eye of the mind.

2. *The judgment.* By which the soul determines as to the quality, &c. of the objects presented to the understanding. This power is either exercised in determining the abstract properties of things, or in comparing one thing with another, and then drawing its deductions.

3. *The imagination.* By which objects are contemplated through an ideal medium. That power which gives a pictured representation to the thoughts, &c. of the mind.

4. *The affections, or emotions.* Of love—and desire—and hope. Of anger, and fear, &c.

5. *The conscience, or the moral sense.* By which we decide as to the moral right or wrong of actions. Whose conclusions, however, are only infallible when under the influence of divine light and truth.

6. *The will, or self-determination.* By which man decides, and chooses, and acts, as he may be influenced by the motives presented to him. Now, these faculties of the soul, though enfeebled, &c. by sin, yet are essential to the soul, and exercise their power, except in cases of infancy, idiocy, and insanity. Let us, then,

II. ENDEAVOR TO ESTABLISH ITS IMMORTALITY. That is, its undying existence, its everlasting being. We refer,

1. *To its essential nature.* Immaterial, or spiritual. In this it seems to partake of a nature like unto that of the angels; yea, in some sense to resemble the spirituality of the Deity. Metaphysicians have reasoned plausibly from this in favor of the immortality of the soul. We refer,

2. *To the excellency of its attributes.*

The powers we have referred to, seem too high and celestial for the limited range of earth and time. The amazing powers of the soul for sublime spiritual contemplation, and its unwearied activity, seem greatly to strengthen the idea of its immortality.

3. *From its capacity for improvement and enjoyment.* There is no boundary to the growth and enlargement of the mind. Think of Newton, and Locke, and Shakspeare, in their infancy and in their mature years. Mental stores may be amassed almost beyond limitation. The exercise of these expanded powers often sets at defiance years, and disease itself, though generally impaired by the infirmities of the body as their medium of contact with external things. So the capacity for enjoyment is equally boundless. Its desires are ever soaring higher and higher; its delights are ever capable of a greater exquisiteness of bliss.

4. *From the innate desires and general impressions of immortality.* Man seems to abhor and shudder at the idea of extinction. He is emphatically the creature of the future. His wishes and hopes never reach a climax; beyond, beyond, is the watchword of the soul. He is ever longing for that he has not. Even in the enjoyment of God, he seeks for a nearer communion, a clearer knowledge, a fuller enjoyment, than earth can ever yield. Besides, the impressions of immortality seem to have been common to mankind in all ages and countries; few nations in which some idea, however feeble or confused, has not existed of a future state of being.

5. *From the apparent want of wise design if man is not immortal.* Wherefore his lofty powers; wherefore his desires, his progression in truth and purity; wherefore his internal horror at annihilation, which would appear as an anomaly in creation, if he be not destined to exist in another world?

6. *From the essential principles of justice and equity.* God is just and holy in all his ways. He must hate, loathe, and punish sin; he must delight in and reward holiness. But view mankind merely in the mirror of this life, and you behold vice triumphant, prosperous, gay, arrayed in wealth and power, and faring sumptuously every day. You behold Christian virtue poor, scorned, persecuted, dying by the hands of the violent and wicked. Does

God see ? is he holy ? then both characters must be transferred to other spheres, where God will deal with every man according to his character and works.

7. *This subject is demonstrated in the pages of revelation.* Here life and immortality are brought to light ; here all men are represented as candidates for an eternity of bliss, or woes everlasting. The translations of Enoch and Elijah, as illustrated by the Redeemer, Matt. xxii. 31, 32 ; Psalm xvi. 10, 11 ; John v. 28 ; 2 Cor. v. 1–8 ; parable of the rich man and Lazarus.

APPLICATION.

1. *How great the dignity of man !* Even in his ruins, how majestic he appears when contemplated in the immortality of his being !

2. *How great our responsibility !* Living and acting for an eternal state of existence. Travelling towards the boundless regions of immortality.

3. *How joyous the gospel proclamation !* A message of present and eternal life. Tidings of immortal life and glory.

4. *How essential personal religion !*

THE GOVERNMENT OF GOD.

"And at the end of the days, I, Nebuchadnezzar, lifted up mine eyes unto heaven, and mine understanding returned unto me, and I blessed the most High, and I praised and honored him that liveth for ever ; whose dominion is an everlasting dominion, and his kingdom from generation to generation," &c.—DANIEL iv. 34, 35.

OUR text is the language of Nebuchadnezzar after his restoration to soundness of mind. His affliction was happily sanctified to the good of his soul, and he learned to venerate the true and blessed God, and to give homage and praise to his glorious and exalted name. Both the words and sentiments of the text are striking, powerful, and instructive, and convey a truly sublime view of Deity to our minds. But we desire especially to regard them as presenting a lucid and comprehensive representation of the divine government. Our subject directs us,

I. To THE SUPREMACY OF THE DIVINE GOVERNMENT. God the Most High exercises his unconstrained authority over the universe. His throne is exalted in the highest heavens, and his kingdom ruleth over all. He is the God of all the kingdoms of the earth. His kingdom is an everlasting kingdom, and his dominion from generation to generation. Men may possess authority and power, sway sceptres over vast empires. Angels may have power delegated to them. But all right and power is in the hand of the God of heaven and earth. As the creator of all and the sustainer of all,—intimately acquainted with all,—present everywhere by his ubiquity, —having unwearying strength,—an infinity of resources—who so fit for the supremacy of the universe ? How below all righteous contempt do idols appear when contrasted with the God of heaven and earth ! Notice,

II. THE ETERNITY OF THE DIVINE GOVERNMENT. "Whose dominion is an everlasting dominion." How appropriate with the title given to Jehovah in the text, "That liveth for ever and ever." As such he existed before all things. His wisdom and might brought all things into being. With him is no mutability, so that he has ever stood in the same relationship to his works. Of his years there will be no end, so that he will reign forever and ever.

III. THE IRRESISTIBLE CHARACTER OF THE DIVINE GOVERNMENT. "He doeth according to his will, &c. and none can stay his stand." His will is ever in harmony with justice, holiness, and benevolence. His will is his law, his indisputable law. His will cannot be effectually resisted. Angels may dispute it, and man may rebel against it, but in both cases inevitable discomfiture must be the result. How arrogant for created intelligences to arraign it, —for created power to oppose it ! Stubbornness, determination, or combination, can only lead to the ruin of those who exhibit them. The breath of his nostrils would consume them together. Notice,

IV. THE INFINITE EXTENT OF HIS GOVERNMENT. He executes his will in the "army of heaven." The host of angelic intelligences all obey him. His commandments in heaven are received with joy, and obeyed with alacrity and delight. His government extends to the whole earth, with all its inhabitants. None are without, or beyond the pale of his control. Every human being of every nation, color, people, and tongue. All classes and conditions are subject to him. He restrains the wrath of the wicked, and overruleth all the purposes and plots of the ungodly so as to secure the counsels of his will. Besides, the divine dominion is exercised over the material parts and elements of the universe. His government extends over all the inferior creatures. Everywhere he is present, and everywhere his power is exercised and his authority indisputably displayed.

OBSERVATIONS.

1. The divine government is worthy of highest wonder and adoration. How vast, —how high,—how perpetual,—how infinite,—how incomprehensible the idea of one universal pervading Spirit,—observing all, diffused through, and governing all!

2. It is a subject worthy of our frequent contemplation. Much of God is seen in his works, and much in his boundless dominion. Here we may meditate until our minds are filled with the loftiest feelings of awe and admiration.

3. It is a subject which should lead to fervent thanksgiving. "The Lord reigneth, let the earth rejoice." How cheering that the world is not left to the contingencies of chance. Not left to the powerful control of some evil despot. Not left to the unrestrained reign and rage of the god of this world. That wicked men have not the sole reins of government. The great disposer of all events,—the great governor of heaven, and earth, and hell, is Jehovah, the righteous, ever-blessed God.

4. It shows us the importance of religion. For what is religion, but our acquiescence in the will of God? Our conformity to his revealed will? This must tend to our dignity, security, and blessedness.

5. The folly of rebelling against his authority. Let the doom of fallen angels, —the expulsion of our first parents,—the judgments with which he has visited our world; warn the incorrigible of the certainty of final and endless ruin. "Kiss the Son," &c.

6. The certainty of God's universal dominion over our world. By the power of his truth, by the might of his Spirit, he has destined our world to become the kingdom of Christ, and that he shall reign over all, and forever and ever.

DIVINE PROVIDENCE.

"The lot is cast into the lap, but the whole disposing thereof is of the Lord."—Prov. xvi. 33.

In this very expressive proverb we are taught the universal government and superintendence of God. God manages all the affairs of heaven, earth, and hell. His reign is universal. His authority boundless. The universe in all its grandeur, and in all the minuteness of its various parts, is under his exact arrangement. With God there is no chance, nothing accidental. His providence includes the rightful regulation of *every* thing. It even descendeth to lots,—a doubtful matter has to be settled, the counsel of those concerned is insufficient, and the lot is cast into the lap, the finger of God disposeth of it. A case is presented, Acts i. 23, &c. You have all been interested in the case of Jonah, see Jonah i. 7.

Our subject is the providence of God. Consider,

I. The prerequisites of Providence. It presupposes that the world is under control, &c.; under the control of one great presiding First Cause. Now this great, blessed, glorious, and eternal being, is God. And as the moral governor of the universe, he is possessed of every attribute and perfection, as the supreme Jehovah.

1. *Infinite knowledge and wisdom.* He knows every thing. All his works. All things. All intelligent beings. Nothing hidden; nothing obscure. At one glance he surveys all things, from eternity to eternity. As such, all he does is done wisely, infallibly, no improvement possible, &c.

2. *Universal presence.* His influential presence is everywhere. "Heaven of heavens," &c. "Whither shall I flee," &c. He fills heaven and earth. This is the perfection of the sublime. Who can grasp the immense idea, God guiding the path of the seraph in heaven, and superintending the fall of the sparrow on earth?

3. *Illimitable power.* "I know thou canst do every thing;" that is, every thing fit and morally right. He asks, "Is there any thing too hard," &c. "The thunder of his power who," &c.

II. The nature of Providence.

1. *It includes the government, or rule of all things.* He has given to every department of the universe suitable laws. The air is governed by atmospheric laws. Wa-

ter by laws suited to it. Light. So every thing else. These are all God's laws. He originated them all, and he sits at the helm of all affairs, directing all things by the word of his power. The connection of all is pointed out by the prophet, Hosea ii. 21, 22.

2. *It includes the preservation of all things.* To rule is one thing, but to supply the wants of all is another. In providence God does both. Fountain of supply to the universe. Every thing lives by him and through him. Source of life, of being, and enjoyment. Not one creature is independent.

3. *It includes the direction of all things to one grand consummation.* Opposed to God's rule are all fallen angels and wicked men. In providence, therefore, God overrules their evil designs and rebellious acts, and makes even the wrath of man to praise him; and he will, finally, by the conversion or the imprisonment of the ungodly, annihilate all moral evil, and fill this world with holiness and bliss, so that all men shall be blessed in Christ, and call him blessed. This leads us to notice more fully,

III. The extent of Providence. Now the providence of God includes all things, and all acts.

1. *It extends to celestial beings.* Their ranks, offices, stations, and services, Psalm ciii. 20.

2. *It extends to all mere animal creatures.* Now the providence of God is seen both in supplying them with food, and in the diversity of instinct by which they are distinguished. Who taught the bird to construct its nest, and every bird to construct such a one as is best suited for its kind, and all different? To migrate at the proper period from one country to another, and to do it so correctly without chart, or the aid of a compass, to know the right path! Who taught the fish to retrace its course, and find out annually its native rivers and streams? The beaver to erect so scientifically its house? The bee, so wonderfully its cell? and the ant, so systematically its city? How wonderfully they are all supplied with suitable food, which they instinctively seek and find! Look, too, at the distribution of the creatures; those which are most useful and essential to the comfort of man, abound in the densely populated parts of the world, while the deadly and dangerous animals are principally found in solitary parts, far from the dwellings of mankind. The man who is not more stupid than the ox, or more inconsiderate than the ass, must see in all this the wonderful providence of God. We have now,

3. *To consider it especially as it regards the human race.* And that as it respects,

(1.) Our entrance into life, Psalm lxxi. 6, xxii. 9

(2.) Our circumstances and condition in life, Deut. xxx. 9, xxxii. 9.

(3.) Our removal from this life, Job xiv. 5; Psalm xxxix. 4; 1 Samuel xxvi. 10; Eccles. iii. 1, &c.

IV. The Providence of God has often been singularly displayed in the punishment of the wicked. Look at Pharaoh, who had multiplied the grievous burdens of the people of Israel; see the number of his plagues. His most cruel edict—the death of the males. See the river of blood, and the death of the first-born. Behold the finger of God. His final overthrow. Look at Adonibezek; he had been successful as a warrior, but had practised the greatest cruelty. "Three score and ten kings," &c. See the case of Ahab, 1 Kings xxii. 34. Look at Haman, with the bitterest hate he plots the ruin of the Jews; he succeeds in every step, the decree is passed and is irreversible. But God disturbs the Persian monarch—turns the plot upon Haman, and *he* is suspended from the gallows he had erected for Mordecai. Behold Belshazzar; the sacred vessels of the Lord's house had been carried as spoil to Babylon; he appoints a night of revelling and dissipation; the vessels are used in their rioting. In the same hour the invisible messenger records the doom of the monarch and the ruin of his kingdom. Look at Herod,—arrayed in costly vestments, he addresses the people, and receives the honors only due to the true God, and is smitten with the finger of the Lord.

V. The Providence of God is seen in striking interpositions on behalf of his people.

1. *Read the history of Joseph.* See what links in the providential chain! Hated. Sent forth. The dry pit. Sold. See him in Egypt,—in Potiphar's house. In prison. As ruler over all the land. Well might he say, "Now therefore be not angry with yourselves that ye sold me, &c., for God did send me before you to preserve life."

2. *Reflect on the preservation of Moses.* The decree, the birth, the resolution, the method, the rescue, the weeping, the sympathy, the nurse, the education, &c.

3. *Observe one point in the history of Gideon.* Israelites oppressed. Gideon called to deliver. The enemy fearfully numerous. His heart fails, he approaches the camp. Hears a dream related, and is at once inspirited for the conflict, Judges vii. 13.

4. *Look at the basis of David's prosperity and renown,* 1 Samuel xvii. 26. His three eldest brethren are in the army. David is sent with provisions, &c. At this time Goliath is giving the impious challenge. David accepts it, and slays the giant. One or two *historical events.*

In the days of Queen Mary, a person was sent with an edict for destroying the protestants of Ireland. At Chester, while lodging at the mayor's house, he happened to state the nature of his commission. A woman who overheard this, extracted this cruel edict from his possession. On his arrival therefore before the authorities, his commission was missed. He returned and obtained a second, but on his way to Ireland again the queen died. And thus the protestants of Ireland were preserved.

Tyndal's Bible sold very heavily, and was likely to ruin those who had embarked in it, when the Bishop of London, to stay the progress of truth, bought immense quantities up and burnt them: thus Tyndal was relieved, and a second and larger edition was printed and circulated. Let us ask in conclusion,

WHAT USE WE SHOULD MAKE OF THE DIRECTIONS OF DIVINE PROVIDENCE.

1. *We should learn the importance of having God for our friend.* To be on terms of reconciliation with God. To be conscious of his favor. That he who rides on the wings of the wind, and that directs the storm and the tempest, is a being who loves us. The way to God's favor is through Jesus Christ. All Christ's disciples know that they are loved of God. The Spirit of God bearing witness, &c.

2. *We see the great necessity for constant prayer.* "In all things by prayer," &c. For he ordereth all things. He has all resources in himself. The hearts of all men are in his hands. In all circumstances let us pray, &c.

3. *The great ground for confidence and trust.* All must be right when God controls all, and reigns over all. "Trust in the Lord Jehovah forever," &c. The doctrine of a divine Providence is full of consolation, &c.

4. *Let it not be abused by our presumption or ignorance.* God governs the world by two kinds of laws. The material world by physical laws; the intelligent part of creation by moral laws. Now if a bad man obeys the physical laws, he will enjoy the physical benefits. Let exercise and temperance prove it. If a good man violates them he will suffer.

5. *Let us not wonder at the apparent darkness of the divine dispensations.* It must be so to all but God.

MAN.

FIRST SKETCH.

"What is man that thou art mindful of him?"— PSALM viii. 4.

IT seems evident that this psalm was composed during the night season. That the divine psalmist was contemplating the heavens, beholding with sublime interest the starry host, and witnessing the moon speeding her course with her reflected glory and silvery brightness. No science more calculated to inspire with profound awe, or lofty emotions, than that of astronomy. The vastness of heaven's outspread canopy—the splendor and magnitude of the starry worlds—the comprehensive and yet minute laws by which their attraction and course are directed, all these, with many other questions, are adapted to fill us with wonder and astonishment. Is it not next to impossible to consider these things and not to ascend still higher, and raise our minds to the great Creator and upholder of them all? Read David's pious exultation when considering the same theme, Psalm xix. 1–6. From the heavens the psalmist descends to the creature man, and asks, "What is man," &c. Our text contains an important question, and includes a twofold interesting declaration. In our text we have,

I. AN IMPORTANT QUESTION, AND WHAT IT INVOLVES. The question relates to man, and might include a variety of interesting particulars. We ask,

1. *What is man as to his nature?* (1.) We reply, he is a compound being, mate-

ria. as to his bodily structure. Formed originally of the dust of the ground, yet this body is fearfully and wonderfully made. The perfection of animal nature, combining all that is valuable and beautiful in itself. Its erect form, its exalted head, its countenance divine, displaying in all its parts both the wisdom and goodness of God. We cannot enlarge on the anatomical and physiological wonders of the human frame; for were we to do so, any one part, the eye, the ear, the hand, the heart, might supply us with ample matter for a sermon. Let us just name, however, a few particulars. In the human body there are 245 bones, with forty distinct intentions, 446 muscles within; so that the bones and muscles have upwards of 14,000 intentions. Then there are not fewer than 10,000 nerves, with an equal number of veins and arteries. 1,000 ligaments, 4,000 lacteals and lymphatics, 100,000 glands, and the skin contains not fewer than 200 millions of pores, all of which are so many avenues of health or sickness, life or death. Look at this complex, marvellous machine, and see in it the wondrous work of God. The functions of the heart are truly amazing. The heart contracts 4,000 times every hour, and during that period there passes through it 250 pounds of blood; so that the whole of the fluid of life, averaging twenty-five pounds, passes through the whole system of veins, arteries, &c., fourteen times every hour, or about every four minutes. That which distinguishes the human body from the mere animal creation most, is the capaciousness of the brain, and the wonders of the human hand. By this peculiar member of the body, man possesses the advantages of every other creature. With this he digs and explores the bowels of the earth, rises higher than the eagle ever soars, can traverse the whole region of the earth, and float on the waters, and thus circumnavigate the globe. By this he can raise ponderous loads which would crush the elephant, and form instruments of defence against the attacks of all the ferocious beasts of prey. We reply,

(2.) Man is a rational, intellectual being. We do not attempt to draw the line where instinct or reason in the inferior creatures ends, and the superior reason of man commences. There is this difference. Each class of the animal creation have their peculiar instincts, &c.; but the rea-son of man avails him for every contingency, and goes beyond the instincts of the whole animal creation. It has been said, too, that the inferior creation just act as the whole of their respective species have done for generations, no improvement or advancement; while the mind and reason of man are ever progressing, and no limits can be set to the sphere of their operations. Look at the amazing efforts of mind in two or three particulars. By the invention of the telescope he brings worlds before his view, which are millions of miles distant from him. By the invention of the microscope he magnifies and renders capable of his observation creatures the most minute, the existence of which would otherwise never have been known. By the discovery of the mariner's compass, he guides his way across perilous oceans, to the most distant parts of the habitable earth. By exerting his influence over the air, and over fire and water, he makes the elements of nature do his bidding, and minister to his claims. By the invention of printing he gives a kind of ubiquity to his thoughts, and stereotypes his wishes to all generations.

(3.) We reply, man is a moral being; he is rendered accountable to the great Supreme for all his actions, words, and thoughts. He can know his duty, reflect, judge, compare, and freely act; and it is evident that the present is only a probationary state of existence. Such is the nature of man, and furnishes a reply to the first question we proposed respecting him. We ask,

2. *What is man as a responsible being?* Responsibility implies the existence of law, revelation, and ability.

(1.) Man is under law or government. There are laws in our nature, as there is instinct in the brute creation. The law of natural affection to parents, children, friends, &c. Besides, there is the law of conscience, or the impressions of the mind as to what is right or wrong; but this will only act truly and without error, under the influence of light and truth. Neither of these are sufficient. God has, therefore, given man specific laws to regulate all his actions towards himself, mankind, and God.

(2.) This law God has revealed—it is contained in the volume of eternal life, the Holy Scriptures. Here it is spread fully before our eyes. Now this revelation is full, clear, and sufficient.

(3.) There must be ability; ability to understand, and ability to perform. Man must be free to choose or to refuse, or there can be neither virtue nor vice. He is always thus addressed in God's word: "If ye be willing and obedient," &c. "Behold, I set before you life and death," &c.

3. *Man is an immortal being.* This is but the morning of his existence. Indeed, unless he is immortal, there is no such thing as responsibility. Here vice is not generally punished, nor goodness generally rewarded, so that the claims of righteousness and equity demand that man should exist in another world. Many of the ancient pagan philosophers came to this conclusion, and it is fully revealed in the gospel, where life and immortality are brought to light. This is man's seed-time, the period of his minority, the time of his servitude, and he is destined to an eternity of existence in another world. This stamps man's character with immense importance, with unutterable value. But we draw to a conclusion.

LEARN,

1. How necessary that we should know ourselves, and reflect on the great end of our being. What am I? What the claims of God? What my destiny?

2. How important that we should be found doing the will of God. This is the will of God, to believe in Christ, and to obey his commandments.

3. How momentous that we should live for the eternity before us; live accepted of God through Christ Jesus; live in communion with God; live in the exercise of faith and hope.

MAN.

SECOND SKETCH.

"What is man that thou art mindful of him?" —PSALM viii. 4.

IN a previous discourse we considered this question in a physical, intellectual, and moral respect. We directed you to some of the wonders displayed in his body—his moral condition, and the immortality of his being. Thus man stands midway between the inferior animal creation and the holy angels; the connecting link; lord of earth, and heir of heaven; more dignified than the beasts of the field, and but a little lower than the angels. But, in contemplating man as a moral being,

II. WE OFFER SEVERAL ADDITIONAL REPLIES TO THE QUESTION PROPOSED. "What is man?"

1. *That he is not what he once was.* His present state is one of deterioration. He is fallen—not now as when he sprang from the hands of the great Artificer. God made man upright, &c. He created him in his own image, &c. He is not what he was once,

(1.) As to the health and immortality of his body. He was formed for endless duration of being. If God intended to remove him from the earth after a season of probation, it would have been without tasting death. Entire, body and soul, as Enoch or Elijah. Beautiful, vigorous, hale, undying. How altered! poor, weak, fragile, diseased, and exposed to ten thousand attacks of fatal affliction. Life is entered with cries and sorrow. We live in an atmosphere of mortality, and our cradles truly rock us to the tomb. Thus was the human frame wrecked on the sunken shoals of sin and transgression.

(2.) He is not what he once was in his dominions and possessions. See Gen. i. 27, 28. Sin has hurled man from his throne of dominion and rule—exiled him from his domain—banished him from his kingdom. The crown has fallen, the sceptre is departed, and the ferocious beasts of the forest are arrayed in fierce daring against him. They no longer own his control, nor give him tribute. His lovely dwelling-place has been confiscated by his treason, and he is doomed by the sweat of his brow to compel the barren earth to yield him support.

(3.) He is not what he once was in his moral powers. Oh, how awful the contrast! Then arrayed in the garments of purity—harmony within and beauty without. His understanding reflecting divine knowledge—his judgment influenced only by truth—his will cheerfully obedient to God's authority—his conscience serene and happy—his affections spiritual and heavenly; in one sentence, perfectly happy, because entirely holy. Now his understanding darkened—judgment perverse—will rebellious—conscience defiled—affections earthly—and over the whole the evil genius of sin, and confusion, and misery presiding.

(4.) He is not what he once was, in his condition and associations. Then an object of divine love, favor, and fellowship—then often visited by angels—then a monarch. Now under wrath—in league with fallen spirits—a rebel doomed to die, &c.—speeding his way to the grave, and to the abyss of despair. In reply to the question of the text, we remark,

2. *Man is not naturally what he may be.* His fall is not irreparable—his loss not final—his case not hopeless. He cannot regain all he has lost. Not a sound physical system—not dominion over the inferior creatures—not an earthly Eden—not translation to a heavenly world; but he can regain more than a counterbalance to all the ills and woes sin has introduced, through the love of God, in our redemption by Christ Jesus.

(1.) His guilt may be cancelled. Forgiveness is obtained, and published, and offered.

(2.) His nature may be renewed, his heart changed, cleansed, sanctified, by the Spirit and grace of God.

(3.) His soul may be the seat of joy and blissful hope—kingdom of God within—begotten again to a lively hope, &c.—become an expectant of life eternal. Salvation is within his reach; and this includes being an " heir of God, and joint-heir with Jesus Christ."

3. *Man is not what he shall hereafter be.* Now a probationer, in a future state of existence his state will be irrevocable, fixed, and eternal. Whatsoever a man now sows, the shall he reap. Two states are revealed. Man changed and consecrated to God in heart and life until death. Then he will be hereafter exalted to God's kingdom and glory; a companion of angels; a worshipper of the Lamb; a sainted, beatified spirit forever. Not a wrestler, but victor; not a racer, but crowned with the imperishable wreath; not a minor, but an inheritor of the blessedness, &c. How elevated, changed, &c. All his desires met—all his faith realized—all his hopes in fruition—body and soul glorified forever, &c. Man *unchanged* and *impenitent,* how different his state hereafter will be! No admixture of enjoyment, or rest, or hope; no possibility of salvation. Judged, condemned, punish-

ed, and that with everlasting banishment from the presence of God, and from the glory of his power. We ask, then,

4. *What is man as to his responsibilities?* We have already admitted his responsibility. We now add,

(1.) That he is responsible for his faculties and endowments. He must give an account for his rational powers and mental endowments; for their right employment; for their due improvement; to be directed in reference to God and eternity.

(2.) For his privileges and mercies. These are of various kinds. A preached gospel—the favorable openings of providence—continued bestowment of God's bounties, &c. Among these we may also mention, time, with the means of grace, &c.

(3.) For his influence and talents. Not merely to get good and receive benefits to his own soul, but also to bless those in the various spheres where providence has placed him. To do good in the world; to show forth the virtues and graces of the Christian character, &c. Now, this responsibility arises from the fact, that this is his probation, and he is hastening to the eternity of righteous retribution.

APPLICATION.

1. What is your individual state before God? What your hopes and fears? What your true condition before Deity? Is it better or worse than the past? Is it improving, or debasing? Is it rising in conformity to God?

2. Learn the necessity of self-reflection and meditation. What am I? From whence? Where destined? Know yourselves, &c.

3. Next to self-knowledge, and in connection with it, the knowledge of God and Jesus Christ. " This is life eternal," &c.

PARADISE.

" And the Lord formed man of the dust of the ground, and breathed into his nostrils the breath of life, and man became a living soul. And the Lord planted a garden eastward in Eden," &c.— GEN. ii. 7–9.

OUR text goes backward to the creation of the world. It is a part of the Mosaic account of God's wonder-working arm, in giving being to our world, and the creatures which inhabit it. We observe here, that all other accounts of the creation are absurd, many of them monstrous in the extreme. The pagan philosophers knew nothing about it; but each speculated according to his own mind, and the whole of them left the subject unsettled. A divine revelation could alone make this subject known, and the one contained in the scriptures is in perfect accordance with the earth itself, is such as to exhibit the glory of the great Artificer, and commend itself to the intelligence of the human mind. Every step in the majestic work is worthy of contemplation; but our text must limit us to man's paradisaical condition. Observe,

I. The person introduced to us in the text.

II. The place prepared for his reception. And,

III. The enjoyments arising from its occupation.

I. The person introduced to us in the text. This person is man, the last work of God, and the master-piece of the whole. The divine Artificer was God; yet not the Father but the Son, for he created all things by Jesus Christ—" All things were made by him," &c. Man is presented to us in his compound character.

1. In his material animal body. This was formed of the dust of the earth—from the name given to the first man, Adam, which signifies red earth. Yet, even in the creation of his body, there is a dignity of expression which is not used in reference to the mere animal creation. Compare ver. 25 of chap. i. and the text. The body is a wonderful exhibition of divine skill. Some think the idea is that of a potter, who forms upon his wheel the vessel of peculiar elegance and worth. How many subjects press upon our attention in reference to the formation of the body of man! Our origin is the dust. However proud or careful we may be of them, they are but modified dust. They are tabernacles reared for a time on the earth, and they are tending to the dust. " Our fathers, where are they ?" Alas! now mingling with their native earth. Let not this subject be forgotten. But man is presented to us,

2. In the spirituality and dignity of his soul. This interesting casket was but to be the case of a precious jewel; the house of a celestial inhabitant. The words may

originally include the life of the body as well as of the soul, for the Hebrew is, *breath of lives ;* natural life, but especially denoting the existence of the immortal, thinking spirit within. In another passage a more full description is given of the soul, chap. i. ver. 27. Endowed him with faculties resembling his own attributes in his perceptive, reflective, and moral powers and feelings. United to the angelic and animal creation, filling up the wondrous chasm between the two.

II. The place prepared for his reception. This is called Eden, which signifies a place of pleasure. In the Septuagint it is rendered Paradise, denoting a park, or place of trees. Here the atmosphere was that of life, the earth beautified with flowers and trees. " Every tree," &c. An extensive variety, an overflowing abundance, and that of the most delicious kind. This was man's original earthly estate; here were his princely domains. But two trees are especially alluded to.

1. " *The tree of life.*" This tree seems to have been the sign or pledge, between God and Adam, of the continuance of his life and bliss. Partaking of this he would ever be reminded of his felicity and immortality.

2. " *The tree of the knowledge of good and evil.*" By some very strikingly illustrated thus :—The " tree by which the difference between good and evil should be known." From the fruit of this our first parents were prohibited. Here, and here only, was man's responsibility exhibited. This was to be the test of his obedience. We ask, then,

III. As to the enjoyments arising from the occupation of Eden.

1. *Superior earthly dignity.* Adam was God's vicegerent. See the extensive charter ratified by the mouth of Jehovah, Gen. i. 28.

2. *Internal peace and harmony.* The faculties brilliantly reflecting God's glory; the affections, as flames of holy fire, burning in love to God ; the conscience transparent and unruffled. No anxiety, no fear.

3. *Celestial and divine communion.* Angels were the visitants, the companions, the friends of our first parents ; but God himself was their beloved Father, with whom they had sweet and unbroken fellowship. In one word, the glory and the bliss of our first parents were perfect. But we have

remarked, it was a state of probation, and we must leave the calamitous result for future consideration. Learn,

1. *The goodness of God to man.* How appropriate the song of the son of Jesse, "What is man," &c. Psalm viii. 4. The soul, how precious ; do we care for, and seek its restoration to God.

2. *How glorious our world before sin entered.* One vast temple, and every living thing doing homage to the great and unsearchable Deity.

3. *The transitory character of earthly bliss and glory.* The scene has passed away ; the whole aspect of things has altered. Eden is lost—paradise forfeited. *How,* you all know ; and this must be the subject for future discussion.

PARADISE LOST.

"Therefore the Lord sent him forth from the garden of Eden, to till the ground from whence he was taken. So he drove out the man."—GENESIS iii. 23, 24.

OUR subject is, Paradise lost. A subject replete with thrilling incident, and one, too, in which we are all personally concerned. In Adam's original moral dignity and Paradise we see a beautiful and appropriate connection. Here holiness and pleasure were united—purity and honor—allegiance and glory. But when sin entirely transformed the nature of man, he was no longer a fit resident of the peaceful bowers of the holy Eden. Let us then inquire,

I. HOW PARADISE WAS LOST.

II. WHAT THAT LOSS INCLUDED. And,

III. IN WHAT MANNER WE ARE AFFECTED BY IT.

I. HOW PARADISE WAS LOST. It was lost,

1. *By sinful credulity.* From the fruit of the tree of the knowledge of good and evil our first parents were solemnly prohibited. A dreadful threatening was annexed to the violation of God's command. In these circumstances, Eve, the mother of all living, was assailed by the tempter, through the medium of the serpent. He insidiously reflects on God's goodness in refusing this tree. He specifies the wisdom it would impart. He affirms that death should not follow. These were Satan's fatal devices. By the first, he induced discontent. By the second, ambitious curiosity. By the third, daring presumption. Eve gave credit to Satan. By this sinful credulity was Paradise lost.

2. *By unbelief.* The first sin was credulity towards Satan, but unbelief towards God. God had spoken, had made a direct affirmation, and a firm belief in this would have preserved our parents from ruin. But unbelief enshrouded the mind, the back was turned on God's truth, and the forsaking of the truth was the loss of Paradise.

3. *By disobedience.* This sinful credulity and unbelief decided the course to be adopted, and the hand of disobedience reached forth and took the forbidden fruit. Now this was,

(1.) Wilful disobedience. There was no mistake or misconception. The duty was obvious, and the sin was wittingly and wilfully committed.

(2.) It was voluntary disobedience. They had sufficient power to resist and to stand. Indeed, having a holy nature, the balance of moral power was in favor of persevering uprightness. Satan could not force, did not compel. He suggested, but resistance was practicable. He allured, but the mind could turn away. So that the sin was a voluntary act, and not one of necessity or force.

(3.) It was ungrateful disobedience. By it all the bounty and goodness of God were trampled upon. It was rebellion against God. Treason against his government, &c. Observe, then,

II. WHAT THE LOSS OF PARADISE INCLUDED. There was,

1. *The loss of the place.* Eden was man's inheritance. His princely residence. The garden of enjoyment and pleasure. Here was the original paternal estate. As a traitor to the crown royal it was now justly forfeited.

2. *The loss of dignity and dominion.* No longer did he represent the Deity. No longer a monarch subordinate only to God. No longer provided with every luxury without toil. The garden yielded profusely, man had only to dress it, and nature teemed with every needful good. Now, alas! he must toil and dig, and with the sweat of the brow obtain his daily bread. The ground was cursed for his sake.

3. *It involved the loss of bodily vigor and health.* His body now became vulnerable

and liable to sicken and die. Sin sowed the seeds of disease in the whole of the animal system, and now it tended to its native element, the earth.

4. *The loss of the divine favor and image.* The brightness of the mind was bedimmed. The affections were frozen. The judgment perverted. The conscience defiled. The passions in a state of disorder and confusion. God's goodness and approbation were forfeited. The moral crown was fallen from the head. The snow-white robe was exchanged for unsightly rags, and the very elements seemed to war against his comfort and life. The loss was temporal, bodily, mental, and spiritual. We ask,

III. IN WHAT WAY WE ARE AFFECTED BY IT.

1. *We are partakers of the poverty which it involved.* Not heirs of paradise, but of the wild desert. Our patrimony is lost. Not born princes, but slaves. Just as the descendants of a traitor lose all the benefits of the original family estate.

2. *We are the subjects of the defilement it produced.* An evil corrupt nature was produced by their sin. That nature we inherit, both as it regards the body and the mind. Here as in hereditary diseases, &c.

3. *We are liable to the miseries it inflicted.* Trouble, disease, death. Now to these every man is liable, and what sorrow and suffering they include. We do not say that by the first transgression we are liable to the second death. For though the son of a traitor becomes poor, and probably inherits his father's diseases, yet he is not tried and put to a violent death for his father's crimes. But it is equally clear, that as possessors of a defiled nature, we must be renewed before we are fit for the holy regions of heaven. And a neglect of this will expose us to the second and eternal death. Just as the son of a traitor might be required to take the oath of allegiance, and in the case of neglect might justly be supposed to possess the treasonable spirit of his father, and thus share a similar doom.

APPLICATION.

1. *How profitable to reflect on the true cause of all suffering!* Sin.

2. *This condition has become one of personal guilt in every soul present.* We have all erred and strayed, &c. All have sinned, &c. Not one righteous, &c.

3. *The necessity of supplicating and ob-*

taining mercy. We must have it or perish. Have it, or be punished forever. The gospel reveals it. Offers it. Oh, accept it and live.

HUMAN DEPRAVITY.

"The heart is deceitful above all things, and desperately wicked; who can know it?"—JER. xvii. 9.

"Know thyself," is a maxim of great importance. Without this, other knowledge will be of little use to us. Ignorance of ourselves is wilful blindness. It is the traveller preferring darkness to light. It is the mariner throwing away his compass, and leaving the vessel to drive before the wind. The word of God will assist us in this work of self-investigation and self-knowledge. It is a discerner of the thoughts and intents of the heart.

Our text presents a fearful picture of the moral condition of the soul, "the heart is deceitful," &c. Our subject is the spiritual anatomy of the heart. Let us ESTABLISH, ILLUSTRATE, and APPLY the TRUTHS it contains.

I. LET US ESTABLISH THE TRUTH OF THE TEXT.

But first, let the text be analyzed. "*The heart*" signifies here the whole soul—the entire mental man—understanding—judgment—conscience—will—passions, &c. *Deceitful* literally signifies crooked, perverse, and wanting in conformity to right rule; it also signifies false, fraudulent, &c. *Wicked* signifies corrupt, criminal, and wholly evil. Now in attempting to establish these truths, we appeal to three kinds of evidence.

1. *The scripture testimony.* God's statement respecting the inhabitants of the old world is equally true now, Gen. vi. 5. Jesus also testified to the same truth, "out of the heart proceed evil thoughts, blasphemies, murder," &c. Likened to a cage of unclean birds; corrupt fountain; bad tree, &c. It is also said in scripture, "that the heart is not right with God." "Froward to evil." "Full of evil imaginings." "Full of iniquity and hypocrisy." Hard and impenitent, perverse, rebellious, set to do evil. Then we appeal,

2. *The history of the wicked.* Look at it in Cain; in Pharaoh; in the inhabitants

of Sodom and Gomorrah; envious Jews; in Judas; in the monsters who have been curses to society; moral pests; think of Nero, Caligula, and Burke and Hare of modern times, &c. Here you see what man may become. How vile and horrible. Surely, "the heart is," &c,

3. *To the weakness and sins of good men.* We now go from the worst to the best, from the lowest to the highest. Look at Noah, a perfect man in his generation, and yet by excess, he becomes clothed with shame. Look at Abraham, and yet he dissimulates, and sacrifices truth. Look at Jacob, how he overreaches, and, by fraud, robs his brother. Look at Lot, whose righteous soul, &c. Look at Moses, yet passion gains the ascendency, &c. Look at Aaron, joining with the people in the construction of the golden calf. And what shall we say of David, and Solomon, and Hezekiah, and Peter, and most of the disciples,— suns, but sometimes eclipsed—good men, but only men, and though gracious, yet often the victims of sinful influences. Surely, nothing more strikingly proves that "the heart," &c. But let us,

II. ILLUSTRATE THE SAME TRUTH. We shall find the deceitfulness of the heart displayed,

1. *In reference to ourselves.* How often are we deceived by it!

(1.) How often it flatters us, by representing our state as being better than it really is! We may admit our general wickedness and weakness, but how unwilling to enter into detail! How desirous to judge by the more favorable aspects of our character! How ready to magnify our excellencies! And,

(2.) It deceives us by furnishing excuses for our peculiar sins. It pleads our constitution, education, examples, the general influences of those around; the minor character of our sins, &c.

(3.) In keeping us from contemplating the evil consequences of our sins. It shuts out from view death and judgment, eternity and hell. It sings the syren's song, Peace, peace.

(4.) In inducing us to defer repentance, &c. Some future season. The difficulties fewer—opportunities more striking— the aids, &c. more direct.

2. *Our hearts are deceitful to our fellow creatures.* How few would dare the test of allowing a fellow mortal to look within! Who would consent to the removal of the drapery—the withdrawing of the curtain? What attempts to stand well with mankind! What garnishing, concealing, &c. But,

3. *Our hearts are deceitful towards God.* And what madness is this! Look at it in a few instances. Is it not so,

(1.) When we present to him mere external service? He has the lips, hands, feet, knees, our profession, &c., but the spirit, the heart, the lowliness, the humility, &c., are often wanting.

(2.) When we confess our sins, and vow amendment, and yet persist in them?

(3.) When we extol his grace at the expense of justice and righteousness, &c.? "Because sentence against an evil work," &c. Because grace abounds we continue in sin.

(4.) When we expect, although we daily refuse, his mercy? Let these observations suffice. How true our text, &c. But we notice,

4. *The superlative deceitfulness of the heart.* "Deceitful above all things." Sometimes we use the term in reference to material things. We speak of the weather, of the sea. But the heart is deceitful above these. It has misled more, shipwrecked more, &c. Satan is a deceiver, but the heart, under the influence of evil, outvies the prince of darkness, sins against greater love, &c. The heart is the source of deceitfulness, fountain, root, womb—deceitful under all circumstances, prosperity—adversity—health—sickness—life—death— youth—age, &c. It is deceitful beyond our knowledge or description. Who can know it? Not the wisest or the best, &c. God only sees it and understands it. It is deceitful and wicked beyond our power to restore. "Desperately." Human influence and power may restrain and modify, but God alone can heal and renew. He can take away the stony heart, &c., and give a new heart, &c. Let us,

III. APPLY THE TRUTHS OF THE TEXT. Learn,

1. *The text addresses these truths concerning every one present.* Not one can escape. Let none evade. Let every mouth be stopped. Every breast be smitten. "Have mercy upon me, O Lord!" &c.

2. *Surely such hearts ought not to be trusted.* "Whoso trusteth his own heart," &c. Rather trust the charming of the deadly serpent; rather trust the sinking

quicksand. Let us rather loathe ourselves ; cover with sackcloth. But we add,

3. *Let us not be satisfied with such hearts.* They may be cleansed, transformed, sanctified, &c.

> " There is a fountain fill'd with blood,
>   Drawn from Immanuel's veins,
> And sinners, plunged beneath that flood,
>   Lose all their guilty stains."

O let us repair to the cross ! &c. Jesus is able and willing to save, &c. Who will give his heart to God ? This is the only alternative. He will make them the temples of the Holy Spirit, &c. Dwell in them. Fill them with his own peace, &c. Finally, the heart must be fully renewed, or excluded heaven. Blessed are the pure in heart, &c. Be ye holy, &c.

THE LAW.

" Cursed is every one that continueth not in all things which are written in the book of the law to do them."—GALATIANS iii. 10.

I DESIRE on this occasion, to place before you one complete view of the law of God, that we may understand distinctly how we stand connected with it, and the great end it should answer in our experience. Correct views of the law are indispensable to a right understanding of the gospel, and a just knowledge of both is essential to our comfort and salvation. We ask then,

I. WHAT DO WE UNDERSTAND BY THE LAW ? Sometimes the term signifies the divine word, the revealed truths of the holy scriptures, &c. Sometimes the whole of the Mosaic dispensation. But in our text we understand it signifying the *moral law.* A law which God wrote upon the hearts and consciences of our first parents. Which was afterwards written upon the tables of stone on Sinai,—and which Jesus has summed up in two great commandments, Matthew xxxii. 37, &c. Every duty to God and to men is included in these.

II. WHAT IS THE CHARACTER OF THIS LAW ? A summary of this is given by the great apostle, Romans vii. 12. It is *holy,* the reflection of God's holy mind. *Just,* that is, based on rectitude ; not unreasonable, but equitable between man and God, and man and man. *Good,* that is, benevolent, having a kind aspect to those for whom

it legislates, and productive of their happiness.

III. WHO ARE UNDER ITS AUTHORITY ? All mankind. It is the law of God for the human family. For each person, and for every one. None above it—none beneath it. It is the law of the Creator of every one. The law of the Benefactor, &c., of every one. The law of the great Judge, &c., of every one.

IV. WHAT IS THE CONSEQUENCE OF DISOBEDIENCE ? God's curse. That is, every disobedient person is under God's displeasure and frown, and exposed to eternal death. And this curse extends to every transgressor, and for every act of transgression. One sin involves the soul beneath this curse. We ask,

V. WHAT REMEDY DOES THE LAW PROVIDE FOR TRANSGRESSORS ? Our text contains none, and the law of God recognises none,—it cannot relax its claims,—it cannot allow of one violation,—it cannot bless one transgressor. It will not be satisfied with repentance, floods of tears avail nothing. It refers to its purity, &c., and demands satisfaction. It is not met by reformation. It says, Pay me what thou owest ! The law is inexorable. It blesses the obedient, but curses the sinner.

VI. CAN ANY ONE THEN BE SAVED BY THE LAW ? We reply, no, not one. For this reason, There is none righteous, &c. All have sinned, &c. Every man then is condemned by the law, and not one can have any hope from it. We ask then,

VII. WHAT END THE LAW IS DESIGNED TO ANSWER ?

1. *By it we see what are the just claims of God.* Here we behold the extensive and perfect obedience he requires.

2. *By it we are brought under conviction of sin.* By the law is the knowledge of sin ; see Romans vii. 9. That is, living without the *law* there was no impression of evil, no sense of guilt. But when the commandment of God came with power to the conscience, and I saw its just demands, then my sin revived. I saw myself guilty, and exposed to death. All my former hopes at once expired.

3. *By the law all self-righteousness is to be destroyed.* A consciousness of its demands, and our disobedience, clearly show us, that by the deeds of the law no living flesh can be justified. As a criminal by referring to the statute book, would only

read his sentence, so by the law, we read our exposedness to death, and must at once perceive that from the works of the law there is not the least hope of salvation.

4. *The law is to be our schoolmaster to bring us to Christ.* To instruct us as to our duty, our guilt, our peril, our helplessness, and our need of a Saviour. So that when we exclaim, " O wretched man that I am," &c., this then refers us to Christ, who alone can save us from the curse of the law, Romans viii. 3. " For what the law could not do," &c. Here then we have a door of hope,—not on Sinai, but Zion,—not from the law, but the gospel,—not from Moses, but Jesus. Christ hath redeemed us from the curse of the law, &c., Galatians iii. 13. An interest in Christ saves us from all the consequences of sin, both in this life, and that which is to come. From present condemnation—" There is therefore no condemnation," &c. And from endless wrath —" The gift of God is eternal life," &c.

APPLICATION.

1. How do you stand connected with the law ? Some perhaps are alive in their own indifference, &c. to it. Never felt their sins to be a burden, &c. What will you do when the law flashes across your souls in death or judgment ? Others may be seeking heaven by the deeds of the law. How foolish and fruitless ! One sin condemns, and binds over to eternal death. Others I trust are convicted of sin. The law has revived it, &c., and they exclaim in sorrow before God,

" Guilty I stand before thy face,
  On me I feel thy wrath abide,
'Tis just, the sentence should take place :
'Tis just, but oh, thy Son has died !"

Many of you, I trust, are rejoicing in Christ's free and justifying grace. Being justified by faith, &c.

2. Learn how God alone is glorified in our salvation. He has provided for us the Redeemer. " In the fulness of the times God sent forth," &c.

3. Let his love and mercy be exalted.

4. Let all our hopes rest continually on the salvation that is in Christ Jesus.

OUR LOSS IN ADAM, AND GAIN IN CHRIST.

" Therefore, as by the offence of one, judgment came upon all men to condemnation ; even so by the righteousness of one, the free gift came upon all men unto justification of life."—ROMANS v. 18.

IN this chapter the apostle is exhibiting both the ruin and recovery of mankind ; our ruin in Adam—our recovery in Christ. The reasoning more immediately connected with the text commences with verse 12. Both these doctrines are important, and both must be felt in order to the enjoyment of true peace. The diseased only need and seek the physician's aid—the guilty only feel their guilt, and apply to God for salvation. Both these doctrines have been perverted and abused. As to man's fallen condition, it has been said that the reverse is true—that all men are born pure, and if any evil has arisen from the sin of our first parents, it only affects the physical system of man. As to man's recovery, it has been said, that through Christ all will be eventually saved ; hence has been taught the doctrine of the universal restitution of all things, and the final salvation of all the human race. Now, both of these doctrines we consider perversions of God's word, contrary to the genius and spirit of revelation. But there is another class of doctrines the very reverse of these, which we consider equally unscriptural. In reference to the fall, it has been taught, that by Adam's guilt all men not only partake of his depravity, but are chargeable with his sin, and are justly condemned for it ; and, therefore, original sin, it is said, might justly exclude us from heaven, and consign us to perdition. In reference to our recovery it has been taught, that Christ only came to be the redeemer and head of a select number of the human race, and that the rest are without atonement, and, consequently, without hope of mercy. These doctrines are the extremes of each other, and, we believe, are both opposed to the true testimony of revelation. The gospel declaration we conceive to go midway between the two, and this we shall labor to establish. We ask, then,

I. WHAT HAVE WE LOST THROUGH ADAM ?
II. WHAT HAVE WE OBTAINED BY CHRIST ?
Imagination and conjecture we must discharge in both cases, and abide by the declaration of God's word. We ask, then,

I. WHAT HAVE WE LOST THROUGH ADAM ?
It has been supposed that if our first parents had been faithful, that their posterity would have been necessarily happy, &c.

This is not so much as hinted at in the scriptures, and we consider as opposed to the responsibility of the creature, which we believe always to be personal and not relative. But, we observe—we lost paradise, that earthly domain of bliss, &c.— we lost health and immortality, and became exposed to disease and death—we lost our moral glory and purity, and became partakers of the fallen nature of our first parents; as such we became obnoxious to God's holiness, and unfit for his presence and glory. Universal guilt is the necessary result of our depraved nature, for it is natural for that which is evil to sin, and only supernaturally that it can do good and follow holiness. We perceive, thus, that all men are, by their own personal guilt, exposed to the just wrath of God, and he may righteously punish them with eternal death. Such is our reply to the first question. We ask,

II. WHAT HAVE WE OBTAINED BY CHRIST? Now, I reply to this, that unconditional eternal life is not secured to any person; that is, that God will not, on account of Christ's merits, save any man without respect to personal character. But Jesus Christ has obtained for man the means of his restoration to God's favor and likeness, and, consequently, to eternal glory. God's holy law Christ has honored and magnified —he has also paid its penalty by the sacrifice of his own life. Thus the law of God has been rendered illustrious before angels and fallen spirits—through Christ's atoning merits God can now be just, &c. God does not grant eternal life on the ground of works, but as a free gift, through Jesus Christ. And God has determined that all who come to him by Christ shall receive the forgiveness of sin, and the spirit of grace and holiness, to renew their hearts, and enable them to do the will of God, &c. Now, this offer of eternal life is the grand subject of the gospel—"this is the record," &c. Christ has placed the whole of our race, therefore, in a condition of salvation. There is no reason, on God's part, why all men may not be saved, &c. But we must also advance another truth following this— that men, so far from being losers by the fall, may be gainers even in an eminent degree.

(1.) We stand not now on the responsibility of our own strength, which in Adam failed, but on the promised grace of Christ.

Christ's fulness of wisdom, and power, and ability are all mine. How superior to a creature's ability, however distinguished!

(2.) The loss of earthly good and glory are more than compensated by the glory and felicity of a future world. For paradise, heaven—for the visits of angels, the temple in which they dwell, &c.—for the pleasures of sense in Eden, the beatific vision of God in glory—heaven instead of earth. Now, this gracious advantage is the high privilege of all men; all men are eligible, and on terms within the reach of all. To deny this is to contradict the spirit and letter of the text, and also verse 20. I would remark, in conclusion,

1. Your loss in Adam has been aggravated by your own guilt. All have sinned—all, therefore, are exposed to death and perdition.

2. In Christ there is opened to you the door of hope and mercy. Will you enter? You may if you will. God says this; with you, therefore, is the alternative. God says ask—seek—knock. He says, come. The Spirit and the bride say, Come, &c.

3. Let the Christian exult in the grace by Christ Jesus. His life-boat is vastly more safe than the bark of Adam's original responsibility. Oh, yes! here is grace abounding to the sinner's weal and the glory of God.

4. All the lost are self-ruined. Yes! every one.

MAN'S HELPLESSNESS, AND GOD'S COMPASSION.

"None eye pitied thee, to do any of these unto thee, to have compassion upon thee; but thou wast cast out into the open field, to the loathing of thy person, in the day that thou wast born. And when I passed by thee," &c.—EZEK. xvi. 5, 6.

OUR text contains a description of the original condition of the house of Israel, and the surpassing condescension and compassion of God towards them. This is followed by a recital of the apostacy and sins of the people against the goodness of the Lord their God. The fearful picture concludes with the announcement of God's mercy and grace, notwithstanding their transgression against him. The text, however, is very applicable to the original state of every human being; and, contemplated as such, it is calculated to fill us with the spirit of humiliation, adoration, and praise. Observe,

I. OUR NATURAL ESTATE. This is most fitly represented,

1. *As polluted.* " Saw thee polluted." The fact of man's defilement by sin is abundantly established by the declarations of the word of God. All men are transgressors, and every kind of transgression defiles and pollutes the soul. The understanding is polluted by ignorance, the judgment by error and falsehood, the affections by earthliness and self, the conscience by wilful disobedience ; so that the prophet's description of Israel is truly applicable to the unrenewed, unconverted children of men, Isa. i. 5, 6—" The whole head is sick," &c.

2. *As outcasts.* " But thou wast cast out." Sin and holiness cannot have communion with each other. The blessed God cannot be pleased with impure and polluted man. Thus angels were expelled the mansions of glory ; thus Adam and Eve the abodes of Eden ; and thus sin exiles every one of its victims from the divine presence and favor. The sinner is said to be afar off ; alienated, &c. by wicked works ; as rebels, outcasts from his kingdom ; as prodigals, far from our heavenly Father's house ; dwelling in darkness and the shadow of death.

3. *As unpitied.* " None eye pitied thee." Angels are as holy and just as they are kind and benevolent. They could not feel for traitors against their God—could not delight in rebel spirits, or have complacency in iniquity. Fallen spirits rejoiced in ruining the hopes and blighting the prospects of mankind, and man had no pity towards himself. Deluded and perverted in all his faculties and powers, he saw not his shame, and felt not his misery.

4. *As necessarily perishing.* Dying of disease, of weakness, of exposure ; dying for want of help. Consider the figure of an infant thus cast out—its helplessness—must perish. So our ruin had been certain, and unavoidable, and eternal. Notice,

II. THE COMPASSIONATE REGARDS OF GOD TOWARDS US. He is represented as passing by and observing the condition of fallen, polluted humanity, and exercising mercy towards them. These regards,

1. *Were the result of rich and spontaneous mercy.* No reasons to induce Deity—

none in the aspect of the sinner—none in the cause of his ruin—self-destroyed—none in his solicitude for deliverance—none in the return he could make. It was mercy originating in mercy, for mercy's sake alone, that caused him to bend over our ruined race. These regards,

2. *Were expressed towards us in promises of love.* " I said unto thee, Live." How analogous, too, the threatening was ! Dying thou shalt die. But God, who was rich in mercy, when he saw our ruined state, promised deliverance and restoration. From the entrance of sin to our redemption, God filled the mouths of prophets with assurances of his grace and favor. By faith Abel and the patriarchs, and fathers, and prophets, looked through the promises given for the mercy of God to eternal life. These regards,

3. *Were embodied in the person of the Mediator.* That we might live he chose a Mediator. He sent him as the fountain of life. He came and proclaimed it. " I am come that ye might have life," &c. " I am the resurrection," &c. Yea, Jesus, as the exhibition of God's love, died in the stead of the ungodly, and bore in his own body our sins upon the tree. The poet has beautifully presented this to us :

" Plunged in a gulf of dark despair,
    We wretched sinners lay :
Without one cheering beam of hope,
    Or spark of glimmering day.

" With pitying eyes the Prince of Peace
    Beheld our helpless grief ;
He saw ; and, oh ! amazing love !
    He ran to our relief."

The gospel just reiterates these regards, assuring us that God sent his Son into the world not to condemn, &c.

4. *A believing reception of God's merciful arrangement brings life into the soul.* God now sends his messengers to invite the outcasts to live—to offer them life—to persuade them to have it, but to have it in Jesus, and in Jesus alone ; and he that believeth the messenger of grace lives. God justifies him freely—saves him from condemnation—regenerates his heart by his quickening Spirit—raises to a new and holy life of faith in the Son of God, &c. ; and this life is perfected and consummated in eternal glory. The gift of God is eternal life. This is the record that God hath given unto us, &c.

APPLICATION.

1. *Learn the wretched state of our fallen species.* How necessary to see this clearly, and feel it intensely.

2. *The unsearchableness of God's mercy.* God only knows the love of God to man :

" 'Tis mercy all, immense and free,
    For oh, my God! it found out me "

3. *That salvation is of grace.* From first to last. The grace of God bringeth, applieth, and consummates the work.

4. *The claims of Deity on our gratitude, love, and obedience.*

THE DISTINCTIONS IN THE GODHEAD.

" In the name of the Father, and of the Son, and of the Holy Ghost."—MATT. xxviii. 19.

DIVINE revelation makes known to us one living and true God, and prohibits all worship being paid to any being except Jehovah. But the phraseology employed obviously presents the one Jehovah under certain distinctions, involving the idea of a plurality in the Godhead. This distinction has been generally denominated the Trinity—Father, Son, and Holy Ghost. The doctrine has been controverted in all ages, and numerous are the theories which men have endeavored to maintain on this deeply profound, and confessedly difficult subject. The advocates of the trinity may be arranged under several distinctions. So also the opponents are diversified in sentiment, from the high Arian to the low Socinian. Our present purpose is to exhibit some of the representations of this subject as given in the infallible records of inspired truth.

I. IT IS OBVIOUS THAT A THREEFOLD DISTINCTION IN DEITY IS NOT IMPOSSIBLE. We have many symbols of this in nature : the sun—the light, and heat thereof; man—body, soul, and spirit. Grotius thus illustrated the doctrine :

" May we not some such thing in mankind see ;
  LIFE, REASON, WILL, in one are three ;
  Are Father, Son, and Spirit equal ? they
  With equal might one sceptre sway."

It is presumptuous to say, that there cannot be three persons in the Godhead.

II. THE OLD TESTAMENT WRITINGS LEAD US TO THIS CONCLUSION. In the very first page of the sacred oracles it is written, " In the beginning God created," &c. The Hebrew word is in the plural number.

Again, " Let *us* make man,' &c. " Behold, the man is become as one of *us*," &c. Gen. ii. 22. " Let *us* go down," &c. Gen. ii. 7. The Jewish benediction—" The Lord bless thee and keep thee ; the Lord make his face to shine upon thee ; the Lord lift up his countenance upon thee," &c. Numbers vi. 24, &c. The same view of Deity pervades the writings of the prophets. See Psalm xlv. 6, 7, cx. 1, cxxxvi. 1–3 ; 2 Sam. xxiii. 3 ; Isaiah vi. 8, also verse 3 ; Isaiah xlii. 1, xlviii. 16, lix. 19, 20 ; Zech. ii. 10, 11.

III. THE WRITINGS OF THE NEW TESTAMENT EXHIBIT THIS TRIUNE DISTINCTION. See it in the baptism of Jesus, Matt. iii. 16, 17. See it also in several striking expressions in the teaching of Christ, John xiv. 16, xv. 26 ; Acts i. 4, 5 ; especially as connected with the great commission, Matt. xxviii. 19. It is often incidentally exhibited in other portions of the New Testament writings. See Acts v. 30–35 ; Stephen's vision, Acts vii. 55, x. 38, xx. 27, 28 ; Rom. v. 5, 6, xv. 30 ; see also the apostolic benediction, 2 Cor. xiii. 14.

IV. THE DIVINE WORKS ARE ASCRIBED TO EACH OF THE TRIUNE PERSONS.

1. *Creation.* " In the beginning God created the heavens," &c. By the " Word" all things were made, &c. By " his Spirit" he hath garnished the heavens, Job xxvi. 13 ; see also Psalm civ. 30.

2. *The work of inspiration.* " God shall reveal this unto you," Phil. iii. 15. " The revelation of Jesus Christ," Gal. i. 12. " The Holy Spirit shall teach you all things," John xiv. 26. " God spake unto the fathers by the prophets," Heb. i. 1. " The word of Christ," Col. iii. 16. " Holy men spake as they were moved by the Holy Ghost," 2 Pet. i. 21.

3. *The work of holiness.* " Sanctified of God the Father," Jude 1. " He that sanctifieth," &c., Heb. ii. 11. " Sanctified by the Holy Ghost," Rom. xv. 16.

4. *The work of raising the dead.* The Father raiseth up the dead, John v. 21 ; Rom. iv. 17 ; 2 Cor. i. 9. Christ raiseth the dead, John v. 21, xi. 25. The Spirit raiseth the dead. " It is the Spirit that quickeneth," John vi. 63. We observe,

V. THAT THE ESSENTIAL TITLES AND ATTRIBUTES ARE GIVEN TO FATHER, SON, AND HOLY SPIRIT.

1. *Eternity.* " The eternal God," Deut. xxxiii. 27. The Son—Before all things,

Col. i. 17. The Spirit—The eternal Spirit, Heb. ix. 14.

2. *Omnipresence.* "Do not I fill heaven and earth, saith the Lord," Jer. xxiii. 24. The Son—"Filleth all in all," Eph. i. 23. The Spirit—"Whither shall I go from thy Spirit," Psalm cxxxix. 7.

3. *Omniscience.* "Known unto God are all his works," Acts xv. 18. The Son—"He knew all men," &c., John ii. 24. The Spirit—see 1 Cor. ii. 10, &c.

4. *Power.* "Power belongeth unto God," Psalm lxii. 11. Christ—"All power is given unto me," &c., Matt. xxviii. 18. The Spirit—"Through the power of the Holy Ghost," Rom. xv. 13.

5. *Wisdom.* "Wisdom and might are his," Dan. ii. 20. The Son—"In him are hid all the treasures," &c., Col. ii. 2, 3. Holy Spirit—"He is the Spirit of wisdom," Isaiah xi. 2 ; Eph. i. 17. It is clear, from this great variety of scripture quotation, that the scriptures recognise a plurality in the godhead, and give to each the titles and perfections of proper Deity.

OBSERVATIONS.

1. With what reverence and profound veneration we should study the nature and character of God! How awfully sublime is the theme—how utterly incompetent we must be to find it out to perfection—how essentially requisite holy fear and humility of mind in its investigation!

2. We should labor to ascertain the connection between the divine persons in the godhead, and the exercises of devotion and worship. We are to come to God through the Son and by the Holy Spirit. We are thus, also, to praise God, and to pray to him. The Father is chiefly the object of worship, Christ is the way, and by the Spirit we worship him in spirit and in truth. God our Father—God our Redeemer—God our Comforter and guide.

3. Divine honors are to be equally given to Father, Son, and Holy Spirit.

4. Let us labor to obtain and enjoy the love of the Father, the grace of the Lord Jesus Christ, and the fellowship and communion of the Holy Spirit.

> "To Father, Son, and Holy Ghost—
> The God whom we adore—
> Be glory, as it was and is,
> And shall be evermore."

THE DIVINITY OF CHRIST.

NO. I.

"Who is over all, God blessed for ever. Amen."
—Rom. ix. 5.

It is impossible by any legitimate mode of interpretation to apply the words of the text to any other than the Lord Jesus Christ. And if they apply to Christ only, then it is evident that they clearly establish the perfect Deity of the Saviour. It cannot be supposed that the apostle would indulge in rapturous flights of imagination at the expense of the essential truths of religion. So that we must either expunge this striking portion of the word from the pages of truth, or the divinity of the Lord Jesus is fully and irrefragably exhibited. But a doctrine of such moment does not rest on one isolated text however clear, peremptory, and conclusive. It is a doctrine diffused through the volume of inspiration. It is a prominent truth of the sacred writers. Let us then explain, establish, and apply the subject. Let us,

I. Explain what we mean by the divinity of the Saviour. It is obvious that some mysterious distinction exists between the Son of God and the Father; and between the Son of God and the Holy Spirit. Yet the distinction does not affect the unity of the Father, Son, and Spirit. And the divinity of Christ clearly involves oneness of essence, nature, and glory with the Father; that is, equality with the Father in majesty, dignity, and power. We cannot enter upon the various hypotheses regarding the expression "Son of God," as to its proper eternity, or as to its application to Christ in his incarnate state; or as to the pre-existence of the human soul of the Redeemer. We believe the scriptures to teach the uncreated, divine, and perfect godhead of Jesus Christ.

II. Let us establish this truth. Our evidence is varied and immense. We refer,

1. *To the testimony of the writers of the Old Testament scriptures.* In the forty-fifth psalm as applied to Christ by the apostle, "Thy throne, O God," &c. In the sixty-eighth psalm, "The chariots of God are twenty thousand," &c. This is also applied to Christ, Eph. iv. 8. The seventy-second psalm is also clearly a prediction of Christ's kingdom and glory. See espe-

cially the seventeenth verse to end. In the seventy-eighth psalm it is said, "Israel tempted the most high God." Let this be compared with 1 Cor. x. 3. Compare also the eighty-ninth psalm with Col. i. 15; Rev. xix. 16. So also the ninety-seventh psalm, ver. 7, with Heb. i. 6; see also Isaiah vi. 1, &c. vii. 14, viii. 13, 15, ix. 6, &c. xl. 32, xl. 9, 10, xlv. 22, lii. 7, liii. 13; Micah v. 2; Jer. xxiii. 5, 6; Dan. vii. 13; Zech. ii. 10, &c. xiii. 7; Malachi iii. 1. Observe,

2. *The testimonies of Christ to his own divinity.*

(1.) Observe the confessions made to, and of him. John the Baptist, John iii. 35—Nathaniel, John i. 49—Matthew, John xi. 27—Peter, John vi. 68, 69; Matt. xvi. 13. The devils, Luke iv. 41. Voice from heaven, Matt. v. 16, xvii. 5—Thomas, John xx. 26.

(2.) Observe his own direct statements: "No man hath ascended," &c. John iii. 13. "And now, O Father, glorify thou me with the glory," &c. John xvii. 1. "Before Abraham was," &c. John viii. 56, &c. "For where two or three," &c. Matt. xviii. 19. "He that hath seen me," &c. John xiv. 9. "All that the Father hath are mine," John xvi. 15. "I and my Father are one," John x. 30. "That all men should honor," &c. "I am Alpha," &c. Rev. i. 8; John v. 12, 13.

3. *The apostolic testimony to the divinity of Christ.* The dying testimony of Stephen, Acts vii. 55, 60. The prayer of the apostles respecting the lot cast for the election of an apostle, Acts ii. 24. "Jesus Christ is Lord of all," Acts x. 26. "Being exalted," &c. Acts ii. 53. Observe the distinct exclamations of Peter, "Everlasting kingdom of the Lord Jesus Christ," 2 Pet. i. 11, also 2 Pet. i. 1. "To him be glory," &c. 2 Pet. iii. 18. James—"Lord of glory," chap. ii. 1. Jude—"Denying the only Lord God and our Lord Jesus Christ," ver. 4, see Whitby on this passage. "To the only wise God our Saviour," ver. 25. Paul —"The Lord of glory," 1 Cor. ii. 8. "The Lord from heaven," 1 Cor. xv. 47. "That he might fill all things," Eph. iv. 9. "Let this mind be in you," &c. Phil. ii. 5. "It pleased the Father that in him should all fulness dwell," Col. i. 19; see Col. ii. 3, ii. 9. John—"The word was God," John i. 1. "Hereby we perceive the love of God," &c. 1 John iii. 1. "This is the true God," &c. 1 John v. 20. "And on his vesture and on his thigh a name written, King of kings," &c. Rev. xix. 16.

OBSERVATIONS.

1. If these passages do not establish the divinity of the Saviour, then it is impossible to understand the writings we term the holy scriptures. They are ambiguous beyond all the writings ever given to the world. There is no principle of interpretation that can lead us to their true signification. But believing the word of God to be a revelation and not a mystification, then at once we must perceive that the divinity of Christ is one of those doctrines which of all others is most prominently declared. Prophets, evangelists, apostles, all concur in their testimony to this subject.

2. Christ can have no claim upon our confidence, if he be not truly divine. The legitimate reading of his own word, his own teaching concerning himself, evidently was designed to make himself known as co-equal with the Father, and the divine Son of God with glory and power.

3. A proper view of this subject is essential to a right direction of Christian conduct. A divine Saviour must have a claim upon us that it would be presumption for any created being to assume. We may venerate and esteem a human saviour, but we can only adore, and trust, and worship a Saviour who is divine. Prayer, and faith, and hope are only meet to Jesus on the ground of the supreme Godhead, and essential Deity.

4. The incomprehensibility of the doctrine is no argument against its truth. Equally so is the existence of one eternal Jehovah, it is one of the confessed mysteries of revelation. "Great is the mystery of godliness," &c. "Then to the law and to the testimony," &c. "Search the scriptures," &c.

THE DIVINITY OF CHRIST.

NO. II.

"Who is over all, God blessed for ever."—ROM. ix. 5.

IN a previous discourse we have examined the testimony of prophets, evangelists, and apostles, concerning the divinity of Jesus Christ. We also adverted to the declarations of Jesus himself. We now proceed to establish the same truth.

1. *From his divine works.* The works which are ascribed to God, and beyond the power of any creature, are fully and frequently ascribed to Christ.

(1.) Creation. Of the Word that was made flesh, it is written, "All things were made by him," &c. John i. 3; "by whom are all things," &c. 1 Cor. viii. 6; "by him were all things created that are in heaven," &c. Col. i. 16; "by whom also he made the worlds," &c. Heb. i. 2.

(2.) Universal dominion. He is Lord of all, "the Father hath given all things into his hands," &c. "By him all things consist," Col. i. 16, 17. See Phil. ii. 9, &c.

(3.) Resurrection of the body. "As the Father raiseth up the dead, even so the Son quickeneth whom he will." "The dead shall hear the voice of the Son of God, and live," John v. 21, 25. "I will raise him up at the last day," John vi. 40. "Who shall change our vile body," &c. Phil. iii. 21. "I am the resurrection and the life," John xi. 25.

(4.) The judgment of the world. "The Son of man shall come in his glory," &c. Matt. xxv. 31. "The Father hath committed all judgment," &c. John v. 22. "The judge of the quick and dead," Acts x. 42. "God hath appointed a day," &c. xvii. 31. "We must all stand before the judgment-seat of Christ," Rom. xiv. 10.

(5.) The bestowment of eternal rewards, and the infliction of everlasting punishments. "I give unto my sheep eternal life. Then shall he say to them on his right hand," &c. Matt. xxv. 34. See also, to the wicked, ver. 41. Mark viii. 38.

2. *From his divine perfections.*

(1.) Omniscience. "Jesus knew their thoughts," Matt. ix. 4. "He knew all men," John ii. 2. "Thou, Lord, who knowest the thoughts of all men," Acts i. 24. "I am he who searcheth the reins and heart," Rev. ii. 23.

(2.) Omnipresence. "Lo, I am with you always," &c. Matt. xxviii. 18. "Wherever two or three are gathered together," &c. See John iii. 13.

(3.) Omnipotence. "To him be power everlasting," 1 Tim. vi. 16. "The Almighty," Rev. i. 8. "Christ the power of God," 1 Cor. i. 24.

(4.) Immutability. "Jesus Christ, the same yesterday, to-day, and forever," Heb. xiii. 8.

(5.) Eternity and self-existence. "I am Alpha and Omega," &c. "The first and the last." "I have power to lay down my life," &c. John i. 18. "As the Father hath life in himself, so hath he given to the Son to have life in himself," John v. 26.

3. *From the divine homage and worship presented to him.*

(1.) He, with the Father, is the proper object of prayer and invocation. "Not every one that saith to me, Lord, Lord," &c. Matt. vii. 21. "With all that call on the name of the Lord Jesus," Acts xxii. 16. Thus Paul besought the Lord thrice, 2 Cor. xii. 7, 9. Thus Stephen's dying request. See also, 2 Tim. ii. 22. Rom. x. 12, 14.

(2.) He is the proper object of adoration and praise. The Father gave the mandate, "Let all the angels of God worship him," Heb. i. 6. He hath also determined, "That all men should honor the Son, even," &c. John v. 22, 23. "At the name of Jesus every knee should bow," Phil. ii. 1, &c. "I thank Christ Jesus our Lord," 1 Tim. i. 12. "Unto him that loved us," &c. Rev. i. 5, 6. "And they worshipped him," &c. Luke xxiv. 50, 52. Observe also the celestial hosts all unite in highest praise to Christ, Rev. v. 3–13, and vii. 10. Nothing can be added to give weight to this indisputable array of divine testimony to the true and proper Godhead of Jesus. Let us then,

III. APPLY THE SUBJECT. Learn,

1. The dishonor done to Christ, by robbing him of his divine character. It involves some measure of unbelief, often the result of unsanctified reasoning. Must grieve the Father, is ungrateful to the Son, and reflects on the Holy Spirit, who has so fully exhibited the Deity of Christ.

2. Learn the claim Christ has on our confidence and love. He demands an entire, undivided trust. Our supreme love. He claims the throne of the heart.

3. Learn the duties we owe to him. Attention to his word; obedience to his authority; regard to his ordinances; delight in his service; zeal for his glory. We should live to him, and die to him, and thus forever be the Lord's.

4. The fulness of blessing there is in the divine Saviour. His power is all-sufficient to aid in every time of need, &c. Grace is an inexhaustible fulness. "Full of grace," &c. "Unsearchable riches of grace," and everlasting treasures of glory

are hid in him. What a desirable friend! What a glorious Saviour! "He is all, and in all," &c.

5. The terribleness of Christ as an enemy. His wrath is terrible, &c. He will break his enemies in pieces, &c.

CHRIST THE MEDIATOR.

"For there is one God, and one Mediator between God and men, the man Christ Jesus."— 1 TIM. ii. 5.

OUR text relates to one of the most important subjects of revelation, and that which is the very essence of the gospel— the mediation of the Lord Jesus Christ. It is of great importance to have scriptural and clear views of this all-essential doctrine. It is a doctrine inseparably identified with our peace, and comfort, and salvation. It is the great cardinal pillar of redemption, the very keystone of the arch of Christianity.

Let us then ascertain,

I. THE PERSON OF THE MEDIATOR.
II. THE WORK OF THE MEDIATOR. And
III. THE RESULTS OF HIS MEDIATION.

I. THE PERSON OF THE MEDIATOR. Now on this subject I desire to present to you the leading divisions of sentiment which have been maintained and taught. We refer,

1. *To those who teach the manhood of Christ only.* Who represent Jesus as never existing prior to his birth of the virgin, and that he stands only at the head of the created servants of God, and the divinely appointed author of the Christian religion, as Moses was of the Levitical economy. This is the Socinian doctrine.

2. *To those who teach that Christ is the highest and first-born of every creature.* Made before all worlds, and therefore more glorious than any of the angels. Yet only a created being, &c. This is Arianism.

3. *To those who taught that there is but one person in the Godhead.* That he descended into the virgin, became a Son, and accomplished our salvation, then diffused himself on the apostles in tongues of fire, and was thus denominated the Holy Ghost. This is Sabellianism.

4. *Those who teach that there is one person only in the Godhead, viz. Jesus Christ.* And that he came into the world to glorify

his human nature, by making it one with the divine, and that the human nature itself is now divine. This is Swedenborgianism.

We believe that the scriptures teach a doctrine respecting the Mediator, essentially distinct from each and all of these, viz. That in the Godhead there are three persons, Father, Son, and Holy Ghost. That God sent his Son, who clothed himself with our nature and became God and man in one person. That Christ was God, is evident *from the titles given to him,* "Immanuel," "God is with us," "The mighty God," "Thy throne, O God," &c. *From his perfections of omniscience,* &c. Omnipresent, &c.—"Wherever two or three are gathered together." Eternally,—"Before Abraham was," &c. "Alpha and Omega," &c. *From his works.* Creation—providence—judgment. *From the homage and worship,* &c. "Let all the angels of God," &c. "Worthy is the Lamb," &c. Yet it is evident that he is distinct from the Father and the Holy Ghost, John xiv. 16, 26, xv. 26, xvii. 1, 24; Matt. xxviii. 19. But our text asserts the manhood of the Saviour. This needs no confirmation. "God sent his Son," &c. But there was a necessity why he should be both.

1. *That he should be man,*
(1.) Having the nature of those for whom he mediated.
(2.) That he should be under the law.
(3.) Be capable of suffering.
(4.) That he should be able to sympathize.
(5.) That he should be a perfectly holy man, without sin or spot.

2. *That he should be God.*
(1.) To have power to redeem, &c.
(2.) To have power over the devil and death, to give infinite value to his obedience; the service of any mere man could only have availed for himself.
(3.) To be an object of absolute trust to all his believing people. Such is the person of the blessed Mediator.

II. THE WORK OF THE MEDIATOR. To mediate, is to interpose between two who are at variance, and endeavor to effect reconciliation. Sin separated man from God. From his allegiance,—image,—and favor. Sin clothed Deity with the vestments of righteous indignation and wrath. Man thus became not only fallen, but in peril of endless death. God could not allow sin to go unpunished, without falsifying his character, and throwing confusion into the universe. Yet his mercy triumphed towards us in that he provided a Mediator. So that the *gift* of Christ was the *effect* of God's love to the world. The work of Christ, then, has two distinct aspects.

(1.) To lay a solid foundation for the exercise of God's love with honor to the divine government and laws. He appeared, therefore, as a man, and the law demanded from him perfect obedience. He gave it—yielded every jot and tittle it demanded. He thus honored the great Lawgiver in all his blessed perfections. He offered his own precious life as a substituted sacrifice on behalf of a guilty world, that the penalty of the law might be fully met. He thus bore our sins in his own body on the tree. He conquered the enemies of man—Satan, death, and the grave. Thus God's love could honorably flow to man.

(2.) In his work he had to bring men to God. As mediator he obtains a time of probation for the guilty. He issues the proclamation of his grace in the gospel. He sends down the Holy Spirit to renew and sanctify the believer. He presents the persons and services of his people to God as their High-priest and intercessor. This then is the work of Christ as mediator.

III. THE RESULTS OF HIS MEDIATION.

1. *A glorious display of the purity and compassion of God.* God is now displayed as the just God, and yet the Saviour. Hating sin, yet loving the sinner. Pouring out his wrath, yet freely dispensing his mercy.

2. *Salvation is now freely revealed and offered to mankind.* Now the gospel may be indeed styled the good news, the glad tidings. " Through this man is preached unto you remission of sins," &c. " This we know and testify," &c. Now Christ is held up to a lost world as the way, and the truth, &c.

3. *The impenitent are now without excuse.*
" No mortal hath a just pretence,
To perish in despair."
The soul's ruin is now connected with the rejection of Christ. For those who despise him there is no more sacrifice for sin.

APPLICATION.

1. How beautifully Christ's mediation harmonizes with the gospel plan of salvation ! Now we have not to do with God directly, but with God in Christ. To be

saved we must place our interests in his hands. This is believing, trusting, appropriating, &c.

2. We learn that there is but one Mediator: No other way or name, and no other intercessor. It is anti-scriptural to pray to saints or angels. Christ is the one Mediator.

3. Let us rejoice in the light and glory of the gospel.

THE PREDICTED CHARACTER OF CHRIST.

" Behold, my servant shall deal prudently, he shall be exalted and extolled, and be very high. As many were astonished at thee ; his visage was so marred more than any man, and his form more than the sons of men : so shall he sprinkle many nations, the kings shall shut their mouths at him : for that which had not been told them shall they see, and that which they had not heard, shall they consider."—ISAIAH lii. 13, &c.

OUR text is a distinct subject from that discussed in the previous parts of the chapter, and evidently ought to have formed a part of the 53d chapter of the evangelical prophet. It is most clearly a prophecy concerning the Messiah. It relates both to his official character, sufferings, exaltation, and conquests ; and as such is replete with deeply interesting matter for our profitable meditation. Observe,

I. THE OFFICE OF CHRIST. God's servant. " My servant." The same phrase is used in 40th chapter, 1st verse. Christ in his mediatorial character, was God's servant, while in his essential glory, he was God blessed forevermore.

1. *Hearken to his own declarations.* "The Son of man came not to be ministered unto," &c. " I must work," &c. " I came to do the will of my Father." Even at twelve years of age he said, " Wist ye not," &c. So at the end of his life, he said, " I have glorified thee," &c., " have finished the work," &c. Christ ever recognised himself as God's servant.

2. *Observe how he discharged the office of servant.* Here we are struck with,

(1.) His fidelity. He was faithful in all things—never omitted one of the requirements of his Father ; did all his will, and that perfectly.

(2.) His zeal—His Father's honor and glory ever melted his ardent soul. " The zeal of thy house," &c. This feeling consumed his sacred spirit. How it burst forth in the temple, &c.

(3.) His perseverance. He held on his course with undeviating constancy ; never turned aside ; was faithful unto death. The text refers to,

(4.) His prudence. The word in the margin is "prosper," but our translation would lead us to view one striking feature in his office—the wisdom which distinguished his course. Now this shone forth as the light of the sun at noonday. In his discourses to his disciples—in his replies to his enemies, "never man spake like this man." Never could entangle him, &c. Infallibility marked all he said and did. The subject leads us,

II. To THE SUFFERINGS HE SHOULD BEAR. "As many were astonished." All Christ's engagements were astonishing—his sayings —his actions ; but the words evidently refer to his sufferings. That a personage so illustrious, should be so abased.—So glorious, should appear so poor.—So holy, should be so reproached.—So powerful, should endure so much.—So heavenly, should drink of the cup of sorrow so intensely, &c. "His visage was so marred," &c. Hear the predictions of the prophet, all of which were so literally fulfilled. Psalm xxii. 6, &c. ; see also 3 and 4 of the next chapter. How bitterly was he calumniated ! How maliciously he was persecuted ! How basely was he treated ! How cruelly he was tortured ! Especially in Herod's hall, and when preparing him for his ignominious death, he might well exclaim, "I am the man who hath seen affliction," &c. "See, is there any sorrow," &c. The lions seized his soul ; the waves went over his head ; the storm beat upon his spirit. Observe,

III. THE EXALTATION OF CHRIST. "He shall be exalted," &c.

1. *Christ was exalted.*

(1.) In his resurrection from the dead. "Him did God raise up, for it was impossible that he should be holden," &c. He spoiled the projects of the powers of darkness, in bursting the prison-house of the grave. "I am he that was dead," &c.

(2.) He was exalted by his elevation to the right hand of the throne of God. "He ascended on high," &c. God said, "Sit thou on my right hand," &c. "Him hath God exalted," &c.

2. *He shou'd be extolled.* That is,

praised—his character celebrated, &c.—Now,

(1.) Angels extolled him as their Lord, heralded him back again to his kingdom and glory, "Open the everlasting doors," &c.

(2.) John heard all the celestial hosts of heaven extolling him in their anthems of praise, "Worthy is the Lamb," &c.

(3.) His ministering servants and people extol him on earth.

> "'Tis all our business here below,
> To cry, Behold the Lamb."

He is fairer than the children of men.

(4.) He shall be extolled by his redeemed saints forever. "Daily shall he be praised," &c. "His praise shall sound from shore to shore," &c. The last sounds that shall be heard in reference to our world will be the voice of praise to Christ. "Hallelujah ! for the kingdoms of this world," &c.

3. *He shall be very high.* Exalted to the throne of supreme authority, power, and glory. Thus he was beheld by Ezekiel—above seraphim and cherubim—receiving the homage and obedience of all in heaven and on earth. Notice,

IV. HIS GRACIOUS CONQUESTS.

1. "*He shall sprinkle,*" &c. He does so,

(1.) By his doctrines. His blessed word falls as the rain, distils as the dew, &c.

(2.) By his blood. When these doctrines are received, then man partakes of the merits of his death, and the cleansing virtues of his blood. The blood of Christ is called the blood of sprinkling.

(3.) By his spiritual blessings. The outpourings of his Holy Spirit, and the rich communications of his mercy and love.

2. *He shall silence the opposition of kings.* These shall oppose the gospel, and employ worldly power and authority against it. But he shall overturn, &c. See Psalm ii. 12. See the change as exhibited, Psalm lxxii. 10.

3. *His achievements shall be unprecedented and wonderful.* "For that which had not been told," &c. Now two things shall particularly astonish.

(1.) The simplicity of his means. Not by carnal weapons, not by human power, not by armies, &c., nor by science, but by the word of grace, and the messengers of salvation ; by the foolishness of preaching, &c.

(2.) The completeness of the results. Effective, deep, and universal changes. Men renovated—society altered. Ignorance banished—crime annihilated—misery extinguished. Purity, joy, and bliss diffused. The days of heaven upon earth.

1. Are we the friends or enemies of the blessed Saviour? Do we despise, reject, deride, reproach, &c., or do we hail, receive, and delight in him? All men act now as his friends or foes.

2. Has he sprinkled your hearts with the blessings of his grace—his word—his blood—his Spirit?

3. Are you aiding Christ in his triumphal career? Accelerating the conversion of the world? The soldiers of his cross?

4. What bright visions are yet to distinguish the cause of the Saviour! "Blessed be the Lord God of Israel," &c.

THE MORAL BEAUTY OF THE REDEEMER.

"Thou art fairer than the children of men; grace is poured into thy lips; therefore God hath blessed thee forever."—Psalm xlv. 2.

None of the sacred prophets wrote more fully, clearly, or sweetly of the Saviour than Jesse's son, the sweet singer of Israel. He was richly imbued with the spirit of prophecy, and was favored to see, in predicted visions, much of the glory and preciousness of the Messiah. He wrote much of his sorrows and humiliation, but he wrote much, also, of his joy and triumph. Of these, the 74th, and the psalm from which our text is selected, have a distinguished pre-eminence. His soul was greatly elevated, and powerfully excited, when he composed this wondrous psalm, " My heart," &c. The original conveys the idea of his emotions being extremely wrought upon, so that his fervid passions boiled within him. My theme is royal—" I speak of the things," &c.; my subject so copious, so richly overflowing, that my fingers inscribe the celestial strains with vehement rapidity—" My tongue is the pen," &c. The title of the psalm is peculiarly interesting—" A song of loves"—of the pre-eminent love of the King-Messiah to his church, and the reciprocated love of the church to

her royal head. Our text is addressed directly to him—" Thou art fairer," &c. Observe, the text refers to the beauty of Christ's person, the graciousness of his address, and the blessedness of his reign.

I. The beauty of Christ's person. " Thou art fairer," &c. Beauty has been defined—an assemblage of graces that please the eye. Let us consider this in its application,

1. To the body of Jesus. No doubt our first parents, in reference to their bodies, were perfect personifications of all that is lovely and beautiful. Sin has defiled, and polluted, and corrupted the whole man. When we refer to the mystical manner of Christ's conception, and that the body of Christ was free from all taint of human depravity, we may safely conclude that, as the second Adam, he was arrayed in perfect health and beauty. As such, although Christ had all our sinless infirmities, yet his body seems to have been secured from disease, even as his remains were preserved from corruption. How affecting, then, the account which is given of the influence of his griefs and sorrows! See Isaiah lii. 14; so, also, liii. 2, 3, &c. But how different did that countenance appear when transfigured on the Mount, shining brighter than the noonday sun—and when he turned it on his persecutors in the garden—and when the officers fell as dead men at his feet! But, consider the beauty of Christ,

2. In reference to his mind. In him dwelt all the depths of wisdom and knowledge. The whole universe, in all its vastness and glory, was open and transparent before him. All the grandeur of the celestial temple was familiar to him. He knew all that the angels knew, or felt, or desired. He knew the mind and heart of Jehovah. No one knew the Father but the Son. How infinite his knowledge! How perfectly glorious his mind! We consider this beauty,

3. In reference to the moral, or holy nature of Christ. In this he was abstract purity—humanity in a glorious state of entire perfection. No weakness, no error; guile was not found in his lips. Holy, undefiled, and separate from sinners—" Fairer than the children of men." Moses, in all these respects, was fair and distinguished; but a greater than Moses is here. One is the servant, the other the Son and Lord. David was justly celebrated as the ruddy son of

Jesse, and how great his intellectual and moral attainments; but here is David's Lord and Saviour, the one a sweet star of the Jewish night, the other the bright orb of gospel day. Solomon, for the fame of his wisdom and glory, stands out in the pages of revelation; but Jesus is infinitely wiser, and greater, and more glorious than Solomon. Daniel was a person of peculiar knowledge, and beauty, and goodness; but his highest honor was to be one of the train of prophets who testified of the sufferings of Christ, and the glory that should follow. Could we abstract all the excellencies of holy men and prophets, and concentrate the whole as in one focus, we should not have a millionth part of the beauty and glory of the blessed Messiah. In the highest possible sense, he was fairer than the sons of men—the fairest among ten thousand, &c. Let us consider,

II. THE GRACEFULNESS OF HIS ADDRESS. "Grace is poured," &c. For his great mediatorial work, Jesus was anointed with the oil of gladness. The Holy Ghost rested on him in all his unbroken plenitude—"Not given by measure," &c. The result of this grace, as poured into his lips, is described by John—"He was full of grace and truth." Now this was true, both as to matter and manner. Listen to the matter: I go to the beginning of his ministry, Luke iv. 16; see also John vii. 37. Look also at his manner. How he influences the woman of Samaria! She forgets her water-pot, &c. How he attracts and softens the officers—"Never man," &c. How he draws forth the eulogium of Nicodemus—"We know that thou art a Teacher," &c. How he melts the heart of the woman who was a sinner—how he discourses with the sisters of Bethany—how he delights the multitudes of the illiterate with his charming goodness, and interesting parables, so that the common people, &c.—how the eye of sorrow looked to him—how the ear blessed him—how the people exclaimed in rapturous songs, "Hosanna, Blessed is he," &c.

III. THE BLESSEDNESS OF HIS REIGN. "Therefore God hath blessed thee," &c. He ever enjoyed the delight and supreme love of the Father. God testifies to this during his ministry on earth. He displayed this in raising him from the dead, &c.; see Phil. ii. 6, &c. He hath constituted him Lord and Christ—given him the honor

of angels, and adoration of all the redeemed in glory. Look at the splendid vision of the apocalypse, Rev. vii. 9.

APPLICATION.

1. Learn the supreme excellency of Jesus Christ.
2. How is he in the estimation of your hearts, thoughts, conversation, &c.?
3. The great end of the ministry and church is to exhibit and exalt the Saviour.
4. We proclaim this Saviour to all now present.

THE MIGHTY SAVIOUR.

"Mighty to save."—ISAIAH lxiii. 1.

EXPOSITORS have expressed some difficulty in giving a full, clear, and harmonious explication of this splendid portion of Isaiah's prophecy. Some have fancied there was a reference to Cyrus, whom God raised up to be the scourge of Israel's enemies; others have thought that it refers to the victories of Judas Maccabeus; but a careful examination of the whole paragraph must necessarily limit it to the Messiah. To no other is the language applicable, especially verses 4 and 5. Then, if it refers to Jesus, it has been disputed as to whether it refers to his passion and conflict with the rulers of this world, and the powers of darkness, or to the conquests he should obtain in the latter days, in the overthrow of unbelieving and impenitent nations. The whole passage seems best to apply to the Saviour's conquests over our spiritual enemies, when, by his sufferings and death, he redeemed us to God, and vanquished our hellish adversaries, when he uttered those exclamations of victory, "Now is the judgment of this world," &c.; and, especially when he cried with a loud voice, "It is finished," &c. But, whatever may be the design of the prophet, our text evidently belongs to the Saviour, and contains one great and glorious truth, that Jesus, our Redeemer, is "mighty to save." The might or power of Christ to save will appear,

I. IN THE DIFFICULTIES HE HAD TO SURMOUNT. These difficulties had relation,

1. *To the divine character.* God's holy, righteous character required the punishment of the guilty. His truth required i

—his government required it—the love and approbation of his holy creatures required it. Deviation from right—connivance at sin—indifference to the government of the universe, would have thrown all creation into confusion.

2. *To the power of our adversaries.* The myriads of hellish hosts had usurped power and authority over the world; had possessed themselves of the heart of man; held him in Satanic thraldom; bound him with chains of darkness, and fetters of rebellion; filled him with hate and treason against God and holiness.

3. *To the depravity of the sinner.* His sin had transformed him into the child of the devil; he became disordered and vile in all his faculties and powers; the crown fallen, the glory gone. "From the crown of the head," &c. Robbed, stripped, half dead, ready to perish, &c. Christ, by his divine might, overcame all these impediments, and removed every difficulty.

(1.) He glorified all the divine perfections in the human nature he assumed. Honored the law, &c.; glorified the government of God.

(2.) He overcame the powers of darkness—asserted the supremacy—caused them to fear, and tremble, and fly—bruised the head of the devil.

(3.) He opened the fountain for the dying sinner—a healing fountain of life and mercy:—

> "The dying thief rejoiced to see
> That fountain in his day;
> And there may I, though foul as he,
> Wash all my sins away."

Christ so controlled events, as to make it righteous and merciful for God to save, &c. Levelled every mountain, exalted every valley, made crooked things straight, &c. When these difficulties are considered in all their formidable character—difficulties which all the angels in heaven could not have removed—it will be clear that Christ is "mighty to save."

II. IN THE COUNTLESS MULTITUDES OF THOSE HE REDEEMED. To save one from extreme peril, from the most imminent danger, would have been great; but Jesus redeemed a world. All the past ages were interested prospectively in his mission and death—all at the period when he lived—all the future ages, even from the first man to the last of woman born, of all ages, coun-

tries, climes, and tongues. "This we know and testify," &c. Think of being surety for untold millions—bearing the guilt of the world—having accounted to him the iniquity of us all. A soul, enduring its own guilt, sinks into the black abyss, and descends lower and lower to all eternity. Now, he took the transgressions of the whole species, &c.; and, in bearing the huge mountain of our world's sins, proved that he was "mighty to save."

III. IN THE DEPTHS OF MISERY FROM WHICH HE RESCUED, AND THE HEIGHTS OF FELICITY TO WHICH HE ELEVATES, THE SUBJECTS OF HIS GRACE. To ascertain the extent of these we must know something of the wretchedness of the sinner's state—something of the pain, shame, remorse, fear, &c.; of the anguish of the sinner's death-bed; of the horrors which burst on them in the eternal world; the dreadful crisis of appearing before the bar of Deity—the fearful sentence—the eternal doom—those shades of night—those scenes of despair and agony. Then contrast this with the eternal glory of the beatified, the scenes of paradisaical blessedness, the throne, the crown, the robe, the vision, the rapture, the overflowing joy, the endless blessedness, &c. In this we especially discern the mightiness of Christ to save. It is seen,

IV. IN THE VARIETY OF CHARACTER DELIVERED AND EXALTED BY HIS SAVING GRACE. It is always a mighty work to convert, even where there is morality, amiability, &c.—even where there is education, and the impress of good example, &c.; but how much greater does it appear, where there is the most palpable ignorance, the most disgusting grossness, the most inveterate enmity, the most hardened unbelief. Look at the sneering skeptic; look at the superstitious pagan; look at the abandoned profligate; yet myriads of these he has saved. He can deliver from the most reckless and extreme state of depravity—Manasseh; the woman that was a sinner; the thief on the cross; Saul, &c.; myriads of idolatrous heathens, &c.; what have we not seen, &c.

V. IN THE INSTRUMENTALITY HE EMPLOYS. By the suspension of the laws of the universe; by angelic instrumentality, &c., we might expect great results. But he works by moral power—moral influence in the word—the power of truth and love—by the all-influential energy of compassion—he draws, allures, &c. Look at the gospel; behold the ministry, &c. These are the agency, &c. Things apparently foolish and weak, &c.; yet in his hands mighty, &c.

APPLICATION.

1. *Our subject is full of hope to the lost and despairing.* Christ is mighty to save, &c.

2. *Consolation to the Christian.* Mighty to keep and preserve, &c. How necessary and essential this.

3. *Terror to the impenitent.* He is mighty to destroy. How terrific the great day of his wrath, &c. "How shall we escape," &c.

EZEKIEL'S VISION OF CHRIST.

"And above the firmament that was over their heads was the likeness of a throne, as the appearance of a sapphire stone; and upon the likeness of the throne was the likeness as the appearance of a man above upon it. And I saw," &c.— EZEK. i. 26, &c.

No man hath seen God at any time. Yet the glory of the Lord has often been displayed to the children of men. It was manifested to Moses and the elders of Israel, Exod. xxiv. 9. "Then went up Moses and Aaron, Nadab and Abihu, and seventy of the elders of Israel, and they saw the God of Israel, and there was under his feet as it were a paved work, a sapphire stone, and as it were a body of heaven in its clearness." It was seen also for the space of forty year⁓ in the pillar of cloud and fire, &c. It was seen resting over the mercy-seat in the tabernacle, and at the dedication of the temple the smoke of the presence of the Lord filled the house. It was seen also by Isaiah, in his resplendent vision of the celestial temple, when he saw the Lord high and lifted up, and whose train filled the heavenly place. The visions of John in Patmos, often embraced exhibitions of the divine magnificence and glory. None however of the revealed displays of God's glory surpass that with which Ezekiel was favored, and which we have read as our text. Let us consider,

I. THE GLORIOUS PERSON WHICH THIS VISION REVEALS.

II. THE RESPLENDENT THRONE ON WHICH HE SITS. And,

III. THE GRACIOUS PRINCIPLES ON WHICH HIS GOVERNMENT IS ADMINISTERED.

I. THE GLORIOUS PERSON WHICH THE VISION REVEALS. The description given embraces three things.

1. *His likeness to humanity,* ver. 26. It is clear it was a vision of the anointed Messiah. Most of the manifestations of God's glory assumed this form. When God appeared to Abraham, there were three in the likeness of men, but one of them is styled the Lord, and reveals the purposes of his wrath. To Jacob, and wrestled with him in the fashion of a man, "but he had power with God." To Joshua over against Jericho with his sword drawn, &c. He was captain of the Lord's host, and Joshua worshipped him. To Isaiah in the vision we have referred to. For the evangelist quoting it, says, "These things spake Esaias when he saw his glory." So now Ezekiel when he beheld the glory of Jehovah describes it as the appearance of a man. But with the aspect of humanity, notice,

2. *His peculiar magnificence and glory.* Ver. 27. Light and fire have ever been the chief emblems of Deity. He is the Father of lights, &c. The Lord God is a sun, &c. These might denote his knowledge—purity—justice. His character is transparent holiness. Mark,

3. *His likeness to Jehovah's glory.* Ver. 28. "The likeness of the glory of the Lord." How harmonious this vision with the records of revelation as to the divine glory of Christ! Hear the apostle, "We beheld his glory, &c. "Who was the brightness of his glory, and the express image of his person." Hearken to Jesus when he replied to Philip, "Show us the Father," &c. "Whoso hath seen me, hath seen the Father." How dim the vision of those who read these things, and see nothing in Jesus but the man, the creature! How frigid and poor the doctrine which places him on a level with prophets, &c.! How insipid the gospel of which he is not the sun and glory! But how suitable this revelation to our state as sinners! The Saviour is God, Jehovah's fellow. How great, glorious, all-sufficient! Here we can trust, and build, &c. But are we not alarmed? Can we see his face and live? Yes, for his was the likeness of a man, "God with us." God in our flesh. God our kinsman and redeemer. Notice,

II. THE RESPLENDENT THRONE ON WHICH HE SITS. Here our words must be few and carefully uttered. Observe,

1. *The position of the throne.* Beneath were seraphim and cherubim, &c. But above the firmament, &c. Having supremacy—the pre-eminence, &c. Our immortal poet has finely paraphrased it—

> "Eternal power, whose high abode
> Becomes the grandeur of a God ;
> Infinite lengths beyond the bounds
> Where stars revolve their little rounds.
>
> The lowest step above thy feet,
> Rises too high for Gabriel's seat ;
> In vain the tall archangel tries
> To reach the height with wond'ring eyes."

Notice,

2. *The magnificent appearance of the throne.* Ver 27. Here we have the symbols of grandeur and majesty, indicating by such figures the glory of the divine government. Also the equity and purity of his administration. He reigns in righteousness and in truth. "Justice and judgment," &c. Besides, with him all is transparent, no confusion, no darkness. The whole, too, is mellowed down by the appearance of amber and the sapphire stone. Goodness reigns throughout. Love sways the eternal sceptre. Only terrible to the incorrigibly guilty, but of tenderest pity to them who love him. We proceed to notice,

III. THE GRACIOUS PRINCIPLES ON WHICH HIS GOVERNMENT IS ADMINISTERED. We mean his moral government in connection with our race, ver. 28. Read a parallel representation, Rev. iv. 3. The first refers to the rainbow—destruction of the old world. Guilt—wrath—destruction—world swept away, &c. Terror and dread would agitate the sons of men, &c. The appearance of a cloud would inspire with alarm, be ominous of peril. God therefore thus covenanted with Noah, Gen. ix. 11, &c. How beautifully applicable to the gracious administration of God in our guilty world ! Sin had exposed to vengeance. Judgment might have visited. God might have taken his bow of justice and his arrows of wrath. But mercy triumphs. Grace superabounds. Love prevails. He unstrings the bow, turns it upward. No arrow is seen. It becomes the emblem of reconciliation. It spans the whole heavens. Embraces the whole world, and is suspended in the gospel as the symbol of peace and mercy. It

is irradiated with all the perfections of Deity. "Mercy and truth meet together, righteousness and peace," &c. It is over the throne of Deity, and from it arises a voice as the sound of many waters. Shall we not hearken to it, "As I live, saith the Lord God," &c. "God so loved the world," &c. "For he sent not his Son," &c. Beneath are myriads of spirits clothed in white robes. Hark ! they sing in loud accents, "honor, and glory, and power, and riches, and wisdom, be unto the Lamb," &c.

APPLICATION.

1. *What elevated conceptions we should have of Jesus !* The most high God demands supreme worship and honor for him, yea, the reverence and obedience of the whole creation. Honor equal to his own, &c.

2. *The subject is full of encouragement to the contrite sinner.* This is the age and dispensation of mercy. You may see God in Christ and not die, yea, approach and live. "Let us come boldly to the throne of grace," &c.

3. *Our subject is full of terror to the incorrigible sinner.* The mediatorial reign of mercy will end. The bow will be strung again. The quiver will furnish arrows of ruin. God will arise, and then wo, wo, wo, to his enemies. Then how terrific the appearance of the Lamb. "Then will they cry to the hills," &c. "For the great day of his wrath," &c. Oh ! then kiss the Son before he is angry, &c.

> "Flee to the refuge of his cross,
> And seek salvation there."

And do so now, this night. For, behold, now is the accepted time, now is the day of salvation.

THE BENEVOLENT MISSION OF CHRIST.

"For God sent not his Son into the world to condemn the world ; but that the world through him might be saved."—JOHN iii. 17.

OF all the discourses delivered by the great Teacher, none exceed in interest and true importance the one which he addressed to Nicodemus, a ruler among the Jews. In the first part, Christ insists on the doctrine of regeneration, or that entire change of heart and life by which a man becomes a new creature, &c. He then expatiates on the grand truths of redemption ; refers for an analogy to the brazen serpent in the wilderness ; and then utters that grand condensed epitome of the gospel, " God so loved the world," &c. Then follows the text, " For God sent not his Son," &c. The text contains two great declarations.

I. IT DECLARES THAT FOR WHICH GOD DID NOT SEND HIS SON, &c. The eternal Jehovah is described as the great source of this amazing transaction—Jesus, the Son of God, as the blessed agent employed to execute his gracious designs—the world the place of his embassy, the theatre of his mighty undertaking. That embassy was not one of wrath but mercy. Observe, the world was in a state deserving condemnation. God could have found ten thousand reasons of condemnation. For its wilful ignorance, they had sought darkness and loved it—for its horrid superstitions—for its gross idolatries—for its awful blasphemies —for its insatiable cruelty—for its avowed rebellion—even the most enlightened part of the world, the favored land of Judea. What causes for condemnation here ! Their perversion of truth—their rejection of prophets—their wide-spread hypocrisy—their natural ingratitude and apostacy—their covetousness and oppression. All these were dark spots, offensive to Deity, incurring his wrath, &c. Yet, he did not send his Son to condemn, &c. ; that is, not as a minister of terror and judgment. In one sense he did condemn—by his holy, spotless life—by his pure and benevolent ministry. But the grand intention is exhibited,

II. IN THE OTHER DECLARATION OF THE TEXT, " BUT THAT THE WORLD," &c.

1. *Might be saved from ignorance and error by his teaching.* He came to bring " life and immortality to light," &c.—to overthrow every false system in the world, whether pagan, or the heresies of the Jews. By propounding the way of life fully, perfectly, yet simply, he left the way to heaven so clear and plain, that a wayfaring man, &c. Hence the common people heard him gladly.

2. *Might be saved from false teachers and models by his life.* There were many teaching philosophy in the celebrated cities of Greece ; various sects among the Jews, Pharisees, and Sadducees, &c. ; not in the whole, one who was worthy of exact and universal imitation. Even the godly among the Jews were frail and imperfect in their lives. He sent his Son, the perfect portrait of his own glory—the perfect model of his own perfections—every virtue, every grace. His holiness was both internal and external. It was complete, lacking nothing. It had no dross, no weakness, no infirmity. As clear as light, as majestic as the sun in the firmament. He could say in all things, " Follow me."

3. *Might be saved from the guilt and effects of sin by his death.* Sin and divine punishment are essentially wedded together —the soul that sinneth shall die. " Cursed is every one," &c. Reverse the decree, and the justice and holiness of God are sacrificed ; execute it, and the world perishes. But God sent his Son to be the Redeemer, to pay a price equal to the claims of eternal holiness and truth. It was the punishment of sin in Christ ; the voluntary victim, the propitiation. He stood in the fearful gap—he took the culprit's place— he bore the punishment in his own body on the tree. Now sin is punished—now God is glorified—and now the world, through him, may be saved. I cannot refrain from quoting a sentence from a work to which we do not often refer for theological illustration, but where this subject is most sublimely explained in one sentence. The immortal Shakspeare says :—

" For all the souls that were, were forfeit once,
　And he that might the 'vantage best have took,
　Found out the remedy."

In the language of the apostle, " For while we were yet sinners, Christ died for the ungodly."

4. *Might be saved from the power and influence of evil, by the communication of his Spirit and grace.* Atonement is made—a way of safety is revealed. But men must know of it—be invited ; for this, there is the gospel of his grace. Before his ascension he said, " All power," &c. ; " Go ye, therefore, and preach the gospel," &c. But the mind must be renewed—a new heart given—the sanctification of the soul effected. " He, therefore, ascended on high, &c. to receive gifts," &c. ; " His Holy Spirit," &c.

5. *Might be saved at death, by their reception into the kingdom and glory of God.* The righteous are blessed in their death, by an abundant entrance into the everlasting kingdom of Jesus Christ being administered unto them. To die is their everlasting

gain. They are with Christ, which is far better. Christ receives them to himself, &c.

6. *Might be saved by a glorious resurrection, and blissful coronation at the last day.* The day of perfect redemption is future. Christ will come again, without a sin-offering ; when he shall appear, we shall be like him, &c. " He shall change these vile bodies," &c. Place his people at his right hand, and give them the crown of glory, &c. " When the chief Shepherd shall appear," &c. " Beloved, now are we the sons of God," &c. Now, all this is included in the great design of Christ coming into our world. There is one part of the text truly important, " Through him ;" that is, Christ. He is the Mediator in and through the whole. Every step in the scale of salvation as it rises higher and higher, it is through him. Saved from ignorance, guilt, depravity ; saved at death, and forever, through Christ, and through Christ only. The next verse shows us the connecting link between our souls and Christ—" He that believeth ;" that giveth his whole heart and soul to receive Christ, trust Christ, and obey Christ ; who becomes his disciple—follower. Unbelief puts Christ from, rejects him—says, " away with him, we will not have him to reign," &c. Let us have the world, riches, honors, pleasures, &c. Sinners render null and void, with respect to themselves, the great designs of God's love, and Christ's sacrifice.

APPLICATION.

1. Contemplate the privileges and blessings of redemption.
2. Avail yourselves of them.
3. Despisers must perish.

THE INCARNATION OF CHRIST.

" But thou Bethlehem Ephratah, though thou be little among the thousands of Judah, yet out of thee shall he come forth unto me that is to be a ruler in Israel ; whose goings forth have been from of old, from everlasting."—MICAH v. 2.

THE prophet Micah was contemporary with Isaiah, and delivered his predictions during the reign of three of the kings of Judah. His prophecies, like those of Isaiah, had especial respect to the kingdom and glory of the Saviour. That which we have selected for this occasion is an ex-press prophecy as to Christ's incarnation, and it points us to the very place of his nativity. How unlike this to the predictions of the heathen oracles, where the sayings of these imaginary deities were so dark and ambiguous, that they admitted of almost every kind of interpretation ! Our text, observe, marks distinctly the place ; and, as there were two Bethlehems in Judea, it gives the particular designation by which that town was called in which the world's Redeemer should appear. The signification of the name is interesting : Bethlehem signifies the house of bread. How applicable to Christ, who was the true bread of life, sent to a wretched and perishing world. Let us consider,

I. THE INTIMATIONS OF THE TEXT AS TO THE PRE-EXISTENCE OF THE REDEEMER.

II. THE PLACE OF HIS ADVENT.

III. THE GREAT END OF HIS APPEARANCE. Observe,

I. THE INTIMATIONS OF THE TEXT AS TO THE PRE-EXISTENCE OF THE REDEEMER. Notice the last clause of the text ; the person who should come forth out of Bethlehem is thus described. It seems to be parallel in sense with that sublime passage in the psalm of Moses, Psalm xc. 2—" Even from everlasting to everlasting thou art God." It is in harmony with that striking paragraph in Prov. viii. 22, and is precisely of the same import with the doctrine, John i. 1. It is the same in spirit, too, with the declaration of Jesus, " Before Abraham was, I am." It evidently invests Jesus with the attribute of eternity. No one is from everlasting but God ; but the text implicitly states this of Christ ; then the fair inference is, that Christ is not only the child born, but the mighty God, &c. " His goings forth," &c. A learned critic says, this form of speech is applied to that which proceeds from the mouth. Jesus is styled, " The Word of God." He went forth, bringing the whole hierarchy of heaven into being ; he went forth creating our world ; and he went forth communing with our first parents in the garden. He went forth for the inquisition of blood, when Abel, the first martyr, was slain by the fratricide Cain ; he went forth in the covenant which he established with Noah ; he went forth in the vision with which Abraham and Jacob were favored ; he went forth to the rescue of the hundreds and thousands of his oppressed ones in Egypt ;

he went forth in the barren wilderness, in the pillar and cloud, &c. ; he went forth filling Solomon's consecrated temple with his glory. In all the arrangements of his providence he went forth, &c. Observe,

II THE PLACE OF HIS ADVENT. "Bethlehem Ephratah." Bethlehem was a small town, six miles southwest of Jerusalem, greatly distinguished for its picturesque situation, and the fertility of its soil. Ephratah signifies fertility. Bethlehem belonged to the tribe of Judah, of whose tribe Christ was. Here we are reminded of Jacob's prophecy, "The sceptre shall not depart from Judah," &c. In this Bethlehem was Christ to be born—the most important event connected with this or any other spot in our world. Bethlehem had often been distinguished before. Here, 1700 years previously, had a tomb been erected over the remains of Rachel, the beloved wife of Jacob, and mother of Joseph. Here Naomi was born ; and to this place Ruth returned with her, who bare Obed, the grandfather of David. This was the birthplace of the son of Jesse, the sweet singer of Israel ; so that Christ was not only the offspring of David, but born in David's city. But the glory of Bethlehem was this : that here was to be first manifested the Son of God, the Redeemer of the world, who came especially to destroy the works of the devil. Mark how the providence of God secured the fulfilment of prophecy. Mary and Joseph dwelt at Nazareth. Nazareth was quite in another part of Palestine from Bethlehem, &c. At this time, Augustus Cæsar issued a decree for the taxing the Roman empire, to which Palestine was now tributary. This was not a money-tax, but an enrolment of the name and condition of life. Joseph, therefore, went, &c., Luke ii. 1, &c. Had not this taxing taken place, or earlier or later ; had not this been Joseph's city, &c., the whole would have been apparently frustrated. But thus it was written, &c. His coming forth at his nativity was with mingled circumstances of humiliation and greatness, of meanness and glory. Look at the parents—the place —dwelling, &c. How lowly, &c. Hearken to the angels—see the star—visit Christ with the Egyptian sages—and how great, magnificent, and glorious. Such was his birth, and such, extensively, was to be the character of his life and mission. But notice,

III. THE GREAT END OF HIS APPEARANCE, AS SPECIFIED IN THE TEXT. There were many ends to be accomplished, but the text refers to the character he was to sustain. He was to be ruler in Israel—to be invested with power, dignity, regal authority, &c. He came to be both a Prince and a Saviour. Hearken to his reply to Pilate before his death, John xviii. 33, &c. This is the key to this part of the text. Christ's dominion is in the souls of men. It is entirely spiritual ; it extends to the whole church, which he hath redeemed ; it shall endure forever. Believers are the subjects—the scriptures the statute-books, &c. His is a rule of righteousness and purity—of goodness and mercy—grace and tenderness—love and salvation.

APPLICATION.

1. *Learn the glory of Christ's nature.* The blessed Son of God. Whose goings forth, &c.

2. *The great design of his advent.* To rule—to set up an empire. He rules all whom he saves.

3. *Are we his subjects, &c. ?* Is he born into our hearts ? Does he sway his sceptre of grace over us, &c. ?

4. *He will destroy all whom he does not rule.*

CHRIST'S ADVENT IN THE FLESH.

"But when the fulness of the time was come, God sent forth his Son, made of a woman, made under the law, to redeem them that were under the law, that we might receive the adoption of sons."—GAL. iv. 4, 5.

ONE of the great mysteries of our religion is the advent of the Saviour into our world. The apostle with all his learning, gifts, and inspired powers of mind, exclaimed, "Great is the mystery of godliness," &c. This illustrious event had long been predicted and promised : the earliest intimation of divine mercy referred to it, "The seed of the woman," &c. Jacob in his blessing on Judah's tribe had recorded, "The sceptre shall not," &c. Isaiah had introduced it with an exclamation of wonder, "Behold, a virgin shall conceive," &c. ; and anticipating it, he bursts forth, "Unto us a child is born," &c. Ages after ages rolled on, until at length, over the favored plains of Bethlehem angels hov erea, and sung to the shepherds, "Unto you is born this day, in the city of David, Christ the Lord." Our text refers to that day, and the great event connected with it. Observe, the person sent—the period specified—the mission contemplated.

I. THE PERSON SENT. " God sent forth his Son, made of a woman, made under the law."

1. *The person was the Son of God.* Angels are sons of God, so are all saints, but Christ is the only begotten of the Father. The sonship of the Redeemer has involved a controversy which commenced very early in the Christian era, and is not yet terminated. The doctrine clearly teaches the pre-existence of Christ. He was sent by and from the Father; he came down from heaven; he had glory with the Father before, &c. It is also evident that Christ essentially partakes of the nature of Deity; that he is really divine, of one essence and glory with the Father—the brightness of his glory, and the express image of his person; "that he thought it not robbery," &c.; that " he is over all, God blessed forever," &c. But the Son of God was sent,

2. *Enshrined in our nature.* The divine glory had dwelt in the ancient tabernacle and temple, but now it became embodied—clothed with our humanity—allied by a most inexplicable union to our nature. Hence the peculiar phraseology of the text, " made of a woman," not born in the usual way, of a woman, but " made," " the seed of the woman." " A virgin shall conceive." Let us just read the inspired account, Luke i. 35. Woman, the first in the transgression, is thus signally honored in the divine conception of the world's Redeemer. Thus, too, the conception of Christ was holy, so that he was perfectly free from all moral defilement and human depravity.

3. *He was subject to the divine law.* " Made under the law."

(1.) As a man he was under the moral law; bound by those precepts of pure equity which are righteous, just, and good.

(2.) As a Jew, he was under the Levitical law, and bound to observe its rites, and offerings, and sacrifices.

(3.) As a surety for man he was obnoxious to the curse of the broken law, and exposed to all its inflictions of wrath. He was born under these, and lived to fulfil these, and thus became a curse for us, although actually he knew no sin. As to the appearance of the Son of God, notice,

II. THE PERIOD SPECIFIED. " In the fulness of the time."

1. *At the time selected in the exercise of God's infinite wisdom.* All times and seasons were his; he knew, therefore, the best and most fitting period for the manifestation of his Son to take place.

2. *At the time predicted in the oracles of truth.* Observe the celebrated prophecy of Jacob, " The sceptre shall not depart," &c., Gen. xlix. 10. Now just at the time of Christ's appearance the civil power and authority of the Jews were usurped by the Romans; they became subject to that great monarchy, and had not the power of putting criminals to death. So also, Daniel had declared that seventy weeks were determined, &c., Dan. ix. 24. So also in Haggai, " The glory of the latter house," &c. Now in that, Christ taught, wrought miracles, &c., and forty years afterwards it was destroyed.

3. *At the most appropriate period, for giving prominence to the Saviour's advent, to the nations of the world in general.*

No other period so well adapted. Not before the flood—not in the patriarchal ages—not during the period of the barbarism which generally prevailed, except in Judea—not during the conflicts of the four great monarchies, but in the learned Augustan age; when the world was at peace—when the evidences of Christianity could be examined by the learned of all countries—when the apostolic Jews could go forth through the known world, &c.—when the world had been prepared by the predictions, the rites, and ceremonies of the Jews, and by the general expectation which seemed universally to prevail—when all other systems had failed to make men wise, and holy, and happy. Observe in reference to the advent of Christ,

III. THE MISSION CONTEMPLATED.

1. " *To redeem,*" &c. Enlargement here is impossible. Allow me to cite a few passages from the records of holy writ. " The Son of man came to seek," &c. " God so loved the world," &c. " This is a faithful saying," &c. He came and " bore our sins in his own body," &c. " Suffered, the just," &c.

2. *To exalt us to an adopted sonship.* By sin, we were outcasts, &c. Aliens under wrath, but being redeemed, we may return

to God, and become his children, "heirs of God and joint-heirs," &c. By a believing reception of the Lord Jesus Christ, John i. 12.

APPLICATION.

1. Are we personally interested in the blessed advent of Christ?

2. Have we realized the blessing of adoption?

3. Are we looking for his second coming?

MANHOOD OF CHRIST.

" That just man."—MATTHEW xxvii. 19.

NOTHING is more self-evident from the scriptures than the manhood of the Redeemer. It is explicitly stated by the apostle, that God sent his own Son into the world, made of a woman, made under the law, &c. Hence also he often spake of himself as a man, and as the Son of man. As such his birth, and life, and death, and resurrection, are all matters of inspired narrative. Let us then consider the nature, the peculiar characteristics, and the importance of the humanity of the Redeemer.

I. THE NATURE OF CHRIST'S MANHOOD. We observe,

1. *That he was not a man after the ordinary generation of human beings.* He was only the Son of man as his virgin mother was one of the descendants of Adam. Hence his conception took place before the marriage of Joseph and Mary, and was produced by the overshadowing of the Holy Ghost. Thus was fulfilled the prediction of Isaiah, that a virgin should conceive, &c. Thus also the emphasis that is laid on Christ being the "seed of the woman." "Made of a woman," &c.

2. *Yet he was a man in the fullest sense of the term.* He was truly human. Had our entire nature. Bone of our bone. Our real brother. Had both the corporeal and spiritual parts of our nature. Not merely like unto, or in the appearance, but in deed and in truth. "Wherefore in all things it behooved him to be made like unto his brethren," Heb. ii. 1, &c.

3. *As a man he went through the various stages of life, and had the infirmities of manhood.* He was born an infant. Passed through childhood. Is presented to us in his youth. Arrived at maturity of years. As a man he was hungry and thirsty, he was weary; as a man he was dejected and sorrowful; as a man he feared, &c.; as a man he could be troubled, and tempted, and perplexed, &c. "Touched with the feeling of our infirmities," &c. Heb. iv. 15. As a man he could die and yield up the ghost.

II. NOTICE THE CHARACTERISTICS OF OUR REDEEMER'S MANHOOD.

1. *He was a holy and just man.* In reference to the conception it is written, "therefore that holy thing which shall be born of thee," &c. Luke i. 35. His whole life was pure and unblamable. No fault was found in him by Pilate, and the revelation to him by his wife was, that Christ was a just man. He had neither original depravity nor practical sin, even guile was not found in his mouth. "Holy, harmless, and separate from sinners." In him God ever beheld his own holiness and truth reflected.

2. *He was a poor and humble man.* Look at his immediate parentage, his reputed father and real mother. His first dwelling a stable, his cradle a manger. His astonishing exclamation, "The foxes have holes, and the birds of the air nests," &c. He became "poor," how poor the tongue cannot express. A servant of servants. His tomb was the property of another, &c.

3. *He was a suffering man.* "A man of sorrows," &c. Grief was his portion through life. He came to mourn and suffer, to agonize and die. His sufferings were predicted; they are minutely detailed, and no griefs were ever like unto his. He came expressly to suffer, &c. Consider,

III. THE IMPORTANCE OF THE HUMANITY OF CHRIST. It was thus,

1. *That he became our kinsman and our brother.* It was necessary that he should know our sinless infirmities. That he should have all the feelings of our nature, and be really and truly man with us, as he was divinely God with God.

2. *Thus he became subject to the divine law.* The law was made for human beings, it behooved Christ therefore to be human that he might be liable to its claims, and thus honor all its holy and righteous requisitions. Hence it is written he was made "under the law."

3. *That he might present himself a sacrifice for sin.* It was the guilt of human

nature that had to be expiated. It was necessary therefore for the surety and sacrifice to have our nature. Christ thus could meet its demands, and endure its righteous inflictions. Thus he could " redeem us from the curse of the law, being made a curse for us," Gal. iii. 13.

4. *That he might exalt human nature, by introducing it into the holiest of all.* See Heb. ii. 17, iv. 14, ix. 20.

APPLICATION.

Let us,

1. *Contemplate human nature.* In its original excellent state. Debased and accursed by sin. Exalted in the manhood of Jesus. And through his death, redeemed and glorified in heaven.

2. *Learn the nearness of Christ to us.* Our brother. The Messiah is our kinsman. We need not then be overwhelmed with fear, or shrink with horror. We may approach and speak to him.

3. *The claims he has on our love, gratitude, and obedience.* Should we not love him when he hath so much loved us, &c. " We are not our own," &c.

EARLY LIFE OF CHRIST.

" And the child grew, and waxed strong in spirit, filled with wisdom: and the grace of God was upon him."—LUKE ii. 40.

OUR text contains the sum of what is related of Christ from his being presented in the temple, to his attaining the age of twelve years. The records of the gospel chiefly refer to his public life and ministry, the work which he came especially to do. The text refers us to four things in the early life of Christ ; these we shall briefly notice, and then observe his subsequent history, to the period of his baptism. Observe,

I. THE FOUR THINGS THE TEXT RECORDS OF THE EARLY HISTORY OF JESUS. We are referred,

1. *To his physical growth.* " The child grew." Increased in physical power. It is not improbable that Christ's body was free from disease, even as his soul was free from pollution. It has also been conjectured that his countenance was remarkable for its dignified benignity. " He was fairer than the children of men." But,

2. *He was distinguished for an increase in mental vigor.* " Waxed strong in spirit." His faculties enlarged and grew in mental power. As a man his mind was as capable of advancement as his body. No doubt all the intellectual powers were possessed by the Saviour in all their perfection.

3. *For the fulness of the spirit of wisdom.* " Filled with wisdom." By observation, reading, meditation, devotion, his mind was filled with true and heavenly wisdom. No doubt this wisdom was peculiarly displayed in his abhorrence of evil, and in his love of holiness.

4. *For the plenitude of the divine favor.* " And the grace of God was upon him." By grace is not meant favor to one unworthy, but complacent delight, and the fullest degree of the divine approbation. Observe how in his subsequent history,

II. THESE FEATURES IN THE CHARACTER OF CHRIST WERE EVINCED. Here too, one short paragraph is all that revelation furnishes. Observe,

1. *His attendance at the holy festival in Jerusalem.* Probably his first visit. " Three times in the year all thy males shall appear before the Lord," Exodus xxv. 17 ; Deut. xvi. 16. The distance from Nazareth was seventy miles. Here was an act of pious obedience to God's ordinances, and one evidence of his attachment to the worship of his heavenly Father.

2. *His conduct in the temple.* How affecting the narrative of the return of his parents, discovering that Christ was not with them ! Their return to Jerusalem, their finding him in the temple, but especially the circumstances in which they found him, " sitting in the midst of the doctors, hearing them, and asking questions." Such was the precocity of his mind, the clearness of his understanding, the readiness of his answers, and the solidity of his judgment, that all who heard him were astonished at him.

3. *His solemn reply to the interrogation of his mother.* " Son, why hast thou dealt thus with us ? And he said, How is it that ye sought me ? Wist ye not that I must be about my Father's business ?" Here his responsibility to God his Father, his recognition of that responsibility, his earnest desire to meet it fully and exactly in all its supreme demands, are presented to our view. Learn, the claims of God are above all, and before all others.

4. *His obedient subjection to his parents.*
He came with his parents to Nazareth, and
was "subject to them." There is no collision of rights between parents and God.
Right obedience is rendered to neither except it is to both. In the temple the things
of God in all their grandeur and holy
majesty weighed down his mind, and absorbed his heart ; but in the house of Joseph and Mary, he was docile, mild, attentive, and obedient, studying their peace,
and cheerfully doing their will and pleasure. Thus Christ became a pattern, an
example of filial piety to the young. There
can be no doubt at this time too, that he
toiled with his hands, assisting Joseph in
the work of a carpenter. Here honest toil
and industry were sanctified by the conduct of the world's Redeemer.

5. *Notice the progression of Christ both
in stature, wisdom, and favor with God and
man,* verse 52. He passed through every
stage of childhood, and youth, to manhood.
His mind enlarged with his bodily growth
—he grew in wisdom daily. Increasing
in holy, heavenly knowledge and understanding. His demeanor was so exemplary,
that his conduct was admired by those who
knew him, and in the favor of the people
he grew daily. God also continued to behold his Son, his elect, and precious one,
with increased favor and delight. Such
was the early life of the blessed Jesus.

APPLICATION.

1. In Christ we have a pattern of early
piety. Let this often be pressed upon the
attention of the young. How delightful
this picture !

2. Here we see the just claims of parents upon their offspring's obedient subjection. This should be cheerful, ready,
constant, and sincere.

3. We see the pre-eminent claims of
God—"Wist ye not," &c. This is the
grand end of life, to serve, and glorify God.

CHRIST'S PROPHETICAL OFFICE.

" For all things that I have heard of my Father I have made known unto you."—JOHN xv. 15.

MOSES had predicted, nearly 1500 years
before the Saviour's advent, that he should
be a Prophet, unto whom God would im-
peratively demand that the people should

hearken. Numerous are the representations also given by the prophets to this office of the Redeemer. Those figures which
represent Christ as a star and as a sun, to
diffuse light, evidently refer to his prophetical character. All those descriptions of
Christ as a teacher, counsellor, messenger,
&c. clearly involve the same idea. At
the commencement of his ministry, Jesus
declared that the Spirit of God was upon
him to this end, and for this work. Let us
ascertain,

I. WHAT THE PROPHETICAL OFFICE IM-
PLIED.

II. ITS CHARACTERISTICS, AS DISPLAYED
IN THE LIFE OF THE REDEEMER.

I. WHAT THE PROPHETICAL OFFICE IM-
PLIED. It evidently implied a divine call—
a divine commission—and divine qualifications. Thus God called Moses, Isaiah, and
Jeremiah. Thus he also sent them forth,
with express messages from himself. Thus
he also qualified them for their important
work. Now, Christ in his prophetical office was,

1. *Chosen of the Father.* Hence David
says, in reference to the Messiah, " Thou
spakest in vision, &c. and saidst, I have
exalted One chosen out of the people,"
Psalm lxxxix. 19. " My servant whom I
have chosen," Isaiah xliii. 10. Thus the
Jews derided Christ, as the professed " chosen of God," Luke xxiii. 35. Peter describes the Redeemer as a " living stone,
chosen of God, and precious." Christ was,
therefore, the object of the Father's choice,
as our Prophet and Mediator.

2. *He was commissioned of God.* Selected for the work, and in the fulness of the
times, " sent forth ;" see the beautiful passage in Isaiah, xlii. 1, &c. On his divine
commission Jesus ever insisted, and laid
great stress. He said, " I am come in my
Father's name," &c. " This is the work
of God, that ye believe on him whom he
hath sent." " For I came down from
heaven, not to do mine own will, but the
will of him who sent me." See also John
vi. 39, 40.

3. *He was qualified by the plenteous
anointing of the Holy Spirit.* Thus, at his
baptism the Holy Ghost descended upon
him ; and hence he also said, " The Spirit
of the Lord is upon me, because he hath
anointed me to preach," &c. Luke iv. 18.
So also that striking testimony, " For he

whom God hath sent speaketh the words of God, for God giveth not the Spirit by measure unto him ;" for it pleased the Father that in Christ should all fulness dwell. He had the continuous unbroken plenitude of the Spirit dwelling within him. Now this qualification, by the Spirit dwelling in him, included,

(1.) A spirit of unbounded knowledge and wisdom. " In him were hid all the treasures," &c. " He knew what was in man"—he knew all things—he knew the Father and declared him—he knew all concerning heaven and immortality.

(2.) The spirit of prescience, so that he could clearly perceive the future. Hence his numerous predictions respecting Judas, and Peter, and the other disciples ; his predictions of his own resurrection—of the destruction of Jerusalem, &c.—of the prosperity of his kingdom—the end of the world, &c.

(3.) Ability to preach and teach—to proclaim God's love, the way of mercy, the remission of sins, &c.—to exhort, entreat, invite, urge, warn, &c.—to illustrate the truth, and apply it to the hearts and consciences of men. Also to teach the true knowledge of the gospel to his disciples—to qualify them for their great work —imparting the knowledge and the power to proclaim among men the unsearchable riches of divine grace.

II. Observe the peculiar characteristics of the prophetical office, as displayed in the life of the Redeemer.

1. *Immaculate purity.* " Holy, harmless," &c. Guile was never found in his mouth. The spotless image of God.

2. *Infallible wisdom.* He could not err. His knowledge embraced every theme, and that with the most positive certainty ; and this power he possessed at all times. The spirit of prophecy abode within him. Notice.

3. *The completeness of his work.* The revelation of Jesus Christ during his life, by his Spirit on the apostles, and in the sublime manifestations of Patmos, completed the system of revealed truth, and finished the canon of the scriptures. As such,

4. *He will have no successor.* He has furnished the church with the oracles of truth, with the ordinances of religion, with purity of spiritual worship, and with a living ministry, who are the voice of Christ to the people. How great, and glorious, and

incomparable is the Prophet of the New Testament dispensation !

APPLICATION.

1. It is our duty and privilege to hear him.

2. To be enrolled with his disciples.

3. To hearken, so as to obey by the power of his grace, and the influences of his Spirit.

THE TEACHING OF CHRIST.

" For he taught them as one having authority and not as the scribes."—Matt. vii. 29.

One branch of Christ's prophetical office was to communicate sacred instruction to the people—to preach the doctrines of salvation, and publish the love of his heavenly Father, to a lost and perishing world. With his entrance on his public work, he began to reveal to mankind the tidings of life and immortality. His instructions were imparted both privately to his own disciples, and publicly to the people, who flocked around him to hear his gracious words. He had just delivered his interesting and comprehensive sermon on the Mount, and it is graphically written. " The people were astonished at his doctrine, for he taught as one having authority," &c. Let us notice the subjects he taught, and how he taught them.

I. The subjects he taught. Now, these subjects embraced the whole of doctrinal, experimental, and practical religion.

1. *He taught the doctrines of religion.* The existence, purity, goodness, and mercy of God ; his own equality with the Father ; the divinity of the Holy Spirit ; man's natural depravity and guilt ; the utter helplessness of human nature ; the necessity of holiness of heart and life. The doctrine of spiritual influence to renew, guide, and keep to eternal life. The certainty of death — the solemnity of judgment — the eternity of heavenly glory, and everlasting punishment of the wicked.

2. *He taught the nature and necessity of experimental religion.* That the seat of religion was the heart—" The kingdom of God is within you," &c. That man must be born again—that the Holy Spirit must dwell in the soul—that the essence of religion is love—love to God, and love to man. That

all forms are utterly worthless without this—and that true religion is progressive, even to eternal life.

3. *He taught the necessity of practical religion.* He stated that obedience was the only evidence of true discipleship—that such as obeyed him were his mother, his sisters, his brethren. He enforced the importance of the law of equity, demanded a pious conversation, and righteous life. He urged heavenly-mindedness, goodness, charity, mercy, &c. " If ye love me," he said, " keep my commandments." But we inquire,

II. How HE TAUGHT THESE THINGS.

1. *With beautiful simplicity.* Illustrating the sublime and lofty themes of heaven and eternity by similes and parables. He drew attention to celestial truths, by speaking of leaven, sweeping the house, seeking the straying sheep, sowing seed, fishing, marriage feasts, &c. Hence the multitude, or common people, heard him gladly.

2. *With direct plainness.* Not uncertain or ambiguous, as the responses of the heathen oracles ; not full of subtle disquisitions, or metaphysical reasonings, as the Gentile philosophers ; not presenting mere conjectural glosses, or rabbinical fables, as many of the Rabbis among the Jews ; but he revealed, illustrated, explained, and enforced his instructions in plain and popular language, opening the eyes of the ignorant, and those who were dwelling in the shadow of death. How direct and plain his sermon on the mount !

3. *He was a faithful and earnest teacher.* It was impossible for him to be listless and lukewarm. He ever had a deep impression of the importance of the work pressing upon him—he ever recognised the pleasure of his heavenly Father, and the value of souls. What a searching specimen of fidelity and earnestness in his address to the scribes and Pharisees, in the 23d chapter of Matthew !

4. *He was an affectionate and tender teacher.* His soul ever overflowed with compassion, so that his words were necessarily full of grace and pity. He rejoiced in the mercy of his mission ; hence how gladly he proclaimed liberty to the captive, &c.— how tender to the woman who was a sinner —how he compassionated the infirmities of his own disciples ! He did not break the bruised reed, &c. Observe his pathetic appeal at the conclusion of his severe address to the hypocritical Pharisees, " **Oh**, Jerusalem," &c. Matt. xxiii. 37.

5. *He was a diligent and persevering teacher.* It is said, he taught daily in the temple. All places and occasions were alike to him. He made it his meat and drink—he was ever about his Father's business. At the end of his life he could say, " I have finished the work," &c. His powers and his moments were all consecrated to God—" I must work while it is called day," &c.

6. *He embodied all his instructions in his own blessed example.* In him they saw his precepts engraven. His spirit—his conversation—his life—all gave force to the duties he urged. Perfect consistency, absolute holiness, and infinite goodness, were ever manifested in the Preacher, so that he presented an example that they should follow his steps. He urged his counsels by saying, " Follow me." " My sheep hear my voice." I need not say that he never erred—that all he taught was pure truth, the whole truth, and taught in the most perfect manner ; and he taught in his own name, and enforced it by his own authority. See this in Matt. v. 28, 32, 34, 39, 44, &c. " I say unto you," &c.

APPLICATION.

1. True Christians are Christ's disciples. They hear him. This is both a duty and a privilege.

2. Whosoever will not hear him must perish. " How shall we escape," &c.

THE MIRACLES OF CHRIST.

" The works that I do bear witness of me."—JOHN v. 36.

So true was the text, that Nicodemus, a ruler of the Jews, acknowledged that they knew he was a teacher sent from God, for no man could do the miracles Christ did, unless God were with him. Both Moses and the prophets attested the divinity of their calling, by miracles. And thus also Jesus referred the unbelieving Jews to the works he did as bearing unequivocal testimony of him. A miracle has been defined an unusual interposition of providence, a counteraction or suspension of the operations and laws of nature. A genuine mircle should also bear the following evidences.

(1.) That it should be palpable to the senses.

(2.) That it should be performed publicly.

(3.) That it should be recorded and made known.

(4.) That such documents should be fairly traceable to the names they bear.

(5.) That the miracle should be connected with some important event or subject of instruction.

(6.) That the witnesses of the miracle should be above suspicion.

(7.) That the witnesses should agree in their testimony.

Now all the miracles of scripture are capable of being thus demonstrated, and especially those of Christ. These tests may be applied to each and every one of them. In reference to Christ's miracles, observe,

I. THEIR VARIETY. Healing by a word or touch all kinds of diseases. Restoring hearing to the deaf—sight to the blind—speech to the dumb—feet to the lame. Removing palsies—fevers—dropsies—impotency—leprosy. Feeding thousands with a few loaves, &c., expelling demons. Stilling the tempest. Raising the dead, &c. Observe,

II. THEIR NUMBER. Not a few, but connected with nearly all his sermons, several at a time. "And whithersoever he entered into villages, or cities, or country, they laid the sick in the streets and besought him, that they might touch if it were but the border of his garment, and as many as touched him were made whole," Mark vi. 56. The miracles of Christ, like his heavenly sayings, are too numberless to be recorded within the compass of the gospel history. With these he began his ministry, and they attested the greatness of the sufferer at his crucifixion. Observe,

III. THE MANNER IN WHICH THEY WERE PERFORMED. In his own name and by his own power. He acknowledged the Father and gave thanks, but exerted his own power, and by his own authority he effected his mighty deeds. To the leper he said, "I will, be thou clean," Matt. viii. 3. To the centurion, "As thou hast believed so be it unto thee," ver. 13. Peter's wife's mother "he touched, and the fever left her," ver. 14. "He rebuked the winds and the sea,

and they were still." He said to the demons, Go, and they went out of the man into the swine. To the paralytic, "Thy sins be forgiven thee," Matt. ix. 2. To the blind man he said, "Be it unto you," &c. ver. 29. As the loaves and fishes passed through his hand he multiplied them. To Lazarus he said, "Come forth," thus evincing that he had all power both in heaven and on earth. Observe,

IV. THEIR PUBLICITY. His miracles were not wrought in a corner, not only were his disciples generally present, but often also the multitude. The unbelieving Jews surrounded the tomb of Lazarus. Several thousands partook of the loaves and fishes. The blind man who received his sight was examined by the Jews. Most of the subjects of Christ's healing power were well known. Deception then was impossible. Christ in all his instructions, and conduct, and deeds, was surrounded by light. His miracles were openly performed, and all might hear and know for themselves. His more private miracles had, at least, two or three to bear witness, as in the case of the ruler's daughter, besides the relatives and friends with whom the restored lived, &c. Observe,

V. THEIR BENEVOLENCE AND MERCY. How striking the contrast between the miracles of Christ and some of those of Moses and the prophets! No supernatural fire was called forth to consume his adversaries. No openings of the earth to swallow his enemies. No destructive energy, to make ensamples of the unbelieving Jews. Like himself and the dispensation he came to set up, they were all gracious and merciful. To heal—to restore—to bless—to make happy—to save. Like the beams of the sun they were joyous, bright, and reviving. He never cursed but once, and that a barren fig-tree growing by the way-side, and hence the property of no one. To do good to the bodies and souls of men, to glorify his Father, and to demonstrate his divine mission were the grand designs of all Christ's miracles.

APPLICATION.

1. *Surely Jesus was the Son of God.* Possessing the power and authority of Jehovah.

2. *His mission was certainly divine.* His works clearly evidence this.

3. *His power and willingness to bless and save remain the same.*

4. *Let the miserable and perishing fly to Christ and be saved.*

THE PRIESTHOOD OF CHRIST.

" Thou art a Priest forever after the order of Melchizedec."—HEBREWS vii. 21.

IN some particulars, both the priests and high-priests typified the priestly office and work of Christ; but in other particulars, Christ's priesthood was essentially different from theirs, and had been most strikingly typified in the priesthood of Melchizedec. We do not purpose to enter on the controverted points connected with Melchizedec; but wish to notice the priesthood of Christ in its general aspect, and then to consider it in its peculiar character after the order of Melchizedec. Notice,

I. THE GENERAL ASPECT OF THE PRIESTHOOD IN CHRIST. Observe,

1. *His divine appointment.* No man took that honor upon himself. To this office Christ was destined, and appointed directly by the Father, Heb. v. 4, &c.

2. *His solemn designation.* The priests of old were set apart by water and oil, with various significant rites and offerings—Jesus by his baptism, by the descent of the Holy Ghost, and his own prayer.

3. *The office of the Priest involved various duties.*

(1.) The revelation of the mind of God —the explaining of the Urim and Thummim, and the ordinary communications of the divine will. Christ revealed the divine character, perfections, will, and glory, in the most full and resplendent manner—with noontide light and meridian splendor, yet with clearness, distinctness, and simplicity.

(2.) The instruction of the people. The priests' lips kept knowledge, and the people sought instruction from their mouths; but both of these features were especially associated with Christ's prophetical office.

(3.) The offering of sacrifices to God. Now Jesus appeared to present the last great, effectual sacrifice of himself—his own blood. See Heb. ix. 9–14, x. 6–12, &c.

(4.) Intercession, and blessing the congregation, Heb. ix. 24. " If any man sin, we have an advocate," &c. " Who ever liveth," &c. He is exalted to bless men, by turning them away from their iniquities, &c., and by the rich impartation of the Holy Spirit—" He hath received gifts for men," &c. Now, for the discharge of these holy duties great were the qualifications of the Redeemer : unspotted purity— boundless knowledge—treasures of wisdom —and riches of mercy and grace. He was the delight of Jehovah—the Lord of angels —the brother of mankind—and the Priest of the universe! Consider,

II. CHRIST'S PRIESTHOOD IN ITS PECULIAR CHARACTER, "AFTER THE ORDER OF MELCHIZEDEC." Now it was so,

1. *In the dignity of his character.* The Son of God, the Prince of the kings of the earth, typified by the kingly character of Melchizedec, " King of Salem," &c.—of greater glory than Aaron and his sons.

2. *In having no predecessor or successor in his office.* See Heb. vii. 1, &c. Thus Jesus came forth, not of the tribe of Levi but of Judah, and according to the oath of Deity, that he should be a Priest forever, &c. Heb. vii. 21. Jesus also abideth a Priest, not being made after a carnal commandment, but after the power of an endless life. In reference to the priests of Aaron they were many, because they were not suffered to continue by reason of death; but Jesus continueth forever, and hath an unchangeable priesthood, Heb. vii. 23, 24.

3. *In the union of the regal with the priestly office.* Priest of the most high God, and yet truly, " King of righteousness." It had been predicted by Zechariah, chap. vi. 13, that he " should be a Priest upon his throne ;" his, is therefore a royal priesthood.

4. *In the virtue and extent of his sacrifice.* The Levitical priesthood was limited to the tabernacle of Israel. They also presented numerous victims, the blood of which had no intrinsic merit in procuring remission of sin, or in purifying the worshipper; but Christ's sacrifice embraced, in its extent of merit, all ages, &c.—the whole race of mankind. " He, by the grace of God, tasted death for every man ;" " And by one offering he hath perfected for ever them that are sanctified," Heb. x. 14.

5. *In the exalted station in which his priestly services are continued.* He has not entered into the holiest place of the earthly

temple with the blood of bulls or of goats, but into the heaven of heavens, the holiest of all, where he has sat down at the right hand of the majesty on high, and where he ever liveth to make intercession for us.

REMARKS.

1. *Christ is now the only true and living Priest.* There is a sense in which men are priests; but it is only in such a manner as comprehends within its range the whole family of God. Believers are kings and priests unto God.

2. *There is only one great sacrifice.* The Lamb of God, slain for the sins of the world. Oh! behold him, and live. Come to this offering, and obtain remission of sins.

3. *There is only one intercessor.* Jesus is the one perpetual advocate, and only Saviour; but able to save to the uttermost those who come unto God by him, &c. Heb. vii. 25.

THE ROYAL CHARACTER OF CHRIST.

" A King shall reign and prosper."—JER. xxiii. 5.

AMONG the offices and works of Christ it was clearly and fully predicted that he should be endowed with regal dignity, and that the government should be upon his shoulders. Hence he is often styled governor, ruler, and prince, in the Jewish prophets; one of these exclaims, " Behold thy king cometh unto thee, he is just," &c. Jer. ix. 9. And in the text, " A king shall reign and prosper." The Jews expected their Messiah to be king, but were disappointed that his kingdom was not of this world. Jesus never denied that the dispensation he came to set up was a kingdom, but he instructed them that it was a gracious and spiritual kingdom; established in the hearts of his disciples, of righteousness, peace, and joy in the Holy Ghost. In his divine power and glory, Christ reigns over the universe, but as the mediator and Lord, he reigns over his universal church. Let us observe,

I. SOME THINGS CONNECTED WITH THE KINGSHIP OF JESUS CHRIST.

1. *He was typified as such.* By Melchizedec, David, and Solomon.

2. *He was appointed king by the authority of the Father.* God said to him, " Thy throne, O God," &c. And again, " I have set my king upon my holy hill." He said to him, " Rule thou in the midst of thy enemies." The Father hath committed all rule, and authority, and judgment to the Son. He hath given all things into his hand. The Father crowned him with glory and honor.

3. *He is the only king over his church.* " Head over all things." The " One Master," or ruler. He hath no fellow in the government of his people. All power both in heaven and earth is given unto him.

4. *His kingdom embraces his universal church.* To all who know him, believe in him, obey him, yielding him homage, and loyal affectionate tribute, honor his statutes, laws, and ordinances.

II. THE CHARACTERISTICS OF THE KINGSHIP OF CHRIST. We notice,

1. *Righteousness.* He is the just one—the holy one of Israel. Hence his empire is one of purity. He came to reveal the way of righteousness, the principles of righteousness, the source of righteousness, and to give the power of serving him in newness of life.

2. *Wisdom.* He is the one " wise God." " The wisdom of God." It was predicted of him that he should " deal prudently." His wisdom involves omniscience, infallibility. He knoweth all things; treasures of wisdom and knowledge are his.

3. *Clemency.* Hence he holds out the sceptre of mercy to his enemies. He designs their restoration to allegiance and bliss. He seeks not to destroy, he came not to condemn but to save. His arrows are truth, and he seeks to slay sin, and rescue the sinner. Hence his merciful proclamations, and overtures of grace.

4. *Love.* He reigns in and over his people, by the exercise of his infinite and unspeakable love. He woos and wins the soul by the exhibition of his love. He commences his reign by shedding his love abroad in the heart. His laws, and ordinances, and requirements, are all the evidences of his love. He is love, and they that dwell in him, dwell in love, and love is the fulfilling of his laws. Observe,

III. HOW CHRIST CONDUCTS HIS ADMINISTRATIONS.

1. *He does so by his word.* This is his royal law; his statute book. It contains his mind, both concerning his friends and

enemies. Here is the charter of the blessings and privileges of his subjects. Here is the revelation of his threatenings to his foes. This word is the highest source of appeal, and nothing in duty, or ordinance, or doctrine, is obligatory unless written here.

2. *By his servants.* These include both angels and men ; the celestial intelligences are ever waiting to know his will, and do his commands. " They are all ministering spirits," &c. His servants on earth are those whom he qualifies to teach and proclaim his word—to administer the ordinances and edify his church.

3. *By his Spirit.* He has obtained the gift of the Holy Ghost ; and he sends down his Spirit to dwell in the heart, to instruct, enlighten, sanctify, comfort, and keep untc eternal life. The Holy Spirit also qualifies men for usefulness, blesses their labors, and renders efficient the means of grace. " When the enemy comes in like a flood," &c. Notice,

IV. The prosperity of his reign. " A king shall reign and prosper." This is illustrated,

1. *By the past.* The early ages of Christianity; its rapid diffusion through the then known world ; myriads converted to the truth, &c.

2. *By a survey of the present.* His word translated into hundreds of tongues—his servants proclaiming the gospel in almost every nation. Fields white to the harvest.

3. *By the certain realization of the future.* Angel flying through the midst of heaven, &c. Christ claiming the heathen, &c. " North giving up," &c. " The kingdoms of this world," &c. " His kingdom shall come, and his will be done," &c. The whole earth filled with his glory. Now this prosperity is certain ; it must come to pass, for God hath spoken it in covenant to Christ, and in promise to the church.

APPLICATION.

1. Are you Christ's subjects ? You are either such or his foes. His subjects know, fear, love, and obey him.

2. He has proclaimed an amnesty to the rebellious. " Let the wicked forsake his ways," &c. " As I live," &c.

3. The incorrigible he will destroy, Psalm ii. 9, to the end.

THE LOVE AND SACRIFICE OF CHRIST

" Who loved me, and gave himself for me."—Galatians ii. 20.

The apostle has been showing that by the deeds of the law no flesh can be justified : that the law was designed to slay the vain hopes of men, and to lead them to Christ, who is the end of the law for righteousness, or justification to every one that believeth. The law makes us sensible of our lost state, and works a death of all prospect of being saved by it, verse 19. Then the apostle shows, that the spiritual life of the Christian is one of faith on the Son of God, verse 20, &c. And he concludes this description in the interesting language of the text, " Who," &c. Let us consider,

I. The person referred to.

II. The declaration made respecting him. " He loved," &c. And by way of application,

III. The use we should make of it.

I. The person referred to. The blessed person is spoken of in verse 19 as Christ, and as the Son of God.

1. *As Christ.* He was the anointed of God ; called, and chosen, and qualified, and sent to be the Saviour of the world. Each of these terms is full of interest. In obedience to the call of the Father, he responded, " Lo, I come to do thy will, O God," &c. As the chosen of God, he was the only being in the universe possessed of every adequate attribute and qualification for the work. Help was laid on him that was mighty, on one that was sufficient. God delighted in him as his elect and beloved. For the immediate work he had to perform, God qualified him by preparing him a body, in which he should tabernacle, Hebrews x. 5. He was also anointed with the Holy Ghost in all his unbroken plenitude—the Spirit without measure was given to him. Then he was sent in the fulness of the times, and he appeared in the place aforetime predicted, and having entered on the fulfilment of his course, he fully glorified his Father in all things.

2. *Son of God.* As such he had the nature of the Father—he and the Father were one—he was " the brightness of his glory, and the express image," &c. Whoso saw him saw the Father. He was of one mind with the Father—he only willed what

the Father pleased, so the Father said, This is my beloved Son, &c. As such he is the most exalted being in the universe—King of kings, and Lord of lords—a name above every name—a throne, &c. All things were created by him and for him, &c. Then consider,

II. THE DECLARATION MADE: "He loved," &c. The text refers to three things,

1. The love of Christ.

2. The sacrifice of Christ, and

3. The appropriation of Christ.

1. *The love of Christ.* Now the love of Christ to man is the frequent subject of holy scripture—it is the very life of the gospel—it was the love of deep compassion —love of intense pity—a love which had the most striking difficulties to overcome— love to an object loveless, worthless, wrath-deserving, without a feature to attract it, "while we were yet enemies," &c., when in a state of pollution, &c. The dimensions of this love are beyond description, the length goes through the range of eternity, the breadth embraces immensity, the height soars upwards to the highest heavens, the depth descends to the verge of perdition.

> "Buried in sorrow and in sin,
> At hell's dark door we lay."

2. *The sacrifice of Christ.* "He gave himself." He became devoted for us. As the ram which Abraham saw in the solemn crisis—as the scape goat, over whose head the guilt was confessed, &c.—as the surety, so Christ took the place of the guilty, and on him was laid the iniquity of us all. *He gave himself,* it was his own act and deed. No man taketh my life, I have power, &c. It was the free-will offering of his own compassionate soul. He had been anticipating it for ages upon ages, he longed for it, &c. *He gave himself.* He brought not a meat-offering, a drink-offering—he gave not silver or gold, but "*himself*," his own soul, his own life, his very all.

(1.) He gave himself to deep humiliation, in becoming a man—made in fashion as a man, a poor man, a slave, or servant of servants.

(2.) He gave himself to reproach, and scorn, and indignation, and maltreatment; to insult, rudeness, contradiction, persecution.

(3.) He gave himself to calumny, hatred, a mock trial, &c.

(4.) He gave himself to *death,* even the death of the cross.

(5.) He gave himself to endure the outpouring of the wrath denounced against sin—he trod the wine-press, he took the cup, and tasted death for every man—he gave his soul a living sacrifice for human guilt —his heart he gave in all the exercise of his mission, and then emptied it of living blood, and shed every drop of it for the salvation of man. Ye are not redeemed with corruptible things, &c. Then notice,

3. *The appropriation of Christ.* He loved " *me,*" he gave, &c. "Me." Let us see,

(1.) Who *may* appropriate Christ? All who belong to our *world.* He is the appointed propitiation for our sins, and not ours only, &c.

All who have gone astray, or are guilty before God. "For on him was laid the iniquity of us all," he came to seek and to save sinners, &c.

All who are included in our species, "For he tasted death for every man." Now all in these several classes may appropriate Christ in his love and merits. But we ask,

(2.) Who *do* really appropriate Christ? Great difference between the may and the do. We know that many do not appropriate Christ. Some are ignorant of him, some disregard him, the mass are wrapped up in unbelief. Many are satisfied with hearing, and reading, or mere profession. They say, Lord, Lord, &c. Myriads in their works denying him, will not own his regal office. But, thank God, some can say with the apostle, "He loved *me,* and gave himself for *me.*" Those who have received Christ by faith, and none else can say this. Faith brings the virtue out of Christ into our souls—it makes Christ all our own, fills our souls with his grace and love, realizes what he is, and what he has done for us—only faith can say, "He loved me," "I live by the faith," &c. We ask,

III. WHAT USE WE SHOULD MAKE OF THIS SUBJECT?

1. *It should fill us with adoring gratitude.* Oh, the love of Christ to me! What a subject for praise and wonder! The love of Christ is the theme of every Christian's rejoicing, and constitutes the song of the redeemed in heaven forever.

2. *Should it not excite fervent love to him?* "We love him because he first loved us," &c. If we had a thousand hearts, he has a right to each and every one.

3. Ought it not to induce examination? Can we with holy assurance appropriate Christ—can we aver our love to him—the doom of those who love him not is fearful. "If any man love not the Lord Jesus Christ," &c.

4. We urge all now present to come and take a saving share in the love of Christ. Be anxious for it, seek its application, its internal communication to your souls.

CHRIST'S SACERDOTAL PRAYER FOR HIS DISCIPLES.

"Father, I will that they also, whom thou hast given me, be with me where I am; that they may behold my glory."—JOHN xvii. 24.

OUR text is a part of our Lord's intercessory address to his Father on behalf of his church and people. He has already prayed for those who were then his disciples, and he now seeks the especial favor of his Father on all who, in after ages, should believe on his name. He prays that these may be one, united in love, even as the Father and Son were one. In our text, he prays for their eternal welfare; that they may be with him, and behold his glory. Consider the persons to whom the prayer refers; the distinction and bliss which Christ solicits for them; and the grounds on which they may rest for its realization.

I. THE PERSONS TO WHOM THE PRAYER REFERS. Now there can be no dispute as to the characters referred to. God has given all believers to Christ, ver. 20. All others reject Christ. Faith apprehends Christ, and receives salvation from him, and through him. The gospel draws the great and momentous line here—believing and non-believing. The believer is justified, accepted of God, and hath the witness in himself. The non-believer is condemned already, &c. Now those given to Christ, are variously described according to the various relations of Christ. As a Shepherd, they are his sheep. As a Captain, the soldiers of his cross. As a Teacher, his disciples. As a King, his subjects. As a Sacrifice, the ransomed by his blood. As to his affection for them, they are called his chosen, his elect, his precious ones. But the radical distinction is this, they are those, who have exercised faith in him, John i. 12. Now as the redeemed of Christ, and as enjoying the blessings of that re-

demption, by faith in Christ, they are given to Christ;—to be perfected in his will,—to be supported by his grace,—kept by his power,—conformed to his image, and finally to be the Saviour's joy and crown forever. Observe,

II. THE DISTINCTION AND BLISS WHICH CHRIST SOLICITS FOR THEM. Now the prayer specifies,

1. Presence with Christ. To be with Christ. This was the joy of the disciples who were favored with his corporeal presence. Sometimes to ecstasy; but this was occasional, limited, and chiefly connected with his sufferings and abasement; strictly, this was Christ with them. But the text refers to their elevation, to be with him in his kingdom and glory, the celestial paradise, his Father's house, where Paul longed to be. His assurance to his disciples was to this effect, John xiv. 1, &c.

2. The vision of Christ. To behold "his glory." The Jews had expected to see the Messiah in worldly glory. The disciples had seen his poverty, persecution, sorrows, &c., but now, Christ wills that they should behold his glory. His glory had been witnessed by Moses and the Israelites, by Solomon and the devout Jews. It had been seen in resplendent visions by Isaiah and Ezekiel. It had been seen by the three favored disciples on Tabor. It was afterwards seen by the disciples when he arose from the dead and ascended into glory; by Paul in his ecstasy; by John in the visions of the Apocalypse. But we presume all were but feeble displays to that which saints shall see in heaven—that which will be the beatification of the redeemed in glory. As far as possible, they will see his glory as the Son of God—the brightness of the Father's grandeur and majesty. They will behold his magnificent throne—see his radiant crown—witness the worship of the hosts of angels, &c.—perceive him exercising universal authority and power, and receiving universal homage and praise—behold him as the moral sun of that vast temple, the light and glory of the heavenly world. And in beholding, they will be the recipients, the participators of the same glory. His reflected light will be their intellectuality, their purity, their blessedness forever.

III. THE GROUNDS ON WHICH THEY MAY REST FOR ITS REALIZATION.

1. It is clearly the will of God. "Fear

not, little flock," &c. God gave them to Christ to be made meet, and to be then received, &c. Not his will that they should perish, &c. God hath given to them eternal life, &c.

2. *It is Christ's fervent desire.* His prayer is peculiarly emphatic. "I will." This is my ardent desire. As the Lord and head of the church, it is his gracious and official pleasure. "Him the Father heareth," &c. Besides, he has died for this end, &c. These are the fruit of his passion and travail. His eternal reward, &c.

3. *From the indwelling of the Spirit in their hearts.* As believers they have the Spirit of Christ witnessing, sealing, comforting, inspiring hope, as the first-fruits, &c. What can be the destiny of such? Not perdition, but heaven; the living water within them shall spring up, &c.

APPLICATION.

1. How needful then to seek conformity to Christ's holy image! If such our expectations, how holy, vigilant, should we be! Grace only can make us meet, &c.

2. The unbelieving wicked could not enjoy the glorious vision of Christ. It would condemn, overwhelm, distract, &c. No reciprocity of feeling.

3. We exhort all to seek a spiritual acquaintance with Christ now, that they may enjoy him forever. "Sirs, we would see Jesus," &c.

BARABBAS PREFERRED TO CHRIST.

"Then cried they all again, saying, Not this man, but Barabbas. Now Barabbas was a robber." —JOHN xviii. 40.

IT has been generally remarked, that land rugged and barren on the surface is most distinguished for the preciousness of its minerals, and that valuable ore is seldom found beneath land that is rich and fertile. We are forcibly struck with the contrast which this presents to the divine word. The word of God is rich and fertile in every part. Its holy surface contains precious and instructive thoughts, and within, it is full of invaluable treasure. It is a deep mine of pure, and rich, and ever-lasting truth. We should never be satisfied, therefore, with the mere letter, but, by meditation and pious study, labor to extract the soul and hidden spirit, which are always lost to the inattentive and careless reader. We present our text as affording a theme in which these observations will be fully borne out. Look then at the text,

I. As TO THE HISTORICAL FACTS WHICH IT CONTAINS. We have in the narrative,

1. *The person denominated "this man."* This was Jesus. A man in common with other men. Born of a woman, &c. A man especially resembling the first man, the second Adam. Without human father,— the perfect image of the glory of God. Yet a man differing essentially from all men. In his all-mysterious union with the divine nature, "God made flesh," &c. A man entirely for our sakes. Love to us caused him to assume our nature. "For though he was rich," &c. In the narrative we have,

2. *Barabbas.* An outcast, a robber, and a murderer. A man of violence and blood. One whose death seemed necessary for the safety of the state. We have,

3. *A multitude of persons.* "They all." Doubtless of all ranks and grades. Scribes, and Pharisees, and rabbis, and publicans, and sinners. A mass of every sort of Jerusalem's inhabitants. We have,

4. *The circumstances of each and all of those presented to us.* Jesus in custody,— Barabbas in prison,—and the occasion when a prisoner must be released according to custom. And we hear only one cry from the multitude. It is, Let Barabbas be free. Not this man,—no, let him be crucified. "Then cried they all again," &c. Well might we pause and wonder, especially if we contemplate the purity,—the goodness, —the sacred character of Jesus, and the infamy and moral degradation of Barabbas, for Barabbas was a robber. Surely truth had left our earth,—surely justice was exiled from the world. Surely holiness had taken an everlasting flight from the abodes of men. Now this is what we term the surface view of this striking text. Let us now dig into this mine of treasure, and we shall observe in this scene,

II. A HOLY DEITY APPARENTLY ACQUIESCING IN THE UNJUST ACCUSATION OF WICKED MEN. If truth, and justice, and holiness be banished from the earth, yet surely they dwell on high. Will not God thwart the envy, malice, and wrath of the Jews? Will he not rescue his beloved Son from those lions and serpents? Will he not vindicate the interests of righteousness and goodness before eternity and heaven? How surprised must have been the devout on earth and the holy in heaven, when the Jews prevailed, and Barabbas was delivered to his friends, and Jesus to the fury of his enemies! The mob, agitated like the ocean in a tempest, with passion and wrath seize the holy and the just, and put him to death. Satan now has triumphed. Fallen demons rejoice. Hell has its carnival of mirth. Christ, though possessing all power, submits, and is led as a lamb to the slaughter. And angels, struck with wonder, gaze upon the scene. Well may we ask, What meaneth this? Who can solve the profound problem? The gospel does it.

Barabbas is the representative of a guilty world. Sunken, depraved, enfettered, condemned, awaiting the righteous retribution of heaven. Deserving to die, and having no means of escaping from the doom. The mercy of God is higher, deeper, wider, and longer, than the guilt of the sinner. Deity exalts his mercy,—expands his compassion, and essays a display of love which should encompass even the rebel man. But how can it consistently be manifested. Substitution is the only remedy. The sinner's nature and condition must be assumed. His wrath-exposed condition must be occupied by another. Who shall bear the due demerit and punishment of guilt. Suffer "the just for the unjust," and by his blood a full, and free, and everlasting satisfaction be made. Christ the blessed one was that substitute. It had been predicted of him seven hundred rolling years aforetime that "He should be bruised for our iniquities," &c. He fulfilled to the very letter the entire compact, and his own benevolent soul harmonized with the decree of the people, although it was against himself, when they cried, "Not this man, but Barabbas." Peter has shown us this harmony, Acts ii. 22, 23. Do you not see then that which appears a vile and bloodthirsty clamor on the surface of this text, is really sweet as heavenly music to the sinner's ear? For if Barabbas be not spared, and Jesus delivered up, we are all unredeemed and must perish forever. While we believingly acquiesce in this declaration, as in accordance with the designs of Jehovah in mercy to our world, yet there is another view in which this scene may be contemplated.

III. WE SEE IN THESE CLAMOROUS JEWS A PERFECT REPRESENTATION OF OUR OWN HEARTS. While we may feel indignant and condemn them, the word and spirit of God turn the condemnation against ourselves, and say to each one present, "Thou art the man." We appeal,

1. *To worldliness.* Is not worldliness in compact with Barabbas, a robber? Think of Lot's wife. Think of the wicked Gehazi. Think of Judas,—of Ananias and Sapphira, and shall we plead for it and prefer it to Christ? We appeal,

2. *To pride.* Is not pride a robber? Robbed angels of their glory,—man of his innocency,—unnumbered myriads of salvation. It is that which God will abase. Which impiously tries to share the glories of Jehovah. And yet how it is pleaded for! How it is idolized! How it is preferred to Christ!

3. *We appeal to unbelief.* Is not unbelief a robber? There is the banquet for the starving, but unbelief will not come. The promise of eternal life, but unbelief rejects it. The opened door of eternal glory, but unbelief locks it, and flings the key into the bottomless pit. The Saviour is at hand to work miracles of grace on all the wretched, but unbelief averts his arm, so that it is recorded he cannot do many mighty works there. And he retires grieving, "Ye will not come unto me," &c. We notice,

4. *All sin is robbery.* Every act of iniquity is a Barabbas. For all these rob God, and destroy the soul. It is the earthworm,—the blight,—the mildew,—the locust. And yet sin is cherished, pleaded for, preferred. Declaim not against the Jews, but let every one smite upon his breast, and say, Here is the Barabbas, the robber, &c.

APPLICATION.

1. We ask then what view do you take of this subject? On what side do you stand? For what plead ye?

2. Barabbas and Jesus cannot both be preferred. One must die. We can have either.

3. Let the Barabbas of our hearts be nailed to the cross, &c. Die, monster!—perish, ingrate! &c.

CHRIST'S ADDRESS TO THE DAUGHTERS OF JERUSALEM.

"But Jesus turning unto them said, Daughters of Jerusalem, weep not for me, but weep for yourselves and for your children."—LUKE xxiii. 28.

THERE is no subject so replete with lessons of high moment as that of the death of Christ Jesus. Here we may employ all our powers—here whole ages might be expended in profound meditation. These are the things which angels desire to look into—the sufferings of Christ, and the glory which should follow. The most profound enigmas, and the most startling paradoxes, are met with here. Look at the sufferer—the most high Son of God, yet appearing as a vile, hated malefactor. Observe, his sufferings were righteous and proper, as the voluntary choice of the sufferer, in the capacity of surety and redeemer, yet as inflicted by men heinous, cruel, and incomparably wicked. See the vicissitudes to which the great and the good are exposed. Six days before he goes from Bethany to Jerusalem; a multitude attend him; the air resounds with joyous acclamation; hosanna is heard from thousands of lips, &c. Now he is treated with marked disdain; the same streets witness the contempt, &c.; the shout now is, Away with him! Both heaven and earth seem to have forsaken him; his friends are all fled; he is hurried to the place of public ignominious execution, as unworthy of life; even Barabbas is preferred to him. In this dark, horrid exhibition, there is seen one beautiful streak of light; there is one interesting incident, which the evangelist records—a number of women who bewailed and lamented for him. Tenderness and mercy had fled from the temple and the priesthood—from the professed pious and devout of the Jews; but it still retained its dwelling in the hallowed sanctuary of woman's heart; and these dared to feel, and to groan, and to lament loudly as the sufferer passed. Our text is the reply of our **blessed** Saviour, "Daughters of Jerusalem, weep not," &c. He, doubtless, referred to the calamities which the unbelief of the Jews would bring upon their nation. The recital of the Saviour's sufferings must affect every heart not petrified by sin. Surely it is not wrong to feel, or to give expression to feeling; but yet the address of Jesus to the devoted women may with propriety be applied to ourselves.

We should chiefly weep for ourselves and for our children. Instead of weeping for the sufferings of Christ, let us weep with him; let our sorrows have the elements of his sorrow; and let us weep on account of the awful results which shall follow to those who weep not at all.

I. LET US WEEP WITH JESUS CHRIST. We need not weep for him because he chose to suffer—because he was able—because he delighted. He longed, &c. It behooved him, &c.; but, especially, because he will suffer no more. We now see Jesus who humbled himself, &c.; exalted, &c.; but we may weep with him. "He was a man of sorrows," &c. Let us look with Christ,

1. *At the insulted perfections of our heavenly Father.* God formed man for his glory, &c.; but how sin insults and despises him. It profanes and blasphemes his name—it spurns his righteousness—tramples on his purity—basely disregards his goodness—returns him hatred for love—disbelieves his truth—denies his being, or sets up rivals in senseless idols. Christ's soul burned with zeal for his Father's glory. Marvel not that his soul was pierced when he beheld the conduct of sinners towards him. Do we revere and love God? then let us weep with Christ.

2. *Let us look with Christ on the violated laws and government of heaven, and weep with Christ.* God's government is perfect, and wise, and good; but sin has thrown the moral world into disorder. Now there is darkness, and confusion, and war, and rebellion, and anarchy. The holy tables are broken and trampled under foot, &c. Think how this must have affected the soul of Jesus. Let us, then, weep with him.

3. *Let us look with Christ at the ravaging effects of sin on our world.* Paradise lost—a sterile wilderness—one great graveyard—nature groaning—human beings suffering. Could the sighs of all who suffer be concentrated! could all the groans be united! could all the tears be collected! Physical torture, mental distraction, moral anguish, all the effects of sin.

4. *Let us contemplate, with Christ, the eternal effects of sin on its votaries.* Consigning the body to the prison of the grave, with a view to a resurrection to shame and contempt—the soul to the black abyss, and to ceaseless tears and endless pain, &c. Christ saw all this, and it moved him to

deepest compassion, filled his soul with anguish, &c. But,

II. LET OUR SORROW HAVE THE ELEMENTS OF HIS SORROW. The sorrow of Jesus,

1. *Was holy.* It arose from his holy nature, and his love of holiness. All sorrow is not such. It may be merely physical, or the result of excitement; but his was that of principle—the pain arising from the rectitude of his nature. Now, true piety involves this—a holy indignation against sin because it is sin, &c.

2. *It was deep, intense sorrow.* Like a mountain it pressed him down—like a sea it swallowed him up; billow after billow, wave after wave, &c. This was the bitter cup he was ever drinking, &c. Now our tears ought to be copious—our hearts deeply affected, &c. "Rivers of tears run down mine eyes," &c.

3. *It was compassionate sorrow.* Discerning between the sin and the sinner; hated the one and loved the other; filled his heart, moved all the yearnings of his nature, &c.; absorbed and became the grand impelling principle of his life, &c.; all love, all benevolence, &c. Let our sorrow have these elements. Let it not be mere indignation at evil, at the shame and degradation sin has effected; but pity and tenderness to the poor sinner.

4. *It was embodied, practical sorrow.* It was more than feeling, it was expressed. It influenced, it produced self-denial. Marvellous liberality—unspeakable suffering—transcendent grace. "Ye know the grace of the Lord Jesus," &c. "He loved us, and gave himself for us." Now, our sorrow ought to be palpable. It should breathe, and move, and live, and labor, and suffer, &c. We should weep,

III. ON ACCOUNT OF THE RESULTS ARISING TO THOSE WHO WEEP NOT AT ALL. Here we may justly begin for ourselves. How little we have wept, as we ought, either for ourselves or our children. Our little love—limited holiness—many sins—often desertion of Christ, &c.; yet we have been little affected. Oh, that we could but feel as we ought, &c. But there is one view of the Saviour's sorrow peculiarly affecting: its influence on every human being will be great and everlasting. Its saving, exalting, and felicitating effects, and also its influence on those who perish. In one, life unto life; in the other, death unto death. Christ did not, could not suffer in *vain.* The blood of Jesus will rest on every human being, either to cleanse or deepen his guilt—either to absolve, or to sink lower in punishment—either to raise to an equality with angels, or to sink lower than lost angels. Nothing so terrific to the lost as the groans of the suffering Jesus—nothing so awful as the cross—nothing so horrible as the recollection of the gospel. Oh! this will deepen fearfully the sufferings of the lost. Now, Christ foreseeing the extreme sufferings of the Jews through their sin, he said, "Weep not for me," &c. Looking as we do and ought, into futurity, in reference to the state of the incorrigible, we should, indeed, "Weep for ourselves," &c.

APPLICATION.

1. *Let our subject lead to right views of godly sorrow.* "For our sins," &c.

2. *Let it lead to deep compassion for the perishing heathen.* Look at them physically—mentally—morally—socially—eternally. Surely we must be affected, &c.

3. *Let our sorrow be genuine and influential.* Let it move our hands, and feet, and hearts. What can we do? What ought we to do? What will we do? Let us do what we can while it will be availing, &c.

THE OPENED FOUNTAIN.

"In that day there shall be a fountain opened to the house of David and to the inhabitants of Jerusalem for sin and for uncleanness."—ZECH. xiii. 1.

ZECHARIAH was a fellow-laborer with Haggai, and materially assisted those engaged in the erection of the second temple. He is styled one of the minor prophets, i. e. one whose predictions were of a limited character contrasted with those of Isaiah, Ezekiel, and Jeremiah. But of the lesser prophets he was most appropriately denominated the sun. His prophecies had respect to the completion of the second temple, the coming of the Messiah, his sufferings and death, the enlargement and prosperity of his church, the conversion of all nations, and the millennial glory of the kingdom of Christ. Our text is a clear and striking prophecy of the death of Jesus as a propitiation for sin. Notice,

I. THE FOUNTAIN SPECIFIED. A fountain is a spring or well of water, but the text employs the term figuratively. It evidently refers to the precious blood of the Lord Jesus. Jesus compared himself to living waters; and as water is the emblem of purity, and is employed to cleanse and purify, so the blood of Jesus is the source of all purity, and cleanses from all sin. But the figure of a fountain is intended to denote,

1. *The fulness and abundance of Christ's merits.* A cistern only contains a limited quantity, and may be easily exhausted, but Christ's merits are as universal as the wants and misery of the world. He is as the ocean for abundance, as the sun, &c.

2. *The continuousness of Christ's merits.* A supply within itself, ever full and overflowing; cannot be any lack, &c.

3. *The perpetual purity of Christ's merits.* Much that is foul and unclean would defile even a pool of water, but a fountain has within itself the means of purification. So the blood of Jesus retains its immaculate nature, all its original holiness and efficacy, nothing can defile it or render it in any degree ineffectual.

II. The opening of this fountain predicted. "In that day," &c. This fountain was,

1. *Promissarily opened to our first parents and the patriarchs.* To our first parents God promised the Saviour. Abel had respect to it in the sacrifice he offered. So all the patriarchs, in their various offerings, had respect to this fountain.

2. *It was opened typically under the law.* All the sacrifices pointed to Jesus and his death. In victims slain a voice spake to the sinner and said, See thy desert, and see the type of him who shall die to save thee.

3. *It was opened prophetically by the predictions of holy men, who testified of Christ.* Thus Isaiah speaks of Jesus as a lamb led to the slaughter, &c. And to him gave all the prophets witness. Zechariah particularly predicted the very act of Christ's atoning sacrifice, xiii. 7, compared with Matt. xxvi. 31.

4. *This fountain was opened really when Christ was suspended on the cross.* It was customary to break the legs of crucified criminals when they wished to accelerate their death. Thus the executioners approached the bodies of Jesus and the malefactors, see John xix. 31. Christ's side is pierced. How wonderful the ways of God!

The soldier had no orders to do it. As his act, it was one of cruel ferocity, wanton barbarism, but here was the finger of God, &c., verse 36, 37, and thus too was the text literally realized, a fountain was thus opened, &c. To this John afterwards refers, 1 John v. 6–8.

III. For whom this fountain was opened. "For the house of David," &c.

First of all *for the Jews*, to the seed of Abraham according to God's promise. He came first to his own. The gospel first offered to them. You will see the wisdom and mercy of this fountain being first offered to the Jews.

(1.) Their day of grace was ending, their privileges closing. This was to be the last great act of mercy before their sun should set, and their national rejection and woes commence. Oh, there was infinite compassion in that command, "beginning at Jerusalem."

(2.) As a test of its efficacy. As the Jews possessed more light, &c., they were the most deeply guilty; therefore if it could save the very murderers of Christ, if the merits of Christ's death were first offered to the conspirators, to the crucifiers of Messiah; and if it could wash out their stains, what nation or people could doubt its virtue afterwards? And it did so. Three thousand, whom Peter charged with the murder of Christ, came to it, and were cleansed from all their iniquities. But,

2. *It was to be opened also to all the world.* "That repentance and remission of sin," &c. Hence the apostle said, "It was necessary that the word of God should be first spoken to you, but seeing ye put it from you, and judge yourselves unworthy of everlasting life, lo, we turn to the Gentiles." Thus Paul says, "To me, who am less, &c., was this grace given, that I should preach," &c.; and in the vision of the Apocalypse the redeemed sing, &c., Rev. v. 9.

IV. The great design to be accomplished by the opening of this fountain. "For sin and uncleanness." The removal of these is the full salvation of the sinner.

1. *He is guilty.* Guilty of sin, exposed to death. Without shedding of blood no remission. How is the sinner to escape? by faith in Christ's blood. "We have redemption in his blood, the forgiveness of sin," &c. The sinner who trusts in that blood shall be pardoned.

2. *Man is defiled, polluted.* His nature

corrupt, a bad head and a worse heart, a polluted spirit. How shall it be made holy? "The blood of Christ, God's Son, cleanseth," &c. "But if we confess," &c. In this fountain we have both justification and sanctification, pardon and holiness.

APPLICATION.

1. Let the believer reflect on his obligations to Christ.

2. Let every unpardoned sinner now come to him, &c., wash, and be clean.

3. There is no other medium of pardon and holiness.

CHRIST'S TRIUMPH OVER THE PRINCE OF THIS WORLD.

"Now is the judgment of this world; now shall the prince of this world be cast out."—JOHN xii. 31.

FOR this purpose was the Son of God manifested, that he might destroy the works of the devil. Isaiah saw the Redeemer as a mighty commander travelling in the greatness of his strength, with dyed garments coming from Bozrah, and exulting in his omnipotence to save. The first promise of a Saviour referred to the great truth that the "seed of the woman," &c. It must never be forgotten that Christ came to emancipate as well as to ransom. To deliver from the power of Satan as well as to be the grand medium of the love of God to man. Our text conveys the idea of a conflict, and affirms on which side victory should terminate. "Now," says Jesus, "is the judgment of this world, and now shall the prince of this world be cast out." Consider, then,

I. SATAN IN HIS PRINCELY POWER AND DOMINION.

II. THE CERTAINTY OF HIS DISCOMFITURE AND OVERTHROW. "Now shall the prince," &c.

III. THE GROUND ON WHICH THE CERTAINTY OF THIS RESTS. "Now is the judgment," &c. Contemplate,

I. SATAN IN HIS PRINCELY POWER AND DOMINION. "The prince of this world." The character, attributes, and powers of the wicked one, are only incidentally referred to in the holy scriptures. But his titles clearly denote his fearful and malevolent character. He is described as a deceiver. The father of lies,—the destroyer,—the murderer,—the prince of darkness,—the prince of the power of the air,— the god of this world. Our text styles him, "the prince of this world." As a prince he is signalized for his power—his allies— his territories. Consider,

1. His power. Probably clothed with all the intellectual grandeur and energy he possessed when one of the shining host. The history of sin is the record of his evil influence.

2. His allies. Are of two kinds,—his fallen compeers called his angels or messengers, spirits equally depraved—fallen— accursed. His allies on earth are wicked persons who possess his spirit, and are committed to the side of evil. In whom he rules, and whom as instruments he employs in the cause of sin.

3. His territory. This includes the whole of our fallen world. No country or inhabited spot where he has not his possessions. His spell rests upon people of every color, climate, and nation. Not one land yet freed from his withering despotism. In maintaining his government in the world he employs the following elements of evil— ignorance—superstition—pride, and cruelty.

(1.) Mental debasement is the first element. His kingdom is the reign of night and darkness. This is essential to its duration. He hates all light and all knowledge. Where he reigns undisturbed, is the region of the shadow of death. "The kingdom of darkness."

(2.) Superstition. To meet the internal craving of the mind for some object of worship, &c., he has invented the whole region of polytheism or idolatry, from the worship of senseless idols to the adoration of demons.

(3.) Pride is the third essential element. The haughty uplifting of the mind against any superior control. Self-deification— haughtiness of spirit, the absence of meekness—humility, &c.

(4.) Cruelty. From the pride of the heart emanate envies, jealousies, strifes, wars, &c. He steels the heart—petrifies— fills with hate—transforms man into a vulture—makes him rapacious—ferocious— revengeful—implacable. Man the curse of his species—the foe of the world. Now we remark Satan's power is that of a usurper. He had seized and by subtlety deceived,—allured from allegiance—seduced, &c. This dominion is nearly as old as our world, and as we have seen, as extensive as the habitations of our race. What an amount of present wretchedness, misery, and wo, has been the result; and how fearful the endless state of wrath to which he has led millions of millions every year, until hell itself might have been supposed to have been filled to overflowing! But the text refers,

II. To THE CERTAINTY OF HIS DISCOMFITURE AND OVERTHROW. "The prince of this world shall be cast out." Not only his territory abridged, and power circumscribed, &c., but totally overthrown. He shall be spoiled, vanquished, and the world freed from his hellish dominion. He shall be cast out, have no spot left for his control within our world; but be tried, sentenced, chained, confined, &c. Now this seems demanded on the ground,

1. *Of the divine glory.* The works of God shall not be eternally marred, and his creation cursed by the usurper Satan. God's wisdom is destined to counteract the plans of the evil one. His power to overthrow his empire. His goodness to rescue mankind from his diabolical grasp. God's glory demands that he should be supreme over all his creatures.

2. *On the ground of the divine purposes.* God has devised a scheme to do all this. He has set his heart upon it. What can prevent its realization? Craft, energy, combination? Surely not! He is wise in counsel, he has said, and it shall be done; devised, and he will accomplish it.

3. *On the ground of the divine truth.* The word has proceede out of the divine mouth. He has been reiterating it for nearly six thousand years. Every jot and tittle must be fulfilled. He has spoken to his Son in solemn covenant, "I will give thee the heathen," &c. He has spoken to his church. "As I live, the knowledge of the Lord shall fill the whole earth," &c. He will speak at the appointed time, and "say to the north, give up," &c.

4. *On the ground of the victories already achieved.* Every saint is a trophy, an instance that the prince of this world is cast out. In all ages he has had these. Early Christian ages—our own country—South Seas, &c. Now these are the streaks of the morning light, and are the prelude of certain and universal day. But observe,

III. THE BASIS ON WHICH THE CERTAINTY OF THIS TRIUMPH RESTS. Christ is evidently laying the great stress of this on his own death. His hour was at hand. "Now is the judgment," or crisis, the momentous period when the effectual step shall be taken. Now the mighty conflict shall decide that Satan's power is gone, and that this world shall be freed from his direful reign. Hence the next verse at once ratifies this view. The death of Christ should be the concentration of all the divine plans, the key-stone of the stupendous arch, the basis of that kingdom which should overthrow the empire of the devil. Now I wish this to be clearly seen,

1. *By the death of Christ a way was opened by which the apostate sinner might return to God and live.* Satan knew God's hatred to sin, and the necessity that he should punish it. He therefore calculated if he could but seduce, that the sinner was inevitably lost. But by Christ becoming the sacrifice, God's justice is satisfied, and yet the sinner may live. Here is God's mercy in Christ, triumphing over Satan's malevolence. Now is the crisis, when a gracious way shall be opened from the gates of hell to the mansions of heaven. Every impediment is to be removed, God be the just God, and yet the justifier, &c.

2. *By the preaching of Christ's death men should be drawn to God.* "And I, if I be lifted up," &c. "The gospel is the power of God to salvation." "We preach Christ crucified, which is Christ the wisdom of God, and the power of God," &c.

3. *By the death of Christ was obtained the gift of the Holy Ghost, who should renew men in the likeness of God.* Here, in connection with the gospel, we have the very agency of God for casting out Satan. The death of Christ was the grand fact of the gospel. The great basis of the good news. Men on receiving its essential truths, receive the remission of sins and the life of the Holy Ghost, who changes the mind. Contrast the influences of the Holy Ghost with the elements of Satan's kingdom. He sanctifies and finally makes meet for eternal glory. Here ability is given to resist the evil one, to glorify God, and to shine forth in all the beauties of heavenly purity.

4. *By the death of Christ the prison-house of the grave should be entered and burst open to mankind.* Satan claimed death as his ally, and the grave as his prison. But now

the crisis was at hand when the Saviour, clothed in the vestment of our flesh, should through death destroy him that had the power of death, even the devil. Here was Satan's territory invaded. His fetters snapped, and a way of escape opened for the prisoners of hope. "O death, I will be thy plague," &c.

APPLICATION.

Our subject is adapted to give right views,

1. *Of Satan and his kingdom.* Powerful —formidable—dangerous.

2. *Of the great Redeemer.* Deliverer from the power of Satan, &c. And the only Deliverer.

3. *Under whose sway do we live?* Who has our hearts—influence, &c. Examine yourselves, &c. "O Jesus, ride on till all are subdued."

4. *Are we co-operators with Christ in his designs of mercy and love?* "He that is not with me," &c. Are you doing any thing? &c. If so, what?

THE CROSS, AND ITS ATTRACTION.

" And I, if I be lifted up from the earth, will draw all men unto me."—JOHN xii. 32.

OUR text directs us to the influence of the death of Christ, in bringing men into gracious contact with the Saviour. In the preceding verse, Christ refers to his triumph in casting out the prince of this world. Both are essential parts of our salvation. We must be freed from the powerful vassalage of Satan; but that is only half— we must be brought to God, and become the happy adopted children of his family. The state of man implied; the great event promised; and the glorious consequences affirmed, are the topics of our text.

I. THE STATE OF MAN IMPLIED. That is, distance. Mankind are invariably described as afar off. Now that is true, of course, only in a moral or spiritual sense; for Christ, in the omnipresence of his divine nature, is in all, and above all, and through all. Sinners, in their unregenerate state, are represented as foreigners—aliens—outcasts—ready to perish—dwelling in the region of death—lost. This is described under the similitude of the wandering sheep, the wretched prodigal, &c. Several pas-

sages of the divine word speak with great emphasis on this subject—"All we, like sheep, have gone astray," &c. There is a perfect contrast in mankind, and in the character of the blessed Saviour. He is pure—they defiled; he is harmless—they guilty; he approved—they condemned; he the reflection of God's likeness—they are of their father, the devil; he delights in holiness and goodness—they in iniquity and evil; he is wise, true, and benevolent; they ignorant, deceived, hateful, and hating one another, without Christ, and without God in the world. Now this is both a state of guilt and misery. Man has destroyed himself—freely strayed from God—forsaken the fountain of living waters, &c. Their misery is internal restlessness and fear, and finally, condemnation and wrath. This is the state of man implied. Notice,

II. THE GREAT EVENT PROMISED. "And I, if I be lifted up." Christ clearly refers to his death. "As Moses lifted up the serpent," &c. Christ does not speak as though it were uncertain or contingent; he had it all in view. This was the crisis or judgment of the preceding verse. Now, in this event observe,

1. *It had been clearly foretold.* Not only the death itself, but the manner of the death: see Deut. xxi. 22; Gal. iii. 13. Now, the erection of the brazen serpent also typified it in the most striking manner. "Even so must the Son of man," &c.

2. *It was connected with the deepest ignominy and debasement.* Only the very vilest of malefactors suffered this death; so that Christ could not stoop lower than this. "He humbled himself, and became obedient unto death, *even* the death of the cross," &c.

3. *It was peculiarly public, and, therefore, capable of universal establishment.* He died in the most public manner. The sentence of the Roman governor is passed—the fact is recorded—no event of ancient times capable of more full corroboration. The time, and the place, and the manner, all adapted to render it notorious and indelible to the latest posterity. Jews and Gentiles, the Roman authorities, are all at hand if the deed is doubted. Observe,

4. *It was an act of self-devotedness on the part of the Saviour.* Possessing infinite power within himself, he could say, no man taketh away my life, &c. "I have power to lay down my life," &c. He was freely passive in the hands of his enemies. He

could have escaped, or have discomfited, &c. But for this great end he was born—he had this ever in prospect—he even longed for it. "I have a baptism to be baptized with," &c.; and, though his humanity seemed to shrink at the last from it, yet, when he had prayed, he was delivered from that fear, and he said to those who came to arrest him, "Here am I." He laid down his life on the cross—yielded it up as an act of devotedness to the eternal interests of our world. When he had received the vinegar, "he cried with a loud voice, and gave up the ghost." Consider,

III. THE GLORIOUS CONSEQUENCES AFFIRMED. "I will draw all," &c. Now, this influence of the Saviour's death is referred to, as,

1. *Attractive.* "I will draw." Now, as an event it was calculated to draw the attention of mankind to it. The character of the sufferer—his miraculous fame—marvellous patience—the phenomena at his death, &c. So we find it. Josephus, the Jewish historian, particularly refers to it; so pagan writers; but the attraction referred to, is that of moral or gracious attraction. It should bring men to Christ; those afar off, &c.; those haters, &c. of Christ. It should attract the hearts and consciences of men—influence their lives and conduct. The idea is that of persuasion, not of terror—not force, &c. "The law was given by Moses," &c., under circumstances of extreme terror, but the gospel should win, &c. We see this exemplified in the sermon of Peter on the day of Pentecost, and the apostles in their first ministrations of peace and mercy. Christ crucified is the most marvellous display of love to the world—the embodiment of infinite grace, &c. Nothing can melt if this fails. "Herein is love," &c. "See there my Lord upon the tree," &c. "They shall look on him they have pierced," &c. This influence,

2. *Is elevating.* "I will draw to me."

(1.) To my cross, as the ground of hope and glory.

(2.) Crucifixion with me. Elevation above the world. The grace of God exalts.

(3.) To Christ in heaven as the object of our love. "Set your affections," &c.

(4.) And, finally, to the enjoyment of Christ in his glory.

3. *This influence is to be universal.*

There is to be nothing restricted in it—not with Judaism for one nation, but for all people. It shall affect all—Saviour of all, and finally triumph over all, and be the instrument of erecting Christ's kingdom from shore to shore, &c. Diffuse Christianity throughout the world, &c.

APPLICATION.

1. *Observe, the cross alone can save the sinner.* "God forbid that I should glory, save in the cross." Here is the one remedy for a world's sin and misery.

2. *It saves, by drawing to Christ.* We must come to him, &c. Misery and death in distance from him.

3. *The church must keep Christ lifted up.*

"'Tis all our business here below," &c.

4. *The world's moral destiny rests upon this.* Never failed—never can, &c.— "Christ the power of God," &c.

PILATE AND JESUS.

"When Pilate saw that he could prevail neth ing, but that rather a tumult was made, he took water, and washed his hands before the multitude, saying, I am innocent of the blood of this just person; see ye to it. Then answered all the people and said, His blood be on us, and on our children." —MATT. xxvii. 24.

HISTORY presents no events at all comparable in importance to the sufferings, trial, and death of Jesus. This is of necessity true, if you consider the dignity of the Saviour, the intensity of his sorrows, and the grand atoning design of his death. In matters so truly momentous, we should not overlook any incident, however apparently trivial in its character; for every event must be considered as a connective link in the great transactions which the Messiah came to accomplish. Our text relates to that part of the Saviour's life when brought before Pilate, and the course that Pilate adopted on the occasion. At this time Palestine was subject to the Roman power, and Pilate was the viceroy, or procurator, under the Emperor Tiberias. His character is represented by the historian as being peculiarly base, sordid, and oppressive. He greatly excited the enmity of the Jews by his obnoxious conduct, especially in introducing effigies of Cæsar, to which he required the Jews to yield almost the homage of divine worship. At one time it is related by Josephus, that he commanded the soldiers to put to the sword a number of Jews for resisting his oppressive enactments. It is to this, probably, Christ referred, when speaking of the Galileans, whose blood Pilate mingled with their sacrifices, Luke xiii. 1. Our text introduces him to our notice as the judge by whom the anointed of God is to be condemned to die. Let us,

I. CONTRAST THE JUDGE WITH THE PRISONER. How different to ordinary cases! Usually the culprit is of the lower and baser class, and the judge one who has been exalted, on account of his integrity and worth, to the judicial station. But here the judge was a pagan—an oppressor—sordid, vain, and ambitious. Look at the prisoner. Think of his divine majesty—the Son of God—the Holy One of Israel. His spotless integrity—his boundless benevolence—his merciful mission. He came to enlighten, to emancipate, to bless, to redeem.

> " Blessings abound where'er he reigns ;
> The prisoner leaps to lose his chains ;
> The weary find eternal rest,
> And all the sons of want are blest."

Pilate was the worst of judges—Christ the Prince of peace ; Pilate sordid—Jesus overflowing with generosity ; Pilate a curse to the people—Jesus the blessing of the wretched ; Pilate, whose name is handed down as execrable to posterity—Christ, whose name will endure forever.

II. CONTRAST PILATE WITH THE JEWS. Odious as Pilate appears, yet he rises in the scale of comparative excellence when contrasted with the Jews. The Jews had superior light. They had the writings of Moses and the prophets ; they were expecting a Saviour ; they had heard and seen the teaching and miracles of Christ. In these, how elevated above Pilate in their privileges ; yet how they sink beneath the Roman governor ! They hate Christ without a cause—they enviously refuse to acknowledge his righteousness and excellencies—they basely bear false witness to convict him—they madly clamor for his life. With insatiable ferocity they persevere, until they obtain his condemnation ; with unparalleled presumption they cry for his blood—the blood of the Holy One—to rest upon them and their children. In the midst of this, Pilate adopted the following course to deliver Christ from their hands :—He publicly declares the innocency of Jesus—

" I find no fault in him at all." He sends him to Herod, that he may be freed from the responsibility of condemning a just man. He wishes Christ to be the object of their national clemency, and hence proposes that Barabbas should die, and Christ be set at liberty. He endeavors to save his life, by delivering Christ rather to be scourged, thinking thus to excite their pity and commiseration. He finally, when all other expedients fail, takes water, &c. This act was strikingly public, and in accordance with a Jewish rite established by the founder of that dispensation, Deut. xxi. 1, &c. Now, in all this we see how superior even Pilate was to the envious and wicked Jews. But,

III. WE WILL CONTRAST PILATE WITH HIMSELF. We have heard his attestation of Christ's innocence—we have seen his expedients to save him—we have witnessed his public refusal to be accountable for his death ; yet, after all, he yielded. He delivers him to death ; he gives authority for the cross to be the instrument of death ; he gives orders to the executioners—to the soldiery ; and, whatever Pilate may think, or feel, or say, or do, Jesus dies by his judicial authority. On the side of Christ was enlisted—the understanding of Pilate—the judgment of Pilate—the conscience of Pilate ; but, on the side of the Jews, and against Christ, were the passions of Pilate—his love of fame—his disregard of justice—his violation of truth. In this act of Pilate, however, observe,

1. *It accomplished the types and prophecies of scripture.* The passage I have read—the whole ceremonial law was fulfilled in Christ. It had been predicted how Christ should be scorned, falsely accused, and condemned.

2. *It established the righteousness of the Saviour.* We have now two evidences of Christ's moral excellency : the testimony of his friends and disciples, even of the apostate Judas ; also of the judge on his trial, " I find no fault at all." " I am innocent of the blood of this just man."

3. *It ratified the condemnation of the Jews.* Thus Providence allowed the Jews to fill up the measure of their iniquity. To exhibit their hypocrisy, avarice ; to their cruelty to prophets and unbelief, they now added the murder of the Son of God. " This is the heir, come and let us kill him," &c.

What do we learn ?

1. *The infatuation of a deceived conscience.*
Conscience strove, spake, and wrought within Pilate ; but he blinded it, silenced it, and soothed it into quiescence. How ? By the water washing his hands, &c. How futile, foolish, vain ! How many are thus guilty, by placing religious rites and forms in the place of practical religion, &c. ; by death-bed confession ; by legacies, &c.

2. *Unrepented sins will eventually ruin their victims.* Thus Pilate, three years after the death of Christ, was deposed for cruelty and banished, and, in horror and wretchedness, committed suicide. Thus the Jews, also, had their prayer answered, "Let his blood," &c. So all impenitent sinners.

3. *There is a fountain open for all sin and sinners.* Oh, every one come to it now, and wash, and be clean.

THE CRUCIFIXION.

"And when they were come to the place which is called Calvary, there they crucified him."—LUKE xxiii. 33.

CHRIST crucified is the grand theme of the Christian ministry ; the great apostle of the Gentiles ever preached this, avowed his determination to know nothing else among men, nor to glory in any thing, save the cross of Christ. Condemned indeed should we feel if this subject should only be published on that one day in the year, which Christians, in past ages, have fixed upon, for the more direct celebration of the death of the Redeemer. All the discourses of the year must derive their power and glory from this subject ; and the daily theme of our meditation must be the work of Jesus, "who loved me and gave himself for me." We may, however, on this occasion, dwell more particularly on the literal facts associated with the death of Christ. The text furnishes us with three striking particulars.

I. THE NATURE OF CHRIST'S DEATH, "He was crucified." Crucifixion was a Roman punishment, and was never inflicted but upon the most debased characters, the most aggravated offenders ; it was, therefore, ever associated with the deepest infamy.

1. *It was generally preceded by scourging.* This was often so severe that the victim died beneath the horrid lash. Our Redeemer was thus scourged—he was bound to a pillar—exposed to the derision of the multitude, and long furrows were made on his sacred back.

2. *The criminal bore his own cross.* This was done to exhibit the justice of the sentence, that he had brought the misery upon himself by his own crimes. How inapplicable to Christ ! Pilate found no fault in him, yet he bore the cross and despised the shame. You remember that when Christ could bear it no further, Simon of Cyrene was compelled to carry it to Calvary ; and in this, he was a type of every disciple of Jesus,

"Shall Simon bear the cross alone,
And all the rest go free?"

3. *In crucifixion, the criminal was nailed to the wood, and then suspended on the cross.* Large nails were driven through the hands and feet, and thus the body was left to endure all the agony arising from the torn and bleeding wounds. Thus it was with Jesus ; those feet which had traversed Judea on errands of mercy, and those hands which had so often been opened to bless the people, were now cruelly nailed to the accursed tree.

4. *A stupifying draught was generally given to the sufferer.* This was composed of medicated wine and myrrh, and was intended to intoxicate, so as to render the sufferer less sensible of pain, see Mark xv. 23 ; this Christ refused ; he would not allow his holy mind to be disturbed by the stupifying potion.

5. *Crucifixion was an exceedingly lingering death, but was sometimes accelerated by other means.* When nailed to the cross a guard was placed to watch the sufferer till he expired, which was not on some occasions for days. Death was hastened sometimes by suffocation, or by breaking the limbs of the victim. You remember in Christ's case, that before the executioners came to do this, he had cried with a "loud voice and given up the ghost." But to make sure of his death, a soldier thrust his spear into the Saviour's side, from which flowed blood and water. Such was the nature of the death of Jesus. Notice,

II. THE PLACE OF HIS DEATH. "Calvary." Sometimes called Golgotha, which signifies the place of skulls. It was the place of execution—the hill of infamy. Around the spot were scattered the bones of criminals who had suffered there. The apostle particularly refers to the place of Christ's death. " without the gate," Heb. xiii. 12. And here we are taught,

1. *That Christ's death was for Jew and Gentile.* Not to be confined to those allied to Jerusalem or Judea.

2. *That the Christian institution had no connection with the Jewish ritual*, but that the whole ceremonial of the Jewish system was abrogated by Christ. We must leave Jerusalem to find the crucified Redeemer.

3. *The place reminds us too of the prominence and publicity to be given to Christ's death.* It was not a secret thing, but open and before the world. Thus, too, is the doctrine of his death to be made known to every people, and nation, and tongue. Christ must be lifted up to the whole world.

III. THE AGENCY EMPLOYED IN EFFECTING CHRIST'S DEATH. Then " they," &c.

1. *The Jews were the procuring agents.* " He came to his own, but his own received him not." The Father sent last of all his Son, but they said, " this is the heir, let us kill him." The Jews falsely accused him, and through envy put him to death.

2. *The Romans were the instruments employed.* The time had arrived when the Jewish power had ceased, the sceptre had departed, so that they could not put him to death. But how striking the contrast between the Jewish religionists, and the Roman pagans! Pilate wished to release him—the Romans had no desire for his death ; but the Jews, his own people, cried until they prevailed, " Crucify him, crucify him," &c.

3. *But in connection with all, we must not forget the purpose of God, the design of heaven.* God had predetermined to give his Son ; Jesus had offered himself as a sacrifice for sin ; he came freely to live, suffer, and die for the world. Yet do not suppose that this influenced the Jews ; moved by wickedness, and that only, they put him to death. But God, in the whole, consulted the glory of his own character, and the salvation of the sinner. Hence, almost every event had been predicted. Thus it was written, &c.

APPLICATION.

1. But for sin Christ had not died. Here are motives for contrition and true repentance.

2. But for his death, there had been no salvation. Here is our only hope of eternal glory.

3. The minister's great work. It is to cry aloud, " Behold the Lamb of God," &c.

CHRIST'S PRECIOUS BLOOD.

" The precious blood of Christ."—1 PETER i. 19.

THE word precious signifies valuable, of great worth.

(1.) It is applied in the divine word to human life. One of the captains sent to seize Elijah said, O man of God, let my life and the life of these fifty servants be *precious* in thy sight.

(2.) It is also applied to the blood and death of the saints, " And precious shall their blood be in his sight." " Precious in the sight of the Lord is the death of his saints."

(3.) It is applied to the divine word, " The word of the Lord was precious in those days."

(4.) To the redemption of the soul, " The redemption of the soul is precious." And,

(5.) To wisdom. " Wisdom is more precious than rubies."

(6.) Loving-kindness of God. " How precious is thy loving-kindness, O God !"

(7.) It is applied to Christ as the foundation-stone. " Behold, I lay in Zion a precious corner-stone," &c.

(8.) To the promises. " Whereby are given to us precious promises," &c.

(9.) To faith. " That have obtained like precious faith."

Finally, it is applied to Christ's blood, " The precious blood of Christ."

I. IT IS PRECIOUS COMPARATIVELY.
II. IT IS PRECIOUS INTRINSICALLY.
III. IT IS PRECIOUS SUPERLATIVELY.

I. IT IS PRECIOUS COMPARATIVELY. Every creature of God is good. He made nothing in vain ; not a leaf, pebble, grain of sand, drop of water. All full of God. We see more of the divine glory in the animal creation. All creatures are precious, so much so, that his wisdom, power, and goodness,

9916

were employed in forming them, providing for them, &c. They are all formed with love of life. How they cling to it! Cruelty is abominable wickedness, insulting to God. God however was pleased, under the old dispensation, to allow some of these creatures to be slain for sacrifices, &c. God in this exhibited the evil and desert of sin, the doctrine of mediation, the provision of a substitute. Now, however precious the blood of these creatures, yet it possessed no real merit in reference to the sin of man.

> " Rivers of oil and seas of blood,
> Alas, they all must flow in vain."

They were but shadows, symbols, types, &c.

II. CHRIST'S BLOOD IS PRECIOUS INTRINSICALLY.

1. *The blood of a human being.* You may learn God's estimate from the price he set upon Cain, Gen. iv. 15. When he spake to Noah, Gen. ix.

2. *The blood of an innocent, spotless being.* Men may deserve to die. " Soul that sinneth," &c. Christ was perfect, no stain, no weakness, no guile.

3. *The blood of a holy, benevolent being.* He was endowed with every excellent quality; just, good, merciful. Every virtue and grace in him in a state of perfection.

4. *The blood of the Son of God.* Christ was the tabernacle of the Deity, all the fulness of the Godhead. A creature is great in proportion to the resemblance to Deity. " Christ is the express image," &c. What value it imparted to Christ's person and work, the life of God's anointed Christ! If all creatures had been sacrificed in earth and heaven, not equal to this. Could easily have created more, but God never had, nor ever will have, but one " only begotten Son," Jesus Christ.

III. CHRIST'S BLOOD IS PRECIOUS SUPERLATIVELY.

1. *Christ's blood made a true and real atonement for sin.* Which no other blood did or could. Animals could not. A million of them not equal to one soul. How could the blood of unconscious, short-lived animals, atone for immortal souls? Angels could not. Sin affected body and soul. No bodies. Besides, a different order. The law was violated by human nature, and human nature must suffer or satisfy the broken law. Man could not. All guilty. Law demanded his life. When he had given that he had nothing left. Now the law demanded obedience, Christ rendered it, and gave his own blood or life for the redemption of the sinner. It was truly human nature, though holy, and therefore possessing infinite virtue and efficacy.

(1.) This atonement extended to all sin. The figurative atoning sacrifices under the law, made no provision for reckless, daring, presumptuous sins ; but Christ's blood extends to all manner of sins and blasphemies, &c.

(2.) This extends its influence to all sinners. Priests of old made an atonement for the congregation of Israel and proselyte strangers. Christ for the whole world. " Christ, by the grace of God, tasted death for every man." " Who gave himself," &c. " And he is the propitiation," &c. And this extends to all ages. Of old the sacrifices had often to be renewed—the great sacrifice once every year. But this reaches from the beginning to the end of the world, eternity to eternity. " Christ was once offered to bear the sins of many," Heb. ix. 28, x. 11, 12, 14.

2. *Christ's blood has given a most illustrious exhibition of the divine glory.* Of holiness—sin pardoned, not palliated. God displayed his great abhorrence of sin. Justice magnified, and iniquity punished. Mercy triumphing in harmony with inflexible righteousness. God inexorably just and yet the Saviour.

3. *His blood has procured for us inexpressibly great and precious blessings.* Forgiveness of sin, peace and reconciliation with God, purity of heart, final victory over our enemies, meetness for eternal glory.

APPLICATION.

Value this blood, apply it, glory in it, exhort sinners to come to it.

THE RESURRECTION OF CHRIST.

" And that he was buried, and that he rose again the third day according to the scriptures."— 1 COR. xv. 4.

THE gospel which the apostle preached, which the Corinthians believed, and by which they were saved, seems to comprehend two great facts, the death and resurrection of the Lord Jesus Christ. To these facts our attention of course is often called. They are facts with which we should be clearly acquainted, and fully conversant. On these, rest the hope of the world. To these the sinner's attention must be directed, and in the exercise of faith in these, he obtains righteousness, peace, and joy in the Holy Ghost. Both the death, and resurrection of Jesus were the subjects of prophecy, and were clearly foretold by himself. Let us then contemplate the resurrection of Christ.

I. IN THE THINGS WHICH IT PRESUPPOSES AND INVOLVES.

1. *It involved his death.* He was condemned to die. He was nailed to the cross. There he was suspended several hours. The executioners pronounced him dead. The soldier thrust his spear into his side, &c. It was evident to the multitude that he was dead. His death was inflicted by the authority of Pilate, at the request of the Jews, and in the presence of the populace of Jerusalem.

2. *He was buried.* His body was requested, and given up to Joseph of Arimathea. It was placed in a new sepulchre, alone. A stone was rolled to the mouth of the tomb, and that was sealed by the Roman signet, and the place carefully guarded by soldiers.

3. *The body of Christ left the tomb.* Did he arise, or was he stolen? If stolen, by whom? His timid disciples, who had all fled when he was arrested, would not have courage. If they forsook a living Saviour, would they have the temerity to steal his corpse? Besides, this would be to charge the Roman soldiers with unparalleled stupidity and inconceivable criminality. Had it been stolen, why was not a reward offered for its recovery? Why not arrest his disciples? Especially, how came it to pass that they allowed them to teach and preach his resurrection?

4. *His resurrection was fully attested.* By those who saw him, who heard him speak, who conversed and ate with him. He was seen by Mary Magdalene, by Peter, by the twelve, by five hundred brethren at once, by Saul on his way to Damascus, &c. He was seen at different times and occasions, seen often, seen when he left this earth with his glorified body, and ascended up into heaven.

5. *These witnesses had no worldly induce-*ments *to testify to a falsehood.* They had never been over-credulous, but unbelieving and slow of heart. They had no interest in being deceived, or in deceiving. It was not for their worldly honor, again to be the disciples of the crucified Nazarene. Poverty, reproach, scorn, persecution, and even death were their only reward. Yet they lived and died bearing witness to the resurrection of Jesus.

6. *In the city of his death thousands in a few weeks became his followers.* Peter openly declared both his death and resurrection. He charged the Jews with murdering the Prince of life, and he boldly stated that he had risen from the dead. Nor was he contradicted. His doctrine came in power and truth to the hearts of the people, and five thousand were soon enrolled under the standard of king Messiah. But let us consider,

II. SOME OF THE THINGS CONNECTED WITH CHRIST'S RESURRECTION.

1. *It was according to the scriptures.* To the type as in the history of Jonah. To the prophecies of the Jewish seers. To Christ's assertion that the temple of his body he would rebuild in three days. Also to his express teaching that on the third day he would rise from the dead.

2. *It was attended with circumstances of peculiar glory.* The earthquake, the rolling away of the stone, the mission of angels, the overwhelming the soldiers with terror.

3. *It was an act of stupendous power.* This was Christ's most sublime miracle. To raise others was supernatural, and evidenced his Godhead. But especially when he had power to take up his own life—to resuscitate his own body, and to exclaim, in the self-sufficiency of his omnipotence, "I am he that was dead, and am alive," &c.

4. *It was an event most necessary and important.* It was essential to the truth of his teaching. To the validity of his Messiahship. To his victories over death, Satan, and the grave. It ratified his engagements. It was the evidence that his sacrifice was accepted, and laid a solid basis of hope on which a guilty world might roll its sin and misery.

5. *Christ thus becomes the resurrection and the life, and the first-fruits of those who slept.* He was the first begotten from the dead. He proved that he had the keys of life and death. And he appeared as the

first sheaf of that countless number who by his Almighty power shall be raised from the dead. He became the plague of death, and the destroyer of the grave. He will put forth his great power in raising his people from the dead in the likeness of his glorious body.

APPLICATION.

1. To you we declare this crucified and risen Saviour. We invite you to contemplate his person, character, and work. Especially regard him as having loved you, died for you, and risen again for you, for your pardon, justification, acceptance, renewal, and everlasting salvation.

2. The Christian has the internal evidence of Christ's resurrection. Christ in his heart, "the hope of glory."

3. Now death has lost its sting, and the grave is but the passage to immortality.

4. Despisers and unbelievers will be raised by Christ to everlasting contempt.

CHRIST'S ASCENSION

"And he led them out as far as Bethany, and he lifted up his hands and blessed them. And it came to pass, while he blessed them, he was parted from them, and carried up into heaven."—LUKE xxiv. 50, 51.

JESUS came into our world that it might be blessed by him and in him. The law, which exhibited the purity and justice of God, was given by Moses; but grace, or the revelation of the favor of God to our guilty race, came by Jesus Christ. Well might angels sing at his nativity, "Glory to God in the highest," &c. Well might they say of him, "Blessed is the womb that bare thee," &c. He came emphatically as the mercy promised to the fathers, to bless men by turning them from their iniquities. His ministry began with the proclamation of blessings to the captives, &c. His sermon on the Mount was full of blessings; he went up and down doing good, and blessing mankind; he died praying for blessings on his murderers; when he arose and met with his disciples he blessed them; and now his mediatory work on earth is finished; he is returning to the presence and glory of the Father; and it is written in the text, that when he had led his disciples out as far as Bethany, he lifted up his hands and blessed them, &c. Notice,

I. THE PLACE OF CHRIST'S ASCENSION. Bethany, a place on the eastern side of the Mount of Olives. Here he had often sojourned with his beloved disciples, Martha, Mary, and Lazarus. Bethany signifies a house of sorrow, and Gethsemane was near to this spot, where he endured his agony. It had also been predicted by the prophet, that he should ascend from the Mount of Olives, Zech. xiv. 4. Observe,

II. THE TIME OF THE ASCENSION. Forty days after his resurrection, Acts i. 4. During this period he was repeatedly seen of his disciples, and gave the most demonstrative evidence of his resurrection, and enabled them clearly to be satisfied as to his identity, &c. During these forty days his enemies had ample time to examine the declarations made respecting his resurrection, and, if false, of undeceiving those who gave credence to them. During this time he also spake many important things concerning the kingdom of God, Acts i. 3. Thus, too, his disciples were prepared for his personal removal from them.

III. THE MANNER OF HIS ASCENSION.

1. *It was visible.* They were beholding him, looking upon him. It was in the light of day. "While they beheld," Acts i. 9. In the presence of a number of witnesses, &c.

2. *It was evidently connected with the ministry of angels.* "A cloud," it is said, received him. Most probably, a cloud of angelic beings. These had announced his conception—sang an anthem of praise at his birth—ministered to him in the wilderness and in the garden. It was they who related the fact of his resurrection, and now—

"They brought his chariot from above
To bear him to his throne;
Clapp'd their triumphant wings, and cried,
The glorious work is done."

It is said, "He was taken up," or "carried"—borne by his attendants, the celestial convoy.

3. *It was while he was in the act of blessing his disciples.* Thus showing that his grace and tenderness had not been chilled by the painful cross, or the gloomy sepulchre. Thus, also, he gave the last proof of his unchanging love to his disciples. How necessary this when he was departing from them; how necessary to cheer and encourage them in the arduous work of preaching Christ crucified to the world!

IV. The place to which he ascended. "Into heaven." The angels also said, "This same Jesus, which is taken from you into heaven," &c. Acts i. 11. He had said, that he should return unto the Father—"To my God and to your God." It is also said, that he is exalted at "the right hand of God," Acts ii. 33. There the dying Stephen beheld him, "standing on the right hand of God," Acts vii. 55. See also Psalm cx. 1; Eph. i. 20. He ascended to that heavenly world from whence he descended, and from which, in like manner, he will come the second time, without a sin-offering, to salvation. Notice,

V. The great ends of Christ's ascension.

1. *He ascended that he might possess the rest and joy promised him by the Father.* "Who for the joy that was set before him," &c. Heb. xii. 2. "Ought not Christ to have suffered these things, and to enter into his glory?" Luke xxiv. 26; Phil. ii. 9; Isaiah liii. 11, 12.

2. *He ascended that he might exhibit his conquests to angels and men.* Hence this event had been anticipated by the psalmist, "Thou hast ascended on high, thou hast led captivity captive," &c. Psalm lxviii. 18; Acts i. 9; Eph. iv. 8. He ascended as "the Bozrah conqueror," Isaiah lxiii. 1, &c.

3. *He ascended that he might take possession of heaven on behalf of his people.* He entered as the Redeemer—as the Head of the church—as the Bridegroom, &c.—as the Forerunner, &c.—as our great High Priest, &c.—"I go to prepare a place for you," &c. John xiv. 1. "Entered into heaven for us," &c. Heb. ix. 24.

4. *He ascended that he might send down heavenly blessings on his church.* "He hath received gifts for men," &c. "Exalted as a prince and a Saviour, to give repentance and remission of sins." Especially to send down the Holy Spirit. "It is expedient for you that I go away," &c. John xvi. 7, xv. 26; Acts v. 31, &c.

5. *That he might carry on his mediatorial work in heaven.* In heaven he appears as our great High Priest, interceding, presenting the persons and services of his people, and sending down the rich effusions of his Spirit and grace. Thus he sustains and perpetuates his kingdom in the world.

6. *That he might exercise his regal au-*

thority until his enemies become his *footstool.* Psalm cx. 1; Matt. xxii. 24; Luke xx. 43; Acts ii. 35.

APPLICATION.

1. *Learn the true dignity and glory of the Son of God.* How exalted! how glorified!

2. *The honor conferred on human nature.* Seated on the right hand of the majesty on high.

3. *The hope with which it should inspire the people of God.*

4. *The certain overthrow of his foes.*

INTERCESSION OF CHRIST.

"He ever liveth to make intercession for them."
—Hebrews vii. 25.

Jesus Christ having finished his work both of obedience and suffering on earth, entered into the holiest of all, where, says the apostle, "he ever liveth," &c. During his ministry here, he interceded for mankind. How sublime, rich, and edifying his sacerdotal prayer! John xvii. How compassionate his dying request! "Father, forgive them," &c. But the full execution of his intercessory exercises was reserved for the heavenly world. In the presence of God he appeared with his own blood, which had been shed for sin, and as the perpetual priest of his church, and the one mediator between God and men, "he ever liveth to make intercession for them." The place—the nature—the objects—and the perpetuity of Christ's intercession are presented to us in the text and its connections. Observe, then,

I. The place of Christ's intercession. That is the heavenly sanctuary, typified under the law, by the holiest of all, Heb. ix. 24. Hence he was predicted of, as a "priest upon his throne." He not only ascended to the right hand of God as a prince, to carry on his government; but also as a Saviour, on whom it devolves to bless his people, and make intercession for them. Thus John beheld him in the midst of the throne, having the appearance of a lamb as it had been slain, Rev. v. 6. Thus as a priest of more exalted dignity than those under the law, he carries on his sacerdotal work in the highest heavens, where " he ever liveth," &c.

II. THE NATURE OF HIS INTERCESSION. To intercede, is to plead on behalf of, and for the benefit of others. In the days of his flesh, Christ interceded by holy, fervent prayers for both his disciples and his murderers. It is matter of doubt, whether he now intercedes vocally or whether his intercession implies only his appearing before God in his mediatorial capacity, and exercising his will that the blessings of redeeming mercy should be imparted to mankind. The poet has said,

> " Five bleeding wounds he bears,
>   Received on Calvary,
> They pour effectual prayers ;
>   They strongly speak for me ;
> Forgive, forgive, they ever cry,
>   Nor let that ransom'd sinner die."

It is evident that the intercession of Christ is identified,

1. *With perfect knowledge and wisdom.* He only asks or desires what is in accordance with the claims of the divine law, in connection with his suretiship for the sinner. His intercession forms a part of that stupendous system which is to fill the world with purity and happiness, and bring eternal glory to the Most High.

2. *It is tender and affectionate.* His bowels yearn over the perishing. His heart is full of tenderest pity and love. He can feel compassionately for the wretched sons of Adam. His pleadings, therefore, are always distinguished by the most rich emotions of goodness and love. No friend, or father, or mother, could ever feel such compassion as glows within his infinitely affectionate bosom.

3. *It is faithful and constant.* The interests of souls are never neglected or forgotten. He does not appear occasionally, but always in the presence of God for us. His immutable fidelity characterizes his intercession. Christ intercedes,

(1.) That the persons and services of his people may be accepted of God. Only in him are we accepted. He is the way both for our personal acceptance and also for the favorable reception of all our exercises and duties, Eph. i. 6 ; Ps. lxxxiv. 8 ; especially see Rev. viii. 3, 4.

(2.) That sin may be forgiven, and the blessings of holiness imparted. " If any man sin, we have an advocate," &c. 1 John ii. 1.

(3.) He prays for the preservation and sanctification of his people. This he did for Simon in the days of his flesh, Luke xxii. 31 ; John xvii. 11, &c. It is also probable that he meets the accusations and charges of the adversary against his people. See Rom. viii. 33 ; Zech. iii. 2–4.

(4.) He prays for their final and everlasting glorification. That they may be perfected in holiness, and then that they may be where he is, to behold and participate in his glory. So that Christ's intercession includes our best interests, both in this world and in that which is to come. Observe,

III. THE OBJECTS OF HIS INTERCESSION. His intercession is not presented on behalf of particular individuals, or select nations, but for the human race. His intercession has chiefly reference to his own people, those who love and obey him, but it is not clear that it certainly excludes the unconverted. He prayed on earth for all who should hereafter believe, and who of course were then not united with his disciples. But his intercession is limited to this life, and embraces neither saints nor sinners who have entered the eternal state. All who come to God exercising faith in the Lord Jesus are most assuredly the objects of his intercession. Observe,

IV. ITS PERPETUITY. It will evidently be coeval with his mediatorial kingdom. The text says, " he ever liveth." The priests of old did not continue by reason of death. But Christ abideth forever, therefore his intercession is continued from age to age, without omission or interruption, and will be successfully exercised until the last ransomed spirit shall be brought to his joy and eternal glory.

APPLICATION.

1. *The subject is full of consolation to the righteous.* To have such a friend—brother —intercessor. One of such dignity—knowledge—power, and love, ever making our cause his own, and advocating all our interests in the heavenly state.

2. *We see how we can come to God acceptably.* He is the way. The advocate ; the one and only Mediator.

3. *Thus our feeble services are well-pleasing to the Father.* In all duties, worship, &c., let us not forget this, and let this be the ground of our hope.

4. *Live in the expectation of enjoying all that Christ asks, throughout eternity.*

THE IMMEASURABLENESS OF CHRIST'S LOVE.

" And to know the love of Christ, which passeth knowledge."—Ephesians iii. 19.

Our text is part of a prayer offered by Paul on behalf of the Ephesian church. Its richness, sublimity, and comprehensiveness, make it one of the most striking passages in the writings of that distinguished apostle, ver. 14 to 19. You will at once see that there is nothing in the subject to limit it to the Christians at Ephesus. Every minister of the gospel would desire this on behalf of his people, and every Christian should earnestly long for this on behalf of himself. " To know the love of Christ." Let us advert,

I. To THE SURPASSING LOVE OF CHRIST.

II. To THAT KNOWLEDGE OF IT WE SHOULD BE ANXIOUS TO ATTAIN. " To know," &c.

I. To THE SURPASSING LOVE OF CHRIST. Every thing connected with Christ is great and extraordinary. His twofold nature—his glorious person—his divine perfections—his wondrous offices—his peerless titles—his amazing work, and his eternal immutability. But the subject of the text is his surpassing love. " The love of Christ, which passeth knowledge." That is, in all its greatness and comprehensiveness, &c. Like the sun we may enjoy its light and heat, yet all its magnificence, and glory, and power, has never been set forth : or as the ocean which may be extensively known in the various shores by which it is surrounded, but which in its hidden depths and mysterious phenomena will remain a profound secret until the last day. Now the love of Christ in all its greatness and infinity is beyond the searching out of created minds, and none can ever know it to perfection. It surpasses all our thoughts and range of knowledge,

1. *In the eternity of its origin.* When did it first move in the heart of the Son of God ? The scriptures only record events as far back as the creation of our world ; with that the love of Christ is evidently coeval. But there is one truly sublime passage which leads us back long ere God brought our world into being, Prov. viii. 23–31. Here then we have the compassionate regards of Christ delighting his spirit in those depths of unmeasured duration which were ante-cedent to the existence of our earth. " It surpasseth," &c.

2. *In the undeserving character of its objects.* Let this be fully considered. Try it even with finite love. Can you conceive of an intellectual person, of pure and lofty morals, of a strong, righteous precision of judgment, compassionating a creature of unmixed vileness, of self-procured misery of deepest hate and malignity of spirit, and one who sought no elevation, desired no mercy, and cared for no deliverance. Yet the reality of this picture is far more striking. Think of the high and lofty One, clad in purity, of infinite equity and truth, yet fixing his regards on a self-ruined and totally polluted creation.

" He saw us ruin'd in the fall,
   Yet loved us notwithstanding all."

Notwithstanding there were countless reasons for not loving us, &c. " It surpasseth," &c.

3. *In the immensity of its cost.* The love of God to us is free, gratuitous, but what did it cost the Saviour ? His temporary abdication of the celestial throne—his descent from heaven—his advent into our world—his assumption of our nature—his deep humiliation and abasement in the flesh —his heart's deepest sorrows and heaviest griefs—his life—his blood—the precious blood of Jesus Christ. And with that the inexplicable travail of his soul. The immolation of his spirit on the altar of eternal justice. The gift of his entire self. To be the ransom—the sacrifice !! Well may we exclaim,

" Amazing love, how can it be,
   That thou, my Lord, shouldst die for me !"

4. *In the comprehensiveness of its extent.* The apostle refers to the extent in four respects :—

Its breadth, comprising in its range the whole world and every creature. " For Christ by the grace of God tasted death for every man."

Its length, reaching from eternity to eternity. The stream took its rise in the ages of eternity, flowed into our world in the first promise, has increased in magnitude, it has rolled parallel with succeeding ages, and will lose itself in the ocean of that eternity before us.

Its depth is to be measured only by the unknown depths of sin, and the still deeper misery from which it has redeemed us. None too low for its embrace, even brands from the burning.

Its height is that of the glories of the beatific vision. The celestial dignity and elevation of the glorified who have washed their robes and made them white, &c. Such then, briefly, is the surpassing love of Christ. Notice,

II. TO THAT KNOWLEDGE OF IT WE SHOULD BE ANXIOUS TO ATTAIN. We should seek,

1. *A gracious personal knowledge of it.* A theoretical scriptural knowledge is very important, but the apostle in one fragment of a sentence has exhibited that which we should covet, " He loved me, and gave himself for me." Now no person in his natural state can experimentally say this. We can say it when the love of God is shed abroad in our hearts, &c. When we have tasted that the Lord is gracious.

2. *To know it in its influences on our own hearts.* The love of Christ is a vehement principle—an exciting, constraining principle. It cannot be inoperative, " We love him," &c. And this love will breathe the atmosphere of peace, and be followed by joy. " Whom having not seen, ye love, though now ye see him not, yet believing, ye rejoice," &c.

3. *To know it in the holy fruits of our lives.* This love begets love. And love to Christ will trust in Christ—honor Christ—obey Christ—deny the world and forsake sin for Christ—surrender all to Christ.

" Love so amazing, so divine,
Demands my life, my soul, my all."

4. *To know it by an increasing experimental knowledge.* To know it more clearly —fully—sweetly,—to know it more in its sway over our hearts and souls. To the attainment of this knowledge,

(1.) Greater regard to the scriptures is necessary. Here this love is detailed—here it is set forth—here are the counsels, purposes, promises, and ratifications of his love. This is the golden mine ; this the celestial atmosphere, &c.

(2.) Closer communion is necessary. Spiritual intimacy will invariably increase it. Distant from Christ, and this knowledge cannot thrive. By speaking to Christ—by meditating on Christ—by setting him before us, we shall increase in the knowledge of Christ Jesus our Lord.

(3.) More fervent prayer is necessary,

" If any man lack," &c. Paul thus prayed for the Ephesians. God the Father honored Christ most generally when Christ was in the act of prayer. So it was at his baptism. On the mount, and when he prayed, " Glorify thy name," and the voice said, " I have both glorified it, and I will glorify it again," John xii. 28.

(4.) Greater zeal for his glory is necessary. Those who honor Christ he will honor, and he has engaged that he will come unto them, and manifest himself unto them, &c. When the heart and life are fully devoted to Christ, the soul shall be greatly enlarged in the knowledge and love of Jesus.

APPLICATION.

1. *This knowledge of the love of Christ is essential.* No salvation without it.

2. *The gospel reveals this knowledge.* Oh read and listen to that revelation. Here the tree of knowledge grows.

3. *Ignorance of the love of Christ will be the soul's eternal ruin.*

CHRIST THE ONLY SOURCE OF ETERNAL LIFE.

" Then Simon Peter answered him, Lord, to whom shall we go ? thou hast the words of eternal life."—JOHN vi. 68.

MANY who had listened hopefully to Christ's teaching became offended with him, and abandoned his instructions, verse 65, 66. Then Jesus addressed the twelve and said, " Will ye also go away ?" &c. Christ put this to see how they were affected by the conduct of the others—persons often act as those around, without reflection, &c. To this interrogation Peter replies, " Lord, to whom," &c. Observe,

I. THE GREAT OBJECT CONTEMPLATED— " Eternal life."

II. AN IMPORTANT QUESTION PROPOSED— " To whom shall," &c.

III. A GLORIOUS TRUTH ASSERTED—" Thou hast the words of eternal life," &c.

I. THE GREAT OBJECT CONTEMPLATED— " Eternal life." What is eternal life ? The existence of the soul and body in a state of felicity forever and ever.

1. *The future existence of the soul.* That it will not die with the body, not be destroyed, nor sleep, but live, and act, and

enjoy—enter upon another world, the region of the blessed—ascend to God, be with the Lord, &c. How supremely important is this, to have a hope of it, to be preparing for it, living for it, seeking it, so as to make the language of the apostle ours, "To live is Christ," &c., to have the portion of Lazarus after he died, "He was carried," &c.

2. *The resurrection of the body.* This was but faintly understood by the Jews, never guessed at by the heathen—Paul at Athens. This is revealed in the scriptures. The ashes we commit to the earth will rise again, not one grain of human dust shall perish. The trumpet shall sound, and the dead in Christ shall rise first, in the morning, with glory, to everlasting honor ; then shall the soul re-inhabit the body, and enjoy,

3. *Everlasting felicity.* The happiness of the saints is not complete till this,—this is the consummation. Then God's presence and glory shall be enjoyed, eternal worship celebrated, eternal bliss possessed. "In thy presence is fulness of joy," &c. "They shall obtain joy," &c.

II. An important question proposed. "To whom shall," &c. It supposes the subject to be entertained, &c., that it is deeply interesting. What can be so much so ?—all other subjects poor and worthless compared. To whom ?

1. *Shall we have recourse to nature ?* The works of the great Creator are resplendent with glory, they are vocal with the praise of their great Artificer, "The heavens declare," &c. Speak of the soul, of guilt, of pardon, of glory, all silent. Ask of immortality, of the resurrection, of eternal blessedness, all is silent, no return is made, &c.

2. *Shall we have recourse to infidelity ?* Why, that either denies or doubts of a future state, it mutters indistinctly about annihilation, it puts out the light of revelation, laughs at the hopes of the Christian, professes to sport with death, judgment, and a future world. Here all is repulsive, chilling, and wretched.

3. *Shall we avail ourselves of Judaism ?* Here is indeed the region of truth, but its discoveries are imperfect, but the dawn of the day ; we linger here waiting for the light of the morning ; we are surrounded with types, and sacrifices, and mysteries ; we are alarmed too with the awful splendor and thunderings of Sinai, until we exceedingly fear and quake.

4. *Shall we go to morality ?* The morals of the Bible are to be the rule of life to the Christian. But do they contain eternal life ? will the keeping one, or any, or all, ensure my salvation ? can I escape the punishment of past sin ? will works of righteousness avail me ? God speaks and says, "By the deeds of the law shall no flesh living," &c.

5. *Shall we go to profession and religious observances ?* Will the name, the form, the routine, the service ? will baptism ? will the Lord's Supper ? will an evangelical creed ? &c. The kingdom of God is not here or there, but within you—no promise of eternal life attached to these.

6. *Shall we seek it by penance, or mortification, by alms ?* &c. Will God be propitious through these ? Will fastings, tears, groans, mortifications ? What says the scripture ? Can we find eternal life anywhere connected with these ? One oblation of all the mere animal creation would not suffice.

> "Rivers of oil, and seas of blood,
>   Alas, they all must flow in vain."

We come again to the text, and consider,

III. The glorious truth asserted. "Thou hast," &c. That is Christ, and we add, Christ only. We observe,

1. *In his lips is the promise of eternal life.* He came to reveal, publish, offer, urge, &c. "I am come," &c. "If any man thirst," &c. "I give unto my sheep," &c.

2. *In his blood is the price of eternal life.* By his sacrifice and death he obtained eternal redemption for us, he laid down his life for his sheep, he suffered the just, &c.

3. *In his hands is the gift of eternal life.* He cancels guilt, he raises to life, "I am the resurrection and the life, whoso believeth," &c.—"God hath given eternal life," &c.—"He is exalted a prince and a Saviour," &c.

APPLICATION.

1. *Who has fled to Christ ?* Received his words, trusted in his death, received the gift. The Spirit within you is the great and sure earnest.

2. *Go not to other sources.* Life, life, eternal life is in Christ. Believe this and obtain it, seek it and live.

3. *Forsake not Christ, you who know his name.* Reply to every tempter, "To whom," &c.

CHRIST THE FIRST AND THE LAST.

(PREACHED ON THE LAST LORD'S DAY OF THE YEAR.)

" I am Alpha and Omega."—Rev. i. 11.

JOHN was the only disciple and apostle of the Saviour who did not suffer a violent death for his Master's sake. He did not, however, escape the persecution and opposition of the world. In old age he became an exile, and was banished to the island of Patmos for his faithful adherence to his Lord and Master. In that desolate island were revealed to him the sublime and splendid visions of this wondrous book. God made Patmos the ante-room of glory, the vestibule of heaven. Christ revealed himself to John in his divine uncreated majesty and grandeur, see ver. 9, 10, &c. Christ, the great theme of the Christian ministry—the life and glory of all evangelical preaching—what subject so suited to the last day of another year, as the dignified announcement, " I am Alpha," &c. Alpha and Omega are the first and last letters of the Greek alphabet, therefore they denote the first and the last, the beginning and the end. Of course they signify both the priority and supremacy of the Redeemer. If Christ claimed this appellation, and had a just right to do so, then his divinity is at once a settled truth. It is clear that Christ is the speaker, see verses 13 and 18. The text is applicable,

I. To THE UNIVERSE OF GOD. Of course I include the entire creation—angels, mankind, the animal creation, and the material world. Of the whole he is the Alpha—he created all things by the word of his power—" Without him was not any thing made." The apostle specifies things both in heaven and earth, &c. Col. i. 16 ; he gave existence to the whole ; fashioned, beautified, arranged, &c., the whole. Of the whole, he is the Omega—the end as well as the source. For his pleasure they were created ; his glory the great end. By him and for him, see Rom. xi. 36 ; Heb. ii. 10. Now Christ has universal rule and authority ; will make all things and all events subservient to his will and glory ; for by him all things consist, and he upholdeth all things by the word of his power. How grand and sublime the idea, that Christ, the Saviour of the world, is the Alpha and Omega of the entire universe, and doubtless will eventually receive the homage of the whole ! The text is applicable,

II. To THE GRAND SCHEME OF REDEMPTION. The purpose of salvation was in Christ—the arrangement was the result of his infinite wisdom—his eye saw, and his bowels yearned—his heart moved—his arm brought salvation. Trace the stream of mercy, and it takes its rise in the infinite depths of his compassion. Trace the ray of hope, and it is found emanating from the Sun of Righteousness, &c. Angels were spectators ; cherubim, &c., heard the announcement, but Christ alone was the Alpha, &c. So also, is he equally the Omega. Salvation refers to him—he is the end of it—the display of his holiness and justice—the exhibition of his righteousness—the transcendent display of his love—the entire revenue of honor and glory return to him—the redeemed are brought to God—the anthems all refer to God—the wise and benevolent designs of God will be consummated in the final completion of the work of redemption. In this there are no co-sharers, no compeers, Christ is the Alpha and Omega. It also applies,

III. To THE VOLUME OF INSPIRATION. Here Christ is the Alpha, &c. It is true in the most literal sense of the term. The volume opens with the displays of his creative power and glory—the Logos creating the world, &c. ; giving nature her laws ; revealing the tenure of man's felicity, &c. ; passing sentence ; revealing the promise of mercy, &c. Take the whole volume, it is the word of Christ. Look at the laws, and rites, and ceremonies, all prefiguring the Redeemer. The prophecies, &c. The gospel narratives. The Acts. The epistles. The revelation of John ; how truly he ends the sacred book, " The grace of our Lord," &c. Our chief view, in reading and meditating on the word, should be to find Christ, to hear his voice, behold his glory, and be conformed to his image. We shall find many illustrious names in its pages, some bearing very prominent positions, but Christ only is the Alpha and Omega. The subject is applicable,

IV. To THE CHURCH. Here Christ is also the Alpha and Omega. The church is Christ's kingdom—his temple—his spiritual house—his mystical body—the purchase of his blood—his ransomed flock—his elect host—his sacred army. He founded it, and is its blessed basis. It derives all life, and vigor, and purity from him ; he sustains it ; " the government," &c. ; because he lives, his people live also. He will be its Omega; by it, he will be glorified and admired, &c., forever and ever. The church has had its apostles, evangelists, pastors, witnesses, confessors, and army of martyrs, but Christ only is its Alpha and Omega. The subject applies,

V. To THE SPIRITUAL LIFE OF THE CHRISTIAN. In your calling, justification, conversion, holiness, &c., joy, comfort, hope, all from Christ as the Alpha. In faith, hope, obedience, love, devotedness, and praise, all to him as the Omega. "The author and finisher of our faith." "Lord, save me," is the prayer of the penitent. "Lord Jesus, receive my spirit," is the prayer of the dying Christian. This subject is applicable,

VI. To THE FELICITY AND GLORY OF HEAVEN. Countless sources of happiness and dignity there; knowledge, purity, rest, communion with all the holy, &c.; but Christ is the Alpha and Omega. He gives admission into the celestial city. He gives the crown. He is the grand object of the beatific vision, "See him as he is." He is the subject of the song. His favor and smile will constitute the happiness of that bright world forever. In heaven he will ever be the Omega, and his eternity will be the date and duration of all its blessedness.

APPLICATION.

1. *What think ye of Christ?* In what estimation do you hold him? What kind of service do you render? What enjoyments derive from him? What improvement in the knowledge, &c., of Christ during the past year?

2. *What madness to reject Christ!* To close the eyes upon the sun—to reject the air—the flowing stream—the staff of life—would be wiser than to reject Christ.

ON THE CONVERSION OF SINNERS.

"Brethren, if any of you do err from the truth, and one convert him; let him know, that he which converteth the sinner from the error of his way shall save a soul from death, and shall hide a multitude of sins."—JAMES v. 19, 20.

THE text refers, doubtless, to the regaining of a backsliding brother: one who has run well, but has turned aside from the way of righteousness. Hence the expression, "err from the truth." At an early period

errors crept into the church of Christ. Some of these were fearful in their influence. Errors as to Christ's Deity, errors as to Christian obedience, errors as to the simplicity of the gospel, &c. There were many false teachers, and these drew the unstable from the purity and obedience of the truth. It was the duty of the pious to endeavor to regain such, to bring them back, &c. We see how Paul labored for the restoration of the Galatians, &c. But the text is capable of a more extended application. We may justly refer it to the duty of the Christian church to endeavor to convert sinners in general. Let us look at it in the extensive and general sense.

I. WHAT IS INCLUDED IN THE CONVERSION OF THE SOUL?

II. WHAT CAN WE DO TOWARDS EFFECTING IT?

III. THE MOTIVES WHICH SHOULD INFLUENCE US TO ATTEMPT IT.

I. WHAT IS INCLUDED IN THE CONVERSION OF THE SOUL? To convert signifies to change, to turn round about. Now this may apply to our views, our feelings, our state, and our conduct. In conversion there is,

1. *A change in our views.* Things are viewed through a new medium, and their aspect is entirely altered. Now a converted person sees *himself*, his conduct, and deserts, as he did not before. He sees sin in its true nature—he sees God in a new character—he views the Saviour, religion, time, and eternity, differently. What he considered light, he now calls darkness—wisdom he now calls folly—good he now calls evil. Just as by looking through certain optical instruments the figures are reversed, so to those converted to God.

2. *A change in our feelings.* It has to do with the heart and all its passions—love, hatred, desire, delight, &c. His soul now loathes his former enjoyments; his former sweets are now as gall and wormwood. He feels differently towards the world and sin, towards the pious, and especially towards the blessed God. "Old things," &c.

3. *A change in our state.* Once in the world—now in the church; once in the broad way—now in the narrow, &c.; a captive—now free; enemy—now a friend; condemned—now justified, and accepted of God. A child—an heir of eternal life.

4. *A change in conduct.* The actions of the life are now counter to what they were. He was prayerless—now he prays; presumptuous—now he fears, &c.; indifferent —now solicitous; disobedient—now from the heart he serves God. He was the slave of Satan, and had the fruit of shame, &c.; now the servant of God, and the fruit of righteousness, &c.

II. WHAT CAN WE DO TOWARDS EFFECTING IT? Now, I mean Christians; not merely ministers, but all who love and know Christ. Now, we cannot illumine the mind with spiritual understanding; we cannot change the will; we cannot wash the spiritual blackamoor white. God must renew, and renovate, and give a new nature, &c. But we can,

1. *Give important spiritual instruction.* Explain and rehearse what we know of religion. Christian knowledge is important. " Go and tell what things the Lord," &c. The disciples were scattered abroad, and went everywhere preaching and teaching the Lord Jesus.

2. *We can employ Christian entreaty and persuasion.* We can persuade them, perhaps, to abandon evil habits—to attend the house of God—to read the Bible—to consider their ways, &c. How many have thus been drawn to Christ by the affectionate kindness of believers!

3. *We can exhibit the characteristics of true piety.* The apostle speaks of persons being won by the conversation of the pious. Our light must shine—the savor of piety be perceived—the fragrance emitted—the spirit diffused abroad. Now this always impresses—always moves. Then we can,

4. *Connect fervent prayer with the whole.* Seek God's special blessing—implore his help—intercede for souls—lay their conduct to heart—travail in birth—be very anxious for it. This will please God, secure his blessing, &c. None ever did so in vain.

III. THE MOTIVES THAT SHOULD INFLUENCE US TO ATTEMPT IT.

1. *There is the possibility of being successful.* It has been done. The text supposes it possible. How great and desirable is such an achievement!

2. *There is the obligation laid upon us.* Obligation of Christ's constraining love; obligation of the Spirit of God within us; obligation of our own consciences; obligation from what others did for us, especially

what Christ has done. " Then I will tell," &c.

3. *We shall obliterate a multitude of sins.* Cause them to be blotted out. Cast as a stone, &c. Trains of evil stayed—plague arrested—curse a blessing, &c. Besides,

4. *Rescue a soul from perdition.* Death —the sentence—the doom—the misery. Everlasting death—devouring flames— eternal burnings, &c. Oh! the felicity of this when we die—appear before God's bar—through all eternity.

APPLICATION.

1. *What reason for self-reproaches!* We are verily guilty, &c. All, every one, &c.

2. *Let us awake to diligence, &c.* Now let bowels of mercy constrain, &c.

3. *Exhortation to the unconverted.* Oh be wise, &c. In this your day, &c.

ON WINNING SOULS.

" He that winneth souls is wise.''—PROV. xi. 30

OUR text directs us to the human soul— the last and great work of God's creative power and goodness. When the earth and the heavens, the sea and the dry land, with their numberless animated creatures, had been formed, then Deity, as the climax of his omnific manifestation, stepped forth and said, " Let us make man ;" and it is recorded, that in his own likeness created he him. The soul's exalted similitude to God's holy image is its highest honor, and this invests it with a glory and a worth which vastly transcend all terrestrial things. But alas! the soul of man can only now be contemplated amid its eclipsed glory and moral ruin. By sin it apostatized and became a wreck. The crown has fallen from its head. Ichabod is now written upon it—the glory is departed. To restore the soul to dignity, holiness, and heaven, is the great design of the plan of redemption. God, in the infinity of his grace and love, has become the help of ruined man ; has set up a plan of reconciliation whence holiness, justice, and truth may harmonize with clemency, mercy, and love, in its salvation. The great remedy is revealed in the gospel. The way of recovery is there clearly pointed out, and God has set up in his church the Christian ministry in connection with the pious influence of his people, for the conversion of sinners to himself. Notice,

I. THE MEANS TO BE ADOPTED FOR WIN-NING SOULS.

II. ON WHOM THE RESPONSIBILITY DE-VOLVES. And,

III. THE WISDOM OF FAITHFULLY DIS-CHARGING THAT RESPONSIBILITY.

I. THE MEANS TO BE ADOPTED FOR WIN-NING SOULS. Now, if we consider some of the circumstances in which the soul is pla-ced, and the influence which may be exert-ed upon it, we shall then clearly perceive what must be done to win souls. We re-mark,

1. *The soul is in darkness, and must be won by the communication of knowledge.*
Man in his revolted condition is in the kingdom of Satan, and that is the kingdom of darkness. Man is represented as being blind—blinded by sin and the power of the destroyer. Now this darkness, or igno-rance, is the blight of the soul—its degra-dation, its misery, its destruction. " For the soul to be without knowledge," &c. " My people perish for lack," &c. To win the soul we must enlighten it—the light of truth must arise upon it—the scales must be taken from the eyes. Man's ruin and help must be detailed—the lamp of heavenly knowledge must be held up to the soul.

2. *The soul is in moral thraldom, and the message of deliverance must be proclaimed.*
The gospel is a message of liberty. It calls to liberty—it proclaims freedom to those who are bound. " Ye shall know the truth," &c. The gospel dispensation is the year of jubilee—the year of release, and announces liberty to the captive.

3. *The soul is under the power of evil, and Christian influence must be employed to dispossess it.* Hence it must be reproved —warned—exhorted—expostulated with— allured. The soul has fears, and these must be aroused ; hopes, and these must be addressed ; desires, and these must be di-rected. Piety has a fourfold influence to exert on men for their good.

(1.) The influence of integrity. An upright conduct—unblameable demeanor— purity of conversation. This will do much.

(2.) The influence of goodness or be-nevolence. The Saviour's heart and mind. Love ennobling, reigning, influencing, &c. It is difficult to resist this.

(3.) The influence of holy cheerfulness. An evident exhibition of the bright radiant influences of true religion on the soul. Melancholy cannot attract—it is the cloud, the desert ; but holy joy is the sunshine, and the verdant scene.

(4.) The influence of kind persuasion. " Come with us, and we will do you good," &c. Affectionate invitation will often do very much.

4. *The soul is incapable of self-restoration, and therefore we must pray for the Holy Ghost to render all other means efficient*
Men may hear and understand the gospel— receive or reject it—be greatly influenced by Christian example ; but the soul must be re-newed by the Spirit of God. He takes away the heart of stone, &c. He translates, &c. from darkness, &c. Thus Paul, "Breth-ren, my heart's desire, and prayer to God is, that Israel," &c. " The effectual fer-vent prayer," &c. Prayer and supplica-tion are to be made for all men, &c. Let us labor to save souls, as if all depended on our exertions, and then pray. as if God did it alone and immediately.

II. ON WHOM DOES THE WORK OF WIN-NING SOULS DEVOLVE ? It devolves pre-eminently on the Christian ministry. They are called, and qualified, and sent out for this great purpose. But it also devolves upon all Christians to make the effort. On parents, as did Abraham, Joshua, David, &c. ; on sabbath school teachers and tract distributors, &c. ; in one word, on all the disciples of Jesus. Their name Christian, like Christ ; their calling, to shine, &c. ; their desire, to do good, &c. ; their talents. however few, &c. Let us notice,

III. THE WISDOM OF FAITHFULLY DIS-CHARGING THAT RESPONSIBILITY. " He that winneth souls," &c. Now, the wisdom of winning souls will appear if you consider,

1. *The value of that which is won.* Who can describe its worth? A city—a king-dom—a world, is as nothing in the scale. He who never erred, has proposed this mighty interrogation, " What shall it profit a man," &c. To win souls is, therefore, the highest wisdom, the most noble of all attainments.

2. *The dignity of those with whom we co-operate.* We move in the same train, and labor with patriarchs, prophets, apostles, &c. They lived, and sung, and toiled, and died, to win souls. We are fellow-workers with angels, for their history is connected

with that of redemption ; they are also ministering spirits, &c. We are acting in unison with the blessed Deity. God was not so glorious, and great, and blessed in creating the world as in redeeming it. His Son, in all the mystery of the incarnation —the depths of his humiliation—intensity of his sorrow and ignominy—the agony of his death, had but one end, to win souls. For this all the arrangements of Providence progress, and will be consummated. The songs of the ransomed will have respect to this, &c. Is it not wise, &c.

3. *The bliss enjoyed by the soul through eternity.* Follow the spirit, &c. into the regions of a blissful immortality. Contemplate its dignity, and joy, and glory, as beatified. Entered on a state of boundless felicity. " In thy presence is fulness of joy," &c.

APPLICATION.

1. *Who are engaged in the work ?* Be constant — active — persevering —devoted. The day of recompense will come. " Be faithful unto death," &c.

2. *Who will now consecrate their services to the Lord ?* What say you, ye young— ye strong—ye with time, &c.

3. *How many here, are yet strangers to Christ ?*

THE MINISTRY OF SALVATION.

" Even as I please all men in all things, not seeking mine own profit, but the profit of many, that they may be saved."—1 COR. x. 33.

THE text is the declaration of the apostle as to the course he pursued in fulfilling the responsible work of the ministry, verse 32. The end of his ministry he specifies in the text, " that they may be saved," &c.

I. THE NATURE OF THAT SALVATION WHICH THE GOSPEL CONTEMPLATES.

II. THE RESPONSIBILITY OF THE CHRISTIAN MINISTRY TO MAKE KNOWN THE MEANS BY WHICH THIS SALVATION MAY BE SECURED.

I. THE NATURE OF THAT SALVATION WHICH THE GOSPEL CONTEMPLATES. What is it to be saved ? It signifies to be delivered—to be delivered from that sinful perishing state in which we are involved by nature. Look at that state in its guilt—in its depravity— in its peril.

1. *To be saved is to be pardoned.* It changes the condition—debt cancelled— cloud blotted out—charges erased. Pardon is *promised*, published, and urged in the gospel. This is the foundation of acceptable piety, to be pronounced righteous by justifying grace. " Thy sins are forgiven," &c. To be saved is,

2. *For the mind and heart to be renewed.* Pardon does not in itself alter the feelings and desires. The depravity is so deep, so entire, so universal, that the heart cannot be repaired, or merely improved—amended ; it must be totally changed—born again —renewed. All old things must pass away. The heart of stone must, &c. God's nature, spirit, and mind imparted.

3. *To be saved is for the soul to be rescued from its peril.* The frown of God— the wrath of the Holy One—the sentence of death—and hell itself. When God forgives, his anger passes away ; no longer under wrath, but favor—delivered from the wrath to come—now a title to everlasting life—names written in heaven—after death, eternal glory—saved into God's family on earth, and into heaven forever.

II. THE RESPONSIBILITY OF THE CHRISTIAN MINISTRY TO MAKE KNOWN THE MEANS BY WHICH THIS SALVATION MAY BE SECURED.

1. *The gospel must be declared, as containing the only way of salvation.* Without this all is darkness—mist—confusion. Not another book in the universe. Ten thousand subjects may be taught, &c., but this nowhere else. Word of salvation. Neither science nor literature can aid us—gospel the only record of mercy.

2. *Jesus must be published as the only deliverer.* No other has the office, nor the ability. Prophets to teach—priests to offer sacrifice—holy men to counsel—angels to minister—but Christ only to save. Stands forth as the sun in the heavens—to all generations, ages, and countries.

3. *Repentance and faith as the appointed means.* They are essentially so—they are necessary to it. Eyes opened—ears unstopped—hearts converted—mind changed —heart penitent, and mercy longed for. Then faith—seeking, finding, resting on Christ. Faith before the cross—before the throne.

4. *Obedience of heart and life as the evidence of salvation.* Not the cause, but the effect—not the root, but the fruit—not the foundation, but the superstructure. Cheerful, willing, entire obedience.

APPLICATION.

1. Have we so preached?
2. Have you so heard?
3. This is the design of the true gospel.
4. We offer it to each and all.

MINISTERIAL ARDOR.

" For whether we be beside ourselves, it is to God ; or whether we be sober, it is for your cause."
—2 Cor. v. 13.

WE are always compelled to regard conduct which is peculiarly striking and prominent. Even the eccentricities of men turn for a time public attention towards them. But where there is displayed great decision of principle, great energy of action, and great disinterestedness of motive, our attention is then excited in a peculiar manner. If we do not approve of the object, we give involuntary homage to men when there is honesty of purpose with nobleness and vehemence of spirit. The worst that we venture to say is, that he may be a fanatic or an enthusiast, but still withal he may be an honest, well-meaning person. Now, to the eyes of both Jews and Greeks, the apostles were just such persons. They were deemed mad with religious enthusiasm, and to this the apostle refers in the text. As Christians we approve, commend, and rejoice in the spirit and labors of the apostles ; but if so, should we not imitate them—imbibe their spirit—breathe their devotedness—exemplify their toil and self-denial ? In one word, should we not exhibit the utmost determination and vehemence of spirit in diffusing the gospel through the world ? We affirm, then, that the cause of Jesus warrants the employment of our utmost energies and powers, even though we are exposed to the charge of being beside ourselves. Let us establish and illustrate this. For proof we refer,

I. To THE MAGNITUDE OF OUR OBJECT. This object is of the highest importance. It is the elevation of human beings to moral dignity, purity, and salvation—lifting up immortal souls from the verge of the pit to the highest enjoyment of celestial grandeur and blessedness. Look at the depraved condition of the human race, especially of the heathen. The mind dark as midnight ; spirit spell-bound by superstition ; heart callous with relentless cruelty ; life one of torture, distraction, horror, wretchedness, and followed by a death of despair. Think of the transformations we seek. Light, liberty, purity, peace, hope, immortality, heaven. What compared with this is mere civilization—national independence—mental culture—earthly prosperity—scientific discovery, &c. Here is the concentration of the glorious, the blessed, the sublime. We refer,

II. To THE VASTNESS OF OUR SPHERE. Even as in ancient days, we may affirm "that the field is the world." Take a map of the world, or a terrestrial globe, and look at the vastness of our sphere. You traverse whole regions of the world, where nothing but darkness and misery reign—China, India, Egypt, Persia, Turkey, South America ; visit the almost brutalized inhabitants of the northern regions ; the aboriginal savages of Africa, &c. In turning round the globe, you see Britain, and parts of America, and here and there an island, where they have the gospel ; but the mass are perishing for lack of knowledge. The world lieth under the rule of the wicked one. Will feeble or tame efforts do any thing to evangelize this sphere ? to illumine these hundreds of millions ? to convert these myriads upon myriads ? If every Christian were wholly devoted either to teach or preach ; if every believer were consecrated entirely to the work, so vast is it, so immense, that our means would scarcely be commensurate to it. A few hundreds of nets are all that are employed to drag this fathomless ocean of its perishing millions. In vindication of the highest zeal we refer,

III. To THE GRANDEUR OF OUR SUBJECT. To effect the glorious end contemplated, what are our means ? what the instrumentality we design to employ ? We answer, the glorious gospel of the blessed God—by the cross of Christ. We purpose no invasion by powerful armies ; we shall send no vessels of war ; no legislative statutes enforced at the point of the bayonet, or the mouth of the cannon. We have arms, but they are the sword of the Spirit—the invincible weapons of truth—the banner of the cross—the standard of mercy—the streamers of peace. Our trumpet sounds to deeds of mercy and love. Simply we carry the gospel of salvation, and preach it to the people. Tell of the Nazarene—his life, death, **resurrection,** &c. Invite them to be reconciled to God. Cry out to them, " Behold the Lamb of God," &c. Is not our subject as simple, beautiful, yet mighty, as the light of heaven ? The melodious angelic song comprises it, " Glory to God in the highest," &c. But will this message effect the great work ? We refer,

IV. To the triumphant achievements of the past. Shall we appeal to the history of the gospel in its early or later days ? We appeal to its origin. This gospel was preached in Jerusalem, the city of Christ's death—the place crimsoned with his blood ; preached by fishermen, &c. See the marvellous results—the conviction and conversion of three thousand under one sermon. Afterwards the number is increased to five thousand. The disciples go forth to other places. They visit Corinth, the most sensual city of the age ; Athens, the most renowned for its multifarious gods ; Ephesus, where the splendid temple of Diana shone forth in its seducing grandeur ; Rome, the imperial city of the world; and everywhere, by the preaching of the cross, souls are converted to the Christian faith, and to the lofty virtues of evangelical morality. Let us now, by one striking transit, come to modern times. Men imbued with the same spirit, yet not possessed of miraculous powers, carry the same gospel to India, and there it breaks down caste, and even proud Brahmins become children in the school of Christ. They carry it to the wilds of Africa—the filthy Hottentots become civil, intelligent, and holy ; to the cannibals of the South Seas, and there a nation is born in a day. Say, then, if the highest zeal is not wisely expended in this great cause ? We advert,

V. To the aspect of the present times. In all parts of the world missions have to some extent succeeded ; but the present aspect of things should excite to the most devoted zeal. The established character of some missions—the great success of others—the opening of new doors of amazing extent—the increased ratio of success in most stations—when caste is broken—when a few dare to do the deed—when native preachers are being raised up, we then seem to have reached the crisis when we may expect to storm the citadel itself. Drops shall be succeeded by showers, and " the little one shall," &c.

VI. To the predicted glories of the future. We are not engaged in a matter of uncertainty ; we have the revealed will of God assuring us of the certainty of success. His word shall not return, &c. " It shall accomplish," &c. Hear the glorious declaration of Deity, " For the earth shall be filled," &c. " I will bring my sons," &c. " He will say to the north," &c. " All flesh shall see the salvation of God," &c. " He shall be praised from the rising," &c. Hear Jehovah's most absolute asseveration : " But as truly as I live all the earth shall be filled with the glory of the Lord." Here then we sow in hope and plough in hope—preach in hope—instruct in hope—pray in hope—believe in hope— give our donations in hope, &c. With such prophecies and promises can we be too ardent and zealous ?

VII. To the limitation of our opportunities. To attempt these sublime objects—to combat this world of evil—to attempt the rescue of these deathless spirits, we have only the short space of a transitory existence. We might well seek antediluvian lives to labor. A *survey* seems enough for our short breath of existence. If we do any thing, there must be devoted, ardent, zealous effort. " Whatever thy hand," &c. " Work while it is called day." This is echoed back from the tombs of past generations—the tombs of the slain warriors in this hallowed cause ; from the tombs of Coke, and Elliot, and Carey ; from the tombs of Mrs. Winslow and Mrs. Judson. " Work while it is called day," &c.

APPLICATION.

1. Are we anxious and earnest in the missionary work ?

2. Who will be so from this hour ?

3. Seek for yourselves what you send to others.

NEUTRALITY IMPOSSIBLE.

" He that is not with me is against me."—Matt xii. 30.

Christ was the most faithful, yet the most tender of all preachers. These were combined in all his addresses. He never failed to pity, yet he also never failed to exhibit the truth to the consciences of his hearers. Having delivered the most soul-searching discourse to the hypocritical scribes and Pharisees, he concludes it with tears, and laments the doom which they might have averted. Surely it should be our constant aim to copy the perfect example of the great Teacher. We would entreat, and reason, and persuade. We would allure you by the precious promises —we would win by heaven's glories— we would attract by the influence of the cross; but if all this should fail—if you still hearken and do not believe—form a part of the public assembly and do not give your hearts to Christ—we then must warn you, and with all fidelity proclaim the language of Christ in your ears, " He that is not with me is against me," &c.

I. WHAT IS IT TO BE WITH CHRIST? It includes several things.

1. *With him in the conclusions of our minds.* The carnal mind concludes very differently to Christ on almost every subject. We know Christ's views of the Father; we know his views of sin—of holiness—of time—of the soul—of eternity— of heaven—of hell. Are we like-minded with Christ—see objects through the same medium.

2. *With Christ in the affections of the soul.* What he loves do we supremely love? What he hates, &c. Do our hearts move with his? our desires with his? Does he in fact draw us after him? his jealousies—his hopes, &c. Now, if Christ's spirit be in us this will be the case.

3. *With Christ in the pursuits of life.* How did he live, and for what? Do we walk in the Lord Jesus? Do we set similar objects before us? aim at similar ends —labor for similar realizations—glory of God and the true good of human beings. He did all his Father's will and work.

4. *With Christ in the endearments of union and communion.* He that is joined to the Lord is one spirit. Christ in you the hope of glory. He manifests himself unto his people, &c. " Behold, I stand at the door and knock," &c.

5. *With Christ in spiritual exercises and conflicts.* Resisting evil—overcoming the world—vanquishing the powers of darkness—praying and laboring against these— setting up and maintaining another kingdom. Are we his soldiers—valiant for the truth—confessing, adorning, and diffusing the truth of his gospel.

II. WHAT IS IT TO BE AGAINST CHRIST? Two classes:

1. *Those who are manifestly so.* Infidels — blasphemers — persecutors — scoffers — the profane and thoroughly worldly—neglecters of his word and ordinances. These need only be named. They have the name of their master in their foreheads; the livery of sin is manifest; their spirit and conversation are conclusive against them.

2. *Those who are not openly, yet who are really so.*

(1.) They who are half-hearted—have some love, some desires, some esteem; but it is not entire. Their hearts are divided —stand midway between the church and the world—follow Christ at a distance.

(2.) Those who are constantly hindered in carrying out their convictions. One is occupied with the worldly, and their salutations and tokens of favor bind him; another with business, and it absorbs—farm, merchandise, &c.; another, the affairs of the family; another, the fear of persecution; others who think secret attachment is sufficient, with Nicodemus.

3. *Those who rest in external observances.* Many pride themselves in their extensive knowledge—in their regular lives—in their attendance on means. How often Christ reasoned with them! " Not those who say, Lord, Lord," &c. " The kingdom of God is not meat and drink," &c. Christ said to Nicodemus, a teacher, &c., " Ye must be born again."

III. CHRIST'S CONCLUSIONS AS TO THOSE WHO ARE NOT WITH HIM. " They are against me." I recognise friends and enemies only—subjects and rebels—lovers and haters. He has no medium class—no medium state—no medium heaven. Now, you who would not be numbered with the enemies of Christ, just let us appeal,

1. *To reason.* Does not reason say you cannot be for two opponents? for light and darkness—sin and holiness—heaven and perdition. Does not reason say, with your views of Christ, you should give him your hearts?

2. *I appeal to conscience.* Your convictions, how often shaken. Under sermons —when reading the Bible—when sick— when at the funeral of a friend—when others have given themselves to Christ.

3. *I appeal to the cross of Christ.* Christ speaks. He says, I loved you, &c. I died for you; for your entire devotedness

to me. He shows his hands—his side ; he groans, &c. Now, what are the claims of Christ? Your lips—your good-will—oh! surely yourselves :—

> " Love so amazing, so divine,
> Demands my soul, my life, my all."

4. *I appeal to the day of judgment.* Christ is now enthroned. He sways the sceptre of the universe. All nations are before him. Behold an assembled world. The countless myriads are divided into four —five—six sections? Oh, no ; but two— the righteous and the wicked—wise and foolish—friends and foes—saints and sinners. What surprise—what confusion— what horror! He exclaims to the disappointed and excluded, " He that is not with me is against me," &c.

APPLICATION.

1. *How important to avoid self-deception!* " Do not err," &c. " Be not deceived," &c.

2. *Will not many resolve to be for Christ to-night?* You must cross the line of demarcation—you must be decided. Now record your vow ; now decide—act, &c.

3. *What can be gained by being against Christ?* What honor ? peace ; happiness ? What in life ? What in death ? What in eternity? Ask yourselves what?

REJECTERS AND RECEIVERS OF CHRIST CONTRASTED.

" He came unto his own, and his own received him not. But as many as received him, to them gave he power to become the sons of God, even to them that believe on his name."—JOHN i. 11, 12.

OUR present subject describes the reception Christ met with when he became incarnate, and made his advent into our world. He was in the world, and we may truly say, that for dignity and mental and moral grandeur the world had never had such a visitant. Yet, it knew him not ; it gave him no deference ; yielded him no homage or respect ; it hailed him with no song of joy ; it knew him not. But the former part of our text is still more marvellous, " He came unto his own," &c. Let us consider,

I. CHRIST'S REJECTION BY HIS OWN, AND ENDEAVOR TO ACCOUNT FOR IT. And,

II. CHRIST'S RECEPTION BY SOME, AND THE ADVANTAGES WHICH FOLLOWED.

I. CHRIST'S REJECTION BY HIS OWN, AND ENDEAVOR TO ACCOUNT FOR IT. " He came unto his own ;" that is, to his own people, and nation, and land. The world's Messiah was to be of the seed of Abraham— of the tribe of Judah—of the royal line of David. He was also to come to their nation—the very city had been predicted in which he should be born. Bethlehem was to be the place of his nativity ; he was to come at a specific time—before the sceptre should depart from Judah, or just at the time that regal power and authority should cease among them as a nation ; and thus he came, and in every iota the prophecies received their exact accomplishment. More, the Jews were ardently expecting him ; all the pious and devout had been waiting for him, and were particularly doing so at the time of his advent ; yet, they " received him not ;" in other words, they rejected him ; they reviled his character—treated him with contempt and scorn—preferred a murderer to him—and at length, with wicked hands, put him to a cruel and shameful death. How surprising this conduct! How can it be accounted for ? Not in any thing connected with Christ, for he was holy, blessed, and the very embodiment of every grace and virtue ; but he became to the Jews a stone of stumbling, and rock of offence. It is written, They were offended in him. This arose partly from,

1. *Fixing their attention on one class of prophecies only.* Those which spake of his regal glory and conquests ; and, interpreting these carnally, they seemed to be ignorant of those which described his humiliation, poverty, sufferings, &c.

2. *They were not prepared for a system of spiritual religion.* They were wedded to forms and rites ; to their ritual, and temple, &c. Their cry was, " We are Abraham's children." " The temple of the Lord are we."

3. *They were filled with desires after worldly pomp and power.* They wished to be freed from the yoke of the Romans, &c. Wanted a Messiah who should have a kingdom of this world—have soldiers, &c.

4. *They were offended at the fidelity of Christ's teaching.* It was too direct—humiliating. It disrobed them of their cloaks of hypocrisy ; it exposed their covetous

ness; it demanded a change of heart—a reformation of life—and holiness both of heart and life. It denounced their self-righteousness, and reproved their skepticism and perversion of their oracles; therefore they received him not. His teaching was luminous, heavenly, divine; but they received him not. His life was one of spotless purity, yet they, &c. His career was one of richest mercy, yet they, &c. His miracles were stupendous and all-gracious, yet they, &c. He was their own Messiah, yet they, &c. Observe, then,

II. CHRIST'S RECEPTION BY SOME, AND THE ADVANTAGES WHICH FOLLOWED. "But to as many," &c. A few did receive him, although the mass rejected him. Observe,

1. *These regarded and believed his message.* They heard, and understood, and were brought to acknowledge him as the Christ—the sent of God. They were satisfied of his divinity, "We know," &c. They believed his word—gave implicit credit to his doctrines—trusted in his promises—and received his person. He described himself as the gift of God; they opened their hearts to him as such. He claimed the character of a prophet, and they yielded full belief to his word. He appeared as their Redeemer, and they trusted in his work and undertaking. He professed to be a king, and they gave him reverence, and yielded obedience to his commands. Sick—they received him as the great physician; poor—as the rich donor of heaven; enslaved—as the great deliverer; lost—as the good shepherd; guilty—as the Lamb of God, &c.; dead—as the life of the world. And in receiving Christ they became,

2. *Identified with him.* As his disciples —followers—sheep, &c. They received his doctrines, precepts, spirit, and kingdom. What were the advantages derived? To them he gave power, or rather right, or privilege, &c. Christ became as we were, that we might become what he was. He being the Son of God, became the Son of man, that we might become the sons of God. Sin had alienated us. We were rebels—ungodly—children of the wicked one; but by receiving Christ, we thus become the sons of God. Those who received Christ were changed, and made partakers of the divine nature. The carnal heart was destroyed—a new heart, &c.— were converted, and became as little chil-

dren—were adopted into the divine family —brought nigh to God—introduced into his gracious kingdom, and became saints, heirs, &c. The blessedness of this condition is exceedingly comprehensive.

(1.) The enjoyment of the Spirit of God. "Because ye are sons," &c.

(2.) An interest in the love and favor of the Father.

(3.) A gracious right to all the benignant mercies of a good providence.

(4.) Heirship to all the promises of the new covenant.

(5.) Angelic attendance and ministration.

(6.) A good hope of future glory.

(7.) A resurrection body, like Christ's.

(8.) A crown and kingdom with Christ in glory everlasting.

APPLICATION.

Are there not three distinctions of character represented by some in this congregation?

1. Some, we fear, are ignorant of Christ; they represent the world, who knew him not.

2. Some, we fear, reject Christ; they know, &c., but do not approve of his doctrines, or laws, or kingdom, and, like the Jews, receive him not. Wedded to forms— a mere name, &c.

3. Others, we hope, like the believing humble disciples, have received him. How transforming were the results; how happy their effects; how dignifying, &c. Be ye followers of God as dear children. Walk in him. Honor the Saviour, &c.

4. All other distinctions will be worthless at a future day. Think of this. Now receive Christ. To reject Christ is ungrateful, wicked, cruel, &c.

THE GOSPEL CALL.

"Many are called, but few are chosen."—MATT. xxii. 14.

THE text is the concluding observation of Christ's in reference to the parable of the marriage feast, and is intimately connected with the exclusion of the man without a wedding garment. It is of the utmost importance that we endeavor to ascertain the true meaning of the word of God. We shall not be likely to do this, unless we take scripture in its connection. Many wild and ridiculous theories have been palmed upon the scriptures. Indeed, almost any thing may be proved from the Bible, if we take the sound for the sense, or if we take verses or sentences without respect to the passages with which they are connected. Let us then ascertain, if possible, the meaning of the words in the text, and see how they apply to this parable.

(1.) *Called* signifies invited. See ver. 3.

(2.) *Many* clearly signifies a great number. First the Jews are included, ver. 3 to 7; then the Gentiles, ver. 9. Christ sends his gospel to the whole world, to every creature.

(3.) *Chosen* signifies accepted, and approved of, in contrast with the man who was excluded for not having on the wedding garment.

(4.) *Few*, is clearly placed in opposition to the great multitude who were called to the wedding feast. In one word, but few sat down to the feast in comparison of those who were bidden. Let us inquire,

I. THE WAY IN WHICH GOD CALLS MEN.

1. *Now God's great method is by the preaching of the gospel.* He sends his servants, as in ver. 3. This is most graphically and powerfully presented to our view, Rom. x. 13–17. Here it is shown, that before salvation there must be calling upon the name of the Lord. But before we can call on him, we must believe in him; before believing is practicable, we must hear of him; we cannot hear, unless some are sent with the message to us. Hence, "How beautiful," &c. "So then faith cometh by hearing," &c. While this is God's general established method of calling sinners, we notice that sometimes he does this,

2. *By the written word—by perusing the truth.* Hence some have taken up the word of God at home, and have thus been led to see their misery and the way of salvation. A tract has sometimes been thus blessed. This has especially been the case among the heathen.

3. *Sometimes God has called by the conversation of his people.* But in this case it has been by their making known the truths of the gospel. Thus the woman of Samaria—her neighbors. God often makes,

4. *The events of providence subservient to this call.* Awful providential events; disappointments in the world; domestic bereavements; bodily afflictions. Now all these may be sanctified, and rendered useful; but every thing will fail of giving comfort and hope to the mind, except the gospel. The gospel is the great primary means of calling sinners to God. We inquire,

II. INTO THE NATURE OF THE CALL ITSELF.

1. *It is a call from sin to repentance.* This is what God says, "Turn ye from your evil ways." "Cease to do evil," &c. "Let the wicked forsake his way," &c. Now this is obeyed in repentance, when sin is discovered to be evil,—loathed,—sorrowed over,—forsaken.

2. *It is a call from the rejection, to a belief of the gospel.* We might inquire, what are the fetters which bind the souls of men? What keeps them from Christ? It is unbelief. This darkens the mind,—stupifies the soul,—keeps eternity out of view,—prevents the mercy of God. Christ could not do many mighty works, &c. Now God requires that we believe in him. "He that cometh," &c. "Without faith," &c. Sincere belief is ever united with godly repentance. Until we believe we shall never give up all for Christ,—nor take up his cross, &c.

3. *From wretchedness to happiness.* Is it not wretched to be poor, blind, naked, diseased, in slavery, condemned, &c.? Such are invited to be rich, to receive sight, raiment, health, liberty, &c. See Christ's first sermon.

4. *From hell to heaven.* We are condemned, and thus heirs of wrath, &c. Journeying to it,—will certainly be turned into it, unless saved by Christ. Now we are invited to flee from it. To receive a title for heaven,—meetness for heaven. "This is the record that God hath given unto us, eternal life," &c.

III. THE EXTENT OF THE CALL. Now to this we may reply, it is universal. It refers to every child of man. See the solemn asseveration of Deity in Ezekiel xxxiii. 11. "God commandeth all men everywhere to repent," Acts xvii. 30. "Go ye into all the world." Now it has been said that this is God's general call. It is not surely meant that God is insincere,—that men cannot obey it. Who will dare thus to charge God? Did ever any guilty soul obey, and was rejected? No, never! Try, and was not able? Never! Yet, mark,

IV. IT IS ONLY PARTIALLY EFFECTUAL. "Few are chosen." Not in the aggregate, for there will be a company no man can number. But comparatively with what might have been. Why few chosen?

1. *Many, like the Jews, sin out the day of their visitation.* "O Jerusalem," &c. "But ye would not." See Prov. i. 24.

2. *Many dislike the terms.* The rich young man,—those who followed Christ for a time, &c.

3. *Many neglect the necessary meetness.* The foolish virgins,—the man without the wedding garment. These are some of the chief reasons.

APPLICATION.

1. God is now calling you. What do you reply?

2. Soon death will call you. Now decide, and humbly hearken to, and obey the invitations of mercy.

3. If you are willing and desirous to come to Christ, depend upon it, you will have the ability, and in no wise will he cast you out.

ON CONSIDERATION.

"My people doth not consider."—ISAIAH i. 3.

THE material parts of the universe are regulated by fixed laws, by which God preserves and governs all things. The merely animal creatures are influenced by instinct, which in many cases seems very nearly to approach to reason. Man is endowed with rational powers, intellectual faculties and his dignity and bliss depend on the right application of these. Now, one of the main stratagems of Satan is to prevent the wise application of these. To induce men to act without forethought or reflection,—or to incite them to act merely by impulse, or feeling, or passion. And by these artifices the great mass of mankind live without thought, and are borne in stupid insensibility to the eternal world. Thus God complains of the infatuation of Israel, "My people doth not consider."

I. LET ME SPECIFY SOME OF THE IMPORTANT SUBJECTS OF CONSIDERATION. To consider, is to think deliberately,—to reflect maturely. And there are many subjects to which our consideration should be attentively and diligently given.

1. *We should consider the character and will of the blessed God.* His works should lead us to this. If you see a beautiful pic-

ture, or piece of sculpture or mechanism, you naturally direct your thoughts to the artist, or mechanist, who has produced them. Now you live in a magnificent and wonderful world. The grandeur of the divine works surrounds you, and ought you not to consider the Creator, the still more wondrous architect of the whole? His relationship to you should induce it. God gave you your existence,—fashioned you, —framed all your members in secret; gave you a reasonable soul. He is your father, your bountiful preserver. Besides, you are ever in his hand,—ever before his eyes,— he ever surrounds you. And he is great, and wise, and powerful, and holy, and just. His love and favor are heaven,—his anger and frown are hell.

2. *We should consider ourselves.* What are we? What our powers? What our capabilities? What our end and destination? What the claims of God? What our duties to others? What the improvement we should make of the present, and what preparation for the future? Are we answering the end of our being, &c.?

3. *We should consider our spiritual state before God.* Is it one of ignorance, or knowledge,—folly, or wisdom,—guilt, or pardon, —condemnation, or acceptance with God? Alienation, or sonship and adoption,—of safety, or imminent peril? Are we heirs of wrath and perdition, or of God and salvation?

4. *We should consider the importance of life.* Life is the seed-time for eternity,— the period of human probation,—the only opportunity of securing eternal blessedness. And how short it is,—how fragile,—how uncertain! How criminal to waste it, to pervert it, &c.!

5. *We should consider the solemnities of death.* "Oh that they were wise," &c. The living know that they must die, but they do not lay it to heart, or consider. Should you not consider its certainty,—its probable nearness,—its truly awful character? Try to realize it,—consider if you were now dying, &c.

6. *We should consider the great concerns of eternity.* The judgment-day. Heaven, with its eternal glories; hell, with its everlasting horrors. Eternity itself, how solemn, how overwhelming! How blissful to the saint; how terrific to the sinner! Eternity! eternity!

7. *We should consider that salvation*

which will fit us for living, dying, and eternity. The salvation, the mercy of God has provided. The salvation, obtained by the Lord Jesus Christ. The salvation, revealed in the gospel. The salvation, which is offered to every sinner. The salvation, which is received by simple faith. The salvation, which delivers from guilt, pollution, fear, and everlasting wrath.

8. *We should consider our present duty and interest.* Men are supposed to care naturally for these. But this care relates merely to the body, and the things of time,—consider whether it is not your duty to obey God,—to serve him,—to live in his fear,—to wait upon him, and glorify him, with your body and soul, which are his. And is not this your interest? " Godliness is profitable to all things," &c. This is moral *freedom ;* and is it not better than slavery ? This is moral *health ;* and is it not better than disease ? This is real and solid *peace ;* and is it not better than anxiety and remorse ? This is absolute *safety ;* and is it not better than to be exposed to eternal danger? Oh, yes; reason, wisdom, experience, all agree it is both your interest and duty.

9. *Consider that there is no substitute for religion.* There are various things which people attempt to make such. But they are all failures, miserable failures. The whole world would not be a substitute,— all ineffectual. " Broken cisterns," &c.

APPLICATION.

Now I urge consideration upon all present.

1. *Some have never considered.* Now begin. Retire and reflect,—weigh and consider, &c.

2. *Some have considered occasionally.* When in the chapel, or sick, or in the house of bereavement, &c. Oh, carry it out. Lay your hearts to it.

3. *There is hope for all who will consider.*

4. *They are hopeless who will not consider.*

ON CONSIDERATION

SECOND SKETCH.

" My people doth not consider."—ISAIAH i. 3.

IN a former discourse we noticed, that one of Satan's chief devices was to keep men from consideration, and we referred to a variety of subjects to which our consideration should be directed. In pursuing the same theme, we now call your attention,

II. TO THE TRUE CHARACTER OF RELIGIOUS CONSIDERATION. And we observe, that,

1. *It should be serious and earnest consideration.* The subjects are too solemn— weighty—to be hastily dismissed. It must not be a mere cursory survey—a rapid glance at these great concerns ; but a careful, deliberate contemplation of them ; just as a prisoner would do who was to be tried for a capital offence ; or as a wrecked mariner how he shall escape a watery grave ; or as a man who is undertaking some momentous journey or voyage. If it be done lightly and hastily it will not profit us, or please God.

2. *It should be connected with prayer.* The exercise will be irksome to the carnal heart. We shall be disposed to give it up, or do it slightingly. Now, the grace of God will give the spirit and feelings necessary for the right discharge of it. Begin it with prayer—continue it with prayer— follow it out with prayer.

3. *It should be connected also with the public means of grace.* Hearken to the divine word as it is read in the sanctuary, and to the preaching of the gospel—Christian conversation, &c. Consideration will not benefit us if God's means and ordinances are neglected.

4. *It should be continued and persevering.* Not too much to devote a portion of every day to it. The last and first moments would be thus profitably exercised, and it must be followed out. Now,

III. NOTICE SOME OF THE REASONS WHY YOU SHOULD CONSIDER.

1. *Because you have powers to do so.* God made you for this end, that you should consider. In neglecting this you despise your own souls—you sink to a level, nay, below the brute creation. They do answer the end of their existence, and they do obey their several instincts. " The ox knoweth his owner." The birds exhibit this in their migrations. The ant, the beaver, the bee, &c., all dispose of their time and means wisely ; but an inconsiderate man defaces the noble faculties within him.

2. *Because it is your duty.* God enjoins it ; he calls you to it—he urges—he expostulates. It is, therefore, to despise God

and rebel against him, if ye will not consider.

3. *It is essential to the possession of true religion.* Various are the ways in which God brings men to himself; by a variety of instruments—by various means, &c.; but none without consideration. Manasseh in prison—Jonah in the belly of the whale —the prodigal in his misery, &c. It is the first great step towards saving religion.

4. *It is never neglected in worldly things.* In entering upon any contract—in buying and selling—in all business engagements— in all secular pursuits. We consider in reference to food and raiment—in reference to our houses—in reference to the body—in reference to our families, &c. Now, are the soul's eternal concerns, the only things not deserving of it?

5. *God may compel you to consider.* By giving you the cup of adversity—by bereaving you of the dearest objects of your hearts—by afflicting your bodies—by embittering all earthly good. Now, is it not better to avoid these corrections, and sorrows, and griefs? I notice,

6. *You may consider when it is too late.* Perhaps on the very verge of eternity, if not in eternity itself. The rich man considered in hell; the foolish virgins considered when the cry was heard; the wicked will consider in the great day of Christ's wrath, when they cry to the rocks and hills, &c. Now, the consideration of the lost in eternity will be in vain—will be bitter beyond description—will be everlasting, and as horrible as it is durable. Let me, in conclusion, urge this subject,

1. *On the young.* Early consideration may benefit you in all respects, and for both worlds.

2. *On those connected with the cares of families.* You may have much to do—be poor, &c.; but do not neglect this great duty. Religion will bless your poverty, and sanctify it. It will assist you in domestic difficulties. You need not be poor in reference to both worlds.

3. *Upon the aged.* Surely you will need no persuasion to consider your years—your experience; all seem to urge it upon you. If still impenitent, reflect with horror on the past, and with intense anxiety on the future. But a step between your souls and death, and, perhaps, hell.

4. *Upon all.* Oh! every one consider, and begin now. Christians, consider more and better.

REPENTANCE.

"Repent ye."—Acts iii. 19.

WE may well hope that serious, deliberate, and prayerful consideration will issue in a change of mind, and a new course of life. Our present subject is repentance— a subject to which the scriptures frequently call our attention, and which is essentially connected with salvation. All pious persons have experienced in their own souls true repentance. All who intend to become followers of the Lord Jesus Christ must become personally acquainted with repentance; and all who do not repent in this life will be the victims of a despairing and unavailing repentance forever. Let us then ascertain in what repentance consists—its evidences—and its necessity.

I. IN WHAT DOES REPENTANCE CONSIST? It includes,

1. *A knowledge of sin.* That we have scriptural views of sin—in its heinousness before God—its offensiveness to the divine law—its great evil—its polluting influences, and ruining power. Many seem not to recognise any thing as sin, except flagrant and vile crimes against the property or life of their fellow-creatures; others mock at sin, or think lightly of it; but with the repenting sinner, sin is viewed as evil, abominable, and deserving of divine wrath.

2. *Conviction of sin.* That this evil affects us; that we are guilty—deeply guilty —guilty in an aggravated degree—guilty beyond enumeration—guilty both of omitting the commands, and violating the prohibitions of God's law—guilty as it respects God, as Lawgiver, Sovereign, Father, Redeemer, &c.—guilty as it respects men. Now this conviction must be deep, startling, &c.

3. *Sorrow for sin.* Not for its consequences only, but for itself as an evil thing. "Against thee, &c. have I sinned." Sinned against God's mercy, forbearance, &c. Now, this sorrow includes what is meant by a broken spirit, and a contrite heart. Mourning for the evils of our hearts and lives. This must not be evanescent, and merely impulse; but abiding, and from a principle of the extreme vileness of all iniquity.

4. *Self-loathing and abhorrence of sin.*
He reflects on his folly, infatuation, &c.;
he now sees things through the right medium, and he exclaims, "I abhor myself,
and repent in dust and ashes." "Not
worthy to be called thy son," &c. Thus
the publican stood afar off, &c. See 2
Chron. xxxiv. 27.

5. *Confession and turning from sin.* "I
acknowledge my transgression," &c. "We
have sinned," &c. Dan. ix. 4. Now, this
confession must be free, and full, and
hearty, and it must issue in forsaking sin,
and seeking the Lord God with all our
hearts and souls. Observe,

II. Its evidences. If we have repented
truly, there will be,

1. *A new state of mind.* God—holiness
—sin—ourselves, &c. will all be differently viewed. Mind, now light under the influence of divine truth; swayed by the
fear of God, &c.

2. *A spiritual conversation.* No man
ever repented, who did not speak of it, and
show it by the fruit of his lips. Worldliness, pleasure, frivolity, will not now distinguish his conversation. There will also
be restitution in all things possible.

3. *Obedience to the truth.* God's word
and law now paramount. "Lord, what
shall I do?" How serve thee—how glorify thee. No longer walking in the broad
way of death; no longer with the heedless
multitude, &c. He seeks the companionship of the pious—attends the ordinances
of the Lord's house—takes pleasure in the
holy exercises of religion.

4. *Union to Christ and spiritual life
through Christ Jesus.* True repentance is
unto life; such, though dead in sin, are
now alive from the dead. "My son that
was dead," &c. Vitally grafted into
Christ, the living vine. Live a life of
faith on the Son of God, &c. Now, these
evidences will be permanent and abiding,
&c. Notice,

III. The necessity for such a repentance.

1. *It is necessary to a right state of our
own minds.* Our powers, and faculties,
and feelings, are all deranged, diseased,
and perverted, until we have repented of
sin. Repentance brings us into that state
for which we were originally destined—
answer the end of our being, &c.

2. *It is necessary to the enjoyment of the
divine favor.* God is rich in mercy, &c;

but we cannot enjoy that, unless we are
likeminded with God. Repentance ensures
his grace, and the communication of his
forgiving love.

3. *Necessary to our own peace and comfort.* No peace without it—no abiding
consolation, &c.; but they that sow the
tears of repentance shall reap in joy; they
that mourn are comforted. "O Lord, I
will praise thee," &c.

4. *It is necessary to our entrance into
heaven.* "Except ye repent, ye shall all
likewise perish." Not a redeemed spirit
in heaven that has not repented; therefore
endless life impossible without genuine repentance.

APPLICATION.

1. *Let me caution against mistakes.* Be
not deceived by a spurious repentance—
that which is merely counterfeit. Partial
reformation from some sins—regret for the
evil we have sustained—the mere assumption of a religious profession, &c.

2. *Let me warn you against delays.* This
repentance is necessary now—future opportunities you may not possess. Many
have resolved and purposed, but have been
ruined by delay.

3. *Let me encourage against despondency.*
You have now space for repentance—opportunity for repentance—the means of repentance—the call to repentance—the rich
promises of grace to aid your repentance—
the certain acceptance of your souls through
Christ Jesus, if you do repent.

4. *Let me remind the impenitent*—That
hell will be the place, and eternity the duration, of the repentance of those who obey
not the gospel of the Lord Jesus Christ.
Oh! awake, awake, and call upon thy God,
that thou perish not.

JUSTIFICATION.

"Therefore being justified by faith, we have
peace with God, through our Lord Jesus Christ."—
Rom. v. 1.

There is no doctrine of the gospel of
greater moment than that of the scriptural
justification of the sinner. Right views
are at the very basis of the Christian
scheme. Error here will lead to other
practical and doctrinal errors, all of which
will be destructive to the best interests of
the soul. I am particularly solicitous,

therefore, that you should most distinctly understand the word of God on this momentous theme. This was the great battering-ram of Luther, by which he shook the doctrinal errors of the church of Rome to their foundation. Imbued with correct notions of this doctrine, it is impossible that hundreds of clergymen of the church of England should have been infected with the pestiferous notions of Puseyism. It is requisite, therefore, that the church of Christ should hold a clear, steady light on this great doctrine; and that every man should perfectly understand it for his own comfort and salvation. Let us notice,

I. WHAT JUSTIFICATION INVOLVES. But a word or two as to the signification of the term. It signifies, to pronounce righteous and free from charge of guilt; and, therefore, demands that the person should be treated as such. It is the opposite therefore of condemnation, and is so placed before us in the Holy Scriptures. Now, scriptural justification involves this truth,

1. *That the person is under law.* That is, responsible to law for his conduct. Now, God gave our first parents a law in paradise; and he has revealed his holy character and will in the moral law, as given on Sinai. This law is holy—in perfect conformity with the divine nature. "Right," or just—quite equitable between God the lawgiver, and the subject to whom the law was given. "Good," or benevolent in its aspect—bearing favorably on the well-being and true blessedness of the subject. It involves,

2. *The transgression of that law.* That the statutes of that law have been wittingly and voluntarily broken; that its high and sacred claims have been violated. This disobedience must have been the personal free act of the transgressor. Scriptural justification involves,

3. *That the transgressor has no means within himself of escaping the punishment of his iniquity.* For the law, of course, had its sanctions and its threatenings—its rewards and its punishments; guilt therefore proved, and of course punishment must follow. Now, the sinner has no resource within himself to avert the curse of the broken law. However ingenuously he confesses—however deeply he laments—however fervently he supplicates—justice demands the execution of the law. He may refer to his obedience to some points; but he that has

offended in one transgression, is exposed to all the vengeance proclaimed against the guilty. He can offer no merit, for he is a culprit deemed only worthy of death; he can promise no future recompense, for his sin has involved him in inability to serve God; he can have no benefit from his fellow-men, for they are all pronounced guilty with himself. "For all have sinned," &c. "None righteous." If mercy were extended as a mere sovereign act, it would seem that the law had been too rigorous, or that contradictory attributes and mutability of mind distinguished the lawgiver. Then, we ask, can sinners be justified? And we notice in reply to that interrogation,

II. THE GROUND OF THE SINNER'S JUSTIFICATION BEFORE GOD. Now, there are two grounds, both of which are essential to our justification.

1. *The meritorious ground.* The sacrifice of the Lord Jesus Christ. "He suffered, the just for the unjust." "He bare our sins," &c. "He suffered for our sins, and rose again for our justification." Now, just observe how this meets the case. The law has been dishonored; Christ, our surety, assumes the nature of man, for whom the law was made, and in that nature obeys it, clearly, fully, and perfectly; he enthrones it on his heart, embodies it in his life, and proclaims it in all its purity and glory to the world; he then meets its penal exactions; it demands the death of the sinner, pronouncing him accursed; he freely lays down his life, and dies in the room and stead of the transgressor. But, did not the law demand the death of many transgressors? Yes; but the infinite worth and preciousness of Christ's blood meet fully all the infinite demands of the law upon transgressors. Now the law is honored, not relaxed; satisfaction is made, not evaded; and now mercy can act in unison, and not in opposition to the holiness of God and his righteous laws. But, observe.

2. *The instrumental means of justification.* "Faith;" being "justified by faith." Now, we have shown that the sinner could not be justified by works. God, therefore, reveals his love to us by the gospel. He assures us of his merciful and gracious disposition towards us, and affirms that he can be the just God, and yet the Saviour. He demands, however, that we should credit his word, and rest on the sacrifice of his Son, for our justification; he demands that

we should plead the death of the Lord Jesus Christ, and come to him, expecting the exercise of his forgiving love in and through him. And this is faith, to believe the record that God hath given of his Son; and all who exercise that faith are at once freely justified from all things, &c. Without this faith we are under condemnation—even the condemnation of unbelief, and the wrath of God abideth on us. Notice,

III. THE RESULTS OF OUR JUSTIFICATION BEFORE GOD.

1. *All our sins are blotted out.* Sins of all grades, and hues, and aggravations, are forgiven; not one charge now against us—no condemnation, &c. Who can describe the preciousness of such a pardon?

2. *Peace and acceptance with God.* Now in a state of reconciliation with God. No longer enemies and aliens, but friends and fellow-citizens; accepted into his favor and family; have his peace upon us, and within us, by the Holy Ghost given unto us.

3. *An interest in all the blessings of redemption.* Now children of the covenant—heirs of the promises—expectants of eternal life—the rich charter of mercy is now ours. "All are yours, ye are Christ's," &c.

OBSERVATIONS.

1. *This great blessing of justification is held out in the gospel to every sinner.* All are guilty—all are redeemed—and all invited to believe. No respect of persons with God. God hath concluded all in unbelief, that he might have mercy on all.

2. *Justification is indispensable to present and eternal salvation.* It is salvation begun, and there can be no admission into heaven except to the justified, &c.

3. *Justification immediately follows faith, and therefore is instantaneous.* The Antinomian doctrine of eternal justification is a gross fallacy—alike opposed to the gospel and common sense. But where faith appropriates Christ, as revealed in the gospel, that instant the great and glorious change is effected.

4 *Justification only affects our state and condition.* In itself it is simply our being pronounced righteous, and thus differs from regeneration and inward holiness; but it is invariably followed by these.

5. *This view of justification gives all the glory to God, ascribes all the merit to Christ, and bestows all the benefits on the believing sinner.*

6. *Urge it on the personal attention of all present.* You have the glorious gospel, in which Christ is set forth as crucified for you. Then believe that testimony.

"Believe, and all your sin's forgiven;
Only believe, and yours is heaven."

CONVERSION.

"And be converted."—ACTS iii. 19.

REPENTANCE is a change of mind and feeling towards God, and invariably results in the conversion of those who are the subjects of it. Conversion is the turning of the soul from its former course of action and pursuit into a new and holy way of obedience to God. A converted man is one who has been turned from darkness to light, and from the power of Satan to God. It is the return of the soul to its original state of allegiance and favor. Let us look at the nature, means, and importance of this change.

I. AT THE NATURE OF THE CHANGE WHICH CONVERSION INVOLVES.

1. *There is a change in the understanding, from darkness to light.* The natural man is blind—dwelling in the region of the shadow of death—a child of night, and of darkness. His ignorance respects all the great moral things of the soul, God, and eternity. Ignorant of his own true state and character; ignorant of God's true nature and perfections; ignorant of the awful responsibility in which he is placed in reference to the eternal world.

2. *It is a change in the judgment, from error to truth.* His perverted judgment formerly called evil good, and good evil; he called sin pleasure, and religion melancholy; he called transgression liberty, and God's service bondage. Now his judgment is entirely altered. He pronounces sin bondage—Satan's service despotism—the paths of wisdom pleasure—iniquity madness; and this will apply to all the high moral principles of true religion.

3. *It is a change in the affections, from carnality and selfishness to love.* The carnal mind—enmity, &c. He hated the things of God—his word—his ordinances—his people—his service, &c. Full of wrath and envy to mankind. Selfishness was predominant—now this corrupt demon is dethroned. Love sways the sceptre—love

reigns in the soul. He loves God, and his fellow-creatures also — he dwells in love, &c.

4. *A change in the will, from rebellion to obedience.* He formerly chose sin—preferred rebellion—selected the way of the transgressor. Now he has turned from these dark ways of sin and death ; he has inquired for the old path—the good old way, and he walks therein, &c. He hearkens to God's word and obeys it. He was once the servant of sin, but now being made free from sin, he is the servant of God, and of righteousness, &c. It is evident, therefore, that conversion involves an entire change of heart and life. It will be seen in all the spheres and relationships in which we move ; it will be visible to the church and to the world. The lion is now a lamb—the raven, a dove—the thorn, a fig-tree—the curse, a blessing.

II. THE MEANS OF CONVERSION.

1. *God's grace is the originating cause.* God's mercy has rendered it possible. Without this, our state, and misery, and destiny would have been fixed and inevitable. His love, therefore, provided the sacrifice through whose merit and worthiness we could return to him. " Return," he says, " for I have redeemed thee." Had he not redeemed us, our return had been impossible.

2. *Divine truth is the instrumental means.* " The law of the Lord is perfect, converting the soul." Christ said to his disciples, " Ye are clean through the word which I have spoken to you," John xv. 3. " Ye shall know the truth, and the truth shall make you free." Now, both the written and preached word may do this, but chiefly the latter. " The gospel is the power of God to salvation, ' &c. Thus the three thousand were converted on the day of Pentecost. Thus the Corinthians, &c. ; see Rom. x. 14–17. Now, remember, divine truth contains the ideas, thoughts, feelings, and will of God concerning sinners ; and it contains matter addressed to the understanding, so as to enlighten it ; to the judgment, so as to free it from error ; to the affections, so as to move, and melt, and win them ; to the will, so that it may choose and decide rightly, &c. If sinners are not converted by this, neither would they, though one should rise from the dead.

3. *Faith and obedience to the truth are essential to conversion.* The sinner is called to hear it—to understand it—to weigh and consider it—to credit it—to act upon it—to obey it with all his heart. We are not to dispute or cavil whether he can do so. God commands it ; and whether the ability be inherent, or communicated by the Holy Spirit, he must do it, or there can be no conversion. Now, the docility, teachableness, credence, trust, and simple obedience of the child, are placed before us as the model to which in conversion we are to be conformed. " Except ye be converted, and become as little children," &c. Notice,

III. THE IMPORTANCE OF CONVERSION.

1. *Conversion is the dignity of the soul ; without it we are debased.* Fallen—wretched — miserable — traitors — outcasts, &c. Crown fallen—glory departed—soul degraded. Conversion elevates, dignifies, exalts to a condition of mental and moral glory.

2. *Conversion blesses, and without it we are miserable.* No peace, or abiding comfort ; no real joy, or true hope. Without it, the victim of anxiety, and remorse, and dread ; with it, there is peace and joy in the Holy Ghost. Christ's own peace, " which passeth all understanding."

3. *Conversion is identified with pardon ; without it we are condemned.* Hence the verse of the text, " that your sins may be blotted out." God has said, if we turn unto him, he will return unto us. " Let the wicked forsake his way," &c. Yes, all the converted enjoy remission of sins, and peace with God, through the Lord Jesus Christ. Without it, every sin rests in all its guilt and heavy penalty upon us ; guilt that will overwhelm at the judgment day, and damn the soul forever.

4. *Conversion is connected with eternal life, and without it there must be the misery of eternal death.* Heaven is peopled with the converted—hell with the unconverted. The one are heirs of wrath—the other heirs of eternal salvation. An unconverted man cannot see the celestial kingdom ; he is unfit for it—could not enjoy it. A man could have no enjoyment from the conversation of those who spake in a language of which he was ignorant ; a sick man no pleasure, although in a region of health ; an unholy man no bliss among the spotless hosts of the beatified ; a man in heaven, hating God, despising Christ, disliking the saints, loving sin, &c., how fruitless of joy would heaven be to him !

APPLICATION.

1. *We address the converted.* Urge gratitude, humility, and continuance in the knowledge, and obedience to the truth.

2. *Urge it upon all the unconverted.* None too good not to require it ; none too evil to be beyond it. Oh, every one reflect and consider your ways, and be wise !

3. *Encourage the anxious inquirer.* What hinders your conversion ? Believe the truth now, obey it now, and be saved.

DIVINE SONSHIP.

" For as many as are led by the Spirit of God, they are the sons of God."—ROMANS viii. 14.

THE terms born of God—born again—begotten of God—regeneration and adoption, are frequently met with in the divine word. Our present subject must of course include the signification of each and all of these New Testament phrases. Let us then endeavor to ascertain,

I. How BELIEVERS BECOME THE SONS OF GOD.

II. THE EVIDENCES OF THAT STATE.

III. THE BLESSINGS IDENTIFIED WITH IT. We ask, then,

I. How BELIEVERS BECOME THE SONS OF GOD ? In their natural state they are described as dead—as carnal—or as children of sin and Satan. A great change, therefore, must be effected before they can become the dignified children of God. The New Testament refers their sonship to two sources, regeneration and adoption ; both of which have respect to man's peculiar state while in his natural condition. As dead in trespasses and sins, they must,

1. *Be regenerated.* That is, begotten from the dead. See 1 Pet. i. 3. Now this communication of spiritual life, even the life of God in the soul, is attributed to, or connected with, three things.

(1.) Born of the Spirit. " Except a man be born of the Spirit," &c., John iii. 5, 6, 8. " It is the Spirit that quickeneth." The holy and blessed Agent by which the heart is changed and renewed is God's blessed Spirit. The prophet describes this at length, Ezek. xxxvi. 26, &c.

(2.) Born of the word. Thus the apostle speaks of those begotten through or by the gospel. The word is obviously the

seed which produces spirit and life. "Being born again, not of corruptible seed, but of incorruptible, by the word of God," &c., 1 Pet. i. 23. " Of his own will begat he us, with the word of truth," &c., James i. 18.

(3.) Born of water. This expression is found in Christ's discourse with Nicodemus, John iii. 5, It is also included in the apostle's address to Titus, " By the washing of regeneration," iii. 5, in connection with the renewing of the Holy Ghost. The great Author of regeneration is God the Holy Spirit ; the means employed, the blessed word of divine truth ; and the external sign of having exercised faith in that word, and experienced the renewing influences of the Spirit, the baptism of water. See 1 Peter iii. 21. But our sonship is ascribed,

2. *To adoption.* When an orphan, or the child of another, is taken into the family, and receives all the privileges, &c. Now the sinner is by nature a child of Satan, and an alien and rebel towards God ; but God mercifully adopts and receives him into his spiritual family, and gives him all the privileges of a child. See Gal. iv. 4, &c. ; John i. 12 ; Eph. i. 5. In adoption we have a new name, are members of a new family, and have, therefore, new associates, &c. Now, as in justification, so in sonship, " We are all the children of God by faith." Notice, then,

II. THE EVIDENCES OF DIVINE SONSHIP.

1. *The enjoyment of the divine Spirit.* " Because ye are sons, he hath sent the Spirit of his Son into your hearts," Gal. iv. 6. " Ye have received the Spirit of adoption, whereby we cry, Abba, Father," Rom. viii. 15. God's Spirit bears witness with their spirits that they are the children of God.

2. *Conformity to the divine likeness.* In a state of sin there is borne the image of the earthly—the image of the evil one. But all who are born of God resemble him, and bear the image of the heavenly. " And having put on the new man, which is renewed in knowledge, after the image of him that created him," Col. iii. 10.

3. *Obedience to the divine will.* Our text instructs us that they are led by the Spirit of God. This is the characteristic of every son—to this there is no exception—this is the very end of their new creation. " For we are his workmanship, created in Christ Jesus unto good works," Eph. ii. 10. " If

we say that we abide in him, we should walk as he walked." It is the nature of the renewed mind to rise upward to spiritual and heavenly things, and to bear fruit unto holiness.

4. *Exhibition of divine love.* This sign is much insisted on in the holy word. " Every one that loveth is born of God and knoweth God," 1 John v. 1. "If we love one another, God dwelleth in us," &c., iv. 12. Our love is to resemble the divine love to us. " That ye love one another, as I have loved you," John xiii. 34. " By this shall all men know that ye are my disciples," &c., ver. 35. Having considered the evidences of divine sonship, let us notice,

III. The blessings identified with it.

1. *An interest in the complacent love of God.* God approves of his children—delights in them—they are his treasure—the portion, &c. His love to them exceeds that of the most affectionate father, or the most tender-hearted mother. " And this love is shed abroad in their hearts by the Holy Ghost," &c.

2. *They are interested in all the blessings and privileges of the divine family.* The rich provision of God's house and table is all theirs. They wear the family robe—possess the family title—enjoy the family guard, " For the angel of the Lord encompasseth," &c.—and have an eternal interest in all the family promises, which are exceedingly great and precious.

3. *Heirs of eternal happiness and glory.* How sublimely this is expressed! " Heirs of God." " Joint-heirs with Christ." "Called to God's eternal kingdom and glory." "It doth not yet appear what they shall be," &c. " They shall inherit all things." Sit on the Saviour's throne, and enjoy the beatific vision, &c., forever and ever. Learn, then,

1. *The Christian's true dignity.* What title, state, or condition, to compare with his ? How petty, puerile, and valueless, all the distinctions of this sublunary world !

2. *The Christian state must be happy.* This is reiterated again and again in the scriptures. It is their highest privilege to rejoice, to rejoice in the Lord always, &c.

" Why should the children of a king
Go mourning all their days ?"

3. *The Christian's responsibilities must be great.* If such be the dignity of their calling, how holy and unblameable should they be in all manner of conversation ! " Only let your conversation," &c.

4. *The Christian's prospects, how enrapturing !* However poor, afflicted, persecuted, despised, yet they are the sons of God, and heirs of everlasting glory.

" Then let our songs abound,
    And every tear be dry ;
  We're marching through Immanuel's ground,
    To fairer worlds on high !"

HOLINESS.

" For God hath not called us unto uncleanness, but unto holiness."—1 Thess. iv. 7.

Of all subjects, holiness is the most truly important to man. In this state he was originally created. To restore him to holiness was the great design of redemption. To effect this, the Saviour opened the purifying fountain of his own blood. To reveal this, and the way of its attainment, is the grand design of divine revelation. The preacher's grand mission is one of holiness. The Spirit of God exerts his influences on the human heart to effect this great consummation. The prayers, self-denial, obedience, and sufferings of Christians, are directly for this one attainment. And heaven itself is invariably represented as the temple of the sanctified, the home of the holy, and the land in which the pure in heart behold God. Surely, then, it is worthy of our serious consideration, and cannot be too deeply pondered by all who are candidates for everlasting blessedness. Let us consider this subject in the spirit of humble and reverent prayer, that God may enable us clearly to understand it, and appreciate it, in all its divine and everlasting importance.

I. Holiness is immediately connected with regeneration. There is no holiness in man previous to this. All scripture testifies to his sin, and depravity, and guilt. There may be intellectuality, external morality, humanity, kindness, amiability, &c., but there can be no holiness. The old heart cannot be holy. Holiness, therefore, begins its spiritual reign when man is renewed in the likeness of the divine image. When he is born from above,—born of God, &c. When old things pass away, and all things become new. When the tree is made good—the fountain pure. We must be partakers of the divine nature before we can reflect the divine likeness.

II. HOLINESS IS THE CONFORMITY OF THE WHOLE MAN TO GOD'S IMAGE. God is not only the source, but the model of purity. Man's original holiness was his being created in the divine likeness. A restoration to that is New Testament holiness. When the understanding is illumined with holy knowledge. When the judgment is influenced by holy truth. When the affections are inflamed with holy love and desires. When the conscience is cleansed from unholiness, and pacified with the holy blood of Christ. When the will is influenced by the holy commands and motives of the gospel. Now thus the heart and soul become the residence of the Holy Spirit, the temple of the living God.

III. HOLINESS WILL BE PRACTISED AND OBSERVED IN THE LIFE. Holy desires, and thoughts, and purposes, and aspirations, will manifest themselves in the life. These will be,

1. *A holy conversation.* A conversation seasoned with grace. A godly conversation,—the fruit of the lips will be holiness to the Lord. Wisdom, and piety, and kindness, will regulate the tongue of the holy.

2. *Holy obedience.* Walking in the fear of God, and in the commandments of the Most High. A delight to do the will of our heavenly Father. Thus the servants of God have their fruit unto holiness. And this obedience will have respect to all the commandments of the Lord. There will be seen what the Lord requireth of his people. "To do justly, love mercy, and walk humbly before God." This obedience will be the voluntary, earnest obedience of the heart, constrained only by love to the Lord Jesus Christ. There will be,

3. *A spirit of holy devotion.* Walking and holding intimate communion with God. Living in the exercise of meditation, praise, and prayer. They will worship the Lord in the beauty of holiness. There will be constant intimacy with the holy exercises of the closet, and devout attachment to the services of the sanctuary. How these were combined in the life of the Psalmist! Ps. lxiii. 1.

4. *Delight in the fellowship of kindred holy minds.* The society of the wicked and friendship with the world will be abandoned. "I am a companion of all them that fear thee," &c. There will be fervent attachment to the persons and company of the pious. "Then they that feared the Lord spake," &c. See also Acts i. 14, ii. 42.

IV. HOLINESS IS PROGRESSIVE. Thus differing from justification and regeneration, which are instantaneous and complete. Holiness begins with the seed, the grain, and grows into the lofty tree. With a little leaven exercising its influence till the whole be leavened. With the morning dawn, which shineth more and more till the perfect day. With the new-born babe, then the young man, afterwards the father in Christ. In all its parts, and graces, and virtues, it is progressive. Knowledge more clear and extensive,—judgment more sound,—affections more mellowed,—conscience more pure,—will more pliant and obedient to God. The life more exemplary, and the whole body, soul, and spirit, more sanctified by the Spirit and grace of God, until they are fully meet for the inheritance of the saints in light.

V. THE MEANS OF HOLINESS ARE VARIOUS. Reading and meditating in God's holy word. Attendance on the public worship of God's house. Constant meditation,—self-communion and prayer. The exercise of growing faith in the Lord Jesus. The daily studying of the example of Christ,—and, through these, the rich enjoyment of the Holy Spirit.

APPLICATION.

1. *How all-important is holiness!* What is our attainment in it? Our desires, &c.

2. *A holy heaven is the final hope of the believer.*

3. *To diffuse the spirit of holiness the great end of the Christian's life.*

4. *The unholy cannot see and enjoy God.*

BELIEF ON TESTIMONY.

"Jesus saith unto him, Thomas, because thou hast seen me, thou hast believed ; blessed are they who have not seen, and yet have believed."— JOHN xx. 29.

AMONG the disciples of the blessed Jesus, we see manifested almost every infirmity that can be seen even now among the followers of the Saviour ; and these failings are ingenuously detailed—not one of their errors is concealed from mankind—the whole truth is fearlessly and prominently exhibited. Look at the ambition of the disciples, desiring pre-eminence, &c. Look at the selfishness of the disciples, "what shall we have," &c. Look at their dulness and slowness of heart, &c. Look at the betrayal of one, the denial of another, and the desertion of all. Then look at Thomas, how marvellously incredible, especially if you consider Christ's previous predictions that he should rise; the testimony given; their character, number, &c. Again, *they* had *seen* Christ, &c. Jesus, therefore, while condescending to his weakness, yet commented on his unbelief, &c. Our text presents two classes of believers, and affirms the superior blessedness of one over the other.

I. Consider the two classes of believers.

1. *Those who believe on the ground of sense.* "Because thou hast seen," &c. You reply, this is necessary and unavoidable. Not so; bigotry, prejudice, and envy, can even overcome the most striking manifestation. A person comes with a great message. His dignity, piety, goodness, are all unquestionable. He seeks neither fame nor riches. Surely his testimony should be received. He can appeal to sacred predictions—he works miracles—he stands forth and does what no other man ever did. You say, "they *must believe*." No! they reject, despise, envy, calumniate, persecute, seek to kill, &c. Others, however, candidly witnessed, and heard, and believed. Now, there is therefore some, but not the greatest amount of virtue in this faith. Observe, then,

2. *Those who believe on the testimony of others.* Now, most things believed must rest on this kind of evidence. The Jews thus believed in Abraham and Moses, whom they never saw, and in David and the prophets. With respect to countries, and persons, and events, we every day thus believe. *The duty* is, to ascertain the possibility, and the reasonableness of the message or fact, and the characters of those who convey it, and the end it is to accomplish, &c. Now, the gospel will bear this investigation—it may be brought to this ordeal. The *facts*, the *writers*, and the *end*, are all worthy of God, &c. There are two additional evidences of the truth of Christianity worthy of our careful attention.

1. *The transformation of character it effects.* The gospel changes the life. It makes the man a new creature; it purifies the fruit of the lip; it destroys the propensity to evil; it converts from darkness to light, &c. Ignorance, irreverence, selfishness, are exchanged for knowledge, devotion, and benevolence. The thorn, becomes a fig-tree; the polluted fountain, clean; the heart and life, changed; the curse, a blessing. Now, this is the unvarying effect on the lives of those who believe it. If a mere invention of men can do this, let disbelievers devise some fabulous scheme, and do the same. Purity can only spring from purity, so that this is an irrefragable proof of the divinity of the gospel.

2. *The consolations it imparts.* It makes its recipients happy. Mourning exchanged for joy—distress for peace—sorrow for gladness—despair for hope. They bless and enjoy God. You say it is delusion—they say it is reality. At any rate it answers the end, and at times when every thing else fails; in sickness and death. It is the testimony of myriads of all classes and conditions, &c. of mankind. Let us now consider,

II. The superior blessedness of those who have not seen, and yet have believed. There is blessedness in the former case; but,

1. *To believe without seeing, evinces greater candor of mind.* And this is in accordance with our faculties and powers. We commend not credulity, for that believes without evidence, and despite of reason. We, notwithstanding, abhor prejudice, for that refuses to inquire and know. Now; candor steps in and says, "State the facts; produce the evidence; allow me to judge and conclude." We ought to believe nothing, however plausible, without this; nor reject any thing, however apparently absurd, until it has been subjected to this process. The Bereans were commended, &c.

2. *This enters more immediately into the nature of true faith.* Real essential faith we distinguish from sight. "We walk," &c. "Faith is the substance of things hoped for," &c.

3. *This kind of faith gives greater glory to God.* Read Romans iv. 14, &c. So also of Noah and Moses.

4. *This is the faith which has been mostly exercised in every age of the world.* Few have seen. Faith in Christ could seldom have any other basis. His ministry only lasted three years; comparatively few,

therefore, saw him. All the patriarchs and prophets to the day of Christ. All believers from the period of his death to the present time. Therefore, very few would be saved, if, like Thomas, they refused unless they saw, &c.

5. *This is the faith which we must exercise in respect to the other great truths of religion.* The kindness of divine providence —the guardian and protecting care of God —the promise of heaven—the crown of celestial glory—the resurrection of the body, &c.—nay, the very being of God, the existence of the Saviour, the intercession of our Mediator; so that if we are now to believe at all, we must have the faith which sees not. The *blessedness* of *believing* is manifold. It *interests* in the promises, for they are all ours. A *bright* hope. Faith gives to hope all its clearness, and power, and *abiding consolation.* Faith brings distant things near. Heaven to earth, &c. *Spiritual fruitfulness.* No real grace or virtue can thrive without it, &c.

APPLICATION.

1. Have you faith in the Lord Jesus? In his person, offices, work, &c. This faith may be increased by reading the scriptures, prayer, &c.

2. We urge believers to receive the testimony given of Christ. Consider its adaptedness to your state, its importance, and then give it your cordial approbation.

3. Believe not, and you exclude yourselves from all the blessings of the gospel. He that believeth not must perish.

A QUESTION CONCERNING FAITH.

"Jesus answered them, Do ye now believe?"— JOHN xvi. 3

No person can have read the scriptures without being impressed with the frequent reference which is made to faith. It is universally held up as one of the very essentials of religion; indeed, the first, great cardinal principle of all acceptable piety. "He that cometh to God," &c. "This is the commandment, that we should believe on the name of his Son Jesus Christ, and love one another," &c. The want of faith deprives of all the blessings of the gospel, and exposes to the righteous wrath

of God. On the other hand, "all things are possible to him that believeth." Then let us examine ourselves by the question Jesus proposes in the text. The subject; the persons interrogated; and the evidences to be adduced, are the three points to which we call your attention.

I. THE SUBJECT OF THE INTERROGATION. It is not knowledge, opinions, feelings, mode of worship, &c., but believing. "Do ye now *believe?*" Let us look at it,

1. *As the credence of testimony.* The scriptures reveal Jesus Christ to us. Full of Christ, of his person, offices, work, &c.; of his sufferings, death; of his mediation, kingdom, reign, glory, &c. Now, do you give the clear and full assent of your mind to what God has testified? Do you without hesitation receive all the record God has given of his Son? Is it enough that God has said it, however sublime, mysterious, and beyond reason? Are you quite satisfied that it should be believed, without demurring, or questioning, or cavilling? Let us look at believing,

2. *As the hearty reliance of the soul.* You are in a lost state. Christ is revealed as one who seeks and saves. Do you rely on him as such? As poor, do you rely on the riches of his grace? As sick, on him as the one physician? As condemned, on him as the surety, the mediator? Do you roll body, soul, and all on him, for time and eternity? withdrawing confidence from every thing, and every person else in the universe? Do you do this without doubting or fearing? Let us look at faith,

3. *In its receiving capacity.* God offers Jesus Christ as his great gift. Have you received him as your wisdom, righteousness, sanctification, and redemption? As your prophet, priest, and king? Have you received the Lord Jesus unto your hearts and souls, as the unspeakable gift of God? Believing includes each and all of these acts. Do you, then, *now believe?* We pass on,

II. TO THE PERSONS INTERROGATED. "Do ye," &c. He put not the question to ignorant persons—to profligate persons—to the worldly; but Christ put it to his disciples. We put it to you, who are called Christians. "Do ye," &c. Look at the form of the question. It is,

1. *Strictly personal.* We cannot answer for one another—not for our nearest friends, &c. To our own master we stand or fall.

Religion is entirely personal. Let us, then, examine and see whether *we* are *in* the faith, &c. To examine the creeds, or opinions, or practice of others is not our province. But, " Do *ye*," &c.

2. *The question also refers to the present.* Most seriously disposed persons intend to believe—expect they will—hope they will. But the future is God's; we cannot presume on a day. But do ye *now ;* are you at this time receiving Christ? If God searches now—tries you now, &c. ; your *present* state. Neither does it refer to the past. Have you *formerly* believed? Can you be safe or happy to trust to past recollections, &c. It is the present to which the text refers.

3. *The text assumes that a satisfactory reply is possible.* That we may say No, or Yes. The whole scriptures go on this principle. Without it we could not apply revealed truth as it is addressed to the Christian. Abraham knew that he believed. The blind man, " Dost thou," &c. Paul, " I know," &c. Now, keep the definition of the subject in view. We say nothing of visions—of marvellous revelations—of fancies and feelings ; but of credence, reliance, reception. Surely this is unanswerable. Then,

III. LET US ASCERTAIN WHAT EVIDENCES MAY BE DEEMED SATISFACTORY.

1. *The recollection of the process by which we were brought to believe.* This state does not come without certain events, &c. A conviction that we do not believe ; a sense of guilt, &c. ; a deep impression of its importance ; the going out of the mind ; the act of the soul on the ground of the divine testimony, &c. Besides, the sermon—the address—the providential event, &c., the mental effort cannot easily be forgotten. A man rescued from the water ; a culprit pardoned at the bar; a person raised from the verge of the grave cannot forget.

2. *The influence that believing exerts on the mind.* If we believe, then we shall desire to *know* more and more of Christ. We shall *love* Christ, &c. It works by love, &c. We shall *hope* in Christ, be grateful to Christ, delight in Christ, &c.

3. *The effect it produces on the life.* Unbelief is connected with rebellion; faith with loyal obedience. One with irreverence, the other with holy fear; one with polluted streams, the other pure ; one, evil

conversation, the other a good, &c. ; one, bad works, the other good works. The life is affected by our unbelief or belief, as the rudder directs the vessel. Obedience and self-denial will ever accompany belief.

4. *Its connection with spiritual enjoyment* Believing, the spirit of adoption and peace is given ; joy is given. The cloud is blotted out ; the thunders roll not, &c. The word of God is different in our estimation ; the ordinances ; the sabbaths. We, who have believed, do enter into *rest*, &c.

APPLICATION.

1. The subject is deeply interesting ; it is of vital importance, &c.; it concerns me, and concerns you all.

2. Let me urge on all who have not believed, the essential importance of doing so. We present you with the writings of evangelists and apostles, and urge you to receive them as concerning you, and heartily to embrace them. Nothing will give you an interest in the great salvation but a living faith.

3. A reference to this subject will often tend to our profit and safety. Do I now believe?

THE PHILOSOPHY OF OBEDIENCE.

" And it shall come to pass, if thou shalt hearken diligently unto the voice of the Lord thy God, to observe and to do all his commandments, which I command thee this day ; that the Lord thy God will set thee on high above all nations of the earth."—DEUT. xxviii. 1.

LAW—Obedience—Blessedness, are the three great topics of our text ; indeed they are the three great principles of revelation. The will of God is law, and all his commandments are the reflections of his holy and blessed character and perfections. It is obvious that an infinitely wise Being must suit his laws to that which is to be governed. Now, moral laws are not suited to irrational creatures, nor mental laws to material things. Mere matter is governed entirely by physical laws—mind, by intellectual laws—moral responsible beings, by moral or righteous laws. Now, these general remarks will apply to all the works of God, and to the divine government throughout the universe. We wish to bring so much of this subject before you as relates to man, and is connected immediately with his present and eternal welfare. Religious people fall into great errors, and expose themselves to many evils, through not having comprehensive and clear views of this subject. Let us, then, with all the plainness of which the subject is capable, look at the laws of God in reference to man, and the advantages to be derived from obedience to them.

I. GOD HAS ESTABLISHED A THREEFOLD LAW IN CONNECTION WITH MANKIND.

1. *We are under physical laws, having material bodies.* The body was originally formed of the earth, and, therefore, is of the earth—earthy. Now, it is clear that the body requires material sustenance—material preservation from evil, &c. Therefore wholesome food, air, exercise, and repose, are necessary to its well-being. It is liable to be injured or destroyed by improper food, air, &c.; exposed to accidents, &c.; therefore prudent care is necessary. Now, a disregard to the laws which regulate the body, will be productive of pain, disease, or premature death. Neglect of the prudential laws may involve in calamity and ruin. Now, it is not obedience to any other laws which will secure health or bodily enjoyment. A man may be very intellectual, and very devotional; but these will neither sustain life, prevent disease, nor avert calamity. Neither is it wise for any man to pray against sickness or peril, if he, at the same time, neglect the laws which affect his physical condition; unless he expects God to be constantly working miracles, and changing the material laws of the universe, on his account.

2. *We are under mental laws, as intellectual beings.* We have capacities for knowledge, and improvement, and the expansion of the intellectual powers. Now, reading, study, investigation, and reflection are essential, just as food, digestion, and exercise are essential to physical health. By these a man may excel in intellectual things, become mentally vigorous and healthy. Now, obeying the physical laws will not make a man wise or intellectual; but obedience to the mental laws, which regulate the mind.

3. *We are under moral laws, as accountable beings.* Now these laws are revealed in the Holy Scriptures. These respect our conduct to God, ourselves, and our fellowmen. In the New Testament economy, all moral excellency is to be based on faith in God; believing the truth of his love to us in Christ Jesus; a belief of his paternal goodness, and merciful and gracious character as our Redeemer. With this is to be connected repentance for past sins; faith or reliance on the great sacrifice of Christ Jesus; turning from evil to good, and walking in the commandments and ordinances of his word, by the promised aid of his Holy Spirit. Now, we may obey the physical and intellectual laws, and yet rebel against God's moral laws, and thus be sinners and transgressors of the holy statutes of the Most High. Let us,

II. LOOK AT THE RESULT OF OBEDIENCE TO THE LAWS OF GOD. Let us take each law, and look at it separately.

1. *Attention and obedience to physical laws will be generally followed by bodily enjoyments, and the comforts of sense.* We say generally, because we inherit many bodily weaknesses and diseases from our parents, which we may not be able to avoid; but these will be materially ameliorated by a strict regard to the material laws of God.

2. *Attention and obedience to the laws of mind, and we may become mentally vigorous.* Grow in knowledge and intellectual power, and thus be fraught with all the happiness and pleasure which intellectuality confers.

3. *But attention and obedience to the moral laws of God, will be followed by moral enjoyments, both in this life and that which is to come.*

Now, by obedience to these, we shall have,

(1.) An assurance of God's favor. This may be established upon this triple foundation. God must necessarily approve of that which resembles himself, and honors his blessed laws. His word assures us that obedience to him shall, through the merits of Christ, secure his approbation. If ye be willing and obedient, &c. In keeping his commandments there is great reward, " Whoso doeth the will of my Father," &c. He will give his Holy Spirit to them who obey him, as an earnest of his love, to witness, &c.; to guide into all truth, &c.

(2.) We shall have tranquillity of conscience; peace within; a heart sprinkled from an evil conscience, &c.

(3.) We shall be interested in all the precious promises. Now, these are bright and numerous as the stars of heaven; refer both to body and soul—time and eternity.

(4.) We shall finally have everlasting life ; a place, a mansion, a throne, at God's right hand ; eternal glory ; celestial joys and pleasures forevermore. But with all these advantages and unspeakable blessings, if we neglect the physical laws, we may have sickness, misfortunes, &c. ; or the mental laws, we may be ignorant ; for there must be obedience to each to secure all the good of the whole.

APPLICATION.

1. *A correct understanding of this subject will enable us to clear the divine government of very much of the suffering of the world.* A very great portion arises from men disobeying God's wise and benevolent laws. Let us not charge God, therefore, foolishly.

2. *We shall understand why our prayers are often not answered.* We ask amiss, inasmuch as we do not act conformably thereto. If we pray for health, and disregard regimen, air, exercise, &c. ; for knowledge, and neglect reading, study, &c. ; for comfort, and do not live in holy obedience to his revealed laws.

3. *The laws which govern us now, will do so forever.* Our resurrection bodies will be freed from the seeds of disease, and living in an atmosphere of health, will never be sick. Our minds free and etherealized in the heaven of light, we shall dwell in high intellectual splendor. The moral powers all holy, will delight in God, in the services of the heavenly temple, and the society of the redeemed forever.

PARADISE RESTORED.

"In whom also we have obtained an inheritance, being predestinated according to the purpose of him who worketh all things after the counsel of his own will."—EPH. i. 11.

WE have previously considered paradise given, and paradise lost.* Our text leads us to the contemplation of paradise regained. Observe the various parts of the text.

(1.) The inheritance is, doubtless, the whole of that salvation which God has provided for a lost world. The consummation of this, is the heavenly state. Eternal glory.

* Pages 53 and 55.

(2.) This inheritance is specified as being in Christ. "In whom," &c., see verse 10. It is said, "This is the true God, and eternal life."

(3.) This inheritance is given to a special people ; those who were predestinated according to God's purpose. God purposed and fore-appointed that all believers, and such only, should have everlasting life, verses 12, 13.

(4.) This inheritance is in present possession ; in title ; in the earnest, or first-fruits. Such are the various portions of this passage of the sacred writer. Let us now consider,

I. THE NATURE OF THIS INHERITANCE.
II. HOW IT HAS BEEN PROCURED. And
III. HOW IT BECOMES OURS.

I. THE NATURE OF THIS INHERITANCE. Now, the inheritance which the gospel reveals to us may be considered,

1. *In its resemblance to that we lost in Adam.* That included,

(1.) The divine approbation. God beheld man with complacency and delight. He was the object of God's favor. The light of the divine countenance was the joyful portion of our first parents. By sin this was lost. God could not thus favorably behold iniquity ; he could not thus approve of a traitor—a rebel. Now, Christ has regained, on behalf of the ungodly, the divine favor. God can look on the guilty through Christ, and justify them freely by his grace. God appears toward our race as a God of love ; not armed with an avenging rod, but holding forth a sceptre of grace.

(2.) This inheritance includes the divine image. Sin effaced this ; man reflected the mind of the evil one, he became possessed of the spirit of Satan. This moral image of God is restored by regenerating grace. Born again ; born from above ; renewed by the purifying power of the Holy Ghost, Col. iii. 10.

(3.) A place in the divine family. The fall was followed by expulsion from Eden's happy scenes. Man became an outcast literally, but still more morally. "By grace man is brought nigh," &c. Eph. ii. 19 ; constituted a part of the family of God. "Because ye are sons," &c. "Behold what manner of love," &c. This inheritance includes,

(4.) Divine fellowship. God had holy intercourse with man ; man had communion with God. Sin dissolved it—broke it off. In redemption it is regained. The soul has access to God; see also 1 John i. 3. This inheritance includes,

(5.) The divine bounty. God's munificence was strikingly exhibited in paradise. How rich the portion he gave to man! But what can equal our gospel inheritance? It includes all possible good. "He now gives grace and glory." "My God shall supply all," &c. "All are yours; ye are Christ's," &c.

(6.) The friendly sympathies and services of the angels. In innocency these were the companions of man; but through sin they were the executioners of God's displeasure. In redemption, they again assume the aspect of friendship and love. They rejoice in the sinner's conversion. They are all ministering spirits, &c. And they conduct believers, when they die, to the realms of glory. Let us now observe in what,

2. *This inheritance is dissimilar to the one we lost in Adam.*

(1.) In many things that was a temporal—in most things this is a spiritual one. That was a temporal Eden—material fruits, &c. This is a spiritual inheritance. One for the mind—one within the soul.

(2.) That was an inheritance on earth. The New Testament inheritance, in its completion and glory, is reserved in heaven, and, therefore, is much more exalted and glorious. Not at God's footstool, but by his side—in his palace. Not a paradise in the region of the material creation, and the lower animals, but with angels, &c.

(3.) That was an inheritance that depended on man's righteous obedience, and rested on himself. The New Testament inheritance is given through the merits of another, and the grace of God is freely given to make us meet for its everlasting enjoyment. No tempter there—cannot be lost. We ask,

II. How has this inheritance been procured? By the mediatorial work of Jesus Christ. We lost the first by the sin of Adam; we obtain the second by the obedience of Jesus. By the first Adam we became poor, and wretched, and liable to death; the second Adam came to give us rest, and peace, and eternal life. Cursed in the first, we are redeemed from the curse by the second. Lost by the first, we are redeemed by the second. Rom. v. 18, "Ye

know the grace of our Lord Jesus Christ," &c. "In the fulness of the times," &c.

III. How this inheritance, this paradise regained, becomes ours. "In whom," &c. This paradise regained does not become ours in a variety of ways. We cannot buy it, or merit it; nor is it given irrespective of any medium.

1. *This inheritance is given to us by God.* And thus the gospel announces it; calls our attention to it; urges our reception of it, &c. But this inheritance,

2. *Is given through faith in Jesus Christ.* Receiving Christ, we become fellow-heirs with Christ. By faith in Christ, we become sons of God, and heirs of eternal life. Jesus and the inheritance go together. Rejecting the one, we also reject the other. "Whosoever believeth," &c. The text speaks of it as being ours, now "obtained." Christians have the title now—the earnest now—and the bright assurance now, of its enjoyment forever.

APPLICATION.

1. *What ground for universal praise.* The new paradise revealed and offered in the gospel.

2. *What cause of Christian rejoicing.* We have experimental possession.

3. *What a subject for blissful hope.* In its blissful consummation in the eternal world.

VALUE OF EXPERIENCE IN MATTERS OF RELIGION.

"He answered and said, Whether he be a sinner or no, I know not: one thing I know, that, whereas I was blind, now I see."—JOHN ix. 25.

THE text is the language of the man who received his sight from Christ, to the cavilling, unbelieving Jews. Nicodemus had said to Christ, "We know that thou art," &c. Of these miracles, some were of the most astonishing kind. That of healing the leper by a word—of raising the dead—and giving sight to the blind. Yet, such was the perverseness and prejudice of the Jews, that they began to discuss the question of Christ's personal holiness, instead of admiring and rejoicing in the wonderful and benevolent miracle which he had just wrought. All these points the young man left the Jews to settle among themselves.

He testified of his own experience—of what he had seen, and heard, and felt. " One thing," &c. Thousands of Christians are, with this person, quite unable to discuss the peculiar points of theological controversy. They may not be able to overthrow the sophistry of the skeptic, nor answer all his objections to the Christian scheme ; but this they can do, they can testify of the power and grace of Christ, and can say, " Whereas I was blind," &c. Our subject is personal experience in matters of religion. Consider, then,

I. THE NATURE OF THIS EXPERIENCE. It is an experience,

1. *Of an entire change.* " Once blind." Ignorant of God and ourselves ; ignorant of the truths and blessings of religion ; ignorant of duties and privileges. This blindness was natural to our former state. " Now see." Eyes opened. Once all dark—now light. Now see our condition—misery—peril ; see our remedy—help, &c.; see the way of happiness and safety. It is the experience,

2. *Of the most important change.* What earthly good to be compared to sight ? One invaluable blessing desired by the blind, that " our eyes may be opened," &c. Important to our enjoyment of God and his works, both of creation, providence, and grace ; to our well-being and eternal salvation.

3. *Of a divine change.* Not a self-effected one ; not one produced by a fellow-creature, &c. 2 Cor. iv. 6.

4. *Of a most merciful and gracious change.* Not deserved—not merited, &c. Free, " without money," &c.

5. *A change effected by the most unlikely means.* The anointing of the clay, &c., seemed likely rather to effect blindness than to cure it. No virtue, either, in the clay, nor the waters of the pool, &c. Therefore it was not an ordinary cure by medicinal means. They were used to test his obedience. Now, the way of salvation by faith in Jesus Christ as a crucified malefactor, was to the Jews a stumbling-block, and to the Greeks foolishness. Learning, philosophy, morality, penance, any thing rather than this. This, however—God's plan—abases the sinner. He cannot glory. God is honored, and man saved. Such, then, is the change experienced. Let us consider,

II. THE TESTIMONY SUCH EXPERIENCE YIELDS, AS TO THE TRUTH OF CHRISTIANITY.

This man bore testimony to the miraculous power of Christ, and in this to his messiahship and divinity. The Jews had the most satisfactory evidence given by him. It could not be illusion, nor wilful deception. He bore about him proof ; he was surrounded by those who knew him, both before and after his recovery from blindness. Now, let us examine the testimony which is given by Christians, as their experience, to the influence of religion on their own hearts.

1. *Their testimony relates to what is personal and conscious.* Not any supposed theory, &c.; but what they know and feel. They know their state is entirely changed, &c.

2. *Their testimony is impartial.* It is not their interest to deceive, or to be deceived. Confers no temporal dignity or advantage ; generally the reverse.

3. *Their testimony is harmonious.* Christians of all ages, and of all ranks, speak of the same things—enjoy the same blessings. It may be objected, that there is diversity of sentiment, and that they are not all agreed. They are agreed as to the reality of religion—as to the blessings they have received. The mode may have differed, as in Bartimeus and the young man ; as in Lydia and Saul of Tarsus.

4. *Their testimony is established by external evidences.* The young man could see. This they might prove or disprove. So Christians profess to be enlightened—now do they walk in light ? to be saved from the power of Satan—now is their life altered ? Is malevolence exchanged for love ? wrath for meekness ? sin for holiness ? Here, then, their fruit is seen, &c.

5. *Their testimony is borne under all circumstances.* If only under exciting occasions, then it would be suspicious. If only in the day of prosperity, also suspicious, &c.; but in solitude—in adversity—in sickness—in death. Myriads have testified with their dying breath, &c.

APPLICATION.

1. *Learn that it is the duty of believers to bear witness for Christ, and of his power to save.* It should be done verbally ; but especially in our tempers, conversation, and lives. Gratitude and love to Christ should induce us. Love to our fellow-men.

2. *Urge the reception of this evidence, and the use of the means the gospel proclaims, upon all.*

3. *The rejection of this evidence exhibits the enmity of the carnal mind, and the power of sinful prejudice in the soul.*

CHURCH FELLOWSHIP.

" And they continued steadfastly in the apostles' doctrine and fellowship, and in breaking of bread, and in prayers."—ACTS ii. 42.

THE previous portion of the chapter describes the sermon of the apostle Peter to the assembled Jews on the day of Pentecost; the effects the sermon produced; and the baptism of those who were converted; and then the order and character of that fellowship which they adopted and steadfastly maintained. On this occasion, we purpose to notice church fellowship, in its nature, duties, and advantages; and meet some objections of those who neglect it.

I. CHURCH FELLOWSHIP IN ITS NATURE.

1. *It is a voluntary fellowship.* When persons unite from free choice; influenced only by truth and love. It presupposes that men are not naturally of this fellowship—not born into it; but come out of the world freely to associate and unite with God's people.

2. *It is a fellowship of faith.* It cannot consist of any really but true believers. Such only have fellowship with Christ; such only are spiritual persons; such only members of Christ's body—branches of the true vine.

3. *It is the fellowship of obedience.* Obedience to the commands of Christ. " Go ye, and teach," &c. " Teaching them to observe all things," &c. Several duties are specified in the text, which belong especially to the church of Christ.

(1.) The apostles' " doctrine;" the great truths concerning Christ and salvation; those doctrines which they had heard and received from the apostles. To hold the truth, and to grow in it, is of vital importance. Not one truth of temporary importance; especially the great cardinal doctrine of salvation by faith in the Lord Jesus.

(2.) " Fellowship;" intercourse of life and heart; where the same exercises are pursued and mutually regarded. But the word also means " communication," or beneficence, Rom. xv. 26; Heb. xiii. 16.

(3.) " Breaking of bread." Or, as the

Syriac version renders it, of the eucharist—evidently the Lord's Supper. Hence, at the origin of this institution, " Christ," it is said, " took bread, brake it," &c., Acts xx. 7.

(4.) " In prayer." Publicly offering up their supplications and intercessions for the blessing of God, and the salvation of the world. In these we see a beautiful exhibition of what a church should be. The first day of the week arrives; the disciples are gathered together; the pastor, or elder, or bishop presides; the doctrines of Christ are expounded, or preached; the truth exhibited. Then the wants of the necessitous are supplied; the gospel influencing the heart, and filling it with Christian goodness and liberality. Then the Lord's Supper is administered—prayer presented—a hymn sung—and the company retire, blessing God, and edified and built up in their holy faith. Steadfast—constant—persevering—regular. Let us look,

II. AT THE DUTIES CHRISTIAN FELLOWSHIP INVOLVES.

1. *The duty of regular intercourse.* " Forsake not the assembling of yourselves together." " As iron sharpeneth iron, so does the," &c.

> " How did my heart rejoice to hear
> My friends devoutly say,
> In Zion let us all appear,
> And keep the solemn day."

Neglect, fraught with evil to the pastor, members, and especially to their own souls.

2. *Exhibition of Christian affection.* This is the command, " Little children, love one another." " Walk in love." Fellowship and love influence each other—promote one another.

3. *Christian admonition and exhortation.* " Admonish one another," &c. " Exhort one another," &c. " Thou shalt not hate thy brother," &c.; nor in any wise suffer sin upon him.

4. *Christian help.* " Bear ye one another's burdens, and so fulfil the law of Christ." Ye that are strong, bear the burdens of the weak; ye rich, the poor; ye wise, the ignorant; ye fathers, the children, &c. " Do good unto all men," &c.

III. THE ADVANTAGES OF CHRISTIAN FELLOWSHIP.

1. *It tends to our improvement.* In knowledge—wisdom—grace—zeal, &c.

2. *To our comfort.* More company; the way more pleasant and lightsome. In **joy,**

some to rejoice ; in sorrow, some to weep ; in straits, some to console ; in difficulties, some to help ; in sickness and conflict, some to visit and cheer, or pray.

3. *It will tend to our security.* Safer, for two are better, &c. Besides, there are many church promises, Eccles. iv. 9.

IV. ANSWER SOME OBJECTIONS OF THOSE WHO NEGLECT CHURCH FELLOWSHIP.

1. *We would unite, if the church were pure.* That it is not, is to be admitted—mourned over—lamented, &c. Never has been. You would have objected to Christ's church, because of the carnal views of the disciples—denial of Peter—betrayal of Judas, &c. I fear such are filled with the spirit of self-righteousness, deceiving their own souls.

2. *Such diversity, we know not which to choose.* But this is not a good reason for neglecting all. Parent's neglecting to educate, or have his child apprenticed, because of so many trades. Take up the word of God, and try them by it ; that most scriptural—most like Christ's, and the first churches. Only one way to heaven, &c.

3. *We can get to heaven without it.* Where is it written ? Perhaps there are those who can ; the sick—the invalid—the exile ; but can you ? If so, what kind of heaven ? For there is fellowship, communion, and perfect bliss in the Christian's heaven. Had you not better be introduced on earth ? Christ says his church is a family—flock—army, &c. Others say,

4. *They are not fit for church fellowship.* Then not fit for the sick bed—for the valley of death—for eternity. Christ can make you so. He desires to do it ; he waits to do it now ; his heart—arm—Spirit, &c., all ready. " Wilt thou be made whole ?"

APPLICATION.

1. *To those now united with God's people.* Be stea fast, &c. Hold fast. Cleave, &c.

2. *To those wavering, now determine.* Do not delay, especially the young.

3. *Sinners, begin to reflect.* Your fellowship with the workers of iniquity is debasing, ruinous, and will terminate in the misery of a crowded, black, and everlasting perdition. Go not with a multitude to do evil, and thus perish forever.

SALVATION IN ZION

" I will place salvation in Zion for Israel my glory."—ISAIAH xlvi. 13.

IT is clear that the 12th and 13th verses refer to the gospel dispensation, and the salvation, or way of righteousness, that should therein be published. By reading Romans i. 16, 17, and, in connection with both, Romans iii. 21. In the gospel, God's righteousness is brought near ; that is, the way of righteousness—the offer of righteousness, &c. That which seemed impossible under the law—and was really so by the deeds of the law—is now adapted to the misery and exigencies of mankind, and offered to all who believe in the name of the Lord Jesus Christ. When the divinely-appointed time arrived—the period described as " the fulness of the times"—then the salvation came. It did not tarry ; it was not delayed ; but God sent it forth in the person of his own Son, who came and redeemed those who were under the law, that they might obtain the adoption of sons. Then follows the text, " And I will place salvation," &c.

I. A DESCRIPTION OF THE CHURCH AND PEOPLE OF GOD. " Zion." " Israel, my glory."

II. THE GRACIOUS DECLARATION. " I will place salvation," &c.

I. A DESCRIPTION OF THE CHURCH AND PEOPLE OF GOD. " Zion." Zion was the name of the loftiest mountain on which the city of Jerusalem was built, and was applied especially to the holy temple, as the place of the assembling of the tribes of Israel. Many very beautiful sayings are recorded of Zion. It is called the " Holy hill of Zion." " The joy of the whole earth is Zion." " Praise waits for thee, O God, out of Zion." " The Lord hath chosen Zion, and there will he dwell," &c. " The Lord bless thee out of Zion." " The Lord loveth the gates of Zion," &c. " Oh that salvation were come out of Zion." Now, these beautiful passages obviously refer to Zion as the ancient church of God —the place of sacrifice and worship, where God manifested his glory. The New Testament church is described by the apostle, " Ye are come to Mount Zion," &c., Hebrews xii. 22. Whatever distinguished Zion of old is still more prominently associated with the New Testament Zion—the Christian church.

(1.) Had they a *priesthood*—we have the great, and last, and perpetual High Priest, Jesus the Son of God, &c.

(2.) Had they a *sacrifice*—we have the one great sacrifice for sin, the Lamb of God, &c.

(3.) Had they the *varied* and *rich furniture* of the tabernacle, and afterwards of the temple—we have the substance of the whole ; a living *altar*—living *bread*—a real *ark*—the true *mercy-seat*.

(4.) Had they the *symbol* of the divine glory—we have the glory itself. " The brightness of the Father's glory, and the express image of his person."

(5.) Had they *prophecy*—we have a more sure word of prophecy, life, and immortality, &c.

(6.) Had they God in their midst ; did he dwell in Zion—we have now the perpetual presence of the Spirit ; abiding with the church forever ; we have the substance, the reality, &c.—the end of the thing signified.

2. *The text also describes God's people.* " Israel, my glory." Now, God is the glory of Israel ; he is the glory of his people Israel. But this is the opposite view. " The church is God's glory ;" the pious, who constitute the true church, are the glory of God.

(1.) For such, he redeemed them. " This people have I formed for myself, that they may show forth," &c. ; and the apostles, " That ye should show forth his praise," &c.

(2.) The church is compared to those things considered great and glorious ; see Isaiah liv. 11. By the apostle John likened to a golden candlestick. The Lord describes his church as his portion, and his people as his jewels.

(3.) By the church, the glory of God is reflected to the world. Her garments are beautiful, like the king's daughter, all glorious within, &c. The mercy, grace, and holiness of God are seen in the church. Hear what the Saviour says : " Herein is my Father glorified, if ye bear much fruit," &c. ; see John xvii. 22. God is denied—his name blasphemed—his works forgotten—his word rejected—his worship refused by the ungodly world ; but he is acknowledged, revered, adored, worshipped, exalted, and glorified by his church and people. What condescension in Deity to represent his people as his glory ! Are there not cherubim and seraphim, and the glorified hosts, too, in heaven ? Yet, he looks down upon his believing, praying, obedient people on earth, and declares that they are " His glory." Now, let us consider,

II. THE GRACIOUS DECLARATION. " I will place salvation." Now, four particulars are included in this sentence of the text.

1. *Salvation.* Included both redemption from evil, and the bestowal of the blessings we need. The salvation of the gospel is salvation from sin and all its accursed effects, and salvation into holiness and all its blessed results. Salvation from guilt —from condemnation—from pollution— from vassalage—from debasement. Salvation into God's favor, love, likeness, kingdom, and glory. Salvation of the soul and of the body. The glorification of the one at death, and of the other at the resurrection of the just. The eternal felicity of both united in heaven forever and ever.

2. *Now this salvation is divine.* " I will place salvation," &c. The salvation of God originated in his eternal purpose of grace and mercy. The exhibition of infinite love. Laid upon his own Son ; brought by his own arm ; published by his own word ; effected by his own Spirit. In every sense it is God's. The contrivance of the eternal Father ; the work of his co-equal Son ; the application of it by the Holy Spirit ; the wonder of angels—the joy of sinners—the confusion of devils—but the *work* of God.

3. *This salvation is to be placed in Zion.* Now, we must look at this subject literally and spiritually. *Literally*—Salvation was placed in Zion. The types and prophecies predicting it were delivered and exhibited in Zion. The germ was planted in the Jewish church—watered with the tears and prayers of the pious, from Abraham to Zechariah and Simeon. Let us read one or two of the passages. " Behold, I lay in Zion for a foundation-stone." Especially Isaiah xl. 9, " O Zion, thou that bringest glad tidings," &c. Obadiah says, " Upon Mount Zion shall be deliverance, and there shall be holiness," &c. Zechariah says, " Sing and rejoice, O daughter of Zion, for lo ! I come, and I will dwell in the midst of thee, saith the Lord." Now all these were literally fulfilled. Christ, the Saviour, was not only a Jew—a son of Zion—but he came to Zion ; he appeared in their synagogues, and streets, and cities, and temple.

He offered his blessing to the children of Zion. After his death, *salvation* was first proclaimed here ; " Begin *at Jerusalem.*" Here were the first fruits of his blessed kingdom — the first converts — the first church ; salvation was *placed* here. But look at the text *spiritually.* Salvation is particularly in his church. Here is the presence of the Saviour, " Lo, I am with you," &c. " Wherever two or three," &c. His gospel and word are here ; his ordinances are here, too, to be perpetuated. In connection with these salvation is chiefly effected. Here, too, the salvation of God's people is completed in their sanctification and preservation from the power of the devil, &c.

4. *The persons for whom this salvation is to be placed in Zion.* " For Israel." To the Jew first, then also to the Gentile. For all partakers of Abraham's faith, whether his lineal or spiritual seed, Gal. vii. 9, and iv. 28. Salvation is for every one that believeth—that receives the testimony, the record given, of God's Son. " Whoso believeth with the heart, and confesseth," &c.

LEARN,

1. *The dignity of the children of God.* " The glory of the Lord," &c.

2. *The responsibility of the church.* In it is salvation. Storehouse of the bread of life ; fountain of living water ; the citadel of the Christian army. On it rests the conversion of the world, and the extension of Christ's cause ; the heathen—the unconverted at home—the rising age.

3. *We proclaim this salvation to every believer to-day.*

ZION, THE PERFECTION OF BEAUTY.

" Out of Zion, the perfection of beauty, God hath shined."—Psalm l. 2.

ZION was a mountain connected with several others, on part of which the temple was erected. This appellation was, however, often given to the whole city of Jerusalem, especially when she was described in her religious character, or in connection with her religious ordinances. " Glorious things are spoken of thee." " Great is the Lord," &c. Ps. xlviii. 1, &c. ; see also Ps. cxxxii. 13. Isaiah also refers to it, xxxiii. 20, " Look upon Zion," &c. Mount Zion, however, was typical of the church of Christ ; and as such, the apostle observes, " Ye are come unto Mount Zion," &c. Heb. xii. 23. It is to this application of the text that we shall call your attention. Observe,

I. A TWOFOLD REPRESENTATION OF THE CHURCH OF GOD. " Zion, and the perfection of beauty."

II. THE GLORIOUS FACT AFFIRMED RESPECTING IT. " Out of Zion, &c. God hath shined."

I. A TWOFOLD REPRESENTATION OF THE CHURCH OF GOD. By the Church of God, we here give the greatest latitude to the term which it can legitimately bear. We mean the congregation of the Lord's people, of every age and country ; the universal family of his children, from the beginning to the end of time. We are to consider this church,

1. *In its representation as Zion.* And as such it may be considered,

(1.) On account of its exalted *visibility.* Mount Zion was elevated above the surrounding country ; seen afar off. Now, this is to be one grand characteristic of God's church. It is to be visible—city set on a hill ; hence often called " the mountain of the Lord," &c.

(2.) As the *chosen* hill of the Lord. " The Lord hath chosen it," &c. It is called the hill of the Lord. " God loveth the gates of Zion," &c. Now, all this in the highest degree will apply to the church. The church is the chosen residence of Deity ; an habitation for God ; the delight of the Lord.

(3.) As distinguished for its *immoveable stability.* See Psalm xlviii. 12, 13. Now, such is the church of God. God its defence and fortress. " The gates of hell," &c. " No weapon," &c. Lived in the midst of combined earthly and hellish foes, yet has survived all her enemies, and she is destined to fill the whole earth with her glory. But Zion is said,

2. *To be the perfection of beauty.* See Psalm xlviii. 2. Now, the church of God is the perfection of beauty,

(1.) In her ministering attendants. The garments of the priesthood were peculiarly striking and interesting. Every part, too, was expressive of God's great designs. The flowing robe—the breastplate—the mitre— the musical bells, &c. ; yet all these were but shadows of the good things of the gospel, Isaiah lii. 7.

(2.) For the virtues and graces of her members. In the world there may be much that is gorgeous and splendid—much that is striking and useful in art, science, and literature, &c. There have been men renowned for patriotism and philanthropy, and some for their stern adhesion to justice and truth. But the perfection of beauty is that heavenly holiness with which Christ clothes his people; the graces of the Spirit. "The fruit of the Spirit is," &c. Gal. v. 22.

(3.) In her delightful and celestial dispensations, ordinances, &c. Look at her on the day of her solemn assemblies! Behold her in her devotional services! In her praises, &c. In her communion at the table of the Lord. In her fellowship.

II. The glorious fact affirmed. "Out of Zion," &c. Then God is in Zion; it is his rest. He dwelt between the cherubim. There was the cloud, &c.; the oracles, &c. Now God hath shined out of Zion.

1. *In the person and ministry of his Son.* Jesus came as the representative of the Deity, full of grace and truth. He came as the light of the world. All the glories of the divine nature shone in his countenance; all subjects became irradiated, &c., by his divine beams.

2. *In the principles and doctrines of the gospel.* Would you see the divine glory? look at the divine mind? Look into the gospel mirror, 2 Cor. iii. 18; see also 2 Cor. iv. 6.

3. *In the spirit and truths of his word.* The entrance of his word gives light; "light shining in a dark place." This is the Spirit's revelation of Jesus Christ. Here the things and glories of Christ are manifested; and by this word dwelling in us we are sanctified and made meet, &c.

APPLICATION.

1. *Are you connected with Zion?* Do you form a part of the holy congregation? Are you sons and daughters of Zion? Born in her?

2. *If so, do you seek her weal, and labor for her prosperity?* Has she your prayers, &c.?

3. *We invite those who are without to unite with the people of God.* Unite in her holy associations, and enjoy her privileges and blessings. "Come with us, and we will do you good," &c.

DEVOTED ATTACHMENT TO THE CHURCH.

"If I forget thee, O Jerusalem, let my right hand forget her cunning; if I do not remember thee, let my tongue cleave to the roof of my mouth; if I prefer not Jerusalem above my chief joy."—Psalm cxxxvii. 5, 6.

It is difficult to decide who was the writer of this psalm, probably Jeremiah; it refers to the period of Israel's captivity in Babylon, and relates the feelings and circumstances of that afflicted people. Former associations and attachments were present in their thoughts and affections, verse 1. Probably the Levites are referred to, who were singers in the temple, but now they have suspended their harps on the willows. Whether they wandered by the rivers to meditate, or were employed to labor, this is uncertain. Thus, in deep adversity, their oppressors required them to sing one of their holy national songs. They remonstrated on the unreasonableness of the demand; it was insulting adversity, adding anguish to suffering. Then the writer breaks forth in the ardent language of the text, "If I forget," &c. It is pleasing to observe the burning embers of this holy patriotism among the Jews to this day, even now they do not forget Zion. And doubtless to that land and city God will assuredly restore them. But Jerusalem was an emblem of the church; the true Jerusalem from above, the mother of us all. Let us emulate the pious Jew in his attachment and exclamation in regard to God's church, "If I forget," &c. Let us consider the nature, the evidences, and the grounds of the Christian's attachment to the church of God.

I. The nature of the Christian's attachment to the church of God.

1. *It is a spiritual attachment.* Church, God's spiritual house—its servants, &c., are spiritual—its inhabitants are spiritual persons—God's Holy Spirit dwells in it. Now one of the fruits of the Spirit is love—love to God, love to the saints, love to the whole church. It is therefore the result of the Spirit's operations on the soul and mind, of the Spirit dwelling in us. Any

other principle, such as display, creed, name, &c., worthless.

2. *This attachment is fervent.* The whole phraseology is of a warm, glowing kind—the affections excited, heart enamored, not mere regard, approbation, or esteem, but devoted adhesion and attachment—an affection like that of a mother to her child, or like a man to his bosom friend.

3. *This attachment is self-denying.* "If I prefer not," &c. In this way the depth and extent of pure affection may be tested. Self is so prominent, that it will reign unless another takes the heart, and then self is crucified. Paul and his righteousness, but afterwards Christ and his cross. What would I sacrifice for Zion?—a little pleasure, a little wealth, a little toil. What can be refused if it be preferred to our chief joy? But this necessarily leads us to the next general topic.

II. THE EVIDENCES OF PRESENT ATTACHMENT TO THE CHURCH OF GOD.

1. *Affectionate remembrances.* "If I forget," &c. Objects of no interest are soon forgotten. The memory retains the things on which the heart is set. The mariner forgets not his home and friends. The miser forgets not his gold. The student forgets not his books. The mother forgets not her child, &c. The patriotic Christian cannot forget the church, the kingdom of Jesus. If distant from her courts, yet he does not forget. If confined in a chamber of affliction, he does not forget; his heart's warmest emotions are identified with her.

2. *Delight in her services.* How differently minded are the worshippers of any Christian sanctuary! With many it is a load, the Sabbath a weariness. With others it is conscientious labor—with others it is a mere form; but with the true Christian it is his delight and pleasure, " I was glad when they said," &c. " I had rather be a door-keeper," &c.

" I have been there, and oft would go," &c.

3. *Exertion for her welfare.* If the attachment is sincere, then, like Nehemiah, the service of Jerusalem will greatly influence the mind. What can I do for Zion? Here am I, Lord, employ me as thou wilt. There will be no fastidiousness, no movements by fits and starts, the heart will influence every faculty and power, both of body and soul. The feet, shoulders, hands, the means, the influence, all, all will be cheerfully consecrated.

4. *Sympathy with its condition.* The law of sympathy is marvellous. How we are affected by the misery of a fellow-creature, but if an acquaintance much more, a dear friend how much more still! Now see this in the case of Nehemiah, ii. 2, &c. But afterwards he was all vigor and exertion in rearing her walls, and then all joy at the completion of their undertaking. This threefold sympathy of sorrow, effort, and joy.

5. *Prayer for her prosperity.* The Christian remembers Zion at the throne of grace. On the arms of faith and prayer he bears it up before God. " Lord, remember Zion." " Answer, and have mercy," &c.

" My soul shall pray for Zion still
    While life or breath remains,
There my best friends and kindred dwell,
    There God my Saviour reigns."

III. THE GROUNDS OF THIS ATTACHMENT. These are very numerous.

1. *It is the Christian's birth-place.* He was spiritually born in her. Ah, he says, I went ignorant, cold, unbelieving, hopeless, &c. The word distilled as the dew, &c.; it opened my eyes, softened my heart, won my affections, renewed my soul; there the Spirit revealed Christ to me, and formed him in me. There I first drew the breath of prayer. " If I forget Jerusalem," &c.

2. *It has been the place of divine manifestations.* Often God has met me there, in perplexity, in sorrow, in bereavements, in distress, in weakness. Often the place of banqueting, of holy visions, of heavenly anticipations. " If I forget Jerusalem," &c.

3. *It is the dwelling of my best friends.* How have I joyed to go up with the sons and daughters of Zion! What sympathy there has existed! Similar necessities, perils, desires, feelings, and similar enjoyments, &c. Heard the sacred word, knelt before the same throne, sang the same praises, met at the same communion. " If I forget Jerusalem," &c.

4. *It is the object of the Saviour's highest love.* Is not Jesus the husband of his church, the foundation of Zion? Hath he not redeemed it? does he not dwell in it? is it not his care, his treasure, his delight, his reward? Engraven on the palms of

his hands, dearer than the apple of the eye. Oh then, "If I forget Jerusalem," &c.

5. *It is the hope of the world.* Church, is the light in the darkness, the salt in the putrescence of impurity, the very pillar of our globe, all visions of future glory are crowned with the church. The waters must go forth—the light, the power, of the Saviour. Then, "If I forget," &c.

1. To the true friends—cherish this feeling.

2. To the indifferent professor—examine, &c.

3. Invite sinners to unite with the church of Christ.

CHRISTIAN SOCIALITY.

"For my brethren and companions' sakes, I will now say, Peace be within thee."—PSALM cxxii. 8.

THE importance of the social principle was recognised by Jehovah in that declaration made at the formation of Eve, "It is not good for man," &c. Based on the conjugal union and resulting from it were the relative compacts, in which the same kindred were united in the bonds of amity together. The sociality of neighborhood or locality was the next form which it assumed. But there is also a spiritual circle of social excellency, in many respects superior to all others; that, based on supreme love to God and unfeigned love to one another. This is referred to in another psalm, "I am a companion of all," &c. Jesus also bestowed peculiar honor on this. When one said, "Thy mother and brethren stand without," he said, stretching his hand over the people, "Whoso doeth the will of my Father," &c. This is frequently included in the metaphorical descriptions of the church—a flock—a family—a company of pilgrims—an army. This is most beautifully described in Acts ii. 44, &c. Let us notice,

I. THE NATURE OF THE CHRISTIAN'S SOCIAL COMPACT. "My brethren and companions." You perceive there is,

1. *Identity of nature.* "Brethren," partakers of the same *spiritual nature;* having the same *heavenly Father;* bearing the same *divine likeness;* being imbued with the same *spirit;* known by the same *holy designation.* "Saints," "children," "heirs," &c.

2. *There is mutual association.* "Companions." Engaged in the same pursuits: travelling in the same road: sharing in the same perils: enjoying the same bliss: feeling the same sympathies! How all these observations apply to the Christian's social circle! They go to the *same ordinances;* engage in the *same exercises;* meet before the *same throne;* are baptized into the *same Spirit;* animated with the *same hopes.* Let us advert,

II. TO SOME OF THE OBVIOUS PECULIARITIES AND DUTIES OF THE CHRISTIAN'S SOCIAL COMPACT. It is a compact not grounded on relative association, or local occurrences. Not established by legislation. This compact of godly people,

1. *Is quite voluntary in its formation.* The result of free choice, the movement of the will and affections. There is invitation on one side, "Come thou with us," &c. There is happy acquiescence on the other, "We will go with you," &c. "This people shall be our people," &c.

2. *It is spiritual in its nature.* Not grounded on mere mental or political principles, but on the enjoyment of the same spirit. Having the same moral nature and desires. Being of one heart and soul. This unity is thus described by the apostle Paul, Eph. iv. 3, &c.

3. *It is connected with mutual obligations.* There must (1.) Be unfeigned Christian love. "Love one another with pure hearts," &c. "Whoso loveth is born of God," &c. "By this," &c. (2.) Mutual sympathy and dependence. "Rejoice with," &c. Hence the metaphor of the human body; see 1 Cor. xii. 13, &c., see ver. 25. (3.) Mutual prayers. Pray ye one for another. (4.) Mutual help. "Do good," &c. How the apostle James urges beneficence and charity! The wise are to be eyes to the ignorant. The strong to bear the burdens of the weak. "Bear ye one another's burdens," &c. (5.) Mutual fellowship. "Forsake not the assembling of yourselves together," &c. The flock cling to one another. "I was glad when they said unto me," &c. (6.) Mutual forbearance. Different degrees of knowledge; different degrees of grace; different dispositions and views. The imperfections of each and all demand this. Let me read that rich assemblage of graces and duties, Romans xii. 6, &c.

III. THE PRE-EMINENT DESIRE OF ALL WHO

BELONG TO THE CHRISTIAN SOCIAL COMPACT. " I will now say," &c. *Peace,* often signifies *harmony, prosperity, happiness.* All these are important to the church of Jesus. Unanimity, not uniformity. *Prosperity,* increase, growth, &c. *Happiness,* the enjoyment of God's favor, celestial light and love, &c. Now it is the pre-eminent desire of all true saints that this peace should be in the church. " I will now say," &c. (1.) I will say it to my own *heart.* I will guard my spirit, and temper, and conversation. I will restrain it with bit and bridle. (2.) I will say to the *church.* By my kind demeanor, courtesy, generosity, cheerfulness, readiness to serve, &c. (3.) I will say it *to* God. Oh, let it be so. I will pray for the peace of Jerusalem. My motto is this, I am for peace. I will labor, &c. Now I will do so for many reasons.

(1.) For my own sake ; that I may dwell in an atmosphere of peace.

(2.) For the Saviour's sake, knowing how it pleaseth, &c.

(3.) For the world's sake. That they may exclaim, " How good and pleasant," &c. " See how those Christians love," &c.

(4.) For my brethren and companions' sake, that they may be happy and useful.

APPLICATION.

1. Let the text be sanctified to those who are brethren and companions in the way to the heavenly Zion.

2. Who will journey with us ? Be our companions and brethren in the holy exercises and enjoyments of religion ?

3. The companionship of the world is false, and sorrowful, and calamitous in its issue.

JEWISH LIBERALITY.

" The children of Israel brought a willing offering unto the Lord, every man and woman, whose heart made them willing to bring for all manner of work which the Lord had commanded to be made by the hand of Moses."—EXODUS xxxv. 29.

ONE of the most striking and honorable features in the character and history of the Jews, was that ardent and devoted attachment they manifested to the sanctuary of the Most High. Three instances are left on the records of inspiration illustrative of this. The first is the case to which the text refers. The second, the munificent liberality displayed in the erection of the temple, and the third when with holy patriotism and zeal they rebuilt that temple under the decree and patronage of Cyrus and Darius. Each of these instances will bear the strictest investigation, and we shall behold in the whole the most elevated, liberal, and fervid zeal, for the house and glory of the Lord. Our subject confines us to the first case on scripture record. Let us consider the object of their regard,— its peculiar characteristics,—and the lesson it suggests.

I. THE OBJECT OF THEIR REGARD. This was the tabernacle which was now in course of erection. Moses in an extended interview of forty days and forty nights with Jehovah in the mountain, received command to erect for the Lord a house. God said, " Let them make me a sanctuary that I may dwell among them." And the work was to be undertaken with solemn consideration. " And look that thou make them after the pattern which was showed thee in the mount." Observe, then,

1. *The tabernacle was of divine appointment and construction.* Expressly revealed and undertaken by divine authority,—Jehovah was its artificer,—the glorious architect. Nothing was left to human fancy or ingenuity. The pattern of the whole was placed vividly before the eyes of Moses.

2. *The tabernacle was designed for the celebration of divine worship.* Here sacrifices were to be presented, — offerings brought,—praises celebrated,—prayers offered. Here the priests and Levites were to be in perpetual waiting. Here sacred festivals were to be held. Divine honors paid. This was to be the centre of attraction for Israel. The place of convocation for the pious. The rendezvous of the godly families of his people.

3. *The tabernacle was the place chosen for the more manifest display of the divine glory.* Just read Exod. xxix. 43, xl. 33.

4. *The tabernacle was the place of blessing to the righteous.* The guilty repaired here, and in connection with confession and supplication, and the offerings they brought, and the faith they exercised, they obtained mercy. God was propitious. He verified his promise, made his name manifest, " The Lord merciful," &c. The impure repaired here, and were cleansed. A variety of washings, and the application of the blood of the slain victims, were employed in the

ceremonial purification of the unclean. The pious here were especially blessed. God directed that the priest should go forth to the congregation and bless them in his great and holy name, see Numb. vi. 22. Now, brethren, not to multiply particulars, we see how beautifully applicable all this is to the assemblies of Christian worshippers. Do we not meet by the divine appointment and authority? Do we not meet to present worship to the Most High? Here is to be brought the sacrifice of a broken heart, &c. Here praise, and prayer, and adoration, are to ascend to the blessed God. Does not God manifest himself here, as he does not, &c. Is it not often our privilege to sing with the poet :—

> " I've seen thy glory and thy power,
> Through all thy temple shine;
> My God, repeat that heavenly hour,
> That vision so divine."

"One thing have I desired," &c. Is not the house of God a place of blessing to our souls? Here we have come guilty, and found mercy. Here wretched, and have been made happy,—sorrowful, and have gone away rejoicing. Has it not been the house of God, and the gate of heaven? He brought us into his banqueting house, &c. Having noticed the object of their regards, let us look,

II. AT ITS CHARACTERISTICS. Observe in reference to the regard manifested to the tabernacle by the children of Israel. That it was,

1. *Cheerful and voluntary.* "Whose heart made them," &c. Here we have the fountain right, no wonder the stream was so. The heart loved and delighted in it, and this made them willing. The heart is the lever which moves the whole man. In religion the heart is every thing. Without it, there is no acceptable piety. No attachment is worth any thing where the heart is not the constraining power. This attachment,

2. *Was palpable and demonstrative.* "Brought a willing offering," &c. The offering was the evidence. God will not have his people to appear before him empty. These offerings had two peculiar features.

(1.) Their variety. "All kinds of work." Look at ver. 21, &c.

(2.) Then the generality or perhaps the universality of the offerings. "Every man and woman,"—the rich and the poor,—the young and the old,—from the highest to the lowest. It could not have been done by the few, but was easily effected by the many. Every heart, every hand, &c. The aged sire, and the little child.

3. *This attachment was generous and munificent.* They denied themselves of their ornaments. They toiled, &c. Gave their best and richest. And what was the result? Look next chapter, ver. 5, 6. I imagine four classes might not be in time. The covetous, the vain, the supine, and the procrastinating. I ask, ought not our attachment to the cause of Christ to be equal to theirs for the tabernacle of Moses? and let this,

III. BE THE LESSON OUR SUBJECT TEACHES.

(1.) They were a highly favored people, the separated people of the Lord,—the peculiar nation. But, beloved, what is your calling and designation? Chosen,—elect, —precious. The jewels of the Lord,— saints of the Most High.

(2.) They had richly participated of the divine mercy. Redeemed from Egyptian bondage,—led through the Red sea.—Dividing, guiding, preserving, &c. But what is your experience? God hath redeemed you not merely by might, &c. But with the precious blood, &c. What hath he not done for you? &c.

(3.) For them he raised up Moses, and Aaron, and Joshua; but his own Son hath he sent into the world for you, &c.

(4.) To them he promised a Canaan,— a land of rest. But for you a celestial inheritance, &c. Nay, your privileges are vastly greater and more precious. They had but the dawn,—the types and shadows; but you have the day, and the anti-type, and the substitute. They had the law, and Moses, and ceremonies; but you have the gospel, and Christ, and the Holy Spirit, &c. I ask, how many feel as they did, and give the same manifestation of it? Alas! some care for none of these things. Alas! some are merely formal. Alas! some are covetous, and give grudgingly. Alas! some act as if God were greatly indebted to them. How is it with you? Give yourselves first, and then the best you have to the Lord's service. Spiritual prosperity must be secured by acting as the Jews did.

THE NATURE AND ADVANTAGE OF GOD'S SERVICE.

"Ye have said, It is vain to serve God: and what profit is it, that we have kept his ordinance, and that we have walked mournfully before the Lord of hosts?"—MALACHI iii. 14.

IT is clear that a very extensive declension had taken place in the professed church of God during the days of Malachi. Our text refers to the state of mind and the conversation of those who were evidently strangers to the root of the matter, and the power of saving piety. Our subject leads us naturally to consider,

I. THE COURSE OF PRACTICAL PIETY.
II. ITS ADVANTAGES, and
III. THOSE TO WHOM IT IS EVIDENTLY UNEDIFYING AND PROFITLESS.

I. THE COURSE OF PRACTICAL PIETY. Real practical piety is the fruit of internal religion, the flowing stream from the fountain of the grace of God in the soul. A right state of heart will produce a right conversation and course of life. Our text gives us a three-fold view of practical piety.

1. *It is to serve God.* Not Satan, or self, or the world. Service of God often includes the whole of religion. It embraces a knowledge of God's will, a love to God's laws, a sincere desire to please God, and earnest effort to conform to his revealed mind. It is to recognise God's right over us, God's claim upon us, and a consecration of ourselves to his glory.

2. *To keep his ordinances.* His appointed institutions. He has always had these. The tree of the knowledge of good and evil. Afterwards sacrifices—solemn fasts and feasts—the rites of the tabernacle and temple. These Jesus honored, and at one of these he began his ministry. He went into the synagogue, &c. Christianity has its ordinances; but they are *few*, *plain*, and *spiritual;* but they are also important; blessings to the spiritually minded; first Christians were earnest. They continued steadfast, &c. Forsaking not the assembling of themselves, &c. In a right state of mind we must love and delight in them. Christ demands it—our profession, our comfort, our safety, &c.

3. *To walk mournfully before the Lord.* Now let it not be presumed that religion is essentially melancholy. We are called to joy and gladness. Let the children of Zion, &c. Rejoice in the Lord, &c. Yet there is a sorrow and mournfulness which is eminently religious.

A contemplation of our own defects, failings, sins, &c.

A contemplation of the condition of many of our friends, &c.

A contemplation of the awful state of thousands around us.

Let us see some examples. "I was grieved because of the transgressors." Absalom caused David many tears, "O Absalom, my son," &c. Jesus wept over Jerusalem. But it is a hallowed *sorrow*, not weakening but invigorating. Sorrow possessing the seeds of joy within it. Sorrow that makes the heart better. Now let us look,

II. AT THE ADVANTAGES OF PRACTICAL PIETY. Now these are numerous—present, temporal, spiritual, and everlasting, but,

1. *It is morally elevating and dignifying.* That which makes man more worthy of the powers he possesses and the station he occupies. It is the honor of man to serve God. It lifts him higher in the scale of being, allies him nearer to angels, to seraphim, &c. It expands the mind, cultivates the intellectual faculties, and betters the heart. "Praise the Lord, ye his angels that excel in strength, ye ministers of his, who do *his pleasure.*" The righteous is more excellent than his neighbor.

2. *It is pre-eminently peaceful in its influences.* In keeping God's commandments there is great reward. "Great peace have they who love thy law," &c.—The peace of the pacified conscience,—the peace of God in the soul. "Peace I give unto you," &c.

3. *It is supremely glorious in its results.* It will ensure a personal interest in all the promises. A sufficient supply of Christian graces. A joyous hope of blissful immortality and eternal joy. "Be thou faithful unto death," &c. "Then he will say to the faithful servant—" Well done, good and faithful servant," &c. Then let us consider,

III. THOSE TO WHOM IT IS UNEDIFYING AND PROFITLESS. The formal Jews thus spake, and doubtless they spake the truth. Now practical piety will be so,

1. *To those who are not adapted to its duties.* Thousands are not adapted to the pursuits of literature or science, &c. So to religion. To serve God we must be renewed in our hearts. Translated out of the

kingdom of darkness. If our hearts dislike God, how can we serve him, or be happy in religious duties? Now this many attempt, and of course they fail, and then they utter the truth of the text, and say, " It is vain," &c. It is so to those,

2. *Who mistake the service God requires.* God does not design we should yield meritorious service—service to deserve his favor, to obtain pardon for sin, and a legal right to glory. Self-righteousness only produces slavery, and binds its vassals in galling chains. Those who place their services in the stead of Christ's merits may well say, " It is vain," &c. And it is so, and so it must be,

3. *To those who try to unite the service of the world and of God.* To be gay in the world, and devout at church. To dance in the assembly of the wicked, and pray in the house of the Lord. To be worldly all the week, and devout on the Sabbath, or to divide the Sabbath between amusements and religion. Such persons will ever feel as the ancient Jews did.

4. *Those who serve God with negligence and inconsistency.* The diligent hand maketh rich. Indolence and barrenness, leanness and dissatisfaction. How often this weakness, languor, and death! How sinful and foolish to blame religion! It is want of it, the neglect of it, &c.

APPLICATION.

1. *Ascertain the true scriptural features of true practical piety.* It must begin by faith in Christ, by which guilt is forgiven, and the soul converted to God ; and it must be matured by the grace of God, and redound to his glory.

2. *Urge all to engage in it.* Her ways are ways of pleasantness and all her paths are peace.

SERVICE FOR GOD REWARDED.

" I have given him the land of Egypt for his labour wherewith he served against it, because they wrought for me, saith the Lord God."— EZEKIEL xxix. 20.

THE way of the Lord is often in the sea ; and his footsteps in the mighty deep. To short-sighted mortals often uttterly past finding out. It would indeed be marvellous if creatures of a day, finite beings, could comprehend the infinite and infallible movements of the Ruler of the universe. God has all resources at command. When he designs the punishment of his enemies he can employ famine, or pestilence, or earthquake, or the devouring sword. Tyre had maliciously exulted in the overthrow and misery of the Jews. God therefore employs Nebuchadnezzar to punish their impiety and heartlessness. Having besieged for thirteen years, he found only a heap of desolated walls. The inhabitants had removed their wealth, and of course Nebuchadnezzar was disappointed ; God therefore says to Ezekiel, verse 18, " Son of man," &c. What is the fair deduction to be derived ? That work for God shall not pass unrewarded. If to enemies, how much more to friends ! We observe,

I. THAT IN CARRYING OUT HIS DESIGNS ON EARTH GOD GENERALLY EMPLOYS HUMAN AGENCY. Occasionally there has been miraculous interposition. Deluge ; Babel ; plagues of Egypt ; angels also, both as instruments of terror and mercy. These are the exceptions ; but let us look at the pacific designs of God. His places of benevolence, &c. He emancipated Israel by Moses and Aaron, &c. Employed Joshua, and Caleb, and others, &c. In erecting the tabernacle the nation was employed, all were invited to help ; so also the people united with Solomon in erecting the temple ; thus too Nehemiah in the erection of the second temple ; so also in the establishment of the kingdom of Christ. He chose men to be his heralds, and afterwards the churches were to diffuse the light, &c. of the gospel. In all ages it has been so ; in the Reformation he did thus ; in the revival of religion ; in Britain at the present period ; missions, schools, tracts, temperance, philanthropy, &c. God worketh by his servants.

II. IT IS IMPORTANT THAT WE SHOULD HAVE CORRECT VIEWS OF THE WORK DEVOLVING UPON US. I assume,

1. *That the whole church is to be an active working church.* Christ says to every converted person, " Go work to-day," &c. If so, then there is work suitable to each ; also in each talents suited to the work. The details of duties are various and abundant. Paul often speaks of the active useful women ; see Romans xvi. 1 and 6 ; Philippians iv. 3.

2. *That we labor to know the will of God as to the department of our labor.* " What wouldest thou have me," &c. Go, preach,

&c. Go, entreat sinners to hear, &c. Go, encourage the attentive hearer ; go, speak to the careless benighted family ; go, teach the young, &c. Go, visit the sick, &c. But I am old and infirm ; go, exhibit the fruits of experience, retire often and pray. Hold up their hands who are toiling. Go, give thy wealth; go, use thy influence, &c.

3. *That we should enter upon work in his fear, and in the strength of his grace.* Many commence from novelty—many with confidence—many from self-righteous views —many because others do—no principle in all this. Fruit will not be good ; to be solemnly impressed as to the duty—to be fearful of ourselves—to depend upon God, &c.

4. *That in working for God, we should be constant, persevering, and humble.* Constant —not by fits and starts of impulse, &c. Persevering ; in good and evil report ; not be weary, &c. Humble ; it is our duty— it is our honor. It unites to angels—all our ability God, &c. " Not unto us," &c. " Not I, but the grace of God," &c. We observe,

III. That work done thus for God, shall not go unrecompensed. Now, we must conclude thus,

1. *From the justice of God.* " God is not unrighteous," &c. But especially from,

2. *His goodness.* He is the best of masters, &c.

3. *From his promises.* Every act of self-denial, every gift of a cup of water, &c. He will reward every man, &c. " For your labor shall not be in vain," &c. But what recompense ?

1. *Present.* Approbation of God. His favor and smile. Our own conscience too. A sense of satisfaction, that we are moving in the sphere of providence, &c. Not living altogether in vain. Besides, the direct effect will be our prosperity ; it will improve, exalt, heighten our enjoyments. God will particularly bless, &c. " More shall be given," &c. Spiritual health, &c. The prayers and the blessing of other persons. They will admire, esteem, supplicate, &c. Especially those to whom we have been useful ; but the recompense,

2. *Will also be future.* God will reward with honoring, satisfying, and blessing, in proportion to our exertions and usefulness. The parable of the talents ; so also Christ's disciples at the last day. " I was an hungered," &c. They that be wise, &c. The recompense will be eternal.

APPLICATION.

1. *Who are working for the Lord?* Maintain purity of motives, simplicity, perseverance, &c.

2. *Who will now consecrate their services?* Noble employment ; present happiness, and future reward.

3. *How wretched the servitude of sin!* " The wages of sin," &c. Oh, renounce that service, and master, and avert the doom.

LARGENESS OF HEART.

" Largeness of heart."—1 Kings iv. 29.

Scripture biography is both instructive and useful. There the lives of men are written by the infallible Spirit of God. The portraits are all true, and real—nothing fictitious—nothing colored by the partiality of friendship—nothing penned under the spirit of prejudice—we see men as God saw and decided as to their principles and character. The diversity of scripture biography is one of its chief recommendations. Men of all grades of intellectual distinction and moral worth, of all stations in life, and of all offices in the church, and in the world. The design of Christian biography is to incite our emulation of the holy, wise, and good, and to warn us against the spirit, conduct, and doom of transgressors. Of those who flourished under the old dispensation, Solomon held a distinguished place. The chapter out of which the text is selected, is describing his worldly magnificence and glory. But how really poor and evanescent all this—his own inscription is " Vanity," &c. But the text contains a higher testimonial, and to one part of this our attention is directed. Let us ascertain,

I. In what largeness of heart consists.

II. The means of its attainment. And,

III. The importance of its possession.

I. In what largeness of heart consists. By the heart we mean the whole soul, including the mental and moral powers. A large heart is,

1. *Evangelically intellectual in its attainments.* This is in fact the very atmosphere of its health and existence. Its powers are

all invigorated, and rendered powerful by the acquisition of knowledge. If this is extensively true of knowledge in general, how much more of that which includes the true knowledge of God, and of Jesus Christ! So valuable was this in the estimation of the great apostle that he made this noble avowal, " Yea, doubtless," &c. " This is life eternal, to know," &c. They that know their God shall be strong and do exploits. This is synonymous with wisdom, which is the principal thing—the adorning of the mind, and the very life of the soul. A large heart will be,

2. *Candid and ingenuous in its conclusions.* A bigoted or prejudiced mind is necessarily stunted and dwarfish. Such a state of mind only observes what passes in the limited range of its own sphere—it only judges of its own things—afraid to look abroad—short-sighted—afraid of excellency where it cannot sanction it. Now, all this is petty, and puerile, and quite opposed to a large heart—a large heart rejoices in excellency anywhere and everywhere— a large heart judges of things in proportion to their true importance—it hopeth all things, believeth all things—it proves all things, and holds fast that which is good— it is not blinded by fond partialities, or fettered by senseless prejudices. This is one true sign of largeness of heart. See it in Moses, when envied by the people, " Would that all the Lord's people were prophets!" See it in the Saviour, " Lord, we saw some casting out devils, and we forbade them,"— " Forbid them not, they that are not against us are with us."

3. *A large heart will be noble and enterprising in its aims.* Now, Solomon transacted all on a mighty and princely scale. Think of the temple ; so also Moses in his office of deliverer of the Jews—so also Nehemiah in rearing again the walls of Jerusalem—so the apostles in attempting the conversion of the world by the preaching of the cross. A little heart only ventures on small matters—a great heart ventures much—aims at much—risks much—expends much energy and resolution. Thus Gideon with three hundred men attacks the countless hosts of the Midianites—thus David challenges the gigantic Goliath—thus Luther dared to attack Rome in her strong holds—thus our forefathers ventured their all for conscience' sake—thus our missionaries dare hazard their lives for the gospel's

sake. Who will say that Carey, and Elliot, and Brainerd, and Schwartz, and Williams, and Moffat, were not men of large heart ? A large heart,

4. *Is generous and liberal in its affections.* Avarice acts like the rust—like the blight—like the pestilence. It affects the features of the face—it affects the gait—it affects the speech. And in all cases it withers and petrifies. Look at the opposite class of feelings. The generous and liberal soul is fat, fair, and comely to look at. The eye bright, and the countenance and the expression benignant, the hand open and expanded ; its gait firm and impressive ; it deviseth liberal things. A worldly, avaricious, sordid heart must necessarily be contracted. Benevolence is the true characteristic of a large heart. Notice,

II. How it is to be attained.

1. *It must breathe a pure air.* The sons of the mountain are esteemed strong and hale. Enlargedness of heart is only attainable by fervent prayer. The soul must often breathe where cherubim and seraphim burn. There must be fellowship with God, communion with the skies. Thus Moses was so great—thus Jacob—thus Elijah. And Jesus has shown us the value and essentiality of this.

2. *It must have nutritious diet.* " Thy words were food," &c. The pure unadulterated word of God. The Bereans— Apollos, mighty in the scripture—Daniel's greatness, " In thy laws," &c. See the spirit of the 119th Psalm. To be great spiritually we must come to this banquet, to these streams, &c.

3. *It must have wholesome discipline.* Moral restraint — self-denial essential — cross-bearing—self-despising. The Christian must be a moral wrestler—a spiritual racer ; self-control. " I die daily," &c. This forms the heroic character ; thus was Moses disciplined in the wilderness ; David, the prophets, the Jews, the apostles, &c. Greatness of heart is not to be obtained on beds of down, in rosy paths, in the calm retirement, on the smooth lake ; but in the desert, on the mountain-top, mid the billows' roar, &c.

4. *It must have heavenly influences.* The sunshine, and the rain, the early dews, &c. God makes great by the communications of his Holy Spirit. He gives strength, and might, and power—he enables us to war—

he renders all mighty and effectual. God has engaged to set his people on high, and to make their hands and their arms strong. To give power to the feeble, &c. Thus and thus only can we have largeness of heart. Observe,

III. THE IMPORTANCE OF ITS POSSESSION.

1. *In largeness of heart there is true excellency.* Not in talents merely—not in titles—not in wealth. Man may have all these—and be petty, little, and mean. But greatness of heart is the true dignity and glory of man. This is human nature in its best and most exalted state. This God beholds and loves, &c.

2. *There is the capacity for much enjoyment.* Capacity for elevated enjoyment must depend on the expansion of mind. Savage and philosopher, child and man. Now greatness of heart enables the soul to receive more, hold more, retain more. A regard to our own interests, to our enjoyments, ought to excite us to labor after largeness of heart.

3. *There are greater capabilities of usefulness.* No mighty movement was ever effected without this. There must be some one having largeness of heart. If not, the plan will fail. The arrangement will be insufficient; largeness of heart gives the power of extensive influence. This is true weight of character. Such men are captains in the cause of Christ—the church of God. The institutions of humanity and religion depend much on men large in heart. They are the pillars of society; they move the masses around them. We should all seek after this. We have many instances in our own history—Wesley, Whitfield, Clarkson, Wilberforce, and Chalmers at present in the church of Scotland.

4. *These are more closely conformed to the image of God.* Vastness or immensity is the idea inseparably connected with Deity. Whether wisdom, power, or mercy. In goodness, God is infinite. Oh, how large, how immense the heart of God! The myriads it embraces—the love that fills it—the beneficence that flows from it—the sun and sea the symbols of it.

APPLICATION.

1. *How the subject condemns many of us.* How contracted, frigid, selfish, useless we are!

2. *The church of Christ presents an enlarged sphere for employment.*

3. *May it excite all to seek after spiritual greatness, true largeness of heart.*

A REMEMBRANCE OF FORMER INIQUITIES DEPRECATED

"Oh, remember not against us former iniquities, let thy tender mercies speedily prevent us, for we are brought very low."—PSALM lxxix. 8.

OUR text contains a prayer suited to the pious under all circumstances and occasions. We cannot possibly feel our unworthiness too deeply, or lament our sins too mournfully before the Lord. Let us then apply the text to our own souls, and in the spirit of sincere earnestness cry unto the Lord, "Oh remember," &c. Observe,

I. A PAINFUL RETROSPECT. "Former iniquities." Two classes. Those which,

1. *Were committed before conversion.* These God mercifully blotted out in the day when we came in penitential faith to his footstool. Yet it is well to remember their greatness and number, and hence how rich the mercy that forgave them. Thus Paul.

2. *Those iniquities which have been committed since our acceptance of God.* "For there is not a just man," &c. "In many things we all," &c. Some of these have been sins of infirmity. Some sins of surprise, by the extreme power of temptation. But many have been iniquities of deliberation. All of them full of evil. We ought not to forget them. Should abase us,—keep us contrite,—excite holy abhorrence, &c. "O wretched man," &c.

II. A PRESENT SENSE OF DEPRESSION. "Brought very low."

1. *Sometimes into a low state of enjoyment.* No relish for spiritual things, &c. No peace or joy, &c. Or,

2. *A low state of despondency.* Hope almost extinct,—soul cast down within us. Doubts and fears prevailing. "I shall one day perish," &c. Faint and dismayed.

3. *A low state of affliction.* Bodily weakness, increase of infirmities, &c. Wearisome days and restless nights, &c.

III. A PRAYER SUITED TO THE DISEASE.

1. *Punishment deprecated.* "Oh, remember not," &c. "If thou shouldest mark iniquity," &c.

2. *The tender mercies of the Lord entreated.* "Tender mercies,"—and nothing so suited to us as this, "He delighteth,"

&c. He has said, "I will have mercy on you," &c. "In the midst of wrath," &c.

3. *Immediate help implored.* "Speedily." The present is always God's time, and should it not be ours? "Prevent us." That is, prevent our ruin, or help us despite of our great unworthiness.

APPLICATION.

1. Let a remembrance of past sins excite to watchfulness.

2. God's mercy,—to gratitude and confidence.

3. The penitent may come now and obtain mercy.

GOD'S BLESSING IRREVERSIBLE.

"Behold, I have received commandment to bless, and he hath blessed; and I cannot reverse it."—NUMBERS xxiii. 20.

THE text is connected with three illustrious orders of persons. The first of these is Balak, king of Moab; Balaam, the wicked prophet; and the Israelites, who were journeying to the land of promise. Balak hated the Israelites, and was anxious to bring evil, &c. Balaam hires himself to curse them; but God frustrated his design, and out of the lips hired to curse, God produced a blessing. Here is the wicked prophet's confession, "He hath blessed," &c.

I. GOD'S PEOPLE ARE BLESSED OF HIM.
II. HIS BLESSING CANNOT BE REVERSED.

I. GOD'S PEOPLE ARE BLESSED OF HIM. So it was with Israel of old. God blessed them by wonderful deliverances, and countless tokens of his favor. His compassionate eye was over them in Egypt; his arm led them out; his bounty supplied their wants; his presence guided—shielded them, &c. God has now his Israel in the world: all the spiritual seed of Abraham; all those who have believed in the Messiah; all who are travelling to a better country. On these his blessing rests. He hath blessed,

(1.) With pardoning mercy.
(2.) With delivering grace.
(3.) With spiritual supplies.
(4.) With all needful good. Now this applies to every age of the world—to every true Israelite.

II. HIS BLESSING CANNOT BE REVERSED.
1. *Wicked men would, but cannot.*

2. *Satan would, but cannot.*

3. *God does not desire to do so, and therefore will not.* We may reject the blessing —backslide from God; but his gifts, &c., are without repentance.

APPLICATION.

1. Are we his people?
2. Then we have his blessing.
3. And this is all-sufficient.

THE CLAIMS OF GOD AND MAN.

" Render therefore unto Cæsar the things which are Cæsar's; and unto God the things that are God's."—MATTHEW xxii. 21.

OUR text is connected with a snare which was laid for the Saviour, and by which his enemies proposed to bring him into collision, either with the Roman power, or into contempt with his own nation, the Jews. Christ displayed his consummate wisdom on the occasion by the course which he adopted. Read the context. He not only, however, delivered himself from the artifice of his foes, but he has left his own example and laws for the guidance of his church to the end of the world. Civil governors have claims, and Christians must cheerfully yield them their due. God has claims, and his demands are most sacred and momentous. Let us then consider,

I. THE CLAIMS OF CIVIL GOVERNMENTS, and
II. THE CLAIMS OF GOD.

I. NOTICE THE CLAIMS OF CÆSAR, OR CIVIL GOVERNMENTS. Now the just claims of civil governments are limited to civil exactions, in opposition to religious or sacred claims. Civil governments rightly demand,

1. *Homage and subjection.* Rom. xiii. 1, &c.; 1 Pet. ii. 13, &c.

2. *Obedience, and tribute or taxes.* Christ did this, Matt. xvii. 27; see also Titus iii. 1.

3. *Thanksgiving and prayer to God on their behalf.* 1 Tim. ii. 1, &c. Now these are the claims of Cæsar and civil governments. But civil governments may demand more than their rights; if they do so, they will be either in matters civil or ecclesiastical; if they levy unjust civil exactions, then as citizens they may be peacefully, yet firmly resisted. Interference

in matters of conscience must also be resisted in our character as Christians. This has been repeatedly done. By the three Hebrews, Daniel, Peter, and the apostles, Acts iv. 18. If governments pass the line, and legislate for the conscience, then they intrude on the solemn claims of Deity. Let us then consider,

II. THE CLAIMS OF GOD. Now these are higher and more momentous in their character ; all things pertaining to conscience and religion are God's.

1. *We are to render to God religious belief and homage.* He alone must be enthroned as God, worshipped, &c., have religious veneration, &c. No man, nor saint, nor angel.

2. *To God must be rendered religious awe and fear.* " Fear before him, all the earth." We are to stand in awe—we are to give him reverence and godly fear. " O fear the Lord, all ye his saints," Psalm xcvi. 4, 9.

3. *To God must be rendered praise and thanksgiving.* We are to bless God, to praise him from day to day, to show forth, &c. He is worthy, &c. " Bless the Lord, O my soul," &c.

4. *To God must be rendered our highest love and delight.* Hence that great commandment, " Delight thyself in the Lord," &c. He is to dwell on the throne of our affections, &c. We are to joy in God, giving him in all things the pre-eminence.

5. *To God must be rendered universal obedience.* Now the laws of God must be read and known, understood and practised. Laws of God of two kinds—moral, such as are essential in the fitness of things—resemble his holy nature. Ceremonial or positive—such as the tree in Paradise, command to Lot, &c., Levitical rites, &c. Under the New Testament two of these stand out. Baptism an ordinance appointed by Christ, resting entirely on his authority. The Lord's supper precisely based on the same kind of authority. Both these are to be held sacred and obligatory on all who love him. Now supp'sing any king or government, or ecclesiastical body, prohibit any of these, and demand obedience to their edicts instead of God's, our text allows of no compromise, you are not to consult your ease or profit, God's claims must be yielded to him only. Our subject places civil and religious matters in their true light, and in their due responsibility. Learn,

1. That the Christian religion is favor-able to order and obedience, but it limits the authority of the state to civil concerns. And,

2. It distinctly exhibits true liberty of conscience. Should not this be dear and sacred to every good man, especially when sanctioned by the spirit of our text.

THE LORD'S NAME PLEADED.

" But do thou for me, O God the Lord, for thy name's sake : because thy mercy is good, deliver thou me."—PSALM cix. 21.

THIS is one of the prayers of the devout and holy psalmist. He is describing the sufferings and persecutions he was called to bear from wicked men, and he then breaks forth in the language of the text, " But do thou for me," &c.

I. THE GOOD MAN IS NOT SUFFICIENT FOR HIS OWN SAFETY AND WELFARE.

(1.) His enemies are numerous and powerful.

(2.) He is sojourning in a world unfavorable to piety.

(3.) He has to do with a nature unfriendly to holiness.

II. GOD IS EVERY WAY SUFFICIENT FOR THE SAFETY AND HAPPINESS OF HIS SAINTS. He can ward off every evil weapon ; he can keep from every evil in the world ; he can carry on the good work of grace within us.

III. BELIEVERS SHOULD BY FAITH AND PRAYER PLACE ALL THEIR AFFAIRS IN HIS HANDS.

1. *In trying providences.* We should use the language of the text, " Lord, do thou for me." Give me light ; incline my feet to the right path ; overrule all for my good.

2. *In deep trouble and affliction.* We are often compelled to be passive—to be silent observers ; to resign all into his hands. Then is the time for God to do for us. He ever works. He can deliver out of trouble — support in it — or make it a great blessing.

3. *How appropriate the prayer of the text to the dying hour !* It has been said, dying is hard work. It is very solemn work. The body sinking—earth receding—eternity appearing. How delightful to feel the language of the text, and to breathe it in our dying prayers !

IV. God's name is the best plea by which we can urge our suit.

(1.) Name often signifies nature. For thy nature's sake. Goodness—love—faithfulness.

(2.) His word bears his name, and is full of promises.

(3.) Jesus, especially bears his name.

APPLICATION.

1. Guard against self-direction, and all self-trust.

2. Commit all to God.

PAUL'S PRAYER FOR THE THESSALONIANS.

"And the Lord direct your hearts into the love of God, and into the patient waiting for Christ."— 2 Thessalonians iii. 5.

Our text contains a very striking exhibition of the doctrine of the Trinity, and also a peculiar instance of prayer being addressed to the Holy Spirit. The Lord—the Spirit—direct your hearts into the love of the Father, and into the patient waiting for Christ. Important as was this prayer to the Thessalonians, equally so is it to us. It is essential to our best interests, that our hearts should be thus directed, &c. Observe,

I. The blessings sought.

II. The Being addressed. And,

III. The importance of the prayer.

I. The blessings sought.

1. *The establishment of the heart in the love of God.* They were not strangers to this emotion, but their increase and establishment in it was desirable. The love of God is the supreme esteem and affection of the soul towards him. It is ever associated with holy fear and veneration; it is always connected with grateful emotions; and is attended by delight in God. When this love exists, the love of self cannot be dominant—nor the love of the world—nor the love of sin. This love is a pure flame, consuming the dross of earthliness. It will also identify the soul with the things of God; with his word—his ordinances—his people—his glory, &c. Now, the heart may be directed more deeply into this love—more intently into it—more delightfully into it—more influentially into it. Meditate more

—read more—pray more—praise more, &c.

2. *The patient waiting for Christ.* Now, the Christian expects the second advent of Christ. It is the object of his hopes—it will be the consummation of his desires; but trials, sorrows, and toil intervene. Hence the necessity of patience—" I will wait all the days of my appointed time," &c. Now, this patient waiting implies prayerful waiting; diligent waiting, "Giving all diligence," &c.; resigned waiting, as the apostle, "I have a desire," &c. "Yet to live is Christ," &c. His ways are best, &c. Labor till he calls to rest, &c. "Be faithful unto death," &c. Observe,

II. The Being addressed. The Lord—the Holy Spirit. Now observe,

1. *He has revealed to us the love of God.* Holy men wrote as they were moved, &c. But for this, we should have been in the direst darkness, &c. Now, who so fit as the Revealer to direct, &c.

2. *He has wrought in us the love of God* —Romans v. 5. " He takes of the things of Christ," &c. He convinces—converts—renews, &c. He kindles the flame, &c. Now, how proper that the same blessed Being who began the good work, should also cary it on in the soul !

3. *All gracious influences are produced by the Spirit of God.* Every holy feeling and desire is wrought by him. He incites, quickens, invigorates, sanctifies. We are sustained—preserved by him. To him must we entirely look for the heart being directed, &c. Patience is also one of the fruits of the Holy Spirit. In trouble he cheers. Observe,

III. The importance of the prayer.

1. *The dangers to which we are exposed.* Heart liable to get cold; worldly influences, &c.; carnal influences; Satan tempts, &c.; love may wax cold; the Laodiceans lost their first love, &c. Now, the things of sight, &c., are fraught with peril, &c. How necessary, then, the prayer !

2. *The value of the blessing supposed.* "Love of God," &c. Now, this is the essence of religion—the root—the basis, &c. If this fails, nothing will be left worth possessing; nothing but leaves, or dry branches, &c. All graces and virtues depend on this. The life of God in the soul.

3. *The enjoyment connected with its pos-*

session. This is the highest degree of felicity, to love the best, &c., of beings, and have it reflected, reciprocated, returned with overflowing measure. This is bliss; heaven on earth, &c. Notice,

4. *The many promises made to those who love God*—John xiv. 21. Indeed, all the gospel promises are connected with this. Just think of one declaration, " All things work together," &c. How desirable—how necessary—how essential to pray, " The Lord," &c.

APPLICATION.

1. *Have you the love of God?* &c. Oh! retain, increase, grow, keep yourselves in the love of God, &c.

2. *Are you waiting for Christ?* Expecting his second advent, &c. Keep the eye of faith and hope steadfast; endure patiently; pray in the language of the text.

3. *Direct the mind of all unrenewed persons to these two important principles.*

SPIRITUAL MANIFESTATIONS.

" Judas saith unto him, not Iscariot, Lord, how is it that thou wilt manifest thyself unto us, and not unto the world ?"—JOHN xiv. 22.

CHRIST is here discoursing as to his departure, and addressing words of peace and comfort to his disciples. The whole chapter abounds with rich consolations. How tenderly, how affectingly he introduces the subject, " Let not your heart be troubled," &c. How full and complete his promise, verse 3, " If I go away," &c. He assures them of the Spirit's comforting presence, verse 16. He then urges continued and uniform obedience, verse 21. On this Judas, or Jude, the same who wrote the epistle, asks, " Lord, how is it," &c. Notice,

I. THE NATURE OF CHRIST'S MANIFESTATION.

II. SOME STRIKING INSTANCES OF CHRIST'S MANIFESTATION. And,

III. THE RIGHTEOUS INFLUENCES OF CHRIST'S MANIFESTATION.

I. THE NATURE OF CHRIST'S MANIFESTATION. To manifest is to show forth; to give a display of himself. Now, Christ has manifested himself,

1. *In the gospel.* Here we behold his glory; here his nature—perfections—works —and offices are all revealed. The scriptures testify of Christ. Here he is manifested to mankind. The gospel is thus called the gospel of Christ—word of Christ, &c. The gospel is the field in which the peerless pearl of great price is to be found.

2. *In the soul.* And this is the special spiritual manifestation of Christ. It is the office of the Spirit to " take of the things of Christ," John xvi. 15. Now, there are many seasons in which Christ is manifested to the soul.

(1.) The day of conversion. Soul has been illuminated—converted—brought to Christ. At last venturing on him by faith, Christ speaks. " Thy sins which are many," &c. " Go in peace," &c. " Be it unto thee even as thou wilt," &c.

(2.) The day of trouble; perhaps of bereavement—of losses, &c.—or bodily affliction, &c. How often has he appeared as to his beloved friends of Bethany, " Thy brother shall rise," &c. Or to Mary, who was sorrowing at the sepulchre, " Why weepest thou," &c.

(3.) In times of imminent peril. Thus Peter, when he was walking on the waves; Paul, when the vessel was in danger. He is better than all their fears, " A very present help," &c. " At my first answer no man stood by me," &c. " Yet the Lord stood," &c.

(4.) In the means of grace. Now, this is especially promised, " Wherever two or three are met together," &c. The Old Testament promises, " Wherever my name is recorded," &c. Hence he engages to beautify the place of his feet, &c.—" To glorify the house of his glory." How often have we seen and felt his presence—" Lord, it is good to be here," &c. " One thing have I," &c.

(5.) In the crisis of death—" Yea, though I walk through the valley," &c. In the day of glory—" Beloved, now are we the sons of God," &c. Looking for that blessed hope, &c. " I will receive you to myself." " Then we shall see his face." We pass on to notice,

II. SOME STRIKING INSTANCES OF CHRIST'S MANIFESTATION. There was,

1. *All the divine appearances in the patriarchal and Levitical dispensation.* To Abraham —Jacob—Moses—Joshua — Isaiah—Ezekiel.

2. *The extraordinary manifestation of Christ after his incarnation.* When transfigured on the Mount; after his resurrection; to Saul of Tarsus; to John in Patmos.

3. *The last manifestation will be at his second advent.* When he comes in his own glory, and the glory of his holy angels. When every eye shall see him, &c.

III. THE RIGHTEOUS INFLUENCE OF CHRIST'S MANIFESTATION. A manifestation of Christ to the soul should produce,

1. *Love to Christ.* A contemplation of Christ should charm and captivate the soul. Thus prophets of old, &c. " My heart is inditing," &c. " He is the fairest," &c.

2. *Gratitude to Christ.* His manifestations are condescending—gracious—beneficent. What should be the return ? " I will praise thee with joyful lips," &c. Every emotion ought to be awakened. " Heart overflowing," &c.

3. *Desires after Christ.* If we know Christ at all, we shall desire to know more. So, if we enjoy Christ, &c. The soul delighting in Christ never can say it is enough. As the poet sang—

" If all the world my Saviour knew,
Then all the world would love him too."

4. *Likeness to Christ.* It has been said that intimacy will produce resemblance. This is especially the case in spiritual things. Close connection with Christ will produce Christ's likeness. The manifestation of the gentle Saviour will produce gentleness ; of the lowly Saviour—humility ; of the loving Saviour—affection ; of the holy Saviour—purity ; of the devotional Saviour—a spirit of sanctity ; of the zealous Saviour—a spirit of devotedness to his cause. Such are the influences of Christ's manifestation.

APPLICATION.

1. *Our subject is one of experience to the Christian.* You have realized the text. Christ has manifested himself, &c.

2. *Remember this is your great privilege.* ' Not unto the world." We must come out of the world. He shines in his own sphere ; in the midst of his own family ; in his own temple, &c.

3. *There are manifestations of wrath as well as mercy.* He will display his vengeance to his enemies, &c. " Oh! kiss the Son, lest he be angry," &c.

IMPORTANT ADMONITIONS.

" Therefore turn then to thy God, keep mercy and judgment, and wait on thy God continually."
—HOSEA xii. 6.

THE text is an exhortation to Ephraim, Judah, and Jacob. But it is of equal importance to us. Worthy of our consideration, and adapted to our improvement and comfort. Religion is not so much a series of disjointed acts, as a gracious spiritual habit of mind, from which will arise affectionate regard, and sincere obedience to the divine commands. Notice,

I. THE RELATIONSHIP BETWEEN THE CHRISTIAN AND JEHOVAH. " Thy God." He is the God of all creatures—the creator and universal ruler of all things. But he is only specifically so to those who know, and love, and serve him. As the God of his people,

1. *He is the object of their reverential awe and fear.* God is greatly to be feared, &c. " Oh fear the Lord, all ye his saints." Let us have grace, &c. As their God,

2. *He is the object of their confidence and trust.* They trust in the Lord with all their hearts ; commit all to him, and into his hands. They view him as God all-sufficient. They trust in him at all times.

3. *He is the object of their delight and hope.* " Delight thyself in the Lord." They delight in all that relates to God ; they delight in his name, word, covenant, ordinances, people, &c. All their hopes too have respect to God. Hope then in him ; for all mercies, and blessings, &c. They hope in the Lord their God—they hope in him for perfect salvation and eternal glory. God is only thus the God of those who are in a state of reconciliation with them through Jesus Christ. Faith in Christ enables us to approach Jehovah as our God.

" My God is reconciled,
His pardoning voice I hear ;
He owns me for his child ;
I can no longer fear ;
But now with confidence draw nigh,
And Father, Abba, Father, cry."

II. THE DUTY. To wait upon God. Now we do this in reading his word. In secret meditation—in prayer, &c. &c. But we do this also when we seek to set the Lord always before us. When our hearts are kept in a pious, watchful state. When a devotional and contemplative state of heart is cherished. Now this waiting is to be continual ; as far as possible incessant. It should be so,

1. *Because we have continual wants which must be supplied.* We are in need continually ; we need light, and peace, and holiness continually.

2. *We are exposed to evil continually.* Hence we require guiding, and keeping, and delivering always.

3. *We have continual duties to perform.* For these we need strength, both of disposition and execution. To love and to practise the Lord's commandments.

4. *God is continually able and ready to bless us.* All times and places are alike with him. Wherever, or whatever the condition, he can and will bless us.

APPLICATION.

1. Avoid neglect of communion with God.

2. Pray that in this you may delight.

THE PROGRESSIVE GLORY OF THE CHURCH.

" Who is she that looketh forth as the morning, fair as the moon, clear as the sun, and terrible as an army with banners."—SOLOMON'S SONG, vi. 10.

BOTH Jewish and Christian commentators have, almost by universal consent, considered this Song of Solomon to have respect to the Messiah and his church. It will be seen that the whole has the appearance of a highly-wrought drama, in which oriental imagery of the richest kind is constantly brought before us. The text is considered to be a vivid description of the admiration of the Messiah for the bride—his church ; and as such we shall consider it on this occasion. Many, very many are the figures by which the church is described. It is likened to a flock—to a family—to a vineyard. Our text compares it to the dawn of the morning—the fairness of the moon—the brightness of the sun—and magnificent as an army with banners. We shall consider this description as representing the church under her various dispensations.

I. THE CHURCH, IN ANTEDILUVIAN AND PATRIARCHAL TIMES, LOOKED FORTH AS THE MORNING. Sin and the fall introduced darkness—the darkness of rebellion, ignorance, crime, and wo. The dark cloud of the displeasure of Jehovah would have rested on our world, had not the pur-

poses of mercy and the designs of love surrounded it. How melancholy the loss of paradise—the expulsion from Eden—the lowering curse—the departure of angels, &c. But just when the darkness became thickest, and the peril most imminent, God revealed the purpose of his grace, providing a Saviour in the person of the woman's seed. This was the break of redemption's day to our world. Believers—thus from Abel to Enoch, and from Noah to Abraham, and from Abraham to Moses—enjoyed this dawn. It was their solace, and hope, and joy. Like the opening morning, there was serenity and peace, and the prospect of a coming day. Of Abraham, it is said, he desired to see the day of Christ ; and, elevated on the wings of a soaring faith, he saw it, and was glad.

II. THE CHURCH, UNDER THE LEVITICAL DISPENSATION, WAS FAIR AS THE MOON. The light was of a different kind ; not so much advancement towards day, as the soft and fair reflected beams of the moon.

1. *The changes of the church's condition seem indicated by this metaphor.* Now in Egypt, oppressed—groaning, &c. ; then free, on her way to the land of rest. Now passing through the channels of the Red Sea, and then crossing the arid desert. Now marching under the guide of the mystic pillar, and then conflicting with her numerous adversaries. Now enjoying of mercy, and then punished by the Almighty for their unbelief, &c. A scene of incessant change. Look at its checkered character in the times of the rulers ; in the days of Samuel, and David, and the prophets.

2. *But it also seems to refer to the variety of her ordinances.* How numerous and dissimilar ! Her feasts and fasts ; her sacrifices and offerings ; her ordinances and services ; her oblations and gifts. How extensive her ritual—one revolving series of ceremonies ; yet how superior her state to the nations around ! There, was dense darkness, or here and there merely suspended a flickering lamp of idolatrous superstition. But,

III. THE CHURCH, IN THE CHRISTIAN DISPENSATION, IS CLEAR AS THE SUN. The moon has gone down—the dawn is superseded—the darkness has passed away. Now the people who sat in darkness, &c. The long-expected era of truth and mercy has arrived. Jesus, the Messiah, is the Sun of righteousness, arising with healing beneath his wings. " The illustrious Day-spring," &c. He burst forth on the horizon of our benighted earth, and he goes forth, exclaiming with sublime energy, " I am the light of the world." The church under this dispensation,

1. *Has superior light.* " Life and immortality," &c. The glorious gospel shines —heaven is opened—the divine character unveiled—the way of mercy opened. Now have we Jacob's mystic ladder, for Christ is manifested as the way to the Father ; he is the one way to glory, immortality, and eternal life. Now the pathway to blessedness is opened to a lost and dying world. " Behold, now is the accepted time," &c. The church now has,

2. *Superior enjoyments.* Greater light, but also greater comfort—better promises —richer gifts—superior influences ; the dispensation of the Spirit, as one of sunshine and blessedness. Now, fogs and mists have passed away ; the rains are over, and the winter passed and gone, and the time of the singing of birds is come, &c.

IV. THE CHURCH, IN HER MILLENNIAL GLORY, SHALL BE MAGNIFICENT AS AN ARMY WITH BANNERS. The term terrible, has been variously rendered. By some, " dazzling" as the starry host—awful as the streamers. In the 45th Psalm, it is equally inapplicably introduced. " Thy right hand shall teach thee terrible things ;" it ought to be wondrous things, or glorious things. So the church, in her latter-day splendor, shall resemble an army with her magnificent and victorious banners. Now, these truths are here implied.

1. *The church has her adversaries.* So has it ever been ; so it now is, and will be, until the approaching of the end. All error is adverse ; all superstition is so: all unbelief—all sin. There are the idolatrous armies of heathen nations ; false systems of pagan worship ; the antagonistical army of Mahomet ; the army of unbelieving Jews ; the armies of corrupted Christian systems ; papacy ; the Greek and Russian churches, and all state, earthly, ecclesiastical hierarchies ; all infidelity and sin ; all the powers of darkness, &c. ; earth and hell—men and devils—ignorance and moral evil.

2. *The banner she displays.* Truth and love. It is implied.

3. *That the advances of the church shall be victorious and triumphant.* Of course,

what is written of her Captain applies equally to herself ; see two passages of Ezekiel. " He shall overturn," &c. Rev. vi. 2. It has been commanded by Jehovah of hosts. " Exalted be ye valleys, levelled be ye mountains," &c. that the glory of the Lord may be revealed. The light shall dispel every cloud of darkness ; truth vanquish all error ; holiness subvert all sin ; peace annihilate all war ; and paradise be regained ; the tabernacle of God set up in our world ; while angels and men all join in one wide-spread chorus, loud as the sound of many waters, " Allelujah ! Allelujah ! the kingdoms of this world," &c.

APPLICATION.

1. *Here hope finds a resting-place for her foot, and solid ground for her anchor, both for the past and present.* Great things have been effected in ancient and modern times—the east and the west, the north and the south.

2. *Our exalted privileges call for corresponding exertions.* Day is the period of activity, &c. Our mercies should make us the devoted followers of Christ. This highly-favored church, we are members of. What does Christ claim ? What have we presented ? What are our resolves ? Who will consecrate themselves ?

3. *The enemies of Christ must perish.* He must reign ; he must conquer ; he will have the dominion, and the glory, and the power. Oh! submit. " Kiss the Son, lest he be angry," &c.

PRAYER AND DELIVERANCE.

" Thou calledst in trouble, and I delivered thee."—PSALM lxxxi. 7.

THE literal reference of the passage is the oppressed state of the Israelites, &c., see Exod. ii. 23. Now, the text is equally appropriate to us. Let us make it our own, and see,

I. TO THE PERIODS OF OUR HISTORY WHEREIN IT IS APPLICABLE.

1. *To our state, when convinced of the evil and danger of sin.* When we saw our ruin—felt our misery—awoke to our danger—aroused to consideration. Then we called earnestly with great anxiety, and God delivered. He sent a message of peace ; burst our fetters ; spake the word

forgiveness; took us out of the horrible pit, &c.

2. *To our state when distressed by trouble of mind.* Perhaps beclouded—harassed—perplexed—soul disquieted, &c. "Then we called," &c. "He caused his face to shine," &c.

3. *To seasons of affliction.* Days of sickness—nights of pain, groaning, &c. Many reasons to desire recovery—"O spare me, that I may recover my strength," &c. He heard, and answered, and delivered. Our text will apply to bereavements—to temptations—to persecutions, &c.

II. The effects the remembrance of this should produce on us. God remembers; we ought, but often do not. It is desirable we should do so.

1. It should make us grateful.

2. It should make us humble.

3. It should make us more dependent.

4. It should make us more believing and confident.

THE CHRISTIAN'S SUPREME DESIRE.

"Wherefore we labor, that, whether present or absent, we may be accepted of him."—2 Corinthians v. 9.

A desire to please and obtain the good will of others, is one of the innate feelings of the mind. When perverted or inordinate in degree, it leads to mental imbecility and vanity. The Jews were charged with "coveting the praise of men," and it is represented as a complete barrier to spiritual dignity and improvement, if we seek honor one of another. A due measure of this, however, is necessary and important. A good name is of great price. To be approved of by the wise and good, is ever worthy of our regard and attention; but this feeling is only rightly influenced when it seeks especially and pre-eminently the smile and approbation of God. This is what the apostle expresses in the text. "Whether," &c. This was the testimony Enoch had, before his translation, that he pleased God. We inquire,

I. What it is to be accepted of God? It involves,

1. *Our justification and adoption into his family.* In the sinful state we are condemned; also aliens afar off. Now we must be reconciled, pardoned, justified free-

ly, &c. Brought nigh. Become his children, &c.

2. *It involves conformity to his likeness.* We must resemble him, have his nature and image. In this we were originally formed, &c. "This people have I formed," &c.

3. *It involves a constant desire to please him.* He must have daily homage, constant reverence, &c. He must be supreme, &c. Be the chief, &c. In all things have the pre-eminence. Thus God will love and delight in us—we shall be his treasures, jewels, portion, inheritance, &c.

II. How this is to be obtained. "Wherefore we labor," &c. Now there must be cultivated,

1. *The spirit of unfeigned humility.* "God resisteth the proud," &c. He abases the self-exalted—he that would be greatest must be as a little child—he dwells with the lowly—he honors those who are little in their own eyes, &c. The lifting up of the heart and imagination grieves him. All glorying and boasting offends his Holy Spirit—such fall into the condemnation of the devil.

2. *The spirit of earnest sincerity.* All pretence, or guile, displeases him. He desires truth in the inward parts. "This people draw nigh," &c. "God is a spirit," &c. There must be the avoidance of mere formality. Harmony between the lips, and heart, and life. What is called uprightness, integrity, thoroughness of character—reality of the graces—not spurious virtues—not mere show, &c.

3. *There must be spirituality of mind.* "To be carnally minded is death, &c., but to be spiritually minded is life and peace." The heart the temple of the Spirit—the exercises performed in the Spirit—the soul hallowed by the Spirit—the communion of the Spirit maintained. Now this is entirely opposed to a worldly spirit, or to a carnal spirit, or to a Satanic spirit.

4. *There must be diligence in the Christian life.* "Giving all diligence," &c. Diligence in the public, social, and secret duties of religion—diligence in prayer—in praise—in reading the word, &c. Diligence in the offices we hold—ministerial diligence, &c. Diligent deacons—diligent members—diligent that we may be found of him in peace. Spirit of apathy, loitering, &c., are displeasing to God.

5. *The exhibition of a spirit of goodness*

and mercy. To do good, as the children of him, who is the fountain of goodness to the world. To imitate his benevolence, and beneficence, and pity, and compassion, and mercy. "Be ye merciful," &c. "Blessed are the merciful," &c. "But to do good and to communicate forget not," &c.

6. *A glowing zeal for his glory in the world.* It is good to be zealously affected, &c. To live greatly, yea chiefly, for this. To be zealous for his name, for his day, for his truth, and for his church and kingdom —a zeal that breathes, and lives, and burns, &c. Something like Christ's. Thus we shall not fail to be accepted of him. Consider,

III. SOME MOTIVES WHICH SHOULD INDUCE US TO LABOR FOR THIS.

1. *Because this is the very end of our being.* All other ends are subordinate to this. To enjoy—to be esteemed of men, and the discharge of the duties of this world, &c., are all inferior to this; the mind adapted to this—powers of reflection—emotions of love and veneration—the eyes, the tongue, and all the senses designed for this.

2. *Because this is the design of our redemption.* He redeemed us to, and for himself—redeemed from our vain conversation or conduct. He has bought us, &c. Not our own, or the world's, &c.

3. *This is the direct tendency of grace within us.* His Spirit within us leads, moves, incites to this—aids to this—produces this—every grace refers to this. Faith glorifies God—so hope—so patience, &c.

4. *This is the true dignity of religion.* To have God's good will, approbation, smile, favor, &c. No honor like this, crown of glory—diadem of beauty—elevation over all the distinctions of the world.

5. *This is the felicity of earth, and the bliss of heaven.* The sunshine of heaven within the soul God loves. God delights in me. The fulness and perfection of this constitutes heaven. No higher bliss for created beings. Christ was transported with it. Angels extol it. The concerts of heaven refer to this. Rev. xix. 4, &c.

APPLICATION.

Learn,

1. *What is the grand object of the Christian life.* Study it—ponder it—aim at it.

2. *Let the sinner seek it.* Through Christ —by faith—just now.

DEPRESSION AND HELP.

"The Lord preserveth the simple: I was brought low, and he helped me."—PSALM cxvi. 6.

OUR text expresses the general experience of the people of God. Who cannot apply it to their experience at one time or other? The life of the Christian is diversified by changes, many of these are of an afflictive character, and tend to bring them into low and sorrowful circumstances, &c. Let us review some of these seasons, and see how the Lord hath helped us, &c.

I. WE WERE BROUGHT LOW BY A SENSE OF OUR GUILT AND DANGER. A state of sin is a low estate of degradation and misery. Horrible pit, &c. Previous to conviction, men are proud and elated. Often self-boasters. The gospel, which goes on the principle of our ruined state, makes men sensible of it before they are delivered from it. See David—Publican, Saul of Tarsus. Prostration goes before exaltation; mourning before joy, &c. He lifts such up, and delivers them.

II. BROUGHT LOW BY BODILY AFFLICTION. How soon is the body diseased—how frail, &c. How often most here have thus suffered; some many times. The Lord helped us—checked the disease—healed the malady—gave back health.

III. BROUGHT LOW BY TROUBLE. Sometimes in business—in circumstances—in family bereavements, &c. The Lord helped us, gave strength, and grace, and comfort.

IV. BY TEMPTATIONS. Often distressing, surprising, &c. Darts—arrows—torrents —sift as wheat, &c. The Lord sustained, delivered, &c. Thus fulfilled his own word, &c.

V. BY DOUBTS AND FEARS. These sink the spirits—darken the mind, &c. Bring very low, almost into despondency. The Lord helped—made his face to shine, &c. Applied some promise, &c.

VI. BROUGHT LOW BY INFIRMITIES AND SINS. All these frailties and sins sink and keep us low, and they would destroy our hope, &c., as they did our peace; but for the help of the Lord. He keeps, restores, &c. Our subject should lead us to gratitude and trust.

ON AN INCREASE OF FAITH.

" And the apostles said unto the Lord, Increase our faith."—Luke xvii. 5.

All who read the scriptures must perceive the great importance attached to faith. It is represented as the first grand step in acceptable piety. "He that cometh," &c. It is represented as the principle of the Christian life. "Now the just shall live by faith." It is represented as giving potency to prayer. "Whatsoever ye ask in faith," &c. It is that which alone can prepare for solemnities of a dying hour. "All these died in faith." Then, our attention may be well directed to the prayer of the text, "Lord, increase our faith." Faith and its increase; prayer to that end; and the reasons on which it is grounded, are the points to which your serious attention is solicited. Our subject leads us to consider,

I. Faith. Faith may be considered as the credit given to testimony. A belief that what is stated is true. Christian faith therefore is the firm persuasion of what God has testified to us in his word. But it also is connected with reliance, truth, or dependence. That faith which is justly denominated saving or evangelical faith, is the credit given to the gospel testimony concerning Christ, and the soul's resting on the foundation there laid, for pardon and eternal life. Now faith must never be confounded with sight, for it has reference to things unseen. Nor with reason, which judges according to its own powers, and capacity, and information; an unscientific Hindoo could never comprehend the nature or possibility of ice. Nor with opinion; I may think this system is right, or give my assent to the other; but opinions are widely different to faith. Nor with impulse, the mere internal emotion or mental excitement. Neither must we separate faith from knowledge, the subject must be revealed, and that revelation known by us before it can be believed. But in reference to faith, notice,

II. Its increase. Faith may increase, —hence we read of weak faith,—of little faith,—and faith as a grain of mustard seed. Faith, like all other moral and spiritual principles and graces, is small in its commencement, and therefore its growth and culture must be sought.

1. *Faith may increase in clearness.* As we apprehend and understand the testimony more fully, so faith becomes more bright. As the character of Christ is more opened to us, will our confidence in him be increased.

2. *Faith may increase in its strength and vigor.* Weak faith falters, wavers, sinks, but by cherishing the principle of faith it grows and obtains a firm hold on the mind. We become settled and grounded in the truth. Adhere more closely and firmly to the founder.

3. *Faith may increase in experimental assurance.* The penitent believes, and is forgiven. Often especial need for faith; he is tempted, believes, and overcomes;—sorrowful, believes and enjoys comfort, &c. These acts are repeated, and thus faith becomes more confident and ripens into experimental assurance. Let us look,

III. At prayer having respect to this especially. Now here let us guard against a common error,—we are not to pray for faith as if the whole rested with God's communications. He has already given us the testimony,—and the great object of faith,— and capacity and power to know and believe. But by spiritual influences he can excite to greater attention,—inspire with higher ardor, give power and success to the means. Cause his sun to shine and his dews to fall. Just as we pray for daily bread, yet toil and labor, and use the means. Such then are the views and feelings we should cherish in seeking an increase of faith. Observe, then,

IV. The reasons on which this prayer may be urged. Consider,

1. *The connection between strong faith, and the fruitfulness of all the other graces.* Just as faith is, so will hope be. So also will love,—faith works by love. And so will be zeal, humility, and patience. Observe, also,

2. *Its influence on our various exercises.* Prayer, praise, reading and hearing, &c.

3. *Consider its essentiality in trying and difficult situations.* When our profession is tested. Perhaps forbidden to profess, or perhaps sneered at, &c. Look at Moses. he feared not the wrath of the king. Look at Peter and John, "We ought to obey God," &c. Or, secondly, when sacrifices are to be made. As Abraham who was called to leave his country and then to offer Isaac, &c. When the mysteries of religion are assaulted. Now as to the sublime

doctrines of Christ's divinity, or the atonement, or the Spirit's influence. Men grasp at these in the self-sufficiency of reason, and laugh, &c. Faith rests on the testimony, God is true, " the mouth of the Lord," &c. Or when suddenly attacked by powerful temptations, as Peter was. When his darts fly in every direction, we resist, steadfast in the faith. " Shield of faith," &c. Or when passing through dark and afflictive dispensations. Little faith will do in prosperity, in the calm, &c. But when adversity, the dark clouds, &c. No fruit on the vine, nor herd in the stall, comforts all fleeing, &c. It was faith that sustained Jacob, and Aaron, and David, and Paul, &c. Or in the midst of old age, infirmities, and approaching death. Faith waits as well as trusts. " I know that my Redeemer liveth," &c. " We know that if this, the earthly house of our tabernacle," &c. He looks steadily and fearlessly at the swellings of Jordan, and sings,

" Fearless of hell and ghastly death," &c.

APPLICATION.

1. Let the increase of faith be earnestly and daily sought.

2. To those who have it not. With all men who have not faith there must be guilt, and wretchedness, and despair. Oh! receive the gospel, &c.

THE PIOUS RESOLVE.

" I will meditate also of all thy work, and talk of thy doings."—PSALM lxxvii. 12.

THE resolution of the text is worthy of our attention, for it is the language of an eminent saint, the pious and devout psalmist. He has been expressing his afflictions and sorrows, and his doubts and fears. He then resolves on the course he would adopt. " I will remember." " Then I will meditate," &c.

I. ON GOD'S DEALINGS WITH US, IT IS WELL TO MEDITATE. And here we shall be struck,

1. *With the graciousness of their origin.* He sought us—condescended to ask our love,—opened his heart and entreated. Oh yes, from him it sprung, and not us. Without worthiness or merit on our part. God's dealings with us are,

2. *Faithful in their continuance.* He has

not left or forsaken,—he has not neglected or forgotten,—has not failed, &c. His dealings,

3. *Have been peculiarly forbearing and tender.* His mercy might often have clean gone. Provoked, he might have given us up. He might in wrath have cut us off as fruitless branches. Oh, how differently has he treated us, &c.

II. THE LORD'S DEALINGS TOWARDS HIS PEOPLE FURNISH PROFITABLE MATTER FOR CONVERSATION. " From the fulness of the heart." Conversation on the Lord's dealings,

1. *Has been the practice of the godly in all ages.* David. " Come all ye," &c. " They that feared the Lord," &c. Woman of Samaria. Disciples going to Emmaus.

2. *It is productive of good to our own souls.* It gives the soul relief. Improves the affections, &c. It is the right and best use of the gift of speech.

3. *It is often beneficial to others.* Who has not been edified by the conversation of the pious? " A word fitly spoken, how good it is!" It may enlighten and save in the sphere in which we move.

4. *It glorifies God.* God's name, and government, and cause, we honor. Silence is often guilt. The two must go together, meditation and conversation.

THE VARIOUS KINDS OF PRAYER.

" Because he hath inclined his ear unto me, therefore will I call upon him as long as I live."—PSALM cxvi. 2.

IT has been well said, that prayer is the breath of the new man—the motion of the renewed heart, and is essential to the existence of Christian life in the soul. A prayerless individual is a rebel in spirit, and robs God of that homage which he has justly claimed from his intellectual creatures. Let us, then, consider the various seasons and times peculiarly appropriate to this exercise. But we first premise, that the Christian will be anxious to cherish constantly the habit and spirit of prayer. It is desirable to unite it with every important act of our lives; to be instant in prayer; yea, to pray without ceasing. We refer,

I. To PUBLIC PRAYER—THE PRAYER OF THE SANCTUARY OF THE LORD. Within the tabernacle and the temple public prayers were regularly presented. Who can read the consecration—the prayer of Solomon, without being affected with the true sublimity and hallowed grandeur which must have struck the congregated worshippers, 2 Chron. vi. 12–21. God said, "My house shall be called," &c. How solemn is the sight of a congregation in the act of prayer! Think of the Being addressed; see the humble appearance of the worshippers—the exercise itself. Who can tell the variety of feelings and emotions agitating the bosoms of the various persons present!

(1.) The minister prays for various orders and classes of *men*. For the disciples of the cross; the tempted—the tried—the feeble—the disconsolate, &c. For the young—for the aged, &c. He prays,

(2.) For various orders and classes of *sinners*. And there is in the congregation a mother, whose son is a prodigal; a father, whose daughter is dissipated—a trifler; a child, whose parents never pray; brethren, whose relations are out of the way, &c. He prays,

(3.) For persons in various *conditions*. For the sick—and some have their best beloved friends on the bed of languishing; for persons who are exposed to peril by sea and land—and some have friends on the treacherous deep, &c. Now, public prayer, designed as it is to be general, finds a response in the various hearts who unite in supplication before God. We,

II. REFER TO CHRISTIAN SOCIAL PRAYER. The Jews had places set apart for prayer. Here it was where Paul and Silas found Lydia; out of the city, "where prayer was wont to be made." The early Christians, too, often assembled together for mutual prayer. These are very important exercises, and deserve the serious consideration of all the members of Christ's church. Now, here we remark, that it is the duty of the brethren to cherish the spirit, and cultivate the gift of prayer. No person should do any thing for God without diligently preparing for it, and doing it in the best possible manner. And what shall I say of the members of the church who ever neglect these sacred and profitable opportunities? What more *necessary* than prayer? What more *beneficial*? We know of no means by which the church can better promote its prosperity.

III. WE REFER TO FAMILY PRAYER. If religious worship should be perpetuated, surely the family ought not to be without it. Joshua said, "As for me," &c. David returned to "bless his household." Even pagans love their household gods and family altars. Now, as to the frequency of family prayer, much must depend on the circumstances of the family. Some pious households have it at morning, noon, and evening; others, morning and evening; and others, only at one of these seasons. At any rate there ought to be family prayer—reading and thanksgiving. Family prayer ought to be exceedingly *simple*, and *easy* to be understood. It should also be *brief*, or children will feel it as a burdensome task. It should also be *regular*. Order and perseverance are essential in every good work.

IV. WE REFER TO SECRET PRAYER. Private prayer is a grand and secret source of the soul's prosperity. It will be the key to public blessings; it is suited to full and free confession; it is a refuge to which we may have instant access. Eminently sanctifying, and enriching, and consolatory to the soul. All the really devout have been distinguished for it. Rules here unnecessary; none but God and the soul present; *at all times*.

APPLICATION.

1. Have we duly regarded these various seasons of prayer, and improved them?

2. Do you discriminate, &c.? This is of the utmost importance.

3. Let heads of families cherish the gift, &c.

4. Let all pray for mercy.

ENCOURAGEMENT TO PRAY.

"Call unto me, and I will answer thee, and show thee great and mighty things which thou knowest not."—JER. xxxiii. 3.

OUR text contains both a warrant and encouragement to pray. The words were addressed by the Lord to Jeremiah in prison; but the spirit of them is applicable to all the saints of the Most High. Prayer is both the duty and privilege of all the children of God—a duty most binding, a privilege most exalting and precious. Let us consider,

I. THE EXERCISE. And,

II. THE PROMISE IN THE TEXT.

I. The exercise. "Call unto me."
Now observe,

1. *Who calls to this exercise?* see v. 2.
We do not wonder that he should call us to
reverence, worship, praise, obey, &c. But
in the text he calls us to pray, to ask blessings, &c., to be enriched by him, &c.
Consider,

2. *Who are called to this exercise?* Jeremiah in the text, all Christians, all the children of God. The text supposes prayer
may be undervalued, neglected, and that
there may be intermissions, &c. We require to be stirred up, the fire may go out,
or the mere form may exist. Indeed, in one
sense, God desires all intellectual, fallen
creatures to pray; he willeth the salvation of all men, &c.

3. *What is the nature of the exercise
itself?* "Call unto me." That is, pray,
ask of me, &c. Now this calling implies
a *firm persuasion* that he exists, that he is
accessible, that he can hear, that he is a re-
warder, &c. It implies also a *sense* of our
need, a desire for the good we want, and
that desire expressed, made known in words
to God. "Call unto me." Now this exercise is not limited to *place*. All places
may be hallowed by the voice of prayer.
Nor to *time*. On all occasions, and at all
seasons, we may make known our supplications, &c. Three times, or seven times
a day. In trouble or in joy, in health or in
sickness, in prosperity or in adversity, in
safety or in peril, &c. Then as to the
manner of calling upon God. Should not
there be *profound reverence?* unaffected
simplicity?—sincere *earnestness?*—hopeful
expectation?—We say nothing as to the
brevity or length, as to extempore or being
aided by useful forms; but let the soul and
iip, the heart and spirit, be given up fully
in the exercise. Notice,

II. The promise in the text. "I will
answer," &c. The promise is two-fold,
"I will answer thee," &c. That is, I will
regard and attend to thy call. It does not
mean that God will invariably grant the
request, or that he will immediately remove
the source of complaint; but the prayer
shall meet with the gracious attention of
God, and, in the end, the suppliant shall be
satisfied. There are two cases of very
immediate answers being given to prayer.
Daniel, see Daniel ix. 20, &c. In the case
of *Peter*, Acts xii. 5–13. In many cases
it is obvious that the answer is delayed, be-

cause we are not sufficiently intent, &c.
But the best results shall always follow
from our supplications. "God will answer." He can do so, he delights to do so,
has he not done so? Then, in addition to
the answer, the promise extends to *the revelation of wondrous things.* It was often in
connection with the prayers of the prophets,
that God revealed his mind and purposes to
them. So, too, the high-priest only received
the communications of the divine will in
connection with sacrifices, offerings, and intercessions. *Solomon*, in answer to prayer,
received the gift of a great and enlarged
mind, so that he is renowned as the wisest
of all mere men. This is the promise, "If
any man lack wisdom," &c. It is also
said, that "believers have received an unction from the Holy One," &c. Now observe, in answer to prayer,

1. *We may expect providential direction.*
"Acknowledge him in all thy ways," &c.
Thus God directed Jacob, gave much wisdom to Joseph, and enabled Daniel to be a
revealer of secrets. God will guide his
people by a right way if they call unto him.

2. *He will enable them better to comprehend the meaning of revelation.* "Open
thou mine eyes," &c. There is such an
infinity of meaning, such wondrous heights,
such depths, such profound mysteries, &c.
It is written, "The secret of the Lord is
with them that fear him, and he will show
them his covenant." Humility of mind
and devotion of spirit, of all things, will fit
us best for a right understanding of the
word and will of God.

3. *God often gives bright anticipations of
future glory.* The most elevated seasons
are those associated with prayer. It was
while praying that Christ was clothed with
his transforming glory. Often saints, when
on the verge of the eternal world, have had
the most rapturous visions of the joys of the
beatified, and the bliss of heaven. One
striking case is recorded in the scriptures.
Stephen, when being massacred, prayed,
and the dying martyr exclaimed, "I see
the heavens opened, and the Son of man
standing on the right hand of God."

APPLICATION.

1. *Does not the subject recommend prayer
to the prayerless?*

2. *Does it not urge a more faithful regard
to it on the prayerful?* It is the bulwark
of our safety, the channel of our supplies,

and that which gives mental and moral greatness to the mind. It is the *priestly work* of Jesus Christ. He ever lives to pray, to make intercession, &c.

THE IMPORTUNATE WIDOW.

" And he spake a parable unto them to this end, that men ought always to pray, and not to faint," &c.—LUKE xviii. 1–8

THE parables of Christ were often designed to illustrate specific doctrines or duties. Several were designed to simplify the profound mystery of redemption in the love of God, and gift of Christ, to the world. The parables of the lost sheep and the marriage feast, were of this class. Others to show the true way of salvation, and the readiness of God to save sinners, as the beautiful parable of the prodigal son. Others the right modes and great advantage of hearing the gospel, as the parable of the sower. Not to proceed farther, our text is designed to urge the duty, and enforce the great importance of prayer. Often the moral or practical inference follows the parable, but here it precedes it. Let us look,

I. AT THE PARABLE ITSELF. Three persons are presented to us.

1. *A judge*, described as unjust—more properly a governor having executive power invested in his own hands. His character, " without fear of God." Under no religious restriction, acting irrespective of God's will or authority, " Nor regard for man." Had no respect to public opinion, treated with contempt the estimate others might form of him. By one of these evil principles he stifled conscience. By the other gave way to the most unjust decisions. Love of money might be his crying sin ; or it might be love of pleasure, mental indolence. A worse character for a judge or governor you cannot conceive.

2. The second character was *a widow*—deprived of the desire of her eyes, the stay of her arm, and the counsellor of her mind. It has been ever accounted a glaring sin to oppress the widow, yet in Christ's time how common ! How Christ charged the Pharisees with devouring widows' houses ! A widow's sorrows and the orphan's tear, have often been produced by the unprincipled and avaricious. This widow had a suit, a case of obvious wrong.

3. The other person introduced is *her adversary*, or more properly her oppressor. " Avenge me," or " decide for me against my oppressor." For a while the judge had no regard. Probably her oppressor had influence or wealth to support him, and she neither. What little prospect of success ! But she perseveres, persists in her plea. Her cry continues to reach his ear till at length he says, &c., v. 4 and 5.

II. LET US CONSIDER ITS DESIGNED APPLICATION. " That men ought to pray," &c. To pray—what is it ? To tell God our wants, and seek his blessing—to pour out our hearts—to make known our requests. Let us look at some reasons why men ought to pray.

1. *Prayer is the language of nature.* All creatures have their respective modes of expressing their wants. The young lions, the birds of the air, &c. The crying of the child. Look at man in imminent peril. Look at man in deep suffering, and how natural is prayer !

2. *Prayer is recommended by sound reason.* Is it not reasonable that a child should depend and seek the aid of the parent ?—That weakness should lean on strength ?—ignorance look up to wisdom ? —penury crave the aid of affluence ? How dependent is man ! How weak ! How ignorant ! &c.

3. *Prayer is an essential part of all religions.* The Mahommedan has his seven daily prayers. The pagan idolater prays. The savage in peril, &c., prays. The American Indian addresses the great Spirit. Shall not then Christians pray ?

4. *Prayer is constantly urged in the volume of revelation.* It is the soul of devotion, and devotion is the very atmosphere of true piety. Examples are placed before us. Abraham, Elijah, David, the prophets, the apostles, &c. The Son of God our divine example. The spirit of prayer, the success of prayer, the various kinds of prayer, are all introduced to us here.

5. *Our necessities should induce us to pray.* What do we not need ? Constant mercy, daily grace, ceaseless help. Weaker than a bruised reed, &c. Our text refers to the adversaries of God's people, v. 7, &c. Our adversaries and oppressors are many : the great adversary, wicked scorners, &c. ; persecutors, &c. Now to contend with these, we are not able. What

must we do ? Appeal to God, commit all into his hands. He will deliver you, justify you, and punish your unrepenting enemies. The text was literally fulfilled in the history of the Jews. In their destruction, &c.

We ask, *What encouragement the text gives to prayer ?*

(1.) Consider the Being we address. Just, holy, good, our Father, Redeemer, Friend, &c., &c.

(2.) Consider our own condition. His children. Redeemed ones, and so much beloved.

(3.) Consider his tender compassion. He invites—he expostulates with us—he delights to answer prayer.

(4.) Consider his great promises; promises for every state and condition, and based on truth, power, and love.

APPLICATION.

1. *To the prayerless.* A state below the heathen. Practical atheism. Never to draw near to God. The wicked through the pride of his countenance, &c. *Notice some excuses*—Forget—cannot—feel sinful, &c.

2. *To those who do pray.* Let there be simplicity, fervor, perseverance.

MUTUAL PRAYER.

" Pray for one another."—JAMES v. 16.

PRAYER has been represented as consisting of a variety of parts. Dr. Watts and others, have shown that from scripture examples we should have respect to adoration, invocation, confession, petition, pleading, intercession, and thanksgiving, in our addresses to God. It is clear, however, that we have few instances where this rule has been fully and systematically observed by those whose prayers are recorded in the sacred pages. While we need not contend for these things as a fixed rule or system, yet it is desirable that we should study the models given in the Bible, and come as near to them as we can. Our subject refers to that kind of prayer called intercession, or in the words of our text, " praying one for another."

I. PRAYERS FOR ONE ANOTHER SHOULD HAVE RESPECT TO THE VARIOUS BRANCHES OF OUR FAMILIES. Parents should pray for their children, as Abraham did for Isaac and Ishmael. As Jacob did for his sons and grandsons. In like manner children should pray for their parents. Do not our offspring need the guarding and guiding blessing of Jehovah ? And do not parents need the sustaining and comforting enjoyments of the divine presence ? Brethren and sisters should pray for one another. Relations and friends should be mutually remembered at the throne of grace. There are perils and sorrows connected with all these associations. Nothing can sanctify them but praying one for another.

II. PRAYERS ONE FOR ANOTHER SHOULD HAVE RESPECT TO THE SPIRITUAL COMMUNITY OF THE FAITHFUL. We should remember our spiritual as well as natural connections. All believers are one family—one seed—one holy house, built up for an habitation of the Spirit of God. Their wants, enemies, and circumstances, are extensively the same. They are one body, of whom Jesus is Lord and head. Then they ought to pray one for another. The apostles were very solicitous to have the prayers of the churches. " Brethren, pray for us," &c. In another place, " and for me that a door of utterance," &c. In return, how often he avows his prayers for the church of Christ, see Rom. i. 9 ; Col. i. 3 ; Phil. i. 3. " Grace be with all them who love the Lord," &c. It is scarcely to be expected, that people can profit by the labors of any man for whom they do not pray. We should not look for a preacher being useful, however he might preach, if he did not pray for his people.

III. PRAYERS FOR ONE ANOTHER SHOULD RESPECT THE NATION IN WHICH WE LIVE. What is called patriotism is often a selfish thing—whenever a people would seek their own prosperity, at the expense of another nation's miseries and groans. Christian patriotism is a love of our country's excellence—a desire for our nation's real welfare and spiritual prosperity—a desire for national intelligence, righteousness, purity, and benevolence. Only such a nation is truly great in the sight of angels and God. In praying for our nation, what a variety of scenes rush before the contemplative mind ! There are the *rich*, the *dignified*, and the *opulent*. What do they need ? Why, every thing. Are they not, as to spiritual things, generally poor, wretched ? &c. Oh ! what peril they are in ! What a change as to their present state, if they die without an interest in the Saviour's love! Hence we are exhorted to pray, see 1 Tim. ii. 1. Then there is *the opposite class* of our fellow-countrymen. The great mass of the poor. The thousands of the sick, and wretched, and dying. Oh, how they need the divine blessing! How we ought to feel and pray for them! There is yet *another division.* The enemies of God. Blasphemers—the haters of Christianity. While we abhor and detest their principles, we should love and pray for their souls.

IV. PRAYERS FOR ONE ANOTHER SHOULD REGARD THE WHOLE FAMILY OF MAN. Our prayers should extend to all men. God's goodness does so—Christ's redemption does so—and so should our intercessions. What a sublime subject for devotional contemplation! A world in arms against God, under the power of the evil one—one dreary desert-savage ferocity, cruel paganism, senseless idolatry, sensual Mahommedanism—blinded Judaism, superstitious forms of Christianity; and only here and there a green verdant spot of purity. What has to be done before the mountains are brought low, the valleys exalted, and the world saved! "Lord, send out thy light and truth," &c. "Thy kingdom come," &c. In this vast world only here and there a Christian missionary. How should we not feel and intercede for them, and for an increase of laborers! Let me urge the exercise of mutual prayer upon you by a few considerations.

1. *We should thus pray for one another because it is the expressed will of God.* It is his command, therefore our duty. "God forbid that I should sin," &c.

2. *We should do so, because it will tend to our own spiritual improvement.* It will tend to soften our hearts—enkindle the tender emotions of sympathy—produce benevolent desires—make us more generous and useful.

3. *We should do so, because it will increase our conformity to Christ.* What a model have we in Christ! How he loved, and labored, and prayed! His last intercession for his murderers. Now, Christianity is Christ's mind in us.

4. *Gratitude for the prayers in which we have been interested should induce us to do so.* You cannot tell what you owe to this account. Eternity alone will develop it. To parents, friends, &c.

5. *It will procure for us the especial blessing of God.* Our affinity will be closer to Deity; our likeness greater; our enjoyments sweeter, &c. Do not forget to pray for yourselves, &c.

THE FERVENT PRAYER.

"The effectual fervent prayer of a righteous man availeth much."—JAMES v. 16.

OUR present design is to exhibit before you the powerful efficacy of those prayers which are earnestly and sincerely offered to the Lord. The profane live without fearing or acknowledging God; the formalist merely says prayers, and is a stranger to the spirit of prayer; the worldling asks, "What profit shall I have?" &c. To the righteous, there is the great assurance of the text, "The effectual," &c. Observe,

I. THE CHARACTER DESCRIBED. "The righteous." This is not one of man's natural characteristics. "None are righteous," &c. "All have sinned," &c. In order to the acquirement of this character,

1. *We must be accepted and justified by God.* Our guilt must be cancelled—all our sins forgiven. No longer culprits condemned, but freely saved by divine grace. This is the basis of all righteousness; this is that evangelical righteousness which we receive by faith in Christ Jesus, Gal. ii. 16.

2. *We must be renewed in our hearts.* A spiritual change must take place in the soul. "Old things," &c. "Born again," &c. "The heart of stone taken away," &c. A new heart implanted. Now this is experimental righteousness, and the root of all genuine holiness; for this includes the indwelling of the Spirit of God, the sanctifier.

3. *There must be righteousness of life.* A regard to God's righteous commandments; walking in his statutes and ordinances to do them. What doth the Lord require of his own adopted children? "Do justly," &c. He that doeth righteousness is righteous. "This is the love of God, that we keep," &c. Consider,

II. THE PRAYER SPECIFIED. Not every prayer, even of the righteous, of which our text speaks; but the "effectual fervent," &c. By some this is rendered, "the inwrought prayer of the heart." It clearly includes,

1. *Internal sincerity.* The opposite of formality; the opposite of double-mindedness.

2. *Impassioned ardor.* The opposite of listlessness; opposite of dulness and supineness. When the soul longeth, yea, fainteth after God. The apostle represents it as travailing in birth. Where the soul is inflamed, and burning with holy desire and powerful emotion.

3. *Importunate pleading.* Where the soul will not have any refusal or delay. Where every thing is argued and urged *with* God; such as his own nature. Promises. Christ's merits, &c. Former mercies, &c.

> " Lord, I will not let thee go,
> Till a blessing thou bestow:
> Do not turn away thy face,
> Mine's an urgent, pressing case :
> No, I must maintain my hold,
> 'Tis thy goodness makes me bold :
> I can no denial take,
> When I plead for Jesus' sake."

4. *Believing perseverance.* To pray with all prayer and perseverance; to keep the eye of faith fixed, and withdraw it not. The hand of faith held out and open, without wavering. With humble boldness standing before the gracious throne, asking until we have obtained the blessing for which we pray. Notice,

III. The results affirmed. " Availeth," &c. That is, they succeed extensively; gain the point; obtain the blessing. Let us cite two or three cases illustrative of this :—Jacob at Penuel, Gen. xxxii. 24–30; Moses at Rephidim, Exod. xvii. 8–12; Aaron and the plague, Num. xvi. 44; Hezekiah and the sentence of death, 2 Kings xx 1. Singular case mentioned in the life of John Knox. It is said Queen Mary feared his prayers more than all the armies of Europe. One night he and several friends were praying together; and as they prayed, Knox said that deliverance was come. He could not tell what, but he felt God was answering their prayers. The next day the news of Mary's death arrived. Let these examples suffice, with the gracious and positive assurance of the Saviour, " Whatsoever ye ask the Father," &c. We see that the effectual fervent prayer of the righteous has availed to the removal of evil—to the staying of wrath—to the ac-

complishing of victories—to the opening of heaven! Who does not see, then, how God has set his broad seal of approbation upon the exercise of prayer?

APPLICATION.

1. *How desirable to be acquainted with the achievements of prayer!* We should study these until we are filled with hope, &c., through believing.

2. *How we should cherish the spirit of prayer!* " I will pour out," &c. How desirable the grace of supplication! How necessary! How important!

3. *Let us endeavor to pray differently.* Aim at the fervent effectual prayer, &c.

4. *See the connection between prayer and character.* The effectual prayer of the *righteous*—such God will hear; and the prayers of such will increase their conformity to the divine nature and likeness. They mutually tell upon one another.

INTERCESSIONS.

" I exhort, therefore, that first of all, supplications, prayers, intercessions, and giving of thanks be made for all men."—1 Tim. ii. 1.

All Christians admit the necessity and importance of prayer. Indeed, prayer forms a part of every system of religion, whether true or false, in the universe. But prayer has a variety of branches, and is presented under various aspects. Our text includes several of these. Supplication signifies deprecation of judgments, or evils; prayer signifies petitions for blessings required; intercessions are addresses to God on behalf of others, for their defence or salvation. I wish us at this time to consider that branch of prayer denominated in our text, " Intercessions." Several questions will tend to open the subject to our understanding, and, I trust, profit.

I. Who is the proper object of intercession? " God." All worship must be given to him. The Father is chiefly to be addressed in prayer. The apostle says, " I bow my knees unto the Father of our Lord Jesus." So Jesus taught his disciples to say, " Our Father," &c. Yet, we have instances of prayer to Christ, who in his divinity is equal with God, and may receive equal honor and worship. Thus Stephen, " Lord Jesus, receive," &c.; and

added, " lay not this sin to their charge."
Yet, viewing Christ as the Mediator, we
say prayer should rather be made to the
Father, in the name of Jesus Christ. All
prayer to angels, or glorified spirits, is derogatory to Christ, and robs him of his intercessory work and glory.

II. On whom does intercession devolve? Upon all the people of God; all
who pray for themselves. Of course, it is
mockery to intercede for others, and neglect prayer for our own souls. All ministers and teachers of religion; all parents
and guardians of youth; all deacons and
officers of the church; all who love God
and their fellow-men. Every Christian is
to be an intercessor for others.

III. For whom should intercession be
offered? Our text replies, "For all men."
Our intercessions are to be as enlarged as
the world, and as minute as every creature. Yet, we must classify if we are to
feel this rightly. Intercessions seem demanded,

1. *For our kindred and friends.* This
should be one part of the family compact—
the golden girdle binding together. Parents for children; children for parents;
brethren for sisters; and relations and
friends for one another. This should follow, and ratify all our acts of kindness,
&c.

2. *For the universal church of Jesus.*
We may be particular and importunate for
our own sanctuary, and minister, and
friends, with whom we commune; we may
be especially earnest for our own denomination; but it is a narrow, contracted, bigoted spirit, if it is thus circumscribed. The
whole kingdom of Christ; the whole church
of the Saviour; every disciple. " Grace,
and mercy, and peace be multiplied to all,"
&c.

3. *For the afflicted portion of mankind.*
I include in this the poor—the widow—the
orphan—the prisoner—the exile—those
thrown on beds of languishing—and the
dying. We know that men are born to
sorrow; affliction is the lot of all; much
that none but God can relieve. All these
suffering persons are members of the body;
children of the same family, &c.

4. *For our civil rulers, and all in authority.* This is expressly mentioned; these
are often objects of envy and dislike; but
religion presents them as objects requiring
our prayers, &c. Their stations are of
very great responsibility; stations of imminent peril; numerous temptations; innumerable dangers; may be instruments
of great good or evil; their hearts are in
God's hands.

5. *In one word, for all mankind.* For
our own nation; its spiritual elevation; its
usefulness; its entire evangelization. For
all Protestant nations, that they may be
leagued in works of righteousness, mercy,
and evangelical effort for the enlargement
of Christ's kingdom. For all papal nations
that they may be restored to the pure religion of Christ. For all Mohammedan and
pagan nations, that they may receive the
true light, " even the saving knowledge of
Christ Jesus."

IV. By what motives may intercession be urged? In each and all of these
respects:—

1. *By the fraternal relationship which exists between all men.* We have all one
Father—one identity of nature—one conformation—one in our dependence on divine
providence—one in our eternal destiny.
Speak not of localities—languages—color
—religious rites, &c.; all are brethren.
The soaring intellect—the grovelling savage—the profound philosopher—the roaming Hottentot—the enlightened Christian—
the cruel cannibal—the crowned monarch
—the starving beggar; yes! all are
brethren.

2. *By the essential principle of the great
law of equity.* " Do ye unto others," &c.
Who does not desire it? I mean, what
rightly regulated and informed mind does
not? Is there not something soothing and
cheering in it? Then let it be reciprocated. Let our intercessions join theirs,
&c.

3. *By the example of the pious.* Behold
Abraham interceding for Sodom; Moses
for the Israelites; David for all flesh. His
dying prayer, " Let the whole earth," &c.
Look at the Saviour's life—a life of intercession; his prayer, " Thy kingdom come,"
&c. His work now, &c.

4. *By the command of God.* The text
rests on the high mandate of the King of
kings. He wills it—approves of it. It is
good and acceptable. Of course, it will
bring down his blessing upon those who
engage it. It will conform us to his holy
mind—assimilate us more to Deity—enlarge, expand, and better our souls. It is
a healthy exercise—a pleasant exercise—

a profitable exercise. Another reason; see verse 4.

APPLICATION.

1. Let us each carry out the spirit of the text.

2. Avoid mere formality in this exercise.

3. Pray for the spirit of fervor and earnestness to be imparted to us.

4. Not forget our own souls.

HINDERANCES TO PRAYER.

"That your prayers be not hindered."—1 PETER iii. 7.

PRAYER is one of the essential exercises of the Christian life. True piety commences with prayer, advances in proportion as this spirit is maintained, and, in the language of one of our celebrated poets, " It is his watchword at the gates of death," &c. How important then to excel in this exercise ; to possess, in a large degree, the spirit of prayer and the grace of supplication. It is especially important to guard against the things which militate against prayer, to set the heart intently on the practice of spiritual devotion, and to avoid every impediment to its constant and fervent exercise. I ground two propositions on the text.

I. THE CHRISTIAN CHARACTER IS DISTINGUISHED FOR PRAYER.—And,

II. THERE ARE THINGS BY WHICH PRAYER MAY BE HINDERED.

I. THE CHRISTIAN CHARACTER IS DISTINGUISHED FOR PRAYER.

1. *Prayer is one of the principles of the Christian character.* A Christian is a child of God. Prayer is both the breath and the language of the new nature. By the imparted Spirit we cry Abba, i. e. Father. Of Saul, as an evidence of his conversion, " Behold he prayeth." The new nature knows its weakness, its necessity, its perils, and therefore it prays. Prayer makes God's ability ours, God's fulness ours, God's omnipotent guardianship ours. Where there is carnal ignorance, there will be no prayer ; pharisaical self-sufficiency, no prayer ; but where there is an enlightened mind, and grace in the soul, prayer will necessarily follow. I observe,

2. *Prayer is a duty of the Christian character.* It is required by the Lord, he wills it, has enjoined it. His authority on this subject is found extensively spread over both the Old and the New Testament scriptures. " He will be inquired of by the house of Israel," &c.—he will have men always to pray, &c., to pray with all prayer, and without ceasing. Prayerlessness is disobedience to God.

3. *Prayer has ever been a prominent trait in the eminently pious.* It is clearly implied in the character given of Enoch and Noah—" walked with God," &c. Doubtless by communion, by daily, constant prayer. Abraham was celebrated for prayer, Jacob and Moses, Elias, David, Daniel, the apostles, and early Christians. Thus, too, how it beamed forth in the life of the Saviour ! he hallowed all his actions, works, miracles, &c. by prayer ; spent whole nights in prayer ; expired breathing forth merciful intercessions, &c.

4. *Prayer is indispensable to the comfort and prosperity of the Christian character.* Without it there must be darkness, coldness, barrenness, joylessness. It keeps up intimacy with heaven, opens the gates of glory, holds audience with the Eternal, wraps itself in the dignified garb of a royal priesthood, breathes the air of paradise, obtains the influences of the Holy Ghost, transfers to itself all the fulness of God. How we might enlarge and amplify on the sweetness, the bliss, the advantages of prayer. But we pass on to notice,

II. THERE ARE THINGS BY WHICH PRAYER MAY BE HINDERED. I need not refer to acts which are positively sinful.

1. *The dominancy of unsanctified temper hinders prayer.* Anger, haste, excitability, &c. All these hinder prayer. Prayer is essentially calm, solemn, meek, kind. The dove is the emblem of the Spirit of God. Not the raven, not the eagle, nor the vulture. Confusion of mind, perturbation of spirit, an agitated, foaming state of soul, is not fit for the divine presence, for holy prostration, for speaking to Deity. God abhors human passion and wrath ; and if we are the victims of these, we may go to the mercy-seat, but the glory will be wanting.

2. *Worldliness of spirit hinders prayer.* Prayer is the ascent of the soul, the celestial rising of the mind, the leaving earth and earthly things behind. For the time

being, the soul is engrossed with the pre-eminent value of the Spirit and eternal things: it exclaims—"Whom have I in heaven?" &c. Worldliness paralyzes, clogs it, binds it to earth, &c.

3. *Strife, or an unforgiving spirit, hinders prayer.* The essential law of the gospel is, forgive and be forgiven. The words of Jesus fully illustrate these two points—strife, Matt. v. 23, &c.; and vi. 14, &c.—an unforgiving spirit.

4. *Levity and a trifling spirit hinder prayer.* Cheerfulness is quite in accordance with the spirit of the gospel; but levity, and foolish speaking, and jesting, are not only inconvenient, but deaden the affections; destroy the fine devotional tone of the feelings, and unfit for the exercise of prayer. This is a great snare to many professors, and often the forerunner to a backsliding state of heart before God.

5. *Neglect of God's holy word hinders prayer.* This is the Christian magazine, his storehouse; here are the promises, the examples, the words, &c.; here indeed are "thoughts that breathe, and words that burn." Sameness and deadness will characterize the prayers which are not supplied with materials from the oracles of God.

APPLICATION.

1. *How necessary to know the hinderances to prayer!*
2. *How important to guard against them, especially the hinderances in our own case!*
3. *Who dare live without prayer?*
4. *Who will now begin to pray?*

PERSEVERANCE IN PRAYER.

"Continuing instant in prayer."—ROMANS xii. 12.

THERE are several passages which convey the same ideas to us with the text. "Praying always," &c.; and when the apostle says, "Pray without ceasing." As to the duty and propriety of prayer there can be no dispute. It is of indispensable importance; it must be the sign of our regeneration and adoption into the divine family; and it must be the closing expression of life's pilgrimage :—

"Our watchword at the gate of death,
We enter heaven by prayer."

There are two special particulars in the text: the frequency and perseverance of prayer.

I. THE FREQUENCY OF PRAYER. "Instant." It cannot mean every moment; this is impossible; but it signifies,

1. *That we are often to be found in this exercise.* David prayed seven times a day; Daniel prayed three times a day; Christ spent whole nights in prayer. These seasons of prayer should be as numerous as we can make them,

"For who that knows the worth of prayer," &c.

2. *That we are regular in the exercise of prayer.* Order and regularity are very important. These are necessary in reference to food, sleep, business, &c. So also in reference to prayer; we should let prayer have its place and season.

3. *That we often engage in ejaculatory prayer.* The expression of desire in some short sentence, or even without words. The *mother*, when directing the affairs of her family; the *father*, when engrossed in business; the *traveller*, when setting out on a journey; the *worshipper*, when going to the sanctuary, &c.

4. *That we cherish and improve the gift of prayer.* By reading, and laying up the prayers recorded in the Holy Scriptures; by often meditating on this exercise; by praying for the spirit of prayer, &c. We are directed,

II. TO PERSEVERANCE IN PRAYER. "Continuing." Not ceasing to pray. We should continue,

1. *Because our necessities and wants continue.* Ever in need—ever dependent; and we are to be supplied through the medium of prayer.

2. *Because our dangers continue.* Enemies without; darts of Satan—the world, &c. Our weakness, &c.

3. *Because our probation continues.* Depending on God, and praying to God, must be parallel with our probation. Cease praying, and our experience would be cheerless; hope darkened; comforts dried up; and the soul perish.

4. *Because the loving kindness of the Lord continues.* He never wearies in supplying; he can and will do more for us than we can ask or think, &c.

APPLICATION.

1. Let believers examine themselves as

to their praying. Is it fervent instant, and persevering?

2. Let us seek largely the spirit of prayer.

3. Let the sinner now begin to pray.

SOCIAL PRAYER, OR PRAYER MEETINGS.

"Where many were gathered together praying."—ACTS xii. 12.

THIS chapter is full of rich and instructive incident. The apostle James had been slain with the sword, and Peter had been cast into prison. The church of Christ exercised incessant prayer on his behalf. No human means seemed to be available for his deliverance; but by believing intercession, an appeal was made to the power and grace of the Eternal. That appeal was effectual, God sent an angel who delivered him from prison, verse 7. On his deliverance he immediately repaired to the house of Mary, the mother of Mark, verse 12. And it is to this place, although midnight, that the text refers. "Many were gathered together praying." This was a special Christian prayer-meeting; and probably it was by the influence of this prayer-meeting that Peter was delivered from prison, and spared to bless the church and the world. Our subject then is social prayer, or prayer-meetings. Let us consider the object, advantages, obligations, and objections, connected with prayer-meetings.

I. THE OBJECT OF PRAYER-MEETINGS. The subject of prayer comes before us in the scriptures as a secret service. "When thou prayest, enter into thy closet," &c. As a family duty, no doubt forming an essential part of family worship in every age of the world. As a part of public worship, "My house shall be called a house of prayer;" so the first Christians continued steadfast in prayer, &c. But prayer-meetings are seasons wherein the members of a Christian church agree to assemble especially for the offering up of their thanksgivings and supplications to God. We have a reference to such a meeting, Acts i. 14. Now the great object is to present prayer to God; but then especially the supplications of those who unite should have reference,

1. To the present outpouring of the divine blessing. Come to God hungry, and thirsty, and weary, and tired, and tempted, and a present blessing should be earnestly sought.

2. To seek the prosperity of Zion. That God may dwell in her, favor her with his richest gifts, choicest blessings, build her up, give her peace and enlargement. "O Lord, arise and have mercy on Zion," &c. —"Now, Lord, send prosperity," &c.— "O Lord, revive thy work," &c.

3. To intercede for the afflicted and tried. Those deprived of the means of grace, those in sorrow, in bereavements, in severely trying circumstances.

4. To supplicate blessings on the other means of grace. The preaching of the word; instruction of the young; the visitation of the sick; the distribution of tracts; the reclaiming of the inebriate.

5. To plead for the conversion of the world. That effectual doors of usefulness may be opened, the general ministry of Christ blessed, useful lives spared, sin dethroned, Christ's kingdom established, and the world saved. Now these should especially be the subject of supplication at prayer-meetings. Notice,

II. THE ADVANTAGES OF PRAYER-MEETINGS.

1. They are adapted to secure the divine favor. Prayer honors God. To meet especially for this, reflects lustre on the ordinance of prayer itself. God must approve. His presence and favor may be confidently expected. "Whatever two or three agree to ask," &c.

2. They are often truly refreshing to those present. Who has not found it a Bethel to his soul? How it elevates the mind, secludes for the time from the sublunary things of the world, brings us near to God! What mercies have been bestowed, and enjoyments communicated in prayer-meetings! Who that has attended often but might say,

"I have been there and oft would go;
'Tis like a little heaven below."

3. It improves the gifts of the brethren who exercise. How many have thus become spiritually intellectual and morally great; how many have been raised up to bless the church, to be eminently useful! Here the talent has been laid out in much fear, and it has become five or ten talents.

4. It promotes brotherly love and union.

Here there is the true spirit of sympathy ; here tears mingle, and joys are interchanged ; here the richest blessings are enjoyed at God's own banquet. Praying together betters the heart, and makes the affections more kindred and kind to one another. Notice,

III. The obligations which prayer-meetings lay upon us. I mean, to attend them regularly, justly to prize them, and hold them in high estimation. I appeal to,

1. *Our numerous necessities.* Are not wants daily pressing upon us ? Do we not need constant supplies ? In constant peril, &c. Surely our exigencies should direct us to the prayer-meeting.

2. *Love to the cause of Jesus.* A large attendance would have a most favorable influence on the cause. They are essentially connected with the prosperity of the church. Love for that, zeal for that, should ever direct our willing feet to the prayer-meeting.

3. *A conviction of the value of divine influences.* God must bless all our efforts if they are to succeed. Here we come after the toils of labor, and the spiritual conflict, to lay the whole before God. " Not by might, nor by power," &c.

4. *To remind us of the services of heaven.* We are travellers, pilgrims, &c. Here we meet in concert, to urge our course towards the temple of the beatified. Eternity will be the duration of that assembly and worship in which we expect to engage. Consider,

IV. Some objections to prayer-meetings.

1. *We can pray at home.* So you ought, and must, but this does not render prayer-meetings unnecessary. Those who love prayer-meetings pray most at home. You might say you can read the scriptures at home, and read sermons at home, thus give up public worship.

2. *Some of the prayers are not edifying.* Perhaps there may be some truth in that, but often the fault is in ourselves. We should not expect eloquence or learning, but simple, earnest, pious supplication.

3. *Our other duties are so numerous.* But how do you act if friends call to see you, or if you desire to enjoy yourselves in any recreation, or if you are sick, &c. These duties then give way, but not for prayer-meetings. Should not every member of the church of Christ, feel it both a duty and privilege to be present as often as possible.

APPLICATION.

1. *A word to those who conduct prayer-meetings.* Guard against those things that render them uninteresting : long prayers, preaching prayers, scolding prayers, unconnected prayers. Prepare, read—especially the Psalms, meditate ; be lively, direct, short, &c.

2. *A word to those who are present and do not engage.* Exercise Christian charity and candor, pray for those who pray, pray with them, &c.

3. *To neglecters of prayer-meetings.* Consider the subject, reflect, and see if it is not for your good to be present.

THE PROSPECT OF THE GODLY.

" Thine eyes shall see the king in his beauty ; they shall behold the land that is very far off."— Isaiah xxxiii. 17.

The literal application of this prophecy is generally supposed to have reference to the deliverance of the Jews from the Assyrian army ; and the happiness and joy of seeing Hezekiah again in his goodly apparel, and freed from the presence of the invader ; and thus be left at liberty to enjoy their own pleasant and goodly land. The history is given, 2 Chron. xxxii. 21. But there is another application of the text which is not, I am sure, a perversion, or misapplication of it ; we mean, to the beatific vision of the King of kings in the heavenly land. We purpose to forget king Hezekiah, and to contemplate only Jesus ; to withdraw our thoughts from the land of Judah, and lift our eyes upward to the heavenly Canaan ; and to contemplate the text as referring to the glorious privilege of all the people of God in a future state. Let us then consider,

I. The glorious prospect before the children of God.

II. The certainty of its realization. And,

III. The preparation necessary for its enjoyment.

I. The glorious prospect before the children of God. " Thine eyes," &c. Now, the prospect respects two things ; the vision of Christ, and the heavenly Canaan.

1. *The vision of Christ.* Christ is King.

His royal personifications are often exhibited in the Holy Scriptures. He was typified as such by Melchisedec, who was king of Salem; he was also typified by David and Solomon, monarchs in Jerusalem; he is often thus described. God says, " I have set my King upon my holy hill of Zion." " I speak of the things which I have made touching the King." " Gird thy sword upon thy thigh, O most mighty ! with thy glory and thy majesty." " Behold the King," &c. " Behold thy King cometh," &c. He was thus inquired of : " Where is he that is born ?" &c. He confessed it : Pilate—" Art thou a king ?" " Thou sayest it ; but my kingdom is not of this world." We see Jesus crowned with glory and honor, &c. He is " King of kings." Prince of the kings of the earth, &c. But he is to be seen in his beauty ; in all his regal splendor and magnificence. Patriarchs and prophets saw him in human form, having the likeness of a man. The Jews saw him in his humiliation, " As a man of sorrows," &c. ; the apostles and disciples saw him in his risen glory ; John saw him in the vision of Patmos, Rev. i. 13, &c. Now, all his people shall see him in all the splendors of divine majesty, &c. His resplendent crown —his majestic brightness. Not as a sufferer ; not with a crown of thorns ; not with a reed ; not prostrated with anguish, &c. They shall see him clearly, fully, eternally, &c.

2. *They shall behold the land, &c.* This was typified by the land of Canaan. Was that a rich and luxurious land ? So this, of banqueting and abundance ; the tree of life, and the rivers of pleasure. A land of freedom, after the slavery of Egypt ? so this, a city of unnumbered immunities and privileges ; no toil, &c. A land of triumph after unexampled warfare ? so this ; here all the inhabitants from earth, who have lived to maturity, were warriors, &c. ; all virtuous, &c. A land of rest after the toils of the desert ? so this is the true rest for the people of God. Was it here that the magnificent temple was erected which God filled with his presence and glory ? so this land is all consecrated ; it is all temple, &c. ; one vast sanctuary. Now, this is the prospect of the persons considered.

II. THE CERTAINTY OF ITS REALIZATION. The text is positive, &c. " Thine eyes shall," &c.

1. *This was contemplated by Christ in our*

redemption. He designed our emancipation from Satan's vassalage, and from the dominion of sin—our deliverance from this present evil world ; and also our elevation to his glorious kingdom, Heb. ii. 10. Hear also his prayer, " Father, I will that they also whom thou hast given me, be with me," &c.

2. *This is repeatedly the subject of the divine promises.* Not to dwell on the promises of the Old Testament, let us look at a few in the New. Christ said, " I appoint unto you a kingdom, even as my Father hath appointed me." " Fear not, little flock," &c. " In my Father's house," &c. " Be thou faithful unto death," &c. " I give unto my sheep," &c.

3. *To this tends the work of grace, in all its influences on the soul.* Our calling—is to God's eternal kingdom, &c. ; our regeneration—" Begotten again," &c. ; our sanctification—" That we may walk with him in white," &c. ; our faith—" To look and realize a better world ;" our hope—" To expect a city," &c.—our affections—" Risen with Christ ;" our hearts in heaven, &c.

4. *A goodly number are now enjoying the fulfilment of these promises, &c.* The patriarchs and prophets ; the apostles and martyrs ; the confessors, &c. ; early Christians ; our fathers, &c. Let us stand on the hallowed ground of revelation, and " Behold the great multitude," Rev. vii. 9 ; also verse 14.

5. *The glory and joy of Christ would not be complete, without the eternal salvation of his people.* We have referred you to his prayer, &c. ; but remember the covenant. " He shall see of the travail," &c. These are his ransomed ones ; these his gracious conquests ; these his joy and crown, &c.

III. THE PREPARATION NECESSARY FOR ITS ENJOYMENT. This may be our application. Nothing is necessary in the way of merit ; or price ; or self-righteousness ; but if we would see the King, &c. then,

1. *We must make him the object of our believing, affectionate regard now.* Looking to him now, &c. ; looking to him in our constant experience ; setting the Lord always before us, &c. The glorified in heaven once followed the Lamb, &c. And this looking must be that of lively faith, fervent love, and cheerful obedience. " If we would see the land," &c.

2. *We must seek and labor for its attain-*

ment. Now they desired a better country, &c. Labor, therefore, to enter, &c. Be diligent, that ye may be found, &c. Travel to it, by persevering in the ways of piety. Go from strength to strength, &c. I conclude with two questions :—

1. *Who are the expectants of these glorious enjoyments ?* Oh ! rejoice ; go on the way to Zion with songs, &c.

2. *Who will now set out on this heavenly pilgrimage?* There need be no exception. None too young—too old, &c. ; none too unworthy, &c. We are journeying to the place, &c.

JACOB'S VOW.

" And Jacob vowed a vow, saying, If God will be with me, and will keep me in this way that I go, and will give me bread to eat, and raiment to put on, so that I come again to my father's house in peace ; then shall the Lord be my God : and this stone which I have set for a pillar, shall be God's house ; and of all that thou shalt give me, I will surely give the tenth unto thee."—GEN. xxviii. 20–22.

How many incidents crowd upon us in this chapter ! Isaac dismisses Jacob that he may escape the wrath of his brother Esau. Having received the paternal prayer and blessing, he departs for Padan-aram, the residence of his uncle Laban. After the first day's journey, he proposes a resting-place for the night. His bed is the earth, his pillow a stone, his curtains the outstretched canopy of heaven. The scenes of that night are then recorded, the vision of the ladder, the address of Deity, and the consoling engagements of God to go with him, to keep him, and to bring him again to his father's land. Then we have the hallowed exercises of the morning, " he rose early," &c. verse 18 ; afterwards the vow which he made, " And Jacob vowed," &c. Observe the vow itself, and the terms of Jacob's stipulation.

I. THE VOW ITSELF. A vow is a solemn engagement made with another ; a religious vow is such an engagement made with God. Vows should relate only to lawful things ; they should be made with great caution, in the spirit of sincere piety, and with prayer, for the assistance of God's grace to perform them. Jacob's vow included three things.

1. *A consecration of himself to God.*

" The Lord shall be my God," I will recognise his claims upon me, I will obey his commandments, I will yield all the homage of my mind, the affections of my heart ; he shall be with me, and to me the supreme ; I will have no other gods than the true God. Pagans have their imaginary deities, their idols ; the wicked worship, some one thing and some another ; one gold and silver, one pleasure, another Bacchus, another fame, &c. But how vain, how foolish, how impious, how ungrateful, for any of these to be our God ! He who made us should be our God, he who preserves us, and in whom we live, &c. ; he who redeemed us by the gift of his Son, he who will be our judge, &c., should be our God.

2. *He engaged to keep a memorial of this consecration.* " And this stone," &c., see verse 18. As a remembrance of the place of audience, no doubt his after devotions would respect that pillar. When he returned that stone should be the memento, &c. So, our consecration to God should often be remembered, in our daily devotions, especially on the Lord's day, in his sanctuary, more particularly at the Lord's table, and especially on such days as this, when we again enter on the religious duties of another year ; at any rate the consecration of ourselves to God must not be forgotten.

3. *A devotion of a part of his substance to holy purposes.* " And of all that thou shalt give me," &c. He recognises God's agency, does not refer to his own skill, or toil, or success, but that " thou shalt give me"—a tenth of this " I will give unto thee." The first instance of this is recorded of Abraham, Genesis xiv. 18–20. Afterwards it was a Jewish rite, for the support of the priesthood ; but as the priesthood passed away with the Levitical economy, so there is no mention of tithes in connection with the New Testament dispensation ; but the principle of devoting a part of our substance is still recognised, and is essential to a right state of heart—it is called a sacrifice—" To do good and communicate, forget not," &c. How can we do it ? To the Lord's cause, by supporting the institutions of religion ; and also to the Lord's poor—" Whoso giveth to the poor lendeth to the Lord." God claims a part of his gifts to us for these purposes. But observe,

II. THE TERMS OF JACOB'S STIPULATION. These terms are strikingly reasonable, and such as Jacob could urge from the divine engagements to him, verse 15,—the divine presence, divine provision, and his return to his father's house.

1. *The divine presence.* "If God will be with me." Moses fervently desired this, and said, "If thy presence go not with us, carry us not up hence." God's gracious presence is necessary to our guidance, it is not in man who walketh, &c.; necessary to our protection, "Keep me," &c. If God be with us and for us, who, &c.—necessary to our comfort.

> "In darkest shades, if he appear,
> My dawning is begun," &c.

This alone can give success to our engagements, &c. If the house is built the Lord must build it, &c. He stipulated,

2. *For divine provision.* Yet see how moderate, bread to eat, &c. He sought not dainties nor luxuries, but necessaries only, having food and raiment, &c. Thus Christ's prayer, "Give us this day," &c. These are all we can reasonably and rightly enjoy; these are pledged, "Thy bread shall be given," &c. "If God so clothe the grass of the field, &c., shall he not much more clothe you." He stipulated,

3. *For his return to his father's house.* This attachment was natural. Now all these points were regarded by Jehovah; he did grant Jacob his presence and kept him, he supplied all his wants, he brought him to the land of his fathers, and that too in peace. See the application of this to the Christian, John xiv. 1–4.

APPLICATION.

1. *Have we avowed ourselves to be the Lord's?* If not, do so now, this service; if so, renew the vow.

2. *God will sanctify such a dedication, and follow it with his blessing.* All needful good here—his presence—bring us to his own house and glory.

THE GOSPEL VISION

A SABBATH SCHOOL SKETCH.

"And the Lord answered me and said, Write the vision, and make it plain upon tables, that he may run that readeth it."—HAB. ii. 2.

IT is probable that Habakkuk lived in the eventful times of the reign of Manasseh, or when that monarch was carried captive to Babylon. The prophecy is one of peculiar grandeur and magnificence; several of the passages are of unrivalled sublimity. But it is evident, that several of his predictions had reference to the gospel dispensation, and the establishment of the kingdom of Christ. Verse 14 clearly points to the glorious establishment of the Saviour's empire in our world. He represents himself as a watchman, he declares his purpose; he will watch to see, wait till God shall speak and direct. He does so. God reveals his mind, directs the prophet how to act. From the quotation of the fourth verse, in three of the epistles of Paul, we feel justified in applying the whole to the revelation which God has given us in the gospel of his Son. Observe, then, the nature, the form, the clearness, and the designation of the gospel revelation.

I. THE NATURE OF THE GOSPEL REVELATION. "The vision." Something which passeth before the sight, scenes which are representative of what shall hereafter be realized. Thus Isaiah's vision of the glory of God in the celestial temple, Isaiah vi. 1; thus Ezekiel, i. 1; thus the scenes described by John as beheld in Patmos. Now the glorious scenes of the gospel dispensation passed before the eyes of the prophets. *As seers* they were allowed to behold and proclaim the events connected with the redemption of our world. The birth, the mission, the life, the sorrows, the miracles, the teachings, the sufferings, the death, the resurrection, and the glory of Christ, were all included in the visions of prophecy. The gospel itself is a vision, to which the attention of mankind is to be directed. It has three distinct features, and in each of these we are deeply concerned. Now the gospel revelation,

1. *Is a divine vision.* A revelation from God; a system of light, emanating from the Sun of righteousness. "God, who commanded the light," &c. The gospel bears its divine impress on it; it has the mind of God in it, the glory of God round about it. Wherever the gospel comes it may be said, "Arise, shine," &c.

2. *It is a vision of mercy.* Not of justice, not of terror, not of wrath. Some of the visions of the prophets represented the judgments of God. Many of John's visions were of this awful character. In the gospel visions, Deity is arrayed in the habiliments of tenderness and mercy; *the Father*

appears bending over his lapsed and miserable creatures, solicitous for their salvation. *The Son* appears as the Lamb slain, bearing away the guilt of the world. *The Holy Spirit* appears in the form of a dove, hovering round the wretched with the olive branch of love and peace. *Angels* appear intensely delighted; and while you behold the scene, there is suddenly heard, in heavenly strains, " Glory to God in the highest," &c. In this vision is written, in burning, indelible characters, " God so loved the world," &c.

3. *It is a vision of hope.* It is encompassed with the word of promise; it is illumined with gracious invitations and precious promises. With this vision is lit up the whole of our sepulchral world; a vision of hope to every nation, and people, and tongue. Of hope to every sinner. The gospel proclaims a ready and all-sufficient Saviour to every child of man. Notice,

II. THE FORM AND CHARACTER OF THE VISION. " Write the vision." Now in every age God has spoken to mankind. He spake to our first parents, to Cain, to Noah, Abraham, Jacob, &c. Now all these communications were precious. But it was the will of God, for the benefit of all the world, that these visions should be *written.*

1. Thus the revelations of God would be more certain, not so liable to be lost or corrupted, &c.

2. More permanent. Written and deposited with the church, all the words of God might be preserved and handed down from parents to children, and from generation to generation.

3. More available. In this way the statutes of God can be carefully consulted and meditated upon; not only hear it in the sanctuary, but study it, &c., at home. Yet how vastly more valuable has the written word become by the art of printing, by which myriads of copies have been multiplied, and the number increased, till the earth may be full of the knowledge of the Lord, &c. Notice,

III. THE CLEAR AND INTELLIGIBLE FEATURES OF THIS REVELATION. " Make it plain," that is, easy to be understood. How necessary this to the unlearned, to the diversified capacities of children, to those who only begin to reflect in old age! Now the Bible does contain scenes of overwhelming grandeur, depths fathomless, heights of celestial infinitude. But the gospel vision

is plain; look at the discourses of Jesus, his parables, prodigal son, lost sheep, good Samaritan, the sower and seed. Look at the commands of the gospel, at the invitations, promises. Hence the common people heard Christ gladly. The way of salvation, how plainly written; like a royal highway, leading from one city to another, so that a wayfaring man, though a fool, may not err. The folly and sin of ambiguous preaching; " Make it plain," do not mystify or embellish, so as to perplex, &c.

IV. THE DESIGN OF THIS REVELATION. " That he may run," &c. This passage is seldom quoted right, generally supposed to read, " That he that runs may read," &c., they put the running first. Now the gospel never will save man, if he remains in a heedless, inconsiderate state, &c.; it must be heard or read with attention. And it is to be so plain, that when a man hears or reads it, he may see the way so clearly as to run in it. Now the great end of revelation is experimental, practical religion. Thus the *cross* is to be lifted up, that men may see and be saved; thus the *pathway* to bliss and glory, that men may run in it, and be guided to eternal life; thus the *name of the Lord* is to be made known as a strong tower, that they may run into it and be saved; thus the ways to the city of refuge were wide and plain, that the manslayer might escape the avenger of blood. For this we preach, that you may be saved. This is the one end of the gospel, the great design. LEARN,

1. *How thankful we should be for the gospel.* Where there is no vision the people perish, &c. We could better spare the stars and the moon, yea, and the sun, and live out a few years in darkness, than be deprived of the Sun of righteousness. How sweet and precious is light, but especially the light of the gospel!

2. *Is the great end answered in all present?* Have you received and obeyed the gospel? Does its light illuminate you? Are you the children of the day? Is your path bright? Do you run cheerfully and gladly? Do you prefer it in your hearts? This is the season of exercise and hope. We should run. Blessings so precious, life so short, opportunities so uncertain.

3. *Sabbath school teachers.* Be admonished and directed by the text. Write the vision on the understandings, memories, and hearts of your children. Be plain, be ear-

nest, repeat, &c. You are not to be satisfied *till they run.* But then you must *allure ;* draw them after you, not stand and point, but say, "Come with us," &c. Who does not see the necessity of all this for the young? Who can tell the share these schools have had in altering the mental and moral aspect of our country? I commend this subject to the children, to the parents, especially to the church of God.

THE SAINTS' AMPLE PROVISION.

" But my God shall supply all your need according to his riches in glory by Christ Jesus."— PHIL. iv. 19.

" GODLINESS," says the apostle, " is profitable unto all things," &c. It not only interests us in the spiritual blessings of divine grace, but secures to us all the favors of a benign providence, and in the world to come introduces us to life everlasting.— " Seek ye first the kingdom of God," &c. True religion requires that we trust God in all things. We are to trust in him forever, for in the Lord Jehovah is everlasting strength. Few passages contain more comfort than the one we have selected for our text—" But my God shall supply all," &c. Notice,

I. THE NATURE OF THE SUPPLY PROMISED. Now this is to meet our *need*, our *exigency*, and *misery*. Now need and wishes may be very different. Need and supposed *wants* may be very dissimilar. We may wish, and imagine we want things which would be injurious, &c. God supplied all the need of the Israelites in the desert, but not all they craved and murmured for. Between need and wishes, there is often almost an infinite disparity. Real necessities are very limited, but wishes may be endlessly multiplied. Now a Christian's need includes,

1. *Sufficiency of temporal good.* David said, "The Lord is my shepherd," &c. "They that seek the Lord," &c. "Their bread shall be given," &c., Matt. vi. 25, 33. Now this also includes all good to our persons and dwellings. "There shall no evil befall thee," &c., Psalm xci. 1, &c. "No weapon that is formed against thee shall prosper," &c.

2. *Supply of spiritual blessings.* Our souls have their wants, &c. We need spiritual bread and spiritual raiment. We

need light, and power, and help. We need protection, support, and comfort. We need grace every moment to aid, and keep, and sanctify, &c. This supply extends to all your need, and it shall be seasonable,—suitable,—ample,—and everlasting. "He will give grace to help," &c. "My grace is sufficient," &c.

II. THE AUTHOR OF THIS SUPPLY. " My God," &c. Just think,

1. *Of his exhaustless resources.* "Riches of his glory." He possesses all things, the universe is his. The sea, and the dry land, —earth and heaven. How vast his territories! How boundless his domain! Never diminished. We have two symbols, the sun and the ocean. Both have met the design of their great originator through all ages. God is the same throughout all generations. Then think,

2. *Of his infallible knowledge.* He knows all your need. He has numbered all your hairs. All your condition is before him. He sees you every moment. Can never be mistaken. Wherever you are, your Father's watchful eye is over you. Think,

3. *Of his infinite goodness.* "He is good, and his tender mercies," &c. He supplies the beasts, insects, &c. All nature. His enemies. "Causeth his sun," &c. Contrast him with your fathers, and if they know how to give good gifts, &c. Especially think of his love in the gift of Jesus. "And if God spared not his own Son," &c. Notice,

III. THE MEDIUM OF THIS SUPPLY. " By Christ Jesus." Christ is the head of his people, and all vitality, and all communion, flow to them from him. Our supplies are,

1. *By virtue of his merits.* Sin cut off the connection between God and man. Christ opened it. By his obedient life, and death, he opened a channel for the love and favor of God. Our life, and all its benefits ; earth, and a.1 its blessings. Heaven and all its glories come to us entirely and exclusively through Christ Jesus.

2. *Through the influence of his intercession.* " God hath exalted him," &c. " He hath ascended on high," &c. His gracious advocacy averts wrath, postpones judgment, secures divine long-suffering, keeps mercies flowing. He makes known all the wants of his people, presents all their petitions, and pleads their cause constantly. All our benefits are through Christ Jesus.

3. *Spiritual supplies are in connection*

with our union to Christ Jesus. "I am the vine," &c., John xv. 1, 5 ; see also John vii. 37, 39. As Christ is one with the Father, so we must be one with Christ, we in him, and he in us, and thus all our supplies will be by Christ Jesus.

APPLICATION.

1. *What comfort the text contains for all the people of God!* "God supplies all our need, will do it, out of his riches," &c. Not according to our merit, but by Christ Jesus.

2. *By humble and believing prayer this supply is obtained.* "Be careful for nothing," &c. "Ask, and it shall be given you."

3. *This supply demands our hearty and unceasing praises.* Should we not in every thing give thanks ? Oh, praise the Lord, for he is good, &c.

4. *Invite the sinner to receive God's pardoning and renewing grace.* "Let the wicked forsake his way," &c.

GOD THE SHIELD AND THE REWARD OF HIS PEOPLE.

"After these things the word of the Lord came unto Abraham in a vision, saying, Fear not, Abraham ; I am thy shield, and thy exceeding great reward."—GEN. xv. 1.

God is every thing to his people that they need. Hence the representations he has given of himself are just adapted to the various circumstances and conditions of his saints. Poor, he is the fulness of their supply. Weak, he is their almighty strength. Ignorant, he is their fountain of wisdom and knowledge. Their inability is met by his sufficiency—their guilt by his mercy, —their unworthiness by his grace. Are they soldiers—he is the captain of their salvation. Travellers—he is their guard and guide ; children—he is their Father and God. Abraham had just been in conflict with the four kings, and God had given the victory into his hands. It is probable his mind was agitated by the events of the warfare. How desirable, how seasonable, then, was consolation and peace ! That was afforded him by the address of God in the text. "Fear not," &c. Observe the peril supposed, the counsel offered, and the promise given.

I. THE PERIL SUPPOSED. Fear is the feeling excited by the approach of suffering or danger. Abraham might justly apprehend this. The Christian life is exposed to this ; our dangers are the repeated topics of this blessed book. There are three sources of spiritual peril.

1. *From the powers of darkness.* Hosts of the fallen angels are engaged in waging war with the saints. Hell is arrayed against the church, and against each member of the church. To this end there are stratagems of allurements. Satan's wiles, his devices, his snares. Thus he ruined the first human pair, and since then countless myriads. His fierce attacks—horrid temptations, the fiery darts of the devil. When he labors to darken, to confuse, to distract, to incite the passions, to lift up to daring presumption, or sink into despair.

2. *From the influence of the wicked.* Their smiles, friendship, truce with God and religion ; or, their persecuting attacks, scoffs, ridicule, envy, hate, violence, &c. Now in some of these forms we shall assuredly meet with peril from the men of the world. We cannot evade or avoid it.

3. *From the weakness and infirmities of our own hearts.* Here extra vigilance is indispensable, were we even arrayed in original purity, or were we established by lofty spiritual attainments. But alas ! our leanness, our weakness, &c. The unsubdued foes within—much for Satan to take advantage of—much to be influenced by the world. Well may alarm take possession—well may dread often surprise, or fear dishearten. Consider,

II. THE COUNSEL PROPOSED. "Fear not." It cannot mean, be not solicitous, or be not vigilant ; but, be not the victim of despondency—of afflictive fears. Be not discouraged, but be strong, magnanimous. Be of good courage.

1. *Fear not so as to be robbed of your comfort.* Fear will do this. Enjoyment and apprehension of danger, are incompatible. Tranquillity and comfort are wedded together. To lie down in peace is impossible,.with great internal anxiety. It is the will of God that we should have an undisturbed rest and peace by the Holy Ghost.

2. *Fear not so as to give advantage to your enemies.* Fear paralyzes—hands hang down —knees tremble — heart fails — the foe rushes in, and the victory is easily attained. Ours ought to be the language of old, "I

will not fear what man," &c. "In the name of God I will do valiantly."

3. *Fear not so as to neglect the means of safety.* Fear confuses, and prudential means of security are forgotten. Reading the word is one, hearing the gospel is another, meditation and prayer are other means, exercise of faith, &c. Now if we neglect these through fear, the enemy must prevail. If we fight, we conquer ; but if we neglect to do so, we are overcome. Observe,

III. THE DECLARATORY PROMISE GIVEN. For so it may be regarded. "I am thy shield."

1. *God is the shield of his people.* This is often presented to us in the word, very often repeated, and doubtless intentionally so. We need it. Shield, a defensive piece of armor, by which the warrior wards off the strokes or darts of the enemy. God is this to his people, their defence. He is the shield of *all* they are or have ; soul, body, family, estate. He is their shield *always ;* God omnipresent, never far off ; round about at all times. *Effectual* shield, nothing can destroy it. "If God be for us," &c. "He that is for us, is more," &c. *Unchangeable* shield. In life, sickness, death. Every instant, no variableness, &c. Think of such a shield, and then ask if fear is not unnecessary.

2. *He will be their reward.* Or "greatly" reward them. Constancy, perseverance, and fidelity, God will reward. The racer shall have the garland—the victor the crown. "Be thou faithful," &c. But there is a rich sublimity about the text. "God will be their reward." His love— his goodness—his peace—his smile. In God is all enjoyment, and this shall be ours. It must therefore be great ; as great as the Godhead. As vast, as high, as profound, as comprehensive as the Deity. "Exceeding" great. Exceeding all we can deserve, or desire, or speak, or think. See that splendid passage, Eph. iii. 20. Then it will exceed all time, and run parallel with eternity itself. What a promise, what bliss, &c.

APPLICATION.

1. *Our subject belongs to the children of God.* To each and all. Oh take it, make it your own ; let it be your beam of joy— your stream of comfort.

2. *The sinner has every thing to fear.* God as judge—as avenger, &c.

3. *Let the penitent lay hold of God's strength and live.* He will say, Fear not, I have blotted out, &c.

MUTUAL SYMPATHY.

"Bear ye one another's burdens, and so fulfil the law of Christ."—GAL. vi. 2.

THE Christian religion is full of glory to God, and full of good-will to man. True religion is heavenly in its origin, and equally heavenly in its tendency. Like that stream which rises first collected from the ocean by the magnetical water-spout, then borne on the wings of the wind to some distant part, and after having descended in rain upon the earth and run in streams until having gained the channel of the river, it is on its passage again to its native ocean. But do you not perceive that in thus retiring to its native ocean, it has fertilized the thirsty earth, and thus has been rendered a blessing both to man and beast ; so true religion while it descends from heaven and leads to heaven, yet it makes the Christian a blessing to every sphere in which he may move in the world. After God blesses a man he always makes him a blessing. Among the range of benevolent Christian duties, is the one in the text, "Bear one another's burdens," &c.

I. THE BURDENS OUR CHRISTIAN FRIENDS MAY BE CALLED TO BEAR, AND HOW WE MAY ASSIST THEM. The figure is a very plain and simple one. A man has a very oppressive load, he can scarcely stand beneath it, his condition and grievance attract our attention, we run to his relief and raise one end, and then the man is relieved and able to bear the rest without pain. Supposing you saw a person in these circumstances, would not common humanity induce you to help ? Then "bear ye one another's burdens," &c. Let us see the burdens our Christian friends may be called to bear, &c.

1. *They may be called to bear the burden of poverty, and we should give them all the aid in our power.* Every age and country, and dispensation, has had its poor. Under the law God made express provision for them. The vast majority of believers are poor. There must be therefore a great deal of suffering amongst the poor in the church of Christ. We shall see how this is to be met, 1 Cor. xvi. 1, 2 ; Acts ii. 44,

&c. This is also spoken of by John, 1 John iii. 17.

2. *They may be called to bear the burden of sickness, and they should have our sympathy and prayers.* None can take away the pain, but, oh, how sympathy lightens the load—how friendly countenances illumine the darkness—how friendly hands impart as it were fresh courage and hope! Then to feel that while we are at the throne of grace, our Christian friends are there, there saying, " Lord, bless our afflicted friend," &c. Why we feel that the affliction will terminate rightly. " The fervent effectual prayer," &c. To have the great Advocate in heaven, and so many advocates on earth, &c. James expressly says, that " the prayer of faith shall save the sick," &c.

3. *They may be called to bear the burden of reproach, and we must assist them by our countenance and support.* Christ has declared, that they that will live godly must suffer persecution. The psalmist exclaimed, " Reproach hath broken my heart." An ungodly world will speak all manner of evil, &c. And sometimes these creep into the church, wolves in sheep's clothing— vicious serpents, of the brood of the devil —busy-bodies, tale-bearers, railers, false speakers. And then the scene spoken of by James is realized, see James iii. 6. Now we are bound to be jealous for the Christian reputation of every brother and sister. Silence when they are maligned is criminal, and the heart that is wounded with the poisoned arrows of slander ought to be encouraged, and bound up, and comforted.

4. *They may labor under the burden of sin, and then must we labor for their spiritual restoration.* See v. 1. See 1 John v. 16. The Lord by Moses has told us what we are to do, Lev. xix. 17. " Thou shalt not hate," &c. Oh, how many have been driven from the church by the unfriendly course adopted by their brethren, and have at last sunk into apostacy, saying, " No man careth for my soul !" How did Jesus act with regard to his disciples who fled— with Peter, &c. How does a father act with his frail children ? How do we act with the diseased members of our bodies, &c. " Brethren, if any man do err from the truth," &c., James v. 19.

II. THE MOTIVE ASSIGNED. " And thus fulfil," &c. The Christian Law is one of " love." This is the royal law, it compre-

hends all others—bears every thing else with it. There are many reasons why we should fulfil this law.

1. *Obedience to Christ.* We call Christ, Master ; but why, if we do not the things he has commanded ?

2. *It will tend to conform us to the mind of Jesus.* " Behold my servant," &c. " He shall not break," &c. He went about bearing the burdens of the sons and daughters of misery. Giving the multitudes food—sick, health—family of Bethany, sympathy, &c.

3. *It will make us exceedingly happy.* God will smile—Jesus bless—the spirit enrich—conscience approve. Heaven in the soul.

4. *We may look for others to aid us if placed in similar circumstances.* " Blessed are the merciful," &c. But he that showeth no mercy shall have judgment without mercy. " For a good man," &c.

5. *Christ will superabundantly reward us at the last day.* Christ is one with all his members. " Head over all," &c. Feeling all the evil and all the good done to every saint.

APPLICATION.

1. Our subject reproves the unfeeling and selfish. 2. Let it excite to compassion and benevolence.

MODERATION IN GRIEF.

" And they that weep, as though they wept not."—1 Cor. vii. 30.

THE apostle has been treating at large on the advantages and disadvantages of the married life, during the state of the church's trial, and also giving full directions for the right development of the relative duties, especially where the husband or wife might be an unbeliever. In the midst of his discourse he suddenly breaks forth in this abrupt yet powerful address. " But this I say," &c. Our sojourn here will at most be but transitory. No condition or relationship in life should cause us to forget the brevity of life, the evanescence of time, and from this we should cultivate a constan moderation of spirit in all the engagemen and conditions in which we may be placed. While we affectionately discharge the duties of the domestic circle, let us remember how liable this scene is to change, and therefore, " let those who have wives," &c. Then he proceeds to the sorrows of life, and says, " and they that weep," &c. Observe,

I. The sorrow supposed. And,
II. The spirit recommended.

1. The sorrow supposed. " And they that weep," &c. By the entrance of sin, the whole creation is burdened with grief and suffering. Man born to sorrow—the world is one wilderness of anxiety—one valley of tears. The sources of sorrow are innumerable. We are vulnerable at all points—exposed in all situations. Perhaps we may look at three or four classes of sorrow.

1. *Personal.* From bodily affliction, pain, and languishing. Many persons scarcely know what it is to enjoy a day's health, a day's physical enjoyment. Weakly frames affected by every change of the weather.

2. *Domestic.* Sorrow from our families and connections in life. Our house not with God as we could desire. Unbelieving, irreligious children, &c. Domestic affliction—domestic bereavements—domestic strife. Or our sorrows may be,

3. *Secular.* Those which arise from the affairs of life. From business distractions, losses and disappointments. Even the pious, with all prudence and care, are often thus circumstanced. Or the sorrow may be,

4. *Spiritual.* From a sense of our own barrenness, weakness, infirmities, sins. From a deep concern for those around us. Solicitude for the church—for the neighborhood—for the world. Think of these four channels of grief, &c. And observe,

II. The spirit recommended. Now mark, it is not to refrain from weeping—does not pronounce it sinful ; tears are as natural and proper as our joys and songs. Weeping has been sanctified by the tears of prophets and apostles, and by the tears of the anointed of God ; for Jesus wept. Religion is not to harden, to render us callous, to make men Stoics. It produces tenderness, renders sensibility more exquisite, &c. But whatever may be the occasion of our sorrow, our weeping should be moderate, even as though we wept not. Let us ascertain when,

1. *Our sorrow may be deemed excessive and immoderate.*

(1.) When it prevents the discharge of the duties of life. When persons sit down to mourn, and forget the claims of their friends, and of society, on their labors and attentions.

(2.) When it causes us to neglect the means of grace, to neglect the Bible, the house of God, Christian conversation, prayer, &c.

(3.) When it eclipses our mercies, and when we neglect to acknowledge the blessings which remain. The mind dwelling only on the troubles and afflictions, and not remembering the blessings which are continued to us.

(4.) When we murmur and bitterly complain. Exhibiting an unresigned spirit. Reflecting perhaps on God.

(5.) When we refuse to be comforted, and allow sorrow, like a disease, to prey on the mind. Injure our health, blighting all our affections, &c. Drowning our comforts, &c. Now in all these instances the sorrow is immoderate, injurious, and offensive to God. Let us inquire,

2. *Why our sorrows should be moderate.* " Or weep as though," &c.

(1.) On account of the number and value of the blessings which we have received. Our blessings have been countless—daily loaded. Days of health—of enjoyment—of happiness, &c. Are these to go for nothing ? " Shall we receive good at the hands of the Lord," &c. A reckoning and survey of these should ever mitigate our grief, and brighten the darkest scenes of sorrow and trouble.

(2.) On account of the overruling providence which has to do with all our crosses. Many of our griefs are directly from the Lord. His appointments, his chastisements ; the rest are permitted and allowed for wise purposes, &c. To weep excessively is to reflect on God—to impugn God—to be dissatisfied, &c. Now are not all his ways wise, righteous, and good ? Then surely we should weep as though we wept not.

(3.) On account of our deserts, which God in mercy does not reward. Let us look at our troubles, how numerous, heavy, deep, keen, &c. But look at your sins. Examine your claims, think how it might have been with you, then ask, " Why should a living man complain ?" " The Lord hath not dealt with us," &c. " It is of the Lord's mercies," &c.

(4.) On account of the pernicious influence of excessive sorrow on the interests of religion. Consider that we profess religion is to sustain, to cheer, to invigorate. But if we sorrow even as others, then religion is dishonored, and inquirers after it discouraged. The history of Christianity has fully exemplified the efficacy of the grace of God to sustain and comfort. Look at the statement, 2 Cor. iv. 8, &c. Now excessive grief blights the graces, and is pestiferous to all the holy emotions of internal piety.

(5.) On account of the transitoriness of all the afflictions of this life. "Affliction endureth but for a night," &c. But momentary. Our sorrows are like passing clouds, flitting, and transient. Then let us weep as though, &c.

APPLICATION.

1. To contend with the troubles of this life, divine grace is pledged and provided. God's grace is sufficient for us under all circumstances, &c. God is our refuge and strength, &c.

2. Have you all wept on account of sin? This should be deep and influential, working repentance unto life, &c.

3. Let us contemplate that bright world, where God shall wipe away all tears, &c.

MODERATION IN JOY.

"And they that rejoice as though they rejoiced not."—1 Cor. vii. 30.

We have previously considered the importance of moderation in the sorrows of life. It is possible to run into the other extreme; to be indifferent to the prudential lessons which trouble should teach us; to be reckless of all events; to sink into a state of apathy, &c. ; or, it is possible to cherish a volatile spirit, and to aim at hilarity of heart, when there ought to be seriousness and reflection. Joy is proper and desirable, in its season. It is as the sunshine of the mind ; but it may be excessive, and thus be baneful in its effects. We should rejoice, therefore, as though we rejoiced not; or in the language of holy writ, " Rejoice with trembling."

I. LET US CONTEMPLATE LEGITIMATE CHRISTIAN REJOICING.

II. SHOW THE PRINCIPLES BY WHICH IT SHOULD BE REGULATED.

I. LET US CONTEMPLATE LEGITIMATE CHRISTIAN REJOICING. "They that rejoice," &c. Now observe,

1. *The Christian is called to rejoice.* Therefore it becomes one of the dignified privileges of the Christian's life—a kind of holy duty. This is repeatedly impressed upon us, &c. It is urged, that we should rejoice in the Lord, and again rejoice, &c. "Rejoice evermore," &c. "Be glad in the Lord, and rejoice, ye righteous, and shout for joy, all ye that are upright in heart." There are many declarations of a similar kind : " Light is sown for the righteous," &c. " We rejoice, in hope of the glory of God." " Whom having not seen, we love," &c. " They that sow in tears," &c.

2. *The Christian has many occasions of joy.* The government of God over all the affairs of the universe—" The Lord reigneth, let the earth rejoice," &c. The beneficent care of God ; the Lord careth for you. To these things should be added, the manifestation of the love of God; a sense of his divine favor ; experimental enjoyment of his blessed Spirit bearing witness, &c. ; the divine engagements on our behalf. To hear prayer—to keep—to guide—to sanctify—to save—and give eternal life. Now, these are all rich topics of rejoicing.

3. *The rejoicing of the Christian glorifies God.* It exhibits his goodness and his grace ; it shows forth his praise ; it is a declaration of the happiness of his service —the easiness of his yoke—the pleasure of his ways.

4. *Rejoicing will be one of the chief elements of glory.* "Everlasting joy shall be," &c. " In thy presence is fulness of joy," &c. " Well done," &c. " Enter thou into the joy," &c. Now, this kind of joy we may fully cherish. But there is another kind of joy which is very different, yet quite lawful, and doubtless that to which the text refers ; a joy arising from the circumstances in which Providence may place us. The possession of health and reason is a just ground of joy ; the possession of a competency ; the possession of domestic peace, and friends ; the possession of the means of mental recreation and improvement; books, &c. Now, to this kind of rejoicing the text, of course, chiefly refers. We

must rejoice as though, &c. Observe, then,

II. THE PRINCIPLE BY WHICH IT SHOULD BE REGULATED.

1. *Temporal rejoicing must ever be subordinate to spiritual joy.* Spiritual health—spiritual understanding—spiritual riches——spiritual peace—spiritual friends—spiritual privileges. Now these must have the ascendency; these the pre-eminence.

2. *We must rejoice in these only as sublunary good.* They want permanence—not abiding; must not rejoice in these as being certain and sure. Who would rejoice much in the passing gleam—over the beautiful, yet fading flowers—over a transitory pleasure?

3. *Our rejoicing must not interfere with the discharge of Christian duties.* It must not prevent prayer—meditation—reading the word—attending on the means of grace.

4. *Our rejoicing must not interfere with the pious exercises of the soul.* There is the exercise of watchfulness—holy vigilance. The exercise of confession of sin; of repentance; daily sorrow for our iniquities, &c. The exercise of self-denial and mortification; the exercise of sympathy with the afflicted, &c. To feel and bear the burdens of our brethren, &c.

5. *Our rejoicing must not exclude the solemnities of religion.* The last and momentous concerns of every responsible being. Death, with its awful realities; judgment, &c. "Flee from the wrath to come." Now, these subjects require peculiar seriousness of mind; they ought not to be forgotten; therefore, we should rejoice, as though we rejoiced not.

APPLICATION.

1. *The joy of sin and sinners is vain and delusive.* Men may rejoice in that which pertains to glare, and the vanity of this world—in its pleasures, riches, fashions; but this must be short-lived. It is ever in direct collision with conscience, and God's Holy Spirit. This is not like the shining sun, brighter and brighter, &c., but a glimmering taper, &c. "The candle of the wicked shall be put out." The joy of the wicked terminates in darkness, &c.

2. *True religion and happiness are connected.* True, intelligent, solid joy, and piety are wedded together. Who, then, is seeking enjoyment? It is here. The kingdom of God is joy in the Holy Ghost. Here are the right grounds of joy.

3. *In proportion to our religion, will be the amount of sterling enjoyment.* Then be diligent and holy, and thus be happy, &c.

MODERATION IN BUSINESS.

"And they that buy, as though they possessed not."—1 COR. vii. 30.

RELIGION is often considered as something distinct from the ordinary movements of life: something for the closet—or for the Lord's day—or for affliction—or death—or eternity. So far from this view being correct, religion is a holy principle, intended to be interwoven with all the affairs of life. It is to be an every day, yea, an every hour concern. It is to be identified, indeed, with the closet—with the sanctuary—with the sabbath—with sickness, &c.; but it is to influence our conduct—to hallow our thoughts—to regulate our desires—and to give integrity and moral excellency to the business transactions of life. Hence the apostle insists, in our text, that in buying, we are to trade in the spirit of Christian moderation. Let us inquire,

I. How A CHRISTIAN SHOULD TRANSACT THE BUSINESS AFFAIRS OF LIFE.

II. How HE SHOULD REGARD HIS POSSESSIONS IN THIS WORLD.

I. How A CHRISTIAN SHOULD TRANSACT THE BUSINESS AFFAIRS OF LIFE. Now, in the business affairs of life,

1. *We must be actuated by the principles of justice and equity.* "Do ye unto others," &c. All extravagant statements in selling, or in depreciating; all attempts to impose on the ignorant, in dealing. Every business transaction should be honorable, open, and upright. The sins of selling and buying are exceedingly numerous, and deeply offensive to God. A good man will abhor all these.

2. *We must not cherish too much eagerness of spirit in business.* Attention, and diligence, and prudence necessary, &c. But this is not to be the mainspring of the soul—the absorbing principle. We read of those who make haste, &c.—who are all avidity, &c. It is requisite to give only a subordinate attention. With many it affects their sleeping, and eating, and enjoyment of life. This is extreme folly.

3. *We must not allow it to encroach on the religious duties of life.* Reading the word—family worship—attendance on the means of grace—a strict regard to the whole Sabbath. Now, it must not rob God of his claims, &c. "Seek first the kingdom of God," &c. "Labor not for the bread that perisheth," &c.

4. *It must not monopolize the affections of the heart.* "Love not the world," &c. A man's trade may be his idol ; supplant God, and eternal things. "Set not your affections on things beneath," &c.

5. *The affairs of business should be transacted in God's fear, and in remembrance of the final judgment.* Every word—every thought, &c., will be judged ; all our transactions in life. How necessary, then, to labor in God's fear—to keep a conscience void of offence, &c. We must stand in company before the bar of God. "God will render to every man," &c. Thus ought we to transact, &c.

II. How WE SHOULD REGARD OUR POSSESSIONS IN THIS WORLD. Now, the profits or riches arising from trade are to be held as though we possessed not ; so, also, all our temporal means. The great truth is, we are but stewards. Nothing is really and absolutely our own. We hold it in trust only, for the discharge of certain duties in life. Our possessions are lawfully expended,

1. *In obtaining for ourselves the necessaries of life.* Food—raiment, and the other needful blessings, for the sustenance of the body, and the improvement of the mind. These claims must be first met.

2. *We must regard the necessities of our families and dependents.* "If any man neglect to provide for his own," &c. In this class, poor and afflicted relatives should have a place.

3. *We must regard the circumstances of the poor and distressed around us.* These we are to consider, remember, and help. God demands it ; they are his poor, and our fellow-creatures. Neglect is sin—unmercifulness, &c. The poor of the church have the first claim, and ought to have the first place.

4. *There are the spiritual interests of Christ's cause and kingdom in the world.* To help those who labor in the gospel ; to circulate the word of life, and consecrate a portion of our means to the glorious kingdom of God's anointed. The gold of Sheba is to be given to Christ. The liberal soul shall be made fat, and by liberal things be established. I never knew a person distinguished for this, who was not specially happy and fruitful. All this is to hold our temporal things as though we possessed not. Now, why should we do so ?

1. *Because they are not the chief good.* They cannot make happy ; not suited to the soul. May have them, and be wretched and miserable. Of the earth, earthy ; refer only to this vile world. What contempt the Saviour poured on these things !

2. *Because they are of uncertain continuance.* Hence called, deceitful—uncertain ; "make to themselves wings," &c. How many have been bereaved, &c. ! Then, surely, the text is wise and proper.

3. *Because they are often spiritually pernicious to the soul.* Often eat as a canker ; blight the moral verdure, &c. Lead to arrogance and self-esteem. Lead to vanity and show ; to worldliness and avarice ; to supineness and spiritual sloth. Exceedingly difficult to be saved with these ; have caused myriads to make shipwreck. How hard for a rich man, &c. All history is fraught with the peril of riches to the soul. How needful, then, the text !

4. *We shall very soon have done with them.* Look at that estate, what owners it has had ; how one has succeeded another, they have all died, and left it behind. "We brought nothing into this world," &c. So it will be with us. The place that knows us now, &c., others must occupy, &c. Then, ought we not to hold, as though we possessed not, &c. ?

5. *We are professedly heirs of the riches of glory.* The spiritual durable riches of eternity ; the inheritance that fadeth not away ; the kingdom that abideth forever, &c. Now these are suitable—sure—ecstatic—everlasting, &c. Ought not these to raise our minds, &c., above the treasures of time ? When heaven is in reversion, it will not be difficult to hold with a loose hand the possessions of time, &c.

"There is my house, and portion fair," &c.

APPLICATION.

1. *Let the subject be the test of examination.* How are we affected and influenced by the business affairs of life, and what hold have the possessions of earth upon us ?

2. *The supreme excellency of religion.* "Godliness is profitable to all things, &c.

"Godliness, with contentment, is great gain."

3. *Let moderation of desire, and affection, in regard to the things of this life, distinguish us from others.* They have no other good, &c. Men of the world, who have their portion in this life, &c. Oh! seek the Pearl of great price. Buy gold, that thou mayest be rich, &c.

THE SUBLUNARY CHARACTER OF THE WORLD, AND THE USE WE SHOULD MAKE OF IT.

"And they that use this world, as not abusing it : for the fashion of this world passeth away."— 1 Cor. vii. 31.

OUR subject is very kindred with that we last considered, buying as though we possessed not. But it takes in a wider range, for it refers to the proper use of the whole world in which we live. In the world, we must have to do with it ; it is the manner and spirit of conducting and regulating this, that the text refers to. We may, we ought, to use the world, but we may not, we ought not, to abuse it. Let us, then,

I. LOOK AT THE RIGHT USE OF THE WORLD.
II. AT THE ABUSE OF THE WORLD.
III. THE REASONS FOR THE USE, AND AGAINST THE ABUSE OF IT, ASSIGNED IN THE TEXT.

I. LOOK AT THE RIGHT USE OF THE WORLD. It is rightly used,

1. *When we contemplate the wisdom and goodness of God displayed in it.* It is everywhere visibly impressed with the finger of Deity ; it is full of design, beauty, and excellency ; it presents endless matter for philosophical and scientific investigation ; its size, its diurnal and annual revolutions ; its place and position in the solar system ; its variety and verdant surface ; its continents and islands ; its oceans and rivers ; its mountains and valleys ; its mineral productions ; its wonders and curiosities ; its atmosphere ; its splendid and star-bestudded canopy ; its bounties and blessings in the form of food, and enjoyments for its millions of inhabitants. Oh, it is a wonderful world ! the whole earth is full of the divine bounty. With all its variety of clime ; with all its tempests, and volcanoes, and earthquakes ; with all its deserts

and wildernesses, it would be a happy, joyous world, but for the existence of human depravity, and the reign of the prince of the powers of the air.

2. *We use it, when we thankfully enjoy the blessings of divine providence in it.* It is not only the region of existence, but of enjoyment ; not only of life, but of pleasure. Now God hath given this as a rich domain to man ; for him he sends the sunshine and the shower ; for him all the variety of the seasons, filling his heart with joy, &c. Now, it is the will of God that his goodness should be received and enjoyed in connection with the exaltation of his blessed name. " Every creature of God is good when sanctified," &c.

3. *We use it, when we make it the place of passage to a better.* It is not our rest, nor portion, nor continuing city. The mariner abuses the ocean if he is always at anchor, &c. The pilgrim abuses the way to the holy festivities, if he rears a dwelling and advances not on his course. The creature abuses God's gift, if he worships it instead of the Creator : so with the world, we are to sail over it to the better land. We are travelling through it to the celestial Canaan ; we are to enjoy its blessings, but adore the Giver, and to allow the gift to allure us to the residence of the great and blessed Donor.

4. *We use the world when we try to improve it by our residence in it.* God is raising it, exalting it, renewing it, but he is doing it by the influence and talents of his people in it. God blesses them, and makes them a blessing. The world is dark, and they are to shine ; polluted, and they are to be its preserving salt ; condemned, and they are to be its intercessors. By their spirit, they are to condemn its sin ; by their lives, to allure to the ways of godliness ; by their influence, to convert its inhabitants ; and by their prayers, to bring showers of blessings on it. Are we making it better ? Are we thus using it ?

II. WHAT IS ABUSING IT ?
1. *Living in it without improvement.* Without increasing in knowledge, without answering the end of our existence in it, without preparing for a better world.

2. *When we thankfully receive its blessings.* Surely God deserves to be acknowledged and praised ; yea, from the rising to the setting of the sun. But how many live without ? These speak of themselves

or their parents and ancestors, but are "without God;" never own him, nor bless him, nor serve him. Surely this is abusing the world.

3. *When we set our hearts upon it.* The love of the world is idolatry; it cannot exist with the love of God; it is a God-dishonoring and God-excluding sin. It will expose its devotees to the doom of the world, be burnt up. We may know if our hearts are on it,

(1.) By our anxieties to get it and retain it.

(2.) By our conversation about it.

(3.) By the time and toil we devote to it.

(4.) By our sorrow at the loss of any part of it. Now these are sure and unerring signs of love to the world.

4. *We abuse it when we live as though we should never leave it.* How many do this; cannot bear to talk or think of leaving it; call things by their own names, and act in all things as though they would never be called out of it. Yet what can be more foolish or idiotic? I refer not to men making a sinful use of it, making it the scene of their ambition, pride, lust, &c. We all know that thus it is abused.

III. THE REASON FOR THE USE, AND AGAINST THE ABUSE, ASSIGNED IN THE TEXT. "For the fashion," &c. The word fashion is taken from the shifting scenes of the diorama, when first one representation and then another passes before you, until the whole dioramic representation is ended. Our own renowned dramatist has beautifully stated this—

"All the world's a stage,
And all the men and women merely players.
They have their exits and their entrances,
And one man in his time plays many parts."

In the world there is a constant change of characters, and therefore it is not to be trusted to, or depended upon. Look at it; now sunshine, then storm; now spring or summer, then autumn or winter; now all gay, then all gloom; now al smooth, then all raging and terrific; now all smiles, then all frowns; now all health, then all sickness; now all joy, then all tears; now all life, then all death. There is the sickly child, and there, the tortured sire; there the gay festive banquet, and yonder the drear sombre tomb; there the mansion of magnificence and splendor, and yonder the cot of squalid misery. Who would love it, idolize it, depend on it? Rather trust the

rising wave, the flitting sunbeam, the passing breeze. Oh no, "the fashion of this world," &c.

APPLICATION.

1. Heaven is the region of stability and eternal blessedness.

2. Seek it, live and prepare for it.

THE DIVINE REQUIREMENTS.

"He hath showed thee, O man, what is good; and what doth the Lord require of thee but to do justly, and to love mercy, and to walk humbly with thy God."—MICAH vi. 8.

THE prophet inquires in the preceding verse in what way and manner he may come with acceptance before God. He then refers to burnt-offerings, &c., and asks if these, if offered upon a grand and extensive scale, will recommend to the divine favor; or, if the offering of human sacrifices, the fruit of the body, would propitiate for the sin of the soul. Now, it is a palpable fact, that among the vilest and most cruel of the human race, sacrifices and religious rites have been presented to their varied sanguinary deities. It is not however these, whether presented on the rural altar, or in the temple of thousands, that can avail, instead of the great practical duties of life. Services, however regularly performed—sacrifices, however costly, God will reject, if the heart is not the seat of devotion, and the life of practical godliness. He hath showed thee, O man, what is good; really, intrinsically good. Good for its possessors and for society; good, as resembling God, the perfection of all goodness. "Do justly," &c. Let us, then, refer to these three essentials of genuine piety.

I. JUSTICE. "Do justly." This, doubtless, refers to our conduct towards our fellow-men. It *includes a right course* of action in the various stations in which the providence of God may place us. As such it is exceedingly comprehensive, and will embrace and be found connected with all the events of life. It includes truth, sincerity, honesty, &c.

1. *There is civil justice.* Existing between rulers and people. Those in authority are responsible for the enactment of righteous laws, and the administration of universal equity. Then, there is loyal obedience and subjection to magistrates and

all in authority. Christ clearly taught this, when he said, in reference to the tribute money, "Render," &c.

2. *Commercial justice, or our conduct in reference to the pecuniary transactions of life.* Now, this includes both buyers and sellers. It is a violation of this to take advantage of the ignorance or the inexperience of those with whom we deal. We never need misunderstand this principle, if we apply Christ's golden rule, "Do ye unto others," &c.

3. *Relative justice.* Now, this extends to the various stations, &c., of life. It includes parents and children, servants and masters, brethren and sisters, &c. Now, on all these subjects the word of God is full and explicit, so that he who runs may understand, &c. Now, to "do justly," must be the constant and unvarying rule in all matters, to all persons, and at all times; in lesser as well as in greater affairs; see Rom. xiii. 7, &c.

II. MERCY. "Love mercy." Now, this includes,

1. *Kindness to the poor and wretched.* This was extensively exhibited under the old dispensation; we have chapter after chapter on it. The poor, the stranger, the widow, and the fatherless, are never to be forgotten. "Blessed is he who considereth the poor," &c. See, too, how the apostle enforced the same, &c. "We should remember," &c. "Pure religion," &c.

2. *Compassion towards our enemies.* Now, this is extremely difficult, as it is the very contrary of what the natural heart would dictate. Not railing for railing; not slander for slander; not evil for evil; not cursing for cursing. See Matt. v. 43, &c.; see also Rom. xii. 17.

3. *Unfeigned charity towards all men.* So that we love all men; would not injure, nay, ready to do good to all; feel interested in all; pray for all; rejoice to promote the happiness of all. Now, this is not to be professed merely, but practised; yea, not only *practised*, but *loved*.

III. HUMILITY. "Walk humbly," &c.

1. *By cherishing self-abasing thoughts of ourselves.* Pride is the natural bias of the mind. There is *spiritual* pride; pride of talent, or knowledge, or merit. All this is odious to God. Jehovah hates it—he loathes it; nothing can compensate for it; it spoils all. We must be abased. Our ignorance —our weakness—our sins ought sufficient-

ly to do it. "Lord, I am vile." "I abhor myself." "Wo is me, for I am undone," &c.

2. *By exalting the divine perfections, and ever glorying in God.* God ought, and must have undivided glory. He will not that any should glory before him. By veneration—by reverence—by praise, we must extol the Lord God, &c. Now, this must be our walk. In secret and in public, the lower we descend in the valley of humility, the higher will be our station in glory.

APPLICATION.

If we would exemplify the text,

1. *The word of God must be our rule.*

2. *The spirit of God, our guide.* "He will lead," &c.

3. *The example of Christ, our model.*

4. *Prayer to God, our constant exercise.*

GODLY SUBMISSION.

"And Aaron held his peace."—LEVITICUS x. 3.

THE ways of God must, of necessity, often be mysterious to us. They are so especially in reference to his own people. Aaron was one of God's distinguished servants. His sons, too, had been favored in beholding the divine glory, in company with Moses, their father, and the seventy elders of Israel. But, alas! they neglected the important sanctities of divine worship, and presumptuously offered strange fire on the altar of the Lord. For this, divine vengeance overtook them, and they were smitten with instant death. To be bereaved of a son, under ordinary circumstances, is a distressing bereavement; but to be bereft of two, suddenly, and by God's visitation of displeasure, is one of the greatest calamities to which a parent could be subjected. Yet, this was Aaron's trial; this cup of anguish he had to drink; and under this severe cross, it is said in the text, "Aaron held his peace." In other words, he bore his affliction with pious submission, as a man of God. Let us inquire,

I. WHAT IS INVOLVED IN THE SPIRIT AARON MANIFESTED.

II. THE PRINCIPLES ON WHICH IT CAN BE VINDICATED.

III. THE MEANS BY WHICH IT MAY BE ATTAINED.

I. WHAT IS INVOLVED IN THE SPIRIT AARON MANIFESTED. We are not to suppose that it was the silence,

(1.) Of Stoicism. Doubtless he felt, and felt keenly.

(2.) Neither was it the silence of haughtiness; disdaining to quail before the Most High.

(3.) Nor yet the silence of melancholy, where the spirit was broken, and hope extinguished.

(4.) Nor yet the silence of terror, from an overwhelming sense of God's wrath. Aaron had seen striking exhibitions of these; but it was the silence,

1. *Of deep anguish.* Not the rolling, noisy brook of lamentation; but the deep stream of affliction, sinking into his heart, overwhelming his filial affections, and absorbing all his parental sensibilities. It was trouble words could not express, nor sighs, nor groans duly indicate.

2. *Of entire resignation to God's will.* He was dumb, and opened not his mouth, for God had done it; and he did not exalt his judgment against that of God, nor doubt the rectitude and wisdom of what the Lord had done. How entire was the resignation! it was unquestioning—unmurmuring. Nature was subordinated to grace, and the parent bowed before the admonitions of heaven. In this Aaron acted with more of the devoted submission of the child, than either Job, Elijah, Jeremiah, and many other of the celebrated saints of the Lord. Consider,

II. THE PRINCIPLES ON WHICH THIS SPIRIT CAN BE JUSTIFIED.

1. *On the ground of God's sovereignty.* Has he not a right to do as he deems fit with the workmanship of his hands? He is the potter, and we the clay. Does he not do according to his will among the armies of heaven? &c. "The Lord killeth, and maketh alive." "Behold, he taketh away, and who can hinder him?"

2. *On the ground of the divine righteousness.* He is righteous in all his ways; not only when he blesses, but when he corrects, or even punishes. He never errs, nor inflicts his wrath beyond the desert. He never acts from whim, nor caprice, nor passion, nor revenge. Justice and judgment are the habitation of his throne.

3. *On the ground of the divine goodness.* God loves to exercise goodness—to bless—to make happy—and true it is, judgment is his strange work. Therefore, when he does so, it is for the maintenance of order and rule in his dominions; and the withholding of occasional displays of his terror would only tend to harden the wicked to the increase of daring sin, and thus the ultimate ruin of a greater number of his responsible creatures. All his dispensations are essentially good, and merciful as well as just. Observe,

III. THE MEANS BY WHICH THIS SPIRIT MAY BE ATTAINED.

1. *Let us contemplate the hopeless condition of fallen angels.* These have sinned, are ruined, and forever damned. How different is our condition! How merciful are the ways of God to men!

2. *Let us remember our guilt.* What is its amount? Who can number his sins? How repeated—aggravated! Each sin has deserved eternal death. All short of that, is grace, &c. No sinner, therefore, is punished beyond his desert. The trial may be keen, heavy, continued; but it is not hell, despair, everlasting wo.

3. *The number of the divine benefits.* How countless—how rich—how free; benefits of nature—of providence—especially of grace. The blessings, too, he has in reversion for the saints. Eternal life; everlasting glory. How few, comparatively, our sorrows and griefs!

4. *The connection between our severest trials, and best interests.* As trials are not contingent, so neither are they without design. Their end is our discipline in holiness, our improvement in divine things. They work for us. "All things work together," &c. Our crosses are blessings in disguise. They are to elicit latent feelings —to strengthen virtues—polish graces— loosen from earth—make us sick of sin— and raise our hearts and desires to the better land.

APPLICATION.

1. *Acquiescing silence honors God.* If we thus honor God, he will assist and comfort. He will lift up—heal—sustain, &c.

2. *Boisterous complainings only aggravate our sorrow.* These can do us no good; but they grieve the Holy Spirit. By these, we reflect on religion, &c.—injure our own souls.

3. *Prayer must ever accompany our resignation.* "Call upon me," &c. "Is any afflicted, let him pray," &c.

4. *All the dispensations of God will be fully vindicated in the judgment-day.* Then his ways and works will appear worthy of his unsullied purity, inflexible truth, and universal benevolence.

VIGILANCE AND SOBRIETY ENFORCED.

" But the end of all things is at hand ; be ye therefore sober, and watch unto prayer."—1 PET. iv. 7.

VERY many of the moral evils of life arise from supposing eternal things to be very distant. This supposition leads to worldliness, to skepticism, to sloth, and indifference. Constant attention therefore to the brevity of life is incessantly urged both in the Old and New Testament scriptures. One very ancient prayer runs thus : " So teach us to number our days," &c. " Oh that they were wise," &c. David prayed, "Teach me how short my time is." Christ often urged this. " Be ye therefore ready." Paul exhorted that they would redeem the time, &c. James, " Boast not thyself," &c. Then our text, " The end of all things," &c.

I. THE SOLEMN DECLARATION.
II. THE ADMONITORY COUNSEL.

I. THE SOLEMN DECLARATION. " The end of all things," &c. It has been supposed that the apostle referred to the destruction of Jerusalem, which was so graphically drawn and predicted by the Redeemer. But it is rather to be supposed that he is referring to the great consummation of all things, especially connecting the text with the fifth verse. Nearly eighteen centuries have rolled round since then, and therefore you doubt the truth and force of the text. But what are 1800 years to eternity ? " A thousand years with the Lord are but as one day," &c. But the force of the text will appear if you remember that death terminates our probation, and then judgment follows. Just as a man who falls asleep, and the hours of night only appear as a moment, when he awakes. So will it be even with Abel, the first who fell asleep, at the end of the world. Besides, at death we enter on our final state, which the judgment will only confirm and not alter. Then, really and truly as near as you are to death, are you near to the end of all the things of this world as they concern you ; and who can say how near that is ?

(1.) Look at the general definitions of human life—at its longest and best, but vanity. A vapor — a thing of naught. " Man that is born of a woman," &c. But a step between any man and death. Our cradles rock us to the tomb. Whoever we be, wheresoever we go, we are travelling to the tomb. Oh yes, as an arrow we are darting through this life, &c.

" Every beating pulse we tell,
 Leaves but the number less."

(2.) Observe how this has been verified in the history of those around you. According to a careful computation, from fifty-six to sixty die every minute ; 3,360 every hour ; 80,640 per day ; 564,000 per week ; 2,257,000 per month ; 29,433,000 per year. Thousands have died in this metropolis, many in this neighborhood—several from this congregation—many of you have lost friends and relatives.

(3.) Is it not reasonable then to suppose your end may be near ? What have you which they had not ? Youth ? why one of our sabbath-school children has perished as the flower ; strength ? many possessed of manly vigor and mature strength ; health ? oh, how soon this withers ; a cold—an accident—a breath of unwholesome air, and the system sickens, and the grave becomes our house ; and when this period arrives, it is the end of this world to us. Its cares, and toils, and riches, and pleasures, and society. The sun shines, but we hail not its light—the wind blows, but we feel not the breeze. The seasons revolve, but we know it not. The noise of business and pleasure is as loud as ever, but we hear it not—the voice of mercy is proclaimed, and the songs of praise sung, and the cry of prayer presented, but we know it not. Now this period may be especially near to some now before God. Consider,

II. THE ADMONITORY COUNSEL. " Be sober, and watch unto prayer." Observe, the duties are,

1. *Sobriety.* Guard against excess, see Eph. v. 15, &c. ; Observe also the words of the Redeemer, Luke xxi. 34. But this sobriety involves freedom from worldly intoxication — from vanity — frivolity, &c. " To be sober-minded," &c. To be found exercising Christian wisdom and prudence. " Brethren, the time is short, therefore," &c.

2. *Devotional vigilance.* I unite the

two, "Watch unto prayer," mere vigilance will not do, nor mere prayer, but both, and both united. So Christ also has wedded the two together. "Watch and pray," &c.

(1.) Watch against Satan, and pray that you may tread him under your feet.

(2.) Watch against the world, and pray that you may be kept from its influence and spirit.

(3.) Watch against your own hearts, and pray for the efficient aids of the Holy Ghost.

(4.) Watch against the seductions of time, and the concerns of this life, and pray for spiritual-mindedness, and a meetness for the realities of eternity.

APPLICATION.

1. To all both parts of the text are applicable. None are exempted from the first declaration, and therefore the latter part is peculiarly appropriate.

2. Let these truths be pondered by every one.

3. Act in reference to them.

FRAILTY AND SINFULNESS OF MAN.

"And we all do fade as a leaf; and our iniquities, like the wind, have taken us away."—ISAIAH lxiv. 6.

DAYS, and times, and seasons, are all instructors of mankind, if they will but hear and consider, and understand. "Day unto day uttereth speech, night," &c. The animal creation also instruct us, the birds of the air, the fishes of the sea, and the insect tribe ; they all obey their respective instincts, and answer the end of their being. The four seasons of the year, are full of wisdom and admonition to the thoughtful observer. Spring is the emblem of youth with all its beautiful prospects and visions of hope. Summer is the emblem of maturity—of man in riper years—the season of activity and toil. Autumn is the emblem of old age, decrepitude, and affliction. And winter of mortality, when man goeth to his long home, &c. Our attention is called to one of the most striking evidences of autumn, the fading of the leaf. Let us consider,

1. SOME OF THE ILLUSTRATIONS OF WHICH THE TEXT IS CAPABLE. Let us look at the sublunary character of empires and nations. Taking a survey of the mighty empires of ancient times, whether the Egyp-

tian, or Assyrian, or Chaldean, or the nation of the Jews, we might have reasoned and inferred as to their perpetual abiding, but they all had their rise, and glory, and decay, and most of them their utter ruin. Their chief capitals, where are they ? Tyre, and Nineveh, and Babylon, where are they ? Palaces razed—buildings levelled—the site of their former occupation disputed. Their glory passed away—Ichaboc written on the countries of which they were the metropolis or chief cities. We see here on a large and mighty scale, the truth of the text. "We all do fade as a leaf." See it illustrated,

2. *In the history of families.* Look what havoc and change is observable in families. Go back to the first family ; see the beloved and godly son a corpse. Look at the family of the friend of God, "Give me a burying-place," &c. Look at the prophet when the mandate is declared. "Son of man," &c. See the horrid slaughter of the infants of Galilee ; and Rachel weeping, &c. The ruler's daughter is dead—the widow's son is borne on the bier to the place of sepulchres—Lazarus has been already interred. What in reference to our own family ? Our devoted anxious parents where are they ? The companions of our early years, where are many of these ? What disruption, what invasion, by the relentless destroyer! No kindred tie can ward off—the most sacred are snapped asunder and destroyed. How true of families !

3. *Observe the personal illustration of the text.* The text equally applies to individuals ; nations and families are of course composed of individuals. Now, what is our life, a vapor — a thing of naught. "Boast not thyself," &c. What have we that is secure, that fades not ? Our possessions are uncertainty in the abstract. Our honors are a puff of breath. Our beauty or comeliness is a superficial tincture exhaled in a single hour. Our strength is lost by a few moments of pain. Our life is a span—our breath is in our nostrils, and we stand in jeopardy every hour. Consider also how true this is of all men. Speak we of the latitudes of the earth—the torrid and the frigid zones are alike here. City and village, savage or civilized. Wealth avails not—dignity avails not—power avails not—influence avails not—even knowledge avails not. Nay, godliness avails not in interrupting the victories of the king of ter-

rors. The sentence is gone forth to every human being, " Dust thou art," &c. The decree is sealed and ratified. " Man that is born of woman," &c. Notice, too, how correctly the falling of the leaf portrays our mutability.

(1.) The falling leaf becomes disunited, and separates from the rest.

(2.) It descends from the branch, and is prostrate on the ground.

(3.) It withers and decays, and returns to its mother earth.

(4.) Some are blown off by the fierce wind and early blast. Others survive to the usual season, and some survive to the verge of winter. So exactly with life; the infant—the youth—the man—and the aged. But how true sooner or later of all ! Observe,

II. The cause which the prophet assigns. " Our iniquities, like the wind," &c. Yes, sin has caused all the separations and disruptions of the universe. Angels from heaven—our first parents from Eden—mankind from God—man from man —body from soul. Sin is the womb of all diseases—the parent of the grave—the opener of hell—the curse of the world. Our iniquities. We need not blame our first parents. We have made iniquity our own ; we have chosen it, adopted it—nourished it—and therefore " our iniquities, like the wind," &c. Then let us attempt an improvement of the subject.

1. *Let us wisely dwell and reflect on what is fading.* Inconsideration will not affect its truth. Ponder, consider, be familiar.

2. *Let us practically act in reference to these things.* Improve time, live usefully, seek the end of our existence and redemption.

3. *Seek an interest in those things which fade not, but are permanent and abiding.* The love and favor of God. The merits and grace of Christ. The influences of the Holy Spirit. A title, and meetness for heaven. Let me urge this on all, and every one. See that the evil is remedied in its source. Sins blotted out, and then we shall live in a better land, &c. Perpetual spring, &c.

EARTHLY VANITIES.

" Vanity of vanities, saith the Preacher: vanity of vanities ; all is vanity."—Ecclesiastes i. 2.

The life and history of Solomon are highly instructive, interesting, and admonitory.

He rises in the horizon of dignity and greatness, as the sun in his glory ; his splendid beams enlighten and enliven the pages of Jewish history ; all seem to indicate abiding greatness and prosperity. But, alas ! his sun becomes obscured ; sins, like dark clouds, intervene ; and his moral history for a length of time becomes afflictive, dreary, and distressing. At eventide, however, it is light. Before the ending of his day, the sun again breaks forth ; and the serious lessons of this book give us every reason to hope, that his return and penitency before God were sincere, deep, and effectual. As a true convert from his worldly voluptuousness, and idolatrous pursuits, he records his experience, and places this sermon as a kind of pedestal, on which a beacon is to be reared, to warn all succeeding generations of the folly and misery of departing from the true living God. Our subject is the leading inscription or text of the whole discourse, " Vanity of vanities," &c. Our text is capable of great abuse and misrepresentation. It may be much distorted, and grievously misapplied. We shall, therefore,

I. Guard the subject from misappropriation.

II. Give it a rational and scriptural interpretation. And,

III. Labor to urge its true and just application.

I. Guard the subject from misappropriation.

1. *The subject is often misappropriated by the disbeliever.* I mean the skeptic—the rejecter of revelation. He contemplates all around him as the result of accident or chance. He recognises no inventive wisdom—no harmonious order—no controlling power—no intellectual design. Seated on the barren rock of infidelity ; excluding Deity from his own creation, he exclaims, in the language of affected indifference, " Vanity of vanities," &c.

2. *The subject is misappropriated by the gay and superficial.* Persons who are truly the butterflies of creation, only they happen to have the form of intellectual and contemplative beings. For these there is no attraction, but in the gay scenes of dissipation. Frivolity is the atmosphere they breathe. Of science, truly so called— philosophy, worth the name—literature,

adapted to enlighten, they are totally ignorant. Speak to these of the solemn verities associated with man's responsibility, and they have no ear to hearken, or mind to observe. They imagine all things must partake of the frivolity of their own pursuits, and consider the text as the best excuse for negligence and irreligion.

3. *The text is misappropriated by the satiated sensualist.* Some give themselves up to work all kinds of voluptuous iniquity with greediness. Ignorant of the true design of animal enjoyments, they expect to live, be hale, and happy, in the hot-bed of putrefaction. At length the mind is overworked—the system shattered—the constitution broken—an immensity of material treasured up for bitter remorse, and protracted pain and horror—and the text becomes their constant exclamation, " Vanity of vanities," &c.

4. *The text is often misappropriated by the unfortunate and distressed.* Persons set out, calculating upon the certainty of pleasure and prosperity ; they only dream of aerial castles standing firm and long. The cherished scheme being realized ; the fair weather, blue skies, and enchanting scenery ; health, friends, riches, enjoyments, are in the inventory of their good, as sure realities. At length come clouds, and storms, and tempests ; one plan is wrecked upon another ; their castles evaporate, their prospects are blighted, and they sit down cynical, morose, disappointed, and cry out, with impetuous and discontented spirit, "Vanity of vanities," &c. Now, it is not necessary that I expose the fallacy in each case I have presented to you. I presume the true state of the matter must be self-evident. Therefore, let us consider,

II. The rational and scriptural interpretation of the text. We premise, none of the divine works are vain ; all He doth is wise, and good, and righteous. All the bounties of heaven are good, and not vain in themselves. This may be said of all that can contribute to the physical or mental enjoyment of man. Knowledge, wealth, society, music, when rightly applied, are not surely criminal. But the text is to be understood thus : that, as man's chief good and spiritual portion, the whole world, with all it presents, is " vanity of vanities." Now, the correctness of this will appear,

1. *If you consider their want of adaptation*

to *man's true nature.* Material things may do for material creatures ; earthly good for mere earthly natures ; but that which is mental, must have a mental good—that which is moral, must have a moral good. Now, riches, honors, carnal enjoyments, might do, were man only material ; had he no spirit, soul, conscience, &c. But to the mind they are chaff, and vanity, and wind ; they cannot satisfy—they cannot fill, for they are not adapted ; they are vanity, &c.

2. *If you consider their mutable uncertainty.* They are ill-adapted, but also insecure. " Riches make to themselves wings," &c. How strange, that man should passionately love and depend on a bird upon the wing ! They are, indeed, uncertain riches. Honor is a bubble—a breath. Only five days intervened between the hosannas, and the cry of " Crucify him, crucify him." Cardinal Wolsey's bitter exclamation has been proved true in ten thousand instances. " Oh ! that I had served my God as I have my king," &c. Pleasures are not ever fragrant ; often they satiate, and then disgust. All these are flitting ; inscriptions on the sand, &c. And what is life itself, that by which we hold the tenure of the whole ? Man, at his best estate, is altogether vanity. Childhood, and youth, and manhood, all, all are vanity.

3. *They do not satisfy the desires, or improve the heart.* Who does not feel his accountability ? Who can obliterate the claims of the divine governor, or utterly bury the admonitions of conscience ? There is the bed of affliction—the hour of death—the day of judgment ; these demand preparation—fitness. What worldly thing can prepare us for them ? Say—is it wealth, titles, wine, festivities, or even general knowledge ? Do they exalt, purify, control the life, assuage the passions, meet the desires, answer the hopes ? Do they array in the robes of virgin purity for the coming of the Bridegroom ? Do they adorn with the wedding-garment ? Do they give a sure hope of a blessed immortality, fit us to die, commend to God, and meeten for glory ? If they do not, then how true the text, " Vanity of vanities !" Is not the interpretation of the text true and just ? Let us, then,

III. Labor to urge a true and just application of the subject.

1. *Let all created good have its right and subordinate place in our estimation.* Food and raiment ; wealth and reputation ; the proper pleasures of life, &c. We demand no monastic seclusion—no corporeal tortures—no cynical life ; but remember, these perish in the using. Call them by their right names ; apply them to their proper end ; be moderate in all things lawful ; and avoid the very appearance of evil.

2. *Let it induce us to seek those which are truly precious and abiding.* Divine knowledge is not vain ; divine riches are not, &c. ; divine honors are not ; divine pleasures are not. A good conscience—God's favor—God's love, &c. ; all these are presented to us in Jesus Christ.

3. *Often contrast the vanity of this world, with the permanent glory of heaven.* There no changes distract—no tempests—no pain, nor sin, nor death, &c. Oh, seek it ! set your affections upon it, &c. Confess that you are pilgrims, &c.

A PRAYER CONCERNING DEATH.

"Lord, make me to know mine end, and the measure of my days, what it is, that I may know how frail I am."—PSALM xxxix. 4.

THIS is one of David's more serious psalms. Generally, he tuned his harp to praise and adoration ; but other subjects were sometimes allowed the precedency. In this psalm, he contemplates his mortality. As a traveller, he looks to the end of his journey ; as a sailor, to the completion of his voyage ; as a laborer, to the conclusion of the day, and the night of death. This is a subject which ought not to be forgotten. It may not be so agreeable as others, but it may be more useful. Thus thought Moses, when he prayed, "So teach us to number," &c., and the text. Observe,

I. DEATH, AS TO THIS WORLD, IS THE END OF ALL MEN. We say, as to this life ; for, though a man dies, yet he shall live again. Death is not extinction—annihilation. It may be said, that the good man only then gins to live ; but it is the *end* as to this rld.

1. *It is the end of all our temporal conns.* Look at the universal toil of human ings. Go to the *mine*, to the *field*, to the

sea, to the *shop*, to the *furnace*, to the *laboratory*, to the *counting-room*, to the *study*, &c., all toil, and this, when not excessive, is advantageous to man. Religion says, a man may be diligent, &c. ; but death is the end. The man's work may *live*, but the artificer, the author, must die. The building, the picture, the book, may remain, &c. Think of this—work for time—live for eternity.

2. *It is the end of our earthly relationships.* How endearing, and sweet, and precious are these ! Look at that family— at that social circle—at that Christian church ; but there is to be a dissolution of these. Parents die, children die, friends die, ministers and people all die. Now two duties. Let us value and love them, and do them good while we have them. Let us not forget their mortality, and idolize them.

3. *It is the end of our probation.* This is the solemn view. We are on trial ; we have talents, blessings and opportunities ; we are stationed here as candidates for eternity. But at death the probation ends ; our talents, and time, and all must be accounted for. Then, we must account for our stewardship—the solemn reckoning, and the reward or punishment. Follow the reflection—I must give an account.

4. *It is the end of our exertions.* Then, we can do no more for our families, the church, or the world. Works of goodness, and devotion, and mercy end. In eternity, no ignorant children, no sick families, no intemperate victims to be reclaimed. As we can do no more for ourselves, neither for others. Reflect, "I must work while it is called day," &c.

II. THIS END WE ARE LIABLE TO FORGET. Hence the text, "Make me to know," &c. ; that is, to remember, to consider, &c. We are liable to forget,

1. *Because the subject is not agreeable to flesh and blood.* Death itself is an evil ; love of life implanted deeply ; in most cases, it produces gloom, &c.

2. *Because other things absorb all.* The mind choked with cares, surfeited with pleasure, or occupied with trifles. Often all the time, all the faculties engaged in other things. Not one convenient season, &c.

3. *Because Satan would have us forget it.* He always tries to blind men as to the future. He would have men ever think of

health and life, and the world. He keeps out of mind the coffin, the shroud, the grave, eternity. Who does not know the truth of this?

III. PRAYER TO GOD IN REFERENCE TO THIS END, IS HIGHLY IMPORTANT AND DESIRABLE. We have referred to the prayers of Moses, &c.

1. *By prayer to God the subject will be kept in mind.* We cannot pray about it, without this. Thus we shall think and consider, &c.

2. *Prayer to God will sanctify the subject to us.* God will teach us, &c.; and his teaching will influence our hearts, &c.

(1.) We shall be deeply impressed with our own frailty, and the uncertainty of life. Measure of our days short; handbreadth; as nothing; altogether vanity; as many entrances for death as we have pores in the body.

(2.) We shall prepare for it, by repentance for sin; by faith in Christ's death; by securing a title for the skies; by walking as strangers, &c.—pilgrims, &c.

(3.) We shall watch for it. "Be ye, therefore, ready," &c. "All the days of my appointed time," &c. Not forget it; but, like the mariner at the mast head, be looking out for the haven of rest, and the shores of bliss.

APPLICATION.

1. *Who does not need to pray thus?* Who has thought rightly, &c., enough on this subject?

2. *Is not the subject worthy the attention of all?* What! the young? How often the flower fades before the noon-day, &c. Man is as mortal at eighteen as four-score.

3. *Those who will not entertain the subject will die twice—yea, forever.*

4. *There is a world where such a prayer will be unnecessary—yea, improper.* No sickness, or death; in the heavenly Canaan, &c.

THE HOUSE OF MOURNING AND THE HOUSE OF FEASTING CONTRASTED.

" It is better to go to the house of mourning, than to go to the house of feasting."—ECCLES. vii. 2.

WE will at once call your attention to the text. Let us,

I. VISIT THE HOUSE OF FEASTING, AND SEE WHAT MAY BE LEARNED THERE. And,

II. VISIT THE HOUSE OF MOURNING, AND ASCERTAIN THE TRUTH OF THE TEXT. That " it is better," &c.

I. WE WILL VISIT THE HOUSE OF FEASTING, AND SEE WHAT IS TO BE LEARNED THERE.

1. *The house of feasting must be described.* Solomon does not mean the house of revelry, scenes of excess, places of sinful pleasure; a wise or good man would never form such a contrast; but there are houses of feasting spoken of with divine approbation.

(1.) There were religious feasts; the feast of the tabernacle, the feast of the passover, the feast connected with the jubilee.

(2.) Feasts of social intercourse and hospitality. Lot made a feast in Sodom when the angels visited him; Abraham made a feast when Isaac was weaned; Isaac made a feast of reconciliation with Abimelech.

(3.) Feasts were spoken of with indirect approbation by Christ. "When thou makest a feast call the poor," &c., Luke xiv. 13.

(4.) The gospel provision is often likened to a feast. "A feast of fat things," &c. Gospel supper.

(5.) Christ honored a feast with his divine presence, at the marriage at Cana in Galilee. There may be seasons therefore when feasts may be seasonable.

2. *Lessons of usefulness may be learned in the house of feasting.*

(1.) We may learn the goodness of God in the provisions of his bounty, and this should inspire gratitude. Every creature of God should be sanctified with thanksgiving.

(2.) We may learn the pleasurableness of the social principle. God has formed us for mutual enjoyment.

(3.) We may learn the joyous character of our religion; not designed to make us wretched, but happy. "Rejoice in the Lord always," &c. We remark,

3. *In going to the house of feasting some cautions are necessary.*

(1.) These visits should only be occasional, or we shall waste our time and means; also enervate both body and mind.

(2.) These visits should be regulated by moderation, even in the enjoyment of the good things of God. In eating, our moderation should be manifest, we should not pamper the flesh, &c.

(3.) These visits must be connected with watchfulness, there are many snares: to foolish talking and jesting, to lightness and frivolity, to vanity and display, to an undue mixture with unprofitable company. Under these restrictions and limitations we may visit the house of feasting. But let us,

II. VISIT THE HOUSE OF MOURNING, AND SEE THE TRUTH OF THE TEXT, THAT IT IS BETTER, AND THEREFORE SHOULD HAVE THE PREFERENCE. " It is better," &c. By the house of mourning is obviously meant the house of bereavement. Where death has invaded, and where the friends are met to attend to the funeral obsequies of the departed; whose house has not been at one time or another a house of mourning? Who has not lost a parent, a wife, a husband, child, brother, sister, or dearly loved friend? With many this has been frequently repeated. How often have we been called to visit the house of mourning! One and another have finished their journey before us, many have gone to their long home, and as mourners we have had to visit their bereaved dwellings. What is to be seen in the house of mourning? The fruit of sin, human nature in ruins, the body prostrate, loathsome, the spirit fled. What a change! I wonder a celebrated poet could ever have composed that hymn,

" Ah ! lovely appearance of death," &c.

What is lovely? To whom? Yet it is good to visit the house of mourning, yea, better, &c. The house of mourning,

1. *Teaches us what we are slow and unwilling to learn elsewhere.*

(1.) Our own mortality. The "living know," &c., and yet act as if they did not. The subject does not impress as it ought, but in the house of mourning it comes home; here we have it in reality before our eyes.

(2.) Our own frailty. We think, though death may come, he is not near,—a great way off. This is one of Satan's delusions, but how often is it torn off in the house of mourning! not only the aged and infirm, but the young and strong.

(3.) The emptiness of earthly honors. What avail titles? honors, renown, talents, learning, &c. ; write them on the coffin plate, engrave them on the marble tablet, &c. How futile, &c.

(4.) The vanity of all earthly things.

Its wealth, its pleasures, music, revelry how empty, &c.

2. *In the house of mourning we see the necessity of brotherly affection and sympathy.* In the house of feasting each one seems happy, all appear independent, to have resources of joy in themselves. But how different in the house of mourning! Here we see our fellow-creatures bowed down, heavy laden, drenched in tears, and our sympathy is called out. We are to aid, to feel, to comfort, to weep, &c. ; and it is well that we should do so. All this softens, subdues, hallows; it tends to tear up selfishness, and to infuse into the heart a spirit of love and generosity.

3. *In the house of mourning the blessings of the gospel are better prized.* "The full soul loatheth the honeycomb." The blessings of the gospel do not attract the gay and the joyous as they ought in the house of feasting. Created good seems then to be in the ascendant. How different when sorrowful and heavy laden; how different when the cistern is broken up, or holds no water; how different when we feel we are dying creatures in a dying world! Now light and peace are desired, now a refuge is precious, now the soul can retire and think and pray. How beautiful now will be the feet of those, &c. Many who in the day of prosperity were trifling and inconsiderate, in the day of adversity have considered. In their affliction they will seek me early.

4. *In the house of mourning we are brought to contemplate the future world.* We are brought to the margin of eternity ; we follow our friends to the very verge, and there they leave us ; we cannot go with them, but our thoughts do so—our feelings—our imaginations ; we seem to come very near to it ; to its gate, and we look through the lattice work ; this is for our good. To be prepared for it ; we must think upon it ; have our thoughts and affections there ; be citizens of it here, expectants here, have our conversation in it, &c. Without these we shall never possess it ; in these respects how much better to go to the house of mourning, &c.

APPLICATION.

1. *Let our subject lead to serious consideration.* To solemn reflection. Brethren, the time is short, &c. Let this be our

prayer, "So teach us to number our days," &c.

2. *Let it lead the Christian to greater spirituality and devotedness.* How diligent we should be ; how earnest ; how intense !

3. *Let it lead the unconverted to immediate decision.* "Awake, thou that sleepest," &c. "I beseech you by the mercies of God," &c. Let the solemnities of religion now impress, &c. Now decide, &c.

THE DECEASE OF THE PIOUS.

" Precious in the sight of the Lord is the death of his saints."—PSALM cxvi. 15.

THERE are four things which are closely and essentially connected with each other. Life and death, judgment and eternity. Every day of life is one towards death, and one nearer to that great day for which all others were made. Death, judgment, and eternity, will just bear an aspect according to our character and course of life. As is the way so will be the end. "Whatsoever a man soweth that shall he also reap." "The wicked is driven away in his wickedness, but the righteous hath hope," &c. Our text relates,

I. To AN IMPORTANT CHARACTER. The Lord's saints.

II. To A SOLEMN EVENT. The death of the Lord's saints.

III. THE INTEREST THE DIVINE BEING TAKES IN THIS EVENT. "Precious," &c.

I. To AN IMPORTANT CHARACTER. The Lord's saints. The term signifies *holy ones ;* but in the original it signifies merciful ones. As mercy is one of the bright attributes of Jehovah, so it is one of the most illustrious graces in the Christian character. But the Lord's saints are distinguished,

1. *As renewed spiritual persons.* None such by nature or education. All men are far from God, &c. Naturally carnal— sold under sin. Aliens—far off, &c. Such must be renewed by the power of the gospel and the influences of the Holy Spirit, before they can become saints. By the Holy Spirit effectually working within them, they are made spiritual—new creatures in Christ Jesus.

2. *As righteous and holy persons.* He who is born of God doeth righteousness. Love to God and love to his commandments distinguish all saints. A righteous life is the only palpable and unquestionable evidence of the saint's true character. But besides righteousness, there will be a seeking after holiness, growing into the divine likeness—conforming to the divine image, &c. We observe,

3. *Saints are peculiar persons.* They differ from the mass. Do not go with the multitude, &c. Their speech betrayeth them. Their maxims, spirit, &c., are opposite to those of the world. Their pursuits and desires, &c., are all different to the world—they are saved out of it. They are pilgrims seeking a better country. Soldiers fighting with the powers of sin. Racers running for the celestial prize. Citizens of heaven, born from thence and thither bound. The text directs us,

II. To A SOLEMN EVENT. Death of the saints.

1. *The most eminent of saints are liable to death.* No amount of piety, goodness, talents, or usefulness, will exempt. No discharge in this war, &c. The fathers, where are they ; and the prophets, do they live forever ?

2. *The death of saints is under the gracious control of the Lord.* The whole of a good man's life is so ; all his hairs are numbered ; all his steps, &c. How much more so his death ! The time, place, manner, &c. The Lord guides through life, and also through the swellings of Jordan.

3. *The death of saints is often a present loss to the church on earth.* The church loses their presence, their prayers, influence, &c. But,

4. *The death of saints is their infinite advantage.* "To die is gain." "Blessed are the dead who die in the Lord," &c. The warfare is over—the race finished, &c. Now the sheaf is ripe—the likeness complete—the majority attained—the probation ended, and the perils over, forever and ever ; now, holiness, intelligence, and bliss, are perfected ; absent from sin, sorrow, and danger, and present with the Lord in the realms of purity, glory, and joy. Observe,

III. THE INTEREST THE LORD TAKES IN THIS EVENT. "Precious," &c.

1. *As such it is especially the subject of his gracious notice and regard.* He always beholds them with complacency and de-

ight, how much more now. He makes all the bed of his people ; he gives light in darkness, &c. He sustains and blesses according to their need, &c.

2. *As such he bestows peculiarly precious blessings.* Often taking down the tabernacle gradually ; often giving a rich experience ; often in mellowing the atmosphere, and irradiating the whole of the horizon, removing every stormy cloud ; restraining Satan, invigorating the graces, giving gleams of glory and draughts from the fountain-head of bliss. In one word, in giving dying grace.

3. *In enabling his dying saints to triumph in dissolution.* It was when dying, that Christ raised the shout of conquest. So Stephen—so Paul—so myriads. This is the Lord's doings, and thus religion, his saints, and especially his own blessed name, are honored and magnified.

APPLICATION.

1. *See the difference between the death of the righteous and of the wicked.* We see it represented in the contrasted scenes of Joseph's dream, where one was elevated to honor, and the other led forth to execution. In the passage of the Israelites through the Red Sea, and the overthrow of Pharaoh, &c.

2. *How different the supports of Deism and Christianity in a dying hour !* What can Deism do for its dying votaries ? Oh, think and reflect.

3. *How different the results of irreligion and piety !* A life misspent, means neglected, soul lost, &c. In the other, the work finished, and the rewards of eternity in sight. Who then will be on the Lord's side ? Young friends, delay not ; oh, let this subject move you ; let it allure you ; now decide !

THE FAITHFUL SERVANT'S REWARD.

" His lord said unto him, Well done, good and faithful servant ; thou hast been faithful over a few things, I will make thee ruler over many things ; enter thou into the joy of thy lord."— MATT. xxv. 23.

THE text is connected with the parable of the talents—a parable fraught with the most important instruction, and one which it is our true interest often to consult and study. In it we are taught our responsibility to God ; that the demands of Jehovah will be in proportion to the talents given, and the means of improvement possessed ; that a period will arrive when we must each render his individual account ; and that God will reward every man according to the use he has made of the talents committed to his trust. Now, the subject presents to our view the result of the divine scrutiny. The servant's accounts are satisfactory, his privileges have been improved, and his master publicly attests it, saying, " Well done," &c. Observe the character, the commendation, and the reward.

I. NOTICE THE CHARACTER REFERRED TO. It is that of servant ; a servant of God. Now, this can only be applied to the Christian ; not to the unconverted sinner, nor to the formalist. Now, in being the servants of God it is implied,

1. *That the service of sin and Satan has been abandoned.* We cannot serve both. In our natural state we are the servants of sin. In repentance we forsake the works, &c., of the devil ; we cease to be the slaves of iniquity ; the yoke of sin is taken from the neck ; and the fetters of our natural bondage are broken off. It implies,

2. *That Christ, and his service, have been cheerfully and solemnly assumed.* Christ invites the sinner to come to him ; to yield himself to him ; to present himself a living sacrifice, &c. Now, this has been done. The mind has assented ; the heart has obeyed. By believing consecration, Christ and his claims have been conceded, and an entire surrender of the soul to him has been made. It implies,

3. *That Christ's authority and commands are fully recognised.* If I am a servant, then Christ is my master. His authority I must own—his laws I must obey. It must be my calling, the end of my life to serve him. I must seek to know his will, and walk in all his commandments. Such briefly is the character. Notice,

II. THE COMMENDATION GIVEN. " Well done, good and faithful," &c. Now, what are the essentials of good and faithful servitude ? There must be,

1. *Diligence.* In opposition to negligence and indolence. An improvement of our time ; a proper regard to duty ; the laying out of our powers, &c. This is often inculcated, "Be diligent," &c. ' Giv-

ing all diligence," &c. The other servant was condemned for slothfulness, &c.

2. *Constancy.* In opposition to vacillation and change. The Christian recognises Christ as his master in all places and at all times. In public; in the domestic circle; in secret, &c. In all his ways he acknowledges, &c.

3. *Cheerfulness.* In opposition to constraint. Not from fear of death and hell, but from love. He is, indeed, constrained; but it is by love, "the love of Christ," &c. He delights to do the will of God; his heart is in it; he loves the master, and loves the service.

4. *Devoted fidelity and zeal.* In opposition to formality and unconcern. He feels the claims of God; he enters into them; he identifies them with his very life; he makes them his own; his first and best powers are yielded to God; Christ has the pre-eminence; the fire of zeal burns on the altar of his heart; he is as faithful even in small matters, as in great ones; he recognises the claims of Jesus to all he is, and to all he has—body, soul, and spirit—time and property.

5. *Perseverance to the end.* He is faithful, even unto death. He serves him in health and in sickness—in life, and to the hour of dissolution. Such is the commendation. Observe,

III. THE REWARD BESTOWED. "I will make thee ruler," &c. Now, this reward includes three things: Dignity, riches, and felicity. It is a reward of,

1. *Dignity.* "I will make thee ruler," &c. Now, this is the general doctrine of revelation, that the saints of God shall be exalted and dignified. God will glorify them before assembled worlds; He will own and confess them. They shall have dominion, be exalted to the station of the angels, and they shall be kings and priests unto God and the Lamb forever. They shall be exalted to thrones, bear victorious palms, and upon their heads shall be crowns of glory that fade not away. A reward of,

2. *Riches.* The riches of grace are now their portion—then the unsearchable riches of eternal life. They are heirs of God, and God shall be their unfailing and everlasting portion. Adversity and want shall be removed forever; have unbounded celestial treasures, and blessings everlasting. It is a reward,

3. *Of felicity.* "Joy of thy Lord."

Now, they have the joys of the Holy Spirit; but this they receive in streams from above. Have it by measure; but there they enter into the joy—bathe in the ocean. Now, they have rays of joy, &c.; there, they are surrounded by the meridian splendor of eternal noon. Now, this joy of the saints will,

(1.) Be proportionate; not all alike. One, two cities; another, five, &c. There are clearly degrees of future glory, "As one star differeth," &c. Three things will bear on the saint's future glory:—

Holiness. Which expands the mind, and gives it greater capability of enjoyment.

Usefulness. "They that turn many to righteousness," &c. And,

Sufferings. "Our light afflictions, &c., work out," &c. "Whoso forsaketh," &c.

(2.) It will be perfect. No mixture—no alloy—no intermission. All sources of sorrow left behind.

(3.) It will be boundless, both in measure and duration. Fulness of joy, and pleasures for evermore.

(4.) It will be the joy of our Lord. Of his *obtaining ;* of his *bestowing ;* the same with his joy, John xvii. 22. "He that overcometh," &c. If we suffer with him, we shall also reign with him; in the enjoyment of him forever and ever. Such will be the faithful servant's reward.

APPLICATION.

1. *Are we the characters?* The servants of Christ.

2. *Are we living and aspiring after the commendation of "good and faithful servants ?"* Are we diligent? constantly zealous? &c. Or, are we indolent? selfish? &c.

3. *How miserable will be the unfaithful servant's eternal destiny!*

4. *Let the devoted servants of Christ anticipate the reward.* Now, you are the happy people; but the fulness of the blessing is to come—the glory is yet to be revealed. Let it incite your feelings and powers; let it enliven your hope; let it cheer your souls:—

> "The thoughts of such amazing bliss,
> Should constant joys create."

5. *Who will be the servants of the Lord?* Who is willing, &c.

IMPORTANT INTERROGATIONS.

" What, then, shall I do, when God riseth up? And when he visiteth, what shall I answer him?"—Job xxxi. 14.

Job—the speaker in the text—is averring his integrity, in reference to his own servants, verse 13. A conscientious man will be considerate of those who depend upon him ; yea, a merciful man regardeth the life of his beast. But, we select the words of the text as referring to a crisis which will be peculiarly solemn and important to every one of us ; that period, when God will rise up and exact from every one an account of his stewardship. There is a passage quite parallel in signification to the text, Luke xiii. 24, &c. I ask, do any present dispute whether God will judge men or not ? if so, revelation must be rejected. This is often propounded for our serious consideration. It is the doctrine of the Old Testament, reiterated by the Saviour, made known by the apostles, and is one of the concluding visions of the Apocalypse. Is it not in perfect harmony, too, with reason, that man should be rewarded or punished according to his works ? Admitting, therefore, these essential principles, we ask, what shall we do ? Let us take the latter clause of the text first. When God riseth up in judgment,

I. WHAT WILL YOU ANSWER ? We put it to the two great divisions of mankind.

1. *We ask you, who are unconcerned and indifferent to religion?* We may assume, that God will require answers to such questions as these :—How have you lived ? What end has your life answered ? How have you employed your talents, opportunities, privileges? &c. What is your present state ? &c. What plea for your guilty condition ?

(1.) *Will you plead your uncertainty as to the nature of true religion?* That you had not demonstration as to the will and claims of God. Not sure as to the truth of the Bible, &c. May not God reply, How did you believe so many things on much slighter evidence ? History, biography, &c. Did you carefully, solemnly weigh the evidences, take pains to be right ? &c. Did you let conscience throw her influence into the right scale ? &c. Did you ascertain how the Bible produced such mighty effects? Could not doubt God's exceeding goodness. Why not love, praise, and worship him ? Is it not plain that you cannot answer ?

(2.) *Will you plead necessity, or circumstances, as the causes of your condition?* Perhaps you say that you had a depraved heart ; peculiar conformation of mind ; extremely ensnaring circumstances and temptations. Now, all this may be true ; but, if you were a judge in a human court, would you take these pleas from a robber, or an assassin ? Besides, God would reply and say, it is not your depravity, but the rejection of the remedy ; not your guilt, but refusal of the pardon ; not circumstances and snares, but despising my Spirit and grace. What then can you answer, when he visiteth ?

(3.) *Will you exhibit your excellencies to counterbalance your sins ?* A good man to your species ; that is, distinguished for humanity—a patriot—lover of your kind— a devoted parent, &c. Two objections to this :—

1. You never designed to serve God in all this. God not in all your thoughts. It was agreeable to your ideas and feelings.

2. You had your reward. Humanity rewards its possessor. Patriotism obtained your own approbation, and that of others. Domestic kindness was returned by the happiness it effected. You did not these things to the Lord, but to yourself, and you had the reward ; but God you neglected—despised.

(4.) *Will you refer to your purposes and resolutions ?* But then they have all been violated. Better not to vow, than to do so, and not to pay them. You had time ; perhaps many years. Means of grace in abundance ; numberless opportunities. A day was given—calls and invitations sent —providences to move you—events all preaching to you. Had you not a reasonable amount of time ? How many had not so much ? Enough for every thing but religion, the soul, and eternity. What will you answer ?

2. *But we turn to the righteous.* What will you answer ? No merit, or righteousness. Will you not refer to the mercy of God—to the sacrifice of Christ—to the plenitude of the gospel—to the efficacy of the Spirit ? Give all the glory to God. Not worthy of the least of thy mercies. Worthy is the Lamb.

" 'Tis just the sentence should take place ;
'Tis just ; but, oh ! thy Son hath died."

We turn now to the second question.

II. WHAT WILL YOU DO ? I ask this of

the unconverted—the unprepared, for the righteous will welcome Christ ; shout, All hail ! Hosanna !

1. *Will you flee ?* But how, or where ? God is omniscient and omnipresent. Cannot conceal, evade, or go beyond his reach and control. All will obey the trumpet's blast ; the sea—hades, &c.

2. *Will you resist ?* Angelic hosts, one of whom slew thousands in a night. Resist the almighty power of God ! the moth could better resist the strength of man ! resist the lightning — the desolating whirlwind ! resist the ocean's roaring tempest ! resist the earthquake—the pestilence !

3. *Will you seek the aid of your fellow-sinners ?* They will be in the like condemnation ; equally powerless—despairing—lost ! Now combination—multitudes, avail not.

4. *Will you appeal to the happy, the redeemed ?* Benevolence will surely be perpetuated in heaven. But if the God of benevolence can punish, then the most merciful will exclaim, " Just and righteous art thou," &c. Will they demur ? Oh, no ! They will solemnly respond, " So let all the enemies of God perish."

5. *Will you throw yourselves on the divine clemency ?* The reign of grace is over—the dispensation of clemency ended. Look at the sceptre—it is pure justice ; no longer pity, &c.

6. *Will you fly to the cross ?* Judea—Calvary, have all passed away. No ; the Lamb is no longer held up for contrition's gaze. The trumpet no longer sounds ; Christ is now judge ; the cross now glitters, as if with fiery indignation to the rejectors—to the unbelievers, &c. Hope and mercy are clean gone forever. What will you do ? Lie down in darkness ; be cast out, &c.

APPLICATION.

1. *But what will you do ?* Avert it now—prepare now—pray now—fear now—repent now—believe now—obtain a hope and title now.

2. *Who will this day ?* Who among you young—you aged ?

FUTURE PUNISHMENTS.

" Fear him which, after he hath killed, hath power to cast into hell."—LUKE xii. 5.

OUR subject is replete with that which is truly solemn, awful, and momentous ; yet it is one of those topics which evidently come within the proper sphere of ministerial duty ; it is a part of the counsel of God. The great apostle said, " Knowing the terrors of the Lord, we persuade men." Before entering, however, immediately on the discussion of the subject, a few prefatory observations may be necessary, perhaps essential.

(1.) That the great and blessed God has a right to make laws for the government of his intelligent creatures.

(2.) That these laws may justly be connected with rewards to the obedient, and with punishment to the disobedient.

(3.) That in the present life it is evident men are not punished and rewarded according to their moral character and doings.

(4.) That there must be therefore another world where the guilty will be punished, and the righteous rewarded.

(5.) That if men are not punished or rewarded in a future state, then the administrations of God are not equitable and just.

(6.) That the scriptures, however, do most clearly and fully reveal such rewards and punishments in the world to come.

(7.) That we can know nothing with certainty on this subject, except what is contained in the word of God.

(8.) Then the word of God only must be our guide and oracle on the fearful subject to which your attention is now invited. Our subject embraces two leading points.

I. WHY THERE IS A HELL, &c. But a word or two as to the signification of the term. In scripture, the word does not always mean a state of punishment, but occasionally the grave, and the unseen world, Acts ii. 31 ; but in most passages it distinctly points to a place of future punishment. Let the following suffice :—" The wicked shall be turned into hell,"&c. " And in hell he lifted up," &c. Now there are three reasons why there should be a hell :—

The first respects Deity. He is a holy being ; he cannot behold iniquity with allowance. Is it reasonable that his enemies should dwell in his sight—share his palace — mingle with his holy hosts ? Think of vile, polluted, malevolent spirits, hating God and holiness, and say if it is not necessary that they should have a world to themselves, and dwell in a state of exilation from God.

Our second reason respects holy beings. There are angels—holy beings—glorified saints. Are these to bear the society of the vile and wicked? If so, the next world, to the righteous, would be vastly worse than this. Now, the godly can retire to their closets, &c.; to the house of God, &c.

Our third reason respects the wicked themselves. Is it not meet and righteous that they should be in a state of restraint, and not allowed to wage eternal war and rebellion against God and his holy government? These reasons will all be illustrated, if we look at our prisons. Who will deny that such places are necessary? Of what avail would be our laws? We say, the honor of the king, and the majesty of his government, require a prison for the lawless and the vile. We say, it is necessary for the safety and welfare of the community at large, or else neither property nor life would be secure. Who would wish to live in society where the most vicious and cruel of mankind range abroad at pleasure? &c. Therefore, that the power of evil may be restrained, the laws regarded, and the rights of the community respected, the prison is necessary. Equally so, and for the same reasons, hell. The honor of Jehovah, the justice of the divine government, the well-being of the righteous, and the restraint of the vile, all demand that there should be a hell. Let us now,

II. Consider the scriptural account of it. It is obvious, that some of the descriptions of the Bible are figurative. "Lake of fire." "Lake that burneth with fire and brimstone;" "where the worm dieth not," &c. I know some have contended for the literal existence of the fire and the worm; but we conceive there are insurmountable objections to those opinions. Among the revealed representations of hell, we have,

1. *The nature of the place affirmed.* It is a prison—a place of confinement into which all the rebellious and unholy are to be thrust. As such, it is stated that it was originally intended for the devil and his angels, Matt. xxv. 41. Men, by uniting with the devil in sin, become his companions, and sharers of the hell prepared for him and his angels. This prison is one of darkness—outer darkness—the darkness of death, &c.

2. *The nature of the misery is also revealed.* It is represented as being extreme—absolute—unmitigated; as horrible as the burning of the flesh with fire—yea, with fire and brimstone. It is described as producing weeping, wailing, and gnashing of teeth. It is represented as a state of utter torment, "I am tormented in this flame." Lost spirits are delivered to the tormentors.

3. *The sources of their misery are also revealed.* The misery of hell will arise,

(1.) From the loss of all enjoyment. There will be no peace, no joy, no happiness for the lost. Not one instant's cessation of horror and wo; not one bright interval; not one cheering moment. The wretched in this life are sometimes cheered by the visits and sympathies of friendship; but the lost will never enjoy that—by the intervention of sleep; but the eye of the lost will never be closed in sleep. All sources of enjoyment and happiness will have fled forever, &c.

(2.) From the infliction of the divine wrath; a sense of God's displeasure; his just and righteous indignation, Psalm xi. 6. "Upon the wicked," &c.

(3.) Earnest and unallayed desires. The representation given of hell in the parable of the rich man; he saw Lazarus afar off. It is highly probable that the lost will see the bright and joyous scenes of heaven—hear their songs—behold their triumph—see the oceans of pleasure. Oh! how they will long to enjoy them! But the desire even for a drop of water will be absolutely refused. Then, too, these wicked desires will remain in all their unsubdued force. The miser seeking gold—the sensualist pleasure—the drunkard his cup. But now they have the burning, feverish desires, but no means of realization.

(4.) From remorse of conscience. Sin will now be seen in all its blackness; seen in the light of the flames of perdition. How, then, will the lost curse themselves! Look at Esau, crying with many prayers for his birthright; but he had sold it—it was gone forever. Now the sinner will see the infatuation of his course. To sell the soul, and heaven, and eternal salvation, for the bubbles of time—for a title—for show, pomp, &c.—an hour's mirth, &c. Every recollection will produce remorse—excite horror. Wealth prostituted; health and strength spent in toiling the way to ruin; talents perverted; pious parents and friends;

but now the gulf between. Bible—but it was neglected; sabbaths wiled away, and gospel mercies not improved; conscience drowned, stupified, &c.; Christ and his cross, &c., despised.

(5.) From the companions of their misery. In hell will be all the vile of the universe, hateful and haters of one another. All the black, debased spirits, that ever cursed the world, with all their propensities and crimes. Think upon them; think of being shut up with fifty of the vilest assassins; but here will be all who ever lived and died in sin, besides the devil and his angels, for whom hell was originally prepared.

(6.) From a sense of settled and eternal despair. For the misery of the lost will endure forever; despair of relief will be the bitterest ingredient in their cup. But many dispute the eternity of the future punishment of the lost. Revelation is explicit.

1. The same words were employed to describe both the one and the other—both heaven and hell. "These," says Christ, "shall go away into everlasting," &c. Again, "where the worm dieth not," &c. The smoke of their torment ascendeth forever and ever.

2. We remark, there is no proof that the punishment will in the least purify the wicked; and if they remain eternally unholy, they will eternally be fit only for hell.

3. God's mercy is pleaded; but we never read of any exercise of it towards the lost, or those of any world but this. Besides, have not fallen angels as much hope on this ground as lost sinners?

4. Here we see the necessity of imprisoning some for life—so long as they live in this world; and this is just and wise. Why not so then in Deity, with respect to the next life? The word of God gives no hope for the lost. How, then, must they feel the pressure of eternal despair! an eternal night; an eternal ocean of waves of sorrow; eternal pain and anguish.

APPLICATION.

1. *We warn all of you against this hell of misery and endless wo.* Oh! flee from it.

2. *A way of escape is opened in the gospel.* You need not one perish. It is the will of God, your salvation, &c.

3. *Deceive not yourselves by forming false ideas of a future state.* Even exclu-

sion from heaven is enough; or by its duration, a thousand years of agony—even that, sufficient to deter.

4. *Let the Christian rejoice, and bless God, who has delivered him from the wrath to come.*

THE UNAVAILING LAMENTATION.

"The harvest is past, the summer is ended, and we are not saved."—JEREMIAH viii. 20.

I SHALL not dwell on the literal application of the text to the distressed and despairing condition of the Jews, to whom it refers, but give it a personal and spiritual bearing on the eternal interests of your soul's salvation; and in doing so, shall particularly dwell on the following propositions.

I. THAT GOD HAS GIVEN YOU THE GRACIOUS SEASONS OF SUMMER AND HARVEST.

II. THAT THESE MAY PASS AWAY UNIMPROVED.

III. THAT THE REGRETS OF SUCH WILL BE AWFUL AND OVERWHELMING.

I. THAT GOD HAS GIVEN YOU THE GRACIOUS SEASONS OF SUMMER AND HARVEST. Summer is the season of opportunity for laboring. Harvest, of plenty for gathering; these are the working and gathering seasons God has given you.

1. *The gracious season of summer.*

(1.) The summer of life; preceded by the spring of childhood. We consider the summer of life to begin with that period when we clearly see and discern between good and evil; much earlier in some than others; now this summer is of diversified length; some of you have had ten, twenty, thirty, forty years of this summer season; some have only a very limited and evanescent summer.

(2.) The summer of reason; thus man is distinguished from the brute beast. He is distinguished for reflection; he can survey, take a retrospect, look on the boundless future; he should be wise, &c.

(3.) The summer of opportunities. To gain knowledge—to receive holy impressions,—to prepare for death—to be meet for eternity.

2. *The gracious season of harvest.* Season of abundant blessings.

(1.) Harvest of knowledge; if ignorant.

it is wilful. The light of the gospel shines; the word of God is possessed; the voice of instruction crieth; the means of improvement provided.

(2.) Harvest of privileges. Sabbaths; sermons; means of grace, &c. How these crowd our years, and months, and weeks; scarcely a day when we might not enjoy and benefit by these.

(3.) Harvest of blessings. The tidings of the gospel, the provisions of mercy in Christ, pardon, acceptance, the prayers of the pious; the Holy Spirit; eternal life, &c. But these seasons,

II. MAY PASS AWAY UNIMPROVED. It was so with the antediluvians; with the inhabitants of Jerusalem; with thousands of others; with myriads in our day, around our doors. Was so with many of you for years; it is so now, we fear, with many present; this will be fearfully exhibited at the last day; then they will cry to the rocks and the hills, &c.; but can we account for it?

1. *Many do not think.* "The ox knoweth its owner," &c. His gross, stupid apathy and indifference; eat and drink, and toil, but never consider either their present state, or future destiny.

2. *They will not forsake their sins.* They love to do evil, it has become their habit. They roll the pleasures of sense &c., under their tongues as a sweet morsel; held fast in Satan's bonds; not convicted, not sorry, not anxious.

3. *They will not believe.* Do not hear as they ought; forget, &c. Do not believe the threats, nor the promises; in sin's hatefulness, and hell's terrors; in God's love, and heaven's glories. Unbelief hardens the heart, blinds the eyes.

4. *They will procrastinate.* Defer the most important concerns, year after year, season after season; from youth to maturity; from maturity to old age; old age to death.

III. THE REGRETS OF SUCH WILL BE AWFUL AND OVERWHELMING.

1. *Sometimes their regrets are expressed in this world.* On the bed of languishing, on the approach of death; often heard it; occasionally persons die in a state of apathy, but often awake just to see the precipice, &c.

2. *They will surely be uttered in eternity.* How fearful the contrast, no light, no probation, no blessings, no means, no ray of hope! These regrets will,

(1.) Be the regrets of intense agony "I am tormented," &c. Agony of recollection; agony of seeing heaven in the distance, agony of self-condemnation.

(2.) Regrets will be unavailing; no space for repentance, no ear for prayer, no fountain, no cross, &c.

(3.) Of black despair. The billows of the ocean rolling in all the fearful raging foam of endlessness. No sound heard, but the wailings of fellow kindred spirits damned, &c., and the terrific exclamations, "Who can dwell in endless fire?" "Who can endure everlasting burning?" &c. "The harvest is passed," &c.

APPLICATION.

1. None would choose this portion.
2. Who would risk it?
3. Who will flee from it? Now is the summer, now is the harvest, &c. Oh! I would call, and urge, and invite, &c.

THE TERROR OF THE LORD, A GROUND FOR MINISTERIAL PERSUASION.

"Knowing therefore the terror of the Lord, we persuade men."—2 COR. v. 11.

THE apostle refers, in the verse before the text, to the solemnities of the judgment day, the judgment seat, the judge, the appearance of every man, and the destinies of each and all. What an awful subject! How solemn and momentous! Now the object of the Christian ministry is to impress these scenes on the minds of men, that holy fear may be produced, and a change of life adopted. Hence he says, "Knowing therefore the terror of the Lord," &c.. Consider,

I. THE TERRORS OF THE LORD AS REVEALED TO US.

II. THE INFLUENCE THIS PRODUCES ON THE CHRISTIAN MINISTER.

I. THE TERRORS OF THE LORD, &c. Now by the terrors of the Lord we understand the exhibition of the justice of God, in the trial of his probationary creatures at the last day.

1. *The day is spoken of as terrible.* "The great day of his wrath," &c. Doom's-day; the day to which all other days now have reference; the day uniting time and eternity; a day often spoken of in the holy

scriptures; the day of God, that great and terrible day,

2. *The appearance of the Judge will be terrible.* Arrayed in all the infinite grandeur of his perfections, "Behold he cometh," &c. "The Lord Jesus shall be revealed from heaven in flames of fire," &c.

3. *The solemnities of the day are terrible.* The erection of the great white throne, the sound of the trumpet's blast, the opening of the graves, the sea giving up its dead, the heavens wrapped together as a scroll, the earth reeling as a drunken man, the sun black as sackcloth, the moon red as blood, the globe experiencing all the throes of dissolution, time ready to expire, the heavens and the earth passing away. Then the universal convocation. All the generations, and tribes, and individuals of mankind, before the eternal tribunal; the opening of the books, the public declaration of every man's sins, the sentence of eternal death, &c. How fearful will be that awful hour! Then shall they cry to the rocks and to the mountains, &c., shall seek annihilation, &c., but the officers of divine vengeance shall bind them hand and foot, &c.

4. *The terrors of the infliction of wrath which shall endure for ever.* Think of the wondrous devouring fire, everlasting burnings, the abiding tempest, the unending storm, the bottomless pit, whence ascendeth the smoke of the torments of the lost forever and ever. Now these terrors are revealed to us; these are the truths of this book. They are just, the holiness of God demands them, conscience attests this. They are certain, God cannot change, &c. We have had some presages of them in the judgments of God on the old word, Sodom, &c.

II. THE INFLUENCE A KNOWLEDGE OF THE TERRORS OF THE LORD PRODUCES ON THE CHRISTIAN MINISTER. "We persuade men."

1. *To hear what God has spoken.* Hear the word of the Lord.

2. *To consider and reflect on these things.* Is it not wise and reasonable?

3. *To believe the declarations of the divine word.* To receive them as truth.

4. *To prepare for this great and terrible day.* Sin invests that day with all its horrors. Then it must be forgiven, forsaken.

(1.) *The Judge must become our friend.* He desires and seeks this.

(2.) *We must give ourselves to his cause and people, and honor him in the world.*

The saints will not only escape, but be openly justified, confessed, exalted, crowned, and glorified. Oh, then,

1. We would *persuade*, because you are reasonable beings.

2. We persuade *each*, as it is a personal concern.

3. *All*, as there is a way of escape for every one.

4. *Now*, because this is the accepted time, &c.

ON CARING FOR OTHERS.

"Am I my brother's keeper?"—GENESIS iv. 9

OUR text was the language of the fratricide of Cain, the first human murderer, the murderer of his brother. God was now holding inquisition for blood. He is in the presence of his Maker and his Judge. A question is proposed as to his knowledge of his brother Abel; to which, in the language of heartlessness, he replies by the interrogatory of the text, "Am I my brother's keeper?" Who can read it without being shocked at the monstrous indifference it evinced? You all stand aghast from such selfish isolation, and Cain is condemned in the court of your consciences. But if Cain was wrong, he was so in principle as well as in expression; and if Cain was wrong, so are all who possess the same spirit, though not extended to the same degree of indifference. We affirm, that every man is bound to feel and care for his fellowman; and to a certain extent, every man is his brother's keeper. We will consider,

I. SOME CASES WHERE IT IS INVARIABLY CONCEDED THAT WE OUGHT TO CARE AND FEEL FOR OTHERS. Now this is admitted,

1. *In reference to parents and children.* How weak, helpless, and dependent, are children! Uncared for, they must perish. A mother's love and attention to her infant child, ever form a subject for the illustration of the tenderest passions of the heart. A father is expected to toil for their subsistence; to pity, to protect, to watch over, &c. And Christianity demands, that parents should train them up in God's fear, labor for their spiritual welfare.

2. *In reference to relatives and friends.* Brethren and sisters are supposed, by their identity of interests, to feel and care for each other. Hence, a brother's neglect

and indifference are justly branded as unnatural. So also when persons are bound in the bonds of mutual regard, connected with the true spirit of friendship. How Jonathan cared for David, &c.

3. *In reference to pastors and flocks.* Here especial affection and regard are properly expected; here love and diligent care are to be evinced. As the shepherd cares for and watches his flock, so the Christian shepherd is to care and watch for souls. How was this exhibited in Paul! how faithful, how tender, how devoted! and this is to be reciprocated. "Brethren, pray for us." "May the Lord have mercy on the house of Onesiphorus," &c. Now these are instances universally allowed. Let us now consider,

II. The legitimate extent to which this principle should be carried.

1. *Should we not care for our neighbors?* Those at our doors; where we are located together. "Thou shalt love thy neighbor," &c. In this way all who compose our families, servants, &c., who work in our shops, &c., those whom we see daily.

2. *Should we not care for our country?* Love of country, or patriotism, has ever been held a distinguished virtue. Desire its freedom, its prosperity, its intellectual elevation, its moral well-being: our fatherland, the country of our ancestors, of our birth, &c.

3. *Should we not care for the suffering?* The poor, fatherless, orphans, widows, the afflicted, &c. We do violence to our nature if we do not compassionate these; humanity demands this. I advance one step beyond.

4. *I ask, should we not care for the world?* This is philanthropy; love to our species everywhere, and a desire to bless our race. All other limits are too contracted; the true circle of goodness is the world; every man of every clime, &c., especially those needing my compassion, requiring my help. If such a one dwell in the sterile frigid regions of Greenland, or in the burning torrid zone, if he cry for my help, I must not ask, "Am I my brother's keeper?" I am bound to care for his bodily weal, I am bound to care for his mental state, for his condition as a man, and a citizen of the world; as an immortal being, accountable with myself to God, &c. My care must be affectionate, sincere, self-denying, &c.

Indifference is criminality, neglect is sin, &c. I notice,

III. The grand considerations which should lead to this affectionate regard.

1. *The oneness of our nature.* "God hath made of one blood," &c.; no alien blood, no captive blood, no ignoble blood, &c. I see in Adam and Eve the original parents of us all; I see an identity enlinking the whole together; I assail my own nature if I inquire, "Am I my brother's keeper?"

2. *We are all dependent on the same Providence.* Whatever is the color, the station, or the class, all hang on God's beneficent care; he gave being to the whole, cares for the whole, gives his sun to shine, &c., his air, his rain, his benefits, &c. Oh yes! in one grand sense they may all kneel and say, "Our Father!"

3. *We are exposed to the same perils.* Perils of adversity, perils of sickness, perils of bereavements, perils of sin, perils of Satan, perils of death; all equally sojourners in the world, all mariners on life's stormy sea, all hastening to the same home of dust, all destined to the same solemn, boundless eternity. I trample on these ties if I inquire, "Am I my brother's," &c.

4. *We are interested in one common redemption.* I delight in that truth of the gospel, "God so loved the world," &c. "He is the propitiation," &c. I would not monopolize the light, the air, the stream, but much less the Redeemer's grace; "Christ by the grace of God," &c. Then by that one precious Saviour, that one great sacrifice, one universal gospel, I cannot disregard one immortal spirit of any country or condition; I insult my Saviour, I trample on the gospel, if I inquire, "Am I my brother's keeper?"

5. *We shall stand before one final tribunal at the last day.*

APPLICATION.

Our text should lead us,

1. *To lay the axe at the root of selfishness,—self-ease,—self-care.*

2. *Let the spirit we have recommended be universally cherished, and we hasten on the jubilee of the world.*

3. *By this we test our true character.*

THE SABBATH.

"If thou turn away thy foot from the sabbath, from doing thy pleasure on my holy day : and call the sabbath a delight, the holy of the Lord, honorable ; and shalt honor him, not doing thine own ways, nor finding thine own pleasure, nor speaking thine own words : then shalt thou delight thyself in the Lord ; and I will cause thee to ride upon the high places of the earth, and feed thee with the heritage of Jacob thy father ; for the mouth of the Lord hath spoken it."—ISAIAH lviii. 13, 14.

THE subject of the sanctification of the sabbath has, of late, extensively engaged the attention of the disciples of Christ. Many persons have professed to doubt the divine obligation of Christians to it ; they say, it was only binding upon the Jews under an inferior dispensation. Now to this subject let us direct our attention for a few moments. The sabbath was instituted during man's innocency in Eden ; afterwards it was placed in the moral code of the ten commandments ; it was associated with the most blessed promises, and its violation with the most terrible threatenings. Its repeal is never hinted at. It is said expressly, "The sabbath was made for man." Not for the Jew or the Gentile, but for the species, for all mankind, even to the end of the world. Now Christ being Lord of all, was Lord of the sabbath. It is clear, that after his resurrection he assembled with his disciples on the first day of the week, and it is absolutely certain, that the apostles and primitive Christians did the same, and have done so through every age to the present time. We fear, then, that all disputes on this subject have arisen more from the heart than the head ; and, on the ground of the divine word, we call upon all who love the Lord Jesus Christ, to remember his sabbath, to keep it holy. Listen, then, to the beautiful statements of the evangelical prophet. Observe,

I. THE THINGS WHICH THE TEXT PROHIBITS. We are,

1. *Not to do our own ways.* That is, not to attend to our own lawful concerns ; not to buy or to sell ; not to work or employ others, except in case of evident necessity and mercy, see Exod. xx. 8, &c. How criminal are those masters and mistresses who forget the spiritual concerns of their servants on this day !

2. *We are not to seek our own pleasure.* It is not to be a day of worldly recreation ; amusements, innocent on other days, are criminal on this : all pleasure-trips, and journeys, and parties, are equally unlawful ; so also all reading of a mere entertaining description.

3. *We are not to engage in worldly conversation,*—" Nor speaking," &c. ; foolish jestings are never seasonable, but conversation about trade, and commerce, and science ; conversation about news, politics, &c., are all unprofitable and improper on this day. We see then the extent of the prohibition ; it includes actions, feelings, and conversation. Observe,

II. WHAT IS ENJOINED.

1. *We are to call the sabbath a delight.* To look upon it as such ; to reckon it not a toil, and not so much a duty and a load as a delight, a privilege, a blessing. Now if we feel and call it so,

(1.) We shall *hail* its approach.

"Welcome, sweet day of rest
That saw the Lord arise,
Welcome to this reviving breast
And these rejoicing eyes."

(2.) We shall *enjoy its exercises ;* we shall feel it to be a day of freedom, of holy pleasure, and enjoyment.

(3.) We shall *reflect* upon it with delight ; recall its scenes, revive its events meditate upon its services, &c.

2. *We must esteem it the holy of the Lord.* The Lord's day ; his holy or sacred day ; hence we shall labor to spend it in a *holy manner,* not negatively, merely avoiding sin, but earnestly seeking holy *influences* and blessings. The reading will be holy, conversation, meditation, songs, praying, &c. Thus we shall labor to keep the sabbath day.

3. *We must call it honorable.* The day God has honored, Christ has honored, saints of old, apostles, and confessors ; and the day the great church of Christ honors : the soul's chief day, day for spiritual things, the sabbath, which is typical of the heavenly rest. God honors it with special promises, &c. Now, if we honor it, it will not be the shortest day ; it cannot be spent in trifling ; we shall give it fully to God and divine things ; we shall labor to exalt God and to extend his glory ; to imitate God, and do good to our fellow-men.

III. THE MOTIVES BY WHICH IT IS ENFORCED. We shall have,

1. *The enjoyment of God.* God will give us real satisfaction and abiding delight ; God will be the portion of the soul, the joy, and the life of the soul. Now is it pos-

sible for the soul to enjoy God without we honor his sabbath? &c.   Think of the smile of God, and the light of his countenance.

2. *God will greatly dignify and exalt us.* "I will cause thee to ride," &c., see chap. xxxiii. 18; Deut. xxxii. 13, "Him that honoreth," &c.

3. *He will give us a rich and satisfying portion.* "Feed thee," &c., with all the blessings of the covenant. Now this is included in one promise, "I will be thy God." All will follow this; this includes both temporal and spiritual blessings; all for time and eternity. All this is ratified by the solemn word of the unchangeable Jehovah, who hath spoken it.

APPLICATION.

1. Let me press this subject upon the solemn attention of the professors of religion; they must make a stand against sabbath profanation; their principles require it, their comfort and usefulness. Be careful in small matters, consider all connected with you; think of the glory of the Saviour, the purity of the church; think of the holy sabbath.

2. Let me entreat sabbath profaners to turn to God; you must displease God, you must be under condemnation, you cannot enjoy religion, you cannot be fit for heaven, your bodies will fare better, your minds, your souls, &c.

3. Let us all improve our sabbaths as they pass along; every one bears its report to the Judge of all; every one will do us good, or render our account more awful. Thousands are now having their last one. "Oh that they were wise," &c.

THE UNION OF PERSONAL AND FAMILY RELIGION.

"But as for me and my house, we will serve the Lord."—JOSHUA xxiv. 15.

How striking the scenes to which this portion of the word of God introduces us. Joshua, the faithful servant of God, who had been the unswerving professor and worshipper of Jehovah during a protracted life, and now mellowed by holy influences, ready for the enjoyment of the blissful reward, ere he gives up his office, and lays down his life, assembles the Israelitish tribes at Shechem, reiterates the goodness of God to them as a people, and urges upon them, in a most earnest manner, the fear and service of the Lord. He appeals to their judgments in this matter, and reminds them that God's service must be voluntary, exhorting them to choose whom they would serve. He then appeals to his own resolution, whatever course others might adopt; he says, "As for me, and my house, we will serve the Lord." We observe,

I. THAT TRUE RELIGION CONSISTS IN SERVING THE LORD. This service implies,

1. *A knowledge of his character and will.* This must precede every other department of God's service. To know God, as revealed in his word; to know his will concerning his creatures.

2. *A right state of heart towards God.* This is not natural to man. Men are at enmity with God—do not love or approve of God—therefore are not disposed to serve him. An entire change of heart is essential; the carnal principle must be slain; a spirit of love and delight imparted; this takes place in regeneration.

3. *A constant waiting upon God.* To learn his mind; to know his designs concerning us; to hear his commands; to be counselled by him.

4. *Sincere obedience to God's authority.* Keeping his statutes from the heart, and walking in his ordinances, &c., to do them. Having his law in our heart, and exemplifying it in our conversation and life. Thus we must personally serve God.

II. THAT PERSONAL RELIGION MUST FORM THE BASIS OF THE RELATIVE SERVICE OF GOD.

1. *This alone will enable persons rightly to understand relative religion.* How can they instruct, direct, counsel their families, unless they know and serve God themselves? Besides, example is equally essential with religious authority and precept.

2. *This alone will ensure the divine approbation.* God will not be pleased with mere forms of piety, or the externals of worship. There must be the entire consecration of the heart to the Lord. God will bestow his blessing, and cause his smile to rest, where there is the true exemplification of his Holy Spirit and word.

III. THAT RELATIVE RELIGION SHOULD EVER ACCOMPANY THE PERSONAL ENJOYMENT OF IT. Here all religious heads of families should feel, and resolve, and act as Joshua.

1. *Where there is true personal piety, there will be the faithful discharge of relative duties.* There will be an eye towards God's authority in all the stations we occupy, whether conjugal, parental, fraternal, or filial. Piety will show itself in the adornments of all the relative spheres in which Providence may place us.

2. *Where there is personal piety, there will be a deep solicitude for the spiritual welfare of our families.* How can it be otherwise? Shall we not value their souls, and hence seek their spiritual well-being? We shall not only desire their present temporal happiness, but their present eternal salvation. Our love is singularly defective if it does not include this.

3. *Where there is personal piety, there will be the means of family religion.* The word of God will be read—family prayer presented—family praises offered—and a family standard of piety maintained.

4. *Where there is personal piety, there will be earnest efforts made to promote family religion.* Family worship, &c., will be followed; serious counsel—affectionate entreaty—scriptural discipline—and fervent private prayer. We shall labor to enlighten the mind, to incite desires after holiness, and thus win them to Christ.

IV. THAT FAMILY RELIGION MAY BE URGED BY A VARIETY OF SOLEMN CONSIDERATIONS.

1. *From the family idolatry of pagans.* If there is family idolatry, surely there should be family religion.

2. *From the family wickedness of sinners.* Families unite to sin against God—to live in vanity—in religious negligence—in dissipation—in worldliness—and sometimes in avowed skepticism. How, then, should Christian families be devoted to the service of God, and the interests of religion.

3. *From the influence of families on churches.* All the active members of Christian churches are mortal. The fathers are going the way of all flesh. Where shall we look but to the families of Christians for the pastors, and teachers, and deacons of the next generation?

4. *From the happy family influence religion exerts.* It irradiates—humanizes; produces peace, comfort, and holy harmony. It is a type of the heavenly state.

APPLICATION.

1. *This subject is especially adapted to Christian heads of families.* To you it particularly belongs. Sincerely consider it, and examine yourselves by it.

2. *In the families of the wicked abideth the displeasure of God.* Let such be warned, &c.

PREJUDICE, AND ITS ANTIDOTE.

"And Nathanael said unto him, Can any good thing come out of Nazareth? Philip saith unto him, Come and see."—JOHN i. 46.

OUR text contains an interrogation and an answer. Both the question and the reply were from good men. Nathanael, a stern, devotional Jew—Philip, a sincere disciple of Jesus Christ. But Nathanael was under the influence of a very common, yet pernicious evil; he was the victim of prejudice. Philip, full of love and joy in having found Christ and meeting with Nathanael, exclaimed, "We have found him of whom," &c., verse 45. Now, when Nazareth was mentioned, Nathanael said, "Can there any good thing come out of Nazareth?" If it had been Rome, or especially Jerusalem, without examination the tidings would have been hailed; but a small, insignificant place like Nazareth, brought out the latent weakness of Nathanael, and hence the exclamation of the text. Philip treated the prejudice of Nathanael most properly. He invited investigation, "Come and see." Our subject, therefore, is prejudice, and its antidote. Let us notice,

I. SOME OF THE PREJUDICES MEN FORM IN RESPECT OF RELIGION. And consider,

II. CANDID INVESTIGATION AS THE ONLY ANTIDOTE.

I. SOME OF THE PREJUDICES MEN FORM AGAINST RELIGION. Prejudice is prejudging, or concluding on any subject, without previous examination. In looking at some instances of its manifestation, we may notice,

1. *The prejudices of skeptical minds against the Christian religion.* In many instances disbelief arises from depravity of heart; but there may be doubts entertained by men who may honestly seek the truth. These doubts respect,

(1.) The necessity of revealed religion.

They say reason is sufficient, as enlightened and guided by the works of nature ; but if so, why have not some of the most profound students of nature found out the Supreme Good, and the way of holiness? If 4000 years had passed over before the dawn of Christianity, had not the world been fairly tried ? Plato and Socrates had propounded their schemes of philosophy five hundred years before Christ ; Seneca was cotemporary with Christ ; Solon, the illustrious Grecian sage, lived nearly six hundred years before Christ ; these had all exerted their talents and influence, and, so far as morals, and purity, and goodness are concerned, in vain. The great themes of religion are guessed at ; they were wandering to seek abodes of pleasure with feeble tapers, surrounded by palpable darkness. Their glimmering rays of reason only made the darkness more visible, and confusion more confounded.

(2.) The prejudices of skeptics also regard the mysteries of revelation. They find heights they cannot reach—depths they cannot fathom — comprehensive subjects they cannot grasp, and hence they reject revelation ; but is it otherwise with nature ? Look at *that* volume. The geologist knows a little—the astronomer a little—the chemist a little—the mineralogist a little—and the zoologist ; but what do they all know together ? Why, scarcely the first elements. Even their most profound professors will confess this. Why, therefore, is it strange that the great and marvellous should extend to the Bible ? If it had been otherwise, they would have said, it cannot be God's book ; it is not great, and grand, and sublime enough. But it is with the Bible as with nature ; light—air—bread—water—all abound, all are accessible ; so the privileges and blessings of Christianity are all clear and simple, so that " a wayfaring man, though a fool, may not err therein."

(3.) The prejudices of skeptics have extended also to the enjoyments of experimental religion. They consider Christian experience as fanaticism, the result of a diseased or fanciful imagination ; they treat it as monomania, and generally connect it with mental imbecility. Surely this is quite prejudging the case. A little reflection would cause them to reason thus : The number of those who experience the joys of religion is very great ; myriads of testimonies ; the various classes of persons ; rich and poor—wise and ignorant—learned and illiterate ; persons of all ages and countries ; persons who had no object to serve, &c. ; persons for many years together ; persons in the article of death, &c.

2. *Let us advert to the prejudices of the formal against spiritual religion.* Many admire religion, as far as attending church and chapel ; a form ; going through the routine of duties and ceremonies ; but all else they call cant, fanaticism, or hypocrisy. Now surely religion, if real, must be internal. Should it not be ardent and sincere ? should it not be precise, and strikingly rigid ?

3. *There are the prejudices of one class and section of Christians against others.* Many are so prejudiced that they see nothing excellent out of the pale of their own sect. Roman Catholics unchristianize all Protestants ; the English church does the same with all Dissenters ; Dissenters often do the same with one another. This spirit has produced intolerance, envy, hatred, persecution, and death. The inquisition, the star chamber, the ecclesiastical courts, are all the offspring of this prejudice. Why can we not distinguish between men and opinions ? Who can doubt the piety of such men as Fenelon, Massillon, and thousands of others of the papal community ? The most rigid dissenter must think of such men as Bishop Hall, and Archbishop Leighton, and Tillotson, and Barrow, and many others, with delight. Where is there a sect but has had its ornaments, and noble, and pious-minded advocates and friends ? We should hate error—have fixed principles—hold fast every grace of truth—but yield to all and every sect credit for the excellencies they may embody, or the truths they may hold. Can we at all account for the existence of prejudice ? It is not always a low, illiterate thing. We find it beneath crowns, and in communion with mitres, and learning, and talents, and even piety. We may, notwithstanding, attribute prejudice,

(1.) *Often to ignorance.* That is, of the subject, person, or thing in question.

(2.) *To education.* Taught certain principles ; imbued with certain predilections.

(3.) *To pride.* We esteem ourselves, and our opinions, more highly than others.

(4.) *To the influence of our reading, and friends.* Consult only, or at least generally, authors and friends who are of our views, &c.

(5.) *To indolent rashness.* Want of diligent examination; precipitancy in decision. Notice some of the evils of prejudice:

1. It is a mental and moral evil.
2. It is an injury to our fellow-creatures.
3. It is an impediment to improvement.
4. It is grievous to God. We ask,

II. WHAT IS THE GREAT REMEDY FOR PREJUDICES AGAINST RELIGION? " Philip said, Come and see." Investigate for yourselves; judge from minute observation. Sometimes there is only one step from prejudice to credulity, i. e. from one evil to another. We remark,

1. *That a fair and candid examination of the scriptures, in most cases will produce conviction as to their divinity.* Sir W. Jones, Lord Lyttleton, Soame Jennings, Hon. Robert Boyle, and hundreds of others, have thus emerged from infidel darkness into the light of gospel day.

2. *A candid examination of the subject of the supreme importance of religion, will lead to the conviction of the great necessity for spiritual and internal piety.*

3. *A candid examination into the excellencies and good of other sects, will lead to the abandonment of sectarian bigotry and hatred.* We shall exercise forbearance—admire the good, &c. We say to all who ask, " Can any good?" &c. " Come and see"—Nazareth, and its great prophet—yea more, &c. See him in the synagogue; see him going forth to work miracles of mercy, &c. Observe him establishing the new dispensation of grace and salvation; opening the gates of paradise to an exiled world; breaking down all national and sectarian barriers; inviting all to be happy; dying to redeem every soul of man. Behold him, despisers! Behold him, ye bigoted Jews! Behold him, ye Gentiles! Sit a his feet; drink the streams of knowledge; obey his commands; be imbued with his spirit; and then reply to the question, " Can any good?" &c.

JOSIAH—A SERMON TO THE YOUNG.

" For in the eighth year of his reign, while he was yet young, he began to seek after the God of David his father."—2 CHRON. xxxiv. 3.

IT is very profitable to listen to wise proverbs and maxims; to hear the counsels of the wise and good; and it should be the study of the young to grow in knowledge and wisdom; but it is still more instructive to observe the personal excellencies of those around us. To see the precepts of the wise, speaking and living in the conduct of the good and pious. Now to this our text calls the attention of the young people present. It refers to Josiah, one of the kings of Judah, and relates, not what he said, but what he did, and what is worthy of your attention and imitation. " While he was yet young," &c. Observe,

I. THE BLESSED BEING REFERRED TO. " The God of David." David was not Josiah's immediate father, but was his predecessor, just as Abraham was the father or predecessor of the Jewish nation. Three hundred and seventy-four years intervened between the death of David and the reign of Josiah; but there are several things worthy of notice in this appellation. " The God of David."

1. *The God who so distinguished and exalted David.* Who found him a ruddy youthful shepherd, and gave him courage and might to slay the vaunting Goliath—who led him through the perils of Saul's court, up to the throne of Israel. Surely promotion cometh neither from the east nor the west, but from the Lord.

2. *The God who was David's portion and joy.* God loved David, and proclaimed him a man after his own heart, and how David exulted and delighted to commune with him and to bless him, of whom he exclaimed, " Whom have I in heaven but thee," &c. "O Lord, thou art my God!" &c.

3. *The God whom David served and celebrated.* He delighted in his law, walked in his statutes, loved his commandments, both privately and publicly sought to exalt God. Died in the enjoyment of the divine favor, &c. The true God of Israel was David's God, and this God was the object of Josiah's pious solicitude.

II. THE COURSE JOSIAH ADOPTED. He sought God. It is said, " he began to seek after God." Now, this supposes,

1. *That he felt his need of God.* Men naturally live without God, disregard him, neglect his laws, &c. Far from him by wicked works; what is worse, most are satisfied with this, do not seek after God.

But Josiah felt his need of God, doubtless felt his sin, his misery, his helplessness without God. Man was not only formed by God, but for him. He is the centre of felicity and blessedness.

2. *That his soul desired God.* As his portion, Saviour, and friend. However rich, we are poor without God. However imaginarily excellent, yet miserable. However surrounded by acquaintance, yet friendless. Now these desires are likened to the feelings of hunger and thirst, like the desire of the tempest-tost mariner for the light of the morning.

3. *That he employed suitable means to find God.* By perusing God's word, for here God is to be found. By worshipping with his people, for here God has engaged to be present. By fervent secret prayer, for to such the Lord is graciously near. Whosoever shall call upon the name of the Lord, &c. Now, doubtless Josiah sought God,

(1.) Earnestly, with all his heart. The promise is to such.

(2.) Humbly, prostrated before God. In sackcloth and ashes.

(3.) With perseverance, urging his suit, pressing his plea, &c.

(4.) Through the promised Messiah. For the pious Jews had reference to the predicted Saviour in their worship and services; now just so must you seek God if you desire sincerely to find him.

4. *Josiah found God, obtained his favor, and lived in his service.* He was successful, he obtained mercy, God loved him, and he loved God. He reformed the manners of the people; put down idolatry, &c., ver. 3 to 7. So that his religion was personal, sincere, and public; it was real, practical, manifest. Now I would,

III. PRESS THE EXAMPLE OF JOSIAH UPON YOUR IMMEDIATE IMITATION. Now, my dear young friends, is it not worth your while to do as Josiah did? Do you not admire his character and conduct? But perhaps you say,

1. *That you are too young.* Not to know good from evil—not to be wise and happy —not to die and be lost forever; besides, Josiah was only sixteen years of age. A time the most critical, often thoughtless. Thousands have begun to serve God as early as your age. Or you object,

2. *My parents are irreligious.* Their example must be bad, &c. Much to be regretted, &c. But Josiah's father was one of the worst of men, read chap. xxxiii. 21, &c. Religion is a personal thing. Or you say,

3. *I am unfavorably situated for religion.* The family, or shop, &c., quite irreligious, they would laugh or jeer, &c. But think of Josiah's difficulties; a complete idolatrous nation, yet he faced the whole, and was religious and good when the multitude were vile; but you say he was a king, then the greater danger, and more were the snares and temptations; or probably you object,

4. *I fear I should not hold out.* With that you have nothing at present to do. You must first begin; but Josiah held out, see chap. xxxvi. 25. God is sufficient for your preservation, &c. He has engaged to keep and sustain you. Thousands began early and held out. John Wesley, Dr. Watts, Whitfield, Doddridge, Matthew Henry, &c., &c. Myriads more. It is more likely that you will hold out if you do begin early. Habits of piety formed, &c. God honored, &c. Now in conclusion, let me urge your immediate seeking of the Lord.

1. *On the ground of your dignity.* It will adorn, be a crown of glory, &c. Elevate the mind, &c. May exalt you even in this life. On the ground,

2. *Of your happiness.* "Her ways are ways of pleasantness," &c. "Happy art thou, O Israel."

3. *On the ground of safety.* Then all will be right. Prepared for all events, ready for life or death.

4. *The miseries avoided.* Sin disgraces, often destroys health, &c. Makes bitter work for after repentance. Urge, exhort, direct.

INSTANT DECISION URGED.

"Choose you this day whom ye will serve."—
JOSHUA xxiv. 15.

JOSHUA was an eminent Old Testament saint, the devoted coadjutor of Moses, and afterwards his faithful successor. He survived Moses twenty-four years; but now his course is finished; he has lived a hundred and ten years; he is ripe for the heavenly garner; he has only to deliver his last dying counsel and then enter upon his reward. He calls for an interesting assembly, verse 1. He recapitulates the events of their history,—he urges personal piety,—avers his own resolution,—refers the matter to their free determination, and calls for their decision. How interesting! How affecting must have been the scene! Let us make it our own, it equally belongs to us. The text clearly contains the following propositions.

I. THAT TRUE RELIGION CONSISTS IN SERVING GOD.

II. THAT MAN IS RESPONSIBLE FOR THAT SERVICE.

III. THAT GOD DEMANDS DECISION AS TO THIS SERVICE. And,

IV. THAT TO-DAY IS THE BEST SEASON FOR CONCLUDING ON THIS SERVICE.

I. THAT TRUE RELIGION CONSISTS IN SERVING THE LORD. We do not by this exclude knowledge, conviction, repentance, faith, &c., but these have essentially to do with our entrance on the divine service. Thus David exhorted Solomon to serve him with a perfect heart, &c. "This is the whole duty of man, to fear God and keep his commandments." Paul says, "I serve God with my spirit in the gospel of his Son." "The blood of Christ shall purge your conscience from dead works to serve the living God." "Let us have grace, whereby we may serve God," &c. "I beseech you, brethren," &c. Now this service includes,

1. *The worship of God.* To bless—adore—praise and extol the Lord. To give him homage, reverence, and thanksgiving.

2. *It includes obedience to his ordinances.* "To walk in his ordinances to do them." To regard with serious attention all the institutions of the gospel. Thus the first church continued steadfast in the apostles' doctrine, &c. It includes,

3. *Practical regard for his moral laws.* These respect God, mankind, and ourselves. To love him, &c. Our neighbor, &c. To devote our souls and spirits to glorify him. The exercise of faith—patience—humility, and self-denial, is of course a portion of the divine service. His word contains the rules by which our conduct, words, and spirit, are to be ordered. The poet sings,

> "Teach me to walk in thy commands,
> 'Tis a delightful road ;
> Nor let my head, nor heart, nor hands,
> Offend against my God."

II. MAN IS RESPONSIBLE FOR THIS SER-

VICE. God never coerces men into it. Will not have the service of constraint. The material part of the universe obey him of necessity. He gives them laws, &c. But man is rational, intelligent, and free. God will only have the cheerful service of the heart. What more clear than the text? "Choose ye." Here are two courses—two ways—God and idols, &c. ; God and sin ; God and the world ; God and self ; God and Satan. God calls on man to decide and act. Now man surely can do this ; if not, he is not free ; if not, he is not responsible. Let us ascertain this from other portions of scripture. See the case of Cain, Gen. iv. 7. Moses and the Israelites, Deut. xxx. 19. So to the Jews, God said, "Turn ye, turn ye," &c. So Christ invited and exhorted, and said, "Ye will not come," &c. "O that thou in this thy day," &c. These passages clearly urge this doctrine on our consciences. If you say that though you may determine yet you have not power to act, forget not that God will give his Spirit to them who ask him, and that if you seek, and knock, and ask, the promises of grace and mercy are full, explicit, and direct. Reject this doctrine, and you are compelled to admit that of fatal necessity, which turns all men into mere machines, and takes the possibility both of virtue and vice out of the world. But every one of us must give an account of himself to God. This responsibility,

1. *Is personal.* For ourselves only. We cannot be so for any other absolutely ; yet there is relative responsibility ; as to the duties of life, &c.

2. *It is universal.* All persons of sane mind ; young and old—rich and poor—every soul now present before God. We remark,

III. GOD DEMANDS DECISION AS TO THIS SERVICE. "Choose ye." To decide,

1. *Is our duty.* God calls us to it. He demands it. He will not allow compromise.

2. *This decision is possible.* Not out of your power. Not impossible.

3. *This decision always precedes a religious course.* This is the turning point. Look at the prodigal, "I will arise," &c. Look at Saul, "Lord, what wilt thou have me to do?" The three thousand on the day of Pentecost. So in all who are converted.

IV. TO-DAY IS THE BEST SEASON FOR

CONCLUDING AS TO THIS SERVICE. " This day."

1. *This day is given us by God for this purpose.* He says, " Now is the accepted time," &c. " To-day," &c.

2. *No other period so adapted.* Distance is widening,—impediments increasing,—difficulties growing,—opportunities wasting. Now God invites—heaven smiles—Jesus beseeches—ministers entreat—the Spirit waits and hovers over your souls—angels attend, &c.

3. *This may probably be the only season.* How many have been ruined by to-morrow! An hour's delay has sometimes brought destruction. "Choose ye this day," &c. O yes, *this* day.

APPLICATION.

1. *Who will respond to the text?* See verse 16, 21. Do you say so? In your hearts—earnestly—humbly—prayerfully?

2. *What will you do if you refuse?* What service? What master? What reward?

EVIL COMPANY PROHIBITED.

" Thou shalt not follow a multitude to do evil."
—EXODUS xxiii. 2.

NOTHING is more evident than that evil is in the world—moral evil—sin. How it originated in the universe is a matter which has greatly perplexed the wisest of mankind. It is one of the secret things, &c. How it was introduced into this world is specifically detailed; the agent—the temptation—the disastrous effects are all very minutely related. Evil is not only in the world, but has spread over its entire surface, and polluted all its inhabitants. To guard us against one of the most fatal sources of its pestiferous effects is the design of the important counsel of our text, " Thou shalt not," &c. Observe,

I. WE HAVE A FEARFUL TRUTH IMPLIED. " The multitude do evil;" that is, the great majority of mankind live in the practice of evil—are transgressing the laws of the Most High God.

1. *Let us substantiate this.* Sacred history attests it, see the condemnation of the old world, Genesis vi. 5 and 6. Only eight persons living in the fear and service of God. Afterwards the nations of the earth walked in the vanity of their darkened minds. Only the Jews had the knowledge and worship of the true God; of them the majority were Israelites only in name. How fearful the state of the world at the advent of the Saviour—the true religion corrupted, and the world lying in the hands of the wicked one. This darkness was partially removed during the first centuries of the Christian era; but afterwards even the Christian system became corrupted, aggrandized with worldly pomp, and then sunk extensively into forms and ceremonies. How melancholy the state of the world at the reformation! How extensively it is so yet; the multitude of nations are yet pagans, and Mahommedans, or savage. Multitudes of persons even of Christian countries are unconverted. The multitude even of our congregations are yet strangers to spiritual religion. Multitudes of all ranks and degrees, of the rich and of the poor, of the learned, of the illiterate, of the young, and of the aged.

2. *Let us account for it.* We do this by referring,

(1.) To the indwelling of evil in the human mind. This is its natural state; to this it is prone; here its feelings, and desires, and actions, are at home. The fountain being corrupt, the streams are necessarily so. The tree being bad, the fruit is such. The soul being depraved, the life is naturally wicked.

(2.) We account for it on the ground of Satanic influence. Men by nature are under his power—his vassals; his influence is exerted therefore within them; he leads them in the way of evil.

(3.) On the ground of human example; children, so soon as they can think or act, have evil placed before them—often neglected—brought up in ignorance and sin.

(4.) On the ground of the sacrifices religion demands; strait is the gate, narrow the way. There is the yoke of obedience, the cross of self-denial, the life of mortification, the crucifying of the flesh—all must be left if Christ be followed.

II. WE HAVE A LAMENTABLE TRUTH SUPPOSED. That men are liable to be influenced by the multitude. This, in some measure, arises from the constitution of human nature. In some persons this tendency is very powerful.

1. *Persons generally act by impulse rather than judgment*—and thus follow the multitude to do evil.

2. *Most persons look up to others*, and are influenced by their actions. The rich are thus, &c., by the poor; the learned by the ignorant; servants observe and imitate their masters and mistresses; children their parents, &c. Friends one another.

3. *To forsake the multitude requires moral resolution and fortitude.* Men are not willing to risk the approbation of those around. Thus it has ever been that men are greatly influenced in their conduct by the multitude. When the people cried Hosanna, the multitude united, and when the priests said, Crucify him, the people cried, "Away with him, his blood be upon us," &c.

III. WE HAVE IMPORTANT COUNSEL GIVEN. "Thou shalt not," &c.

1. *It is irrational.* Carry this out, and in heathen lands you would worship stocks and stones. In uncivilized regions be wild, and devourers of each other. Reason demands reflection—enforces consideration, &c.

2. *It is unscriptural.* God, in every age, and under every dispensation, has demanded the opposite. This distinguished Noah, Abraham, the prophets, the apostles, and the pious in all periods and countries of the world. To follow the multitude is to disobey God—to be the vassals of Satan, and to travel in the dark path of guilt and wo.

3. *It is unsafe.* All evil doers will perish. The wages of sin is death to each and all its servants—broad way, and its crowd of travellers are united to death, even eternal death. A multitude of evil doers cannot avert God's wrath, cannot mitigate each other's misery, and cannot escape everlasting torments—however numerous, each must die alone, and each appear for himself before the judgment seat of Christ, and each hear and bear his own inevitable doom.

IV. THAT SINNERS MAY DESIST FROM THIS COURSE, AMPLE FACILITIES ARE GIVEN.

1. *The right and good way is clearly revealed.* "Thus saith the Lord, Stand in the way and see," &c. Christ announced the narrow way, the way of holiness and salvation. It is a plain path, so that the wayfaring man need not err therein.

2. *Holy examples are placed before us.* "Be followers of those who through faith and patience," &c. Abel, Enoch, Noah, David, Daniel, and the apostles, especially the bright example of Jesus.

3. *Divine grace is promised.* Grace to save from sin, "Whosoever shall call on the name of the Lord," &c. Grace to resist evil—grace to persevere, &c.

4. *The most momentous motives are presented.* Present peace and happiness—joy in death—eternal glory.

APPLICATION.

1. To whom is the text applicable especially?

2. Who have obeyed its wise counsels?

3. Who will do so this day?

AGAINST PROFANITY.

"Thou shalt not take the name of the Lord thy God in vain; for the Lord will not hold him guiltless who taketh his name in vain."—EXOD. xx. 7.

OUR text is one of the commandments given with such solemnity by Jehovah to Moses on Sinai. It is a commandment often referred to in other parts of the sacred writings as one part of the moral code. It is one of universal and everlasting obligation. God addresses it to all his intellectual creatures, and its violation is an act of guilt, that will assuredly involve the delinquent in the displeasure of God. Let us therefore consider,

I. How THIS COMMANDMENT IS VIOLATED.
II. THE REASONS BY WHICH OBEDIENCE TO IT MAY BE URGED.

I. How THIS COMMANDMENT IS VIOLATED.

1. *By heinous acts of perjury.* Calling on God, or appealing to his name for the confirmation of a lie. This is a flagrant act of infamy, and which is justly punishable by the statutes of the land. Often have the guilty been screened, and often have the innocent been ruined, by this kind of perjury. Common lying is generally the precursor to false swearing.

2. *By calling upon God's name to curse ourselves or others.* Imprecations and curses are the most awful instances of profanity. How frequently do we hear men using language of the most profligate character, and associating the name of God with woes of the most horrible description!

3. *All light and irreverent uses of the name of God.* How many well-meaning persons err in this way, and sometimes

Christians interlard the name of God with trifling or worldly converse, who appeal to God on trivial occasions—who talk about God without serious or reverent reflection! We almost fear to illustrate this, yet it ought to be clearly understood. "God knows." "By the help of God." "As sure as God's in heaven." "God help you." "God bless you;" are the usual expressions in the mouths of the most wicked in this great city. How common is this sin! In all its characteristics; among nearly all classes. It is one of our national vices. How God's people should lay it to heart!

II. THE REASONS BY WHICH OBEDIENCE TO THIS COMMAND MAY BE URGED.

1. *It is solemnly forbidden in the text.* Therefore it is clear and binding in its authority. No reader therefore of the Bible can plead ignorance as an excuse for profanity. That law which was given under circumstances of such unparalleled sublimity, says, "Thou shalt not take," &c. Jesus showed the importance of this command by presenting it as the first petition in his divine prayer. "Hallowed be thy name."

2. *Profane swearing strikes at the root of all reverence for religion.* How can God be esteemed, and adored, and venerated, if men use his name profanely? There can be no fear of God—no deprecation of his wrath—no awe of his majesty—no regard to his authority. An irreligious state of heart must be the result; pious feeling, a spirit of devotion, or true seriousness cannot exist with profaneness.

3. *It is a sin extremely unnatural.* We can account for many evidences of depravity. We can understand how men may be gay, or sensual, or worldly, or angry, or even revengeful. May account for almost every sin, however vile and awful; but for profanity, no reason can be assigned. It does not gratify any passion—it does not obtain any enjoyment—it does not procure any advantage—it does not advance its votary to any glory. It is a superfluity of sin. A causeless, stupid, senseless crime against God, even the true and blessed God.

4. *It is a sin that greatly corrupts society.* A spirit of reverence for God, recommends religion. It must tell on society. Its influence will be seen and felt. It will check vice and keep in certain bounds glaring impiety. But profanity curses so-ciety, it blights every lovely thing, it is fearful in its effects on the young, who soon catch the spirit, and imitate what they hear. I add also, it is as indecent as it is vile. An insult to every educated and right-principled member of society.

5. *It is a sin that will fearfully harden the heart.* Hence how common for this class of persons to associate profanity with serious and affecting things! Men have been known to do this in sickness, in pain, when undergoing operations. Soldiers in the field of battle; sailors at sea; persons even in the struggles of death. I believe there is no vice which so excludes all excellency, and opens the flood-gates to all vileness and hardness of heart.

6. *It has often procured the signal wrath of God.* "Because of swearing the land mourneth." To blaspheme God's name was a capital offence under the law, Levit. xxiv. 10, &c. How often has instant judgment fallen upon perjurers, upon wicked persons who have imprecated God's wrath! A man in a village in Scotland, competed with others which could use the most horrid oaths, and was smitten with swelling of the tongue so that he could not draw it into his mouth, and died in three days. Heaven cannot be inhabited by the profane; hell must be their portion, and even there I doubt if the swearer will find a fallen angel so vile as himself.

APPLICATION.

1. *The remedy.* Solemn consideration of the grandeur and glory of God. Consider how angels act, &c. Guard your lips, watch against the rising of your heart; pray for God's Holy Spirit to change your soul: you must be new creatures. Dwell upon the senselessness of the crime, &c.

2. *Let Christians set a striking example in reverencing God's name.* And let their example and influence check bold transgressors, instruct our children, &c.

LIBERALITY AND SELFISHNESS CONTRASTED.

"There is that scattereth and yet increaseth; and there is that withholdeth more than is meet, but it tendeth to poverty. The liberal soul shall be made fat; and he that watereth shall be watered also himself."—PROVERBS xi. 24, 25.

OUR subject directs us to two very opposite courses, and the general consequences of each. The truths of the text are of a very important character ; they include the reactive influences which benevolence and selfishness produce, and are followed by a most cheering and delightful promise to the generous and liberal soul. When we remember that the second great command respects our fellow-creatures, an apology will not be necessary for calling your attention to an entire discourse on these topics ; yet, lest any should conclude, that religion is constituted of those actions which have respect to mankind only, allow me to remind you, that all acceptable piety commences with repentance towards God, and faith in our Lord Jesus Christ ; these, connected with regeneration, form a basis for the structure of personal piety. Personal piety includes supreme love to God, and unfeigned love to our fellow-men. Our text specifies one branch of our love to mankind, and it is beneficence ; observe, then, the contrast instituted, and the promise made.

I. THE CONTRAST INSTITUTED. Observe this contrast,

1. *In reference to the characters introduced.* One is described as a scatterer, that is, one who distributes, a person of feeling mind and generous enlarged heart ; one whose soul is expanded and warm. This character refers to the *habit*, to the prevailing disposition and conduct, not to an occasional act, &c. It includes also *purity* of motive, not an ostentatious giver, who makes it the subject of parade and show. Jesus describes the truly generous as not allowing the left hand to know, &c. This character also implies *perseverance* in well-doing. Abounding and continuing, &c. Now the other is described as a *withholder*, that is, a selfish man. One niggardly, of contracted spirit ; one afraid to distribute of his substance. Who hoards it up, and thus monopolizes what God confers ; views himself as the end, and not the channel of God's bounty ; not like the ocean yielding freely to the water-spout ; not like the clouds which give their plenteous rain ; nor like the earth yielding its increase, &c.

2. *The contrast of the text respects the results arising from the conduct specified.* He who scatters increaseth.

(1.) Now this is often the case, even as it respects temporal blessings. Beneficence often obtains a reward in kind ; God has a thousand ways of securing this. The wi-

dow who dared to share her meal and oil with the prophet, had it miraculously continued to her. It is not often that really benevolent persons sink into want. David's experience was, that he never saw the righteous forsaken, &c.

(2.) It is ever the case in reference to internal enjoyment ; and what is the end of all we have but enjoyment ? Now the good man enjoys what he has. There is God's blessing on it, and with it, and in it ; he has the satisfaction which a truly good and sanctified conscience confers. If spiritual blessings are given in exchange for our temporal benefactions, surely the recompense is ample and sufficient.

(3.) This will surely be the case in reference to an eternal reward. The day is coming when every one shall receive a reward for every deed of goodness and mercy ; when every kind word, and action, and visit, and gift, shall be noticed, acknowledged, and recompensed. We are instructed in this, where Christ says, though the poor cannot recompense, yet ye " shall be recompensed at the resurrection of the just." He that withholdeth tendeth to poverty. There are claims which must have a preference. Our own wants and those of our families, prudent arrangement for the contingencies of life. These things " are meet." But he who withholdeth, &c., more than this, it often tendeth to poverty. Some withhold, because they fear *want*, dare not trust divine providence ; some withhold, because the demands of pride and fashion drain all their resources ; some of a *sordid avaricious spirit*, they are earthworms ; like the horseleech, or the grave, or the sea, they are ever craving ; some withhold on the ground of the *ingratitude* of the poor. All these are so many evidences of a selfish nature. This often defeats its end.

(1.) Such cannot guard against contingencies. Failure of banks, fires, bankruptcies, &c. God can blight every movement ; accidents, afflictions, can drain all dry ; this is not unfrequently the case.

(2.) Then there is always poverty of enjoyment ; however much, it is not enjoyed. Mental sterility, spiritual barrenness, nothing bright or cheering within ; it is the frigid zone, winter, ice, darkness.

(3.) Then such shall be poor indeed at death ; not a title to a better world ; not a jot or tittle can they take with them; they brought nothing into the world, &c. And when the Master demands an account, how fearfully appalling and eternally terrific; such is the contrast instituted. Observe,

II. THE PROMISE MADE. "The liberal soul," &c. That is, he shall flourish, &c.

(1.) God's blessing shall rest on his affairs; see Psalm xxvii. 3, xli. 1.

(2.) God's blessing shall rest on his soul; he shall be happy. He that hath mercy on the poor, "happy is he." God will answer his prayer, Isaiah lviii. 6, 7. His soul shall be very fruitful, Isaiah lviii. 10, 11. Such shall be established in divine things. "The liberal deviseth liberal things, and by liberal things he shall be established." Now we may ascertain some grounds why the liberal soul, &c.

1. *This is the design of our being invested with these blessings.* All things have reference to some end; nothing made for itself. Look at the sun, the moon, the stars, the sea, &c. And God never gave wealth to be locked up in banks or cabinets, but to be diffused, &c. Every thing else is perversion, to scatter is the great design, &c.

2. *There is the benevolent character of God placed for our imitation.* "Be ye merciful as your Father," &c. "Be ye followers of God as dear children," &c. "He is good to all," &c. "With such sacrifices he is well pleased."

3. *There is the divine connection between means and end.* I have spoken of the end of our means. Let us look at the philosophy of using our gifts.

(1.) Take the golden grain, and hoard it up, it will moulder and rot; sow it, and it will yield thirty, sixty, &c.

(2.) Take the power and disposition to communicate knowledge, and your teaching will enlarge, and improve, and enrich your own minds.

(3.) Take Christian instrumentality to do good and employ it, and your ability will increase, and your own souls be abundantly blessed, you cannot fail to get good; just so those who scatter abroad, shall increase. The bread cast upon the waters shall not perish, &c. It is but little we can do; but a short period allotted us; let us then not be weary, &c. And let us, in the midst of all, seek enlarged communications of the divine favor. Let us not trust in our benevolence for acceptance with God. Let humility always clothe us, remembering that at best we are unprofitable servants.

THE SATISFACTION AND ADVANTAGES OF GODLINESS.

"But godliness with contentment is great gain." —1 TIM. vi. 6.

THERE is a very current maxim, of great value and importance, that a contented mind is a continual feast. Without a great degree of this, happiness is utterly impossible. Neither wealth, nor honor, nor the gay scenes of pleasure, can confer real solid enjoyment on the soul of man. To these we may add learning, knowledge, power, and influence; the whole of which may be possessed; and yet as it regards solid bliss, vanity may be written upon the whole, and vexation of spirit. In a thousand points we are vulnerable; to a thousand diseases we are exposed; a thousand events may arise to distract and distress us. Our very breath is in our nostrils, and however earthly good may surround us, we are liable every moment to be exiled by the stroke of death from the whole. We would invite all searchers after true happiness to seek that real blessing in another path. It may assuredly be found and enjoyed; and our text gives us the direction—the infallible recipe. "Godliness with contentment," says the apostle, "is great gain." Let us consider,

I. THE SCRIPTURAL DEFINITION OF GODLINESS.

II. THE TRUE NATURE OF CONTENTMENT.

III. THE ADVANTAGES ARISING FROM THE UNION OF THE TWO. Let us endeavor to give you,

I. A SCRIPTURAL DEFINITION OF GODLINESS. And to a mere definition we must confine ourselves. It necessarily involves,

1. *A saving knowledge of God.* "This is life eternal," to know God in his natural attributes and moral perfections; in his works and government, especially as the Redeemer of the world—as the great source of love and mercy to our fallen race. To know this for ourselves—not because the Bible records it—the preacher declares it, but because we have experienced his power

and truth, and love in our own souls ; because he is our God, and we are his children. Not a learned, metaphysical knowledge of God, but a personal, inward, experimental sense of his grace and mercy. To know him in Christ ; God manifest in the flesh ; Immanuel, God with us, and for us, and in us. Godliness includes,

2. *The indwelling of the Holy Spirit.* "Because ye are sons, or children, God hath sent forth," &c. " The Spirit of God beareth witness," &c. Hence the new covenant promise runs thus :—" I will put my Spirit," &c. " As many as are led by the Spirit of God," &c. " Know ye not that ye are the temples," &c. It includes,

3. *Conformity to the will of God.* The mind conformed—the heart conformed— the life conformed. The mind agreeing— the heart delighting—the life obeying. In this state the thoughts, desires, purposes, expressions, and actions, will be under divine authority and control. To please God will be the great end of life. Enoch had this testimony before his translation, that he pleased God. The apostle said he exercised himself to maintain a conscience, &c.

4. *Devotedness to his service and glory.* The godly desire to make God known ; to show forth his praise ; to extol him and exalt him before men ; to labor with God and for God ; by the entire surrender of all we are and have to his cause and glory. " Glorify God in all things." " Whethei ye eat," &c. " No man liveth to himself."

> " Were the whole realm of nature mine,
> That were a present far too small."

" The love of Christ constraineth us," &c. This is godliness—the godliness of the New Testament ; that which is saving, &c. We now pass on to consider,

II. THE TRUE NATURE OF CONTENTMENT. Now, this implies a state of mind acquiescing in the arrangements of God respecting us, and our lot and portion in the world. It is the opposite of ambition, anxiety, and avarice ; it is equanimity of spirit, arising from an internal approbation of God's government and ways. Of course, there are special seasons when contentment is to be exhibited and proved. We need not wonder that persons should be contented when they have health, prosperity, friends, &c. ; but contentment shines in the fiery furnace of affliction—in the night of adversity, when friends forsake us, or when by death we are bereaved of them. It flourisheth in persecution, in reproaches, in suffering, and in death. In one word, it reconciles the mind to the various circumstances in which God may choose to place us. Now, contentment is not a sullen, mechanical principle ; not a stoical state of mind ; not mere affectation. It is in harmony with the greatest possible sensitiveness ; it can feel and discriminate ; it would prefer ease, and enjoyment, and prosperity ; but it can bend to the burden, bow to the correcting hand, drink the afflictive cup, submit to the severe stroke, or even resign itself to death. Now, a godly contentment is grounded,

1. *On the perfect excellency of the divine character.* God is the sum of all perfection ; pure light, pure goodness. All that is great, and glorious, and wise, and merciful, and righteous, form his divine character. Contentment says, " His wisdom cannot err ; his powerful arm cannot weary ; his plans cannot be frustrated ; his goodness cannot be exhausted ; his love cannot change ; his promises cannot fail ; his righteousness cannot do wrong ; and his tender mercy is over all his works, and it endures through all generations." Godly contentment rests,

2. *On the equity and benignancy of his government.* That government extends to all creatures, and all worlds ; it combines all events. God cannot but reign righteously, for there is no iniquity in him. He must reign bountifully, for he is good to all. Just as the sun cannot shine without diffusing heat and light, so God in all his government must act righteously and benignantly. That righteous and good government, or providence, encircles me and you always, every instant, and in every place. That trial—that cross—that sorrow—that bereavement, was a part of it. " The Lord reigneth," &c., is the song of the Christian. Godly contentment rests,

3. *On the richness of the divine gifts.* What has he not given us ? The earth, the heavens, the sea, the sky, the valley, and the mountain—the vital atmosphere— the light of day. What more ? Life, powers, sensibilities, &c. ; many sources of enjoyment. His revealed will as the guide to immortality ; exceeding great promises ; his own Son—his ever blessed co-equal Son, the Prince of life, and the

Lord of glory. Here the apostle will assist us, "If God spared not his own Son," &c. Oh! read it with emphasis. With this Son, the Holy Spirit, and eternal life, shall we not be content? What higher, what richer, what greater, what more enduring blessings could he have imparted? Godly contentment arises,

4. *From humbling views of ourselves.* As creatures, how unworthy, guilty, polluted, profitless, rebellious, wayward children! What have we merited? What is our desert? If God were to take all he might justly take, what should we have left? Oh! ask and reply to that question.

5. *From a sense of the infinite superiority of spiritual over earthly things.* That spiritual gifts are the perfect gifts; more precious and durable; more excellent, as adapted to the mind and heart; and if these be healthy, and happy, and prosperous, it must be well with us, and if not, it cannot be well with us. Whatever we may possess, we must be wretched and miserable indeed.

6. *From the evanescence and uncertainty of the present state of existence.* Look at the past, like the stream ever flowing—the present, fleeting—the future approaching. We are travelling to the sepulchre, to the divine tribunal, to eternity. The soul will then be all—the favor of God all—its salvation all.

III. THE ADVANTAGES ARISING FROM GODLINESS AND CONTENTMENT. "Great gain." Satisfaction of soul is the result; solid, internal enjoyment; comfort, which sets circumstances at defiance—which is within, a source of blessedness; what the world cannot give or take away; a perpetual feast; an invulnerable defence; an unchanging, radiant prospect; a certainty of blessedness. How great, how superlative, how everlasting this gain!

APPLICATION.

1. Examine yourselves on these two points—godliness and contentment.
2. They exercise a mutual influence on each other.
3. Admonish those who have neither.

AN UNGODLY SPIRIT REBUKED.

"Ye know not what manner of spirit ye are of."
—LUKE ix. 55.

OUR text presents us with a striking instance of the weakness and sinful infirmities of two of the eminent disciples of the Saviour. One of these was the beloved John, who afterwards became so distinguished for meekness and love. Between the Samaritans and the Jews the most deadly animosities prevailed; they even refused to each other the common civilities and courtesies of life. Hence the exclamation of the woman to Jesus, "How is it that thou, who art a Jew, askest water?" &c. Jesus had now set his face to go up to Jerusalem, and on his way had to pass through a Samaritan village, and he sent messengers that they would prepare for him. It is written that they would not receive him, because he was on his way to Jerusalem. They probably hoped that Christ would tarry with them, and decide the protracted controversy about the right place of worship in their favor. When James and John saw this, they indignantly exclaimed, "Wilt thou that we command fire?" &c. Their desire was that they should at once be consumed. They quote scripture in support of it; but wisely they refer it to Christ. The only good thing in it was the interrogation in reference to it, "Wilt thou?" The answer of our Redeemer is the text of this occasion, "But he turned and rebuked them," &c. From this striking and instructive portion of the divine word, we notice,

I. THAT THE PROFESSED DISCIPLES OF CHRIST MAY BE GREATLY INFLUENCED BY A WRONG SPIRIT. Let us,

1. *Notice some instances wherein this is exhibited.*

(1.) In maintaining bitterness of mind to those who have different views of divine truth. How rare it is to see exhibited a spirit of affectionate candor with regard to other sects and parties! Our own opinions are the right, the orthodox ones. To differ from us is to go from the way of truth. A very small variation is sufficient to set them down as heterodox, and perhaps to unchristianize them altogether. If we are compelled to speak well, it is in a cool tone, or with several deductions, which nullify all that has been said. This is sometimes the case in reference to doctrines, or forms of worship; to ordinances, to discipline, &c. Thus the state church treats dissenters, and thus dissenters treat the state church; Roman Catholics, Protestants; and Protestants, Roman Catholics. Now, if Christ were present in this arena of disputation and strife, do you think he would agree either with the churchman or the dissenter in their unhallowed strifes? No! he would say to each, and to the whole, "Ye know not," &c.

2. *It is seen in carrying our dislike of men's sins into dislike of their persons.* We are to hate all evil, both in ourselves and others. We cannot detest too much the pollution which may be manifest in those around us; but this indignation and hatred must not include the person of the sinner. I must hate profligacy, but have compassion on the profligate; hate drunkenness, but feel for the drunkard; hate avarice, but love the souls of the avaricious; hate hypocrisy, but yearn over the hypocrite," &c. When our wrath goes beyond this, we tread unhallowed ground; we become transgressors; and Christ says to us, "Ye know not," &c.

3. *It is seen in cherishing an unmerciful and unforgiving spirit towards our enemies.* Nothing is so pre-eminently exhibited in the divine word as the indispensable importance of love, even to our enemies. We are commanded to put away all malice, and anger, and wrath. Our own forgiveness is even suspended on that of forgiving others; yet, how Christians err in this! How often they are implacable; how often feel and speak evil of their supposed enemies! Sometimes this is done on the most trivial ground—often arising from mere spleen and envy. I ask, is it so with any of you? Do you know of any one towards whom you thus feel? If so, the rebuke of Christ is addressed to you, "Ye know not," &c.

II. LET US ACCOUNT FOR THE EXISTENCE OF THIS SPIRIT. We marvel not at this in unconverted persons, who are strangers to the love of God, and the power of the Holy Spirit; but we expect the image and spirit of Jesus in the regenerated, converted follower of Christ.

1. *It arises from the very partially sanctified state of the heart.* Much of original corruption remains within; much spiritual territory to be possessed; attainments of grace low; the soul frigid and sterile.

2. *It arises from the influence of unhallowed prejudices in the mind.* In some cases imperfect education, or ministerial instruction; trained in an atmosphere of bigotry

and strife; indoctrinated into sectarian principles instead of the principles of the gospel. Hence some ministers and churches are celebrated for bitterness of spirit, exclusiveness of feeling, and party animosity. Often our reading has much to do with it; the word of God a very secondary book; only read authors of our own party and creed, &c.

3. *From self-ignorance and self-deception.* "Ye know not," &c. Know our name, and creed, and peculiarities, but not our spirit. Know the spirit of others, and can condemn it, yet know it not in ourselves. Live without self-examination, with little self-communion, or fellowship with God; thus err and deceive our own souls. We come,

III. TO SPECIFY THE DIVINE REMEDY FOR THIS WRONG SPIRIT.

1. *The cultivation of an humble and lowly spirit.* To see and feel our own unworthiness—our own defects, and failings, and sins. A sense of these will abase, occupy our reflections, confessions, &c. We shall neither have time nor disposition to unchristianize or excommunicate others.

2. *A diligent perusal of the divine word.* Here are admonitions, exhortations, counsels, &c.; here are beacons, as in the text; here our models, &c. Deeply imbued with the spirit of the word will greatly preserve us.

3. *A careful imitation of the example and spirit of Jesus.* His nature—his mission—his life, &c.; all breathe pure, infinite love, &c. His Spirit dwelling in us is religion. How did he feel, and act, and speak? What the design of his mission? What the influence of his love, &c.?

APPLICATION.

1. Attention to our spirit is of the utmost importance.

2. Our own happiness and improvement identified with it.

3. A right spirit only will recommend religion.

ON VAIN THOUGHTS.

"How long shall thy vain thoughts lodge within thee?"—JER. iv. 14.

THE religion which is acceptable to God must be of the heart, it must have its dwelling in the heart, it must sanctify the heart; and from a heart devoted to God, will issue works of righteousness to the divine glory. Hence great stress is laid upon this in the sacred volume, "My son, give me thine heart," &c. "A new heart will I give you," &c. And in the verse of the text, "O Jerusalem, wash thine heart," &c. But our text limits us to one subject or branch of the heart, that is, the thoughts—"How long," &c. By thoughts we mean the exercise of the faculties of the mind confined within itself, in distinction to those operations of the mind, which are embodied in words or actions; therefore thoughts involve the cognizances or perceptions of the understanding, the conclusions of the judgment, the decisions and purposes of the will, and the ideas of the imagination, and the conclusions of the mind in general: but imaginations, desires, and purposes, will comprehend chiefly what we mean by thoughts. Let us consider the thoughts the text refers to, show their vanity, urge their exclusion from the heart, with some directions for securing that object.

I. THE THOUGHTS REFERRED TO. It is obvious that the thoughts must often be engaged in reference to the things of this life. Business, and the lawful concerns of our families, must employ our thoughts. Excess here is only sinful; to have the thoughts wholly absorbed. Now this is the case with many. But of the thoughts which are referred to I notice,

1. *Proud and high-minded thoughts.* When persons think more highly of themselves, &c.; when their defects, &c., are lessened, and supposed excellencies magnified. The human heart is naturally disposed to pride; proud thoughts will lead to a proud countenance and to pride of life.

2. *Thoughts which refer to human applause.* Thinking how we can obtain the goo word and favor of the world; to have the good opinion, especially of those around us, and to bask in the beams of honor. Now these thoughts will also lead persons to a course of action degrading to themselves, and with which hypocrisy will be a main and leading ingredient; such will adopt soft and oily words, and an apparent condescension of gait and conduct.

3. *Worldly thoughts.* Anxiety concerning earthly good, "Why take ye thought," &c.? what shall I eat, &c.? Thus the soul will be chained down to the earth; only contemplate the material good of this life. Those thoughts lead to covetousness, which is idolatry.

4. *Envious and malignant thoughts.* Looking with pain and dislike on the good of others, feeling uneasy at their prosperity, anxious to depreciate their reputation, secretly preparing arrows of enmity to injure them.

5. *Thoughts of speculative wickedness.* When sin is acted in the mind, when evils are lodged in the soul and presented to the imagination, and then fostered in the prolific soil of the human heart. These thoughts are peculiarly prevalent in persons of corrupt imaginations; polluted conversation, and sensual books, greatly tend to this evil. I refer,

6. *To the general dissipation of thoughts.* When there is no mental order or self-government; when the mind is open to every intruding thought, and when the soul is like the channel of a muddy stream, ever receiving, and ever communicating that which is foolish, and trifling, and sinful. I connect with these, those whose thoughts are ever occupied with the mere ideal, always living in a world of fancy; the theatre, and works of fiction, greatly tend to produce and foster such thoughts. Let us,

II. SHOW THEIR VANITY. They are vain,

1. *As they are foolish.* Contrary to a sound understanding and real wisdom. No man can improve, either mentally or morally, under their influence; even as it regards the attainment of real knowledge and enjoyment as rational beings in this life, they are foolish. There are so many sources of mental enjoyment in the works of nature, in wholesome reading, in the discoveries of science, and wonders of art; but how foolish when we reflect that we are candidates for eternity!

2. *As they are empty.* Nothing substantial in them; they afford no real enjoyment, no true pleasure; as well might a man attempt to live on the wind, or in viewing pictures of food and drink.

3. *They are evil in the sight of God.* Our accountability extends to the thoughts— "God searcheth the heart," &c. Every thought is to be brought into judgment; evil thoughts must be forsaken and pardoned, or they will condemn us forever; and evil thoughts are generally the precursors of evil actions; they are often the seeds or germ, &c. We,

III. URGE THEIR EXCLUSION FROM THE

HEART, WITH SOME DIRECTIONS FOR SECURING THAT OBJECT. "How long," &c. ; surely long enough already ; our happiness, safety, and spiritual improvement, are sufficient reasons for the exclusion of these vain thoughts. But how is this great object to be secured ? There must be,

1. *A deep conviction of the evil of these thoughts.* Feel them to be the plague of our souls ; feel them to be our burden, our misery, &c. Nothing can be effectually done without this.

2. *We must be humbled before God on account of them.* They must be loathed, confessed with sincerity and abasement of heart before the Lord ; the soul contrite before the Lord, covered as with sackcloth, &c.

3. *We must seek purification through the blood of Christ.* Christ's blood cleanseth from all sin, even sinful thoughts. It purifieth the conscience.

4. *We must daily supplicate the sanctifying power of the Spirit.* He is the sanctifier ; he gives us spiritual power to resist evil ; he will impart to the soul the things of Christ, and impart his holy mind ; he will enable us to war with these thoughts, &c.

5. *Recognise God's omniscience and cultivate his fear.* Be in that fear all the day long. Remember he is conversant with our thoughts. Pray daily, "Cleanse thou me from secret faults," &c.

6. *Store the heart with the divine thoughts of his holy word.* "I hate vain thoughts, but thy law do I love." "Thy word have I hid in mine heart," &c.

APPLICATION.

1. *Learn the exclusive spiritual claims God has upon us.*

2. *Labor after inward purity of heart.*

3. *Thoughts are only evil when cherished, &c.,*—When they "lodge within us." Reject them if possible on their approach, at any rate by prayer and faith exclude them if they have taken possession.

THE RIGHT EMPLOYMENT OF THE TONGUE.

" Keep thy tongue from evil, and thy lips from speaking guile."—PSALM xxxiv. 13.

WE have considered, on previous occasions, the spirit and the thoughts ; our present subject is the tongue : a subject to which the scriptures often invite our attention. Unless the tongue be under the sanctifying influences of the grace of God, we are told by the apostle that our religion is vain, and that whoso offendeth not in word, that man is a perfect man. A good man, out of the good treasure of his heart, will bring forth wise and useful conversation. But an evil man, out of the bad treasure of his heart, will bring forth only a stream of pollution and death. A wholesome tongue, says Solomon, is a tree of life. Our subject then is the religious use of the tongue. Let us notice, then, what we should avoid ; what use we should make of it ; how we may do it ; and the motives for so doing. In the use of the tongue,

I. WHAT SHOULD WE AVOID ? The text specifies evil in the general—" from evil."

1. *From the evil of impiety and blasphemy.* All expressions against God's character, and glory, and works, and will. All witty citations and perversions of scripture. All jocular uses of the divine word. All rash and speculative speaking on the solemn concerns of the soul, religion, and eternity.

2. *From the evil of profaneness.* All cursing, swearing, and imprecations, taking God's name in vain. "Thou shalt not take the name," &c. All exclamations in which God's name is irreverently used. Many sincere Christians err here. Never use any of the divine titles but with awe and godly fear.

3. *From the evil of falsehood.* Now this is a monster evil—it assumes an almost endless variety of shapes and hues.

(1.) One of its forms is that of slander—when we declare that which is false to injure another.

(2.) Another is that of detraction, when we may not assert any positive evil, but withhold from the real merits of those of whom we speak, or endeavor to fritter away their excellencies, and rob them of their true reputation.

(3.) Evil speaking—when we become the conveyers of evil concerning others without good evidences of its truth ; and also when we needlessly dwell on the infirmities or sins of others—this is severely reprehended in scripture. The backbiter is an odious character. Among other modes of falsehood there is,

(4.) That of false jesting, where persons

invent the ridiculous and the ludicrous, and palm it upon people as truth.

(5.) Falsehood used in trading and business, when an untrue impression is made upon a seller or buyer. Persons are guilty of this in extolling their articles, and others in cheapening them. What a world of iniquity is exhibited to the eye of Deity in the transactions of trade; how few even of professors have clean hands! I refer,

(6.) To flattery, when we desire to gratify persons, by stating excellencies which we do not believe them to possess. Some persons court this, are ever eagerly seeking the company of such, but it lessens not the guilt of the flatterer. We should not only keep ourselves from the evil of falsehood of all kinds, but also from the evil,

4. *Of talkativeness.* The tongue was never designed to be in perpetual motion as the muscles of the heart, or the blood in the veins. Talkativeness is an evil in itself, and also leadeth to much evil. "In a multitude of words there wanteth not sin." Few perpetual talkers have good consciences. There are times when it would be cruel to be silent, but there are surely seasons when it is cruel not to be so.

5. *From the evil of anger and contention.* Wrathful words—words spoken hastily—words designed to irritate, and incense, and provoke. How James refers to this, chapter iii. verse 5, &c. But we ask,

II. WHAT USE SHALL WE MAKE OF THE TONGUE?

1. *Let it be placed under the influences of wisdom.* Let it give utterance to that which is wise, and be the instrument of conveying knowledge. Have something to say when we speak, and something worth saying.

2. *Let it always be identified with truth.* Abhor falsehood as mean and contemptible, but especially as grievous to God, and ruinous to the soul. "Speak the truth one to another," &c.

3. *Let it be the instrument of peace.* Avoid all wrangling, and strife, and contentions. This be your motto, "I am for peace." Let the tongue not be dipped in gall, nor in the oil of dissimulation, but the holy oil of amity and love; "speaking the truth in love."

4. *Let it be the minister of edification.* Use the tongue for the good of mankind,

Col. iv. 6. Speak to instruct—to comfort —to encourage and warn, &c. We ask,

III. HOW WE MAKE THIS USE OF THE TONGUE?

1. *By seeking the sanctification of the heart.* The mouth is the channel for the stream from the inward fountain of the soul. From the state and fulness of the heart the mouth speaketh. If the fountain be pure, then will the streams be so. A heart filled with heavenly wisdom and holy love will ever produce a pious and edifying conversation. As the heart is, so will be the tongue.

2. *By having it under strict government and control.* If allowed to run riot, or left to itself, evil must be the result. A wise man will place under restriction this difficult member. He will discipline it. "Keep it as with bit and bridle," &c.

3. *Exercise Christian vigilance in reference to it.* Have watch as well as guard. Keep a sentinel at the door of thy lips. Be slow also to speak. Exercise caution and circumspection, &c.

4. *Employ it in holy services.* Reading the divine word, prayer, praise, Christian conversation, &c. And let the prayer have especial respect to this difficult member. Now let us glance,

IV. AT SOME MOTIVES FOR THE RIGHT APPLICATION OF THE TONGUE. Because of the connection,

1. *Between the tongue and the conscience.* Is not conscience oftener grieved and defiled by the tongue than any thing else? Who does not know this? If a good conscience is worth having, then "Keep thy tongue," &c. Because of the connection,

2. *Between the tongue and our real prosperity.* "A wholesome tongue is a tree of life," &c. It will exert a favorable influence on the whole soul. On account of the connection,

3. *Between the tongue and our usefulness.* Our influence will greatly depend on this. If this member is extensively wrong we shall do little good in the world. If it be seasoned with the salt of grace we shall extensively be blessings to others. On account of the connection,

4. *Between the tongue and the judgment day.* Words as well as actions will be judged. All that we have said as well as done—every idle word. A falsehood will then cover with shame, and exclude from the heavenly state.

APPLICATION.

1. *Let the subject be the test of personal examination.*

2. *Let it be duly pondered in its momentous bearings on our highest and best interests.*

3. *Let those who are the slaves of an evil tongue seek deliverance by the power of divine truth and grace.* A new heart is essentially necessary.

SPIRITUAL APATHY DENOUNCED.

"Wo to them that are at ease in Zion."—
Amos vi. 1.

Some men are at ease in their sins, though heinous and aggravated, through their consciences being seared and insensible; some are at ease in their indifference to religion, through the absorbing power of worldliness, or through the fascinating pleasures of life; some are at ease through carnal presumption, resting on the exercise of the final mercy of God; some are at ease by the delusions of self-righteousness, depending for acceptance and salvation through the deeds of the law; but to none of these classes does our text refer. It distinctly points to the professors of religion —the visible servants of God—the members of his church. "Wo to them that are at ease," not in the world, but "in Zion"—in the church. Let us define the characteristics; ascertain the causes; and show the evil of this state of mind. Let us,

I. Define the characteristics. And in this definition we shall more especially accompany the description, by showing the evidences of this state of heart and mind. In the church it is delightful to observe the spiritually-minded, the active, the liberal, the zealous followers of Christ. Now those at ease in Zion form the contrast of each of these classes. The apathy supposed in the text is,

1. *Opposed to spiritual-mindedness.* The mind is greatly under the power of the carnal principle; secular and earthly things have the ascendency; communion with God is rare and feeble; devotion at a low ebb; the thoughts, desires, feelings, &c., are of the earth, earthy; the rays of celestial light are but dim in the chamber of the understanding; and the fire of hallowed emotion is almost extinguished on the altar of the heart.

2. *It is opposed to holy activity.* Activity is one of the essential laws of the universe; it is especially so in relation to mind. The powers of the soul were destined for activity. Without this there can be neither health nor vigor. Activity is essential to the welfare of our own souls—essential to the discharge of the duties of the Christian life— essential to the prosperity of the church and kingdom of Christ in the world. Heaven is the scene of holy activity; hell is the theatre of wicked and malignant activity; the world is one field of varied yet incessant activity; and is the church of Christ the only sphere for unconcern and apathy? Is it not painfully evident, that not more than one in twenty are actively employed in honoring the Redeemer, and seeking the extension of his cause?

3. *It is opposed to generous liberality.* We cannot expect persons to be generous and self-denying for that which has no hold upon the heart. Most people will support what they greatly esteem and love; but if the heart is not influenced, there will be no generous liberality. What is given to the cause of God will be doled out on the principle of duty, or propriety, or respectability. Now, such a state of feeling will never provide the means for converting the world. How different this to the first Christian churches! Let me read a passage or two: Acts ii. 44, iv. 3, &c.; 2 Cor. viii. 1, &c. Men cannot be profuse in the family and in the world, in pleasure and luxuries, and calculating in the church, unless they are at ease in Zion.

4. *It is opposed to fervid zeal.* The concerns of personal religion are so great and lofty, that they demand the most intense devotedness of our powers to God. "Fervent in spirit." But besides these, there are the great interests of the cause of Jesus, none of which can be effectually promoted without fervid Christian zeal. All that is great, and glowing, and good in the visible kingdom of Christ, has been produced by the zeal of its loyal subjects, followed by the blessing of God. It was zeal that made our confessors and martyrs; zeal that raised and sustained the Reformers and the Puritans; zeal that gives men the missionary spirit, and supports them in their spheres of self-denial and suffering. We cannot dispense with this spirit, unless

Satan is to overcome, and the world have the ascendency. How criminal, then, is the apathy of that spirit of slumber which rests on many of the professors of religion ! Let us, then,

II. Ascertain the cause of this evil. It may arise from,

1. *Mistakes as to the true nature of religion.* Religion is not only enjoyment and privilege, but duty, labor, and activity. Religion makes a man better and happier, but it also makes him the servant of the Saviour ; a laborer in Christ's vineyard ; a soldier in Christ's army. "I beseech you, brethren, by the mercies of God," &c.

2. *From the feeble influence which the doctrines of the cross produce within us.* These doctrines are calculated to constrain the soul to entire devotedness. "God forbid," &c. "Yea, doubtless," &c. The love of Christ should constrain us, &c. Who does not admire these lines ?

"Were the whole realm of nature mine,
    That were a present far too small:
Love so amazing, so divine,
    Demands my life, my soul, my all."

But do we seriously believe them ? do we feel them ? If not, it is only sentiment— only poetry. Now, the apathy of the formal must greatly arise from the feeble influence of these doctrines on our hearts ; and the cause of this must be, the great distance we live from Calvary. We do not cling to it, look up to the Sufferer, hear his dying groans, feel his love, or we could not be at ease in Zion.

3. *Unnecessary intercourse with the men and things of the world.* The most devout and holy know how chilling this is ; even with the utmost watchfulness it is so. But if this atmosphere is often breathed—if this society is preferred—if much of our leisure time is thus occupied, how can it be otherwise that we should not be at ease in Zion ?

4. *Forgetfulness of our responsibility.* We must every one give an account of himself, &c. ; we are stewards, and must render an account of our stewardship ; we are accountable for our talents, time, influence, property, &c. ; we are accountable for all the good we possess ability to do, in the world and in the church. The day of reckoning will come, and how desirable that we be found faithful—that Christ may say, "Well done," &c. Let us, then,

III. Show the evil of this state of mind. "Wo to them," &c.

1. *It is evil in itself.* Displeasing to God ; grieves his Spirit ; perverts his mercies, &c.

2. *It is evil in its influence.*

(1.) On the persons who are at ease. It renders the soul barren ; it robs it of peace ; it often leads to apathy.

(2.) It is evil in its influence on the brethren ; it is withering in its effects ; it will infect others ; lull others into that state of lethargy.

(3.) It is evil to the church ; takes away its beauty and vigor ; renders its influence almost powerless ; throws it into the shade, and rejoices its adversaries.

(4.) Its influence is bad on the world. Men must see that it is not the religion of the New Testament, of Christ, and the apostles. It hinders the conversion of souls ; hardens skeptics, &c.

APPLICATION.

1. *Let the text be the test of our present condition.* Are we condemned by it ? or do we pass through the ordeal with triumph ? I fear most of us are condemned.

2. *Let it lead to greater devotedness.* All have need of this. Let us aim at this for our own sakes—for the sake of the church —especially for Christ's sake.

REAL SACRILEGE.

"Will a man rob God ?"—Malachi iii. 8.

Robbery—robbery ! Why, you say, the very term has only meaning when used in connection with the most profligate and abandoned portion of society. How insulted any man would feel to be denounced as a robber ; lost to all correct notions of righteousness ; to be desperate, daring, and reckless ; not to regard the rights and feelings of others. How low are such sunk in the scale of society ! Surely, I have not one such person here. But our text seems to charge men with the highest kind of robbery—robbery of God. It has been observed, "To rob the poorest individual is felony ; to usurp the prerogatives or riches of a monarch is treason ; but to rob God is sacrilege." I fear that not only the Jews were guilty of this, but also that many here are not clear in this matter. "Will a man rob God ?" What is it to rob God ? The heinousness of doing so, and its consequences, be now therefore considered.

I. WHAT IS IT TO ROB GOD ? To rob God is to deprive him of any of his just rights. God has a just and equitable claim,

1. *On our homage and reverence.* If his name is profaned, or used with levity, or interlards our conversation, it is robbery of God. Jesus has shown us the importance of this, in making it the first petition of the prayer he taught his disciples, " Hallowed be thy name." Many persons do this through thoughtlessness, &c. God is greatly to be feared, and his venerable name held most sacred.

2. *God has a claim on our grateful love.* We ought to love supreme excellence—the most perfect good. God is such. Infinite love ; eternal goodness and mercy. But see his goodness to us. How striking— bountiful — pitiful — constant — never-failing ! Ought he not to be praised ? Is he not worthy to be praised, &c. But if he is not extolled and blessed, then do we rob God. This is his right and due. Silence and indifference is guilt.

3. *God has a claim upon our obedience.* He is to be served ; with lip and life ; from the heart ; with diligence, earnestness, &c. He is to be served before men. Every omission of duty robs him—every transgression robs him. Who, then, is not guilty ? &c.

4. *God has a claim upon our time.* It is all his gift. Every year—month—day. He requires a portion of it to be devoted to him. He demands the youth of life ; ought he not to have it ? The flower of our days, &c. " Wilt thou not from this time ?" &c. He demands a portion of every day in religious worship, morning and evening ; prayer—thanksgiving—reading—meditation. He demands the day of holy rest ; he did this from the creation ; he did this by Moses in the law ; he received this from the disciples. Who has not robbed God of youth—of daily time—of the sabbath ?

5. *He has a claim upon our means and talents.* I refer to our ability of doing good. Honoring him ; teaching the knowledge of him ; glorifying him ; supporting his cause ; regarding his poor, &c. His interests are to have a high, extensive, and deep place in our affections and esteem. Who has not robbed God of these ? How little he has had ; how unfair a proportion, &c. Reply ye, who is free from guilt ? &c. Consider,

II. THE HEINOUSNESS OF ROBBING GOD.

Now, it is not a light thing ; it is a great sin ; very grievous to him. Measure it,

1. *By the Being we rob.* God ; not only the greatest, most exalted, and blessed Being, but our heavenly Father—our Preserver—our Saviour.

2. *By the persons guilty of it.* Recipients of his bounty—objects of his care — for whom he has given his own Son. Let Satan and unredeemed spirits be so infatuated ; but can ransomed creatures—souls for whom the Saviour died ?

3. *By its glaring rashness and presumption.* Men rob privately in the dark—in hope of escape ; but we rob God when his eye is upon us ; when he is surrounding us ; while he is recording the deed – writing it down against us. What daring —what effrontery—what hardness and infatuation ! Consider,

III. ITS FINAL RESULTS. It has present evil results ; it is unwise ; it is self-injurious. We rob ourselves ; we rob ourselves of his favor, his approval, his love, his blessing, his peace ; but its final results must be calamitous. There will,

1. *Be the arrestment.* He will send his officers, &c. ; bring us before his bar, &c. " We shall all stand before," &c.

2. *There will be the conviction.* We cannot clear ourselves. His own gaze will light up every conscience, and all our guilt will flash before our eyes. This conviction will be public.

3. *There will be the sentence.* Separation from the holy, the elevated, the happy. Doomed to the abode of the devil and his angels ; everlasting blackness and fire. " The wicked shall be turned into hell," &c. I apply the subject by asking, what shall we do to avert the doom stated ?

1. *There must be confession.* Go, and acknowledge your sin. He requires this. Do it humbly—ingenuously—sincerely.

2. *Restitution.* As far as possible. Cannot give him back youth and time ; but now surrender yourselves, body, soul, and spirit.

3. *There must be amendment.* Repent ye, or reform ye. " Cease to do evil," &c. " Turn ye," &c. " If the wicked man," &c.

4. *There must be trust in Jesus Christ* Christ is our Mediator ; the way—the fountain—the sacrifice, &c. Who will surrender himself thus to God ? Seek mercy, and obtain everlasting life.

INSTABILITY

"Unstable as water, thou shalt not excel."—
GENESIS xlix. 4.

OUR text was one of the predictive declarations of the dying Jacob. It related to his first-born Reuben, who on account of an early flagrant transgression was disrobed of the dignity and privileges of the first-born ; but we select the text as containing a great truth, or maxim, equally true whether we consider it in reference to mere mind, or to morals in general. Instability is the great impediment to pre-eminent excellence. The unstable scholar shall not excel in learning ; the unstable tradesman shall not generally excel in worldly prosperity ; the unstable philosopher shall not generally excel in intellectual attainments ; decision, constancy, perseverance, are essential to success. It is just so in religion.

I. LET US SEEK OUT A FEW SIMPLE ILLUSTRATIONS OF THE TEXT.

II. ACCOUNT FOR ITS EXISTENCE.

III. PRESCRIBE A REMEDY.

I. LET US SEEK OUT A FEW ILLUSTRATIONS OF THE TEXT.

1. *We often see this instability in inquirers after religion, and they do not excel in the formation of their moral character.* How many hear the word of God from principle, and often with pleasure, and are not rejecters of the truth ? The word commends itself to their minds, they hear and they feel it ; it produces conviction, emotion, and they resolve to yield themselves to God. How often these feelings are combined with prayer, with deep anxieties, and mental conflict ; but they defer, they allow the internal disquietude to be allayed, they enter on the scenes of domestic duty or business, and then, alas, their averments and resolves all pass away. This is often repeated, week after week, year after year, and the heart still is unchanged and the character not formed. Never far from the banquet, but they do not enter ; always under the sound of the gospel, but they do not obey it. " Unstable as water," &c.

2. *We often see this in professed Christians in reference to a variety of particulars.*

(1.) In reference to knowledge. Instability in scripture reading. There is one hallowed fountain of knowledge, the holy scriptures ; it is our duty, our privilege, to be familiar and mighty here, but the reading of many is distinguished by inequality and instability, and therefore they remain children in understanding ; babes in wisdom ; when they ought to be approaching perfection, they are only acquainted with the first elements of divine truth.

(2.) Christians often do not excel in self-government, through instability in moral discipline. The evil of our nature is only partially removed in regeneration ; then the old man is crucified, but lingering he requires the continual application of mortifying means. The divine direction is, " Work out your own salvation, for it is God," &c. " Mortify your members," &c. " Crucify the flesh," &c. We are to bring ourselves under restraint, &c. Bit and bridle to the tongue, &c. Yet how often is our moral feebleness displayed ; almost as churlish, or morose, or passionate, or frivolous, as when we set out in religion. How is it ? Our discipline has been unstable. By fits and starts ; the rein has now been held tight, and then thrown loose over the necks of our passions, and thus unstable, we could not excel.

(3.) Christians often do not excel in fruitfulness through instability in the means of grace. Our conflicts and trials weaken us. The world is barren ; earthly scenes make us spiritually lean and frigid ; God has appointed the means of grace for our refreshment ; these are the green pastures, the banqueting house, &c. " They that wait upon the Lord," &c. Instability in regard to these necessary and gracious appointments, always causes sterility and barrenness. God is dishonored, and his rich goodness undervalued.

(4.) Christians often do not excel in usefulness through instability in the exercise or cultivation of their talents. An active, persevering employment of our talents is essential to usefulness ; we cannot do much good without this ; we must seek a sphere of labor suited to our talents and time, &c. Enter on it heartily, and perseveringly follow it ; thus we cannot fail to do some good, our power to do good will increase ; additional talents will be given to him that hath. How many act like the man with one talent !

(5.) Christians often do not excel in the enjoyments of religion through instability in the exercise of devotion. A devotional spirit brings immediately into close fellowship with God; this is especially connected with God's favor and loving-kindness; then he will cause his face to shine, &c. Thus we shall be lifted above the petty difficulties of this world. "Our path resemble the morning light, shining brighter," &c. Deserted, or neglected closets, formal prayers, &c., eat out the enjoyment of piety to the core; thus unstable as water, &c. In reference to instability,

II. LET US ACCOUNT FOR ITS EXISTENCE.

1. *It is sometimes constitutional.* This is often the peculiar failing, the besetting sin, the most vulnerable part. Vacillation is often owing to the temperament, and the peculiar development of the individual; it is not however thus beyond remedy, but it will need greater determination, skill, and labor, to master it.

2. *It is often the result of inconsideration.* We do not duly ponder, fully examine, and then lay down those rules which under God's blessing would preserve us from it. A greater regard to a contemplative habit of mind, &c.

3. *Often occasioned by unwatchfulness.* We are too little on our watch-tower. Thus open to the wiles of the adversary, &c. For this evil, let us,

III. PRESCRIBE A REMEDY. In one word, this is the grace of God; by the grace of God we can do all things, and, of course, overcome this evil. Grace will enlighten, restrain, govern, sanctify, make fruitful, useful, happy, &c.

1. *But its need must be felt.* Not labor in our own power, &c. Be conscious of our weakness, &c. Desire it, &c.

2. *But this grace must be sought.* We must ask for it, for this end, fervently, &c.

3. *This grace must influence us.* Not resisted, not neglected &c. But we must co-operate.

APPLICATION.

May our subject,

1. Lead us all to strict examination. Most, I fear, are chargeable in some way, or to some extent, with instability.

2. May we resolve this morning to give ourselves to God with purpose of heart, and to cleave to the Lord with all our souls.

3. To excel should be the desire of all the children of God.

SUPERSTITION.

"I perceive in all things ye are too superstitious."—ACTS xvii. 22

THE truth of the apostle's charge, in reference to the Athenians, is at hand, for to propitiate imaginary deities, they had filled their city with innumerable altars; idolatry had attained a kind of perfection in the city of Athens. Wealth, and genius, and authority, had all been presented at her shrine. In addition to the gods known and famed in their mythology, they had erected one altar to the unknown God. This had particularly struck the mind of the great apostle, and this he made the subject of his discourse. "Whom, therefore, ye ignorantly worship," &c. Superstition is defined, unnecessary fear, and is generally associated with reverence for imaginary beings. Let us glance,

I. AT THE ORIGIN AND CAUSES OF SUPERSTITION. The first superstitious act on record is presented to us in the holy scriptures, in the case of our first parents immediately after the fall, Gen. iii. 7, 8. Here guilt was the cause, ignorance or blindness was the result, and superstitious means of safety the scheme they adopted. How foolish and futile to cover themselves from the eye of omniscience, or to flee from an omnipresent God! We present this as the general basis of all superstition, ignorance of the word and works of Deity. As men are in darkness, and are strangers to these, they will be superstitious; as they emerge into the light of revelation and true knowledge of the works of God, they are freed from this baneful and distressing curse. Notice

II. THE UNIVERSALITY OF SUPERSTITION.

1. *It has darkened by its dreary mists all countries and ages.* The ancient Jews, though favored with the light of a partial revelation, were not free from its idolatrous apostacies. Egypt may be termed its nursery; here it was cherished in ten thousand forms. At one period, they had 30,000 imaginary deities. Their two leading gods were Osiris and Isis,—thought to be the sun and moon. They also worshipped the ox, the dog, the wolf, the hawk, the crocodile, and the cat; they likewise adored trees, plants, and roots; the country was full of temples and priests; they taught the doctrine of the transmigration of souls, &c., and their lives were one round of ab

surd usages, rites, and customs. The ancient Carthaginians worshipped a variety of deities, especially Celestis, likewise called Urania, or the moon ; and Saturn, known in scripture by the name Moloch. It was this monster idol, in whose burning arms the children were sacrificed, while their dying agonies and shrieks were drowned by the noise of drums and trumpets. Two hundred children were at one time sacrificed to this sanguinary deity. The Persians worshipped the sun, and paid divine honors to fire ; but all ages and all countries, whether civilized or savage, have had their absurdities and superstitious customs. Neither war nor peace—ignorance nor learning—philosophy nor art—poetry nor music, could remove the baneful curse of superstition from the world.

2. *In the modern history of the world, superstition has held the empire of mind in its debasing and cruel grasp.* Let us look at this in three or four aspects. In reference,

(1.) To witchcraft. James the First wrote a learned work on witchcraft, and our English parliaments legislated for the punishment of this crime with death. Witchfinders were appointed in every district. A variety of ignorant and wicked modes of testifying the accused were adopted. Three thousand were put to death during the long parliament ; in various parts of Germany not fewer than a hundred thousand—in England altogether not fewer than thirty thousand in two hundred years. Sir M. Hale, that upright and pious judge, condemned two to be burned in 1664, and two were executed in Northumberland so late as 1722.

(2.) To soothsaying and astrology. That is, the belief that the destiny of persons is influenced by the planets under which they are born. Gross superstition ! The Romans, Chaldeans, Assyrians, Egyptians, Greeks, Arabs, and the Brahmins of India, have all been devoted to this supposed art. In Europe astrology has been patronised by crowned heads, and by whole bodies of the learned. Dr. Dee, the author of the prophecies of the destruction of the metropolis, was a distinguished man in the time of Queen Elizabeth, and richly patronised by her majesty. In our own times we see the influence of this in our astrological almanacks, and the eager avidity with which every predictive pamphlet is bought and read. Allied to this, and built on it, is the whole mischievous fabric of fortune-telling, and yet thousands of otherwise intelligent persons give this their countenance, even in our own enlightened day and times.

(3.) The superstitious application of the unknown laws of nature. Eclipses of the sun or moon were viewed with horror, and there are recorded instances of learned persons, who, on such occasions, have fainted with fear ; comets were judged to be omens of wars, earthquakes, famine, or pestilence. The northern light at one time filled beholders with alarm, and their imaginations often fancied they beheld horsemen, and chariots, and armies. The flitting lights on waste and damp lands were considered presages of peril ; so also a variety of easily accounted for events ; the ticking noise of a little insect, by many is called the death-watch ; the screech owls screaming at the window—the dog howling in the night—the curling of the melting tallow in the candle—the falling of salt, &c. ; so also the whole round of lucky or unfortunate days.

(4.) The superstitious rites associated with religion. It is the belief of some, even of the Protestant community, that at the baptism of a child the devil is cast out. Is it much better to imagine that the application of a little water to the face changes its nature, regenerates it, &c., as now taught by many in the church of England? Look also at the consecration of burial grounds—the tolling of church bells at the death of parishioners who desire it : in one word, look at every rite, and custom, and ceremony mixed up with religious worship, which is not clearly taught in the Bible, and no other term can be appropriately given to them than that of superstition.

III. The evils of superstition. These are manifold.

1. *It prostrates and degrades the exalted powers of the mind.* Mental slavery, night and darkness of the soul.

2. *It never leads to holiness.* Indeed superstition steps forth to take the place of genuine piety, and dispenses with repentance and obedience, &c., and gives shadows, and thus it cheats and deceives the mind.

3. *It is destructive to real peace and enjoyment.* Superstition has nothing bright or radiant to cheer. No, its temple is darkness—its spirit cruelty—its influence is terrifying.

4. *It keeps men from the one true way of*

salvation. One of Satan's chief instruments. Conscience, &c., demands religious interposition for its relief; Satan therefore gives it vanity, and lies, and superstition.

IV. THE REMEDY. We present it in one word—" knowledge."

1. *Knowledge of the divine works.* The light of natural philosophy, and the discoveries of science, have done much to lessen the superstition of our country; no one now faints at an eclipse, or dies of fright at the appearance of a comet. But,

2. *A knowledge of God's word. Here is pure truth.* All, every word simple truth—appropriate truth; it is sent for our deliverance. Oh, abide by it; seek its enlightening influences; let it dwell in you; obey it; believe, and worship, and live according to this book. One great truth. The Son of God was manifested that he might destroy the works of the devil; of these superstition is one. It will teach you what to fear, and how to exemplify it. God, death, judgment, wrath to come. Let me urge this upon you. To you is the word of this salvation sent. God now commands all men everywhere to repent, &c.

THE CHARACTER AND BLESSEDNESS OF THE GODLY.

" Blessed is the man that walketh not in the counsel of the ungodly, nor standeth in the way of sinners, nor sitteth in the seat of the scornful. But his delight is in the law of the Lord; and, in his law doth he meditate day and night. And he shall be like a tree planted by the rivers of water, that bringeth forth his fruit in his season; his leaf also shall not wither; and whatsoever he doeth shall prosper."—PSALM i. 1–3.

THIS delightful portion of the Old Testament, denominated the Psalms, contains an inexpressibly rich mine of precious treasure. And these treasures are of the most diversified character. It contains a portion of almost every variety the Bible presents to our view. It is descriptive and preceptive. It contains odes and sacred songs. It has both its praises and its prayers. It directs to duty, and exhibits the goodness and mercy of God in the promises he has given to them that love him. It exhibits the terrors of divine wrath to the wicked, and opens to the child of God a bright and glorious passage to eternal glory. This delightful book opens upon us with the language of blessing, and to this we now direct your prayerful attention. In this description of the godly man, notice,

I. THE EVILS WHICH HE AVOIDS. Here three terms and three representations are placed before us.

1. *He walketh not in the counsel of the ungodly.* Now by the ungodly, we are to understand those who are more especially negatively wicked. That is, who may be free from notorious vices, but who are not the recipients of the grace and Spirit of God. Now there may be great external decency, and yet the heart in an ungodly state. The child of God does not walk in the counsel of these. He is not governed by their suggestions. Does not unite in their associations. He cannot do this, for two must be agreed, if they walk together.

2. *He standeth not in the way of sinners.* Now life is often represented as a course or way. Every act is a step in this way. —Now the way of the sinner is evil, a way of transgression. It is a broad way,—a way that declineth,—a way of darkness, and which terminates in the gulf beneath. Now the godly man does not stand in this way. His course is the narrow up-hill track, a way of light and comfort, and which leads to Zion's hill.

3. *He sitteth not in the seat of the scorner.* This is a most flagrantly wicked and presumptuous condition of mind. It is one expressive of deep depravity, reckless madness, and desperation. The scorner laughs at piety, treats religion with contempt, and ridicules the people of God. This is the most awful state of wickedness, and is generally the prelude to the just judgments of God. Now observe the degrees which the text presents to us, and their connection with each other.

(1.) Men listen to the counsel of the ungodly, and walk in their fellowship.

(2.) They go on until they can take up their position in the way of the practically evil.

(3.) Then they become hardened and infatuated, until they can mock at sin, and treat with scorn the condition of the pious.

II. THE COURSE WHICH HE PURSUES. And here we have,

1. *His delights.* That which is the highest source of enjoyment to him. And this is the sure index to the character, " He delights in the law of the Lord," in the holy scriptures; which contain the

revealed will of God to man. The word of God is precious to all his people. Job said, " I have esteemed the words of his mouth," &c., Job xxiii. 12. David said, " The words of thy mouth are better to me than thousands of gold and silver." See Psalm cxix., which is full of the thoughts of the Psalmist on this subject.

2. *His practice.* He meditates in it day and night. Now to meditate, is to consider its meaning ; to weigh it ; to revolve it over in the mind. Now this is necessary to rightly understanding it, and benefiting by it. This is his constant practice. Day and night, morning and evening, when engaged in the affairs of the day, or perhaps when retired to his bed, his heart would silently dwell on the wonders of the divine law.

III. THE HAPPINESS HE ENJOYS. He is described as " blessed ;" that is, he is made happy in the favor of God. Now this blessedness is described in several respects.

1. *In its spiritual fruitfulness.* " Like a tree," &c. " He shall neither be barren," &c. " He shall be strong and flourishing, in the courts," &c. He shall have his fruit in " season." Grace and strength according to his state, &c., of affliction—prosperity, &c.

2. *In the constancy of his profession.* " His leaf shall not wither," &c. He shall hold on his way,—stand fast in the faith of the gospel,—hold fast his profession, —not go back.

3. *Divine success shall attend all his engagements.* That is, all his spiritual engagements shall be blessed ; and all his temporal affairs shall be connected with the benign influence of the providence of God. " All things shall work together for good," &c. See this beautifully illustrated, Psalm xxxvii. 3–6, and xxiii. and xxiv. 37. Such is the happiness of the godly man.

APPLICATION.

1. *See the connection between holiness and devoted attention to the divine word.* Verse 1, you see what evils he avoids ; and verse 2, you see how this is done. Christ thus prayed, " Sanctify them by thy truth," &c.

2. *See the connection between daily meditation in the law of God, and spiritual prosperity.*

3. *Learn one great cause of spiritual weakness and barrenness.* Neglect of the law of the Lord. How often do you read it ? How frequently meditate ? &c. entreat you to find time for this. Be Bible Christians. How rich the revelation we possess compared with David's portion ! We have the prophecies, gospels, the Acts of the apostles, epistles, &c.

THE CHRISTIAN'S ORIGINAL STATE.

" Wherefore remember . . . . that at that time ye were without Christ."—EPHESIANS ii. 11, 12.

THE apostle is calling the attention of the Ephesians to the consideration of their former condition previous to their salvation by Jesus Christ. He refers to several particulars—Gentiles, aliens, strangers, hopeless, and without God in the world. He introduces this list of their miseries by the language of the text. At that time " without Christ." Our text refers to the believer's original condition, and calls his remembrance to it.

I. THE BELIEVER'S ORIGINAL CONDITION. " Without Christ." This description applies to all mankind, however diversified their natural state in other respects.

1. *Without the saving knowledge of Christ.* Do not know him in his dignity—graciousness—merits—value, &c.

2. *Without an experimental interest in Christ.* Not stones built upon him ; not members of his body ; not branches of Christ the living vine ; not living by faith in him, and by him.

3. *Without love to Christ.* Not prizing him as the pearl of great price ; not esteeming him " the fairest among ten thousand," &c. ; not acquainted with Peter's feelings, " Lord, thou knowest," &c.

4. *Without regard to his authority.* Not recognising his lordship ; not owning his authority, sceptre, laws, &c. ; living as if there were no Christ, &c. Now let me remind you that such a state is one,

(1.) Of extreme evil. It is a sin against the infinite love of God ; against the unceasing mercy of the Redeemer. Base ingratitude, &c.

(2.) Of great misery. Slaves, diseased, wretched.

(3.) Of imminent peril. Out of Christ ; no hope ; heirs of wrath and hell. Exposed to eternal death. The text calls the believer,

II. To REMEMBER HIS ORIGINAL STATE.

1. *To remember it, and be humble before the Lord.* No room for spiritual pride. O think of the rock, and the hole of the pit, &c.

2. *To remember it, and celebrate it with thanksgiving.* The Christian should rejoice in Christ always, and in every thing give thanks.

3. *Remember it, and compassionate those who are still in that miserable condition.*

4. *Remember it, and consecrate ourselves to the service of the Lord.*

THE DIFFICULTIES OF SALVATION.

" And if the righteous scarcely be saved, where shall the ungodly and the sinner appear ?"—1 PETER iv. 18.

THE scriptures often present truth to us by way of contrast. This is a powerful way of impressing the mind. Truth and error, holiness and iniquity, heaven and hell, are often thûs placed before us. In this way characters, and their necessary destinies, are often drawn in the inspired records of revelation. " Say ye to the righteous it shall be well," &c. " The wicked shall be driven away," &c. " These shall go away into everlasting punishment, but the righteous," &c. Such is the spirit of the text. " If the righteous scarcely," &c.

I. NOTICE THE CHARACTER. " The righteous." Now those who are represented in the New Testament as being evangelically righteous, are such,

1. *As are justified by the grace of God.* Not now guilty transgressors, but forgiven and considered righteous, and treated as such through faith in Christ. Until thus justified we are guilty, unrighteous, condemned before God. " For Christ is the end of the law for righteousness to every one that believeth," Rom. x. 4. " Wherefore the law was our schoolmaster to bring us unto Christ, that we might be justified by faith," Gal. iii. 24. Such,

2. *As are renewed in righteousness by the Spirit of God.* This is effected in regeneration, when God takes away the stony heart, &c. ; when we are born of the incorruptible seed of the word of God, born of the Spirit ; when all old things pass away, &c. ; when, as the workmanship of God, we are created anew unto good works. Such,

3. *As are righteous by conformity of heart and life to the law of God.* When sanctification is begun, and carried on in the soul, and where the life yields the fruit of righteousness to the glory of God ; when we know, and love, and do the will of our Father who is in heaven. Now this is the character. Notice,

II. THE IMPORTANT TRUTH IMPLIED. " That the righteous scarcely are saved." Not saved without difficulty. Before we enter upon this, observe,

1. *There is a cheering truth expressed.* That the righteous *are* saved. Now they are delivered from the reigning power, and from the guilt and condemnation of sin, and they have a title to eternal salvation ; their names are written in heaven ; they are children and heirs of God and eternal life ; they have the earnest of glory in the grace dawning within them ; they have the first fruits, &c.

2. *There is amplitude of provision, and sufficiency of means for their salvation.* The grace of God is abundant ; the love of Christ passeth knowledge ; the influences of the Spirit possess almighty energy ; and as to means, there is the light of revelation, ordinances, promises, a throne of grace, intercession of Christ, &c. Yet mark, the salvation of the righteous is,

3. *Connected with great difficulty.*

(1.) The reception of salvation is so. The kingdom is likened to a pearl, and all must be sold to possess it. To a feast, and all must be forsaken to come to it. The gate is strait ; the kingdom of heaven suffereth violence, &c.

(2.) To retain present, and obtain eternal salvation is difficult. Look at the enemies of the Christian, the spirits of darkness, Satan and his host, the darts and the wiles of the devil ; look at the situation of the Christian, in a world hostile to God ; in arms against heaven ; the seat of Satan ; to the Christian it is a field of warfare, and how many are slain ! a restless sea, and how many are wrecked ! enchanted ground, and how many are bewitched with its fascinations ; a race-course, and he must agonize to the goal of death. Look at the Christian's weakness, how infirm, how imperfect, what little strength ! Need you wonder then that he is saved with difficulty ?

Not one Christian that ever entered heaven had an overplus of grace; not one, too much holiness.

III. THE SOLEMN QUESTION PRESENTED. " Where shall the wicked and ungodly appear ?" I need not stay to define who are signified by the wicked ; and the ungodly means all who are strangers to the saving grace of God, who have not the Spirit of God, the image of God, who do not love and obey God. Now if the *pardoned* and *regenerated* are scarcely saved, where shall the *guilty* and *depraved* appear ? if those who *fear* and obey God are, &c., where shall the *impious* and *profane* appear ? if those who *deny* themselves are, &c., where shall the *profligate ?* &c. ; if those who make religion their *business* are scarcely saved, where shall the *neglecters* and *despisers* appear ? if those who *believe* and *pray* are scarcely saved, where shall the *unbelieving* and *prayerless* appear ? Finally, if those who *do good*, and labor to follow Christ are scarcely saved, where shall the *servants* of the *devil*, who do evil, appear ? I leave these observations to your solemn and deliberate consideration ; let reason reply, let conscience reply, let scripture reply. They will appear at the left hand of God. The end of the wicked and ungodly must be despair and eternal wo ; none can escape who neglect this great salvation.

APPLICATION.

1. *Let the subject deeply impress you with the momentous meaning of the term* SAVED. Delivered from the wrath and misery of hell, and lifted up to heaven and eternal glory.

2. *Let the subject command all your energies and powers.* You cannot do too much, or sacrifice too much, in order to your salvation. See what men do for earthly glory, and for the riches of this world.

3. *Let the sinner and the ungodly now yield themselves to God.* There is mercy with God, &c. He invites, he promises. " Let the wicked forsake his way and the unrighteous man his thoughts, and let him return unto the Lord, and he will have mercy upon him," &c.

THE SAINT'S PROSPERITY THE DELIGHT OF JEHOVAH.

" Let the Lord be magnified, which hath pleasure in the prosperity of his servant."—PSALM xxxv. 27.

OUR text contains several words which may properly form topics for our present meditation.

I. THE CHARACTER TO WHOM THE TEXT REFERS. " His servant." Angels are the servants of the Lord. Jesus, the Mediator, became the servant of the Lord. All saints are such. " Being made free from sin, ye became the servants of God," &c. Jehovah, and the prince of darkness, divide the world. Only two classes ; servants of sin, and of holiness. God's servants,

1. *Know his will.* Have ascertained wherein his pleasure consists.

2. *Wait upon him.* Appear before him to inquire—to ascertain his pleasure, &c. Their eyes are directed to the Lord.

3. *Obey his word.* His word is law ; they have respect to all his commandments ; delight in the law of the Lord.

4. *Depend upon him.* He gives them sustenance. He feeds, clothes, protects, rewards, &c.

II. THE PROSPERITY SPOKEN OF. This is not worldly prosperity ; that is often the bane and ruin of the individual. But it is,

1. *Advancement in divine life.* Growing in conformity to God ; rising higher in spiritual attainments, &c. ; from the child to the man, &c.

2. *Vigor of the divine graces.* Faith strong—hope bright—love increasing—humility deepening, &c.

3. *Increase of divine peace.* " Peace flows as a river," &c.

4. *Usefulness in the divine cause.* Honoring God ; establishing his kingdom, &c.

5. *Satisfaction with the divine portion.* Real enjoyment. " Godliness with contentment," &c. " Happy art thou," &c.

6. *Expectation of the divine glory.* " Looking for that blessed hope," &c. ; waiting for the appearing of the Lamb.

III. THE DECLARATION MADE. " The Lord taketh pleasure," &c. He delighteth in the prosperity of his servants.

1. *He takes pleasure in making provision for it.* Our prosperity is of the Lord. All fruitfulness from him, &c. Now he has made ample provision.

2. *He takes pleasure in imparting the blessings.* He waits to supply ; he expostulates. " Hitherto ye have asked nothing," &c.

3. *He takes pleasure in observing their prosperity.* This is his delight, to see the

results of grace ; the fruits of the Spirit ; his own likeness, &c.

APPLICATION.

1. Let his servants magnify and bless his name.
2. Be faithful and persevering.
3. Who will become servants to God ?

THE WAY AND MANNER OF ACCESS TO GOD.

"In whom we have boldness and access with confidence by the faith of him."—EPHESIANS iii. 12.

By the fall man has become darkened, and his heart alienated and estranged from God. Sin keeps man separated from God, and exposes him to his severe displeasure. In redemption we are brought near to God. By the death of Jesus we have a new and living way opened into the holiest of all ; now God can descend to the sinner, and the sinner ascend to God. Jesus is the ladder, or the way of access, between man and God—between heaven and earth. Now, this is the subject of the text. Notice,

I. OUR ACCESS TO GOD. It is only applicable to the believer. "Without faith," &c. We have especial access to God in three exercises :—

1. *Prayer.* Prayer is speaking to God, telling God our need, making known our requests, seeking his favor, &c.

2. *Praise.* Is celebrating the divine goodness ; thanking God for his mercy and grace ; speaking to him, and extolling his name ; the overflowing of the grateful soul in the divine presence.

3. *Meditation.* This is the soul's silent intercourse with God ; the mind contemplating, reflecting, and thinking upon God. Now, these may be separate or united exercises of the soul ; they may be public, domestic, or private. Our access to God should be frequent, so as to recognise God always, and in all things. Notice,

II. THE MEDIUM OF OUR ACCESS TO GOD. "In whom," &c. That is, in Christ, see verse 11. Now, Christ is the medium and depositary of all spiritual blessings.

1. *God only holds intercourse with men through Christ.* "I am the way," &c. "One God, and one Mediator," &c. Of old, God would only be approached through the medium of sacrifices. "Without shed-

ding of blood," &c. All these typified the Lord Jesus, the true and perfect sacrifice for the guilt of the world. There is but one way to the holiest of all—whether we come there to praise, or pray, or meditate—and that is the way consecrated for us by the blood of Christ.

2. *Sinners must be in Christ, to have comfortable access to God, and be accepted of him.* "In whom." We must be personally accepted in the Beloved before our services can please God. God does not demand any spiritual services from men until they are spiritually in Christ. The first great demand of God is, that we believe in the name of the Son of God. This brings us into a vital union with Christ. "There is no condemnation," &c. And then we are privileged to have access to God, by our union to his Son.

3. *Faith in Christ's person and work must distinguish each act of access to God.* The life of a Christian is a life of faith. Faith is not to be an occasional act of the soul, but the soul's constant exercise. When we approach God we should ever feel our personal *unworthiness*, and this should lead us to exercise faith in the *dignity* of Christ's person. We should feel our constant *guilt*, and this should lead us to trust in Christ's *death*. We should feel our *unfitness* to come before God, and this should lead us to depend on Christ's intercession at the right hand of God. Thus faith must always be exercised in our access to God.

III. THE SPIRIT IN WHICH GOD DESIRES US TO APPROACH HIM. With "boldness." This is enjoined, "Let us, therefore, come boldly," &c., see Heb. x. 19. Now, this is not to be irreverent, unhallowed boldness—not self-righteous, self-complacent boldness—not presumptuous boldness ; but it must be with the boldness of confidence—with holy freedom and liberty of speech—with the boldness of expectation that our suit will be heard and received. Now, this boldness of the believer in his access to God may be grounded,

1. *On the nature of the Deity.* The Being we approach is not a despot—not a malevolent Being ; his nature and his name is love. He is only terrible to incorrigible sinners. "He is the Lord merciful," &c. We may have boldness,

2. *From his divine relationship to us.* He is our Father—our spiritual Father. "As a Father," &c. "If we being evil." &c.

The child fears not—doubts not; so, when we go to God, let us remember it is our privilege to address him as " Our Father," &c.

3. *From the delight he expresses in his people having access to him.* God is displeased if we have not frequent access. He invites us to live to him, and in him—the fellowship cannot be too close. He invites us to draw near—He allures, &c. The great end of all blessings is to draw us closer to God.

4. *From the presence of Christ in the holiest on our behalf.* Jesus is the officiating High Priest ; his incense is ever ascending ; all power is in Christ's hands ; the Father always heareth him, &c. " We have an advocate with the Father."

5. *From the remembrance of past instances of success.* Never did the Lord falsify his word, forget his promise, or turn away the seeking seed of Jacob empty. He has been better to us not only than our fears, but has done for us better than we ever asked or thought.

APPLICATION.

1. *Urge the ungodly to immediate reconciliation.*

2. *Let the believer exult in his privilege of access to God.*

3. *Let holy, fervent boldness and confidence characterize our approaches to him.*

CONSTANT REJOICING.

" Rejoice in the Lord alway : and again I say, Rejoice."—PHIL. iv. 4.

IT has ever been one of the most common and powerful objections to Christianity, that it is opposed to the present happiness and enjoyment of mankind. Now this has been of immense injury to the Christian cause, especially in preventing young and lively persons giving it their attentive consideration. Dr. Watts had respect to this objection in those admirable lines—

" The sorrows of the mind
   Be banish'd from this place ;
  Religion never was design'd
   To make our pleasures less."

Now, this objection is truly fallacious. It originates in two misapprehensions.

(1.) As to the nature of rea joy. The silly mirth of the tavern or of the inebriated party, is mere noise, mere chaff ; such joy reason itself cannot commend.

(2.) As to the gloom of the religious ; now that is not always gloom which appears so. There may be seriousness of countenance, and a solemn state of mind, yet no gloom. Who can think of God, of death, and of eternity, and not be serious ? The gloom of the pious, when real, does not arise from religion, but often from a deficiency of it, and the sufferings arising therefrom, &c. See that parent, he appears gloomy, he feels for his children. That woman, her countenance is sad, her husband is a mocker. No ! true religion enforces and produces real, solid, abiding joy. The Christian has many causes of rejoicing ; works of nature—of providence —of redemption ; his own state, privileges, &c. ; but there is one pre-eminent, the text supplies it, " Rejoice," &c. Notice,

I. THE OBJECT OF THE CHRISTIAN'S REJOICING. " Rejoice in the Lord." All Christian duties and privileges have respect to the Lord Jesus Christ. He is to be preached ; we are to believe in him ; to be baptized into him ; found in him ; here in the text, to rejoice in him. " Rejoice,"

1. *In the perfection and glory of his person.* Our Redeemer is the Lord of Hosts ; the mighty God of Jacob. Immanuel, God with us. " Unto us a child," &c. He is the Lord of angels ; object of eternal worship and praise ; the king of glory ; the fairest among ten thousand, &c.

2. *In the completeness of his work.* He has wrought out a perfect righteousness— he has overcome our foes—he has redeemed us to God—he has finished his saving arrangements.

3. *In the offices he fulfils.—He is our prophet.* A teacher from God. The great apostle and prophet of whom Moses, &c. Of the last and most perfect dispensation. *Our priest,* he has offered an acceptable sacrifice unto God. Ever intercedes, &c. *Our king.* Oh think of his goodness, graciousness, potency, glory. " Grace is poured into his lips," &c.

4. *In the tenderness of his sympathies.* " He is touched," &c. He does not break the bruised reed, &c. " As the head," &c. ; never forgets, nor neglects, &c.

5. *In his inexhaustible fulness.* The believer entirely depends upon him. Out of his fulness, &c. ; if it failed, what would

become of his church? We read of the unsearchable riches of his grace.

6. *In the immutable perpetuity of his regards.* "Having loved his own," &c. Whatever, or whoever fails, he will not. Our own condition will alter, but not his grace, &c. "The same yesterday," &c. This is the rock of triumph to the godly.

II. THE CONSTANCY OF THE CHRISTIAN'S REJOICING. "Alway: and again I say," &c. We doubt not that we should rejoice in prosperity, when we are happy, &c.; but this is not alway. We are to rejoice,

(1.) Under persecution. See Matthew v. 11, 12. *Acts 5:40 & 41*

(2.) In temptations. See James i. 2, 4.

(3.) In keen afflictions and fiery trials. 1 Peter iv. 12. Hence some were tortured, &c. Not accepting deliverance. "Alway." "For all things work together," &c. Let us notice,

III. SOME OF THE REASONS FOR THE CHRISTIAN'S CONSTANT REJOICING.

1. *It is a duty which we owe to God.* Not left to our own will, &c. He says, "Rejoice," &c. "Rejoice evermore." He says, "Arise, shine," &c.; besides, his Spirit produces this, "The fruit of the Spirit is joy," &c., Gal. v. 22.

2. *It is an exercise most profitable to ourselves.* Hear what the wise man says, "A merry heart maketh a cheerful countenance; a merry heart doeth good like a medicine." "And the joy of the Lord is our strength."

3. *It will do honor to our profession and recommend religion.* It is said of some that "every one had the countenance of a king;" of the disciples, "they took knowledge," &c. Moses bore the radiance of the divine beauty on his countenance. Spiritual rejoicing will recommend religion to those who are without. Seeing this, they will say, "We will go with you," &c.

4. *It will be preparatory to the enjoyments of heaven.* Heaven is the region of felicity. "In thy presence is fulness," &c.

> "The hill of Zion yields
> A thousand sacred sweets," &c.

APPLICATION.

1. *Learn the superiority of the joys of religion to all other joys.* Divine—spiritual—real.

2. *Invite the inquirer after bliss, to Jesus.* Are you weary? Are you thirsty? Are you saying, "Who will show us any good?"

3. *How joyless the state of the condemned sinner!*

THE TEMPTATION OF PETER.

SKETCH I.

"And the Lord said, Simon, Simon, behold, Satan hath desired to have you, that he may sift you as wheat; but I have prayed for thee, that thy faith fail not; and when thou art converted, strengthen thy brethren."—LUKE xxii. 31, 32.

IT is said that "whatsoever things were written aforetime were for our learning, that we through patience and comfort of the scriptures, might have hope." Our text is one of those portions of the divine word, replete with useful instruction, and is well adapted to promote our spiritual security and well-being. Among the disciples of Christ, Peter occupies a very prominent and distinguished place. He was a bold, ardent, and devoted follower of the Saviour. He was one of the most distinguished of the apostles, and had the honor of opening the kingdom of Christ, both to the Jews and the Gentiles. By the characteristics of his mind he was exposed however to danger. Hence by his very spirit and temperament, he was in danger of impetuosity and rashness; an evidence of this immediately follows the text. "And he said unto him, Lord, I am ready," &c. His want of humble fear and his lamentable fall are beacons to us, and address us in the language of the apostle, "Let him that thinketh he standeth, take heed lest he fall." Observe in the text. A dangerous enemy referred to; the design of that enemy specified; the gracious intercession of Christ affirmed; and a subsequent duty enforced.

I. A DANGEROUS ENEMY REFERRED TO. That enemy is "Satan," who is justly described as our adversary, accuser, murderer, destroyer, &c. The character of Satan is fearfully exhibited in the history of our world. He was the tempter, who by the serpent seduced our first parents; he was the instigator of Cain to slay his brother Abel; he has been exerting his spiritual power to ruin and destroy human beings from that period to this. We see his hatred of the holy and the happy in the case of Job, chap. i. ver. 6, 7; see Zech.

iii. 1, &c. We have also recorded his vile and impious attack on the Messiah, the Son of God, Matt. iv. 1, &c. Against this enemy we are incessantly warned. " Your adversary, the devil, goeth about," &c. " Resist the devil," &c. " Above all, take the shield of faith, by which ye may quench,' &c. Now this enemy,

1. *Is insidious in his attacks.* He is a spirit, and therefore, without notice, can have access—be in our dwellings—near our persons—inflaming our spirits, &c. Hence his subtlety is often the subject of scripture remark.

2. *Malevolent in his designs.* To blight, curse, destroy; to becloud the understanding, pervert the judgment, inflame the passions with evil, and pollute the conscience. He hates purity and happiness, and therefore labors to efface them.

3. *Persevering in his attacks.* It would appear, that for thousands of years, he has been pursuing his cruel avocation, and he is still going about, &c. He assails the young convert—harasses the aged Christian—and often only ceases his temptations on the dismissal of the soul to the regions of light.

4. *Fearfully successful in his efforts.* He keeps the mass of mankind in his hellish thraldom. God of this world—prince of the power of the air, &c. His temptations keep myriads from godly decision, and unnumbered hosts of the followers of Christ have apostatized through his hellish devices. Such is the enemy presented to us in the text. We have,

II. THE DESIGNS OF THIS ENEMY SPECIFIED. " Desired to have you," that is, desired to have the people of God under his power—directly exposed to his fiery darts —in his cruel grasp—that he may sift, &c.—exercise them with the most trying and harassing temptations. If possible, that they may utterly fail, and faint under the process, and thus be regained to the standard of sin and death. In tempting and sifting the people of God, he endeavors often to suggest,

1. *That they have no interest in the divine mercy.* That their faith and hope are counterfeit; that their joys are merely animal excitement; that theirs is false security; that they are yet in the gall of bitterness, &c. Thus he labors, that they may cast off their confidence in which they have great recompense of reward. He suggests,

2. *The hardness of God in his providence towards them.* He refers to the prosperity of the wicked; how they flourish as the green bay-tree, &c. No sorrow, no bands in their death, &c. Asaph was severely sifted on this subject, Psalm lxxiii. 1–17. He urges,

3. *That God has withdrawn his consolations.* That our deadness, formality, hypocrisy, &c., have provoked the Lord, and therefore that he has abandoned us. Often the pious thus sifted, have cried, " Hath the Lord forgotten to be gracious," &c. " Is his mercy clean gone," &c. Or he excites,

4. *To indifference on the ground of divine mercy.* That the Lord will not be rigid with his people. That the divine partiality will overlook their infirmities. That they may sin, because grace doth abound; and perhaps he exhibits the failings of Abraham, of Moses, of David, of Peter, &c., and says, it is presumption to expect to be more holy than these. Let me just refer to certain circumstances, under which we give Satan great advantage in his temptations, and which are presented in that part of the history of Peter to which our text refers.

(1.) Great self-confidence, trusting to our experience—courage—wisdom, &c. &c.

(2.) Unwatchfulness. Being at ease. Spiritually indolent. Not on our guard.

(3.) Unnecessary admixture with the world. Sinful society. Worldly, trifling intercourse—Satan's ground. All these in Peter's case. I conclude by reminding you,

1. *That Satan desires to have you.* Each and all.

2. *That you are not ignorant of his devices.*

3. *To put on the whole armor of God.*

THE TEMPTATION OF PETER.

SKETCH II.

" And the Lord said, Simon, Simon, behold Satan hath desired to have you that he might sift you as wheat; but I have prayed for thee, that thy faith fail not; and when thou art converted, strengthen thy brethren."—LUKE xxii. 31, 32.

THE admonition of Christ to Peter, we should have supposed would have effectually preserved him from the perils to which he was exposed—an admonition so plain, so earnest, so emphatic—but alas! the sequel of his history proves the contrary. With the warning fresh in his mind—with the courageous avowal yet hanging on his lips, the Saviour's hour of arrest arrives. He is seized by the violent band, and, at first, Peter magnanimously draws his sword, &c., forgetting that moral and not physical courage was demanded on the occasion. Christ is hurried away to the Jewish tribunal, and now Peter's defalcation commences, but Peter followed afar off; he then rashly ventures into the society of Christ's enemies, and afterwards falls into the snare Satan had laid for him, denying with oaths and curses that he knew the Messiah! Alas! how frail is man! How brittle his resolutions! How evanescent his goodness! "Like the morning cloud," &c. Let us now consider,

III. THE GRACIOUS INTERCESSION OF CHRIST. "But I have prayed for thee," &c. Here Christ stands before us in his character as the great High Priest of our profession. To pray for his people,

1. *Was necessarily connected with his office.* He has left us a rich instance in his prayer for the disciples, &c. John xvii. Doubtless he often prayed for his disciples when he spent whole nights in solitude, and secret devotion. And now "exalted to the right hand of the Majesty on high, he ever lives to make intercession," &c. In this exercise Christ delighted, and therefore his prayer would be earnest, tender, and faithful. His prayer,

2. *Was that Peter might not apostatize from the faith.* Peter evidently had faith in Christ—was a true and real believer, and Christ desired that he might not utterly cast off his trust and adherence to him. But how does this agree with the result? Peter's faith was suspended—ceased to exercise its sustaining influence—did not repel the dart of the enemy, nor preserve him from sin. But Peter did not entirely and fully apostatize. He did not yield himself up to evil; desert C'rist's standard, and go over to the enemies cause. Sudden as was his sin, equally so was his contrition. Deep as was his guilt, still deeper his sorrow. Though cast down he was not destroyed; hence there is an immense difference between one gross sin, and entire apostacy. The best of men have been overcome by the former, without yielding to the latter. Observe,

3. *Christ's prayer was successful.* He obtained for Peter grace that held him even

when over the gulf; that rescued him from the lion's mouth, from the very grasp of the destroyer. Peter became penitent, believing, and was restored to God's favor and mercy. He was reconverted. Lifted out of the mire and clay, &c. "Restore unto me the joys," &c. "If any man sin," &c. Notice,

IV. THE SUBSEQUENT DUTY ENFORCED. "When thou art converted, strengthen thy brethren." Now let us ask,

1. *How he was to do this?*

(1.) By the exhibition of his own example. He would be a living trophy of the efficacy of the grace of God—its power to raise and restore. His own spirit would be inspired by the experience he had previously known; his love and gratitude would correspond in some degree with the mercies he had enjoyed. Thus his humility, his gratitude, and his zeal would have a favorable influence on his brethren.

(2.) By his instructions and counsels. He who had felt the severe, trying power of the enemy—who had reaped the grief and anguish of his own sin in departing from God—who had been arrested by the gracious look of the Saviour, surely would be best fitted to enlighten, admonish, and counsel others. Such would be most earnest in warning others.

(3.) By directing them to the only source of restoration. His fall and misery had brought him to know the power of Christ in saving, healing, and comforting. How he could speak of this! how enlarge and expatiate on it! how urge it! and in this way he could strengthen his brethren. He could do it,

(4.) By personal exertion on behalf of the fallen. If our sins and falls do not make us compassionate and pitiful, and solicitous for our fellow-erring Christians, it is strange indeed. Who that had fallen like Peter, could be harsh, and censorious, and indifferent to the brethren who had been overcome by temptation. "Brethren, if a man be overtaken in a fault," &c. "They that are strong should bear the infirmities of the weak," &c.

(5.) By fervent prayer to the Father of mercies on their behalf; as Christ did for Peter, Christians are to do for each other. See James v. 16; 1 John v. 15, 16, &c. We inquire,

2. *Why he was to do it?*

(1.) Gratitude to the Saviour. This is

the best expression of it, to "strengthen the brethren." To exhibit his mind to them. Feel and pray, &c., as he did.

(2.) Love to the brethren. Feeling for them, knowing the misery of a fallen state, grief and distress of sinning against Christ.

(3.) Zeal for the cause of Christ. Would we have Satan to triumph—the church to be injured—the wicked to conquer? Surely not. It is lamentable when they fall, but worse when they remain in the pollution of their sin. Restored, they often are most valiant for Christ, &c. So Peter.

APPLICATION.

1. *Learn the mutability of the best of saints.* All frail, weak, &c.

2. *Learn the solace and security of the righteous.* The love and intercession of Christ.

3. *The necessity of repentance and reconversion.* Tears—confession—supplication —change of conduct, &c.

4. *How the church should treat the fallen.*

PRESERVATION FROM THE DESTROYER.

" By the word of thy lips I have kept me from the paths of the destroyer."—Psalm xvii. 4.

MAN'S present state is one of probation. Here he is on trial for eternity ; here his principles will be tested by circumstances, and by the temptations of the evil one. But for his salvation and preservation God has made ample, available provision. Of their own ability no one could avoid and escape the influence of Satan's temptations. This terrific enemy by his subtlety, his untiring perseverance, would involve in ruin the most devoted, &c. Now the Psalmist tells how he kept himself, &c. " By the word of thy lips," &c. Let us make some observations,

I. ON THE DESTROYER.
II. HIS PATHS.
III. OUR MEANS OF PRESERVATION.

I. ON THE DESTROYER. The destroyer is Satan. His name is peculiarly appropriate. A murderer from the beginning. He destroyed himself, and his compeers in the first sin. He destroyed our first parents, and brought death, &c. His work is to destroy. He is a most successful destroy-er ; myriads, &c., of all ages, and countries, and classes.

1. *He destroys man's moral dignity.* Debases—brings from his lofty original state. Casts down—dims the fine gold. Transforms the sovereign into a slave ; heir of glory, into an outcast. Removes the halo of glory, and covers with shame and ignominy.

2. *He has destroyed our portion.* Our original Eden with its plenitude of blessedness. Beggared our race ; involved in treason ; then proscription, and confiscation, and poverty followed. Portion of health, also gave sickness and pain, &c.

3. *He destroys the body.* Introduced death, made a sepulchre of the world. Smote that beautiful temple of God ; caused it to decay and fall, and moulder in the dust. Go to the beds of the dying, &c. Go to the grave-yard, &c.

4. *He destroys the soul.* Makes it morally wretched here. Appals it with guilt ; exposes it to wrath ; deludes, poisons it ; entices it into the black pathway of wo ; and finally triumphs in its everlasting condemnation and misery. Draws it down to the everlasting abodes prepared for himself and his angels.

II. HIS PATHS. Only one way, broad, dark, downhill, delusive, &c., way of sin. But in this way are many paths.

1. *There is the path of skepticism.* Rejection of truth—of divine revelation—of God's existence—of providence—of the divine claims, &c.

2. *The path of the scorner.* Who sneer and treat with ridicule serious and eternal things. Fools who mock at sin.

3. *The path of the pleasure-taker.* Lovers of pleasure more than God ; who run into excess and riot, &c. Those who are found in the scenes of mirth, in the ball-room, &c.

4. *The path of the worldly.* Who love the present evil world ; who seek its treasures only ; live on it and in it. Children of this world, creatures of time and the present.

5. *The path of the trifler.* Who understands and feels, &c., but still treats God and the soul as inferior objects. Who is not duly affected, not decided, &c., wile away means, opportunities, and life itself.

6. *The path of the self-righteous.* Who turn from the gospel and the cross of Christ, and lean to their own righteousness, &c. Trust in themselves, like the Pharisees of

old, &c. All these, with many others, are the paths of the destroyer.

III. OUR MEANS OF PRESERVATION. " By the word of thy lips," &c. The word of God is the grand instrument of our safety, &c. Let us see this established from other portions of the scriptures, Psalm cxix. 9 and 11 ; Psalm xxxvii. 31. I observe,

1. *The word of God is the means of our deliverance from these paths.* God's word proclaims liberty, &c. " Ye shall know the truth," &c. Christ's words deliver from the power of Satan, &c. The preaching of the gospel is the power of God, &c. The destroyer cannot resist the almighty word, &c.

2. *It also guides those whom it delivers.* " Thou shalt guide me," &c. It reveals the way of life, shines upon it, &c. Makes our duty plain, exposes the snares, &c. Preserves from Satan's devices.

3. *It preserves those also whom it guides.* " Kept by the power of God," &c. Commend you to God and the word of his grace. It sanctifies, &c. ; thus Christ employed it as the sword, defensive and offensive, " Thus it is written," John xvii. 14, 19. Now in addition to the instrument of safety, there is its use, its application ; " by the word ;" by its perusal ; by meditating on it ; by applying it in faith ; by it being prayerfully employed.

APPLICATION.

1. *Let us not forget our peril.* Watch, &c. Be vigilant, &c.

2. *Remember our remedy.* Be familiar with it, &c.

3. *Urge all to escape, &c.* The way is open, you are invited, warned, entreated, &c.

SAINTS THE TEMPLE OF GOD.

" For ye are the temple of the living God."—2 CORINTHIANS vi 16.

THE term temple is one which peculiarly designates the habitation of the Godhead. Hence the heaven of heavens is in glorious reality the most holy place, and is the proper, essential temple of the universe. But the word, as you are aware, was applied to that magnificent structure erected by Solomon, and which is so often referred to in the Old Testament scriptures. To the first there was added the second temple,

to which the prophet Haggai referred, " The glory of the latter house," &c. To this temple Christ went up in his youth— and this he purified by the expulsion of the buyers and sellers—and the destruction of this he clearly foretold. The word temple may, by a spiritual application of the term, be applied to the whole New Testament church ; but our text applies it to individual Christians, and so it is used in several parallel passages ; 1 Cor. iii. 16, and vi. 19 ; Eph. ii. 21 ; and 1 Pet. ii. 5. Now, let us on this occasion,

I. CONSIDER THE RESPLENDENT SIMILITUDE.

II. THE PRIVILEGES INVOLVED IN IT. And,

III. THE DUTIES ARISING FROM IT.

I. CONSIDER THE RESPLENDENT SIMILITUDE. Now, when we say the Christian is the temple of God, we observe the appropriateness,

1. *In its construction.* It was of divine devisal ; its form, its plans, &c., were all of God. He was the architect and artificer ; the emanation of his own good, wise, and holy mind. Now, the salvation of the soul, involving its restoration from sin, and misery, and death, was entirely of God ; his own infinite skill devised the whole scheme. It was the bright emanation of his holy and compassionate mind, not the production of human knowledge and power, &c.

2. *In its erection.* The materials,

(1.) Originally unfit, distant. So in reference to human beings—carnal, defiled, far off. These materials were,

(2.) Prepared and rendered suitable ; so the soul enlightened, purified, and converted, &c. ; brought nigh.

(3.) In this a suitable instrumentality was appointed ; not miracles, but means. God could have done it by either ; so he employs his servants, his word, his ordinances ; men of rare gifts and powers. &c.

3. *In its dedication.* When finished, the temple was dedicated, publicly, devotionally, entirely. Just so the Christian. To this we are repeatedly called. " I beseech you, brethren, by the mercies of God," &c. This is called putting on the Lord Jesus ; confessing Christ before men ; making a good profession. Now, this must be done publicly before men ; devoutly ; with

fervent prayer ; entirely ; consecrating our whole selves, &c. The similitude is seen,

4. *In its moral magnificence.* The grandeur of the temple filled with wonder and amazement ; overawed, when completed, &c. Now, there is a moral magnificence in the Christian character. How changed. What a transformation ; were we to say from a brute to an angel, it would not do justice to it. A rebel, now a friend ; an alien, now a child ; a curse, now a blessing ; the palace of demons, now the dwelling of God ; truth in the place of error ; knowledge instead of darkness ; wisdom in the place of folly ; purity instead of defilement ; righteousness instead of sin ; heaven instead of hell. Now, let us consider,

II. THE PRIVILEGES INVOLVED.

1. *The divine recognition.* He owned the temple—called it his—put his name on it ; thus it was hallowed and glorious Now, so does God treat his servants ; he calls them his own—gives them his name. " My sons and my daughters," &c. ; my people ; my jewels.

2. *Divine residence.* God dwelt in the temple ; his glory filled it. He was there addressed in prayer and praise ; he was consulted, worshipped, &c. Now, all this is the privilege of the saint. " Dwell in you," &c. " We will come unto you," &c. We may commune, speak his praise, seek his mind, &c.

3. *Divine benediction.* God's blessing was eminently in it, and on it, and for it. Prophecies and promises. " My heart and mine eyes," &c. " Whereby are given to us great and precious promises," &c. God's blessing is upon his people. Now consider,

III. THE DUTIES ARISING FROM IT. Now, the following, selected from many, must suffice :—

1. *Purity.* The temple was to be holy ; not for profane use—not for carnal purposes. Now, God cannot delight in us except as we are pure. The conscience, affections, &c., must be holy to the Lord. Now, we must seek after this, labor for it, &c.

2. *Constant service.* The fire was not to go out ; the worship was to be incessant ; the offerings regular. Now, he requires this from us. " Pray without ceasing ; rejoice evermore," &c. Our offerings, too, must be constant ; the offering of a

broken spirit, &c. ; our liberality to his cause, &c.

3. *Reverential awe and hallowed tranquillity.* The worship was to be with fear and reverence. God is greatly to be feared, &c. Fear before him, all his saints, &c. ; peace, &c., is indispensable ; God is not the author of confusion ; we must put away all wrath, &c. ; the spirit of the dove and the lamb.

4. *Reflection of God's glory.* The Jew went up and beheld the symbol of Deity ; he shone forth there. Now, we are thus to be reflections of God's likeness ; the world should see God in us. " Take knowledge of us that we have been with Jesus," &c. " Epistles read and known," &c. " Show forth his praise," &c. Now, these are the duties.

APPLICATION.

1. *What reason for humiliation and shame!* Are there not idols in this temple —impurities—disorder ? &c. Let us bow down before the Lord ; seek a fresh consecration, &c.

2. *Subject full of God's condescension.* " Will God dwell ?" &c. " To that man will I look," &c.

3. *The soul of the sinner is Satan's seat.*

4. *Who will now become the temples of the Lord ?*

DAVID'S REGRETS AND CONSOLATIONS.

" Although my house be not so with God, yet he hath made with me an everlasting covenant, ordered in all things, and sure," &c.—2 SAMUEL xxiii. 5.

THE whole history of David is fraught with instruction. It was a most astonishing series of sunshine and cloud, of darkness and light, of prosperity and adversity, of sorrow and joy ; but in the great providence of God he had now reached the margin of life. He had crossed the desert, and the goodly land was before him ; he had weathered the storm, and the haven was in view ; he had fought the good fight, and the crown glittered in prospect ; he was uttering now his last words—his dying sayings, and they were worthy of the illustrious prophet, the royal monarch, and the highly-favored servant of the Lord. Let us consider the regrets, the experience, and the happiness of David, as expressed in our text.

I. OBSERVE HIS REGRETS. "Although my house," &c. The expressions of the text are elliptical : something is implied more than we read. He evidently meant that his house was not so,

1. *As it ought to be.* The family should resemble the celestial abodes of the blessed ; full of God's light—the residence of the divine favor—the scene of divine obedience —the circle of divine love ; in one word, what Joshua resolved, " As for me and my house, we will serve the Lord." But in David's family there were jealousies, envyings, bickerings, disobedience to parents, rebellion, and almost every foul thing that could reflect the perdition beneath.

2. *It was not as David had desired it to be.* He had, doubtless, longed for the highest well-being of his family. His example had reflected the earnest piety of his own soul ; his influence, his prayers, &c., doubtless had been incessantly offered ; but instead of spiritual fertility, there was barrenness ; instead of order, confusion ; instead of holiness, sin.

3. *Yet it was as many of the families of the righteous have unhappily been.* Who can reflect on this without grief ? The first family had within it Cain, a fratricide ; Noah's family had within it Ham, the father of the Canaanites ; Abraham's family had a mocking Ishmael ; Isaac's, a profane Esau, &c. Then look at the sons of Aaron and Eli, and so of many others of the servants of God ; but still the grief and regret was not the less. To how many does it apply here ? How few the exceptions—how exceedingly rare ! Can we account for it ? We would refer,

(1.) To the truth that piety is not hereditary. The Jews erred in this, " We are the children of Abraham," &c. No ! religion ever was, and ever will be, personal.

(2.) It often arises from the glaring imperfections and weaknesses of pious parents. Children often reason that religious persons should be faultless ; they expect perfection, and the contrast is so striking. Our religion is so scanty, so feeble, light so glimmering, example so irregular, that children stumble, are prejudiced against religion, and perhaps rush into the world. We are not sure that one glaring inconsistency will not do more to harden them, than a year's propriety of conduct to do them

good. Let this admonish every parent present who professes religion. There may be many things in your families to pity, but perhaps much more to blame. But observe,

II. DAVID'S PERSONAL EXPERIENCE. " Yet God hath made with me an everlasting," &c. He, doubtless, referred to the covenant of redeeming mercy, with which he was experimentally acquainted. Now this covenant, or agreement, is the great act of God in offering mercy to mankind, through the person and work of Christ, who is the Mediator of the new covenant. Now, this covenant is the subject of revelation, especially of New Testament revelation. To this covenant David had given his believing assent. He had applied it with all its blessings to his own soul, so that it became experimentally his. God allows all who believe to have the same interest in it, and happiness from it, that David had. Now, of this covenant he affirms,

1. *That it is everlasting.* Not only everlasting with regard to time, but in God's own mind and purpose before all time. This redeeming thought was part of his gracious design from all eternity. So is it everlasting in its duration. It was parallel with all time, and extends to all eternity ; it is a covenant never to be annulled ; it elevates its participants to everlasting dignity and joy ; its grand promise is eternal life.

2. *It is ordered in all things.* As such, its mediation, its promises, its dispensations, its conditions, are all arranged and settled ; nothing confused, &c. ; like all God's works, reflecting his own order and harmony. The whole plan reflects God's infallible wisdom, and is certain to accomplish what he designed ; for, observe,

3. *It is secure.* Men may violate covenants—God cannot ; they may fail for want of ability, &c. Adverse circumstances may thwart ; but this is sure—on a rock. It has been assailed, forsaken, &c. ; but it is still sure. Hell and devils are in league, &c. ; but it is sure,

(1.) To glorify its Author.

(2.) Reward the Mediator.

(3.) Save all believers.

(4.) And overthrow all its foes. Now, though David's house was not so, &c., yet from this experience observe,

III. THE HAPPINESS HE ENJOYED. This happiness arose,

1. *From the salvation he realized.* **In the**

covenant was " all his salvation." Salvation from past guilt and wrath, from pollution, from condemnation ; salvation into God's favor and kingdom ; salvation even in death ; salvation, including the opening grave and eternal glory. So is all our salvation in this covenant ; and so also from this all true and genuine happiness flows. No substitute for this ; this is the one thing.

2. *From the satisfaction he expressed.* " All my desire." It was the pre-eminent thing, the absorbing, &c. ; that which made up for every deficiency ; that reconciled to every lot ; that which was the end of life itself. Other things might be subordinately desired and valued ; but this chiefly, this always, &c. " The Lord is the portion of my soul," &c. Nothing but an interest in God's covenant can or ought to be all our desire. " Whom have I in heaven but thee ?" &c.

APPLICATION.

1. *Learn to expect relative and domestic disappointments.* Here are our sweetest joys, or our keenest sorrows. Every home is not a sanctuary from toil, and trouble, and guilt ; our houses are infected with the plague of sin.

2. *The responsibility of the parental office.* Tears and lamentations are worse, if possible, than hypocrisy, if we do not seek the salvation of our children. If you do not instruct, how can you mourn their ignorance ? If you do not impress, and influence, and pray ? &c. Do think of these things, &c. We shall all be constrained to do so before we leave our families. Let that hour often be anticipated ; it will benefit us, &c.

3. *Think and feel for the children of the irreligious.* This one end of sabbath school tuition, to care for the children of the poor.

4. *Are you interested in this covenant ?*

5. *Death-bed hopes must rest on this covenant alone.* Not on creeds, works, usefulness, &c.

THE LAW OF LIBERTY.

" But whoso looketh into the perfect law of liberty, and continueth therein, he being not a forgetful hearer, but a doer of the work, this man shall be blessed in his deed."—JAMES i. 25.

OUR text, and the preceding verse, refer to the manner of hearing the divine word—

and this is, indeed, a subject of great importance. It is important to take heed what we hear, and also how we hear, and likewise as to the results of our hearing. Some only hear with the external ear; they know what words we speak, but do not labor to comprehend the sense and signification. Others hear for the time, and try to understand ; but when the benediction is pronounced they conceive all is over, and pay no further attention. Others hear, and retain a general knowledge and remembrance, but do not apply it to their own hearts and consciences, nor practise what they hear; but the good hearer " looketh into the perfect law," &c. Our text contains,

I. A STRIKING REPRESENTATION OF THE DIVINE WORD.

II. A TRUE PORTRAITURE OF THE CHRISTIAN HEARER.

I. A STRIKING REPRESENTATION OF THE DIVINE WORD. A threefold description.

1. *A law.* Law of God ; the legislative enactments of King Messiah ; the revealed will of God ; the moral rule of action, given by one who had authority—Jehovah ; binding upon those to whom it is addressed ; promulged for their instruction and benefit; sanctioned by rewards and punishments Now this law,

2. *Is perfect.* As it is,

(1.) The law of a perfect Lawgiver.

(2.) A perfect rule of life. It ensures all that relates to the mind, lip, and life.

(3.) As it is perfectly equitable. Pure; free from all error ; no weakness or imperfection ; nothing overlooked, &c.

(4.) Perfect, as it relates to all states and circumstances in which men are placed. The monarch, the subject, the prince, and the beggar ; all civil and social relationships are embodied.

(5.) It is absolutely sufficient ; it needs no addition ; cannot be improved.

(6.) Because it is the standard of all perfection. All other laws are good or bad as they resemble this.

3. *It is a perfect law of liberty.* Now three ideas here :

(1.) As a law of truth and equity, it frees the mind from the bondage of ignorance and error. " Ye shall know the truth," &c.

(2.) As a law of love and mercy, it brings us into the liberty of God's forgiving grace.

(3.) As a law of holiness, it frees the soul from the dominion of sin. "The law of the Lord," &c., see Psalm xix. 7. Our subject gives us,

II. A TRUE PORTRAITURE OF THE CHRISTIAN HEARER.

1. *He gives intense regard to the divine word.* Looketh, as the cherubim did, into the ark which contained the divine law. He does not give it casual or superficial attention, but intense and earnest; see this set forth, 1 Peter i. 10, &c. This is his spiritual habit, his Christian course. "He looketh" into it.

2. *He extensively retains what he hears.* "Not a forgetful hearer." The memory of persons differs exceedingly; liable to infirmities and decay. Not necessary to retain the words, but the sense and meaning. How many are forgetful hearers! Is it not because they are not sufficiently interested? because they do not labor to remember? because they are not judicious in reference to hearing? Three simple rules:

(1.) Prepare for hearing by prayer, &c.
(2.) Be wakeful and intent in hearing.
(3.) Be deliberate and silent after hearing; avoid unnecessary talking for at least a few minutes, that it may sink into the mind.

3. *He exemplifies the word in his life and conduct.* "A doer of the work." Conforms to the law; obeys what is spoken; endeavors to live the truths of the divine word; walks in the good way, &c.; and in this he perseveres, for he "continueth therein." He follows on to hear, and learn, and to know, and do the will of God. The Christian hearer,

4. *Is a blessed, or happy character.* "Blessed in his deed." In this course he enjoys God's favor and blessing; the end of hearing is answered; his soul delights in the word; it is the joy of his heart; he is truly blessed; this has a good influence on him in the various eventful scenes of life.

APPLICATION.

1. Let us try ourselves by the text.
2. What reason for improvement.

THE CHRISTIAN'S REGARD FOR AN UNSEEN SAVIOUR.

"Whom having not seen, ye love; in whom, though now ye see him not, yet believing, ye rejoice with joy unspeakable and full of glory."— 1 PETER i. 8.

THERE is, in real religion, a mutual reciprocated feeling between God and his people. Religion is said to consist in knowing God, and God is said to know his people. To be known of God is to be approved and accepted of him. Religion is represented as essentially including love and delight in God; and God has stated, in the most affectionate forms of expression, his love and delight in his people. The Christian dwells in God, and God dwells by his Holy Spirit in the hearts of his children. The Christian honors God, and whoso honoreth God, doth he also honor. Our text refers to three of the leading features of genuine spiritual piety.

I. FAITH IN AN UNSEEN SAVIOUR.
II. LOVE TO AN UNSEEN SAVIOUR.
III. JOY IN AN UNSEEN SAVIOUR.

I. FAITH IN AN UNSEEN SAVIOUR. Faith is contradistinguished from sight. Thomas believed only upon palpable evidence, when to doubt were impossible. The apostles and first disciples saw Christ; he tabernacled among them; they beheld and heard, &c.; yet, as regarded his divinity, his true Messiahship, they had to believe as his life and miracles testified of him. The saints, before his advent, had to believe on the ground of promises, prophecies, and types. These pointed to Christ, and giving full credit to these, they saw the day of Christ, and rejoiced and were glad. The followers of Jesus now have the record of the gospel, the testimony of the various evangelists and apostles; he is no longer in our world, living a life of spotlessness, teaching and performing miracles of grace and mercy. Faith believes the record which God hath given of his Son, receives it as a truth worthy of all acceptation, exclaims with Peter, "I believe that thou art Christ;" with the woman of Samaria, "This is indeed the Christ;" with the centurion, "Surely this is the Son of God;" with Thomas, "My Lord and my God." Believing is realizing Christ in all his offices, work, and grace; accepting him as God's gift, looking to him as the Lamb, building on him as the foundation, fleeing to him as the refuge, trusting in him as the only hope, &c. Now believing on such evidence, is what we do every day in other matters. In books of voyages, &c., in works on history, &c., in ancient biography, &c., lives of Alfred the Great, Socrates, Alexander, &c. Now on the record of the New Testament writers we thus believe in the Lord Jesus Christ. The next principle recognised is,

II. LOVE TO AN UNSEEN SAVIOUR. "Whom having not seen ye love." Now love to this unseen Saviour is grounded on a belief,

1. *Of his character as revealed in the divine word.* In him is every thing lovely and excellent; purity, truth, meekness, goodness, patience, grace. Desire of all nations; fairest among ten thousand, &c. This love is grounded,

2. *On a belief of what he has done for us.* Pitied us, &c. He hath redeemed us, &c., given himself for us, lived, sorrowed, died for us. Oh, who can have such claims as Christ?

" Were the whole realm of nature mine," &c.

3. *On a belief of the relationship and offices he sustains towards us.* He is our elder brother by choice, &c. He is our unfailing friend; he proved himself a friend in need, &c. He is our surety, took our place; our advocate, he ever liveth, &c. "We have an advocate with the Father." He is our life, the life of our souls, &c.

4. *We love him on the ground of faith in what he has engaged to do for his people.* What has he done already? Who can recite it? What is he doing? Oh, draw aside the veil, and look into the holiest of all, &c. But we now ask, what has he engaged to do? to keep, to guard, to sanctify, to support in death, to crown with glory, to confess us, &c., to give eternal life, &c. Believing all this, surely we may exclaim, "Whom having not seen we love." But,

III. WE REJOICE IN AN UNSEEN SAVIOUR Faith works by love, and both are productive of joy.

1. *We rejoice.* This is the spiritual habit of the soul, to joy in God, to rejoice in Christ Jesus. It is said the disciples were glad when they saw the Lord. To find Christ and know him is matter of great joy. The woman and silver penny, &c. The disciples going to Emmaus. Now this is joy peculiarly spiritual; joy of heart, really felt and experienced. It brightens the countenance, nerves the soul, fills the mouth with holy praise.

2. *This joy is beyond expression.* Can-

not be told; words not to be found; speech too poor; requires another language, a seraph's tongue, &c.

3. *This joy is full of glory.* Joy from God's glorious mind, the joy of God; joy of the glorious gospel, joy full of the impress of Christ's glory, joy anticipating endless glory, a ray from the noontide light, a draught from the celestial fountain, a bunch of Canaan's grapes; the earnest, the first-fruits of that glory which shall be revealed, &c.; not full of anxiety, distress, or fear, but full of glory.

APPLICATION.

1. *Do you believe in Christ?* Have you received Christ, ventured all upon him? &c.

2. *Do you love Christ?* Do your thoughts, lives, &c., attest it?

3. *Do you rejoice?*

EARNESTNESS IN RELIGION INDIS-PENSABLE.

" And from the days of John the Baptist until now, the kingdom of heaven suffereth violence, and the violent take it by force."—MATT. xi. 12.

THE Saviour had just passed a high eulogium on John the Baptist, but had also stated that the least in the kingdom of heaven, &c. John was greater than any of the prophets in the dispensation in which he lived, and the office which he discharged; but he only heralded the Lord's anointed. He saw the dawn of the day, but the least of the Saviour's disciples was greater, more ennobled and favored by being in the kingdom, enjoying Christ, and sharing in the blessings of his reign. The Saviour then refers to the excitement which had been produced by the preaching of the Baptist. From his day the kingdom of heaven suffered violence. He went forth and called men to repentance, great multitudes heard and obeyed, and were baptized; and this eagerness still continued, for while the Jewish priests, and scribes, and Pharisees rejected the Saviour, the people, especially publicans, and harlots, and outcasts, pressed into the kingdom of God. The kingdom of heaven, or the New Testament dispensation, is still upon the earth, it reveals the same privileges, and offers the same blessings now to us, &c.; and it must be accepted in the same way. Let us then consider,

I. THE NATURE OF THE VIOLENCE WHICH MUST BE EMPLOYED.

II. THE MOTIVES WHICH SHOULD IMPEL US TO EXERCISE IT.

I. THE NATURE OF THE VIOLENCE WHICH MUST BE EMPLOYED. By violence, we understand moral energy and fire. The idea is that of a person pressing through a crowd, or an army storming a citadel. Now the violence necessary to securing the blessings of salvation includes,

1. *A violence of resolution in opposition to vacillating inconstancy.* Many resolve and re-resolve, and yet do not advance. Their resolves are like the morning cloud and early dew. They say, they will go into the vineyard, but do not. Now this procrastination is the ruin of thousands. To attain the blessings of the gospel, there must be determinate violence; a vehement decision; a making up of the mind. Set your heart and soul, &c.

2. *This violence includes thorough self-denial, in opposition to ease, and self-indulgence.* Nature loves ease, apathy, self-indulgence. Christ demands mortification, self-denial, and cross-bearing. No man would enter the list of wrestlers with folded arms; no one compete for the wreath, and give way to luxury and enjoyment. We are to strive to enter in; literally, agonize. Self must be chased out of all its retreats and fastnesses. The old man must be crucified if Christ is to benefit us.

3. *This violence includes the effort of the whole soul in opposition to a divided heart.* God will be found of us when we seek him with the whole heart. Often the understanding, judgment, and conscience, agree, but the affections and will are opposed; now thus success cannot be realized. A double-minded man, or a man of two minds, is unstable, &c. There must be resolution, self-denial, and concentrated effort. Every faculty and feeling must enter on the work, &c.

4. *There must be the violence of ardent prayer in opposition to listlessness of desire.* The desires suited to those who would enter the kingdom, are described by hungering and thirsting, panting, fainting, &c. "My soul followeth hard," &c. There must be importunity. Knock, seek, appeal, cry out, plead, persevere. Languor can do nothing, the throne must be stormed. "I will not let thee go." This importunity is urged by Christ in the parable of the importunate widow, &c. Exemplified in the Syrophenician woman; need I add, that this ardent prayer must fasten itself by faith on the divine word. Rely on the testimony God has given, &c. Hold by the horns of the altar, &c.

II. CONSIDER THE MOTIVES WHICH SHOULD IMPEL US TO EXERCISE THIS VIOLENCE.

1. *The resistance with which our spirits have to contend.* Our own hearts will resist—unbelief, reigning sin, indolence of spirit, &c., enmity to God. The world will resist us by ridicule perhaps, or by interposing its spirit, and maxims, and enjoyments; especially its honors, pleasures, &c. Satan will resist us. When the father brought his afflicted child, who was possessed, Satan threw him down, &c. He will not tamely resign his palace and throne; now it is only by violence that we can succeed in overcoming the resistance.

2. *From the pre-eminent value of the object to be attained.* "A kingdom." The Persian monarch promised Esther to the extent of half his kingdom, but this is a whole kingdom, and a heavenly one; kingdom of grace here, and kingdom of glory forever. In this kingdom there is dignity, and riches, and enjoyments. An inheritance, a crown, dominion, and pleasures for evermore, a kingdom of eternal glory, everlasting felicity; is it not worth striving for? See how men strive for a morsel of bread, few riches, few honors; and what are all these but toys and bubbles, &c.

3. *On account of the limited period of effort which is afforded.* There might be some show of reason for indifference and ease, if we had a thousand years, or even a century. But our probation is most absolutely short, and exceedingly uncertain. We cannot boast of the morrow, cannot tell what a day may bring forth, &c. The poet has very solemnly said,

> " Lo, on a narrow neck of land,
> 'Twixt two unbounded seas I stand,
>   Secure, insensible;
> A point of time, a moment's space,
> Removes me to that heavenly place,
>   Or shuts me up in hell."

To-day, then, how earnest and violent ought we to be!

4. *On account of the awful loss we shall*

sustain if we do not gain it. But two states of existence hereafter; kingdom of glory, and kingdom of darkness—heaven and hell—paradise and perdition; and there is no way of gaining the one and shunning the other, but that specified in the text. Oh, then, is it not all-important, &c. This is a reason high as heaven, deep as the abyss of wo, and long as eternity. "The kingdom of heaven," &c.

APPLICATION.

1. To those who possess it, and are of it. This termination must be carried out. Show the same diligence to the end, &c.

2. Who will enter the lists for the kingdom of heaven, and now? We invite and urge all.

3. The thoughtless and indifferent must perish.

THE WORK OF RELIGION PERFECTED BY GOD.

"The Lord will perfect that which concerneth me: thy mercy, O Lord, endureth for ever: forsake not the work of thine own hands."—PSALM cxxxviii. 8.

PIETY is not the exhibition of any separate virtue or grace, but the union and harmony of all the graces in their due proportions, and well-regulated influence on the character and life of the possessor. For instance, it is not mere magnanimity, but holy heroism, mingled with circumspection and godly fear; it is not merely resolute confidence, but implicit trust, associated with vigilance and solicitude; it is not faith alone, but faith which produces good works, fruit of righteousness; it does not so look up to God as to forget the use of means, and unites these with fervent prayer for the divine blessing. We are led to this train of thought from the spirit of the text. See the confidence of the Psalmist, "The Lord will," &c. But that confidence is followed with earnest supplication. "Forsake not," &c. But let us consider the general tenor of the text. And we notice,

I. TRUE RELIGION IS THAT WHICH CONCERNETH US. It is emphatically the one great and supreme concern and end of life; it is the one thing needful. Not a vain thing, for "it is our life." Whether we consider the nature of the soul, our responsible condition, the uncertainty of life, the probable nearness of death, the solemnities of judgment, and the awful realities of eternity—religion is that which especially concerneth us. If so, then,

1. *It ought to be our first concern.* "Seek ye first the kingdom of God." This is the basis of all happiness and security, ought to be laid first; first in life, first every day, first in preference to all other things.

2. *It ought to be our chief concern.* Not only first, but most prominent. Exercising our chief thoughts, meeting our chief desires, influencing our chief actions, &c. It must have the ascendency if it is to prosper. Religion, if at all secondary, will decline. As the heart is one of the chief vital organs of the body, so the affections surrendered to God, must be chiefly swayed by his Spirit and grace.

3. *It must be our personal concern.* Friends may do much for our religious comfort and welfare, but only when our own personal exertions are put forth; none can repent for us, pray instead of us, meditate for us, enjoy or serve God for us. Religion is essentially personal, and every one must give an account for himself to God.

4. *It must be our constant concern.* Religion is not to be impulsive, but habitual. The healthy exercise of the mind; the daily rising of the emotions to God. Persevering obedience to the divine laws. "Rejoice evermore, pray without ceasing," &c. Daily walking in the path of duty; growing in the divine likeness; warring the good warfare; faithful unto death; "always abounding in the work of the Lord," &c. Stability and perseverance essential to our salvation. We notice,

II. THAT TRUE RELIGION IS THE WORK OF GOD'S HANDS. Our concern, and God's work.

1. *God made all the arrangements necessary to our being religious.* Exercised his compassion—sent forth his Son to redeem us—given the Holy Spirit—commanded the heralds of truth— pened a way in his providence for our he ring the gospel, &c., &c.

2. *Religion in the soul is the direct production of divine influence.* Are we enlightened? "God who commanded the light out of darkness," &c. Are we converted? "He turned us from darkness," &c. Are we regenerated? "He hath begotten us again," &c. Are we justified?

We are "justified freely by his grace."
"His workmanship, created anew to good
works."

3. *Religion depends on the communications of his grace.* Jesus said, "Without
me ye can do nothing." "He that hath begun the good work will carry it on," &c.
He laid the foundation, and will bring on
the head stone. All our comfort and
strength, &c., are from God. But notice,

III. TRUE RELIGION IN THE BEST SAINTS
IS YET IMPERFECT. "The Lord will perfect that," &c. Supposing all the graces
of religion in the soul, they are only in a
progressive state ; none perfect. Who is
perfect in knowledge ? In faith ? In patience ? In obedience both as to matter and
manner ? In love ? In resemblance to
Jesus ? How true of each and all, "There
is yet very much land to be possessed," see
Philippians iii. 12, &c. We observe,

IV. FOR A CONSUMMATION OF RELIGION
EVERY TRUE CHRISTIAN IS SOLICITOUS. They
know and feel their imperfections ; they
mourn and grieve ; they long and desire.
Now this solicitude is accompanied with
consolation and hope ; and this consolation
and hope rest,

1. *On the divine engagements.* "The
Lord will perfect," &c. He has engaged
to do it. Given many promises. He will
never leave nor forsake his people. He will
be with them in the waters, and in the fire.
"In six troubles," &c. This consolation
and hope rest,

2. *On the unchanging mercy of God.*
"Thy mercy, O Lord, endureth," &c.
God's engagements are all founded on his
mercy, and not our worthiness. The mercy
of the Lord is from everlasting to everlasting, &c., &c. Now his tender mercies
are especially exercised towards his saints.
This consolation and hope rest,

3. *On the unfailing efficacy of prayer.*
Hence the prayer, "Forsake not the work,"
&c. "God will be inquired of." All the
saints of God have been sustained, &c.,
but none without prayer. Prayer is God's
ordinance, and he has ever honored it.
"The fervent effectual prayer of the
righteous availeth much." All the saints
of the Most High have been eminent for
prayer ; Abraham, Jacob, Moses, David,
the apostles, &c. All the glorified in
heaven can attest, that praying breath was
never spent in vain. Let our subject,

1. *Lead to individual examination.* Are

we concerned about true personal religion ?

2. *Let the subject cheer the servant of
God.* "He will perfect," &c. Then
throw away your fears. "His mercy endureth," &c. Then exercise hope and
confidence in him.

3. *Let the subject incite to devotional diligence.* The use of God's appointed means
in the spirit of humble, continuous prayer.

THE BELIEVER'S APPROACH TO GOD.

"Oh that I knew where I might find him ! that
I might come even to his seat : I would order my
cause before him, and fill my mouth with arguments."—JOB xxiii. 3, 4.

OBSERVE from these words,

I. THE PLACE OF APPROACH SPECIFIED.
"His seat."

II. THE MANNER OF APPLICATION ADOPTED. "I would order my cause," &c.

III. THE MODE OF PLEADING DETERMINED.
"I would fill my mouth," &c.

I. THE PLACE OF APPROACH SPECIFIED.
"That I might come even to his seat."
The seat or throne of Jehovah is in the
heaven of heavens, infinitely above the
seats of cherubim and seraphim. We
should ever have three views of the seat of
Jehovah.

1. *Its grandeur.* See Isaiah vi. 1–3.
"I saw also the Lord sitting upon a throne,
high and lifted up, and his train filled the
temple. Above it stood the seraphim ;
each one had six wings ; with twain he
covered his face, and with twain he covered
his feet, and with twain he did fly. And
one cried to another, and said, Holy, holy,
holy, is the Lord of hosts ; the whole earth
is full of his glory." See also Ezekiel i.
26–28. "And above the firmament that
was over their heads was the likeness of a
throne, as the appearance of a sapphire
stone ; and upon the likeness of the throne
was the likeness as the appearance of a
man above upon it. And I saw as the
color of amber, as the appearance of fire
round about within it, from the appearance
of his loins even upward, and from the appearance of his loins even downward, I
saw as it were the appearance of fire, and
it had brightness round about. As the appearance of the bow that is in the cloud in
the day of rain, so was the appearance of
the brightness round about. This was the

appearance of the likeness of the glory of the Lord. And when I saw it, I fell upon my face, and I heard a voice of one that spake."

2. *Its purity.* God dwells in the holiest of all ; the purity is such, that the heavens appear as if unclean before him. He sits upon the throne of his holiness. Justice and judgment are the habitation of his throne. The seraphim and cherubim continually cry, "Holy, holy, holy," &c. Now the grandeur of his seat might overwhelm us, and the purity of it fill us with terror as guilty sinners before him. Considering the throne or seat as such we might exclaim,

"Lord, what shall earth and ashes do ?
We would adore our Maker too ;
From sin and dust to thee we cry,
The Great, the Holy, and the High."

But there is another feature connected with the seat of Jehovah, and that is,

3. *Its graciousness.* "It is a throne of grace." Now here we come to God through Jesus Christ the propitiatory. Through the person and work of Christ, God can be just, and yet the justifier of the ungodly. This should never be forgotten in prayer. "There is one God," &c. "We have an advocate," &c. Now as a throne of grace the sinner may approach, the unworthy may draw near, obtain mercy, and find grace to help, &c. Observe,

II. THE MANNER OF APPROACH ADOPTED. "I would order my cause," &c. In presenting our cause before God, we must ever keep in view,

1. *Our utter unworthiness.* Job in one place confessed that he was vile. Should we not all feel thus. See the example of David, "Hear my prayer, O Lord, give ear to my supplications, in thy faithfulness answer me, and in thy righteousness, and enter not into judgment with thy servant ; for in thy sight shall no man living be justified." Psalm cxliii. 1, 2. We cannot be too conscious of our nothingness and sinfulness before God. In ordering our cause we must have respect,

2. *To the spirit of true sincerity.* "God is a spirit," &c. Lord, search me and try me, and "see if there be any way of wickedness in me, and lead me in the way everlasting," Psalm cxxxix. 24. Then in ordering our cause before God, there must be,

3. *Submission and obedience to his will.* We may express our darkness, helplessness, and misery ; we may call upon God to hear, and help, and deliver. but after all we must lie in his hand, wait his time, and be satisfied that what he doth shall be best. Notice,

III. THE MODE OF PLEADING DETERMINED. "I would fill my mouth with arguments." Now God leaves his people to plead before him. A fervent wrestling spirit, he will not, he cannot despise. Now there are many arguments which we may plead before God.

1. *There is the argument of his universal goodness.* He is good to all, and his tender mercies, &c. He blesses all his creatures. He clothes the grass, and feeds the ravens, causes his showers to fall upon the ground of the wicked, &c. If so, how much will he bless his own children, the objects of his love !

2. *There is the argument of his engagements and promises.* Now the engagements of God, relate to the *keeping* of his saints ; to their preservation. To *giving* them all needful good. That he will *hear* all their cries, *deliver* them from all their enemies, *supply* all their wants, and never, never *leave* or forsake them. Such are powerful arguments. "Hath the Lord spoken, and shall he not perform ? Hath he said it, and will he not bring it to pass ?"

3. *There is the argument of his past loving-kindness.* Shall we not plead what he has done ? He has been our *help* from our birth. He was our *benefactor* in youth, &c. What has he not done for us ? How richly, freely hath he blessed us ! Now we ought not to forget his past loving-kindness. We should plead it with gratitude, and infer, believing from it, his power and willingness to help us.

4. *There is the argument of his work within us.* Our desires for his presence and favor arise from the motions of his Spirit in our hearts. These longings are his own implanting. He has sent the Spirit of his Son into our hearts, and this Spirit excites our longings after him. " For we should know not what to pray," &c.

5. *There is the argument of the advocacy of his Son.* Christ has died and risen from the dead, yea, he hath ascended, and ever lives to make intercession for us. "We have an advocate," &c. "Him the Father heareth always."

APPLICATION.

1. *Let me urge all anxious seekers of Christ to go to the seat of God.* He waits to save. He is ready to pardon.

2. *Here is the Christian's true resource in time of trouble.* Imitate Job. Say, "O that I knew where I might find him!" Then go to his seat, "Cast your burden upon him," &c.

3. *How truly wretched is a prayerless state!*

CHRISTIAN UNITY URGED.

" Endeavoring to keep the unity of the Spirit, in the bond of peace."—EPHESIANS iv. 3.

SIN has not only made man hostile to God, but has set one man in battle array against another. Shortly after Adam sinned against God, did his first-born slay his brother; and from that period of his foul deed of hatred and blood to the present, strife, and war, and revenge, have thrown their deep shade over the history of our world. Sin in its chief essential element is discord. It divides, separates, confuses, and distresses. Now those who are converted are not perfectly freed from all the remains of the carnal mind, and therefore in them are roots of bitterness which distract the hearts of the pious, and produce division and disunion among the friends of Jesus. In apostolical times, we see an instance of this between the holy Paul and Barnabas, who were greatly imbued with the Holy Ghost. This existing spirit in the visible church has led to various schemes for the promotion of greater affection among Christians. Yet up to this day divisions and distractions of the church continue. The only sure balm for the healing of these rancorous wounds is found in the text, " Endeavoring to keep," &c. Our text refers to the true principle of unity, and to the right method of maintaining it. The text refers,

I. To THE TRUE PRINCIPLE OF UNITY. " Unity of spirit," not,

(1.) Denominational unity; where the members of a sect are allied by a certain name, creed, form of worship, &c. Which of the hundreds of sects, like Aaron's rod, shall swallow up all the rest? Not,

(2.) By an attempted uniformity. Before this can be effected, all minds must be uniform; all modes of education; all books, and reading, and study. Variety is the law of the universe, and is quite accordant with general unity. As the rays of light are formed of every color of the rainbow. As the various stars all present the splendor of the firmament. As the various gases combine in the atmosphere of life. As the various objects are all necessary to form the picturesque of the landscape. As the several features are essential to the beauty of the countenance. A tame and general uniformity in the church would be an anomaly in the universe. Not,

(3.) By extra liberal concessions. When persons are willing to forego any view of truth, &c., for the sake of visible harmony. Unity, even of the right kind, is too dearly paid for if purchased by the sacrifice of one grain of truth. No, the principle of the text is unity of spirit. And this spirit is the Spirit of the Lord Jesus Christ. " If any man have not the Spirit of Christ," &c. Now supposing all Christians to have this, then there must be unity of spirit. Color language, creed, mode of worship, will not, cannot prevent it. Now this unity of spirit involves,

1. *True spiritual affection.* Love one to another—love to all saints—love unfeigned —love that will produce sympathizing care, beneficence, tenderness, pity, and mutual prayer. Love in deed, and not merely in word.

2. *This spirit is essentially a spirit of humility.* Pride is the great cause of contention. Men never can be united, while they stand on the stilts of their own preconceived superior excellency. The man who says, " I am more righteous than thou," will always say to his brother, with the same breath, " Stand off!" But if we think of ourselves in the spirit of Christian humility, we shall be prostrated together in the dust; and thus before the footstool of God's mercy, the spirit of unity will be felt, and cherished.

3. *This spirit must ever be a spirit of kindly forbearance.* See verse 2. How often this is urged on our careful attention, Col. iii. 12, &c.; Rom. xiii. 1, &c. Thus only can the spirit of Christian unity be really promoted. But notice,

II. THE RIGHT METHOD OF MAINTAINING IT. Now this method is

1. *Personal.* We are to " keep the unity of the Spirit," &c. Every man for

himself. Not legislators to do it, or synods, or sects, but each Christian must keep his own spirit, and maintain that unity of feeling, that true catholicity of heart, which will abhor distraction and division. This method is associated with,

2. *Decided effort.* " Endeavoring." It will not come as a matter of course, but rather the opposite ; therefore we must endeavor ; strive for it ; labor for it ; read for it ; pray for it ; exhibit it whenever and wherever we can do so. This method is identified in the text,

3. *With a pacific compact.* " In the bond of peace." We are to consider ourselves and all true Christians, united in holy bonds of fraternal amity. We are to keep that bond inviolate. Use all methods for the bond being more close, and dear, and strong. Our motto must be, " I am for peace." Our spirit must be that of peace. We must seek the wisdom that is peaceable. We must especially pray that the heart may be engarrisoned, or kept by the peace of God, &c.

APPLICATION.

1. A firm and persevering regard to divine truth is compatible with this spirit.

2. A decided maintenance of the principles of true Christian liberty alone can lay a broad foundation for this peaceful unity.

3. Legitimate exertions for the removal of the corruptions and abuses of Christianity, will not break the Christian unity, however it may affect the unity of the denominations of the universal church. Luther—the puritans—Wesley—the Free Church of Scotland—dissenters in their present efforts, therefore, are not condemned by this subject.

CHRIST'S PRAYER FOR THE UNITY OF THE CHURCH.

" That they all may be one, as thou, Father, art in me, and I in thee; that they also may be one in us, that the world may believe that thou hast sent me."—JOHN xvii. 21.

NOTHING is oftener repeated than this, " There is only one church." The Roman Catholics loudly utter this ; the church of England ; and the various bodies of dissenters. It seems to be a settled principle amongst most Christians ; but then, each sect arrogates to itself the exclusive title of the one church, and some do this to the exclusion of all other Christians. There never was a period when it became Christians to understand this subject more than at the present. Our subject leads us directly to it. It was the solemn prayer of the blessed Saviour, and reiterated three times in the course of his intercessory address to the Father, verses 11, 21, 22.

What is the church of Christ ? The great body of believers scattered over the face of the world.

Is the church one ? In one respect, indeed, it is. All converted, renewed persons are members of Christ's spiritual body ; but in its visible aspect it is divided and torn—church against church, sect against sect, &c. This cannot be pleasing to God ; it is explicitly opposed to Christ's prayer ; it weakens the influence of Christianity ; it must ultimately cease, and the text will eventually be accomplished. Before we enter upon our subject, we ask,

(1.) When and where did divisions commence ? At Corinth ; see 1 Cor. i. 12.

(2.) The cause of divisions ; 1 Cor. iii. 3.

(3.) From that day the church of God has been the seat of disputation and variance.

I. To WHAT EXTENT IS UNION IN THE CHURCH OF CHRIST POSSIBLE ?

II. HOW MAY WE CONTRIBUTE TO IT ? And,

III. WHY WE SHOULD DO SO.

I. To WHAT EXTENT IS UNION IN THE CHURCH OF CHRIST POSSIBLE ? Absolute, minute, and universal oneness is, perhaps, impossible with imperfect and erring beings; but true Christians may be united,

1. *In spiritual affections.* Love is the very essence of religion ; one main feature in the child of God ; an essential principle in the mind renewed by divine grace. Surely it is not indispensable that persons should in all particulars hold all our sentiments to entitle them to our affection. The good Samaritan displayed kindness and generosity to the poor Jew. Love to the whole family of God is necessary to the existence of true religion, " By this shall all men know," &c. We should be united,

2. *In mutual supplications.* " Pray one for another," &c. This we are to do for all men, but especially for the family of Christ. If in error, we should seek for

their spiritual enlightenment; if weak, for their being strengthened. Now, fervent intercession for the whole church is calculated to beget greatness of soul, and catholicity of spirit.

3. *In ardent efforts for the extension of Christ's cause.* If Christians would forego their jealousies and bigoted animosities until the great common foe were conquered, they would have little to do in the end but join in the song of triumph. There is ample for all to do. The field is the world —dark, besotted, dreary, perishing. Should not all unite for its salvation? Ignorance, skepticism, profligacy, stupor, worldliness, &c.

4. *In holy emulation to glorify God.* Persons lose sight of this in seeking their own sectarian purposes. Few ask, " How does God view it?" Will he be pleased? Will it honor his word—please the blessed Spirit—exalt Christ? Self, alas! has the place of God—our opinions—our modes of worship, &c.—our denominations. If God were constantly before us, we should not be able to see these in a light of such magnitude. The sun would render the stars invisible; the sea would render the little rivulet perfectly insignificant. All Christians may unite to glorify God to this extent. Without sacrifice of truth, or compromise of principle, all thus may be one. We ask,

II. How MAY WE CONTRIBUTE TO THIS UNITY OF THE CHRISTIAN CHURCH?

1. *By cherishing the Spirit's holy influence.* His motions tend to unity. He heals; he binds up; he harmonizes. We cannot drink deeply of this stream without there springing up the same spirit of love and unity.

2. *By setting the example of Christ before us.* Of him it is said, " He pleased not himself." How we should remember his numerous exhortations to humility and condescension, " Whoso will be greatest must be as a little child," see also John xiii. 14.

3. *By using always purity of speech.* Not using sectarian language; not the garbled expressions of this or that denomination. Many may be known by their prayers—by their modes of conversation. In Christ's kingdom there is only one language—the language of pure revelation; and this ought to be so spoken, that none should know what meeting we attend, or what sectarian name we bear; and in the latter

days there will not be three hundred religious dialects as there are now. Human phraseology has done much to make divisions, and more to keep them up. To this, I add,

4. *Let us treat all Christians with candor and respect.* Let us excel in courtesy. While we honor all men, let us especially honor the friends of Jesus everywhere, and on every occasion. We ask,

III. WHY WE SHOULD LABOR FOR THE UNITY OF THE CHRISTIAN CHURCH?

1. *Because it is the will of God.* This ought to suffice. What parent does not love this in his family? God much more in his church.

2. *Christ prays for it.* It is one of the desires of the soul of the Saviour. He travails for this, and without it will not be satisfied.

3. *It will tend to our strength and comfort.* " Union is strength." It is more, it is comfort; it is the luxury of enjoyment.

4. *The world's condition demands it.* " That they all," &c. A divided church cannot convert the world. We must be united before we conquer; then, and then only, we shall prevail. We shall not silence the infidel, or assist the doubter, until we are united ourselves.

APPLICATION.

1. *The condition of the church is calculated to fill us with grief.* Weeping and sorrow might well fill our souls. The church of Rome—Puseyism, &c.

2. *This unity must be personal.* Associations, &c., can do little.

3. *Let us think of the unity of heaven.* No discord there; there all are one, &c.

THANKFULNESS.

" And be ye thankful."—COLOSSIANS iii. 15.

WE ask,

I. WHAT IS INCLUDED IN THANKFULNESS?

1. *A right appreciation of the benefits God confers.* Think of his dignity, and of our unworthiness.

2. *A sincere value of the blessings bestowed.* Every gift of God should be prized.

3. *Fervent acknowledgment to God for his goodness to us.* The heart must move the tongue, " Open thou my lips," &c.

The tongue never so truly well employed as in blessing God.

4. *Affectionate obedience to God for his benefits.* "What shall I render?" &c. He asks our hearts and lives.

II. On what grounds should we be thankful?

1. *Our relation to Deity.* His creatures —his dependents—his children.

2. *The mercies bestowed.* Temporal and spiritual. Life—preservation—privileges —redemption, &c. What are,

III. The considerations that should excite to this duty?

1. *Its reasonableness.* All creatures have some mode of expressing their delight. Harmony of the spheres; birds of the air, &c.; fields, rivers, winds, &c.; especially superior beings—seraphim, &c.

2. *Its pleasurableness.* Some duties painful; self-denial, &c. This luxurious; essence of joy—light of the soul, &c.

3. *Its profitableness.* Health of the soul. It gives vigor—pleases God, &c.

4. *Its durableness.* The very atmosphere of heaven. Will endure forever and ever.

JEHOVAH'S DESIGN WITH RESPECT TO HIS PEOPLE.

"This people have I formed for myself; they shall show forth my praise."—Isaiah xliii. 21.

The text refers to the seed of Jacob, the literal house of Israel. You are well aware how obviously it is true in reference to that nation. God resolved to deposite his truth and worship with one special people. Accordingly, he called Abraham to be the father of this nation, and he gave him many great and glorious promises, and formed his seed into a people for himself, that they might show forth, &c.; and as a nation, they did show forth, &c. In their laws, in their worship, in their deliverances, &c., they did show forth the praises of God. But on account of their apostacy God excluded them from their distinctive place as his elect, and diffused his goodness to the nations of the Gentiles. Thus the apostle speaks, Rom. xi. 17, 20; the church of Christ now enjoys the appellation of "The people of God." Whether Jews or Gentiles, or both, to them the text will appropriately apply, "This people," &c.

I. The people referred to. That is, the people of God, sometimes called saints, the righteous, the servants of God, the children of God, &c. Now of this people we notice,

1. *They are a saved people.* Not only redeemed, but saved. Christ is the "Saviour of all men, but especially of them," &c. The apostle says, "By grace are ye saved," &c. Not shall be, &c., but are, &c., see Titus iii. 5; 1 Cor. i. 18. They have felt the efficacy of divine grace; tasted and handled the things, &c.; have been delivered from the wrath to come; justified, renewed, adopted, and sanctified, &c.; saved from sin to righteousness, from darkness and sin into the knowledge, favor, love, and image of God.

2. *They are a peculiar people.* So they are described by the apostle. Not like others, they are not of the world, unlike the world, they are only pilgrims and sojourners. Hence their manners and customs, their costume and speech, their spirit and temper, their conduct and pursuits, are all peculiar to themselves; it must be so, it ought to be so, the opposite would be evil, &c. Now in addition to this,

3. *They are a distinct people.* There are many peculiar people in the world, who are yet of the world. But this people are distinct and separate. A people in the world, but unconnected in heart, in life, in conversation, in profession. Christ's army in a world which is in arms against him; Christ's vineyard in the waste-howling desert, &c.; Christ's disciples following his steps, &c.; crucified to the world, &c. Notice,

II. The formation specified. "This people have I formed," &c. Consider,

1. *The nature of this formation.* Formed into a "people." God did not intend believers to be isolated beings, he designed they should be collected, united, a people. Hence they are likened to a family, flock, company of travellers, congregation or church, city, nation. Only in this way can they exercise their graces, &c.; exhibit Christianity in its social influences, and extend it in the world. Beautifully likened to the human body; 1 Cor. xii. 14, 20. Observe,

2. *The Author of this formation.* "I have formed," &c. It is divine, it is of God. The church is God's husbandry, God's building; he gives the same Spirit

to all, but a diversity of operation, that each may add to the comfort and prosperity of the whole. Hence the term, " The church of God." God's collecting, calling, saving, uniting, keeping, &c. Notice,

III. THE END CONTEMPLATED IN THIS FORMATION. "For myself," &c. God is the first cause, and the great end of all things. He could have existed alone, but it pleased him to form the universe, &c., he made all things for himself, &c. Now he has formed the church especially for himself. It is called his rest—his dwelling—his delight ; and he designs that they " should show forth," &c. They do this,

1. *By exhibiting the effects of his gracious operations.* They are internally different, but this cannot be seen except by God, but its effects are seen, the fruit is different. "What fruit ?" &c. " But now being made free," &c. "Took knowledge," &c. The sick whole, the lepers are now cleansed, curse a blessing, the dead alive, &c.— " They show forth," &c.

2. *By laboring to diffuse his glory.* They live and act for this, pray for it, &c. "Let the whole earth," &c. They seek the glory of God, in heart and life identified with it, &c.

3. *By pious resignation to the divine appointments.* Happy in affliction, calm in peril, peaceful in death. See how Job glorified God ; see the apostles and first Christians ; see every poor, and sorrowful, and dying Christian.

APPLICATION.

1. *Of what people are you personally a part ? of the world or the church ?*

2. *Let the people of God think of their high vocation, and the end of religion, " To show forth," &c.*

3. *God will be glorified in the punishment of the finally impenitent.*

ZION'S FUTURE PROSPERITY.

A MISSIONARY SKETCH.

" For Zion's sake will I not hold my peace, and for Jerusalem's sake I will not rest, until the righteousness thereof go forth as brightness, and the salvation thereof as a lamp that burneth."—ISAIAH lxii. 1.

IT is not quite clear whether the prophet is speaking in the text in his own name, or in the name of Jesus, the true Messiah and Head of his church. We rather view the text, however, as that of Isaiah, whose heart burned with holy zeal for the enlargement of the church, and the diffusion of the divine glory. But the sentiments uttered are truly worthy of all the servants of Jehovah, in every age of the world. Every faithful minister of Christ will earnestly appropriate the language of the prophet as his own, and exclaim, " For Zion's sake," &c. We would further ask, why should not the text be expressive of the feelings of every Christian ? All who have tasted that the Lord is gracious—all who are identified with the progress of divine truth, and feel compassion for deathless souls, may well utter, with deepest emotion, the sentiment of the text, " For Zion's sake," &c. In this last and most extensive sense, we shall view this beautiful passage on this occasion. Observe,

I. THE LIMITED AND OBSCURE CONDITION OF THE CHURCH IMPLIED. By Zion and Jerusalem, we understand the spiritual church and kingdom of God. The figures of the text involve the idea, that this church requires extension and additional glory. Now, what is the true state of the church of God, even in this late era of the world's history ? We fear that the true church of Christ in all lands, including the professors of all Christian denominations, would not be more than twenty millions, and probably not so many. Of course, I do not reckon all the nominal Christians of the world. Of Mahommedans, there are about 160 millions ; of Jews, nine or ten millions ; and 700 or 800 millions of benighted, perishing pagans ; while regions of the earth are yet dreary, sterile, and the very regions of death. Even in Europe, there are vast masses with only the flickering light of papal superstition, or the equally dim and sickly rays of the Greek church. Two thousand five hundred years have transpired since Isaiah penned the text, and yet what extensive domains of darkness and wo are still lying in the hands of the wicked one. Satan is yet the prince of this world. How circumscribed the church of God ! How little is yet known of her spiritual power and glory ! Even in the countries. of her greatest prosperity, the majority of the people are at variance with her holy principles, and strangers to the felicity and blessings she confers. Observe,

II. The truly noble spirit averred. "I will not hold my peace," &c. "I will not rest." Here silence, and indolent inactivity are disavowed. How, then, can we speak and act for the extension of the righteousness and salvation of the gospel economy?

1. *The Christian minister can speak in the exercise of his public duties.* One part of our public work is to present to you the prophecies which relate to the travail of Christ's soul, and the subjugation of the world to his cross. His office is included in that commission which commanded the preaching of the gospel to every creature. It devolves upon him, therefore, to keep this subject in view; to dwell upon it in his ministrations; to unite the friends of Jesus in this great work. While he preaches and teaches Christ to those at home, he must ever remember the perishing millions abroad.

2. *Sabbath school teachers should impress this on the children of their charge.* The minister must act upon the generation that now is; the Sunday school teacher on the generation rising up—on those who are to be the pastors, deacons, and members of the church in the succeeding generation. The Sabbath school must be the nursery of the missionary spirit. It has already sent scores into the missionary field; and if well indoctrinated in the truths of universal philanthropy, it will be the army of reserve for extending the hallowed crusade of mercy and grace through the world.

3. *Parents should also train up their families in the missionary spirit.* It should form a part of household conversation; the condition, misery, and claims of the heathen should be early instilled into the mind of the young and rising generation; information from time to time should be imparted; their pity elicited, their compassion drawn forth, their generosity excited. Thus every Christian family, in its social character, should be enlisted on the side of missions.

4. *All Christians should speak with God in prayer.* In the short epitome of prayer left us by Christ, two petitions directly bear upon it: "Thy kingdom come," &c. It was predicted that the Redeemer's glory should engage the petitions of his pious followers. "Prayer shall be made for him continually." Now, our prayers should often embrace this great subject. We

should plead, and supplicate, and wrestle with God; we should press our suit, urge our requests, &c.; be intent, and earnest, and believing. We should remember what promises we have to plead—what reasons to incite us—what instances of success to cheer us; especially we should remember, how in our prayers we are one with God. His covenant, his engagement, both to Christ and his church, are most specific on this subject. Therefore he will hear and approve of our intercessions. But earnest prayer to God,

5. *Must be followed with corresponding activity.* "I will not rest." God will not convert the world by miracle, nor by the abstract influences of the Holy Spirit, but by the means which he connected with his kingdom at the beginning. "This gospel of the kingdom," &c. By the diffusion of the truth, &c. Did all the followers of Christ speak and pray only, it would necessarily be inefficient. Besides, without corresponding effort, it would be hypocrisy towards God, and a mockery of the heathen. Men must go into these dreary regions of the world; then they must be sent and supported; they must have Bibles, and tracts, and schools; then the church at home must be active and liberal. "If they descend into the mine," as Carey said, "those at home must hold the rope." If they go forth in the war, we must provide the ammunition; and those who do not this ought never to speak or pray about Christian missions—of course I mean if they have the least ability to help. Notice,

III. The reasons on which the magnanimous resolve of the text is grounded. "For Zion's sake." "For Jerusalem's sake." There are several reasons implied in the one avowed.

1. *For the sake of the God of Zion.* That his glory may fill the whole earth; his name be everywhere adored, his laws obeyed, and a revenue of praise from all his creatures be presented.

2. *For the sake of the King of Zion.* He has given Christ to be "Head over all things to his church." Christ is set as God's holy king in Zion. Now, the sorrows and sufferings of Christ were to be rewarded by universal empire; see Isaiah liii. 10, 11, "And I, if I be lifted up." Love to Christ, and sympathy with him, should excite us to say, "For Zion's sake," &c.

3. *For the sake of the church itself.*
When the visions of prophecy are realized,
then will be the jubilee of the church—her
consummated glory—her final triumph.
Do we not desire this? long for it? Has
not the church been a peculiar blessing to
us and our families? Should not gratitude,
therefore, influence us? If not, let love
of self do it; for the prosperity of Christ's
kingdom involves in it our prosperity. We
cannot speak, and labor, and give to the
cause, without deriving incalculable blessings to our own souls.

APPLICATION.

Address,

1. *Those whose spirits harmonize with the
prophet of old.* Who feel the emotions, and
express their desires and resolutions as
he did.

2. *Those who are not acting in concert
with the text are so far at variance with the
Redeemer.*

3. *The claims of missions are loud and
comprehensive at the present period.* We
live in the last times; our facilities are
numerous; the openings of providence signally striking and wide. Let us not
slumber, then, when the day is breaking,
when the momentous triumphs of the cross
must be close at hand, &c.

4. I might refer largely, and last of all
—*To the truly miserable and pitiable condition of the heathen.*

JOY IN SORROW.

"As sorrowful, yet always rejoicing."—2 CORIN-
THIANS vi. 10.

THE text, and the whole paragraph, refer
to the apostles, and the first preachers of
the gospel. In it we see the toil, and suffering, and peril to which the ambassadors
of Jesus were first exposed. Several portions of the passage are presented in the
way of paradox, &c., see verse 9, &c. The
text is equally applicable to all the disciples
of Christ, in every age of the world. Of
all such it may be said, "As sorrowful,"
&c. Let us look at several particulars in
which the text is especially exemplified.
It is true,

I. IN RESPECT TO THE ADVERSE AND AF-
FLICTIVE SCENES OF LIFE. This world to
the Christian is a valley of tears—a howling wilderness—a stormy ocean; many
things to disappoint and try the Christian.
The ordinary troubles of life, in which they
share with their fellow-men; peculiar afflictions to which they are liable as Christians. Now these are *many.* "Many are
the afflictions of the righteous." "It is
through much tribulation," &c. These
often involve the friends of Jesus in sorrow
—often cast down and dispirited on account
of the way; but in these there is cause for
constant rejoicing.

(1.) Their afflictions are limited and light.

(2.) Their enjoyments numberless.

(3.) Their support constant and efficient.

(4.) Their trials salutary and useful.

(5.) Prospect of a world where they
shall be for ever unknown.

"When I can read my title clear," &c.

II. OFTEN SORROWFUL ON ACCOUNT OF
THEIR OWN IMPERFECTIONS AND INFIRMITIES
AS CHRISTIANS. So little light; so little
confidence; such a wavering hope; so
little strength; so often turned aside from
the path of duty; so listless in devotion;
so unfruitful, &c. Now these are real
causes of sorrow to the sincere Christian.
But even here there are *reasons for always
rejoicing.*

(1.) That there is the least genuine
grace.

(2.) That God is so condescending and
tender. "As a Father," &c. "He knoweth," &c.

(3.) That Christ sympathizes and intercedes for us.

"He knows what sore temptations mean,
   For he has felt the same."

(4.) That there are provisions of grace
to meet all our need.

(5.) That there is a fountain always
opened, and the promise, "If we confess,"
&c.

III. OFTEN SORROWFUL, WHEN ANTICI-
PATING THE SOLEMNITIES OF DEATH AND
JUDGMENT. The Christian recognises his
stewardship, &c. He knows he must die,
and give an account. When his Lord
calleth, he will have to surrender it up.
There is, too, the act of dying, and the
reality of judgment. Feeling his unprofit-
ableness he dreads, and perhaps almost
despairs; fears the ordeal and the issue.
But we should always rejoice, for,

(1.) Dying grace is pledged; **and never**

has the pledge been broken, and the soul deserted.

(2.) Death is a conquered servant, not a reigning tyrant.

(3.) The Judge is our brother and our friend. Reverse the text. Sinners rejoice, and yet are really sorrowful.

IV. OFTEN SORROWFUL ON ACCOUNT OF OUR CONNECTIONS IN LIFE. Those who have tasted of the grace of God cannot be indifferent to their relatives and friends. So far from this, they long and pray for their salvation. How often they see no hope of their desires being granted! Perhaps enemies, mockers, or careless, &c. ; entirely indifferent. Now this is a cause of sorrow. Yet there are some grounds of rejoicing :—

(1.) We are only responsible for the use of means.

(2.) While mercies and privileges are continued there is hope.

(3.) All our friends and kindred are not in this state.

V. OFTEN SORROWFUL IN REFERENCE TO THE CHURCH OF CHRIST. So little real, abiding good effected ; so many only have a name ; so many very occasional in regard to the means, &c. ; so many not using their energies for the weal of sinners ; so many who go back ; so few full of hope, and faith, and zeal, and good works. Yet here we may also rejoice that,

(1.) There are some who do honor to religion ; who love the ordinances ; who are full of love and the Holy Ghost ; who are ripening for a better world.

(2.) Some who are useful, and consistent, and persevering.

(3.) That the Lord is very good to his people, and fills his poor unworthy servants with all needful good, &c. ; and that he will not cast them off, nor forsake, for his name's sake.

VI. OFTEN SORROWING ON ACCOUNT OF THE WORLD—THOSE WHO ARE WITHOUT. Whose eyes are grieved for the transgressors ; whose eyes weep, because men keep not God's law. " Oh ! that the wickedness of the wicked," &c. Yet, we rejoice to see so many blessed institutions for the young, for the poor, for the ignorant, for benighted neighborhoods, for the intemperate, &c. ; and that some good is done, some are converted, &c. One such instance is precious *beyond the value of the world.*

APPLICATION.

1. *Learn the mixed state of the present world.* Light and darkness, joy and fear, &c.

2. *Seek supremely a better world.*

3. *Look for the mercy of God.* " Be diligent," &c.

HEAVEN UPON EARTH.

" As the days of heaven upon earth."—DEUT xi. 21.

WE often speak of heaven ; the way to it is by evangelical obedience to God's word. Often we desire heaven : we need not wait till we die to enjoy it, we may have heaven now, heaven in our hearts.

" The men of grace have found,
    Glory begun below ;
Celestial fruit on earthly ground,
    From faith and hope may grow."

Let me call your attention,

I. To THE LITERAL REALIZATION OF THE TEXT. " The days of heaven upon earth" were enjoyed by our first parents in Eden. Paradise was a striking type of heaven. So heaven is called, and we read of its streams, and of its tree of life.

1. *Paradise was the region of purity, and so is heaven.* It is the holy city. Nothing that defileth can enter into it.

2. *Paradise was the abode of honor and dignity, and such is heaven.* All there are ennobled, dignified. Possess dominion, glory, and honor.

3. *Paradise was the scene of happy communion, and such is heaven.* Angels, and God himself conversed and held intercourse with our first parents, and saints and angels have one blest and endless communion in heaven.

4. *Paradise was the seat of delightful pleasures, and such is heaven.* There are the rivers of pleasure. Oceans of delight. Fulness of joys, and pleasures for evermore. Paradise indeed was strikingly typical of the heavenly world. Let me now call your attention,

II. To THE SPIRITUAL REALIZATION OF THE TEXT. Now this is enjoyed by the members of Christ's mystical and spiritual church. Observe,

(1.) The gospel dispensation is called the kingdom, or reign of heaven. " Repent ye," &c. Thus he says the kingdom of heaven suffereth violence, and the violent take it by force. To Peter he said, " I will give to thee the keys of the kingdom of heaven." Observe,

(2.) The description given of the gospel church, as contrasted with the old dispensation, is exceedingly interesting and appropriate, Heb. xii. 18–24. Now it is in the true spiritual church of Christ, that we have the days of heaven upon earth.

1. *We have a heavenly king.* He came down from heaven. He is Lord of heaven. The light and glory of heaven. Is worshipped and adored by all the hosts, &c.

2. *We have heavenly blessings.* The calling is called a heavenly calling, Heb. iii. 1. " Heavenly gifts," Heb. vi. 4. " Blessed be the God and Father of our Lord Jesus Christ, who hath blessed us with all spiritual blessings in heavenly places in Christ," Eph. i. 3.

(1.) Divine peace is the peace of heaven ; and this peace Christ gives to all his disciples. " My peace I give," &c. " The peace of God," &c.

(2.) Our joys are heavenly. " Whom having not seen, ye love ; in whom, though now ye see him not, yet believing, ye rejoice with joy unspeakable and full of glory." 1 Peter i. 8.

(3.) All our supplies are heavenly. " Every good gift, and every perfect gift is from above, and cometh down from the Father of lights, with whom is no variableness, neither shadow of turning," James i. 17. All the holy influences of the Spirit descend from heaven. Our bread is from heaven, and the streams of which we drink flow from between the throne of God and the Lamb.

3. *We have heavenly communion.* Every exercise connected with Christian fellowship is heavenly.

(1.) Prayer is the united flame of devotion ascending to heaven.

(2.) Praise is the grateful incense arising and mingling with the ascriptions of the heavenly hosts.

(3.) At Christ's table we feed upon the bread of heaven, and eat together of the true manna which descends from heaven. How appropriate the lines of the poet.

> " Happy the souls to Jesus join'd,
> And saved by grace alone ;
> Walking in all his ways, they find
> Their heaven on earth begun."

4. *We have heavenly delights and anticipations.* How often have we enjoyed the Spirit as an earnest or first-fruits of the heavenly inheritance ! How often experienced the rapture of Peter, " Lord, it is good to be here." How often had some of the kindred feelings of Paul's ecstasy, " Whether in the body, or out of the body," &c. How often felt raised almost up to heaven, until the imagination has seemed to behold the gates and the scenery of the new Jerusalem ! We have exclaimed, " This is none other than the house of God," &c. How often would we have given the preference to be absent from the body, and to be present with the Lord ! Surely these are as the days of heaven upon earth. Observe,

III. The FUTURE GLORIOUS REALIZATION OF THE TEXT. This earth is not to be Satan's seat forever. Not the scene of sin and wo and the curse forever ; not to be the grave-yard of the redeemed forever ; it is destined to a glorious renovation. To be lifted up from the degradation of the curse. To be the seat of moral loveliness, and become the garden of the Lord. To cease being the walk of prowling beasts of prey, and become the abode of the innocent and the happy ; to cease to be the field of blood, and become the land of peace, when the nations shall not learn war any more, and when nothing shall hurt or destroy in all God's holy mountain. " The wolf also shall dwell with the lamb, and the leopard shall lie down with the kid ; and the calf and the young lion, and the fatling together ; and a little child shall lead them ; and the cow and the bear shall feed ; their young ones shall lie down together : and the lion shall eat straw like the ox. And the sucking child shall play on the hole of the asp, and the weaned child shall put his hand on the cockatrice's den. They shall not hurt nor destroy in all my holy mountain : for the earth shall be full of the knowledge of the Lord, as the waters cover the sea," Isaiah xi. 6–9. " Violence shall no more be heard in the land, wasting nor destruction within thy borders ; but thou shalt call thy walls salvation, and thy gates praise. The sun shall be thy light no more by day ; neither for brightness," &c.

(1.) Now, all this is certain, because it hath been pledged in the solemn covenant of the Father with the Son.

(2.) It is certain, for it is written in the

unalterable volume of truth, that " the whole earth shall be filled," &c.

(3.) It is certain, for the beginning of the conquests have been achieved, and now, " He who hath many crowns upon his head, is going forth from victory to victory." Now by way of application, we ask, How may we contribute to bring about the blissful consummation ?

1. *We must become the subjects of heavenly grace.* Every converted soul is one restored to the heavenly reign of Jesus. So much sin and misery blotted out ; a source of evil stopped, and a source of good opened. The image and spirit of the wicked one are erased, and the image and spirit of God exhibited. Now this is the first step, then,

2. *We must exhibit heavenly graces and dispositions.* Where we move we must try to produce a heavenly atmosphere, heavenly influence, the holiness of heaven. We must reflect the goodness of heaven, we must diffuse the kindness and mercy of heaven.

3. *We must devote all our energies and means to promote heavenly institutions.* There are two mighty interests contending for the supremacy, for the universal triumph. It is not difficult to see on what side the various institutions are allied. We know the tree by its fruits. There is the preaching of the gospel ; there are meetings for prayer ; there are tract and visiting societies ; there are Bible and missionary societies. Now are we giving all the weight of our influence to these institutions ? Are we supporting and praying for them ? All can do the latter. " Thy kingdom come." Do we internally long for it ? By the employment of means, shall there be as the days of heaven upon earth.

4. *You are all contributing to, or hindering the coming of Christ's kingdom.* Which is your position ? How are you acting ? Let us see how we really stand before God.

PRESENCE OF GOD IN HIS HOLY TEMPLE.

" But the Lord is in his holy temple : let all the earth keep silence before him."—HABAKKUK ii. 20.

THE feelings of the mind are necessarily differently impressed by the circumstances in which we are placed, and the scenery by which we are surrounded. Go to the house of social festivity, and there joy and gladness are the only elements which will appear appropriate or be excited by it. Go to the house of mourning, and how very apposite the sentiments, and the emotions felt! Go to the house of legislature, there the interests of the nation, the efficiency of statesmen, and the principles of politics, necessarily engross the mind. Go to the hall of science, and there the wonders of nature, and the productions of art, lead us to the heights of admiration, or into the depths of profound inquiry. Go to the court of justice, and see human nature degraded in fetters, exiled, or doomed to death ; and another class of feelings differing from all the preceding are produced. Go to the palace of royalty, enter the throne-room, see the splendid equipage and dazzling trappings of earthly greatness, &c. Envy or ambition, and thoughts of human grandeur, will have the ascendency. I desire to introduce you into an assembly, more deeply interesting, instructive, and solemn, and yet more elevating than any of these ; it is the temple of Jehovah—the house of the living God. That to which the text refers, " But the Lord is in his," &c. There is a threefold temple inhabited by Jehovah. The heaven of heavens ; the temple seen by Isaiah and John, &c. ; the temple of the sanctified heart. " With that man," &c. " Know ye not that ye are the temple," &c. The assembly of his saints. " Wherever two or three," &c. To the last our attention will be confined.

I. WHAT THE DECLARATION IMPLIES.

II. THE DESIGNS OF HIS PRESENCE.

III. THE IMPRESSION IT SHOULD PRODUCE.

I. WHAT THE DECLARATION IMPLIES. It does not limit the divine presence. The heaven of heavens cannot contain him. He fills immensity. " Whither," &c. His spirit pervades all creation ; but it refers to the especial presence of God in the rich condescensions of his grace. God is there by the ubiquity of his nature ; but he is there especially,

1. *By the revelations of his mind.* The assembly of saints is to be the pillar and ground of truth. Here the word of God is deposited. Anciently in the ark were the two tables of the law. Now the law and the prophets, and the gospels, and the letters of the apostles—the completed

canon of truth. Now here is God's mind, and will, and purpose. His statutes and blessings, &c. Just as the sovereign is often said to be, where his will is proclaimed, &c.

2. *God is present by his ordinances.* The ordinance of praise respects him, and recognises him as near. So adoration and prayer, so baptism and the supper. These have his impress upon them.

3. *God is present by the power of his Spirit.* The Spirit is the gift of Christ to the church. "I will send the Spirit of truth," &c. "He shall abide," &c. "God is a spirit," and must be worshipped as such, &c.

II. THE DESIGNS OF HIS PRESENCE.

1. *The design of inspection.* He tries the heart and the reins ; he examines the motives, &c. ; he observes the conduct, the expressions, the thoughts ; he sees who sincerely bows the knee, &c. His eyes see all, and all perfectly.

2. *The design of gracious assistance.* He is present to help his people—to calm—to enlighten—to incite—to open the heart and lips, &c. To impart the hallowed fire to our souls, &c. To open the ear, and loosen the tongue, &c.

3. *The design of seasonable consolation.* God has engaged to comfort his people "in Jerusalem." "Even as a mother," &c. "Comfort ye, comfort ye," &c. A sense of sin is felt, &c. The mind depressed, &c. Trouble encountered, &c. God listens to their plaints and moans ; he hears the cry of his people, and imparts seasonable consolation.

4. *The design of effectual co-operation.* God allows us to be considered co-workers with himself: but our labors will effect nothing without his blessing. He gives efficacy to all means—to prayer, to preaching, &c. As the means involve the conversion of souls, the establishment of saints, and the furtherance of the gospel, the Lord is present to secure, by his Holy Spirit, these great and momentous ends. Then in reference to the divine presence, we ask :

III. WHAT IMPRESSIONS SHOULD IT PRODUCE ?

1. *Reverential awe.* "Let all the earth keep silence." Can divine worship be too reverently regarded and conducted ? Is it reverent to come in late ; to rush in so as to disturb ; to gaze about—to be listless—to sleep—to cover the head before you get out

—to talk about worldly things at the door &c., &c. We forget that "the Lord is in his holy temple," &c. It should produce,

2. *Devout preparation.* We go to meet the Deity, to see him by faith—to hear him speak—to speak to him—to be blessed, &c. Then we should prepare, so as to be collected, quiet, thoughtful, &c. "Take off thy shoes," &c.

3. *Deep spiritual humility.* If God is in his temple, then he alone should be exalted. As all the stars disappear from our vision before the rising sun, so God is the great Sun of righteousness, &c. The people are as nothing, but dust, &c. The minister, &c. God all in all. How abased and lowly we should be ! We should bow down and worship. Body and mind should be prostrated before him.

4. *Great encouragement.* We cannot fail in our object. Every good can be obtained, every evil avoided. God possesses an infinite fulness of blessedness for his people. Other things may fail—friends absent—minister not equal to his usual state, &c., but God is in his holy temple, &c.

APPLICATION.

1. *Learn the dignity of Christian worship.* To come immediately before God, &c.

2. *The value of a mediator.* We need a days-man, an intercessor, &c.

3. *The importance of revelation.* To know how to come, &c.

4. *The value of the Spirit.* To assist our infirmities, and help in every time of need.

THE GRACIOUS END OF CHRIST'S MISSION INTO OUR WORLD.

"For the Son of Man is come to seek and to save that which was lost."—LUKE xix. 10.

THE mission of Jesus to our world was associated with astounding wonders and inexplicable mysteries. Never in any respect was there any thing like it. Warriors have visited countries, but their footsteps have been marked with blood, and their career with misery and death ; travellers have explored distant regions, but their object has been to discover the wonders of nature, or monuments of art ; philanthropists have occasionally gone forth on errands of humanity and mercy, and have given of their profusion to the sons and daughters of misery ; but Jesus, the blessed Messiah, came into our world to bear the fetters, to submit to the shame, and to endure death for a race of guilty rebels, and by suffering, concentrated in his own person, what they deserved, to seek and to save that which was lost. Let us briefly advert,

I. To THE DISTINGUISHED PERSONAGE REFERRED TO. "The Son of Man." And here we are led to consider the incarnation of the Son of God. Jesus is often described as the Son of God, Lord of Glory, &c. But as Mediator, it behooved him to assume the nature of man ; and thus it is written, " God sent forth his Son," not in his essential and glorious form, but " made of a woman," &c. Hence he took upon himself not the nature of angels, but was of the seed of Abraham. Several reasons why Jesus became the Son of man :—

1. *As Mediator, he must be interested in both parties.* Hence he was God with God, and man with man.

2. *That he might suffer and die for man.* The divine nature could not suffer.

3. *That as kinsman, he might have right to present himself a ransom, &c.* Here the same nature suffers that had sinned, and was condemned.

4. *That he might be an example to his people.* Enduring their infirmities ; living, &c., with the same nature, in the same world.

5. *That he might sympathize with them as their great and tender High Priest, &c., in heaven.*

II. NOTICE THE EMBASSY OF THE SON OF MAN. " The Son of Man came." Three questions will elucidate this :—

1. *From whence did he come ?* He came from heaven, the palace-royal of Jehovah ; from the throne of the Father ; the glory of the celestial state. He had ever been with the Father ; was as one brought up with him ; by him had all things been created, &c. He was the first-begotten of God— the first-born of every creature—the delight and fellow of the Father—the righteous Lord, and heir of all things ; he came from the heaven of heavens.

2. *Where did the Son of Man come to ?* He came to this fallen, benighted, and miserable world ; a world in a state of sinful revolt, misery, and death. What condescension ! What grace ! How he abased

himself, &c. He made his footstool his dwelling-place ; he came not on a transitory visit, but to be a citizen of it ; to live in it for more than thirty years.

3. *In what manner did he come ?* Not with regal pomp ; not with a train of celestial attendants ; not in grandeur ; not to dwell in its palaces, &c. A poor village was his birth-place ; a poor virgin his mother ; a stable his first residence. He took upon him the form of a servant ; he came not to be waited upon, and ministered unto, but to be the servant of servants.

III. THE GREAT END OF THE SAVIOUR'S ADVENT. " He came to seek," &c. Now, here is a distinct reference to the state of the human family. " Lost." Not in the absolute sense ; not irrevocably. Some emblems may assist us here.

1. *Look at that sheep which has left the fold.* It is straying on the dark and distant mountains, exposed to every beast of prey. Such was our state. " All we like sheep," &c. We never should have returned ; we should have wandered on, in endless mazes lost.

2. *Look at the mariner.* His vessel has driven against the hidden shoal—has become a total wreck ; he has escaped to the summit of a barren rock. Is he not lost ? He cannot long survive—cannot recross the trackless deep. Such the state of man.

3. *Look at that sickly, wretched being.* The leprosy has spread its desolating foulness through the whole system ; no remedy, &c. ; the disease is deepening and spreading. Is he not lost ? So man became defiled. " From the crown of the head," &c.

4. *Look at that malefactor.* He has committed some capital offence—has been tried, convicted, condemned. Is he not lost ? He is in the eye of the law a dead man. So sin had involved us in guilt, and brought us under condemnation ; the black curse of eternal death hovered over our miserable world. Thus, brethren, we were lost. Now, the end of Christ's mission was to seek and to save that which was lost. As the kind shepherd, he followed the straying sheep, &c. ; he traversed the dreary mountains, &c., and prepared a fold for his straying flock ; he visited the desolate mariner on the rock, and brought close to him the life-boat of salvation, and freely offered to conduct him to the regions of bliss, and shores of immortality ; he came to our hos-

pital world, and brought a balm—the balm of health and life—to heal the leper, &c. ; he came to the condemned prisoner —took his place—bore his doom—died in his stead—suffered the just for the unjust, &c.

APPLICATION.

1. *Herein we see the condition of all men by nature.* A condition from which the grace of God hath provided deliverance.

2. *Are you found of Christ ?* Restored —saved.

3. *The incorrigible wanderer will be lost forever.*

4. *Now urge the acceptance of Christ upon all present.*

CHRIST THE LIGHT OF THE WORLD.

" I am the light of the world."—JOHN viii. 12.

OF all the material creatures which God has made, light is the fairest and most striking emblem of himself. God is light —the Father of lights, and in him is no darkness at all. Light is also one of the metaphorical titles of the Redeemer, and with John it was a favorite comparison. In him " as the Word," or Logos, " was life, and the life was the light of men." Jesus also adopts the same expression in reference to himself, " I am the light of the world." The emblem is exceedingly appropriate on account of the purity of light, on account of the joy which it diffuses, but chiefly as it is the source of manifestation. By it all things are discerned ; without it, yet having the organs of sight, we perceive nothing. Jesus is the great Sun of the universe—the fountain of light and life. We observe, then, that light is the emblem of life ; and,

I. HE IS THE LIGHT OF BEING TO ALL HIS CREATURES. Light is the symbol of life— darkness of death. The state of things before his creative power was exerted was dark and void, and light was the first creature he spake into being. It is probable that the light of existence is as extensive as the universe—that everywhere living beings exist. Throughout all his animated works, he is the light. He gave life to every thing, and he holds the life of every creature in his hands. In him all things live and move, &c. ; the glow-worm and the man, the insect and the angel, the imperceptible animalcule and the seraph. Light is the emblem of knowledge, and,

II. HE IS THE LIGHT OF INTELLIGENCE TO ALL RATIONAL BEINGS. He has given each the instinct or reason best fitted to its nature, &c. He has endowed the mind of man with all its lofty powers ; with understanding, judgment, memory, and all the capacities with which it is ennobled. The still greater, clearer, and more elevated powers of angels are all conferred by him. Light is the emblem of joy and gladness, and,

III. HE IS THE LIGHT OF THE GOSPEL. As a revelation of God's mind ; it is called the glorious gospel of the blessed God, because it is irradiated by the beams of the Son of God. He brought life and immortality to light. Take Christ away, and we have no gospel. What was the condition of the world when Christ was not known ? Dark ! dark ! Darkness covered the earth, and gross darkness the minds of the people ; so dark that neither philosophy, nor science, nor literature could remove it. In this benighted condition, man could obtain no certain knowledge,

1. *As to the true God.* Hence the whole scene of idolatry ; hence the unnumbered deities. Every thing was appealed to, and worshipped by some as God ; sun—moon —stars—the sea—rivers—the wind—fowls of the air—beasts—fishes—creeping things. Hence, too, idols formed of wood, and stone, and clay, &c. Christ revealed the true and living God. " No man hath seen God," &c. As the Father of mercies, and the fountain of compassion, tenderness, and love. The world was dark,

2. *As to human sin and misery.* And Christ made this manifest ; and he presented himself in contrast to the world, a perfectly holy being ; but, most of all, he showed how they could be pardoned and removed—how the guilty could be forgiven and delivered from it. So dark were mankind, that they had adopted cruel rites to obtain this. He presented the Father, and the returning prodigal ; the publican, &c. ; himself as a sacrifice for sin. The world was dark,

3. *As to the supreme good.* Some had looked for this in pleasure, some in knowledge, &c. Christ showed that it consisted in the enjoyment of the love of God ; a right state of heart towards God and towards

men; in one word, "Love." Dwelling in love, &c. The world was dark,

4. *As to futurity.* The state of departed spirits he revealed. Heaven of bliss—hell of wo; eternal life, and eternal death; also as to the body, its resurrection by the mighty power of God. We observe, light is the emblem of hope, and,

IV. Christ is the light of the Christian's character and expectations. "God who commanded," &c. He has opened their eyes, and now they see; he has given them day—the day of salvation; he is in them as their light. "The day star hath arisen in their hearts." Once darkness, now light, &c.

> "He is our soul's bright morning star,
> And he our rising sun."

Light is the medium of beauty, and,

V. He is the light of the church. The language of Isaiah may be applied to the church, "Arise! shine," &c. The church is not in darkness, but in light. The church is a city set upon a hill; all her light is from Christ. He is the sun—the centre of all her light and glory: he reflects his glory upon her; he bespangles her firmament with the stars of his right hand, &c.; he causes the spirit of light and comfort to dwell within her; and the course of his church is to be increasingly radiant and glorious, until the light of the moon be as the light of the sun, &c., and the whole earth be filled with her glory. Light is the emblem of glory, and,

VI. He is the light of heaven. Rev. xxi. 23. On Tabor, the apostles were overwhelmed with his effulgent rays, &c.; but in heaven he shines forth infinitely brighter than the sun; illumines the celestial temple, so that there is no night there.

APPLICATION.

1. *How many are in darkness!* Of ignorance—sin—unbelief. Christ is the light of the world. Why tarry far off? Why remain children of night and darkness? &c. Awake, &c.

2. *According to our fellowship with Christ will be the Christian's light.* Nearness to Christ and we have light, hope, joy, &c. Labor,

3. *To bring others to the light.* Every Christian should feel that,

> "'Tis all his business here below
> To cry, Behold the Lamb!"

REVERENCE CLAIMED FOR CHRIST.

"Having yet therefore one son, his well-beloved, he sent him also last unto them, saying, They will reverence my son."—Mark xii. 6.

Our subject relates immediately to the Jews, and their rejection and murder of the Messiah. It also directs our attention to God's judicial dealings with them as a nation, and the election of the Gentiles to their privileges and blessings. The Saviour also here predicts, or rather applies an ancient prediction to himself; see verse 10, "And have ye not read?" &c. Our present design is the consideration of the words of our text as they will properly apply to us. Observe, then,

I. The dignified character of Christ. "God's well-beloved Son." This representation presents Jesus to us,

1. *In his divine nature.* God's one Son. Angels are called sons of God; saints are the sons of God; but Jesus is God's one Son—a Son in a very different sense to angels or saints; for to which of the angels did he ever say, "Thou art my Son," &c. For when he bringeth in the first-begotten into the world, &c., Heb. i. 5, &c. Christ, as the Son of God, possesses a oneness of nature with the Father, "I and the Father are one." "Whoso hath seen me hath seen the Father," &c. He also possesses an equality of glory, &c. He thought it not robbery to be equal with God, &c. He is over all, God blessed for evermore. His name, his power, his dignity, &c., are supremely pre-eminent. Observe, Christ is placed before us,

2. *As the object of the Father's delight.* "His well-beloved." It is written, "The Father loveth the Son," &c. Thus did Isaiah prophesy, xlii. 1. At his baptism, God proclaimed his love when the heavens were opened, &c. "This is my beloved Son," &c. This was repeated at his transfiguration; see also in Christ's sacerdotal prayer, John xvii. 24. Notice,

II. The mission of Christ. "He sent him also." God had sent his prophets and ministering servants to teach, to warn, and reveal his will to his people; but, last of all, he sent his Son.

1. *From whence?* From his own bosom. "No man hath seen God at any time; the only begotten Son, who is in the bosom of the Father, he hath declared him." He enjoyed inexpressible glory and joy with the Father before the world was; but from

heaven's dignity and bliss he was sent forth, and came down to us.

2. *To whom was he sent?* To a world of sinners. First of all, to his own; to the Jews, the seed of Abraham; to the house of Israel; but also with an express design for the benefit of the world.

3. *For what was he sent?* To be the Saviour of the world; to restore men to the favor, image, and enjoyment of God.

(1.) He came to destroy the works of the devil, and set up the kingdom of heaven on earth.

(2.) He was sent to illumine a dark world by the doctrines of the gospel.

(3.) To recover an alienated world by his power and grace.

(4.) To redeem an accursed world by his death upon the cross.

(5.) And to purify a polluted world by his spirit and blood. It was an embassy of pure, infinite, inconceivable love and grace.

III. THE REVERENCE GOD DEMANDS ON BEHALF OF HIS SON. He said, they will reverence my Son, i. e. treat him with deference, with supreme respect; give him their obedience. Let us ascertain,

1. *The manner in which this reverence should be evinced.*

(1.) By adoring love of his person. This is what angels give him. "Worthy the Lamb," &c. How rapturously David wrote and sang, Psalm xlv. 1, 2.

(2.) By cheerful obedience to his authority. Christ must be regarded in his princely authority. No reverence without obedience—the cheerful obedience of the heart. When one said, "Thy mother and thy brethren are without," he said, "Whoso doeth the will," &c.

(3.) By studious imitation of his example. He hath left us an example, "My sheep hear my voice." If we say that we have received him, we should walk as he also walked.

(4.) By ardent zeal for his glory; making Christ's interest our own; living to spread his name and praise; seeking the prosperity of his kingdom and cause in the world; having one heart with Christ in all his spiritual designs.

2. *The grounds of this reverence.* They are very many.

(1.) Think of the glory of his person. The supreme God; the King of kings; Jehovah of hosts; the ruler of the universe.

(2.) Contemplate the purity of his character. The source of perfect holiness; light, and beauty, and perfection of Christ; not one spot or frailty; the Holy One of Israel.

(3.) The riches of his grace. Not only purity, but purity embodied in love, in goodness. Mercy is the radiant bow of his throne; mercy, that has astonished heaven; mercy, infinite, boundless, eternal. Herein is love, that he laid down his life, &c.

(4.) The preciousness of his benefits. By reverencing him we enjoy his favor, love, communion, spirit, grace, and glory.

(5.) The terribleness of his wrath; see it in the history of the Jews, and read Psalm ii. 11, &c. Rev. vi. 12.

APPLICATION.

1. *Address sinners.* Rejection of Christ will involve you in endless wrath and ruin.

2. *Saints.* Aver your reverence for Christ. Not only cherish it, but exhibit it. Fearlessly profess him before men, and ever live to the glory of his name.

GOD'S CALL TO THE SLEEPER.

"Awake, thou that sleepest, and arise from the dead, and Christ shall give thee light."—EPHE-SIANS v. 14.

VARIOUS are the similitudes employed in scripture to describe the state of the sinner. He is represented as an alien, a rebel, an outcast, a captive; as diseased, blind, wretched, and lost. He is spoken of as deceived and perishing. Our text describes him as asleep, and also dead. Let us consider,

I. THE SINNER'S AWFUL STATE.
II. GOD'S GRACIOUS CALL.
III. THE GREAT PROMISE.

I. THE SINNER'S AWFUL STATE. Asleep and dead, or perhaps the Spirit designs the sleep as the sleep of death, a deadly sleep, a sleep tending to death. Now this deadly sleep is characterized by the following striking symptoms.

1. *It is a state of darkness.* In sleep the organs of vision are closed; there may be the rays of light, the beauties of nature, &c., but they are not seen. Such is the condition of the soul, in a state of darkness; without true and saving knowledge; ignorant of himself, of God, and of the

things that belong to his peace. He has the capacity, and there is the revelation, the light of the gospel shining, but he sits in darkness, and in the shadow of death.

2. *It is a state of insensibility.* Asleep, the person hears not, enjoys not; he is temporarily dead to all around him. Such is the state of the sinner; he hearkens not to God; he enjoys him not; a thousand blessings are near him, but he has no taste nor desire for them.

3. *A state of inactivity.* In sleep all the limbs are at ease; no desires formed; no plans laid out; no work effected. Such is the state of the sinner as to all moral and spiritual labor. He labors not for the bread, &c.; he agonizes not for the crown; he strives not for the goal; he works not out his salvation; he flees not from the wrath, &c.; he walks not in the way of holiness; he prepares not to meet his God.

4. *A state of illusion.* Sleep is the season of dreams, of vain and vapid imaginations. How striking these dreams often are! how vivid! how like reality, truth, yet all illusive. A state of sin is one of illusive dreams. Afflicted with the plague of sin, yet they dream of health; poor, dream of riches; debased, of dignities; wretched, yet dream of bliss and joy; condemned and in the way of ruin, yet dream of heaven and eternal life; life ebbing, they dream of years to come. Who can describe the dreams of sin and sinners?

5. *A state of peril.* Asleep, they are no longer able to watch and defend themselves. Now the horrid assassin and murderer wend their cruel way to shed blood. How many have slept only to awake in eternity; so also from accidents, fire, storms, &c.; also from disease and sudden death. So exposed is the sinner; exposed every moment to the just displeasure of God; thus while Belshazzar was feasting; thus while the rich fool was planning; thus while Herod was deified.

6. *This sleep is a state of disease.* Not natural and healthy sleep, but the result of disease, the effect of moral depravity. Hence it becomes more profound, more universal, more unexcitable, till it terminates in eternal death. Sleep of death, ending in death everlasting. From this state men never awake themselves. Observe,

II. GOD'S GRACIOUS CALL. It is God speaking in the text, and he is speaking in mercy with a view to our salvation. Not as he will speak at the last day, when his voice will awake the dead, and shake the universe. God thus calls,

1. *By the various circumstances and events of life.* Often by adversity—by affliction—by bereavements—by the example and advice of friends—by instances of his displeasure, sudden deaths, &c.

2. *By his blessed word.* By the word written and preached. Most read or hear it read, and how it describes our state, &c.; how it calls to repentance, &c.; how it urges salvation. But especially by the preaching of the word. The minister goes forth expressly to warn, arouse, and exhort. Have you not been called hundreds, yea, thousands of times? "If any man have ears," &c.

3. *God calls by the admonitions of conscience.* Who has not felt the inward conviction, the inward rebuke, the inward warning? &c. Now thus God calls men, but to what?

(1.) To awake; to shake off the lethargy; to arouse themselves; to exercise their powers; "Consider your ways," &c. To reflect, &c.

(2.) To arise from the dead; to forsake the position of sleep and death; the company and state of the dead, &c. Illustrate it by a person who has taken some powerful opiate; or some one who has been overcome by intense cold, and where sleep would be death. Now power is ever given to obey.

III. THE GREAT PROMISE. "Christ shall give thee light."

1. *The blessing promised is light.*

(1.) The light of saving knowledge.

(2.) Of true peace and joy by the forgiveness of sin.

(3.) Of holiness. "A new heart," &c. Become a child of light, &c.

2. *The source of the blessing is Christ.* Christ is appointed to this. It is his work, &c. In the days of his flesh, &c. To many here. Whosoever cometh, &c.

3. *The manner of its bestowment.* "Shall give." All his blessings are gifts. Free, rich, meritless, suit all cases, &c.

APPLICATION.

1. *We call upon the sinner to awake.* Now; in earnest.

2. *Warn the Christian against lethargy.* "Let us not sleep as do others," &c

ON STRIVING WITH GOD.

"Wo unto him that striveth with his Maker."
—Isaiah xlv. 9.

The sinner is variously represented in the writings of this holy book. The idea of rebellion is one of frequent recurrence. A sinner rebels against God's authority and dominion. The sinner is frequently styled an enemy, and this is evident both from his heart, and tongue, and life. The heart is in a state of enmity, &c.—the tongue impiously exclaiming, "Depart from us, for we desire not," &c., and wicked works distinguish the ungodly man. Very frequently the sinner is described as fighting against God, or contending with him, and this is the idea of the text, "Wo unto him," &c. Let us notice,

I. The manifestation of this strife.
II. The evils of such a course.
III. The final results.

I. The manifestation of this strife. To strive is to oppose, and in a variety of ways sinners exhibit opposition to God. There is,

1. *The unblushing opposition of infidelity.* Nothing can exhibit more daring wickedness than infidelity—denying God. Excluding his existence or government from his own world. To say there is no God! or to affect to say so, or to reduce him to an indifferent spectator of his works and creatures. In connection with infidelity there is the rejection of the scriptures, and boasting of the sufficiency of nature to teach us virtue and religion. What part of nature? Or what can we know of moral right, &c.—of evil? &c. Apply this to truth, to honesty—to prayer, &c. It is all mockery, you might as soon expect a child to learn to speak by hearing the winds. No! the rejecter of the Bible will not find another oracle of truth in the universe. How devoted this class of individuals are in prosecuting their work! How eager to dissuade others from their adherence to the Christian religion!

2. *The fearless transgressions of the bold and daring in iniquity.* Those who drink in iniquity as an ox, &c. Who lay aside all the restrictions of conscience and the respect of the virtuous around them. Who give themselves up to every evil way and work. Whose language is filthy and brutal. Who have no fear, nor shame, nor sense of their responsibility, and who are in fact demonized by habitual sins.

3. *Those who resist the providential dealings and interpositions of God for their salvation.* Providence subserves the designs of grace. The movements of the divine government are often full of instruction—often act as warnings and beacons. Adversity, sickness, and bereavements are often employed to lead to thought and consideration, to reflection, repentance, and personal religion. The resistance of these is striving against God. If these do not soften they harden. Some metals melt while others harden in the furnace. God hedges up the way of some, that in their afflictions they may seek him; if they do not, they must break through and fight against him.

4. *Those who will not yield to the overtures of the gospel.* The gospel proclaims men enemies, and seeks their return to friendship; traitors, &c.; wanderers, &c.; and urges, "Be ye reconciled to God." "Agree," &c. "Be at peace," &c. The gospel proclaims an amnesty; but of course it is on the principle of throwing down their weapons and ceasing to strive and rebel. Whoso persists in unbelief strives against God—yea, against the riches of his grace.

II. The evils of such a course.

1. *It is full of infatuation.* It cannot be vindicated upon the principle of reason or propriety. It is evidently a sign of the mind being blinded by the wicked one. Either the faculties of the understanding and judgment are in entire darkness, or they are wofully perverted. There cannot be greater madness or more complete folly than to strive against God.

2. *It is fraught with evils to our own souls.* It acts negatively in excluding the greatest blessings God has to bestow. "Your sins have withholden good things," &c. It excludes the divine favor, peace of conscience, and a hope of immortality. It deprives us of all the rich communications of heaven. Besides, it acts positively to our injury. It degrades the mind, it hardens the heart, it sears the conscience, it fills with fear. "The wicked flee," &c. It converts conscience into a gnawing worm. It often makes life insupportable, and drives to delirium or to despair.

3. *It is full of ingratitude.* Look at the child that despises and treats irreverently his parent. How you feel indignation to

rise, &c. That child is the sinner who strives against his Maker. Look at that befriended individual who calumniates and seeks the ruin of his patron and benefactor —conspires against his property and life. Look at that ransomed slave who unites with the bloodthirsty enemies of his benefactor, &c. But all figures must fail in the illustration. But in reference to striving against God, notice,

III. ITS FINAL RESULTS.

1. *We cannot injure Deity.* We might injure a potsherd like ourselves. Even a weak man may injure a powerful one. But God is too high for the arrows of the sinner's rebellion. We cannot baffle, or confuse, or disturb his felicity. Neither,

2. *Can we benefit ourselves.* Who hath hardened himself against the Lord and prospered? Who indeed? Is there any case on record? The man who strives against God converts the pure stream into a deadly current, the wholesome air into a pestilent atmosphere, and all the enjoyments of life into sources of wretchedness and misery. It blights all the soul's prospects of felicity forever. Nor can we,

3. *Escape the triumphs of the divine judgments over us.* One must prevail. We cannot; then God will; and his prevailing will be our wo. "Wo unto him," &c. The vengeance of God is the direst wo, and it must be endured; the wo of his displeased and incensed countenance; the wo of his righteous sentence; wo of his fiery indignation which shall consume the adversaries; wo of everlasting misery as the desert of iniquity; wo unto him—to each and all such. To the beggar and the monarch; to the great and the small; to the learned and the ignorant; to the young and the old; to all and every one.

APPLICATION.

Probably there are four descriptions of character here.

1. *The strivers against God, who are indifferent, perhaps reckless.* Oh think and stop in your career, &c.

2. *Those who occasionally relent and hesitate.* Allow those good emotions to prevail. They are heaven's distilling dews. "Grieve not the Spirit of God," &c.

3. *Those who are suing for mercy.* Oh now exclaim, "I yield, I yield, I can hold out no more," &c.

4. *To the children of God.* Rejoice in your religious experience, and labor for the weal of others. Feel for others,

" Oh tell to all the world around
  What a dear Saviour you have found."

REFUGE OF LIES.

" And the hail shall sweep away the refuge of lies."—ISAIAH xxviii. 17.

NUMEROUS are the stratagems of Satan to ruin souls. In some he effects this by hurrying them on in the broad way of open transgression; in others by rendering them the victims of some peculiar constitutional sin; as pride, cruelty, oppression, avarice, &c.; in others by inciting a spirit of disbelief to the truth. "The fool hath said in his heart, There is no God." In others by inducing inattention to the things of the soul. But our text leads us to contemplate the false refuges to which he causes others to betake themselves. Observe, sinners often feel the necessity of a refuge; they frequently betake themselves to refuges of lies; such refuges will be ultimately swept away.

I. SINNERS OFTEN FEEL THE NECESSITY OF A REFUGE. This arises sometimes from,

1. *An internal sense of guilt.* Unless in cases of utter obduracy, transgression and remorse are ever wedded together. Even Pagans have felt these workings of conscience, these pangs of guilty torture. Under these, men sigh for peace, long for rest, and earnestly desire a refuge.

2. *From the calamitous events of life.* Sudden adversity, domestic bereavements, visiting the open grave of some friend; bodily indisposition, mental disquietude, &c.

3. *From the supposed nearness of death.* How men, who mock at religion in health, quail at the approach of death! How Voltaire trembled in a storm, how anxious then to have deliverance, to obtain a refuge!

4. *Under the alarming influences of the preached word.* When the truth has flashed across the mind and startled the conscience. Thus Felix, and thus thousands. How lamentable that these impressions and convictions are often so fleeting, so evanescent; but still more so when they flee to sources of false security. Notice then,

II. SINNERS FREQUENTLY BETAKE THEMSELVES TO REFUGES OF LIES. Of these notice,

1. *Partial reformation of life.* Giving up the grosser sins of which they have been guilty : intemperance, avarice, profanity, wrath, injustice, fraud, &c. Now the amputation of a member, when the whole body is diseased, is fruitless.

2. *A general regard to Christian morality.* To the outward acts of obedience. If parents, parental regard to their children ; if children, filial obedience ; discharge of the social duties, general uprightness, external decorum, propriety of speech, a rigid regard to truth, all of which are good in their legitimate sphere and extent.

3. *An outward profession of religion.* Punctual regard to public worship, a proper regard to ordinances, a name among the people of God, zeal against infidelity and rreligion. Then we may notice,

4. *A prominent and public sectarian spirit.* Rigid adherence to party, and sect, and creed ; violent anathematizing all others ; great ardor in the public events of the church to which they belong. " Come, see my zeal," &c.

5. *Distinguished generosity and charity.* Liberality to the poor, works of beneficence, enrolled among the compassionate and benevolent. " Give their goods to feed the poor," &c. Now all these are often only refuges of lies ; all these may engage a man's anxious attention, and the root of the matter have no place in his heart. We may add,

6. *A general reliance on the mercy of God.* A kind of self-confident persuasion that God is good, that he will not punish, an indefinite resting on his clemency, forgetting his righteousness, purity, truth, &c.

III. SUCH REFUGES WILL BE ULTIMATELY SWEPT AWAY. They will be so,

1. *In a dying hour.* Then the mental vision often becomes peculiarly acute, the moral sense keen and distinct, and the honesty of the Spirit throws off the tinsel mask, which is now manifestly worse than useless. How poor and worthless is self-righteousness, in all its possible extent, to a spirit just stepping into the presence of the holy God ! A queen of England, although professing to be " defender of the faith," and having bishops at her control, felt this, and died in circumstances of unutterable alarm.

2. *In the morning of the resurrection.* Then all classes and distinctions will be reduced to two. None but the righteous will have a part in the first resurrection.

Others will rise with shame, confusion, and horror, to everlasting contempt.

3. *In the decisions of judgment.* God will judge all men in righteousness. The wicked and the righteous will be separated, as a man separateth the sheep from the goats ; no pretence will avail, no disguise, no plea, no stratagem, no importunity, no effort to flee, &c. All refuges of lies will be swept away.

APPLICATION.

1. Warn against these destructive schemes and wiles of Satan.

2. Exhibit the one only refuge, Jesus Christ, who delivers from the wrath to come.

3. Urge instant faith in him; " Count all things but loss," &c. All who believe in him are secure for both worlds ; to this refuge repair every one, earnestly, and now.

————

GOD'S SOLICITUDES FOR MANKIND.

" Oh that there were such an heart in them, that they would fear me, and keep all my commandments always, that it might be well with them, and with their children forever."—DEUTERONOMY v. 29.

OUR text refers to God, and his ancient people Israel. At the time of the giving of the law, under the influence of fear, and no doubt in the full sincerity of their hearts, they had said to Moses, " Speak thou unto us all the words that the Lord our God shall speak unto thee, and we will hear it and do it." God approved of their holy determination, but knowing the deceitfulness of the heart, he says, " Oh that there were such an heart in them," &c. Jehovah had the concern for Israel he has for you, he desires you to possess sincere and unfeigned piety, that religion, which will benefit you forever, and be a blessing to your posterity after you. We shall ground several propositions upon the text.

I. TRUE RELIGION IS INSEPARABLY CONNECTED WITH A PECULIAR STATE OF HEART. " Oh that there were such an heart," &c. The state of the heart naturally is evil ; an evil root, an evil fountain. It is described as a heart of stone ; cold, hard, unyielding, deceitful, &c. ; it is described as proud, self-willed, and carnal. Now, with this state of heart there can be no piety. This heart, therefore, must be renovated, so as to become a new heart, flesh instead of stone, spiritual instead of carnal, contrite instead of callous, lowly instead of proud; in one word, it must be renewed and made spiritual, cleansed, &c. "Old things," &c. This is a very important consideration, the basis of acceptable religion. "My son, give me thy heart," &c.

II. A RIGHT STATE OF HEART WILL BE CONNECTED WITH THE FEAR OF GOD. Many dare God, insult, blaspheme, &c.; many never think of God, &c.; many regard him with horrific dread. All these states of mind are equally contrary to religion. A right state of heart will produce fear, reverential fear, holy fear, filial fear. "The fear of God" is often used for the whole of religion. His perfections, works, glory, judgments, should all inspire this fear.

III. A RENEWED HEART WILL BE EVINCED BY EVANGELICAL OBEDIENCE. Not will-service, not self-righteousness, not meritorious obedience, but evangelical obedience, as the fruit of a right state of mind, the effect of faith, the obedience of love. Now this evangelical obedience should be evinced in two ways.

1. *By its universality.* "All my commandments." They are all right, wise, good; all of them are important and necessary; ye cannot be right-minded and wish to choose, &c. "Ye are my friends if ye do whatsoever," &c.

2. *By its perpetuity.* "Always." Most men do what is right occasionally, but our obedience must be constant. "Always,— in season and out of season, in prosperity and adversity, under reproach, persecution," &c.; at all rates and hazards, "Be faithful unto death," &c.

IV. TRUE RELIGION IS ESSENTIALLY CONNECTED WITH OUR WELL-BEING. "That it might," &c. Now this is true,

1. *As to our present well-being.* It is well for the body and the soul, for the mind and the heart. It exalts—improves—blesses—comforts—saves, &c.

2. *As to our future well-being.* It shall be well with the righteous, "They shall be mine," &c. They are heirs of glory. "Shall see the King in his beauty," &c.; they shall die in peace, and dwell with God forever. "When flesh and heart fail," &c.

V. JEHOVAH IS SINCERELY CONCERNED THAT THIS RELIGION SHOULD BE OUR INDIVIDUAL PORTION. Hence his declarations—

provisions—invitations—forbearance, &c. His nature disposes him to this, his glory also.

APPLICATION.

1. *Learn the true characteristics of acceptable religion.* Renewed heart, fear, and evangelical obedience.

2. *Learn the desirableness of true piety.* Our welfare, &c.

3. *The influence of true piety on our posterity, &c.*

4. *The inexcusableness of those who are irreligious, &c.* "Oh that," &c.

THE PRIDE AND OBSTINACY OF THE SINNER.

"The wicked, through the pride of his countenance, will not seek after God."—PSALM x. 4.

Two points in theology we deem of essential importance; they cannot be too highly estimated, too seriously pondered, or too frequently considered. The first is this, all good is from God; he is the one source of light, and purity, and bliss. Whatever excellency or enjoyment pertains to men, God is the author, and the whole glory belongs to his name. The second is, that the evil and misery of man are of himself, and that all the blame of his wretchedness and ruin is his own. This is often exhibited to us in the scriptures, &c. Two or three passages shall suffice. "I have called," &c. "Ye will not," &c. "Whatsoever a man soweth," &c. And also the text. The text contains a character to be defined—a line of conduct to be explained—and the cause which is assigned for that conduct. The text contains,

I. A CHARACTER TO BE DEFINED. "The wicked." We are too apt to apply the term to the notorious—to the profligate, &c. There is one view I wish to impress upon you, that the absence of real piety involves the charge of wickedness. We are not to judge by the opinions of men, by human laws, but by the scriptures of divine truth. I ask not the magistrate of the district—I ask not the persons you travel with—I ask not your neighbors, or friends, or family; but I inquire of the oracles of eternal truth. Do you believe in the Lord Jesus Christ? Do you enjoy and obey the influences of the Spirit? Do you love God supremely?

Are you spiritually minded ? Do you seek first and chiefly the kingdom of God, &c. ? Are you actuated by the holy principles of the gospel ? If not, however intellectual, you do not know God ; or moral, you do not serve him ; or amiable, you have not his mind ; or religious, yet you have not the Spirit of Christ Jesus ; unless the heart has been renewed, and the mind of the Saviour imparted, we belong to the class described in the scripture as being wicked. How many then of this character are now before God in this assembly ? Do I belong to it, or have I been saved from it ? Observe in the text,

II. A LINE OF CONDUCT WHICH MUST BE EXPLAINED. "Will not seek after God." Let some truths premise our remarks here. Men are alienated from God by sin. All men have forsaken him. God is willing to be sought by his wandering children. He desires their return ; he employs means for it ; many by these means have returned and sought God, and obtained mercy. But the wicked will not seek, &c.

1. *They will not seek after the knowledge of God.* "Some men," &c. All other knowledge they admire, extol, &c. They would be ashamed to be ignorant of letters —of general science—of literature, &c. But they know not God, &c. ; neither will they seek in the volume of eternal truth to attain this knowledge. No time, or talent, or opportunity, given to this. Created things, but not the Creator. Sublunary, but not the immortal. Often frivolous, &c., but not the supreme good.

2. *They will not seek after reconciliation with God.* They have rebelled, transgressed, &c. God is displeased with their conduct—they are under sentence of wrath, yet they act and live as though they were secure. No sincere anxiety to enjoy the favor of God.

3. *They will not seek conformity to God's likeness.* Most men desire to resemble some one or some class. The ambitious, the rich, the influential ; but they care not to resemble the divine holiness ; aim not at attaining the image of God. They do not love or admire spiritual purity, therefore will not seek to possess it.

4. *They do not seek after fellowship with God.* "God is not in all their thoughts." They desire not communion with God either in public or private ; they say, "Depart from us, we desire not the knowledge of thy

ways." They seek this in reference to kindred spirits ; they commune with nature and art, but not with God. Let us notice,

III. THE CAUSE OF THIS PROCEDURE WHICH THE TEXT ASSIGNS. "Pride." Undue esteem of self. Arrogant estimation of their own powers, &c.

1. *Pride hates the view which the scriptures give of human nature.* It will not have man dethroned. Will not allow his total depravity—his helplessness—misery, desert, &c.

2. *Pride approves not of the divine supremacy.* Each carnal heart would rule —hold the reins—sway the sceptre. Likes not God's control. Approves not being subordinate in every thing to Deity.

3. *Pride often rejects the way of salvation.* As a free gift, all of grace. It says, Let me do something—excel and win it— strive and conquer for it—suffer and earn it—work and pray for it.

4. *Pride objects to the means connected with salvation.* Contrition, confession, abasement, restitution, lowliness, &c., of heart, confession of Christ before men.

5. *Pride dislikes the universality of salvation.* Murmurs that the vilest, &c., should be equally welcome ; or the poorest—or the most illiterate. It would have a dispensation to itself—a respectable religion, a peculiar kind of service, not vulgar, &c.

APPLICATION.

1. *Have you sought after God?* In truth. Earnestly and prayerfully.

2. *Or are you indifferent?* What is the cause, &c. Is it pride ? Examine, be particular, faithful, minute, &c.

3. *The threats to the proud are fearful.* Publicly disgraced, brought low, &c. ; covered with shame, &c. No distinction in the great day, either of rank, or talent, &c.

4. *All are now invited to seek after God.* "Let the wicked forsake his way," &c.

GOD'S GRACIOUS INVITATION TO SINNERS.

"Come now, and let us reason together, saith the Lord: though your sins be as scarlet, they shall be as white as snow ; though they be red like crimson, they shall be as wool."—ISAIAH i. 18.

IT is scarcely possible to conceive of a more interesting and delightful exhibition of the love and mercy of God, than is presented to us in these words ; unless they had been found in the volume of eternal truth, we might justly have doubted their veracity. For the speaker in the text is Jehovah, a Being infinitely happy and glorious in himself, whose felicity and dignity cannot be enlarged or diminished. He needs not, on his own account, the return of the sinner to himself ; besides, he is the offended party. It is his authority which nas been slighted. His laws violated—his goodness abused—his holy image effaced. How marvellous, then, that he should stoop to ask reconciliation with poor wretched man, the rebel and traitor against heaven ! Yet so it is. " Come now, and let us reason together," &c. Notice,

I. THE CHARACTERS ADDRESSED. Now the characters are not such as excel in moral excellency, but the reverse, the debased, the vilest and most degraded of sinners, represented, in their iniquities, as being like unto scarlet or crimson. How apt are we to think that such are too low to be raised up, too defiled to be made clean, too far alienated to be reclaimed ! Whatever we may think, these are the invited in our text, and these are the characters we are now to contemplate. Who then are included in the description ; their sins being as scarlet, &c. Now it includes,

1. *Those whose sins are glaring and manifest.* There is much invisible evil in existence. Much hidden in the deep recesses of the soul. Much that the eye of man or angel never sees. There may be hidden thoughts of impiety, and blasphemy, and infidelity, and anger, and malice. But externa circumstances act in the moral world as the shore to the ocean, limiting and bounding its waters. Now a great many of the ungodly are thus restrained, and it is well for society and the church of Christ that it is so. But we find numbers who have gone beyond this boundary, who are not ashamed of their iniquities. Who countenance wickedness in public places and bear the mark of the beast in their foreheads. Many revel in iniquity. Drink it in as the ox drinketh water. Loudly blaspheme. Openly debase themselves, and glory in their shame. The sins of such are as scarlet or as crimson.

2. *It will apply to those whose iniquities are especially productive of much evil and misery.* To those who are ring-leaders in sin ; those who constrain others to do wickedly ;

those who are champions of vice ; ridiculers of piety, and who labor to throng the road to hell with their fellow-sinners ; and here let me refer to those who are heads of families. Your children and domestics look up to you ; they will extensively be, what you appear to be. You create the deadly atmosphere they breathe, you poison the waters they drink. What cruelty such display to their families ! You swearing, you drunken heads of families, you who have ruined your children.

3. *It will apply to those who have sinned against great privileges and mercies.* Now it cannot be doubted that many who are in a condition of darkness would have been otherwise, had they possessed the privileges which others have enjoyed. Thus Christ said, " Wo unto thee, Chorazin ! Wo unto thee, Bethsaida," &c. As it is with nations and cities, so it is with individuals. How many have had privileges and mercies of a high character ! I place among these pious parents. You had their example, their prayers, their best counsels, their dying entreaties. I place religious society. You have moved in a circle favorable to piety ; you have seen religion embodied, &c. A faithful ministry. You have had the gospel in purity, plainness, and affection. I place also striking providences. God has met you in affliction, in bereavements, &c. What did you say, resolve, and vow before God ? And what have you done ? Are you not ingrates, promise-breakers, mockers of God ?

4. *It will apply to backsliders.* Such as have once been enrolled in Christ's army, but who have deserted and gone over to the camp of the devil. Who once prayed, but now have refrained, &c. What an awful state ! What grief you have caused to the church ! How you have dishonored Christianity, and wounded the Saviour in the house of his friends ! How infidels have scoffed ! How the world has been hardened ! Poor miserable apostate ! are not thy sins " as scarlet, yea, as crimson," &c.

5. *It will apply to aged transgressors.* Those who have grown gray-headed in the service of sin. Old age is unnerving that arm, which has ever been lifted up against God. Oh think of the course you have pursued ! Think how countless your sins ! Think how unnumbered your provocations ; and yet you are adding to the dye and making it deeper and deeper. What hard-

ness of heart ! What callousness of spirit ! What thoughtlessness of soul ! " Your sins are as scarlet," &c. Observe then,

II. THE INVITATION JEHOVAH PRESENTS. "Come and let us reason," &c. He wishes to have your state and condition tested by reason. He gives you the opportunity of self-defence ; he is willing to hear all your motives, and arguments, &c. Now will you come to God, and reason with him ? What will you say ?

1. *You cannot plead ignorance.* You have been conscious of the evil of your ways. Reason, conscience, scripture, condemn you. You have known better ; your eyes have been open. You have seen the evil, and yet have chosen it.

2. *You cannot plead necessity.* The Jews of old said, they were sold to do evil ; that is, they could not avoid it. Now, if any of you imagine this, it is the grossest self-deception ; it cannot be the will of God that you should do evil. This is horrid and impious indeed. You have sinned freely, it has been your own act and choice.

3. *You must plead guilty.* And in doing so you must cast yourselves upon the mercy of God. If guilty, and if all the evil and blame is with you, then God must be clear, and you condemned. What then must be the result, must sentence go forth ? Not if you will,

4. *Plead the merits of Christ.* Here is the sacrifice for sin. Here your hope, your plea.

" 'Tis just the sentence should take place—
'Tis just, but oh ! thy Son has died."

Now in availing yourself of this plea, all that God requires is repentance and faith. Confess and forsake sin, and believe on the Lord Jesus Christ. If you do this, then notice,

III. THE GRACIOUS PROMISE GIVEN. " Though your sins be as scarlet," &c.

1. *All your sins shall be blotted out.* Every one both of omission and commission. All your sins of heart, lip, and life ; from the first to the last. Blotted out as a cloud.

2. *You shall stand accepted in Christ.* He shall behold you in Christ as righteous. Look at the hue and the dye of the guilty sinner ; when accepted look again. Not one mark, not one spot, not one charge.

3. *By sanctifying grace you shall be made fit for glory.* He will give you a new na-

ture, and make you really and perfectly holy. " Without spot or wrinkle," &c. And this shall be followed,

4. *By the gift of eternal life.* Rom. vi. 23 ; 1 John v. 11.

APPLICATION.

1. *Let me urge you all to come and reason with God, and do it now.* There is salvation for every one.

2. *If you will not come, you will be without excuse.*

3. *You must come to him in death and judgment.*

TERMS OF DISCIPLESHIP.

" Then said Jesus unto his disciples, If any man will come after me, let him deny himself, and take up his cross, and follow me."—MATTHEW xvi. 24.

To perfectly holy beings it must be a source of indescribable pleasure to obey God. The faculties and powers of such intelligences only find a proper sphere of exercise in the divine service. To hearken to God, to do with the most fervent zeal his will, is the highest enjoyment of which they are capable. Now, the very reverse of this is true when applied to depraved, polluted creatures. Sin, then, is the end of their actions, and in that they have carnal delight and pleasure. Sin in such cases is natural, even as the stream must be foul where the fountain is corrupt— the fruit worthless, when the tree is evil. Religion, therefore, does violence to the carnal mind ; self must be crucified ; and, from the necessity of the case, no man can be a disciple of Jesus unless he deny himself, &c. Observe the course prescribed ; the advantage with which it is connected ; and the means of its exemplification. Notice,

I. THE COURSE PRESCRIBED. Three things are noted by the Redeemer :—

1. *Self-denial.* " Let him deny himself." Self is often ignorant, presumptuous, confident, wayward, &c. Self seeks gratification, ease, and exaltation. Now, all these are the fruit of sin, and contrary to God and holiness. There cannot be religion with self-satisfaction—with self-righteousness—with self-pleasing. Just as in taking the nauseating draught, violence is done to the taste—or in the painful am-

putation of a member, violence is done to the feelings ; so, in serving God, the old man, the flesh must be crucified ; self must be subverted ; and the will of God become the supreme law of the mind.

2. *Reproach and suffering.* " Let him take up his cross." The cross is the symbol of ignominy and pain, and there can be no genuine evidence of piety without bearing the cross. This cross is often composed of the envy and reproaches of the wicked —the false accusations and persecutions of those who hate the Redeemer and his holy cause ; and so long as the world is under the power of Satan, it will harass, defame, and, if possible, injure the followers of Jesus. This Christ expressly stated to his disciples ; and the experience of all true Christians establishes that scriptural statement, " That it is through much tribulation," &c.

3. *Imitation of the Saviour.* " And follow me." Jesus is the example of his people. " He hath left us an example," &c. " My sheep hear my voice." We must follow him in a conscientious regard to the ordinances and commandments of God ; in a public avowal of holiness to the world ; in the hallowed exercises of pure devotion ; in the discharge of the practical duties of the Christian life ; in a life of continued activity and benevolence ; in patient resignation under suffering. Christ must be set before us. " Looking unto Jesus," &c. Notice,

II. THE ADVANTAGES WITH WHICH THIS COURSE IS CONNECTED.

1. *A dignified union to Christ and his people.* By coming out from the world, Christ will receive us. He will admit us to enjoy union and fellowship with him ; have a place in his spiritual family ; be numbered among his disciples ; have a relationship to Christ more exalted than that of the highest angel in heaven.

2. *A saving interest in his favor and love.* He will grant us the full and free remission of all sin ; impart the spirit of adoption ; give us internal tokens of his approbation ; " Manifest himself," &c. ; see John xiv. 23, xv. 1, &c.

3. *A constant supply of his all-sufficient grace.* Without this the Christian's life could not be sustained. His grace alone is sufficient for us ; this he will freely and abundantly pour out. His love to us, his engagements, the experience of all saints,

confirm this. He desires to bestow it in all its refreshing plenitude.

4. *A participation of his glory forever.* " If we suffer with him, we shall also be glorified with him." Observe Christ's express declaration, " Whosoever, therefore, shall confess me," &c., Matt. x. 32. Hear his sacerdotal prayer, " Father, I will that they also whom thou hast given," &c. John xvii. 24 ; Rev. iii. 5, 21. Now, a faithful regard to the course prescribed will eventually terminate in glory, immortality, and eternal life. We inquire, then, in reference to this course,

III. THE MEANS OF ITS EXEMPLIFICATION. How shall we deny ourselves ?

1. *By obtaining a nature suited to the work.* The heart must be renewed ; new spirit imparted, &c. By faith in Christ Jesus we become the sons of God, and partakers of the divine and holy nature.

2. *By seeking the aids of the Holy Spirit.* The Spirit will enable us to crucify the flesh, to forsake evil, to imitate Christ. He will guide, sanctify, establish, keep.

3. *By the continued exercise of faith.* " The just shall live by faith," &c. I am crucified with Christ, &c. By faith the Old Testament heroes conflicted and overcame.

4. *By having a single eye to the divine glory.* God will then honor, and support, and bless us ; fulfil all his word, &c., guide by his counsel, &c.

APPLICATION.

1. Here is encouragement for the Christian.

2. Hope for the penitential inquirer.

3. And admonitory warning for the formal.

MAINTENANCE OF THE CHRISTIAN PROFESSION.

" Let us hold fast the profession of our faith."—
HEBREWS x. 23.

THE apostle, in the previous verses, has been exhibiting Jesus Christ in his sacerdotal character. He represents the church as the house of God, over which Jesus is the great High Priest. He exhorts believers to an experimental acquaintance with his saving benefits, " Let us draw near," &c. He then enforces the importance of

Christian stability, "Let us hold fast," &c. Consider,

I. WHAT THE CHRISTIAN PROFESSION INVOLVES. It involves,

1. *A saving knowledge of Christ.* Ignorance of Christ unfits for a profession. The gospel was written, and is preached, that men may know Jesus Christ. "This is life eternal," &c. "I count all things but loss for the excellency of the knowledge of Christ Jesus our Lord." We would see Jesus, is the inquiry; and then it should be, We have found him, &c. Jesus Christ in you, the hope of glory.

2. *It involves trust and confidence in Christ.* "Profession of our faith." Faith receives Christ—builds on Christ—unites us to Christ—and makes Christ all our own. Faith is the vital act of the soul, by which we commit all our concerns into his hands; expect from him and through him every blessing here; and finally, eternal life.

3. *It involves a public attestation of our approbation of Christ.* To profess, is to show forth—to exhibit—to let others see and know that we are the Lord's. It is to take his name as our badge—belong avowedly to his cause; to wear the livery of Christ; to speak the words of Christ; to show the spirit of Christ; to seek the glory of Christ; to be his witnesses—his confessors; to go forth without the camp; an opposite course to his enemies, and quite distinct from the formal and indifferent.

4. *It involves obedience to his ordinances and commands.* "My sheep hear my voice, and follow me." "If ye love me, keep my commandments." The promise is, that he will put his law into our hearts, and that we shall walk in his statutes and ordinances to do them. This is not the obedience of fear, or of toil, but of love and a willing mind. "The love of Christ constraineth us." Now this profession Christ demands, if a man will be his disciple, that he should take up his cross and follow him. He said, "Whosoever is ashamed of me, I will be ashamed of him," &c.

II. BY WHAT IS A CHRISTIAN PROFESSION OPPOSED? This opposition is implied, not expressed; but the exhortation is pointless without this. Now, this profession,

1. *Will be opposed by our adversary, Satan.* "Simon, Simon, Satan desires to have thee," &c. "Your adversary, the devil, goeth about seeking whom he may devour." His wiles—darts, &c.

2. *An ungodly world will oppose this profession.* "Marvel not that I said unto you, that the world will hate you." Christians have been hated, and persecuted, and reviled, and mocked, and put to death in all ages. If ye were of the world it would love you, but it now hates you; often worldly friends and relatives; a man's foes are often those of his own household.

3. *The remains of evil within us will oppose this profession.* An indolent heart; self-love; pride; ease; the flesh will war against the spirit; spirit of discontent, &c. But,

III. HOW IS THE CHRISTIAN PROFESSION TO BE MAINTAINED?

1. *By holding fast to the sanctifying word of truth.* "I have no greater joy than that my children walk in the truth." "Sell it not." "Let the word of Christ dwell in you."

2. *Let us hold fast to the means of grace;* see verse 25. God has appointed the church to be a social compact—to form a united bulwark to the enemy. In the means of grace, we meet with God and take courage. Here we are refreshed for our journey; here we brighten our armor; here we stand on the mountain-top, and get a glimpse of the land which is afar off; here we drink of the brook by the way, and lift up our head.

3. *Let us hold fast to the person and work of the Saviour.* "He exhorted them all that with purpose of heart they would cleave unto the Lord"—adhere to him. "Except ye abide in me, and I in you," &c. Christ is our life. We walk in him, and derive all our grace, &c., from him. We must be nothing, and Christ Jesus every thing. Christ the Alpha, and the all in all; Christ our foundation—way—dress—food—pearl —joy—song—glory, &c. In salvation it must ever be, "None but Christ; none but Christ!"

4. *Let us hold fast to believing prayer.* Be instant in prayer, praying with all prayer. "Pray in faith, nothing doubting." Pray in secret. "Pray always," &c. Notice,

IV. THE IMPORTANCE OF CARRYING OUT BOTH THE LETTER AND THE SPIRIT OF THE TEXT.

1. *It is very important to those who are without.* "The world." If we give up our profession infidels and blasphemers will rejoice, worldlings will be hardened, form-

alists satisfied, inquirers discouraged. The mischief may be everlasting.

2. *It is important to our fellow-Christians.* How distressing to see those who walked with Christ turn aside—to see the soldiers of Christ desert! It tends to damp the zeal of the friends of Zion. How painful for the apostle to say, "Demas has forsaken me," &c.; how distressing to Moses to see the thousands of Israel sinning and perishing in the desert! But,

3. *It is all-important to ourselves.* If we go back, Christ's soul will have no pleasure in us. If, after we have put our hands to the gospel plough, we look back, we become unfit for the kingdom. Give up the profession of faith, and hope goes, peace goes, Christ goes, and heaven goes; for only he who endures to the end shall be saved.

APPLICATION.

1. *For the maintenance of this profession there is ample provision made.* Jesus says, "My grace is sufficient for thee."

2. *Remember your state before you professed the Saviour.* At that time when you were without Christ, and without hope, &c.

3. *Think of your enjoyments in religion.* Of the pleasures you now possess, &c.

4. *Look to the end.* The goal—the crown—the kingdom. Life is fast ebbing, time is receding, eternity approaching. Oh! then, hold fast.

5. *Who will resolve to profess Jesus now?* You half-hearted, you undecided, you seekers after bliss, now determine.

ENCOURAGEMENT TO THE TEMPTED.

"There hath no temptation taken you but such as is common to man; but God is faithful, who will not suffer you to be tempted above that ye are able: but will with the temptation also make a way to escape, that ye may be able to bear it." —1 CORINTHIANS x. 13.

IN this chapter the apostle is referring to several events in the history of the Israelites; and especially to the evils into which they fell. He then notes that these things were written for our admonition, &c., see verse 11. He then draws this important practical inference, "Wherefore," &c., ver. 12. Then he speaks of the temptations to which they might be liable, and assures them, "There hath no temptation," &c. Observe,

I. WHAT IS SAID CONCERNING THE TEMPTATIONS OF THE BELIEVER. It is clearly intimated,

1. *That believers must have temptations.* Now the term signifies to try, and often refers to the assaults of our enemy, the devil. The snares by which he endeavors to destroy the soul. It signifies also the opposition or enticements of evil men, and it includes the trials into which God may bring his people. In the text it must be confined to the first two of these, viz. the evils to which we may be exposed from Satan, and an evil world. Now these will ever be opposed to the happiness and holiness of the people of God. It is Satan's nature to deceive and destroy. "In the world," &c. "Marvel not," &c. Exemption is not to be expected, indeed, is not desirable. "Count it all joy," &c. James i. 2, &c. Indeed, without these we cannot be conformed to Christ. We must share in his sufferings, if we would participate in his glory. "Whosoever overcometh," &c. Now this implies temptation and opposition.

2. *It is affirmed that our temptations shall not be uncommon.* "There hath no temptation," &c. Now this is a great mercy. This ought greatly to cheer us. We shall only drink of the common cup. Have to do with the common evils, &c. We are apt to imagine our condition worse than that of others. There never was but one who could truly say, "There is no sorrow like unto my sorrow." Let me hear your complaints, in reference to your trials and temptations, which of them is uncommon.

(1.) Are you tempted to horrid and gross evils? Think of Job, who was tempted to curse God and die; think of Jesus, who was tempted to idolatry—to the worship of the devil.

(2.) Are you tempted to despond through a sense of your unworthiness,—see Abraham, the friend of God, yet he calls himself dust and ashes. Job exclaims, "Behold I am vile," &c. Isaiah, "Wo is me." Peter said, "Depart from me," &c.

(3.) Are you tempted that your trials are severe and greater than others? Look at Jacob, Aaron, David, Job, the first Christians.

(4.) Are you tempted to doubt the efficiency of prayer? Think of Paul, who prayed thrice, &c. Remember the importunate widow. Perhaps you merely wished. God desired to excite you to holy ardor, &c.

(5.) Are you tempted that God will forsake and leave you ? See the case of Job, xxiii. 1–10. See Asaph, Psalm lxxvii. 7, &c. Observe,

II. WHAT IS SAID CONCERNING THE FAITHFULNESS OF GOD TO HIS TEMPTED PEOPLE. "God is faithful." His truth and will are not affected. " I am the Lord, and change not." He is of one mind, &c. All the saints of past generations exclaim, " O Lord God, faithful and true !" One act of unfaithfulness would shake the confidence of all the saints and angels in heaven. He cannot be otherwise. Now the faithfulness of God will be seen in his goodness to his tempted people, and that in three respects.

1. *Temptation shall always be proportionate to your strength.* " Who will not suffer you to be," &c. He knows your frame, &c. He remembers your state. He watches the fire and the floods. He apportions the medicine, &c. What consolation there is in this !

2. *He will ever provide a door of deliverance.* " Also make a way of escape," he did so to Abraham, in the ram caught. Never allow us to be shut up in temptation. See the case of the Israelites on their way to the Red Sea, when he divided the waters. When there is no other, there is always a way upwards. "Call upon me," &c. Psalm cvii. 11.

3. *Until his people are delivered, they shall have strength to be able to bear it.* He will uphold and strengthen, as he did Paul. '' My grace is sufficient," &c.

APPLICATION.

Let the Christian remember,

1. *Life is a state of trial, and we shall have grace sufficient for it.*

2. *Eternity a state of reward, and glory will amply compensate for the sorrows of life.*

3. *Let not temptations drive you from Christ, or produce apathy and carelessness as to your spiritual state.*

BELIEVERS, STRANGERS, AND SOJOURNERS.

(ON THE LAST EVENING OF THE YEAR.)

"For we are strangers before thee, and sojourners, as were all our fathers; our days on the earth are as a shadow, and there is none abiding."
–1 CHRONICLES xxix. 15.

OUR text is the declaration of David, and is found among his last words. He lived to a good old age, therefore his testimony is the language of experience ; he was a man both of knowledge and wisdom, therefore this saying should be treasured up Besides, he had reigned forty years over the nation of Israel, so that this is a royal saying. But he was a holy man, one in whom dwelt the spirit of inspiration ; he wrote as he was moved, &c., so that this is God's saying to us through David. The truth expressed in the text is a general one ; it has been realized in every age of the world ; so that we cannot err in applying it to the present time and occasion. We remark, however true,

I. THAT THE TEXT IS NOT THE LANGUAGE OF MANY OF OUR FELLOW-MEN. They are the children of this world—the creatures of time ; all their actions and arrangements, maxims, plans, spirit, &c., have to do with this world. They read and think, they buy and sell, &c., build, &c., only in reference to time. Absorbed in the things of time, they are strangers to heavenly and eternal things. Yet, whether they will or not, they must sojourn only for a season ; the stream of time is bearing them onward, &c. " The place that knows them now," &c.

II. THE TEXT HAS BEEN THE LANGUAGE OF THE GODLY IN ALL AGES. Abraham, when treating for a burying-place, said, " I am a stranger and sojourner," &c. ; the patriarchs, who died in faith, are represented as confessing that they were strangers, &c. ; Peter exhorts the scattered Christians of his time to pass the time of their sojourning here in fear, &c. ; the Christian recognises this truth.

1. *He feels that he is a stranger.* His affections, &c., are not here ; he uses the world, but does not love it. As a traveller, his heart is fixed on his home ; as a mariner, on the haven above.

2. *He acts as a stranger.* He conducts his affairs as such ; he buys, &c. ; he rejoices, &c. ; he does not entangle and absorb his mind, &c. ; he sits loose, &c. Then he has to do constantly with his intended residence ; his prayers go there, his hopes, his desires ; he receives intellectuality from them ; he is preparing himself for that world ; he has a title ; he has the nature of the inhabitants ; he is meetening for it.

3. *He speaks as a stranger.* His lan-

guage is that of Zion; he speaks of Christ and spiritual things; his language shows that he is a stranger, &c.

4. *His dress is that of a stranger.* Garment of righteousness. He is seen and known by the works which men behold; his dress is not that of worldly vanity and show, but the righteousness of his Lord and Master.

III. As a sojourner the Christian's state is deserving of peculiar attention.

1. *It is exceedingly uncertain.* "It is as a shadow." It may be a flitting, transient one, or more lengthy, but it is not to be reckoned upon, or trusted to. At best it is but a shadow.

2. *The Christian's time here is short.* As a swift post; as a weaver's shuttle; as an eagle; as a vapor; as a thing of naught.

3. *The Christian's removal hence is certain.* No one's time is abiding. God dwells in one endless duration without change; but man must quit this state of being. "I know that thou wilt," &c. "The living know," &c. Nothing can reverse that solemn, stern decree, &c.

4. *But we add, the Christian's sojourn is ever under the divine direction and care.* He does not wander at random; he is not the creature of chance; he is not without a guide and guard. The providence of God is all these, and infinitely more to him. God illumines his way, directs his steps, supplies his wants, chases away his fears; he conducts by his counsel, and afterwards receives into glory. We notice, finally, the Christian sojourner's removal hence is always his advantage. On earth he is distant from his inheritance, friends, and complete dignity. "To live is Christ, but to die is gain." "Mark the perfect man," &c. An abundant entrance is administered, &c.

APPLICATION.

1. *To the man who does not feel the text.* Let me entreat you to pause, and think, and weigh its truths; let the year pass in review. How many of your friends and acquaintance have died? Do not shut your eyes and ears; this will not avail. Love the world as you may, you must leave it; you cannot stay, nor take it with you. Seek a better; from this hour do so; your lease may almost have expired.

2. *To the Christian stranger.*

(1.) Be vigilant, that you do not imbibe the spirit of the world.

(2.) Exhibit the joys of Christianity in your experience. "Thy statutes shall be my song," &c. "Return to Zion singing," &c. "The joy of the Lord," &c. This will recommend your Saviour and his religion.

3. *Let us do all we can for the improvement of the world.* There is very much to be done. What ignorance, wretchedness, sin, &c. Shine; do good; diffuse the graces of religion; exert Christian influence.

4. *Especially let us labor to take others with us to heaven.* "Come with us," &c. Let our present meditation embrace God's blessings, that we may be thankful; God's grace and sufficiency, that we may trust in him; our sins, that we may be contrite, &c.; the great remedy, that we may come to it, &c.

THE RENEWAL OF THE INWARD MAN.

"For which cause we faint not; but though our outward man perish, yet the inward man is renewed day by day."—2 Corinthians iv. 16.

The text refers to the sufferings of the apostles, and their being overruled for the good of the churches, and the glory of God. He then refers to their preservation and continuance in their holy calling. "For which cause we faint not," &c. Observe,

I. Of what the apostle speaks. "The inward man," signifies the mind or soul, that living, intellectual being which thinks, and wills, and desires, &c. All moral qualities and responsibilities have to do with the soul. The body—the outward man—is the mansion of the inward man. The senses and members of the body obey the supreme dictations of the soul. Now, the inward man has its desires and necessities. It is capable of exhaustion and weakness; it is vulnerable, and may be injured; or it may be diseased, and it is exposed to spiritual death. Notice,

II. What the apostle declares concerning it. He says, it is renewed. The word signifies to restore, to invigorate, &c. Now, the Christian's toils, conflicts, sufferings, and temptations, produce weakness, fatigue, &c.; therefore the soul of the Christian requires to be renewed, or he would faint and be overcome. Now, we require,

1. *The renewing of our desires.* The hungering and thirsting to be kept up ; desires after God and holiness, &c.

2. *Our affections.* Our love to God, and his word, and ordinances ; love to his holy precepts.

3. *Our ability and spiritual strength.* Power to resist evil, to walk in the way of the Lord, to go onward in the Christian conflict. Now, this renewal of the inward man must be *constant,* "Day by day." Thus the body is renewed day by day ; thus, by dews and showers, the earth is renewed day by day. We ask,

III. How GOD RENEWS THE INWARD MAN DAY BY DAY.

1. *By the communications of his word.* God's word is spiritual food, milk, honey, water, &c.

2. *By the visitations of his Spirit.* His Holy Spirit revives, quickens, strengthens, &c.

3. *By blessings on the ordinances.* "They that wait," &c. How necessary,

(1.) That we feel our need of this. And,

(2.) That we humbly, yet believingly, seek it by daily prayer.

SELFISHNESS.

"For all seek their own, not the things which are Jesus Christ's."—PHILIPPIANS ii. 21.

OUR text is to be understood as involving a very general censure, but not in reality a universal one. Most persons act very extensively under the influence of selfishness. Very few, compared with the multitude, crucify self, or rigidly practise the true spirit of self-denial. Now, there is a principle of self-love which is lawful, and which is planted in our nature for the very wisest of purposes. Every man has an innate love of life, of happiness, &c. We are not to be indifferent to these things ; but love to these things may become so inordinate, and so absorb our feelings and thoughts, as to transform us into the characters condemned in the text, or as described by the apostle, when writing to Timothy, "Lovers of their own selves." Let us consider some exhibitions of this spirit— trace it to its source—notice its evils—and recommend the means of deliverance from it.

I. LET US CONSIDER SOME EXHIBITIONS OF THIS SPIRIT. It is seen,

1. *In a desire to obtain self-gratification.* This gratification may consist in the pleasures of sense—in amusements of the world —or in mental recreations ; but, whatever may be the choice, if the spirit is occupied in arranging, and contriving, and carrying out expedients to meet its own absorbing desires, then is it evident that selfishness is predominant.

2. *In seeking to assume self-dominion.* Love of power is not confined to legislators and men of rank ; it is often seen in the tyranny of the village schoolmaster ; in the arrogance of heads of families ; in masters and mistresses ; in ministers and officers of the church. Now, let this be the ruling passion, and selfishness is evidently predominant.

3. *In intense eagerness for popular applause.* Some would be monopolizers of the good-will and praises of mankind ; constantly panting after the approbation of their fellow-creatures ; seek with deep solicitude the honor that cometh from men. The most vain and censurable methods are often adopted to obtain this end. The joy of such is suspended on the verdict of popular opinion.

4. *In a craving after the possessions of the world.* This is a very common passion, and one of the worst; to seek their own temporal prosperity in preference to every other object. This spirit of covetousness has been known to trample upon all rights, dissolve the dearest ties, and adopt the most odious measures for the sake of gain. A thirst for gold is one of the most debasing passions that can pollute and pervert the soul. Now, these are the most common exhibitions of the spirit of selfishness. Let us,

II. TRACE THIS SPIRIT TO ITS SOURCE. This is expressed in one word—depravity. It arises from the moral derangement of the powers—from the undue elevation of one of the feelings of the heart over the higher and more noble faculties of the soul. We see it as the master-spirit in the first transgression. Was it not this that prompted the desire to take and eat of the fruit of the tree of knowledge of good and evil ? and this perverted, diseased nature, has been handed down to all the posterity of the first guilty pair. Hence it is the natural bent of the fallen nature—the necessary tendency of the corrupt mind; and hence the universality of its manifestation in all ages, classes, and countries; the mass seek their own; all grades of human beings are distinguished for it. It is the plague-spot of our world, and the bane of the family of man. There may be customs, and usages, habits, &c., all favorable to it; but the spring of this stream is man's depravity, the evil state of the heart. Let us note,

III. ITS EVILS. These are legion. Look at it,

1. *In its influence on the mind and heart of its victims.* Its very tendency is to deface the image of God; to dry up the fountain of goodness in the soul; to demoralize the man; to wither its moral beauty and loveliness; to spread o'er it the foul plague spot. It robs it of its enjoyment, prevents its growth and expansion, and eclipses its glory.

2. *Observe its influence on society.* It either isolates, or binds men together in clannish bands, or in base and unprincipled confederacies. Let it be carried out to its full length, and it would leave weakness unaided, misery unpitied, wretchedness unregarded, ignorance unlamented, and all the sorrow and grief of our world uncared for. A man of this kind is often the curse of the domestic sphere, the bane of the neighborhood, the iceberg of the church, and the barren fig-tree of the world.

3. *It is one of the anomalies of the universe.* God has created all creatures and things to have a mutual influence for good on one another. The angels live not for themselves; the sun shines for the benefit of the solar system; the wind blows, the rivers run, the ocean moves, the earth feeds, all nature exercises her functions for relative principles and ends; there is not one isolated, self-destined operation in the universe.

4. *It is totally unlike God.* "The Father of lights, from whom proceedeth every," &c. God exists to diffuse blessedness; he reigns for this; all his attributes have respect to this; all his works, and ways, and word, &c. Especially, how unlike God manifest in the flesh, &c.; how unlike the anthem of the angels at his birth; his life, his death, &c. Observe,

IV. THE MEANS OF DELIVERANCE FROM IT. The renewal of the mind and soul; the entire sanctification of body, soul, and spirit; the indwelling of the Holy Spirit in all his guiding and controlling influences. Thus the fountain will be made pure, the tree good, &c.

APPLICATION.

1. The existence of this spirit in the church is owing to the low spiritual state of believers.

2. Against it all Christians should prayerfully strive.

3. It can have no existence in the heavenly world.

THE EVIL OF SPIRITUAL IGNORANCE.

"That the soul be without knowledge is not good."—PROVERBS xix. 2.

OUR text is one of the concise proverbs of Solomon. Most of these brief sentences contain a great fund of thought, and they have this especial recommendation, they are easily committed to memory, and the impression they make is often long and vividly retained. The ancients were famous for conveying their doctrines and principles in this condensed form. The Proverbs of Solomon, as they are unrivalled in beauty and excellency, so they stand forth as being indited under the inspiring influences of God. They are divine, therefore they are true. And they are generally as important as they are true. Of all these proverbs there is not one of greater moment than that of our text. "That the soul," &c.

I. LET US ILLUSTRATE AND ESTABLISH THE TRUTH OF THE TEXT. Before we enter on the chief point, we offer a few preliminary remarks. By the soul we mean the intellectual, thinking part of man. That spiritual, reflecting, undying, and dignified inhabitant of our frail and perishing bodies. Knowledge signifies perception, illumination. The opposite of ignorance and darkness of mind. Now knowledge may either be associated with that which is temporal, or metaphysical, or moral. It may either be speculative or practical. Knowledge of nature, or science, or art, is good, and desirable, and important. But that knowledge which is pre-eminent is religious knowledge. Knowledge of God and his will; knowledge of ourselves, our condition, our duty, our privileges and blessings, our destiny; knowledge of Jesus Christ and his great salvation. This is the excellency, the essence, the perfection of knowledge. This is all necessary and necessary to all; it is so always, and will be so forever. A man may be wise, and good, and happy, without other kinds of knowledge, but none can be so without this. Then it is to spiritual and divine knowledge that we shall limit our subject on the present occasion. Now for the soul to be without knowledge is not good, because,

1. *It frustrates the end of our being.* The soul was formed for knowledge just as the sun for the communication of light. And as the bed of the ocean for the reception of the water, so the soul to be the depository of knowledge. Thus did Adam appear when formed in the image of his Creator. One grand and chief resemblance was in the intellectual faculties with which he was endowed, and the knowledge with which God invested him. The senses of the body are designed to be the inlets of knowledge as to the things around us. The eye, the hand, the taste, the smell, the hearing; the soul has its powers too; the understanding, by which we perceive and know; the judgment, by which we conclude as to the properties, &c., of the things we contemplate; the imagination, which colors and presents objects before us in their ideal forms. Memory, by which we retain and keep fast the things perceived and known. Now these powers avail not, they are perverted, if the soul be without knowledge, &c. " That the soul," &c.

2. *Because it is its degradation and debasement.* Knowledge is one of the glories of the divine nature; so it is also the dignity of man. In the fall, man lost much of this; darkness spread its fell mists over the soul; darkness pertains to the world beneath and exposes to its shame and contempt. Knowledge pertains to God and heaven, and makes us partakers of the glory of God. Without knowledge, man the monarch becomes the slave, the savage, the degraded creature of the material earth, and the companion of animals and beasts that prowl upon its surface. Not to know God and his will and works is the deep prostration of the creature of his image and his favor. For the soul, &c.

3. *Because it is its misery.* How pleasant, how cheering is its light! How sweet to behold the works of God, to look abroad on the fair face of nature, &c. Now to be without knowledge is to be blind, for knowledge is the sight of the soul; knowledge is the food of the soul, and without it, it must starve and die; knowledge is the health of the soul; ignorance is the disease and leprosy of the soul. View that being enslaved, blind, starving, diseased, and then you have a faint representation of the soul without knowledge.

4. *Because it is the guilt and condemnation of the soul.* Ignorance, especially to those under the privileges we possess, is sinful: it is criminal. We have the means, the facilities of knowledge. God requires us to possess it. If we are without divine knowledge, it is because we have disliked it, neglected it, and wiled away our opportunities and mercies. In the night none can see or discern the beauties which surround them; but ours is the day; the day is the period of light. Jesus proclaims himself the light of the world. We blame men not for being strangers to languages, to philosophy, to science, or art, without the facilities; but men may have moral intellectuality, spiritual knowledge. It is in the scriptures; it is published from day to day, and it is highly criminal not to know God and Jesus Christ whom he hath sent. Not to know ourselves and our destiny; not to know the day of our visitation. It is not good,

5. *Because it will be the death, the total ruin of the soul.* For the children of ignorance and darkness walk in the way of darkness, and their end will be blackness and darkness forever. " My people perish for lack of knowledge." The soul without knowledge is unfit for the enjoyment of God, and incapable of participating in the bliss of heaven. A person may have a volume of superior merit before him, but of what avail is it if he cannot read it? He may be surrounded with the most splendid scenery, but what avails it if he is blind? An essential prerequisite for heaven is the saving knowledge of God; this is life eternal. Heaven is the region of knowledge; the world of eternal light and day. Let me, then,

II. ASK WHAT ARE THE PRINCIPLES WHICH OUR SUBJECT INVOLVES.

1. *The lamentable condition of those who are spiritually ignorant.* How many of these dwell around us! Are there not such in this assembly? The state of such

is truly pitiable, dark, condemned, perishing.

2. *The high estimation in which we should hold the privileges we possess.* We have the book, emphatically the key of knowledge ; the whole mind of God to man ; the guide to happiness and heaven. We have the messengers of knowledge ; the preachers of the gospel are sent forth, that their lips may dispense knowledge. All the ordinances of religion are adapted to this end. We have many especial facilities which no age of the world ever had ; abundant streams flowing from the press ; means of instruction, especially schools. How different to our forefathers !

3. *The responsibility of the church of Christ to diffuse the knowledge of God abroad.* Believers are to shine, &c. We are to labor, holding forth the word of life, &c. We are to train up the rising age, &c. We are to pray, " O Lord, send out," &c.

APPLICATION.

1. *Have you this knowledge ?* If so, grow in it, &c.

2. *If not, seek till you possess it.*

THE SCRIPTURAL INSTRUCTION OF
THE YOUNG.

" And these words which I command thee this day, shall be in thine heart : and thou shalt teach them diligently unto thy children, and shalt talk of them when thou sittest in thine house, and when thou walkest by the way," &c.—DEUTERONOMY vi. 6-9.

OUR text is found in connection with a paragraph of peculiar weight and sublimity. Moses, that distinguished servant of Jehovah, is rehearsing to the people of Israel the high commandments of the Lord ; he introduces the subject in the following striking and powerful manner ; " Now these are the commandments," &c. Here you will perceive duty and privilege, obedience and reward, are united together. He then calls for their special attention. " Hear therefore," &c., verse 3. This exclamation he repeats, when referring to the unity of the Godhead, verse 4 ; he then lays the basis of his exhortations in the especial religion of the heart, verse 5 ; and then immediately builds upon it the duties prescribed in the text. " And these words," &c. Let us consider the subject to which

the text refers ; the duties the text enjoins ; the mode of performance the text recommends. Now we have to notice,

I. THE SUBJECT TO WHICH THE TEXT REFERS. " And these words." Now the text may mean the entire law and will God had made known to Moses, and then revealed to the people, or to the immediate paragraph which precedes the text ; but we may justly apply the text to the sacred scriptures in general. To the lively oracles both of the Old and New Testaments ; the Bible in its comprehensive and complete character, including Moses and Christ, the prophets and the apostles. Now the scriptures contain a revelation of all essential truths ; a summary of all Christian duties ; a charter of all desirable blessings ; it is the true guide to the knowledge of God, salvation, immortality, and eternal life. Emphatically the book of books, and to all who desire it, the record of salvation. It gives light to the ignorant, wisdom to the simple, and peace to the unhappy ; it converts the soul, guides the feet, and sanctifies the heart ; it is the pilgrim's staff, and the warrior's sword ; the mine of wealth, and passport to glory ! What a subject ! A book, which has God for its author—truth for its matter—and salvation for its end. We pass from the subject,

II. TO THE DUTIES THE TEXT ENJOINS. It is the scriptural instruction of their children ; to teach them the words of God and salvation. Now look at this in several lights.

1. *Our children are naturally ignorant of these things.* None, by mere dint of natural effort, ever found out the true knowledge of God ; uninstructed, therefore, they will grow up in mental and moral darkness.

2. *In these things our children have a deep interest.* They have minds capable of instruction, the capacity for knowledge. There seems to be an inherent desire for knowledge ; it is the very atmosphere of the soul's health and well-being. The true wealth of our children depends greatly on their acquisition of divine knowledge ; their happiness essentially depends upon it ; their usefulness in this life ; and what is most of all, their eternal salvation. " My people perish for lack of knowledge."

3. *For the instruction of our children we are responsible.* I deny that this responsibility rests anywhere to the exclusion of

the parent ; on him it rests. "Thy children," and as much as it rests upon them to provide food, and raiment, and medicine, &c. The care of the mind as well as of the body is committed to them, and the one is infinitely more weighty than the other. Parents may not in every case be able to teach their children, but then they must see that it is done. In our sabbath-schools, the church of Christ provides for those who cannot have Christian instruction at home, and also to aid those parents who are thus laudably engaged. Now we proceed to consider,

III. THE MODE OF PERFORMING THIS DUTY THE TEXT RECOMMENDS. The text enjoins,

1. *The possession of experimental religion in the teacher.* "These words, &c., shall be in thine heart." A mere mechanical teacher must have mechanical skill—a mental teacher, intelligence—a moral teacher, the principles of true morality in his own soul. The Christian teacher aims not only at informing the mind, and storing the memory, but amending the heart. A knowledge therefore of true religion only, can qualify the instructor for his work. The heart is the moral lever, to give weight and efficiency to the counsels of the lip ; the heart only can make us earnest, and intent, and solicitous. Now this applies to all moral instructions. Parents, guardians, sabbath-school teachers, &c. The text enjoins,

2. *Diligence in the execution of this work.* It is not to be done cursorily, or with indifference ; not by spasmodic throes, but by continued efforts ; the difficulty of the task renders diligence indispensable. The variety of the instructions to be conveyed to the mind, and the short period allotted for the execution of the task. Only the diligent will extensively succeed. We have enjoined,

3. *Frequency of effort.* Observe the detail of times and seasons, presented to us in the text. The first part of the day is to be thus occupied. This is to engage our attention through the day, "When thou sittest," &c. This is to be identified with our recreations, "When thou walkest by the way." This is to close all the other duties of the day, "When thou liest down." Now there are spiritual subjects, suited to each of these times and occasions ; to be wise and apt in their use is very desirable. The text enjoins,

4. *Simplicity in the mode of instruction* I think this is included in the phrase, "Thou shalt talk." Nothing is more foolish, and of course useless, than to attempt to convey instruction to children, by orations or set speeches and addresses. If we are to instruct, to impress, to interest, we must talk. Bring down both words, ideas, and style to their capacities ; this is a most desirable attainment, and essential to extended success ; and in this how beautifully Christ the great teacher stands forth as our perfect model. Our efficiency may be easily tested, if we will catechize our children on the points in which they have been taught, and see if they have clearly and distinctly understood them. We add,

5. *Patience and perseverance.* All children are not equally quick, and apt to learn ; the mind, in some cases, is slow of development. Now such instances must not be despised ; they especially need our aid, and compassion for them should induce patient perseverance. To impart knowledge to the juvenile mind has been fitly compared to the pouring of a fluid into a long, narrow-necked bottle, where care, patience, and attention, and perseverance, are all requisite. But we observe,

6. *All instructions must be followed by fervent prayer.* Prayer should precede, accompany, and follow our efforts.

APPLICATION.

Our subject I fear is,

1. *The condemnation of many parents present.* Do not trifle with God's commands. You must meet your children at the last day. Our subject,

2. *Shows us the importance of sabbath schools.* These are the true seminaries of the church of Christ. These are the hope of the world.

3. *Efforts for instructing the young should meet with the generous and cheerful support of the pious.*

KNOWLEDGE, OBEDIENCE, AND FELICITY.

"If ye know these things, happy are ye if ye do them."—JOHN xiii. 17.

WHAT is true religion ? Is not the question important ; is it not necessary ? None will dispute its importance or necessity. One replies, true religion is being of the true church; and he limits this true church to his own denomination. Another replies, true religion is having sound opinions and views; and those are religious who of course agree with the sentiments he professes. A third replies, true religion is the regular observance of Divine worship, and a general regard to Christian morals. We reply to each and all of these, and say a person may be invested with each of these, and yet not be religious at all; he may belong to the purest Christian communion; he may hold the most orthodox sentiments, and he may lead the most exemplary life, and yet be a stranger to spiritual, practical godliness. True religion is beautifully delineated in the text; it is triune in its nature—knowledge—practice—felicity. If ye know, and do, then happy are ye. We notice, then,

I. In order to true religion there must be knowledge. "If ye know," &c. Ignorance is one of the foul antagonists of religion. It is pernicious and ruinous to the soul; it is a foul libel on man, and a still fouler libel on religion, when utterance is given to this maxim, that "ignorance is the mother of devotion." No! ignorance is the mother of crime, and wretchedness, and wo, and it may be of superstition, but knowledge is one of the essential principles of religion.

1. *There must be a knowledge of the true God.* His nature, character, will.

2. *A knowledge of the scriptures.* A persuasion of their inspiration and truth; a knowledge of their contents, especially those parts which relate to our salvation.

3. *A knowledge of ourselves.* As fallen, sinful, polluted, helpless. To know the plague of our own hearts, &c.

4. *A knowledge of Jesus Christ.* As the sent of God—the true Son of the Most High—Mediator, &c. Of his gospel. What it reveals, and offers, and requires; now it reveals God's mercy; it offers salvation; and requires repentance, faith, and holiness. Surely a knowledge of these things is essential to true religion.

II. In order to true religion there must be obedience. "Not every one that saith, Lord, Lord," &c. Neither knowledge nor talents will do without obedience. "Ye are my friends," &c. Now in doing these things,

1. *We must have respect to the will of God, as the rule of our obedience.* Not fancies, or feelings, or impulses, or the conduct of others, but the direct revelation of God. Have respect to all his commandments.

2. *We must do these things with humility of mind.* Not in the way of merit and self-righteousness; but with all lowliness, &c.

3. *We must do these things with cheerfulness and affection.* From a sense of grateful love to Jesus Christ. Not from fear or constraint.

4. *We can only do these things in the strength of divine grace.* God must work both to will and to do. Not us, but the grace of God within us.

5. *Our obedience in doing these things must be constant and persevering.* Endure to the end, &c. We must be so found doing when Christ shall call us. Labor to the end of the day of life. Faithful unto death, &c.

III. That religion identified with knowledge and obedience, will certainly be productive of felicity. "Happy are ye." We do not say it will secure riches, or honor, or wealth, or worldly friends, but it will tend to create happiness.

1. *There will be the happiness of a rightly regulated mind.* Chaos, and confusion, and night, exchanged for light, order, and day. A new creation in the soul. Old things have passed away, &c. God the soul's centre and rest.

2. *There will be the happiness of internal peace.* Peace with God—peace with conscience—peace with all men. The peace of God will keep and rule.

3. *There will be the happiness of conscious safety.* To have guilt cancelled—fetters burst; wrath removed. No longer under the curse, &c., but have the testimony of the Spirit, that we are children of God—now accepted.

4. *There will be the happiness of cheering hope.* Hope is the telescope of the soul—our anchor in storms—our staff in our pilgrimage. Hope of victory, full salvation, and eternal life. Hope of heaven. Good, bright, solid hope. Begotten again to a lively hope, &c.

5. *The happiness of divine communications.* Grace in every time of need. Heavenly visitation, especially in secret duties, public ordinances. Oh yes! happy are ye. Truly so; increasingly so and shall be eternally so.

APPLICATION.

1. *To the religious.* Is your religion of this threefold kind ? Light in the mind—practice in the life—joy in the spirit. Are you not greatly deficient in each of these ?

2. *Invite all to know, obey, and enjoy.* The means of knowledge you have, grace to obey is promised, and happiness must ensue.

ON OUR OWN MIND.

" Should it be according to thy mind ?"—Job xxxiv. 33.

Few, if any, of the human family ever endured such severe trials as Job ; and his unyielding confidence in God, his patience, and his humility, are left on record for the instruction of the afflicted of God's people unto the end of the world. We do not marvel that in some things he betrayed the infirmities of a man. The suspicions of his friends as to his integrity were calculated to hurry him into some expressions of haste, and to the adoption of some expressions in self-justification, which otherwise he would not have employed. Our text is the appeal of Elihu, and follows a very fine exhibition of that spirit which should attend us in our sorrows and trials, verses 31, 32. He then asks, " Should it be according to thy mind ?" I observe,

I. WE ARE NATURALLY ANXIOUS THAT THINGS SHOULD BE ACCORDING TO OUR MIND. This is a general, if not universal feeling. Sin entered our world on this principle, and by it, is extensively perpetuated. You see it in all ages ; even children wish to have their own minds ; see the headstrong youth ; the young man ; the person of mature years ; the aged ; all evidence this ; all strive and contend for this ; you see it in all stations, the rich and noble and affluent ; but the same feelings extend to the poor, and the indigent. The learned and the illiterate are both living examples of this. This is the broad palpable mark of the profane ; and it is the spot and infirmity of the religious and true servants of God.

II. WE ARE TOTALLY UNFIT FOR DECIDING IN THE THINGS WHICH CONCERN US. We are so because we are more influenced by passion than reason ; because we are so darkened in our understandings and judgments ; because we are at best so short-sighted ; because we are so influenced by sense, and present things. If things were left to our minds, we should never choose trials, disappointments, crosses, afflictions. bereavements. We should not be able to determine on our removal out of time. We should not court temptation, and chastisement, &c. Now all these are indispensable to our well-being, fruitfulness, and future safety. How well then is it for us, that we are not left to determine for ourselves ! Besides our minds are so unsettled ; we are so fickle, and vacillating. The mind we had for things years ago, is now altered. Our present mind will be modified, altered, or probably entirely changed by circumstances. Then how futile to desire that things should be according to our minds !

III. IT IS IMPOSSIBLE THAT THINGS CAN BE ACCORDING TO THE MINDS OF ALL PERSONS. Each one desires his own mind ; but almost every one comes in collision with his neighbor. Now amongst ten thousand various minds, which is to have the ascendency ? It is evident, that not more than one or two can be gratified out of the whole. So that all having their own minds is an impossibility. Why, men are not agreed on any one subject. Every man seeks his own things ; confusion and clashing interests distract and divide our world. A scene of discord vastly worse than that of Babel, would rack and torture our world, if every man had liberty to obtain his own mind.

IV. How MANY HAVE BEEN RUINED BY HAVING THEIR OWN MIND ! Our first parents. The inhabitants of the old world resolved, in spite of the warnings of Noah, to eat and drink, &c., and were so found when the flood came. Lot had his own mind, when he selected the well-watered plain of Sodom for his abode ; Pharaoh would have his own mind, and the sequel of his history is found in the overthrow of himself and hosts in the Red Sea ; the children of Israel would have their own minds in the wilderness, and their apostacy and ruin was the consequence. Now, I appeal to you : Should children have their own minds ? should culprits and malefactors ? should violent, wrathful persons ? If so, what misery and horror would fill our world ! Is it not a fearful truth, that men choose the way of death and hell, and thus perish forever, in having their own minds?

V. IT IS INFINITELY BETTER THAT ONE PERFECT MIND SHOULD CONTROL THE UNIVERSE. Such a mind has God. It is clear, all-seeing, pure, wise, good, and just. He comprehends all, knows all, and can direct all things to a glorious consummation; he is ever of one mind, and never changes nor varies; his power is boundless, his resources infinite, his plans infallible. How delightful, then, that God reigns—reigns in heaven, on earth, and through the universe! His kingdom is an everlasting kingdom, and he ruleth over all.

VI. IT IS OUR HAPPINESS AND REAL WELL-BEING TO BE SUBJECT TO GOD'S MIND. Religion says, "Thy will be done." In heaven all are agreed on this subject; not a discordant sentiment or feeling; and all do it. True religion leads to this. In conversion the sinner bows to God; as piety increases, the will of God is more clearly understood, and more cheerfully obeyed; the language of healthy and sincere Christians is just that of the Redeemer, " Not my will, but thine be done."

VII. CERTAIN THINGS MAY ASSIST US IN COMING TO THIS STATE OF MIND. A persuasion of our own incompetency, " It is not in man that walks to direct," &c.; a retrospect of God's goodness in reference to our past concerns, " Goodness and mercy have followed us," &c.; the daily presentation of our desires to God, " In all thy ways acknowledge," &c. " Commit thy way to the Lord," &c.; a conviction of the transitory character of earthly things, fashion of this world passing away—a looking to the things that are eterna..

THE WORSHIP OF THE HEAVENLY HOST.

" And the host of heaven worshippeth thee."— NEHEMIAH ix. 6.

OUR text is connected with the solemn address of the Levites on a day of fasting and especial worship. It contains some of the most sublime thoughts that can possibly occupy the human mind. " Then the Levites," it is recorded, " said, Stand up and bless the Lord your God forever and ever; and blessed be thy glorious name, which is exalted above all blessing and praise. Thou, even thou, art Lord alone, thou hast made heaven, the heaven of heavens, with all their host, the earth, and all things that are therein, and thou preservest them all; *and the host of heaven worshippeth thee.*" The contemplation of superior greatness and goodness has a tendency to elevate and improve the mind, and to inspire the soul with feelings of the loftiest and holiest emulation. Hence we are repeatedly called upon in scripture to consider the lives of those who have been distinguished for godliness, and to make them ensamples for our imitation. The apostle Paul calls upon us to consider the Old Testament worthies, that we may be followers of them who through faith and patience now inherit the promises; and the blessed Redeemer, in that inimitable prayer which he taught his disciples, also directed their thoughts to the holiness of angels— for that is clearly implied in that part of the Lord's prayer, where we are to pray that God's will may be done on earth, even as it is done in heaven; in other words, that man may be as holy, as spiritual, as obedient as angels; and, while Jesus Christ came expressly to shed his blood for human transgression, and turn aside the justly incurred wrath of the Most High, he also came to be our ensample, and " he hath left us," says the apostle, " an example that we should tread in his steps." Our subject leads us to contemplate the angels of God, for it is quite clear that our text refers to angelic beings. Sometimes the term " host" is used in scripture to represent the stars; the starry host; the planets, those numerous magnificent worlds, which God has created in the immensity of space around us; but it is evident our text refers to intelligent beings—to those happy and blessed creatures, who were formed previous to our world's existence, and who have retained all their beauty, and dignity, and purity, and who are incessantly worshipping the God of heaven. Therefore, in our thoughts and meditations let us leave this earth, and travel upward to a higher state, even to the holiest place of all. Let us venture in the exercise of imagination, and by the power of faith, to ascend to that world where God has his immediate throne, and his resplendent dwelling-place; and there, by the assistance of our text, let us contemplate all the host of heaven worshipping God. Let us dwell for a little,

I. On the host itself.

II. On their employment. And,

III. The practical uses we should make of it.

I. The host itself. The existence of a class of beings, usually denominated angels, is obviously established in scripture. Reference is often made to them both in the Old and New Testament scriptures.

(1.) As to the *nature* of these beings. They are spirits—pure spirits; not clothed with material forms as man. "Who maketh his angels spirits," &c.

(2.) As to their *character*. They are described as perfectly wise, "Angels of light." As good and holy. They are said ever to be hearkening to the voice of God's word; to do his will. Holy angels; without spot; no imperfection.

(3.) Their *number*. Thousands of thousands; analogy from other parts of the creation.

(4.) As to their *orders*. They are called by very expressive titles—thrones, dominions, principalities, powers. We read also of archangels, seraphim, and cherubim. Some of the ancients thought there were nine orders, others eight, others four, and that the angels were under the dominion of archangels. We read, too, of Michael and his angels. We proceed to notice,

II. Their employments. They serve God; do the bidding of Jehovah. All eye to see—all ear to listen—all heart to love—all wing to fly; but, doubtless, one chief employment is to worship God. In scripture, we have some splendid exhibitions of this, Isaiah vi. 1, 2, Rev. iv. 6, 11. Now, their worship is lofty and dignified, holy and fervent, earnest and sincere, cheerful and incessant. We add, that with the angelic host there are united the spirits of the redeemed, who are made perfect; the souls of holy patriarchs and prophets, apostles, and confessors, and martyrs; and all who have died in the faith and hope of the gospel. Many of our friends and kindred; many of all ages and generations, countries, &c.; elevated to the society, and worship, and joys of the angels. One celestial corporation; one glorious assembly; one vast and happy family. The worship of the heavenly host differs from ours in many respects,

1. *As to the place.* The heaven of heavens; the holiest of all; throne of God in the midst; Deity immediately with them.

2. *As to its character.* More pure and spiritual; nothing gross appertaining to them; nothing indolent and lethargic; spiritual in the highest degree; burning with fervor; brilliant with intelligence; transparent with sincerity.

3. *It is peculiarly humble and lowly.* They stand before the throne as cheerful and ready attendants; they bow down before God, &c.; say nothing of themselves; cast their crowns before him, &c.

4. *Their worship is chiefly praise and adoration.* They extol God, bless him, praise him, adore, &c. All unite in one sublime chorus, "Blessing and power," &c. All their wants are supplied; no prayer; no confession; no supplication; no deprecation.

5. *Their worship is uninterrupted and eternal.* Day and night, &c. Filled with God; absorbed with God; rest in God; nothing above or beyond. Theirs is the fruition—the perfection of bliss.

6. *They seem to identify their worship with the works of God in connection with our world.* That is, they rejoice and adore God in the various displays of his glory with which they are favored. At the creation they sang together; they were the messengers to the patriarchs and prophets; attended at the giving of the law; announced the birth of the Redeemer; sang o'er the plains of Bethlehem; ministered to him in his temptation and agony; hailed his resurrection; were his convoy, &c.; rejoice in the conversion of sinners, &c.; will unite in the lofty acclamations of the glorified in heaven forever.

III. The practical uses to which our subject may be applied.

1. *It should inspire us with holy emulation.* To resemble them in their character, disposition, and employment.

2. *To think of them in our worship.* Could we then be cold and formal? How dignified, how precious, how sweet is divine worship!

3. *To rejoice in their friendship.* Bless God for their ministering to us. So to live,

4. *That we may be their companions forever.* Let us remember the gracious declaration of the Saviour—that his saints shall be equal to the angels. If so, how poor is this world! how inferior to our great destiny! how unworthy of our attach-

ment! and how necessary is Christian diligence! how indispensable holiness of heart and life! how precious, the fountain opened, &c. There is another world, where there are hosts of angels, fallen, miserable, despairing, &c.; where they hate, blaspheme, and gnash their teeth, &c. " Choose ye, which shall be your companions forever."

NEW YEAR'S COUNSELS TO THE GODLY.

" Fret not thyself because of evil doers, neither be thou envious against the workers of iniquity. For they shall soon be cut down like the grass, and wither as the green herb. Trust in the Lord, and do good; so shalt thou dwell in the land, and verily thou shalt be fed. Delight thyself also in the Lord; and he shall give thee the desires of thine heart. Commit thy way unto the Lord; trust also in him, and he shall bring it to pass."— PSALM xxxvii. 1–6.

OUR subject this morning may be properly denominated New Year's counsels. In the merciful providence of God, we have entered upon another year. These divisions of time are calculated to make impressions upon our minds;—and it will be well for us if these impressions are of a useful character, and if their influence is effective and permanent. I cannot conceive of a series of counsels more adapted really to do us good, than those which we have read, and which form the introductory part of this rich and beautiful psalm. Let us consider these counsels as they are presented to us in the text.

I. NOT TO BE PERTURBED OR ANGRY WITH THE WICKED. I have used the words perturbation and anger, as expressing the meaning of the word " fret." The Psalmist means, do not get your own souls into disorder and confusion, and lose temper and murmur, because of wicked men. Let us however not mistake this counsel. He does not mean that we are to be indifferent to the wicked and their course. The good man is to abhor sin, and hate every evil way; he is to pray, " Oh let the wickedness of the wicked," &c. " May thy will be done on earth," &c. But how often do men transfer their hatred of sin to the sinner; and how often do we allow our minds to be confused and irritated, and thus we add our sin to the sin of the wicked! We are in danger of showing a Pharisaical

spirit, and acting as judges of others. We are in danger of assuming a prerogative which belongs to God alone. Look at the apostles James and John, who prayed for fire to consume those who did not receive their message. Forget not Christ's rebuke. " Ye know not what spirit ye are of." We are in danger of envying the wicked. " Neither be thou envious." Perhaps the blasphemer is in purple, and the man of prayer in poverty; the ungodly in the mansion, and the pious at his gates; Agrippa on the tribunal, and Paul in chains at the bar. Well, so it is, and it may often perplex us; but real Christianity precludes envy. To envy, is to sin; it is a fruit of the flesh; it is to destroy our own peace; it will corrode and eat out all enjoyment. " Then fret not, neither be envious," &c.

(1.) Because every man is accountable to God. Leave it with Jehovah.

(2.) We are sincerely to pity and commiserate their state; but if we are perturbed, and angry, and fretful, we cannot do so, &c.

(3.) Think how transient is their present state, verse 2. " For they shall soon be cut down," &c. What would you think of a person, who should visit a prison, where men under sentence of death were crowded together; and suppose the prisoners seemed merry, were clothed gorgeously, and gave each other high-sounding names. Would you fret or be envious? Impossible! would you not weep, would not your hearts ache, &c.? verses 9, 10.

II. WE ARE TO CONFIDE IN GOD, AND IMITATE HIS BENEVOLENCE. " Trust in the Lord," &c.; that is, depend on God—lean on the Lord—look to him for every blessing, &c.

(1.) Trust not in *yourselves*.

(2.) Trust not in *men*. Rich men or princes. " Cursed is the man that trusteth in man."

(3.) Trust not in *riches*, or any of the adventitious circumstances of life. The world is a sea in ceaseless motion. Trust only in the Lord, and trust him wholly, and fully, and always, and for every thing, and forever. Trust the riches of his grace— and the kindness and sufficiency of his providence; and God shall protect thy life, and satisfy thee with food; all things needful will be supplied; God will be thy friend and refuge. " And do good." To the bodies and souls of those around you.

Console the afflicted, relieve the widow, remember the poor, and offer Christ to all.

III. WE ARE TO MAKE GOD THE GREAT OBJECT OF OUR SUPREME JOY AND LOVE. "Delight thyself," &c. Give God our first and chief regards. Look to him as the great source of all blessedness; as the fountain of blessings; meditate on his blessed character and perfection; live near to him by daily prayer and communion; seek his glory in all things; labor to exalt and please God. Do as Noah did, as Enoch did, as Abraham did, as Daniel did, as Jesus did, who ever pleased him. "And he shall give thee," &c. He shall make thee happy, &c. Every heart desires this; every soul thirsts and pants for it. Well, you shall have it; you shall feel his own peace keeping you, &c. His joy elevating, &c. His love shed abroad, &c.

IV. GIVE EVERY THING UP TO BE MANAGED BY THE LORD. "Commit thy way," &c. The course of a person's life is his way. Two things are included.

1. *Our providential course.* The affairs of life. These we cannot manage ourselves. Boast not thyself of to-morrow. Look at that child in a vessel at sea; what would it do? Look at that stranger in a distant land with his guide. Look at that person with a case of legal difficulty. Now as a child commits itself to the captain of a vessel—as the stranger to his guide—the man with his suit to the advocate or counsellor—so we are to commit our way to the Lord, &c. Give up all for him to manage, &c.

2. *Our gracious and spiritual course.* The care of our souls. Our best interests, &c. He will manage it rightly, &c. Keep all secure, and bring us to eternal glory. All shall end well, everlastingly well. Let us regard these counsels. Meditate on them, and practise them, &c.

APPLICATION.

1. Admonish the thoughtless.
2. Warn the unbelieving.
3. Direct the inquirer.

CHRISTIAN ESTABLISHMENT.

"Now he which stablisheth us with you in Christ, and hath anointed us, is God."—2 CORINTHIANS i. 21.

DIVINE grace exerts a uniform influence on the human heart. The manner in which grace operates is very diversified, the instruments also various; but there is a similarity in the effects on the hearts of all who believe. The apostles, although inspired and distinguished by wonderful endowments and miraculous gifts, were still on the same level with other saints, as to the necessity and influence of grace on their souls. This is seen in the text. Now, "he who stablisheth us," &c. Let us look,

I. AT THE BLESSINGS EXPERIENCED.

(1.) Established. There is of course a necessity for this. The tree planted must have time, &c., to take root and be established. The foundation laid, must have time to rest and settle, and be established. The seed sown must have space for sinking into the earth, taking root downward, and being established in order to fruitfulness, &c. The mind must have time to embrace truth and reflect upon it, &c., before man can be established. So with divine grace; time, means, and influence are necessary before Christians can be established.

(2.) Christian establishment is very necessary. It is necessary to our spiritual prosperity. To be moved and unsettled is to be incapable of religious improvement. "Unstable as water," &c.

(3.) It is necessary to our comfort. Vacillation is as wretched as unprofitable. Real peace, and fickleness, are incompatible.

(4.) It is essential to our safety. To be moved from the hope, &c., is to decline and apostatize. Ye did run well," &c. How essential—how important to be established; and this should include establishment in *knowledge*—divine knowledge—knowledge of Christ, and the way of salvation—knowledge of the great doctrines of the gospel, &c. To be men in knowledge. In *faith.* For faith to be strong, invulnerable, &c., that it may not fail. In *love*—love to God—love to his holy law—and in compassionate love to all men. In *obedience;* cheerfully and with heartfelt delight to obey God. To delight to do his will. In our *profession.* A city elevated, impregnable, set on a hill.

II. THIS ESTABLISHMENT OF THE CHRISTIAN IS IN CHRIST. "In Christ." All our privileges and blessings, &c., arise from our being in Christ. Our first parents had no stability in a state of innocency, much less can we in our own imperfect frail nature ; but in Christ our security is firm and sufficient. In his meritorious sacrifice we nave the established favor of God to us. In his intercession the establishing influences of his Spirit. In his example, the established model for our perseverance. In his fulness, establishing grace in every time of need. The tree must have good soil. The Christian tree is planted into Christ. The stone of the structure must have a good foundation—Christ is the foundation stone—built on him—rests on him, &c.

III. The author of this establishment is God. Now he, &c., "is God." Not ourselves, yet we must use the means. Not ministers, yet we must take heed to the word preached. Not angels, yet we may rejoice in their ministrations ; but God is the source. "Every good gift," &c. Then three things are necessary.

1. *Dependence.* Trusting God. Believing God. He who does so shall never, &c. He will keep him in perfect peace.

2. *Prayer.* Seeking God's blessing. Waiting upon him. Imploring his daily help.

3. *Praise.* Grateful acknowledgment of the past, &c. Giving thanks continually to his name.

APPLICATION.

1. The most mature Christian still has need of deeper establishment.

2. Young Christians and new converts should be particularly solicitous for it.

THE ANOINTING.

"Now he which stablisheth us with you in Christ, and hath anointed us, is God."—2 Corinthians i. 21.

Various are the figures by which the Holy Spirit is represented in the holy scriptures. He is compared to the air or wind. "The wind bloweth," &c. So when it rested on the apostles, &c. Thus God breathed into man, &c. So Christ to his disciples, after his resurrection, said, "Peace," and breathed on them, &c., John xx. 22. To fire ; thus it rested on them as cloven tongues of fire. "But ye shall be baptized," &c. "Quench not the Spirit," &c. As water. "If any man thirst," &c. He spake of the Holy Spirit, &c.

So also to oil. He shall be anointed with the oil of gladness, &c. ; this is the idea the text contains. Believers are anointed of God, viz. : anointed with the Holy Ghost. See the uses to which oil was applied, and you will at once observe the propriety and beauty of the text.

I. The sick were anointed in order to healing. In the beautiful parable of the good Samaritan, oil and wine were poured into his wounds. See also James v. 14. Now in these is set forth the healing influences of the Holy Spirit. It is the work of God's Spirit to heal the broken hearted, Isaiah lxi. 3.

II. The weary were refreshed by the application of oil. In hot climates this was often indispensable to real comfort. It tended to cool and refresh the debilitated system. Thus David exclaimed, "Thou hast anointed my head with oil," &c. Thus Christ commended the penitent woman who poured on him the precious oil, and said to Simon the Pharisee, "My head with oil thou didst not anoint." Now the Holy Spirit refreshes the soul, revives it, inspirits it, and gives real vigor and comfort.

III. Oil was used to beautify the countenance. One of the blessings acknowledged in the 104th Psalm is, "oil which maketh the face to shine." Now the Holy Spirit beautifies the soul. "He will beautify the meek," &c. David's prayer is to the point. "Let the beauty of the Lord our God," &c. Grace is the true beauty of the soul, it confers beauty which is pleasing to God, and abiding, and heavenly.

IV. Oil was used in anointing for sacred offices.

1. Kings were anointed with oil. Believers are made kings unto God, they are destined to reign with Christ forever, to wear eternal crowns, to have an everlasting inheritance.

2. Priests were anointed with oil. Believers are a royal priesthood. Spiritual priests offering up spiritual sacrifices to the Lord. This qualifies them, and sanctifies their services, both of praise and prayer.

3. Prophets were anointed. "The Spirit of the Lord is upon me." Every Christian is to teach Jesus Christ. To witness for Christ, and by their conversation, and spirit, and life, to glorify Christ. The Holy Spirit must enable them to do this. Thus believers are anointed of God.

APPLICATION.

1. Examine yourselves.
2. Seek this.
3. Honor the anointing.

BEING SEALED.

" Who hath also sealed us."—2 Corinthians i. 22.

In our last discourse, we noticed the anointing of the Holy Spirit, and referred you to the Spirit's operations as likened to oil, on account of their healing, refreshing, beautifying, and consecrating influences. The apostle presents us, in the text, with another figure on the same subject. The Spirit is compared to a seal, and believers are represented as receiving the impression of it in their hearts. A few remarks on the use of seals will elucidate the subject to our minds.

I. Seals were made use of to ratify and render authentic important documents. We have a reference to this in a civil contract, Jer. xxxii. 9, &c. ; in reference to a national covenant, Nehemiah ix. 38. Now the gifts of divine grace, especially the blessings of the new covenant, are by the Spirit sealed over to believers ; for the laws of this covenant are represented as being written on the hearts of believers, and to these the seal of the Spirit is attached.

II. Seals were used to discriminate and mark property. Hence slaves had a mark of their own ; valuable things had the impress of their owners' seals ; see Ezek. ix. 4 ; Rev. vii. 2, &c. Now, it is by the spirit we possess, that our real character is truly known. If we are sons, or children of God, then God hath sent the Spirit of his Son, &c. " The Spirit itself beareth witness," &c.

III. Seals were designed for the preservation of jewels, and other objects of value. Thus, cabinets of jewels are closed, and have the seal of the proprietor upon them ; thus, the stone rolled to the mouth of the sepulchre was sealed, &c. ; thus, confidential communications are sealed. Now, thus does the Spirit seal believers. " They are his jewels," &c. ; his epistles. He only knoweth their value ; the world knoweth them not. He knows and preserves. " None of them have I lost," &c. Our preservation and security are entirely of God. By the power of the Spirit are we kept, through faith, unto eternal salvation.

IV. By the seal some image or device is impressed. There is one prayer in the Canticles, " Set me as a seal upon thine heart, and upon thine arm," &c. Now, the seal is the Spirit of God, and bears the full likeness of Deity ; a spirit of light, truth, holiness, love, &c. In this image man was created. By the Holy Spirit this is renewed in the heart of the believer. He bears the impression of light, of truth, of holiness, of love. As the impression on the wax corresponds with the image on the seal, so the heart of the believer bears the impression of God's Spirit, and is thus sealed by it.

APPLICATION.

1. *Men exhibit the likeness of the spirit by which they are impressed.* Wicked men that of Satan. There is the impression of ignorance, delusion, iniquity, malevolence, &c. See this described, Gal. v. 19, &c.

2. *How we should cherish and honor the Holy Spirit.* By prayer, holy meditation, watchfulness, humility, and love. " Grieve not," &c.

3. *The subject affords much comfort.* Sealed to the day of redemption. How consolatory ; how adapted to inspire hope, joy, &c.

THE EARNEST.

" And given the earnest of the Spirit in our hearts."—2 Corinthians i. 22.

We have previously considered the Holy Spirit under the figures of oil and a seal ; we now have a third metaphorical representation, under the idea of an earnest. The word has reference to the hiring of servants, who at the period of their engagement receive a small sum of money, by which the agreement is ratified, and as the pledge of the reward, or wages, that shall be hereafter given. Now, the Holy Spirit is given to those who become the servants of God, on their reception into the divine family ; and this gift is the earnest of what God will hereafter bestow upon them. This is more fully seen in Eph. i. 13, 14. We observe,

I. The earnest is the same in nature with the final reward. This is essential to an earnest. Now, the Holy Spirit is thus, in the blessings he imparts, an earnest of eternal life; for this is the final gift—eternal life. Observe, then, some of the features of resemblance. The gift is,

1. *Everlasting spiritual existence, in opposition to the death of the sinner.* Now the earnest is the living spirit in the soul; spiritual life begun. "It is the Spirit that quickeneth." This is the living water—the life of God within the soul.

2. *A reward of light.* Eternal noon-day splendor. Heaven needs not the light of the sun or moon, &c. God is the light of it; no night there. The Spirit dwells in the mind as a spirit of light; by it we are light in the Lord. "God, who commanded the light," &c. No longer darkness, &c.

3. *The reward is one of perfect purity.* No sin in heaven, the holy place; holiest of all—perfectly so. The Spirit dwells in the people of God, as the spirit of sanctification, transforming, purifying, cleansing, and making meet for the purity of heaven.

4. *The reward is one of celestial victory, and eternal triumph.* The upright have dominions, crowns, &c. "Unto him that overcometh," &c. Now, the Spirit dwells as an earnest in the heart of them; he imparts courage to the mind—power. By the Spirit, as with a sword, we slay all our adversaries. Our present conquests are those of the Holy Spirit within us.

5. *The reward is one of perfect love.* The infinite love of God to us, and the perfect love of God within us. Now, the Spirit dwells in the heart as an earnest of this. "The love of God is now shed abroad," &c. The Spirit enkindles, sustains, and perfects this love.

6. *The reward is one of unceasing joy and bliss.* There we shall obtain joy and gladness, &c. "Fulness of joy," &c. The Spirit dwells in the heart as an earnest of this. The fruit of the Spirit is joy. As the indwelling Comforter he produces this. It is sometimes unspeakable and full of glory. Thus we see as an earnest, it is of the same nature as the reward. Yet,

II. IT IS INFERIOR IN DEGREE. But a small portion of that reward. Now we know only in part; now very partially sanctified. It is but as the first sheaf to the great harvest—the drop to the shower —the dawn to the day.

III. IT IS THE GUARANTEE OF THE WHOLE. The rest must follow the earnest, unless the promiser dies, loses his ability, or acts unjustly. These are contingencies which cannot apply to Deity; therefore the earnest he gives of the Spirit, pledges most inevitably the whole reward.

APPLICATION.

1. *Have we the earnest of the Spirit? &c.* Do we possess a new spirit, different to what we formerly had? a spirit delighting in God, his word, ordinances, prayer?

2. *Let us rejoice in it.* How precious in itself, and also in reference to the eternity before us.

3. *By faith in the gospel, the Holy Ghost is imparted as an earnest.*

SCRIPTURAL ASSURANCE, &c.

"I know whom I have believed, and am persuaded that he is able to keep that which I have committed unto him against that day."—2 TIMOTHY i. 12.

TRUE religion is of heavenly origin, and is at utter variance with the spirit and principles of this world; true religion generally exposes its possessors to persecution and trouble for Christ and conscience' sake; but true religion has within itself the elements of comfortable experience, sufficient to sustain the mind in the deepest sorrows and severest afflictions. Let us see these verities exemplified in Paul. His religion was of God—the light and truth of heaven, and it was essentially different to every form of religion then in the world. As a Christian, Paul suffered the loss of all things for his Lord and Master. How long and afflictive the catalogue of his sorrows! but the internal principles of divine grace caused him to rejoice in all his tribulation, and at last to lay down his neck for the testimony of Jesus. This brings us at once to the text. Now a prisoner—ready to die. "For the which cause," &c. Our text is expressive of the essentials of evangelical experimental religion, and in that light we shall consider it.

I. A KNOWLEDGE OF CHRIST IS THE FIRST GRAND ESSENTIAL IN EXPERIMENTAL RELIGION. "I know whom," &c. The knowledge of Christ is the essence of knowledge; it is knowledge of the highest and most precious kind. Knowledge of letters—of science—of nature—of languages, all are valuable, but none to compare to the knowledge of Jesus. What say the scriptures? " This is life eternal." "Yea, doubtless," &c. But this knowledge of Christ must,

1. *Be scriptural.* Know him as he is revealed in the holy, living word; the scriptures testify of Christ. We know nothing rightly, perfectly, unless we appeal to the sacred testimony. His nature, person, offices, work, and glory, are all exhibited. The Bible is the word of Christ; the field of the precious pearl; the mirror where Christ is visibly beheld. But this knowledge,

2. *Must be personal.* "I know." Not my minister, or my teacher, or my friends; but my understanding, my judgment, my mind, and spirit are acquainted with Christ.

3. *It must be saving.* Know him as my Redeemer, by the freedom into which he brings my spirit, "If the Son make you free," &c.; by the forgiveness of my sin, " He came to give the knowledge of salvation by the remission of sin;" by his purifying grace, "If I wash thee not," &c. Thus, the blind beggar might know much by hearing of Christ, but much more when Christ had said, "Receive thy sight." Thus, the Samaritans knew something from the woman who had talked with Christ, but much more when they came to him. Such know Christ, who can say, "We have found him of whom," &c. "My beloved is mine." "My Lord and my God."

II. FAITH IN CHRIST IS EVER CONNECTED WITH THE RIGHT KNOWLEDGE OF JESUS. "I know *whom* I have believed." Believed what?

1. *What Christ has said.* Said of my sinfulness—my misery—my ruin. My help is in himself; what he has said; his love, and grace, and readiness to save. Believed what? Why,

2. *What he has done.* Became a man, and poor; suffered, died, rose again, and ever lives, &c. Believed what?

3. *What he has promised.* Present mercy; sufficient grace; eternal glory.

III. FAITH IN CHRIST SURRENDERS THE CHRISTIAN'S ALL INTO CHRIST'S HANDS. The salvation of the soul may be justly considered as comprising the Christian's all, for this is really and truly every thing; but the entire person of the Christian is committed—soul and body. The believer gives himself; his whole undivided self.

(1.) To be preserved and kept by the power of God.

(2.) To be fully laid out for Christ's glory.

(3.) To be sanctified and fitted for future bliss.

IV. THE CHRISTIAN IS FIRMLY PERSUADED OF THE SECURITY OF THAT WHICH IS COMMITTED TO JESUS. Whence arises this persuasion?

1. *From the ability and love of Christ.* His heart is set upon the eternal salvation of his people, and he has all power to do it. He can work, and none can hinder; this will be Christ's eternal joy and reward.

2. *From the past experience of Christ's goodness.* What has he not done? Look at guilt cancelled—debts forgiven—iniquities cleansed—blessings pure and divine imparted—mercies continued. Past safety; past help.

3. *From the unvarying testimony of the saints in all ages.* Was Enoch disappointed? or Jacob? or David? or Simeon? or Stephen? or the martyred saints now in heaven?

V. THE CHRISTIAN HAS ESPECIAL RESPECT TO THE LAST DAY. "Till that day." He refers to the same, verse 18, in reference to Onesiphorus; a day in which Christ will vindicate, confess, and publicly reward his disciples; the day of the saint's coronation, reward, and glory. Then Jesus will surrender all that has been committed to him, and say, These I have pardoned, sanctified, and kept, and not one is lost save the son of perdition.

APPLICATION.

1. *Have you this knowledge and firm persuasion?* Are you looking to that day?

2. *Let each one commit his all to Christ.*

HOW TO TREAT OFFENCES.

"Moreover, if thy brother shall trespass against thee, go and tell him his fault between thee and him alone," &c.—MATTHEW xviii. 15–18.

THE best of men are but partially sanctified, and therefore are surrounded by infirmities. Such being the case, intercourse cannot be kept up without offences; such will occur, even among the great, and the wise, and good; but New Testament direction is fully, explicitly, and clearly given, how we should act under these circumstances. The directions are the very opposite of the feelings of the human mind, contrary to our carnal hearts, and contrary to the course very often taken. Persons often, when offended, become morose and reserved, avoiding the person ; or they become vindictive, and try to injure them ; or they become angry, and express in passion their displeasure. All this is wrong, evil, to all concerned. Observe the method Christ has laid down.

I. The trespass supposed, whether accidental or designed. Whether it regards reputation, or property, or feelings, &c. Then, the direction given :

II. Seek a private interview. That he may explain, if possible. Better adapted for him to confess. More faithfully and affectionately admonished. State to him plainly, candidly, yet kindly. The motive ; you may gain, convince, convert him to a friend, deliver from sin.

III. If this fail, take one or two more. Let them be unobjectionable persons—peaceable persons—prudent persons. These are to witness, and aid by their counsel and influence. If this fail,

IV. Bring it to the church. Let the brethren decide. Do so for these reasons.

1. For the offender's sake. He may hear the church.

2. For Christianity's sake.

3. For the world's sake, that they may see we are neither indifferent nor malevolent. If he refuse to hear the church, then he must,

V. Be removed from Christian communion. This is the last act, and if this is rightly done, it is ratified in heaven, verse 18. Do not let us neglect this order. You object. He is not worthy of all this, &c. This is troublesome, &c. ; but it is your duty ; Christ demands it !

ADMONITION.

" Admonish him as a brother."—2 Thessalonians iii. 15.

To admonish, signifies to warn, to reprove gently, &c. The context supposes that some might disobey the epistle, and he then states the course that should be pursued, verse 14. Observe,

I. In the church of Christ there will be cases requiring admonition. Always been so. So with the apostles, and with the purest church in the world. Ignorance, imperfect graces, temptations, &c., all tend to this. Men drawn aside, &c.

II. On whom does the duty of admonition devolve.

1. *It devolves on some persons officially.* On ministers and elders of the church ; on parents and teachers.

2. On the experienced venerable Christian. In some instances, on all believers.

III. The way in which admonition should be given.

1. *The admonitor should be free from the evils on which he admonishes, or his admonition will be powerless, &c.*

2. *He must select an appropriate place and opportunity.*

3. *He must do it in the spirit of Christ, and not in his own spirit.*

4. *He must do it confidentially, and not make it the subject of conversation.* Where admonition fails, there must be rebuke, and if that fails, it must be told to the church.

IV. Motives by which this duty may be enforced.

1. *The relation of the person admonished.* He is our brother ; so we ought to feel and care, &c. If sick, or in danger, &c. How much more when the soul, &c.

2. *For the sake of the church of Christ.* We would not that men should apostatize, &c. Satan triumphs ; world rejoices, &c.

3. *For our own sake.* We should be condemned, if we saw a man on the verge of peril, and did not cry out, &c. We shall be guilty, &c. Objections to this duty,

1. *It more properly belongs to the minister.* He cannot know every instance, &c.

2. *It will give offence.* Much depends on the spirit, &c. I know persons who constantly do it, and do not offend.

3. *We feel it painful, &c.* But it is not the less necessary, &c. Let all Christians do so to those who are without. Let us warn, entreat, &c.

THE WEAK, &c., COMFORTED.

" A bruised reed shall he not break, and smoking flax shall he not quench."—Matthew xii. 20

Our text must be particularly familiar to every one who reads with attention the holy scriptures. We first meet with it in the forty-second chapter of Isaiah's prophecy ; and here in the gospel by Matthew, we see its direct and appropriate application to the Messiah, the friend of sinners, who came expressly to seek and to save, &c. Let us inquire,

I. WHAT THE METAPHORS IN THE TEXT SIGNIFY. And,

II. WHAT THE DECLARATION IN THE TEXT INCLUDES.

I. WHAT THE METAPHORS IN THE TEXT SIGNIFY. The metaphors are two, but alike in spirit and signification.

1. *The bruised reed.* May refer to the musical reed, extensively used by the eastern shepherds while tending their flocks ; or it may refer to the common reed, which is easily blown down and crushed. In the one case, the musical reed ceases to yield melodious sounds if crushed, or the common one to be of any use when bruised.

2. *The smoking flax.* Refers to the wick of the lamp, which is just expiring for want of oil, when light is scarcely emitted, and when the odor is offensive. Both metaphors refer to the same spirit, character, and state.

1. *They may be appropriately used to denote the broken-hearted penitent.* The soul crushed with a sense of sin, and an awful apprehension of the divine wrath ; the heart which has yielded before the hammer of divine truth ; the pierced contrite heart; the lowly abased spirit, where all self-exaltation is dethroned ; the whole soul bowed down before God. When the tongue confesses, and the soul loathes its sinful state.

2. *They may perhaps indicate, more directly, a weak and imperfect state of grace.* A low state of spiritual attainment. Where there is little knowledge—little vigor—flickering hope—much weakness and instability, confidence and peace only very imperfectly enjoyed. Or,

3. *A condition of extreme trouble and distress.* Afflictions sometimes bring us low ; troubles and trials, especially if they come wave after wave. When the clouds appear after the rain—keen tempest, &c. Let us notice, then,

II. WHAT THE DECLARATION OF THE TEXT INCLUDES. Observe, it is negative. He will not break—not quench. The shepherd finds his reed crushed, and as he can easily supply its place, he breaks it and throws it aside ; or the husbandman sees he reed beneath his foot, and disregards it.

The flickering light, or merely smoking flax, is extinguished. Not so Christ. He will not break, &c.

1. *He never has done so.* The history of the church contains not one instance ; the history of his life, not one case. See how he acted to his disciples—to the afflicted poor. All was pity, kindness, compassion, mercy, gentleness. So you all have felt it, to you.

2. *He never will do so.* For it would be contrary to his nature—to his office—to his delights and enjoyments.

3. *He will do the very opposite of this.* He will bind up and restore—he will heal and strengthen—he will encourage and revive—he will raise up and enliven. Then our subject,

1. *Encourages the timid and fearful.* Christ is as compassionate as he is great— as tender as he is glorious. Go to him by prayer. Cast your souls upon him.

2. *None shall be destroyed but the impenitent.* And because they despise the Saviour.

CHRISTIAN HOPE ACCOUNTED FOR.

" And be ready always to give an answer to every man that asketh you a reason of the hope that is in you, with meekness and fear."—1 PETER iii. 15.

TRUE religion must not only be enjoyed, but professed ; Christ is to be put on ; we are to confess him before men ; our light is to shine for the good of others ; we are to be Christ's witnesses, and confessors to the people. In doing this, the water of life within us springs up, and sends its stream abroad for the good of all around. But more is required of us than even profession ; we are to stand forth to vindicate the religion we profess ; we are, if necessary, to be disputants in the cause of Christianity ; we are to " be ready," &c. Four propositions will bring the subject of the text before us.

I. CHRISTIANS HAVE A HOPE WITHIN THEM. Hope is the expectation of future good ; it differs, however, from wishing, or desiring. It is an expectation grounded on what is possible and probable, yea, the certainty of what is satisfactorily established. Christians are the children of hope ; unbelievers the slaves of fear. The apostle thus speaks,

" Blessed be God," &c., 1 Peter i. 3. The Christian's hope has respect to four things:

1. *An interest in the arrangements of a benignant providence.* The God of providence is the God of grace. Those who are the subjects of his grace are especially interested in a kind and beneficent providence. Of such Christ speaks, when he says, " The very hairs of your head," &c. " The ways of such are ordered by the Lord." " The Lord keepeth them in the hollow of his hand." " If they commit their way to him," &c. " No weapon formed against them," &c.

2. *A full supply of all spiritual blessings.* This supply includes all that they can possibly need, in every condition of their pilgrimage to a better world. Their hope embraces that gracious declaration, " My God shall supply," &c. " The Lord God is a sun," &c.

3. *A safe and blessed dissolution.* Christians have not always an easy transition ; not always a triumphant one ; but always a safe one ; one of peace and hope. " The righteous hath hope in his death."

4. *A certain glorious resurrection, and eternal life.* The hope of eternal life is the grand consummation—the glorious issue—the full redemption of body and soul forever.

II. CHRISTIANS HAVE REASONS FOR THE HOPE THAT IS WITHIN THEM. These reasons are many ; but we refer to the three chief :—

1. *A persuasion of the truth of God's word.* They hope for these things, because they are revealed in the scriptures—published and offered there. There the foundation, the medium, and the certainty of salvation, both present and eternal, are made known. Now, the Christian believes most firmly the truth of this volume ; he considers it as God's own word, and he rests on it as an immoveable rock. " The grass withereth, the flower fadeth, but the word of the Lord endureth forever." Another reason is,

2. *The experience of true religion in the soul.* There is the harmony of their experience with the word of God. They have tested the gospel. It is represented as a word of light—and they are enlightened ; a word of power—and their rocky hearts have been broken ; a word of mercy—and their guilt they feel to be cancelled ; a word of purity—and their evil hearts are cleansed ; a word of comfort and joy—and they have peace ; the word of Christ—and Christ is now within their hearts, the hope of glory. Another reason is,

3. *The concurring testimony of all believers.* The experience of one Christian is in the main the testimony of all ; the general external and internal effects are the same. Persons of all grades, &c., profess to know, to feel, and to enjoy the same. Hence, in the mouths of many witnesses is the reality of religion established.

III. CHRISTIANS MAY BE CALLED UPON TO GIVE A REASON OF THEIR HOPES TO OTHERS.

1. *Fellow-Christians may ask this for their own edification.* " They that feared the Lord," &c.

2. *Penitent inquirers may ask, for their direction and encouragement.* " They shall come seeking, &c., inquiring their way to Zion," &c.

3. *Infidels may ask, to scoff and rail at religion.* To mock ; to gainsay. Now observe,

IV. TO THESE INQUIRERS WE ARE TO GIVE AN ANSWER.

1. *We must be able to do it.* Not ignorant of the great grounds and principles of our faith and hope. Religion not a blind thing, &c.—not mere feeling.

2. *We must be ready to do it.* Have the mind to do it. Not be afraid, nor ashamed, nor reluctant, &c.

3. *We must do it in a right manner.* " With meekness." A calm, quiet spirit ; a modest manner. Not ostentatiously ; not self-complacently ; but with meekness. " With fear ;" that is, solemnly—seriously ; with reverence for God and the truth. Not flippantly ; not with levity, &c.

APPLICATION.

1. *Let the Christian rejoice in his hope.* How rich, blessed, and certain ! It ought to lift him up ; make him always rejoice, Rom. xv. 13.

2. *This hope is within the reach of all.* Christ is the hope ; he is offered to you, &c.

3. *Do not reject Christianity until you have a substitute.*

PENITENCE AND EXPECTED MERCY.

" Who can tell if God will turn and repent, and turn away from his fierce anger, that we perish not ?"—JONAH iii. 9.

Our text relates to Nineveh. Nineveh was a dark, benighted, pagan city, densely populated, and aggravatingly wicked. To this city, Jonah, the prophet, was sent to preach repentance, ere their sins brought upon them the destroying wrath of the Most High. On the preaching of Jonah, the people were convinced of their sins, and fasting, repentance, and prayer were presented to God, that his wrath might be stayed. This humiliation was general, from the king on the throne to the poorest of the city. The king also set the people an example of pious penitence, verse 5. Observe the connection between the text, and the sermon of Jonah, verses 3 and 4. How wise and admirable was the course the Ninevites adopted! What an example for Christian nations and cities! Let us see how it will bear on the condition of every sinner now before God. Three propositions will open the subject to our minds and hearts.

I. As fallen beings, we have all greatly sinned against the Lord.

II. That wrath is threatened against every transgressor. But,

III. There is every reason to believe that sincere repentance may avert the doom threatened.

I. As fallen beings, we have all greatly sinned against the Lord. This is the unvarying doctrine of the scriptures. It applies to all mankind, of every age and nation; of course, it applies to every person in this congregation. When the mind has been enlightened, it is seen and felt. Ignorance of this truth argues that great darkness overspreads the mind. How important that every one should know the plague of his own heart: general statements not enough. To know, to feel, and confess I have sinned, and done wickedly.

1. *We have sinned.* Against both tables of the law—by commission and omission; against the divine government; against redeeming love; against the economy of grace; against the glorious gospel; against the Holy Spirit; against the light and convictions of our consciences! Who can plead exemption? Not one.

2. *We have all greatly sinned.* Both in number, magnitude, and aggravation. Against great light, and great mercies; against a great God; against repeated re-

solutions. Our sins are like a great mountain—a great cloud—a universal disease. Our sins have been of ingratitude, rebellion, and treason, for all sin includes these. Then many have sinned for years, many years; through youth, through maturer years, even to old age. Well would the lamentation of Isaiah suit us, " Wo is us! wo is us!"

II. That wrath is threatened against every transgressor. God necessarily disapproves, hates, and abhors all sin. As a just and righteous sovereign and law-giver, he is bound to punish it. His word contains his denunciation against every persevering, impenitent sinner. This wrath involves three things:—

1. *God's righteous disapprobation in this life.* His face is set against the wicked; he is angry with them. Say unto the wicked, it shall be ill with him. " He that believeth not," &c. Every day and moment God is displeased, justly displeased with the sinner.

2. *His curse in the hour of dissolution.* " The wicked are driven away," &c. " The candle of the wicked is put out," &c. His death brings him into the presence of his Judge. How fearful is this! How intolerable the idea!

> " What scenes of horror and of dread
> Await the sinner's dying bed;
> Death's terrors all appear in sight
> Presages of eternal night!
>
> " Tormenting pangs distract his breast,
> Where'er he turns he finds no rest,
> Death strikes the blow, he groans and cries,
> And in despair and horror dies."

3. *His fearful wrath through all eternity.* Let a few passages suffice here. " The wicked shall be turned into hell," &c. " Upon the wicked God shall rain fire and brimstone, and a horrible tempest." " Whosoever was not found written in the book of life, was cast into the lake of fire." " These on the left hand of the Judge shall go into everlasting punishment," &c. There shall be weeping, and wailing, and gnashing of teeth, and there the worm dieth not, nor is the fire quenched. Oh, think of eternal horror, eternal pain, eternal agonies, eternal despair! But I hasten with joy,

III. To observe that we have every reason to believe that sincere penitence may avert the destruction threatened. Literally, God is not a man that he should repent, &c. He is of one mind, the same yesterday, &c. "I am the Lord, and change not." But this is a settled principle in his moral government under the gospel, that sincere penitence shall avert the deserved wrath. Observe, this is,

1. *Peculiar to the gospel.* The law does not recognise this; it says, Obey and live; disobey and die! It will not be satisfied with sorrow or amendment; indeed, it cannot. But the gospel reveals a Mediator between God and man; one who has propitiated by his death; one who has borne the desert of sin. A surety, and through his merit, God can be just, &c. "Through this man is preached," &c. The penitence which is effectual,

2. *Must be the effect of the truth upon the conscience.* We have a beautiful instance in the case of the three thousand on the day of Pentecost. They heard, understood, felt, cried out, and became the recipients of the divine mercy. Thus the word acts as a hammer, &c. Christ crucified is to be preached in connection with this. "They shall look on him," &c.

3. *This penitence must be deep and sincere.* Not a mere emotion; not a transitory sensation; not a slight impulse, but a sincere feeling in the whole soul. The ardent action of the whole mind. See it in the penitent woman, her shame, her tears, her contrition.

4. *It must be influential.* Work repentance, or change of mind and life. Bring forth fruits meet, &c. The case of the Ninevites. Humiliation, fasting, confession, prayer, &c. Now such penitence shall avail.

(1.) God has said it. "To that man will I look, who is of a contrite spirit." "The sacrifice of God is a broken spirit," &c. "Blessed are they that mourn."

(2.) Sacred history, and the experience of the whole church of Christ, establish it. When did it not prevail? When was the penitent spurned, rejected, cast out, denied? Who ever perished, however vile, worthless? &c.

APPLICATION.

1. There is no alternative between penitence and death.

2. Now consider, reflect, and live to God.

3. To all is the offer of mercy sent.

GOD'S PARDONING MERCY CELEBRATED.

"And in that day thou shalt say, O Lord, I will praise thee; though thou wast angry with me, thine anger is turned away, and thou comfortest me."—ISAIAH xii. 1.

It is evident that the preceding chapter relates to the reign and kingdom of Messiah. The latter end of the chapter clearly relates to the ingathering of the Jews— a time yet to come—a period which will be the spiritual jubilee to the tribes of Israel, and the beginning of the millennium to the world itself. The text refers to the happy and delightful expressions of grateful confidence, which shall be ascribed to the Lord God of Israel. "And in that day," &c. Now while this is clearly the meaning of the passage, yet it is capable without any torturing of a personal application. The text may be assumed by every believer— by every spiritual child of Abraham; as such we shall treat it on the present occasion. We have,

I. A PREVIOUS STATE REFERRED TO. "Thou wast angry with me." When we speak of anger in Deity, it is not to be supposed that he is influenced by passion as we are. The term indicates his disapprobation and determination to punish. This disapprobation, &c., is never excited towards any beings, but in accordance with his settled equity and holiness of character. God is righteous in all his ways, and just in all his dispensations. We notice,

1. *That man's character and conduct, while in his natural state, are such as justly to expose him to the divine anger.* What does God survey in the sinner? Ignorance, unbelief, enmity, malevolence, impurity. Not a redeeming trait, &c. Not a lovely feature. His conduct is exceedingly displeasing to God; he returns not for the mercies received; he acknowledges no divine benefits, he reverences not God, he yields no obedience; he does not what God justly and reasonably expects from his rational creatures. Then he breaks his laws, violates his statutes, and does those things which God has sacredly forbidden to be done. In addition to this, he abuses his long-suffering, and despises his mercy. He rejects the gracious message of the gospel, and puts to death again the Son of God. We ask,

2. *How may rational intelligent beings be*

sensible that they are the objects of the divine anger? "Thou wast angry with me." Now this is clearly revealed in God's holy word. "God is angry," &c. He has expressed it in the most striking and varied language. "His face is set against them that do evil." Then this is ratified by the workings of conscience. Let any one do good secretly, and contrast his state of mind with the feelings arising after the commission of secret evil. In both cases, the cognizance of man shall not be included. What a difference! day and night—bliss and anguish—heaven and hell, do not form greater contrasts.

3. *The divine anger is of all things most to be deprecated.* Only observe what has been the effect of the divine anger to impenitent sinners. Think of the old world; of Pharaoh and the Egyptians; of Sodom, &c. View it written in indelible and awful characters in the history of the Israelites. See the scriptural definitions and figurative representations. It is a desolating flood—a horrible tempest—a devouring fire; nothing can resist it—nothing alleviate it—nothing extricate the victims of it; and to the finally incorrigible it will rage with desolating and eternal fury. But notice,

II. The DELIGHTFUL CHANGE EXPERIENCED. "Thine anger is turned away," &c. This change is experienced in a two-fold form.

1. *The divine displeasure is removed.* "Anger turned away." The cloud blotted out; no longer under condemnation, &c. This necessarily supposes a change in the creature. His enmity and opposition to God have ceased; he has seen the evil of sin; confessed and forsaken it; and believed in the Lord Jesus Christ. A state of unbelief involves us beneath the divine wrath; a state of faith brings us from this dire condition. God abhors the high and proud spirit; but he looks in pity upon the lowly and contrite.

2. *The divine favor is enjoyed.* "Thou comfortest me." We cannot stand in a neutral state with respect to Deity. The instant his anger is removed his favor is enjoyed. This comfort is the light of the divine countenance—it is the possession of the Holy Ghost; the dove of peace and comfort hovers over the soul. Now guilt, remorse, and the burden of sin are gone, and there is in their stead the smile—the blessing of God. This comfort is real, not visionary; suitable, abiding, and inexpressibly precious; and it is associated with all good, both in this life and in that which is to come. It is the precursor of everlasting felicity. Observe,

III. The GRATEFUL RETURN PRESENTED. "I will praise thee." Acceptable praise includes,

1. *The offering of a thankful heart.* It must arise from within; it must have to do with the affections of the soul. Heart gratitude is alone real, and that which God will receive.

2. *It must be free and spontaneous.* "I will." Not I ought, or should, but "I will." I feel borne away with the principle of grateful love to God. This feeling fills the soul; absorbs all its faculties.

3. *It must be constant.* Never out of time, or unreasonable. "In every thing give thanks." In secret; in the domestic circle; in the social means of grace; in the public ordinances, &c. "I will praise thee every day," &c. Praise God always, in health and sickness, death and eternally.

4. *It must be practical.*

5. *It will be eternal.* "Unto him who hath loved us," &c.

APPLICATION.

Let the text be,

1. *The test of our state.* Can we use it? Is it so with us? Is God our reconciled friend?

2. *The test of our spirit and conduct.* Do we love and bless God? Is it our delight to do so?

3. *Let it be attractive to the convicted, mourning sinner.* There is a way to divine peace, and to real and heavenly comfort. Christ is that way. Come now to God through him.

PREACHING CHRIST

"Whom we preach."—COLOSSIANS i. 28

IN the erection of a building, one of the chief and most important matters is the foundation; for if the foundation fail, how can the building stand? In the construction of an arch, the key-stone is that which holds the whole in security. Most systems have their main principles, their cardinal truths. In the human body, some parts are vitally important ; in our existence, bread is the staff of life ; but you ask, what mean these disconnected observations ? I reply, in preaching, Christ is all this to the excellency and value of the sermon. Our discourses are evangelically deficient if Christ is not the foundation—the key-stone —the grand principle and essential truth of the Christian system—the true, living bread of the world. In preaching or suffering, Christ was all to the apostle—" We preach not ourselves," &c. He avowed his desire not only to win Christ, but to have fellowship with him in his sufferings. All his epistles are full of Jesus Christ. This is pre-eminently the case with this epistle. He dwells on his sacrifice, dignity, &c., and then adds in the 27th verse, " To whom God would make known," &c. We preach,

I. ALL CHRIST.
II. CHRIST TO ALL.
III. CHRIST ALWAYS. We preach,

I. ALL CHRIST. In other words, a " whole Christ." We claim for him,

1. *The highest dignity and glory.* He was the angel of Jehovah's presence to the Jews, and he is to us Christians, God over all, blessed, &c. He holds no inferiority to the eternal Father, but claims perfect, essential, unbounded, and everlasting equality. " He thought it not robbery," &c. He is " Immanuel, God with us." His throne is the highest, at the Father's right hand,—the throne of the universe. His authority is illimitable. He created all things—upholds all things—preserves all things—and by him all things consist. On his head are many crowns ; the ascriptions of the redeemed, and of seraphim and cherubim, are incessantly given to him " whom we preach." Notice,

2. *We preach him in his perfect humanity and abasement.* A true man ; made like unto his brethren, &c. ; bone of our bone, &c. ; really the second Adam ; and in his abasement, we refer to Bethlehem— the stable—the manger—poverty—slander —persecution—at last death. " He humbled himself to death, even the death of the cross." He died as a thief, or a murderer ; on a cross between heaven and earth —between two malefactors, &c. " Whom we preach,"

3. *In the glory of his offices.*

(1.) Divine offices as ruler, &c. ; but especially his mediatorial offices, as the prophet and apostle of the world.

(2.) As a priest, presenting one sacrifice for man's transgression.

(3.) As the King of Zion, establishing an empire of truth and righteousness, of peace and love on the earth. These offices meet a world's wants.

i. Dark ; he illuminates it by his truth.

ii. Lost ; he saves it by his death.

iii. In rebellion, he subdues and governs it by his grace. " Whom we preach,"

4. *In his sacrificial obedience and merit.* In his divine and human natures he possesses infinite dignity ; in his obedience and righteousness, God's eyes rest on immaculate holiness. His blood has expiatory virtue, and his life once offered removes the curse, and rolls it from our world. The whole is expressed by Isaiah, " All we like sheep," &c., and sung by the redeemed, " Unto him who loved us," &c. " Whom we preach,"

5. *In his illustrious triumphs.* He triumphed over error by his doctrines ; over temptations by his endurance ; over malice by his meekness ; over diseases, death, and devils, by his miracles ; over sin by his death ; over the grave by his resurrection ; and over souls by his gospel and love. Who does not unite with the poet,

" Oh ! Jesus, ride on, till all are subdued," &c

But,

II. WE PREACH CHRIST TO ALL.

1. *All stand in need of Christ.* None righteous, &c. ; none sufficient to save themselves ; no other Saviour for any. Wisdom, righteousness, sanctification, redemption, and eternal life, are nowhere but in Christ. " Whom we preach to all,"

2. *For he is the Saviour of all.* Brother of all ; lived for all ; died for all. He has the nature of all in the holy place. " Whom we preach to all,"

3. *For he has sent his gospel to all.* The world is the extent of his commission :—

" Wide as the world is his command,
Vast as eternity his love."

" Whom we preach to all,"

4. *Of every class and rank.*

(1.) Civil—monarch, beggar, rich, poor

(2.) Mental—philosopher, illiterate, civilized, savage.

(3.) Moral—the orderly and the rude,

the correct and the profligate, the best and the worst; also to all ages. We invite children to sing their hosannas to Christ: we entreat the aged to take Jesus in their arms by faith, &c.

III. WE PREACH CHRIST ALWAYS. We desire Christ to find a place in every discourse, and to be its life and glory. "We preach Christ,"

1. *As the essence of all doctrines.* Justification; regeneration; sanctification.

2. *As the substance of all blessings.* Pardon; peace; hope; joy.

3. *As the beginning and end of all duties.* Obedience begins with believing in him, and ends in living to him.

4. *As the model of all virtues.* His life and conversation quite perfect. Practical essons of humility, self-government, lowliness, courtesy, gentleness, fortitude, goodness.

5. *As the sum of all enjoyment.* Ask the forgiven penitent, "I will praise," &c. Ask the tranquil believer, "The peace of God," &c. Ask the dying Christian, "To die is gain." Ask the beatified spirit, "With the Lord to enjoy him; to see him as he is."

APPLICATION.

1. *Is Christ yours?* Have you received him? Does he dwell in you?

2. *Are you Christ's?* Your hearts, lives, possessions—all.

3. *Who will become Christ's to-day?* For to you is the word of this salvation sent.

THE HELP OF GOD FOR HIS OWN CAUSE PLEADED.

"Arise, O God! plead thine own cause."—PSALM lxxiv. 22.

TRUE religion identifies a man with the things of God. No man who loves God can live to himself, &c. A good man is concerned for the divine glory. His feelings are depressed or exalted, as God is honored or despised. True piety throws its powers of vision through the universe, and rejoices in all that reflects the mind of God, and weeps over the misery, and sin, and ruin which darken so many portions of our world. In the midst of the evil that exists, he perceives the nand of God working, resisting the violence of Satan, circumscribing the limits of human wrath, and giving exercise to the powerful ele-

ments of truth and holiness. Beholding this, the good man's energies are aroused, his spirit encouraged, his ardor excited, and he gives utterance to the prayer of the text, "Arise, O God!" &c. We remark,

I. GOD HAS A CAUSE IN OUR WORLD. The affairs of the universe are in his hands. Our world is a part of that universe. He made it; he upholds it; he governs it. It is under his cognizance; regulated by his agencies, &c. But morally, our world is in a state of revolution. Satan introduced into it the elements of moral evil. By it, it became the region of crime, darkness, misery, and death. To counteract this revolt, and remove its effects, God mercifully set up a cause in our world—a remedial system—a system of restoration to truth, holiness, and salvation. Now, this cause is based on the redeeming love of God; on the mission of Christ into our world; on the setting up of Christ's kingdom, so as to overthrow the kingdom of the evil one. The cause of God and his church are the same. The church is to be the instrument for carrying out Jehovah's designs. God, by his Holy Spirit, dwells in the church, and thus perpetuates and gives efficacy to its influence and exertions.

II. THE CAUSE OF GOD IN OUR WORLD IS DISTINGUISHED BY CERTAIN STRIKING CHARACTERISTICS.

1. *It is distinguished for its knowledge.* Cause of light, and therefore it is bearing down the darkness of the world. Ignorance is the citadel of Satan's kingdom. God is light; diffuses light; makes his church the instrument of light. The seven churches of Asia were likened to seven golden candlesticks. "Ye are the light of the world." "Cities," &c. The church is to arise and shine, &c. Now the word of the divine truth is the light of the church.

2. *It is distinguished for its holiness.* The church is separated from the mass, and is holy to the Lord. Called to holiness; invested with holiness; to exhibit holiness. Thus it is to condemn the sin and defilement of the world, and like salt to save it. from corruption and ruin.

3. *It is distinguished for its benevolence.* It embodies the sentiments of the song of the angels at the birth of the Redeemer, "Glory to God," &c. Its aspect towards heaven is purity—towards earth, goodness. Now sin produced misery to man; to his body and spirit; to man personally, rela-

tively, &c. Religion breathes love, peace, goodness; it exercises candor, mercy, compassion, pity, and tenderness; it sacrifices self, and lives and works for others. Now, the influence of this benevolence is to diffuse happiness through our world. As sin has rendered man a curse to his fellow-creatures, religion makes him a blessing.

III. THE CAUSE OF GOD, THOUGH COMPRISING MANY ELEMENTS, IS YET ONE. Tyranny and despotism have cursed our world, crushed many thousands beneath their cruel yoke. Liberty, therefore, is the cause of God; freedom of limb and conscience are the unalienable prerogatives of man. War has made our earth drunk with the crimson fluid of life, and is opposed to God's glory and man's well-being; peace, therefore, is God's cause. Ecclesiastical systems of error have been the bane of the church, and, riveted by state authority, have been one of the heaviest drags on the chariot wheels of the gospel; church purity, therefore, is the cause of God. Now, in the gospel of the Saviour are two principles, which, if imbibed and carried out, would overthrow every evil, and bring about the consummation of every good—the love of God, and the love of man; one as a burning flame ascending to Deity, and the other as a benignant sunbeam shining upon the world. All real good in the world is identified with God's cause.

IV. THE CAUSE OF GOD IS GREATLY IMPEDED AND OPPOSED. Opposed by all the moral evil in the world; by all the power of Satan. Impeded by the apathy of its professed friends; impeded by human systems, creeds, and earthly influences; by the want of devotedness, prayer, and faith of Christians.

V. PRAYER TO GOD ON BEHALF OF HIS CAUSE IS THE CHURCH'S DUTY. What examples we have in the history of the church, where the ardent piety of its people was thus displayed! How Moses interceded; how David supplicated, &c.; how Jeremiah prayed and wept; how Paul agonized; how devotionally fervent were the early Christians, the Reformers, the Puritans; Knox, and others; and how eminently godly persons do so now! Thus to pray is pleasing to God—really profitable to ourselves. Such prayer has many promises on which to rest; such earnest prayerfulness has generally preceded and accompanied the revival of religion.

VI. GOD CAN MOST EFFECTUALLY ANSWER THE PRAYERS OF HIS PEOPLE. Now, he can do this by the signal acts of his providence, or by the especial influences of his grace, or by both harmonizing with each other. Hence observe how he rescued his people from Egypt; how he delivered the Jews from the wicked plots of Haman; how he turned back their captivity by Cyrus; how he has overthrown empires, raised up instruments, and restricted human wrath and passion; how he has made the wrath of man to praise him, &c.; and how he has opened doors of usefulness; given men the powers to adopt varied kinds of instrumentality; how he has raised up remarkable agents—Luther, Wickliffe, Knox, Wesley, Whitfield, &c. But we anticipate the full triumphs of his cause by the universal diffusion of his truth; by the erection of the cross, " And I, if I be lifted up," &c. Providence subserving the means of grace; and this shall be " until the kingdoms of this world," &c. " Till the knowledge of the Lord," &c. " Till all flesh shall see his salvation."

APPLICATION.

1. *Who are with Christ in this cause?* How are you feeling and acting? What doing for its extension? &c. Oh! labor and pray.

2. *Who are indifferent?* More concerned about their own temporal affairs.

3. *Who are opposed to it?* That is a fearful position. We urge you to abandon it. Seek the mercy of the Lord, that you perish not, &c. And now shall not this be our prayer, " Arise, O Lord!" &c.

ON A REVIVAL OF RELIGION.

" Wilt thou not revive us?"—PSALM lxxxv. 6.

To revive signifies to restore; to increase; and a revival of religion supposes its previous existence. The necessity and importance of religion we do not stay to establish. It is presumed that this is felt to be of the very highest moment; of both individual and general interest; essential to man's best interests both in time and eternity. Observe what our text supposes.

I. THE COMPARATIVE LOW STATE OF RELIGION. We use the term comparative, because that which is only a low state of religion with one, may be ardor contrasted with that of another. Look at this subject in relation to,

1. *Individuals.* What a limited state of knowledge, faith, peace, hope, joy, &c.; what little devotedness; what formality, earthliness; what selfish manifestations; what feebleness of action for Christ and his cause; how little of the mind of Christ, and the power of high-toned piety.

2. *As to churches.* Here, also, great diversity of state; but take the more prosperous. How few really enlisted in active support of the great movements of the age. How few of the most flourishing churches inspired by glowing zeal; living in all things to God, for souls and eternity.

3. *As to the universal church of Christ.* In its catholic aspect. How feeble its instrumentality—how limited its resources—how contracted its sphere — how few its leading master minds and its members, as contrasted with the subjects of the kingdom of Satan—how little effected—how very much to be done. What solicitude, therefore, should it excite among Christians of all sections of the church.

II. THE IMPORTANCE OF A REVIVAL OF RELIGION.

1. *To each individual Christian.* It will be their dignity, elevation, riches, and true felicity. This is their fertility and meetness for eternal glory.

2. *To the great cause of the Redeemer.* Its beauty, vigor, grandeur, extension, and consummation, all depend on the revival of religion.

3. *To the world at large.* How are its darkness, guilt, misery, and wo to be removed without a revival of religion? The spiritual salvation of the world hangs upon it.

III. THE MEANS TO BE ADOPTED FOR SECURING A REVIVAL OF RELIGION.

1. *An increase of personal piety among the disciples of Christ.* This applies to every Christian, especially in humility, faith, and benevolence.

2. *A better organization of the friends of the Redeemer.* The army is large, but the real active force exceedingly few. In churches comprising hundreds, perhaps not more than one in ten is really engaged in active effort for the extension of the Redeemer's kingdom. Some system of division of labor, &c., must be adopted to remedy this great evil.

3. *The removal of certain great impedi-*

ments. The disunion of real Christians; the overthrow of sectarianism, &c.; temporal poverty, and excessive physical toil. We must expect and labor for this. Civil freedom and happiness are favorable to true piety, and its revival throughout the world. It is to be regretted that persons in our own country have so little time to spare for mental and moral improvement. Tyranny and oppression will all be swept away as the truth of the gospel wins its widening course. Ecclesiastical secularities are also great impediments.

4. *The united prayer and self-denial of the church.* Prayers more direct and fervent—more pleading—more agonizing.— Prayer meetings for this end more common, and better frequented. Christians more self-denying. A willingness to give up our own feelings, &c., for the honor of Christ, and the extension of his kingdom.

IV. THE PROBABLE SUCCESS OF THESE MEANS. " Wilt thou not ?" &c. That God is willing to answer this appeal is evident; for,

1. *He desires it.* It is asking for what is agreeable to him. His bowels yearn over this miserable world; his affections are upon it; he wills the salvation of each and of all.

2. *God has engaged for its accomplishment.* How many the predictions; how great, and radiant, and glowing the promises! and not one shall fail. The celestial heavens are bestudded with them. A galaxy; a milky way.

3. *God has revived his cause in answer to prayer.* His word records instances of such a kind. Two instances must suffice: Neh. viii. 16; Acts iv. 31. In Scotland, in the sixteenth and seventeenth centuries; in England, Ireland, and Wales, in the eighteenth century. Then what ground of hope there is; what reason to unite and plead, " Wilt thou not ?" &c.

APPLICATION.

1. *Who feels the propriety and force of the text ?*

2. *Will you pray, and labor, and toil ?* Assist to remove the impediments, and to keep the machinery in motion.

3. *It will be effected by us, or without us.*

4. *See what persons do for sin and false religions.* Pleasure-takers; infidels; pagans.

JEHOVAH'S GRACIOUS DECLARATION CONCERNING THE WICKED.

"As I live, saith the Lord God, I have no pleasure in the death of the wicked."—Ezekiel xxxiii. 11.

I know not of a more solemn yet interesting passage in the holy scriptures, than the text we have just read in your hearing. Whether we consider the speaker, or the solemn declaration given, it demands our most serious and prayerful consideration. The speaker is Jehovah, the eternal and ever-blessed God, the fountain of purity, and goodness, and truth. The declaration relates to the death of the sinner. Not the death of the body, but of the soul, that which includes the righteous infliction of wrath in the world to come. The death of deaths; the death that never dies. The declaration affirms that this is not the pleasure of God. He has not appointed, or decreed, or necessitated it. He does not desire it. He confirms this by a solemn asseveration or oath, "As I live." Notice,

I. To whom the text refers.

II. The evidences by which it is confirmed.

III. The impressions it should produce upon our minds.

I. To whom does the text refer? "The wicked." The transgressor. We readily believe that God wills not the death of the righteous. He cannot do this. But the text refers to the very opposite of these. Those who are far from God. Haters of God. Disobedient, &c. Now the term includes all who are unrenewed in their hearts. Hence, in the sight of God, all who are in their natural state are such. But the text will apply,

1. *To the flagrantly wicked.* Notorious sinners. Men who have exceeded those around them in crime. Daring, desperate, prominently vile. Bearing the mark of the beast in their foreheads. Who glory in their shame. Yes, our text applies to the very vilest of these.

2. *To the aged wicked.* God does not will the death of the hoary-headed rebel. He whose childhood was folly — whose youth was riotous—whose maturer years were criminal, and whose old age is evil and perverse, yet in the eternal death of him, God does not delight.

3. *The influentially wicked.* He does not delight in the death even of the ringleaders of evil; yet this is a fearful state to be in. Alluring others to dreary regions of wo. To be champions for vice; to spread the deadliest poison around; to mature others for endless torments; yet these are included in the gracious declaration in the text. Of these, then, none are excluded, no, not one of the countless myriads of the human race.

II. The evidences by which it is confirmed. How does it appear that God has no pleasure in the death of the wicked?

1. *In not leaving the sinner to the results of his crimes.* God had only to be passive and leave the sinner to his own ways. Guilt made man anxious, wretched, and miserable. Like poison, it would have worked death—as fire, it would have consumed the spirit. Had God left man the prey of his own freely chosen evil, he must have been eternally lost. God's interference was for the sinner's recovery, it was essential to his rescue, and consequently establishes the truth of the text, that God has "no pleasure in the death," &c.

2. *The marvellous provision for man's restoration is another evidence.* God made provision for the salvation of man, that provision was the sacrifice of his own Son. He laid our iniquity upon him. He transferred the sufferings of the guilty to the holy and just One, who suffered for us, that he might bring us to God. This provision is truly marvellous, it surpasses understanding. It is too high, too vast, too sublime, too profound, for human comprehension. The whole economy of redemption exhibited in every unfolding of it the great truth of the text. Wherefore the abasing advent of the Son of God? Wherefore the sorrowful and afflictive life, the cruel and shameful sufferings, the intense agonies, the inexplicable passion, the bloody and ignominious death of the holiest person in the universe, if God delighted in the death of the sinner? The song of Bethlehem— the doctrines of Jesus—the sufferings of our substitute—all, all testify that God "has no pleasure," &c.

3. *The gracious principles on which salvation is tendered is a further evidence of the truth of the text.* To show the divine solicitude for man's welfare, the blessings of salvation are brought down to his moral exigency and condition. Every impediment is removed. Every blessing prepar-

ed, and God only requires the acceptance of his mercy, on his own gracious terms of appointment. No oppressive toil—no hard exertions—no painful penances—no preparatory self-preparation. The object of his hope is lifted up, and he has just to look, and as Moses, &c. The bread of life is presented, and he has but to receive it. The fountain of healing is opened at his feet, and he has but to step in. The proclamation of liberty is made, and the door of emancipation is opened, and he has but to go forth and enjoy the liberty and happiness of the children of God. Here then we see in the adaptedness of the gospel provision, that "God has no pleasure," &c.

4. *The long-suffering of God, and his forbearance to the impenitent, further ratify the truth of the text.* Every sinner deserves to die. God could justly punish with death on the first rejection of his gospel. God has power to do it. The sinner is always in his power. But how does the Lord act towards the wicked? He restrains his wrath—he bounds his vengeance—he extends the reprieve, he does vastly more than this, he keeps in activity a variety of means for his rescue and salvation. He sends days and years of these—he sends sabbaths and ordinances—he sends ministers and friends—he sends promises and threatenings —he sends comforts and afflictions, and all for what? That the wicked may not die, to exhibit his unbounded mercy, and to prove that he has no pleasure in the death of the wicked. We shall only add,

Finally, the solemn asseveration or oath in the text. An oath is a solemn, deliberate affirmation, made as before God, and calling his cognizance to what is attested. Jehovah cannot testify before a greater, for he is the only God, and beside him there is none else; but to vindicate his tender mercy and compassion for the welfare of the wicked, he stands forth, and before angels, men, and devils, he proclaims by his own eternal immutability, "As I live," (not only in myself, by my eternal self-existence, but as the fountain of life and being to the universe itself,) "I have no pleasure in the death of the wicked." Let us briefly notice, then,

III. THE IMPRESSIONS IT SHOULD PRODUCE UPON OUR MINDS.

1. *We should be impressed with our own personal responsibility.* Many would cavil with circumstances, and reason about ne-

cessity, and thus remove the blame from themselves, and affirm his desire for our destruction. Every man must give an account, and God will reward every man, &c.

2. *We should be affected by God's gracious conduct towards us.* What love and mercy is here exhibited! It ought to melt the hardest heart. It ought to constrain the most desperate rebel, &c.

3. *We should co-operate with God so as to secure the great salvation.* Nothing is requisite but to act with God. To will as God wills; agreement here will secure present reconciliation and eternal happiness.

4. *We should do all in our power to prevent the wicked from dying.* Every minister. Every Christian, feel, pray, labor, &c., or we are not like God.

ADAM AND EVE.

"So God created man in his own image: in the image of God created he him; male and female created he them."—GENESIS i. 27.

THE history of our first parents cannot but be interesting in whatever light it is considered. Of their nature we are partakers. In the results of their conduct we are involved, and therefore from their example and history, valuable instruction must be derived. With the leading events in their lives scripture is replete, and therefore to its divine and authentic records let us appeal. We may contemplate them,

I. IN THEIR PRIMEVAL PURITY AND BLESSEDNESS. The offspring of God; made by him, and for him; but especially formed under peculiarly interesting circumstances. The last and fairest of the divine works—the result of the divine council— and formed in the divine likeness — created with a spiritual nature, immediately proceeding from God, chapter ii. 7. Intellectual, holy, happy—in their understanding, reflecting the divine knowledge —in their judgment, the divine truth— in their affections, the divine goodness— in their conscience, the divine purity—in their will, the divine dominion. All the faculties and passions nicely balanced. All their powers in a state of transparent beauty and harmony. God enthroned in their affections, adored in their spirits, and obeyed in their lives. In their earthly condition, having the supremacy over all terrestrial creatures; invested with entire, indisputable dominion; the earth their domain; Eden their royal abode; angels their friends and companions, and all creatures their willing and obedient servants; above all, God their joy and supreme good. In this state they had ability to abide. Subject to Deity by a law the most easy, beneficent, and practicable; but alas! how soon is this picture of moral beauty and felicity reversed. Behold them,

II. IN A STATE OF TEMPTATION AND PERIL. Tempted by the devil. Tempted to disbelieve God in reference to the forbidden fruit—tempted to disobey his explicit commands—tempted to exalt themselves to an equality with God. These temptations were addressed to the weaker vessel, when alone, and alas! they were successful and prevailed. She beheld, and hearkened, and desired, and ate. Adam also from her received the fruit of sin, and fell into the same condemnation. With this act fled innocence, peace, and purity. Shame was the immediate result, and fear and dread followed in its train; thus sin and wo were introduced into our world. Observe them,

III. UNDER ARREST AND EXAMINATION. By the darkness of their minds, they had supposed it possible to flee from God. How foolish, how futile! His voice arrested them. Their fear and shame are confessed, chapter iii. 10. The heart-searching interrogation is presented. "Hast thou eaten," &c. Self-justification — man throws the blame on the woman, and the Being who had given her to him. " The woman whom thou gavest me," &c. And then reluctantly the admission, "I did eat." The woman throws the blame on the serpent. Ah, sin was found so degrading and miserable, that its perpetrators were most anxious to disown it. And now notice them,

IV. RECEIVING THE RIGHTEOUS SENTENCE OF GOD. On the woman was pronounced sorrow in conception and child-bearing, and subjection to her husband, verse 16. To the man toil, perpetuated through the course of his existence. "In the sweat," &c., ver. 19. And on both, the dissolution of the body. " Dust thou art," &c. And now the seeds of death began their operation, influence, &c. Every step was one towards the house appointed for all living; but in addition to this sentence, sin had effaced the moral beauty and excellency of their spiritual nature. The

gold, alas, how dim! the fine gold how changed! The crown of dignity had now fallen from their head, and the sceptre of royalty from their grasp. The spirit was bereft of its virgin purity, and the moral glory had departed; instead of peace was anxiety; instead of joy, remorse; instead of tranquillity, distraction; instead of health, disease; instead of the divine smile and approbation, the holy displeasure of God. Notice,

V. THEIR EXPULSION FROM THE ABODE OF HOLINESS AND BLISS. As traitors their inheritance was forfeited, as rebels they were excluded those peaceful scenes of purity and joy. God himself exercised the sentence. "So he drove out the man," &c., and a flaming sword prevented their access to the tree of life. Now, alas! sinners, polluted and wretched, and expelled the paradise which had been prepared as a residence of dignity and enjoyment. But observe them,

VI. AS THE SUBJECTS OF GOD'S MERCIFUL INTERPOSITION. In the midst of wrath, mercy was remembered. Compassion triumphed over judgment; and when the cloud of punishment seemed so black and terrible as to exclude all hope, a ray of celestial light streaked the agitated horizon, and a promise of redemption and deliverance given in those joyous words, that the woman's seed should bruise the serpent's head. Doubtless religious instruction and direction were given. The mode of access to God revealed; the way of their gracious acceptance clearly made known; and the terms of their final salvation fully detailed. Let us,

1. Mourn over the evil of sin.

2. Rejoice in the remedy provided. And,

3. Personally seek the salvation the gospel proclaims.

FAITH AND SACRIFICE OF ABEL.

" By faith Abel offered unto God a more excellent sacrifice than Cain, by which he obtained witness that he was righteous, God testifying of his gifts: and by it he being dead yet speaketh."— HEBREWS xi. 4.

How awfully prolific and rapid in its dire progress is sin! The first man born into our world was a murderer; not only a murderer, but a fratricide—the murderer of his brother. How greatly mistaken was the mother of all living when, at the birth of Cain, she exclaimed, " I have gotten a man from the Lord," imagining that he was the promised seed who should bruise the serpent's head. Her second son was a martyr, and one destined to lead the van among those who suffered death for the testimony of Jesus. Our subject however this morning refers to his faith, and the sacrifice he presented to God. To this then we would call your serious and prayerful attention.

I. ABEL OFFERED SACRIFICE UNTO GOD. The immediate and precise origin of sacrifices is not revealed. It is exceedingly probable that when God revealed the promise of a Saviour to our first parents, he gave them direct instructions on the subject of sacrifices, and we have no doubt the skins with which he clothed them were the skins of animals which had beeh thus presented. Animal food was not then allowed. To slay animals expressly for their skins is improbable, but to suppose the beasts slain for sacrifice, and the skins thus appropriated, seems reasonable, and leads us at once to the very probable institution of sacrifices. Doubtless God revealed the nature of the sacrifices, and the symbolical end they were to answer. Abel's sacrifice was the firstling of his flock. A lamb, the best and most choice his flock could yield. This was afterwards incorporated in the Jewish ritual as the great annual offering. The victim which Abel presented was slain. Doubtless a rude altar of stones was erected, and on this the lamb was presented to God.

II. ABEL'S SACRIFICE WAS MORE EXCELLENT THAN CAIN'S.

(1.) Now we presume it was the offering prescribed by God. God will not own or bless will-worship. In religion God leaves no room for fancy or human invention.

(2.) Abel's offering was better, as being more suited to a sinner. Homage, reverence, gratitude, &c., become holy beings, something more is necessary from the guilty. A sinner requires a mediator, a way of access to God. Cain's sacrifice only savored of natural religion. God's claims as a Creator and Benefactor must not be forgotten ; but we must never forget, as guilty beings, that we need pardon, and as polluted, a laver of purification. Praise and veneration will not do instead of repentance, confession, and faith.

III. ABEL OFFERED HIS SACRIFICE IN FAITH. And his faith,

1. *Would regard his own unworthiness and guilt.* " The whole have no need of a physician," &c. The act of killing the lamb, would lead him to reflect on the just desert of sin. By sin came death. " Here I see the claims of God's offended justice and broken law, thus my life might have been poured out."

2. *His faith regarded the great sacrifice of which his lamb was but an emblem and a type.* The ancient sacrifices were designed to keep up and prefigure the great propitiation for sin. The ancient saints rested not on the victims slain, but on the Lamb of God, who should be offered in the latter days for the sin of the world.

3. *His faith would regard his own interest and dependence on that sacrifice.* He offered the sacrifice for himself, he felt personally concerned. Here he rested his hope, and believed God would accept him through the promised Messiah. He believed what God had testified, and on that great Victim he rested all his expectation of God's favor, and eternal life.

IV. GOD TESTIFIED HIS APPROBATION OF ABEL'S SACRIFICE. " He obtained witness," &c., " God testifying," &c., see Gen. iv. 4.

1. *How did God witness?* He could have done so by an audible voice, but doubtless by fire consuming the victim. Some commentators render " he had respect,"— " kindled with fire." This was the way in which God accepted the sacrifices under the law, see Lev. ix. 24.

2. *What did God witness?* " That he was righteous." Offered what pleased God ; obeyed God's sacrificial law ; but it doubtless means that he was justified, forgiven ; that God expressed his favor, and accepted him through the great sacrifice ; that his heart was penitent, humbled, believing.

V. ABEL BY HIS FAITH AND SACRIFICE STILL GIVES INSTRUCTION TO MANKIND. " By it he being dead," &c. Now in what does Abel instruct us ? He saith,

1. *That sinful man may have access to God.* Can man approach a holy Being ? Will he not perish ? No, God is accessible even to the guilty, the sinner may bow down and not perish, " for his mercy endureth forever." He saith,

2. *That the way of sacrifice is the only way which God approves.* " Without shedding of blood," &c. All our blessings are

through Christ's death. No pardon or holiness without it. He saith,

3. *That faith is essential to acceptance.* Unbelief insults God—rejects his mercy. Throws discredit on his word. Faith trusts all and every thing, where God has laid the only foundation. As the poet has sung,

" Believe, and all your sin's forgiven ;
  Believe, and you are heirs of heaven."

4. *That true religion may expose to severe suffering.* It may cost us our wealth, liberty, reputation, yea, life itself. "If a man will lose his life," &c. It cost Abel his. He was slain by his brother.

Finally, it teaches us, that God's favor will amply repay for all it may cost. Abel paid a great price, but was. it not worth it? You do not doubt it. Myriads have paid the same, and not one has ever regretted it. Not one that would not cheerfully pay the same cost again. Go through the whole army of martyrs, behold them in their white robes, see their glittering crowns, their waving palms. Ask you, who are they ? These are they " who came out of great tribulation," &c. If they had a thousand lives, they would sacrifice them all for Christ— all for salvation—all for eternal life. Believers, cleave to Christ. Sinners, come to him and live.

CAIN

" And bare Cain, and said, I have gotten a man from the Lord."—Genesis iv. 1.

Such is the brief account of the entrance into our world of the first of woman born. The first promise had inspired our progenitors with the hope that Cain was the woman's seed who should bruise the serpent's head. Little did they think that that child was to be the cruel persecutor and murderer of his brother, and that age upon age must pass away before the appearance of the incarnate Redeemer of the world. Let us just glance at the leading particulars in the life and character of Cain. Observe,

I. HIS PECULIAR CONDITION AS THE FIRST-BORN CHILD. What anxieties he would occasion ; what attention elicit ; what hopes and desires excite ; the first infant, with all the accompanying weakness, &c., of that state. How dignified in his parentage, notwithstanding their fall, &c. ; how copiously towards him would maternal kindness flow ;

how every action would be observed ; how his growth and advancement towards maturity watched, &c. Notice,

II. HIS RURAL OCCUPATION. " A tiller of the ground." Though the eldest of Adam's progeny, yet he was not nursed in the lap of luxury and indolence. Industry is an honor to any man, however exalted. His labor was of a useful kind, adapted to increase his physical health and enjoyment. He had before him the beauties of nature —around him the wonders of creation— and above him the glorious heavens, in the height of which sat enthroned the Maker and Lord of the universe. His occupation was favorable to meditation, to seriousness, and communion with God. It was adapted also to promote gratitude to God, and dependence upon the communications of his rich and essential blessings on the culture of the accursed ground. The earth he tilled proclaimed the injury it had sustained through sin, and also would admonish him as to his final dusty bed. Consider him,

III. AS AN UNACCEPTABLE WORSHIPPER. It seems highly probable that God had revealed to our first parents the nature and character of that service he would require from them ; and, doubtless, the offering of sacrifices was an essential part thereof. Thus the worshipper would be led to perceive the evil and desert of sin, and to look forward to the great sacrifice which should in the end of the ages take away the sin of the world. But Cain's offering " was of the fruit of the ground," in which God was recognised only as the Lord of nature ; a mere acknowledgment of his being and government, such as holy creatures might with propriety have presented. But neither Cain's spirit nor worship had the least reference to his sinfulness, or the necessity of divine mercy. In this it is contrasted with that of Abel, verse 4. As such, it was rejected of the Almighty. Observe him,

IV. AS A VICTIM OF FRATERNAL ENVY AND MALEVOLENCE. He discovered that his offering was rejected, while God honored Abel by a gracious acceptance of the sacrifice he had presented ; and now envy —that foul Satanic passion—took possession of his soul. It is said, " He was very wroth, and his countenance fell." His soul disdained his God, and hated his brother ; he indignantly abhorred him for his excellence, and the worst of all feelings now rankled in his bosom. Alas ! he was now the slave of the destroyer, that wicked one, who was a murderer from the beginning. A great proportion of the crime and misery of our world is to be traced to the sin which had now full possession of the soul of Cain. We are called to view him,

V. AS A GUILTY FRATRICIDE. God had expostulated with him on his wrath, and sullenness, and envy; he had cleared himself of partiality, and had assured him that if he did well he should be accepted; he had thrown the responsibility entirely upon him, see verse 7; but it was all in vain; the demon of hate still kept possession, until at length " he rose up and slew his brother." Thus did the influence of Satan and man's depravity prevail; thus did excellency and real piety suffer; and thus did the accursed earth drink in the precious blood of one of the saints of the Most High. Abel had lived in the divine service and favor; was hated and persecuted for his superior and godly spirit; died a martyr; and was the first of the human race to realize the blessedness and glory of the eternal world. Observe,

VI. CAIN A GUILTY CULPRIT IN THE PRESENCE OF THE SUPREME JUDGE. How overwhelming the solemn interrogation of Jehovah, " Where is Abel, thy brother?" the cool and wicked falsehood he uttered, " I know not;" the heartless, evading question, " Am I my brother's keeper?" then the solemn declaration of God, " What hast thou done? the voice of thy brother's blood crieth," &c.; the pronouncing of the curse, " And now art thou cursed from the ground," &c., verses 11, 12. His misery now filled him with horror, and overwhelmed, he exclaimed, " My punishment is greater than I can bear." Divine mercy was richly mingled in God's dealings with him. He was allowed to live; his life was pronounced sacred, verse 15; his punishment was evidently limited to this life; his after-life is not stated; but we fear he remained a child of the wicked one.

1. Unbelief is one of the reigning principles of the carnal heart, and is full of evil fruit.

2. How fearful a sin is envy; how to be guarded against.

3. How essential is the fear of God.

4. How all-important an interest in Christ Jesus.

GOD'S TESTIMONY CONCERNING ENOCH.

" By faith Enoch was translated, that he should not see death; and was not found, because God had translated him; for before his translation he had this testimony, that he pleased God."—HEBREWS xi. 5.

IN every age and dispensation, God has had his illustrious servants exhibiting to all around the power of religion, and the beauties of holiness. In the first age of the world, there was the pious Abel, the first of the noble army of martyrs; in the period which intervened between that time and the flood, there was the holy Enoch, of whom our text speaks; at the time of the deluge, there was the righteous Noah. So we see that each period, however dark and wicked, had its pious luminaries, its sacred stars, which lit up the moral hemisphere, and showed men the true pathway to a blissful immortality. We now direct your attention to Enoch. Observe,

I. HIS PERSONAL HOLINESS.
II. HIS INTERNAL ASSURANCE.
III. HIS GLORIOUS REWARD.

I. HIS PERSONAL HOLINESS. This is thus expressed by the Holy Spirit: " And Enoch walked with God." In the Greek translation of the Old Testament scriptures, it is rendered the same as in our text, " He pleased God." Three things have ever been requisite in pleasing God:—

1. Faith. " By faith Enoch," &c. " Without faith it is impossible," &c. Faith is the firm persuasion of the truth of a testimony or record. To reject or disbelieve such a testimony, is to make the person testifying a liar, the greatest possible insult you can offer. This is what unbelief does to God. He that believes not the record God has given, &c., makes God a liar. How horrible the idea! What God testified to Enoch we know not, or how; whether by vision, an audible voice, or by immediate inspiration. Whatever was the method of God's communicating his testimony, Enoch believed God; he believed all the Lord testified; and this was the basis of all his religion, the root of that pious tree which bare such holy fruit, and was finally transplanted to the blissful regions of the heavenly paradise. In pleasing God there must be,

2. Affectionate communion. God must be supremely loved—the object of our

soul's delight; he must have the palace of the heart—the throne of the affections. The soul was originally created for this; capable of it; and this must be the centre around which the mind must revolve, and the end to which all its delights must tend. Thus God will be in the thoughts, in the imaginations, in the mental exercises of the mind. He will be with us, and we shall be with him, in secret, in public, by the wayside, by day, and by night. We shall have continual fellowship and spiritual intercourse with him. In pleasing God there must be,

3. *Constant and progressive obedience.* "Be followers of God as dear children." We are to imitate Deity. Thus Christ, the good shepherd, says, "My sheep hear my voice, and follow me." God's voice must not only be listened to, delighted in, but also obeyed; and there must be constancy in this; it must be the wont and custom, the habit and practice. There must also be advancement; going onward. The child can walk but feebly, or a little at a time; but it gains strength, and then can do so easily and more extensively.

II. HIS HAPPY ASSURANCE. "He had this testimony," &c. Now, we may be assured of having the approbation of another in several ways. Take the case of a child and its father, or the subject and sovereign.

(1.) Now, if either give certain commands in which they exhibit great interest, and to which they attach great importance, then by obeying those commands, and carrying out those designs, we rationally conclude that we possess their approbation.

(2.) This will be still more forcibly deduced, if we feel that we have the same spirit, enter heartily upon the same pursuits. Thus, supposing the emperor of China is sincere in his denunciations against opium, every Englishman must please him who labors to prevail with our countrymen to abandon that traffic. Now this may be still more effectually ratified,

(3.) By a written, or a verbal attestation. Let a child show the father's letter wherein his approval is attested, or state the sentiments he has uttered; let the subject refer to his king's eulogy, and then the matter is placed beyond all doubt. The Christian has this threefold testimony :—

i. He compares his life by the divine word, and he reads his conformity to that.

He sees some faint resemblance in that infallible mirror.

ii. He searches his own spirit, and he feels that it agrees with the Spirit of God; with God's desires and delights; and in this, that it is the opposite of what it was.

iii. God's Spirit imparts the approving light of his countenance and breathings of peace, just as when Christ visited his disciples, and breathed on them, and said, "Receive ye," &c. The apostle says on this subject, "Because ye are sons," &c. Gal. iv. 6; Rom. viii. 14, 16. "For as many as are led," &c. This testimony is exceedingly valuable,

(1.) As it regards our safety.

(2.) As it regards our comfort; for both of these entirely depend on having this testimony, &c. Observe,

III. HIS GLORIOUS REWARD. "Was translated," &c. This is sometimes spoken of in reference to character and state. "Translated from the kingdom of darkness," &c.; but here it refers to the removal of Enoch from this world to the heavenly glory. "He was not," &c. He did not remain on earth; he was not found in his usual sphere; it is probable his friends were surprised when they missed him, and knew not whence he was removed. God, however, declared that he had taken him, or in the words of our text, "translated him." He was thus exempted from the stroke of death; he was delivered from the corruption of mortality; he entered not the house appointed for all living; his remains did not see corruption; but it is clear that he underwent some important change to fit him for the joys of immortality. 1 Cor. xv. 50.

APPLICATION.

1. *Learn the doctrine of a future state of existence.* And in respect both of body and soul. This is but the dawn of our being—the infancy of our existence; the body shall live again. There are already three glorified bodies in heaven—Enoch's, Elijah's, and that of our blessed Redeemer. These are the first-fruits of a glorious harvest.

2. *The sure path to a blessed immortality.* Walking with God, and thus having the testimony, &c. Believers, cherish this. Sinners, be anxious for this, &c. Let all think how important it will be in the day of death and of judgment.

3. The great, essential principle of saving religion is faith.

THE FEAR AND FAITH OF NOAH.

" By faith, Noah being warned of God of things not seen as yet, moved with fear, prepared an ark to the saving of his house ; by the which he condemned the world, and became heir of the righteousness which is by faith."—HEBREWS xi. 17.

WE now proceed to contemplate the third distinguished worthy presented to our notice in this illustrious chapter of the believing heroes of Old Testament history. The same striking encomium is passed upon his devoted spirit and conduct as on that of Enoch ; see what is said of Noah, in 6th chapter of Genesis, 9th verse, &c. Our text, however, refers to the great leading events in his life ; his deliverance from the flood, which God brought upon the old world. This is very concisely, yet clearly presented to us in the words of the apostle, " By faith, Noah being warned," &c. In reference to Noah, notice,

I. THE WARNING HE RECEIVED. We read the warning, Gen. vi. 13, 14. The cause of this awful threatening was the universal spread of deep-toned iniquity and corruption, Gen. vi. 1–5, 12. The nature of the threatening was the universal destruction of all flesh. This God threatened he would accomplish by a flood of waters, verse 17. This warning related to *unseen things.* There was nothing to indicate this in all the range of nature around him. The sky, and earth, and sea wore their usual aspect. The man of observation might look round, and yet nothing confirmed the intimation ; the man of science might appeal to the laws of nature, &c. The worldlings of that day would not spare one hour to examine the question, nor the men of pleasure have one scene of banqueting less; the great mass of the people would ridicule and laugh at the folly of the eccentric, fanatical Noah ; yet, despite of all this, the warning was received in the spirit of pious reverence by that godly man. Notice,

II. NOAH'S CONDUCT IN REFERENCE TO THIS WARNING.

1. *He believed God.* He regarded the threatening as coming from the faithful and true Jehovah. Faith in God's testimony was the spring of Noah's conduct. This is the basis on which the structure of his after life was built.

2. *His faith produced fear.* He feared the evil threatened—the wrath denounced. God is greatly to be feared ; his wrath is terrible. This is the characteristic of the Lord's people, that they have his fear before their eyes. " The fear of the Lord is the beginning of wisdom." They are in the fear of the Lord all the day long.

3. *His fear was connected with active obedience.* He obeyed God. God told him how he might escape by the construction of an ark, Gen. vi. 14. Here the duty was formidable, expensive, connected with great toil, and which would expose him to general contempt ; but his faith was operative. " He prepared the ark," &c. ; as prescribed by God ; the identical vessel in all things, as God had ordered. His obedience was *full, minute,* and *explicit,* see verse 22. " Thus did Noah ; according to all that God commanded him, so did he." This is genuine, acceptable, saving religion. Notice,

III. THE REWARD WHICH FOLLOWED THE PIOUS COURSE NOAH ADOPTED. We see the importance of *believing God's word,* and thus fearing his wrath, and gratefully accepting the method of escape he has provided. Two things specified :—

(1.) He condemned the world; his preaching, and practice, and building the ark, all condemned the world ; left it excuseless ; justified God's dispensation.

(2.) He became heir of righteousness ; that is, he became before God and men a righteous character, and therefore entitled, through the mercy of God, to the reward which had been promised. But the reward itself,

1. *Consisted in his own preservation.* He escaped the vengeance of God ; his life was spared, the greatest earthly blessing he could enjoy ; and this was but a shadow of the great and eternal salvation which as a righteous man he would enjoy forever.

2. *His family were also interested in the deliverance.* God often blesses individuals for the sake of others. There is a real blessing in being piously connected ; but that will not save, if they personally reject the piety of their relatives ; see the case of Lot and his daughters, &c. The advantages and privileges are greater ; but if abused, their condition is the more signally awful. Noah's sons, and their wives, evidently obeyed Noah, regarded his commands, went with him readily into the ark,

&c., and thus were delivered with him. Oh! how joyous to be saved, and those related to each other, all saved together.

APPLICATION.

1. *God has revealed the certainty of a future judgment.* He has recorded the method, and the sublime grandeur of the great day; he has reiterated this solemn warning; of this we see no indication. The scoffer asks, Where is the promise? &c. Men generally neglect and despise it; but the day will come. The flood was delayed 120 years, yet it came at length; so will the final day of God.

2. *God demands your belief of this great and solemn warning.* He calls you to fear, &c.

3. *He has revealed a way of safety.* His Son is the ark; the door of this ark is open; he urges you to enter; on this your safety depends; no other way. Are you believing—fearing—obeying?

4. *Are you laboring for the security of your children? &c.* They are all equally welcome with you; but each must personally enter.

ABRAHAM'S BELIEVING PILGRIMAGE.

"By faith Abraham, when he was called to go out into a place which he should after receive for an inheritance, obeyed; and he went out, not knowing whither he went. By faith, he sojourned in the land of promise, as in a strange country, dwelling in tabernacles with Isaac and Jacob, the heirs with him of the same promise. For he looked for a city which hath foundations, whose builder and maker is God."—HEBREWS xi. 8–10.

AFTER God had frustrated the Babel builders, and confused their speech, sacred history refers us to the origin of distinct nations, and the fact of God choosing Abraham to be the father of the Jewish people, and one whom God engaged to bless and make a blessing. To this eventful period the text refers; see Gen. xii. 1, &c. Thus Abraham acted through the influence of faith. He believed God; he forsook all for God; he went where God directed; he considered himself but as a stranger; and, finally, he looked for a more fixed and abiding habitation.

I. ABRAHAM BELIEVED GOD. For this he holds a most eminent and exalted station in the sacred pages of truth; so much so, that he has the honored appellation of "father of the faithful." His confidence in God was so full, and entire, and unshaken, that he was styled the friend of God. Now, as faith is the foundation of every holy work, in proportion as this is strong and vigorous, will every virtue thrive, and flourish, and bear fruit. It is like gold, the most precious of all metals; but we are enriched according to the abundance we possess of it. Weak faith is valuable; but it is strong faith gives glory to God. Weak faith will walk safely on a calm lake; but strong faith will not sink in the tempest or the storm. How desirable it is to believe God! all God says, and at all times. Faith has an eagle's wing, and an eagle's eye; it can rise to the greatest possible elevation, and it has a lion's courage amidst confusion and persecution; even when the sea roars, and the earth shakes, it sits with firm security, and sings "defiance to the gates of hell!"

II. ABRAHAM FORSOOK ALL FOR GOD. His own country; his father's house. In this,

1. *He gave up what he possessed for that which was promised.* He had an interest in his father's house, and his own country. These were in hand, in possession; and, doubtless, were far from being despicable. He left, however, his own land, and his father's house, for that which was named in the promise.

2. *He gave up the present for the future.* Present subsistence, and present patrimony, for some good to be hereafter bestowed. Now, in these we see the nature of the demands religion makes. Abandonment of our carnal possessions and pleasures for those which God promises; to give up the society of the world for the church; to resign present profits for future advantages; to lose sight of earth and time for heaven and eternity. Abraham became as it were isolated from the world to be united to God; a true picture of spiritual religion. We cannot enjoy the world and God; nor love both; nor serve both. We may use the world; but it cannot be pre-eminent, and God be glorified.

III. HE WENT WHERE GOD DIRECTED. True religion has,

1. *An ear to listen to God.* "Speak, Lord, for thy servant heareth." God spake

to Abraham, and he reverently heard the will of God propounded to him.

2. *Feet of cheerful obedience.* Having heard and understood, he " obeyed." Acted as God directed ; walked as he chalked out the way. God said, This is the way, and Abraham walked in it.

3. *Unsuspecting surrender of all into the Lord's hands.* " Not knowing," &c. God knew, and this was his comfort, &c. It is not necessary for a passenger to understand navigation to reach the port, &c., in safety ; or for a child to know the way, when its father holds its hand ; or the patient, anatomy or medicine, when the skilful physician is present.

IV. ABRAHAM CONSIDERED HIMSELF A STRANGER. As such he acted and lived. He conducted himself as a dying man in a dying world ; he knew this was not his rest, or home, or portion ; and this is precisely the spirit we should feel and cherish. A little reflection might convince every one of the propriety of this. This world is merely a land of passage : eight hundred millions are ever crowding its surface ; but they are all moving. " One generation passeth away," &c. Some are just leaving it—others just entering—but all are moving. Hence life, as a river, is ever emptying its countless drops into the ocean of eternity.

V. HE LOOKED FOR A MORE FIXED AND ABIDING HABITATION. Here he recognised his own immortality ; he associated with future existence a union with kindred spirits ; he beheld above not a desert but a city —the city of God—the new Jerusalem— the palace of Jehovah. He saw its foundations were firm ; yea, firmer than a rock, the very being, and purposes, and perfections of God sustaining it. Its grandeur was worthy of its artificer. " Builder and maker is God." He looked for it by faith, and daily hope, and constant prayer ; he reckoned upon it as his own ; he lived in reference to it ; and daily felt himself getting nearer and nearer.

APPLICATION.

1. *Have we obeyed God, and given up the sinful pursuits of the present world ?*

2. *Are we walking by faith or sight ?* Abandoning present temporal gain, for future spiritual and eternal glory.

3. *Urge all to set out.*

4. *Believers to persevere, &c.*

JACOB WRESTLING WITH THE ANGEL

" And Jacob was left alone ; and there wrestled a man with him until the break of day. And when he saw that he prevailed not against him, he touched the hollow of his thigh ; and the hollow of Jacob's thigh was out of joint, as he wrestled with him."—GENESIS xxxii. 24, 25, &c.

THE patriarchs and early saints possessed not the valuable direction of a written revelation. In that early age there were none especially inspired either to teach or prophesy to the people. To make up for this, God often revealed himself to his saints, especially by visions and dreams of the night. Oftentimes too did Jehovah appear and discourse with them, assuming sometimes the form of a man, and at other times the appearance of an angel. Jacob was favored with two of these especial manifestations. At Bethel, where he saw the ladder reaching to heaven, and on the occasion to which the text refers. Notice,

I. THE CIRCUMSTANCES IN WHICH JACOB WAS PLACED.

II. HIS MYSTERIOUS CONFLICT.

III. HIS WONDROUS VICTORY.

IV. THE BLESSINGS BY WHICH IT WAS FOLLOWED.

I. THE CIRCUMSTANCES IN WHICH HE WAS PLACED.

1. *He was returning into his own country.* He left it through fear of his incensed brother. More than twenty years had passed over. His return was under God's direction, ver. 9. " In all thy ways acknowledge," &c. " Commit thy way," &c.

2. *His brother was announced as coming in wrath to meet him.* He had wisely and piously sent a message of kindness to Esau, v. 3, &c. ; but his resentment was aroused, and Jacob is informed of his hostility, &c., ver. 6.

3. *He had prudently arranged his temporal concerns.* His peril seemed awfully imminent. What could he do ? (ver. 7.)

4. *He had fervently poured out his soul to God.* He followed up all with earnest prayer. He pleaded God's promises, ver. 9 to 12. Having done this, he sent over the brook his flocks, and also his family.

5. *He was now enjoying devotional solitude.* " Alone," so far as mortal beings were concerned. " Alone," to press his suit with God. " Alone," to confess his

sins, and to open all his heart to the Lord. Notice,

II. HIS MYSTERIOUS CONFLICT. This conflict was mysterious indeed ; we have nothing like it on record. It was not merely mental. His body and soul were engaged ; but who was the glorious being, &c. " A man," says the text ; but in verse 28, he is said to have " power with God." See Hosea xii. 4, 5. None other than Jehovah Jesus. God in the appearance of humanity. God anticipating his incarnation, &c.

(1.) How unequal the conflict !

(2.) How protracted ! lasted for several hours.

(3.) To show the weakness of Jacob, and his own power, he touches him and disjoints the hollow of his thigh ; but still Jacob maintains the struggle.

(4.) He solicits permission to retire. " Let me go, for the day breaketh." How easily he could have done so ! but he honors Jacob's perseverance, and elicits his strongest faith. God will not oppose physical might to moral power. He allows moral influence to prevail.

(5.) Mark, Jacob resolves not to yield without the blessing. " I will not," &c. What pious valor, decision, energy, perseverance ! And now observe,

III. THE WONDROUS VICTORY HE ACHIEVED. God allows omnipotence to yield to the influence of faithful prayer. In token of the victory,

(1.) He obliterates his former name. No more Jacob, i. e. Supplanter, the sins and frailties of the past blotted out, see chapter xxvii. 34, &c.

(2.) A new name is given, " Israel," a name of honor and holy distinction. " One who has power with Jehovah," one who has prevailed with the divine majesty of heaven and earth. The title was one of great honor, and everlasting renown ; a name too which should descend to thousands of thousands, and to generations then unborn. Then notice,

IV. THE BLESSINGS BY WHICH IT WAS FOLLOWED. Verse 23. " And with men," &c. This victory was the assurance that men should not overcome or destroy him, the less victory would certainly follow the greater.

(1.) The mind of Jacob was filled with sublime yet sweet conceptions of God's glory. He called the place, " Peniel," &c.

(2.) He marvelled at his own preservation. " And my life is preserved."

(3.) The wrath of his brother was turned aside. His heart was in the Lord's hand, and he subdued and softened it. " If a man's ways please the Lord," &c.

(4.) He retained, however, the sense of his weakness. " He halted upon his thigh." Lest he should be exalted above measure. To keep him prostrate before the Lord, &c.

APPLICATION.

1. *The marvellous potency of prayer.* How wondrous its achievements ! What hath it wrought ?

2. *The secret of its power is fervor.* Persevering fervor. What was emblemized by Jacob's wrestling ? Not fainting ; not ceasing ; but pleading, and pressing our suit. Let us long for, and seek the spirit of prayer, and the grace of supplication.

3. *Let the prayerless now see the value of prayer.*

PHARAOH AND JACOB.

A SKETCH FOR THE AGED.

" And Pharaoh said unto Jacob, How old art thou ?"—GENESIS xlvii. 8, 9.

OUR text introduces us to one of the most striking scenes of Old Testament history. We have before us three distinguished individuals ; the monarch of Egypt ; the prime minister, raised by extraordinary providences from a captive to that exalted station ; and the devout Jacob ; the man who, as a holy prince, had power with men and with God, and who was named Israel because he prevailed. Joseph is introducing his venerable and beloved father to Pharaoh, who with affable condescension and kindness, thus addresses the hoary headed saint, " And Pharaoh said unto Jacob," &c. Let us consider the question, the reply, and the lessons it suggests.

I. THE QUESTION ASKED. " How old art thou ?" We observe this is,

1. *A very common question.* How often it has been asked in our hearing, of us, and from us to others ! We may generally form some idea, but not always correct, some persons look much younger. Read the account of Moses, Deut. xxxiv. 7. Also of Joshua, xiv. 10, &c. ; others look aged early—labor,

sorrow, constitutional weakness, afflictions, &c. Some become old early by emaciating sins, &c. The wicked often do not live out half their time.

2. *This question is interesting.* How marvellous is life! The wonder is that we live, not that we die. How mysteriously is life sustained, what pulsations! what inspirations and respirations of the lungs! how many vessels have to be acting so that the machinery may not stand still! as the poet says,

" Our life contains a thousand springs," &c.

besides, the dangers are so numerous, &c.

" Dangers stand thick through all the ground,
 To push us to the tomb;
And fierce diseases wait around,
 To hurry mortals home."

3. *This question is solemn and momentous.* It is connected with great responsibilities, mercies, privileges, opportunities, gratitude, improvement, and duties demanded; oh! weigh this, and then how momentous life becomes! But, also, because it is connected with eternity; our cradles rock us to the tomb; whatever we do, wherever we be, we are travelling to the grave; yes, and to eternity.

" Lo! on a narrow neck of land,
'Twixt two unbounded seas I stand," &c.

To elderly persons, how affecting this should be to you; the morning and the afternoon, the spring and the summer are gone, and the evening and the autumn are passing away. Observe in reference to this question,

II. THE ANSWER GIVEN.—Mark,

1. *The age specified.* 130 years, a very extended age, yet it was short when contrasted with his predecessors; his father Isaac lived 180, his grandfather 175, his great grandfather 205, and many of the antediluvians approached to 800 and 900 years; yet 130 to us appears very long. In the time of Moses, the great majority did not survive 70, and now a generation is computed at 30 years; these are statistics well worthy of our consideration.

2. *He represents his years as being few.* There is the most marked difference in past time and the future; how short a period is a year in the retrospect! Ask the aged, and they all agree, that a long life is as nothing; one says it is as yesterday, another says it is as a tale, &c., a mere vapor,

man's life is but **as a shadow, a flitting** cloud, &c.

3. *He describes his years as being evil.* That is, years of sorrow and affliction. Jacob's were so in many cases. His own private anxieties—exiled when a youth, servant for twenty years to his uncle, much domestic trouble. There stands the tomb of Rachel; then Joseph is in his opinion slain; his sons, some of them profligate others cruel, most of them ungodly. In his old age exposed to adversity through famine; he was the man who had seen trouble; fears within and fightings without; and this is a fair sample of human life; most of you know it. A wilderness a rough sea—a perilous desert.

4. *He describes his whole life as a pilgrimage.* " The days of the years," &c. I like this form of speech. We should not forget that our years are formed of days we cannot tell what a day may bring forth " So teach us to number our days," &c Altogether it is a pilgrimage. Incessan. change—mutability itself—a continuou progression. Not at home in the body " strangers," &c. Thus the saints have always felt. " They confessed," &c. Now let us notice,

III. THE LESSONS WHICH IT SUGGESTS.

1. *Let us form a true estimate of life.* It is short and sorrowful. Let us settle this in our minds, we shall then treat the world as such, and expect such treatment from it.

2. *Let us ascertain if the great ends of life are accomplished by us.* The ends for which we should live.

(1.) For ourselves. To secure our own salvation and spiritual improvement.

(2.) For the good of others, our families, the church, and the world.

(3.) For God. To glorify Him, to show forth our love and gratitude, &c. He formed us for this, &c.

3. *Let me ask the elderly if they are distinguished for the graces and virtues which should distinguish old age.* Should not such excel in knowledge, experience, patience, self-command, spiritual-mindedness, charity, &c., such should be ensamples and counsellors to the young, &c.

4. *Old age without piety is a fearful state.* Think of the sins of sixty or seventy years, of the abused blessings, and neglected privileges; what a mountain of guilt, &c. Travelling from God and heaven towards

perdition, how awful your influence on others, &c.

5. *The aged sinner may be forgiven.* God's patience yet waits, His mercy still lingers. Thě door is still open, but do not delay or trifle. Be intent, &c.

6. *May all present set out on the heavenly pilgrimage.*

ESAU.

"Lest there be any fornicator, or profane person, as Esau, who for one morsel of meat sold his birthright," &c.—HEBREWS xii. 16, 17.

VERY much has been improperly said and inferred respecting Esau. By some he has been represented as the type of the abandoned, and as bearing the broad seal of God's eternal reprobation. Surely such forget, that by representing him as hated of God and predestined to wo, with all feeling minds they must enlist pity for his wretchedness, and sympathy on account of his doom. Thus reasoning, God has been greatly dishonored, and, in opposition to his solemn asseveration, he has been declared a respecter of persons. The literal scriptural account will vindicate Jehovah, and throw all the blame on Esau himself. Hating and loving, in the words of scripture, often signify ardent, and less devoted affection. Jesus says, "Except a man hate father and mother, wife and children," &c. So it is said, "God loved Jacob, and hated Esau." God's disapprobation of Esau was owing to the profanity of his character, and to that the text refers.

I. LET US LOOK AT ESAU'S PROFANE BARTER, AND CONSIDER THOSE WHO IMITATE HIS CONDUCT. Esau, as the first-born of Isaac, possessed many privileges, and was heir to many blessings. These privileges were two-fold.

1. *Temporal.*

(1.) He had pre-eminence of authority and power over the rest of the family.

(2.) He had a double portion of the paternal estate.

2. *Spiritual.*

(1.) From the first-born, before the law, descended the priesthood of the family.

(2.) Of him and his seed was the Messiah to spring.

(3.) He was first to receive the especial blessing of the father, which was uttered in the spirit cf prophecy, and was associated with peculiar and precious promises. Now, ĥis birthright he sold. The circumstances are given to us, Gen. xxv. 29, &c. Was not this an extremely foolish barter? To prefer one plain meal to his birthright? How can it be accounted for? It was the result,

1. *Of inconsideration.* He did not ponder and weigh the matter; he acted hastily, &c.

2. *Appetite was another cause.* So powerful that he could not restrain it until food was prepared, &c.

3. *An irreverent depreciation of spiritual things.* He held the birthright in low esteem; he was a worldly and carnal man. A small amount of piety would have given to it a high sense of value. He was deficient alike in personal piety towards God, and filial piety towards his father; the two are often wedded. Such was the profane barter; but many have acted as unwisely, and with equal profanity. Look at Gehazi, the servant of Elisha, who for a number of garments lied to Naaman and his master, and became the subject of a fearful leprosy; look at Judas, who for thirty pieces of silver, &c.; look at Ananias and Sapphira, who to retain a portion of their property, lied to the Holy Ghost; look at Herod, who dared to receive the flattering homage of the crowd, and was eaten up of worms. All these were bad bargains, equally with Esau's. Are there none here who are acting with equal profanity? Those who sell themselves for vanity; seek the applause of their fellow-creatures, &c.; make this their God. Those who sell themselves for money; for this will do any thing; they sacrifice truth, honesty, goodness, &c.; all is devoted to this, &c. Those who sacrifice themselves on the altar of pleasure; lovers of pleasure, &c. Those who exchange their souls for rioting and excess; in most cases these bargains are worse than that of Esau. He did obtain a good— a meal; he had his hunger alleviated; but how often the sinner receives evil, and evil only, for the fearful price he pays. We have more light than Esau had, &c. He regretted; but not so with many around us, &c. This leads us to notice,

II. ESAU'S UNAVAILING REPENTANCE. He evidently altered his mind—saw his folly— labored to undo the deed. He was very urgent, and sorrowful, and intent; but his repentance,

1. *Seems to have been carnal in its motives.* He regrets not his depravity ; he acknowledges not his sin ; he does not abase himself before God. Doubtless, the worldly part of the blessing was what he chiefly deplored.

2. *His repentance was too late.* The word was pronounced ; Isaac could not recall it ; the blessing was irrevocably transferred. Esau's repentance, I fear, is but too common in the stead of repentance unto life. We may exclude one sin for another ; we may abandon a sin on account of its influence on our health, or reputation, or property ; we may give up vices from necessity, not having the power of gratification ; we may do so through sheer dread of future consequences, and not from dislike to the sin ; we may alter our mind when it is too late ; the conscience may become seared and callous ; the Spirit may cease to strive ; put it off till the door is shut. Many have wept on their death-beds in vain ; many in the prison-house of hell, for " there is weeping, and wailing, and gnashing of teeth," &c. Then what is the application of the whole ?

1. *Let me glance at your condition.* You have an immortal spirit of amazing powers, &c. ; you are responsible to God ; you are sinful, exposed to death, but redeemed. Christ has opened a way of life. The gospel reveals it, &c. You can accept, or reject.

2. *Let me glance at your duty and interest.* Now to accept of the blessing of salvation. This year, though nearly finished ; this night, though almost ended, by earnest prayer and faith turn to the Lord. Let the soul's salvation be preferred to all things.

3. *Let me exhort you in reference to the sins and dangers of this season.** Now is a time of peculiar danger, frivolity, mirth, carousing, indolence, &c. Oh ! be on your guard, especially you young persons. You who have made a Christian profession, let your consistent conduct reprove and silence gainsayers.

THE CHOICE OF MOSES.

" By faith Moses, when he was come to years, refused to be called the son of Pharaoh's daughter ; choosing rather to suffer affliction with the people of God, than to enjoy the pleasures of sin for a season. Esteeming the reproach of Christ greater riches than the treasures in Egypt ; for he had respect unto the recompense of the reward." —HEBREWS xi. 24-26.

AMONG all the illustrious Old Testament saints, Moses occupies the most dignified and promising place. His whole life was one of signal and illustrious events. The impression that he made at his birth, by his captivating beauty, so that his parents resolved to save him, not fearing the edict and wrath of the king ; his amazing preservation, when floating in the fragile ark on the waters of the Nile ; his favorable reception into the palace of Pharaoh, under the auspices of the king's daughter ; his amazing privilege of obtaining learning and influence in the court of royalty ; but now we no longer watch the workings of providence for him, but we see him also operating with that providence, and taking his stand with his afflicted countrymen after the flesh. There were many then living who might sway the sceptre of Egypt, but probably only one in all things fit to be the emancipator and ruler over Israel. To this our direct attention is called, " By faith," &c. You are aware how the Israelites entered Egypt during the time of Joseph ; how they multiplied, so as to become an immense people ; how they were cruelly entreated and oppressed by their tyrannic taskmasters ; how their increase was attempted to be bounded by the destruction of their male children ; and now the crisis of deliverance is drawing near. Moses is to be the great agent in God's hand. " And by faith," &c. Observe,

I. THE CHOICE MOSES MADE.

II. THE THINGS MOSES SACRIFICED.

III. THE TIME IN WHICH HE MADE THIS CHOICE AND SACRIFICE. And,

IV. THE GREAT PRINCIPLE BY WHICH HE WAS ACTUATED.

I. THE CHOICE MOSES MADE. He chose,

1. *The condition of his afflicted countrymen.* Men generally aspire to the society and circle of those above them ; men generally choose the society of the affluent and influential, or of the intellectual and cultivated. His countrymen were poor, in the lowest walks of life ; they were slaves in the direst bondage ; they were treated as the refuse of the nation. Not noble after the world's reckoning ; not rich ; not walk-

---

* Preached during Christmas festivities.

ing in the paths of honor, or literature, or science ; but slaves groaning in bondage ; yet he chose them—became one with them ; as he could not at once raise them to earthly dignity, he descended step by step, and became their friend, and companion, and brother. Before you censure Moses, do not forget they were the people of God ; the objects of God's smile, and love, and care ; and were destined to act a more remarkable part in the drama of the world's history than any other nation under heaven.

2. *He chose religious reproach.* " The reproach of Christ." Literally, of the Messiah. The Israelites were the descendants of Abraham, and Isaac; and Jacob. Unto them God had promised to send the Messiah. These prophecies and promises they cherished ; in them they trusted ; for these they hoped. No doubt their services and conversation respected the coming of the Messiah ; and for this belief and worship they were reproached. The Egyptians were idolaters, ignorant of the true God ; therefore the Israelites were despised, and reviled, and scorned, and treated as fools and fanatics. True fervid piety has ever thus been treated. But the reproach of Christ, is it not better than to be reproached by God, or the reproach of conscience ? Now this was the choice of Moses. Observe,

II. The things Moses sacrificed. Now by these we are to determine the heroism, the patriotism, the piety of the act. He was not shut up to the condition of the Israelites, or to the reproach of Christ ; he had worldly glory, wealth, and pleasure at his command.

1. *He sacrificed the dignity of a prince.* He had been the adopted of royalty ; but he severed the connection, and refused to be called the son of Pharaoh's daughter ; he traced his lineage back to Israel, and to that stock, though now in poverty and oppression, he adhered. Survey the contrast ; a prince-royal—and a slave. Yet he despised the one, with all its authority and glittering show, and preferred the other. A sceptre did not fire his ambitious eye ; a throne did not absorb his thoughts ; a crown did not elicit his desires.

2. *He sacrificed the riches of royalty.* Egypt at that time was one of the oldest and wealthiest monarchies ; her coffers were full of treasures ; as a royal prince, they were within his grasp ; but the golden

dust of the nation, the crowns and diadems of the court, corrupted not his soul, nor fascinated his heart.

3. *He sacrificed the pleasures of a palace.* And what sensual enjoyments were not within his reach ? What could mind devise, or heart desire, or imagination conceive, which were not at his hand ? These pleasures of sin formed the atmosphere of his royal residence ; these flowers of enjoyment grew at his feet ; these retreats of gratification were ever at his command ; but he magnanimously, and in the fear of his God, sacrificed the whole. Observe,

III. The time at which he made this choice and sacrifice. " When he was come to years." He was now forty years of age ; in the very prime and vigor of life. It was not, therefore, a mad eccentricity of youth, much less the cynical declaration of old age, satiated with enjoyment ; but when he could best reason upon the value both of his choice and sacrifice. He had long enjoyed the dignities and the honors of royalty ; he was now nearer to the climax of earthly glory ; he was now possessed of sufficient experience to determine with wisdom, &c.; his resolution and conduct we have placed before you. Well may we inquire, therefore, as to,

IV. The great principles by which he was actuated. These are placed in the text :—

1. *Faith.* " By faith," &c. He believed to be of the seed of Abraham was truer dignity, than to be the son of a pagan princess ; he believed to be one of God's poor people was more exalted, than to be the sovereign of an idolatrous nation ; he believed to be the reproached, as one hoping in the Messiah, was better than to enjoy the smiles and plaudits of the courtiers of a palace ; he had faith in God, as a true God, and in the Messiah he had promised. Another principle,

2. *Was sanctified self-interest.* " He had respect," &c. He knew of the prophecies and promises connected with the faith and service of God. Now, this faith weighed the grandeur of the honors, and riches, and enjoyments of Egypt in the right scale ; and he found it better for him thus to choose, and thus to sacrifice. Egypt's royal honors and treasures were but for a season ; the short span of life ; evanescent ; " For the fashion of this world," &c. He saw, too, that poverty and reproach, &c., were

also very transient; but he saw the rewards of faithful obedience to Christ as having reference to heaven, and to eternity; that they were celestial and everlasting; " He, therefore, had respect," &c.

APPLICATION.

1. *I ask, was his choice wise ?* I appeal to the honors he had on earth; I appeal to the communications of heaven; to the revelation of the divine glory; to Pisgah's top; to the heaven of heavens. Nearly 4000 years have transpired since the decease of Moses; where are the honors, treasures, and enjoyments of Egypt? Where the renowned Moses ?

2. *Then imitate his conduct.*
3. *Act upon the same principles.*
4. *And ensure the same high reward.*

THE BURNING BUSH AN EMBLEM OF THE CHURCH.

" And the angel of the Lord appeared unto him in a flame of fire, out of the midst of a bush : and he looked, and behold, the bush burned with fire, and the bush was not consumed."—Exodus iii. 2.

OUR text relates to a series of wonderful persons and events : Moses, the great Jewish lawgiver, and deliverer of the children of Israel; an Angel, yet not one of the ordinary intelligences, but obviously the uncreated and ever-blessed Son of God, verse 4; an interesting phenomenon — a bush enveloped in flame, and yet unconsumed; that phenomenon symbolizing the condition and preservation of the seed of Abraham, who were now enduring the sore and grievous oppression of Pharaoh in Egypt, and yet by the providence of God were sustained and preserved. But we have selected the text with a view to its application to. the church of God in all ages, and desire to ground upon it the following propositions :—

I. THE TRUE CHURCH OF GOD IS NOT ASSOCIATED WITH EARTHLY GRANDEUR AND MAGNIFICENCE. What is the emblem in the text ? The lofty oak—the towering cedar ? no; the bramble bush, of apparently mean and low appearance. Nothing in it to please the eye; nothing to fascinate the imagination; nothing to attract the notice of the intellectual and great. But what is God's church ? Why, what it ever has been, and must be—the body of those who believe in God, and obey him. Now wherever these are found, in whatever class of society or nation, they are the true church of God. Of course, there never has been a nation of such; and therefore never, in the true sense of the term, a national church of God. Now, the truly and sincerely pious have ever formed the minority of any and every sectional denomination, and as such, have always been among the despised and contemned of the human family. Ask the opinion of the world respecting this pure, unsophisticated, spiritual piety, and they laugh at it, deride it; ask the nominal members of the visible church; they despise them, and look with contempt upon them as fanatics, puritans, and righteous overmuch. Few of the members of the church of Jesus are found in king's houses; few in the mansions of the noble; few among the great and renowned of this world. Even yet the church of God is a little flock, and appearing to the eye of sense as one of the things that are not. The present position of the church is like that of the bush in the desert. Where was this marvellous phenomenon seen ? Not in heaven; not in Eden; but in the desert. Behold the sterility and dreariness, and see the moral aspect of the world; behold the dangers of the desert from beasts of prey, and awful storms, and see the imminent perils which surround the earth in which we live. But allow me to remark, that the church of God is in this world for the world's advantage. The church of Christ is the very conservation of the world. It bears it up; life-boat; hospital for its morally diseased; illumines it with the light of hope, and by its sanctifying influence shall finally make it to bud and blossom as the rose; see Isaiah xxxv. 1, &c.

II. THE CONDITION OF THE CHURCH HAS EVER BEEN THAT OF TRIAL AND SUFFERING. It was planted amidst persecution; and was not one of its earliest members a martyr to the envious feelings of his brother ? Behold it afterwards assailed with the ridicule of the old world; then riding on the bosom of the waters of the deluge; then mourning under the despotic decree in Egypt; afterwards in captivity by the waters of Babylon; now emerging into notice beneath the wings of the Sun of Righteousness, but immediately hated and persecuted to the death of the Messiah; after the death of Christ, apostles, confessors, and unnumbered hosts of its disciples, moistening the very soil of the world with their blood; passing through ten fiery persecutions, until hell had exhausted its resources of torment, and the world appeared one vast aceldama, or field of human gore. But allow me to refer to one peculiar and fearful instance of suffering to which the church of God has been exposed. No sooner was the Christian religion secularized, than it became the instrument of torture and oppression. Liberty of conscience was assailed; spiritual purity despised; and the best and worthiest of its members galled and injured by those in the earthly ascendency. What myriads have been persecuted to the death by papal Rome! The woman of Babylon is dyed scarlet with the blood of the martyred saints! Every state church has been a persecuting church. How was it that the rivers of Scotland became like the crimsoned Nile of Egypt? By prelacy, which was thrust upon the people at the point of the bayonet, and by the mouth of the cannon. What has been the state of conscientious Nonconformists in England? In 1662, two thousand ministers were ejected on St. Bartholomew's day from the church of England, because they could not assent and consent to every thing in the Book of Common Prayer. An act was passed, that no man should hold an office of civil trust, unless he took the sacrament at the church of England; another act, that no congregation of more than five adults should meet for worship except in the church of England; another, that no minister should live within five miles of a borough or city, and that schools should not be taught except by ministers of the church of England. During the reign of Charles II., eight thousand persons died in prison, and from that period to the restoration, fifty-two thousand more. Pagans have persecuted the church of God; Mahometans have done so; the world has done so; but not all together a hundredth part with the persecution that has been exercised by the dominant party over the sects who could not conform to her principles and forms. How has humanity thus been disgraced—religion rendered odious to the heathen—skepticism confirmed! How have demons rejoiced, and, if possible, angels wept! What a book of martyrs will be opened in the day of doom! What a scroll of lamentation, sorrow, and wo will then be spread before an assembled world!

III. THE CHURCH OF GOD HAS WITHIN IT THE ELEMENT OF PERPETUITY. "Not burnt." Not consumed. Look at this,

1. *As a striking fact.* Is it not so? How wonderfully the church of God flourished in Egypt—has flourished in all ages; the fire has purified, but never consumed. It has survived all opposition; has had earth and hell against it; and yet lives, yet prospers; the gates of hell have not prevailed, &c.

2. *For this there is a sufficient reason.* God was in the bush; he spake out of it. This is the secret of its life and perpetuity. His wisdom has baffled the counsel of the wicked; his arm supported the church; he took away the consuming principle from the fire; made the wrath to praise him, &c., Psalm xlvi. 1, &c. Where are the enemies of the church of God? Where Pharaoh? Balak? Herod? Where the Roman emperors? Where Julian? Where the judges of the Inquisition? Where the officers of the Star Chamber? Where the impious Bonner? the iron-hearted Jeffries? Where are they all? Gone down to the grave with infamy! "So let all thine enemies perish, O God!" &c. But where is the church? Living—prospering—growing; extending its boughs to the South Seas—to Australia—to China; and is destined to become a universal praise throughout all the earth.

APPLICATION.

1. *Understand the nature of Christ's church.*

2. *Abhor persecution.* Value and hold sacred all the precious boon of liberty of conscience.

3. *Look to Jehovah for success.* He can help, and he will; he ever has done so.

4. *Sympathize with the persecuted and the tried.* The true church is yet exposed to suffering; as in France, Switzerland, Scotland, &c.

THE MYSTERIOUS PILLAR.

"And the Lord went before them by day in a pillar of cloud, to lead them the way; and by night in a pillar of fire, to give them light; to go by day and night."—EXODUS xiii. 21.

THE dispensation of Moses was a dispensation of miracles; the manifestation of God to Moses was miraculous, when he revealed himself to him in the burning bush; it was by successive miracles God compelled Pharaoh to let the Israelites depart from Egypt; and the history of Israel, from leaving Egypt to entering Canaan, was but one chain of wonderful events. This morning we select one of these divine manifestations for the subject of our meditation. " And the Lord went before," &c. Let us consider it,

I. LITERALLY AS A DIVINE INTERPOSITION ON BEHALF OF THE ISRAELITES.

1. *The pillar of cloud was miraculous, or supernatural.* It was not a common cloud, but the cloud of the divine presence; that which veiled from them the grandeur and overwhelming glory of God. God has generally thus shrouded himself, when he has held audience with his people. It overspread the mountain; it filled the holiest place in the tabernacle; it covered the mercy-seat; it filled the temple, &c. So it was now the symbol of God's presence with his people.

2. *It was the constant and infallible guide of Israel.* Hence its appearance was altered to suit the alternate seasons of day and night. It never left them; no, not for a moment. By day, it was a *cloud ;* by night, as a pillar of *fire.* God is an ever present and ever suitable help to his people. He is with his people at all times, and under all circumstances. Day of prosperity, night of adversity; day of health, and night of affliction; day of life, and night of death.

3. *This pillar was the defence of Israel.* Hence, when in peril from the Egyptian host, instead of being in front of the camp of Israel, it removed and went behind, and intervened between them and their enemies. All our security is of God. We should have no might against our foes, if the arm of the Lord was not on our side. See the sufficiency of the defence; the omnipotent Deity. Before the Egyptians could have injured Israel, they must have overcome Jehovah. Well might the church sing, " The Lord is on our side, therefore we will not fear," &c. " The Lord of hosts is with us," &c.

4. *The pillar of cloud and fire was the joy and confidence of Israel.* How delightful to know that God was for them; to have with them the token and sign of his presence. Nothing can be equal to a sense of the gracious presence of God. If so, I cannot err—I cannot faint—I cannot be destroyed; all must be well. The form of the cloud was calculated to produce this confidence. It was a pillar; not like other clouds. There was the appearance of order and arrangement, of firmness and stability. The providence of God is subservient to the designs of grace, &c.

5. *The pillar of cloud, &c., was the oracle of the Israelites.* From thence came the voice of God to Moses, verses 15–26. See Exodus xxxiii. 9. Now this clearly shows us, that if we are to secure the guidance and protection of God, we must hearken to the voice of the Lord; we must obey the word of the Lord. Now, God no longer speaks to us from the cloud; but the apostle says, " We have a more sure word of prophecy," &c. 2 Peter i. 19. Let us consider the pillar, &c.,

II. AS TYPICAL OF THE LORD JESUS CHRIST.

1. *It typified the constitution of Christ's person.* Symbol of God's presence; in it dwelt the Deity; it was the garment of Jehovah. So God came to us in the person of Jesus. " His name shall be called Immanuel." " God with us." " And the word was made flesh," &c. Now, the cloud was the emblem of Christ's body; hence " God was manifest in the flesh."

2. *It typified Christ's redeeming work.* The pillar of cloud was connected with the deliverance of Israel, and the overthrow of their enemies. " So Jesus came to save his people," &c. One exceedingly appropriate passage, Luke i. 68–72. In doing this, he delivered us from the bondage of iniquity, &c. He also came that " he might destroy the works of the devil." Observe,

3. *It typified Christ as the light and guide of mankind.* Jesus is described as a " light," &c. He said, " I am the light of the world." He came to reveal the way to God—the way to heaven. He marked the path through this world to eternal glory. So fully he did this, that he said, " I am the way," &c.

4. *It typified Christ's glorious presence with his church.* When his church was sent forth in the persons of the apostles and disciples, he said, " Lo! I am with you," &c. And to the church he is all and in

all. He guides—protects—cheers; he is its glory, and its defence; he is the oracle of the church. God says to his people, "Hear ye him." The word and ordinances are the signs of his presence.

APPLICATION.

1. *Let the subject greatly encourage the people of God.* Christ is with you. He will never leave; he will conduct to glory. Believe, love, and obey him.

2. *He is the only director to glory and eternal life.*

MANOAH AND HIS WIFE.

"And Manoah said unto his wife, We shall surely die, because we have seen God," &c.—JUDGES xiii. 22, 23.

BEFORE the time of Moses and the prophets, God often manifested himself to the patriarchs, by appearing in the form of a man, or by visions of the night; afterwards, these supernatural appearances became more rare. A few visits, however, are recorded. Among these is the striking instance to which the text refers; see verse 3, &c. This vision was repeated, verse 8, &c. It is obvious from the name assumed, that this angel of the Lord was the Son of God, his name being "Secret, or Wonderful." We see in this subject an exhibition of weak faith and gloomy fears; and of strong faith and cheering hope.

I. WE SEE THE EXHIBITION OF WEAK FAITH AND GLOOMY FEARS. "We shall surely die," &c. Here Manoah was evidently bound by the fetters of a superstition, which has prevailed in all ages, that supernatural appearances were premonitions of death. We do not marvel that sinful beings should be agitated and alarmed. There was a time when angels conversed with our first sire, and when our parents held joyous communion with God; but sin dissolved the fellowship, and clothed man with the garment of sin, and shame, and fear. Where unbelief reigns, or where faith is feeble, a view of the divine character and glory is calculated to overwhelm the soul if you,

1. *Contemplate the divine holiness, and our own pollution.* God spotless; man depraved. "From the crown of the head," &c. Contemplate,

2. *The divine justice, and man's guilt.*

One swaying a sceptre of righteous, impartial equity; and man laden with guilt, his sins crying for vengeance.

3. *The divine truth, and our excuseless condition.* The edict has been declared, that "The soul that sinneth shall die." Shall God lie, or the sinner be punished?

4. *The divine ability and our helplessness.* God has power to execute all he has said. If he resolve, we cannot escape.

5. *The divine conduct in reference to the guilty, and our equal guiltiness.* He has stepped forth to punish; he has whet his glittering sword; he has poured his vengeance—and why not upon us? Why should we escape? Now, in all these points weak faith reasons, and that plausibly, against itself. "We shall surely die," &c. Let us now turn our attention to the display,

II. OF STRONG FAITH AND CHEERING HOPE. "But his wife said," &c. Now here we see the very opposite reasoning and inferences from the same premises and facts. The reasoning of Manoah's wife refers to three particulars:—

1. *She concludes favorably, from the acceptance of their sacrifice.* "If the Lord," &c. Now, the acceptance of the offering was evidently a token for good. It has been so in all generations; it was so with Abel, &c. Now, the Christian may reason thus, from two important considerations:—

(1.) From God's acceptance of Christ's sacrifice. All previous ones derived their virtue from this. Christ has presented an effectual and all-efficient one. "It speaks better things," &c. This the Christian pleads, and from this derives his hope.

(2.) From God's acceptance of us through this sacrifice. "The sacrifices of God," &c. Now, the Christian has presented this; he has laid himself on the sacred altar; "God has mercifully heard and accepted," &c.; but if he had resolved to destroy, he would have accepted neither.

2. *She concludes favorably, from the revelation he had made.* This to her was a most interesting revelation, and it was evidently one of great favor. Now, thus the Christian also may reason. God has revealed his mind to us, and it is emphatically a revelation of mercy and hope; a revelation of grace and compassion. The scriptures were given that we might have abundant consolation, and good hope.

3. *She reasoned favorably, from the promise which the angel gave ;* verse 5. Now, the revelation which God has given us is also one of great and precious promises ; and these promises all meet in Jesus Christ, the great deliverer, and are all yea and amen, &c. Our deliverance from evil, by his power and grace, is the leading promise, and is associated with a series of promises referring both to time and eternity. Now, surely these are striking evidences that God does not mean to destroy us.

APPLICATION.

1. *That the germ of religion is confidence towards God.* To believe his love to us ; to receive it ; to trust in it ; venture our souls fully on it. This is the province of faith. How desirable, therefore, that it should be strong and vigorous !

2. *We often see striking displays of Christian confidence and courage, where we least expect to see them.* We should have expected strong faith in Manoah. He should have been the shield to his wife's fears, &c. ; the stronger vessel ; but morally he is the weaker, and his wife has to reason away his fears and dread. This is not the only instance. We see the like in the holy women who dared to go with Christ to the cross, &c. Priscilla, in concert with her husband, undertook to teach even the eloquent Apollos the way of the Lord more perfectly.

3. *Have we a lively and cheering hope in the mercy of God, through Christ Jesus ?* Let me urge this upon you. How necessary this is ! We preach to you for this. Do you feel this ? Have you confidence in God's love ?

BOAZ AND RUTH.

" And Boaz answered and said unto her, It hath fully been showed me, all that thou hast done unto thy mother-in-law since the death of thine husband ; and how thou hast left thy father and thy mother, and the land of thy nativity, and art come unto a people which thou knewest not heretofore. The Lord recompense thy work, and a full reward be given thee of the Lord God of Israel, under whose wings thou art come to trust."—RUTH ii. 11, 12.

IN the days of the judges of Israel, a man of the name of Elimelech, with his wife Naomi, went to reside in the land of Moab in consequence of the famine which prevailed in Bethlehem Judah. During his residence there, his two sons married with the daughters of Moab ; the name of one of these was Ruth, the person addressed in the text. It came to pass in this mutable and dying state of things, that both Elimelech and his two sons died, and thus Naomi, Ruth, and Orpah were left to exclaim, in the bitterness of the grief of widowhood, " Lover and friend thou hast put far from us, and our acquaintance," &c. Naomi determined to return to her own people, and Ruth, who evinced the deepest affection for her, resolved to accompany her. When Ruth was advised to act as her sister-in-law had done, she exclaimed, " Entreat me not to leave thee," &c. i. 16. Ruth did accompany her, and her kindness had been made known to Boaz, a rich and near kinsman with whom she had now her first interview, and who thus addressed her in the text. " It hath fully," &c. We design to accommodate the subject to those who abandon the world and unite themselves with the church of God. Observe,

I. THE ABANDONMENT. She had forsaken her country and friends. Every believer in the day of his conversion must do the same. We must abandon,

1. *Our original state and condition.* Metaphorically we are said to be far from God. Aliens—outcasts, ready to perish. We are in the region of the shadow of death. On the dark mountains of iniquity. Now, like the prodigal our steps must be retraced. We must not remain in the land of rebellion, in the enemy's country. Like Abraham, we must come out, &c. Like Ruth, we must take our departure.

2. *We must abandon associates and friends.* " And hast left thy father," &c. We cannot be confidential bosom companions of the ungodly, and yet love and serve God. The friend of the world is the enemy of God. Religion is entirely personal. A man must be so for himself ; he cannot take his acquaintances with him, and therefore must go without them ; he cannot take his family ; mother, wife, &c. Suppose Ruth had tried this ; her efforts would have been vain, they did not see as she did, nor feel as she did. We must not therefore wait for others, but be in earnest for ourselves. When one wanted to go and bid adieu to friends, Christ said, " If any man love," &c. So when one wanted to bury his father, he said, " Let the dead," &c. Now we observe,

(1.) That this abandonment is difficult. It is not congenial to flesh and blood; it is therefore represented as a sacrifice. " Present yourselves," &c. " Strive to enter in," &c. And it is so difficult that we notice,

(2.) It can only be done by faith. Abraham did it by faith; so doubtless did Ruth. Faith recognises the peril of our state, the necessity of repentance, &c. A faith losing sight of present pleasure and riches, for future pleasures, and enduring treasures of righteousness. By faith Moses did thus. Consider minutely his case. Observe,

II. THE CHOICE. " And art come unto a place," &c. Now in choosing the people of God for our people we resolve,

1. *To conform to their maxims and habits.* To walk with them; to unite with them in their duties; to adopt their costume; to speak their language, and to be incorporated with them in all their services and engagements. We resolve,

2. *To share their burdens and perils.* This is the end of society, to sympathize and aid each other. " Bear ye one," &c. Thus it is in the body, the hand assists the foot, &c. Thus Ruth had identified herself with Naomi; now this can only be done by cherishing a liberal and benevolent spirit, feeling our kindredness, &c. This choice may properly include,

3. *A desire to participate of their various blessings.* If Ruth resolved to leave all for Naomi, why not enjoy Naomi's advantages? " We will go with you," &c. Yes, and we say to those who are without, " Come with us," &c. There is no monopoly in spiritual blessings, there is bread enough and to spare. We do not envy the new convert the fatted calf, &c. Notice,

III. THE PRAYER. " The Lord recompense thee," &c. We ought to pray for one another; especially for young converts. Now this prayer is,

1. *Very comprehensive.* " Recompense." " A full reward." The blessings of the God of Israel were princely; satisfying; delighting the soul; inconceivably precious. God oftentimes gives a recompense in kind; he did so to Ruth; he did so to Job; at any rate they shall have the principal, and a hundred-fold interest in the world to come. This prayer is,

2. *Certain in its realization.* The Lord can fulfil it; he will fulfil it. His nature disposes him; his promises pledge him. His Son intercedes, &c.

3. *This prayer was connected with a congratulatory declaration of safety.* " Under whose wings," &c. How checkered is the dream of life, and how exposed is man to danger! God is the pavilion, &c. Our rock, and fortress. Under his wings we may indeed trust; here is comfort and security. Who will harm you? &c. " The Lord God is a sun and shield," &c.

APPLICATION.

1. *How desirable that providential visitations should be sanctified!* The death of Ruth's husband was the means of her uniting with God's people.

2. *How necessary to cherish and perfect good desires!* She thought, resolved, acted. Have you done so?

3. *Decision in religion will have its reward.* " As long as he sought the Lord," &c.

ELIJAH'S SINFUL FLIGHT.

" But he himself went a day's journey into the wilderness, and came and sat down under a juniper tree: and he requested for himself that he might die," &c.—1 KINGS xix. 4.

NOTHING is calculated to edify us more than an acquaintance with the experience of saints who have gone before, and who, having borne the burden and heat of the day, have entered into rest. We are exhorted " to be followers," &c., but how can it be, unless we are intimate with their history, and study their character? Elijah was a very illustrious servant of God. His life is full of the marvellous, and we wonder how persons, who have received a religious education, can prefer the reading of works of mere fiction to the astonishing facts recorded in the prophet's life. Our subject, however, presents him to our notice under unfavorable circumstances. His sun at this time, if not eclipsed, is overcast with dark and intercepting clouds. To profit by the theme the text supplies, let us inquire,

I. WHAT WAS THE STATE OF MIND HE DISPLAYED. We perceive a display,

1. *Of great fear.* The preceding chapter relates his signal triumph on mount Carmel. It details the extraordinary success of prayer—the prayer of Elijah. The heavens, which had been as brass, nad sent down refreshing rain on the previous dry and

parched earth; but now he is unnerved, his courage fails, his heart sinks, his spirit drops. At what? At the oath of the impious Jezebel. Read from the first verse to the text—he who stood before four hundred and fifty idolatrous priests, and had commanded them to be slain, as you will see in the fortieth verse of the previous chapter, now begins to fear, and manifests the utmost dread.

2. *We observe manifest impatience.* He is evidently fretting himself. His spirit is ruffled—the equilibrium is lost—the nicely poised balance of feeling is deranged, and his whole demeanor indicates haste, restlessness, and rashness. Doubtless he was weary and exhausted by his journey, but to give himself up to haste, was decidedly wrong. How necessary is self-government and self-possession! How delightful in patience to possess our souls—to be passive in the hands of Deity! Elijah had previously displayed amazing perseverance, but faith and patience seem now both to fail.

3. *He presented an unhallowed prayer to Deity.* Many have supposed that he had had intimations of his translation, but being now out of humor with his condition, says, " I forego the superior transit, let me die," &c. We do not say that this desire is always unhallowed. Paul said, " he had rather depart," &c. The mariner may wish for the haven, the prisoner for liberty, the traveller for his home ; but it is not right to desire, except in deference to God's will ; rather with Job, say piously even in great suffering, " I will wait," &c., than seek it by prayers not authorized. We have no such directions. No promise to such a prayer. Elijah had much to experience, much to teach, and much to do, before his labors could terminate. Let us, then,

II. ENDEAVOR TO ACCOUNT FOR IT. We do this on the ground of human infirmity, infirmities which attach to the good, and the holy, and eminently pious. Elijah was a moral sun, and yet there are spots upon the sun. We have no spotless examples but one, who, though he was made sin for us, yet knew no sin. It is amazing, too, that the failings of pious men have ever been in those points of character for which they were most eminent. Look at Abraham, ingenuous, implicitly trusting in God, and yet concealing the truth respecting Sarah to Pharaoh, and who fell into the same sin precisely with Abimelech after-

wards. Look at Lot, whose righteous soul was vexed, &c. ; and yet in solitude became the victim of sin, and that sin incest. Look at Moses, the meekest man ; see his condemnation of the evil spirit of his countrymen, and yet the sin that excluded him from the land of promise, was rashness and impetuosity. Look at David, the man of inward purity,—after God's own heart, and yet he falls into the polluted snare of sensuality. Look at Peter, the heroic disciple who avows his resolution to live and die with Christ, yet first follows afar off, and then denies, &c. Look at John, the loving disciple, yet he was one who prayed that fire from heaven might consume the Samaritans, because they received them not. Now these were not mere accidents, but a continuous series of proofs that good men may not only fail, but fail in the very things for which they are pre-eminent. This may arise,

(1.) From too much self-confidence. We fear this or that sin, but feel assured that we shall not fall into others. And this,

(2.) Causes unwatchfulness. Our excellencies and virtues require watching. We are vulnerable all over. No part can be left unguarded with safety. Let us consider,

III. HOW WE MAY IMPROVE BY IT.

1. *It should lead us to diligent self-examination and circumspection.* Prove ourselves, &c. Try to ascertain our real state. Be faithful, &c. Be jealous, &c. Take heed to our spirit and temper, &c. Oh, yes! on the temporary defection of Elijah, it is written, " Let him that thinketh he standeth, take heed lest he fall."

2. *It shows the importance of continually depending on the grace of God.* His grace is sufficient. Not our knowledge, or talents, or graces, or experience, &c. He is to us God all-sufficient, &c.

3. *It points out the value of Christian magnanimity.* " Add to your faith, virtue, or courage." " The fear of man bringeth a snare." How necessary are holy resolutions! " Be strong, quit yourselves like men." " Be strong in the Lord," &c. How happy when, like Joshua and Caleb, we can be vigorous and hopeful ; or, like the three Hebrew worthies, and Daniel, firm and invincible ; or, like those described by the apostle, who accepted not deliverance, that they might obtain a better resurrection.

4. *It may console Christians when bowed down by a sense of their infirmities.* Our adversary suits his wiles to our circumstances and feelings. When confident, he would incite us to presumption—when depressed, he would sink us to despondency. Let feeble saints remember Elijah, and not be swallowed up with sorrow, and especially Elijah's God, who is as pitiful as ever, who knows our infirmities, and remembers that we are but dust.

Finally, *Our subject shows us the worth and propriety of that prayer,* " Hold thou me up, and I shall be safe."

ELISHA'S ENEMIES AND GUARD.

" And when the servant of the man of God was risen," &c.—2 KINGS vi. 15–17.

THE faithful servants of God in all ages have been hated, and often put to death on account of the obnoxious messages they have had to deliver to the enemies of Jehovah. How great must have been the wrath of Pharaoh when Moses delivered to him the demands of God, in reference to his oppressed and suffering people ; but he feared not the wrath of the great king, &c. So you remember how Elijah was called to deliver the most unwelcome truths to Ahab and Jezebel, but in the fear and strength of God he dared to do it. This has been the command of God, that they must declare faithfully his truths, whether men will hear or forbear. Elisha had been fulfilling his prophetical duties faithfully in reference to the king of Syria, and he came therefore with horses and chariots, against the man of God. Elisha's servant, having risen early, beheld the warlike host, and came to his master, saying, " Alas !" &c. And he answered, " Fear not," &c. Let us consider several propositions, by which the text may be rendered instructive and edifying.

I. THE PEOPLE OF GOD ARE SURROUNDED BY A HOST OF ENEMIES. The aspect of those seen in the text was exceedingly terrible. " A host," &c. Their appearance too was warlike and formidable, " horses and chariots." I take no notice on this occasion of the enemies within, the legion of doubts and fears, &c. Nor of our adversaries in the world. " Marvel not that the world hateth you." But there

is a host of fallen spirits ; Satan and the powers of darkness. We wrestle not with flesh and blood, but with principalities and powers, and spiritual wickedness in high places. The leader of this host of spiritual foes, is described as our adversary ; the destroyer, the prince of darkness—the devil ; he is likened to a roaring lion, &c. He is in league with all the fallen spirits to do evil, to war against God and to destroy souls. There are several features in this host of malevolent spirits of an awful kind.

1. *Their invisibility.* Not observed by our eyes. May injure us unnoticed ; may direct all their missiles unperceived.

2. *Their power and energy.* Angels excel in strength ; fallen spirits doubtless possess it in an awful degree. In the case of Job, by a great wind they smote the four corners of the house, so that it fell to the ground ; in the case of bodily possessions, how it brought to extreme wretchedness and misery those who were its victims !

3. *Restlessness and activity.* It is probable, that as spirits, they weary not, know nothing of fatigue ; so that they can keep up incessant hostility. Then there is,

4. *Their extreme malevolence and hatred to us.* Inspired with deepest envy ; full of bitter hate and wrath ; longing to destroy and tear to pieces ; desiring to blot out all excellency, and involve in misery, black and hopeless as their own, all the creatures of God.

5. *Their access to the mind is another fearful faculty they possess.* They can act upon the understanding, judgment, imagination, passions, &c. This is clearly expressed when in reference to wrath, &c., we are called not to give place to the devil.

Finally. *There is their number.* It has been conjectured that the countless myriads of the redeemed are destined to occupy their vacated thrones. The poet has said in reference to them,

" They throng the air, they darken heaven,
    And crowd this lower world."

What a fearful enemy ! We remark,

II. THAT A CONTEMPLATION OF THIS ADVERSE HOST IS CALCULATED TO PRODUCE FEAR. And his servant said, " Alas ! my master, how shall we do ?" &c. Our fears may arise,

1. *From a sense of our own weakness.* Our knowledge cannot grapple with their intelligence and craftiness ; our power of

resistance with their deadly missiles. The lamb is not more unable to combat the lion, or the dove the vulture, than man these evil foes. How shall we do?

2. *From a conviction of our tendency to evil.* They worsted our parents in their original purity. How inferior our ability! We have the very seeds of evil within us. Much ignorance, and error, and unbelief, and superstition, and fear, and passion. Their fiery darts ignite these elements of sin. We have traitors within the citadel, who would open the gates and betray us. Hearts of unbelief, &c.

3. *From the recollection of those who have been ruined by this host.* Our world has been made to resemble a valley of dry bones. The number of those slain is thousands of thousands; many of these we have known; need we wonder, therefore, that the people of God should exclaim, "Alas! what shall we do?" We observe,

III. THAT GOD HAS ABUNDANTLY PROVIDED FOR THE SECURITY OF HIS PEOPLE. "The mountain was full of horses," &c. God is the great defence and protection of his people; the munition of rocks. He is as a wall of fire, &c. Then, in addition to this, he has appointed a perfect panoply of spiritual armor for our defence; this is described by the apostle Paul, "Put on the whole armor of God." But our text introduces another kind of defence; it is that of angels; the spirits of light and glory; the hosts of heaven, &c. You know it is written, "The angel of the Lord," &c. "He will give his angels charge," &c. "Are they not all ministering spirits," &c. It is also written, "Who maketh his angels spirits, and his ministers a flame of fire." These were often employed to serve the patriarchs—to instruct, counsel, and deliver the prophets; they were now the body-guard of Elisha; they are often the watchers, keepers, and deliverers of the saints. This is a cheering consideration, when we reflect on the presence of the evil malignant spirits, that however terrible, yet around our path "there are horses of fire, and chariots of fire." But we observe,

IV. GRACIOUS ASSISTANCE IS ESSENTIAL TO OUR RECEIVING COMFORT AND ENCOURAGEMENT FROM THE DEFENCE GOD HAS APPOINTED. The servant saw the foe, but not the guardian host. A striking exhibition of the influence of fear and unbelief. We fear and tremble when the eye of faith is closed; but we exclaim by faith as Elisha did, "Fear not; for they that be with us," &c. Now to realize this, and have confidence from it,

1. *God has given us his word.* He has filled it with declarations of love and mercy; full of promises, &c.; and we must open our eyes and believe these, if we would have spiritual consolation. A believing view of the scriptures will enable us to exclaim, "They that be with us," &c. He has,

2. *Promised us his Holy Spirit.* By the Spirit we shall be instructed in the warfare, &c. Equipped for the conflict. It is thus written, "When the enemy shall come," &c. Now this must be believed and personally realized, and then we shall exclaim, "They that be with us," &c. He has,

3. *Given us striking examples of delivering goodness.* Look at Jacob fearing the wrath of Esau—look at the Israelites in the wilderness—look at David exposed to the envy of Saul—look at Daniel, &c.—look at Peter in prison, &c. What do these things teach, but the same truth, "They that be with us," &c.

APPLICATION.

1. *The Christian life is a warfare.*

2. *God is the strong tower and refuge of his saints.*

3. *Faith in him will render us invincible.*

DAVID'S DISTRESS AND CONSOLATION.

"And David was greatly distressed; for the people spake of stoning him, because the soul of all the people was grieved, every man for his sons and for his daughters: but David encouraged himself in the Lord his God."—1 SAMUEL XXX. 6.

IN reading the text, a variety of scripture passages are forced upon our remembrance: "Man that is born of a woman," &c. "Many are the afflictions of the righteous," &c. "It is through much tribulation," &c. Many of David's psalms come to us bedewed with the tears which were shed when they were composed. The history of our text shall be the introduction. At a time of difficulty, David fled into the land of the Philistines, and dwelt with Achish, king of Gath; the king gave David Ziklag for his abode; a war broke out between the Israelites and the Philistines, and Achish

sought David to aid him in the warfare.
Here were two extreme difficulties: he
must fight for his benefactor, and against
his country—or for his country, and against
his benefactor. In either case, gratitude
or piety would have been sacrificed. The
lords of the Philistines, however, jealous
of him, refused him as their ally; therefore, he returned back. But mark the
scene he beheld, when he reached his residence, verse 1, &c. Let us consider,

I. David's great distress.

II. The nature and source of his encouragement.

I. David's great distress. Look at
several particulars :—

1. *It was a severe domestic calamity.*
Their city burnt—property perishing—but
chiefly the captivity of their wives and
children, taken by a rude, violent, lawless
soldiery; exposed to suffering, violation—
probably death. The absence of our friends
is often a sore trial; their afflictions exceedingly painful; their death one of the
severest strokes of providence; but, I ask,
would not death be preferred to such a captivity as we have described? How exposed we are to relative afflictions! In
proportion to the extent of that relationship,
they are so many channels of grief; in
proportion to our tenderest regards there is
the possibility of the greater anguish and
deeper sorrow. The loss of a Joseph—of a
Rachel—of a friend like Jonathan—of an
only son, &c.—of a beloved brother; but
here, by one fell swoop of adversity, their
wives, and their sons, and their daughters,
were seized by an ungodly and excited
army.

2. *It was a sudden and an unexpected
calamity.* Sometimes we have premonitions and signs of coming sorrow; then
there is time to prepare, to anticipate, and
to fortify the mind by serious and pious
contemplation; but this was sudden and
unexpected. He was returning to his home,
and expecting to find his habitation in
peace; expecting a hearty welcome, a kind
reception; especially to enjoy the sweet
and tender reciprocation of domestic affection. But, alas! how blighted were his
hopes—how sorrowful his countenance—
how overwhelmed his spirit. A city in
ashes—dwellings in ruin—beloved friends
borne into captivity. What could exceed
the shock? what embitter such a cup?

what deepen such a trial? You do not
wonder at David's distress. View him as
a man—as a husband—as a father—as a
child of God. His distress was natural, in
accordance with true piety, and with the
most generous feelings of kindness and benevolence. Hence observe,

3. *The immediate effect of this calamity;*
verse 4. Their grief was loud; it vented
itself in wailings, &c.; it flowed in tears;
it exhausted the physical strength; they
could weep no more. Ah! cries and tears
are the resource of nature, which, if block-
ed up, would often produce the sullenness
of deep melancholy, the ravings of phrensy,
or the instant disembodiment of the spirit.
Tears, and cries, and groans, are the natural results of sorrow, affliction, and distress. Happy when it does not become the
sorrow that worketh death. We turn from
the distress,

II. To the nature and source of his
encouragement. Observe,

1. *The great object of his encouragement
and comfort.* God; the Lord God; the
ruling Jehovah of the universe. He went
at once to the Great Supreme. A link in
the chain of providence seemed to burn with
calamity. He went upward to the Being
in whose hand was the whole chain. To
whom could he so well refer as to the God
whose presence is everywhere — whose
eyes observe all—whose power is above all
—whose righteousness regulates all—and
whose resources include all things in the
immaterial or material parts of the universe? But observe,

2. *The interest he personally had in that
great object.* One word here of infinite
value. "His God." See you not the difference between the God, or their God, and
my God. Look at the beautiful address,
Psalm lxiii. 1 :—

> "The God that rules on high,
>   And thunders when he please;
> That rides upon the stormy sky,
>   And manages the seas:
> This awful God is ours,
>   Our Father, and our Love," &c.

3. *The grounds of his encouragement and
confidence in God.* I need not say more of
the perfections of God, or his relationship,
&c.; but we may add to these,

(1.) *His government.* He knew that all
things and events were under God's control, and that he was a wise, just, and good
God. "Though clouds," &c.; though ob-

scure, or dark, &c., yet always right. He knew that none could seize the reins, or prevent the rule of Jehovah, or defeat his designs.

(2.) *His especial and particular providence.* That this government especially had respect to the righteous. If he cared for the grass, &c.—for the lions—for the ravens—and for sparrows, then still more so for his people—" The very hairs of their head," &c. " The Father knoweth that ye have need," &c. Objects of especial love, and divine delight.

(3.) *In his gracious declarations.* Look at the figures he has chosen. Walls of Jerusalem ; shield ; tower ; refuge ; pavilion, &c. Father's paternal care ; mother's tender love ; an unchanging friend, &c.

(4.) *In his great and precious promises.* None of these speak of 'exemption from trouble, but support in it—deliverance from it—sanctification of it—happy influence, and glorious issue out of it.

(5.) *In his past experience of God's love.* God had done great things for him. Read the preceding portions of his history ; the events of his life. He is now called to review this, and then he encouraged himself in the Lord, &c.

APPLICATION.

1. *We may have distresses similar to David's.* Why and wherefore, if it be the will of God, should we be exempt ?

2. *We may have David's consolations.* David's hopes were not blighted. He sought to know the will of God ; he adopted means, and regained his family and his friends. Therefore,

3. *There is never any need for despair.*

4. *How wretched they who have deep trials, and no religion !*

DAVID AND HIS HOST IN THE CAVE OF ADULLAM.

" And every one that was in distress, and every one that was in debt, and every one that was discontented, gathered themselves unto him ; and he became a captain over them."—1 Samuel xxii. 2.

Our text relates to a literal incident in the life of David. From fear of Saul, he had taken refuge in the cave of Adullam, and here he was joined by those of his own family, and his father's house. Here, too,

he collected together a small army, and our text describes the character of those who fled to his standard, " And every one that was in distress," &c. We design to apply the subject, by way of accommodation, to one greater than David, even to David's Lord, and to those who became soldiers under the Captain of Salvation. Notice,

I. The description of those who gathered themselves unto David. And,

II. What he became unto them.

I. The description of those who gathered themselves unto David. " And every one," &c. Now, this description will particularly apply to those who, sensible of their misery, come to Jesus Christ for life and salvation. We apply the passage to the awakened conscious sinner, who is bowed down by penitency at the foot of the cross. Observe, they were such,

1. *As were in distress.* There is such a thing as worldly distress, and worldly sorrow ; these often work death—drive to distraction—involve in ruin. There is distress arising from bereavements, &c.— Thus David, " I am distressed for thee, my brother Jonathan," &c. ; Rachel weeping, &c. Distress arising from bodily affliction : wearisome days, sleepless nights, &c., severe pain, &c. ; but the distress of the penitent arises from none of these sources. It is distress of soul for sin ; distress, like the psalmist's, when he discovered himself in the horrible pit, &c. ; like the publican's ; like the prodigal's, " I have sinned against heaven," &c. ; godly sorrow for sin, &c. Observe,

2. *They were such as were in debt.* Or, as it may read, every one that had a creditor. Now, every sinner is a debtor to the justice of God. We were bound to serve and obey, and we have all trespassed. From the goodness of God, we have received unnumbered blessings, and have not returned, &c. ; the mercy and forbearance of God, we have not improved, &c. Our debt is great, immense, overwhelming, what we can never pay. Observe,

3. *They were discontented.* In the margin we have a better rendering, " Bitter of soul." This would arise from their reflecting on their debt and distress. Were destitute of enjoyment ; almost overwhelmed ; anxious for deliverance ; in a state of desperation. Now, the awakened sinner

feels thus. He is bitter of spirit; his heart is sad; his condition deplorable; darkness surrounds him; he is filled with anxiety, "What shall I do to be saved?" &c., weary and heavy laden, he intensely longs for rest; he groans for freedom, &c. Now, it is said that they gathered themselves to David.

(1.) They had evidently heard of him, and where he was; so have those who are awakened, &c. You have read of Christ, and heard of Christ, and the tidings have been such as to interest you.

(2.) They know their condition could not be worse. Now this is generally felt by those who seek the Lord; they are perishing of hunger; a change must be rather favorable than otherwise.

(3.) They therefore hoped, and gathered themselves unto him; they ventured, and came to him; they had thought, reflected, considered, resolved, and now they act. So it is with the anxious soul; prayer is poured out, hope is cherished, faith exercised; the hand is stretched out, and laid on the head of the sacrifice:—

"'Tis just the sentence should take place;
'Tis just; but, oh! thy Son hath died."

(4.) Observe the subjection which is expressed, "They gathered themselves unto him," that he might be "over them." Were subject to him. It is thus only we can come acceptably to Jesus; it is thus only Christ will receive us. We must be under his authority and laws. As the disciple is under his teacher; as the subject is under the sovereign; as the patient is under the physician; as the child is under the parent, we must yield ourselves to the Lord, &c. Notice,

II. WHAT HE BECAME UNTO THEM. "He became a captain over them." That is, their head, leader, and commander; he undertook their cause. All the ideas included in the similitude of captain, are amply sufficient for a discourse; we shall, therefore, notice the happy results arising from gathering ourselves under Christ, and Christ becoming a Captain over us.

1. *He delivers from distress.* The weary and heavy-laden find rest; the prodigal finds a home; the traveller, a refuge; the friendless, a friend; the poor, the bread of life.

2. *He discharges our debt.* Insolvent; nothing to pay; owing more than ten thousand talents; yet when we come to him trembling for the consequences, he says, "Be of good cheer, thy sins are forgiven thee." He frankly forgives all; he is exalted a Prince and a Saviour, &c.

3. *He gives true content, peace of soul.* He takes away the cup of bitterness; he takes away the gall and the wormwood; he takes the restlessness and anxiety away, and says, "Peace I give unto thee, my peace I leave with thee," &c. He implants that kingdom in the heart, which is not meat and drink, but righteousness, joy, &c. Let us inquire, Have you gathered yourselves to Christ?

1. *Some of you have.* Then our subject is one of happy experience. Cleave to Christ; honor and extol him.

2. *Some of you are doing so.* Be determined; be prompt; venture on him, &c.

3. *Some have not decided.* Unto whom will you go? or how will you bear the distress, the debt, the bitter spirit? Oh! think, consider, repent, &c., and do it now.

MEPHIBOSHETH.

"And the king said, Is there not yet any of the house of Saul, that I may show the kindness of God unto him? And Ziba said unto the king, Jonathan hath yet a son, which is lame on his feet."—2 SAMUEL ix. 3.

NOTHING is more calculated to give us just views of the things of time, than seriously contemplating the movements of the providence of God. Just views of divine providence would make us sober, serious, prayerful, and contented. We often live for years without at all thinking of the way in which the Lord our God hath led us. This is both unwise and unprofitable. The word of God contains many striking exhibitions of the wonders of providence, both in the history of nations and individuals. The history of the people of Israel is one vast chain of connected wonders. Their formation, their rise, their glory, their decline, their dispersion, and yet their preservation, furnish ample materials for meditation and astonishment. How interesting in this respect is the history of David! What a life of joy and sorrow, honor and humiliation, good and evil! In his life there are some of the finest displays of real goodness and tender feeling the word of God contains. An instance of this sort is contained in the narrative connected with the text. Let us glance at the more prominent things which it contains.

I. OBSERVE THE MUTABILITY OF WORLDLY GREATNESS. About thirty-four years before this, you will witness the appointment of Saul as the first king of Israel. Many things of the most flattering kind connected with him. His majestic appearance; his sacred anointing; his possession of another spirit from God. He had a rich kingdom, a powerful army, and a numerous family; but what changes have transpired! He apostatizes from God; he becomes a curse to the people; his life is laden with trouble, his heart tortured with envy, until he becomes the victim of despondency, and finally, he expires by his own hand; his numerous family are scattered; and in a few years only one individual of the royal race of Saul is to be found. Let it teach us the evanescence of earthly things; how uncertain is worldly glory and grandeur!

II. OBSERVE THE EFFICIENCY OF THE FAVOR AND BLESSING OF GOD. And here we must contrast David with Saul; and if you look back to his history, you find him dwelling with his father in rural life—a shepherd; but God brings him out of obscurity —gives him a noble spirit—introduces him to the court as he who had slain the impious Goliath. The same care follows his steps, delivers his life often from jeopardy, and finally places him on the throne of Israel. Who does not see the providence of God in all this? It could not have been, had not God been with him. "God's blessing maketh rich," &c.; his favor is better than life. Observe,

III. THE EXHIBITION OF A TRULY MAGNANIMOUS SPIRIT IN DAVID TOWARDS THE HOUSE OF HIS BITTEREST ENEMY. "Is there any yet?" &c. For what purpose? That I may erase them from the earth? that I may sit secure on my throne? that I may revenge the unrelenting malignity of Saul, their father? Oh, no; but that I may show him kindness. This is true magnanimity, real greatness. It has been said, to do good to those who love us is natural; to do evil to those who do us good is devilish; but to do good to those who do us evil is godlike. It is imitating Him who "causeth his sun to shine," &c.; it is imitating the blessed Redeemer, who died for his enemies, and who employed his dying breath in pray-

ing for his murderers, "Father, forgive them," &c. Oh! how hard a lesson, but how necessary! "Love your enemies," &c. "Bless them that curse," &c. "For, if ye forgive not," &c.

IV. WE SEE A STRIKING INSTANCE OF GENUINE AND DISINTERESTED FRIENDSHIP. Friendship is the affection of kindred hearts and minds. It never existed in greater purity and ardor than between David and Jonathan. Who can read the ode composed by David on Jonathan's death, and not be affected: " How are the mighty fallen in the midst of the battle ! Oh, Jonathan ! thou wast slain in thine high places. I am distressed for thee, my brother Jonathan; very pleasant hast thou been unto me : thy love to me was wonderful, passing the love of women," 2 Sam. i. 25, 27. Now, this friendship did not die with Jonathan; see verse 1. And here the son of Jonathan is brought under the monarch's notice, &c. This reminds us of the dealings of God with sinners. God is graciously disposed to us through the merit of Jesus. It is the language of divine benevolence, &c.; it reminds us of what Christ expects from us. We profess to be his friends. If so, what would we not do for Christ? How we would honor him, clothe him, entertain him, &c. This we cannot do; but we have his friends all around us—his children; and he says, "Whosoever giveth a cup of cold water," &c. "As much as ye do it," &c.

V. WE SEE A REMARKABLE INTERPOSITION OF PROVIDENCE ON BEHALF OF THE FATHERLESS AND AFFLICTED. In the first instance, God had provided this afflicted child with a friend in Machir, verse 4; and now he is received into the palace of David.

APPLICATION.

Observe,

1. *The reward of pious benevolence to the seed of the godly.* Jonathan had been David's friend in the day of adversity, and God blesses and befriends Jonathan's son through the medium of the same David. God will not forget pious benevolence and liberality.

2. *The advantage of pious ancestors.* There was nothing in Mephibosheth to call for all this; but there was in his father Jonathan. Who can tell what blessings we inherit through the influence of our godly predecessors? see Psalm ciii. 17; Prov. xiii. 22.

3. *We are reminded of the rich provision of the gospel for the humble, penitent sinner ;* verse 7, to the end. A sense of unworthiness, and a believing reception of the message of grace, will ensure to us all the blessings of life and salvation.

DAVID AND HIS FAMILY.

A SKETCH FOR HEADS OF FAMILIES.

" And David returned to bless his household."— 2 SAMUEL vi. 20.

OUR subject is to heads of families a subject of great importance on very many accounts. The family is composed of distinct individuals, each having their own responsibility—parents, children, servants, masters, &c. The family (I mean the Christian family) is connected with the church of Jesus Christ—indeed ought to be a church in miniature. The family is also connected with the world ; and the influence of every family is for the good or evil of mankind in general. True religion qualifies man for every sphere. It makes him first a good man ; then a good relative character ; a good citizen ; and a blessing to the world. The example in the text is one of very great interest in reference to our subject. David had been very piously and actively engaged during the day ; he had brought the ark of the Lord into the city of David ; he had been filled with the spirit of holy joy and exultation ; and then he concludes the whole by returning to bless his household. We inquire, then,

I. IN WHAT WE MAY BLESS OUR HOUSEHOLD. We cannot bless the members of our families with saving grace ; we cannot convince, convert, or sanctify them ; but we can use those means which under God are most likely to be efficient in obtaining these all-important results.

1. *We must establish family order and discipline.* And nothing can be really well done without these. The merchant adopts a system of order ; the student the same. The gardener does not throw his seeds at random, or leave his ground open and exposed, without fence, &c. Every family should be regulated by the laws of order, and be under wise arrangement ; each should know their place, and keep it. In some families, children rule ; in others, servants ; and in many, there is no rule at all. To extract comfort from such dwellings would be a miracle indeed ; besides, it is the greatest mischief to the individuals themselves. They become spoiled and ruined, unfit for society, and often pests to the world. Not much good can be done without order, and to this, discipline must be added. Tempers, dispositions, and actions must be brought under restraint, and, if needs be, punished. How many are ruined through indulgence ! I do not plead for the instant use of physical correction, but for the due use of authority, and parental restraint. Eli's sin was, " his sons made themselves vile, and he restrained them not."

2. *We must set up domestic worship, and regularly maintain it.* God has declared that his curse rests on the families who call not on his name. Joshua said, " As for me," &c. So " David returned," &c. Family worship should include reading the scriptures, prayer, and praise ; it should be regular ; should include the whole family ; be simple, and short. Singing will generally make it attractive to the younger branches.

3. *We must exhibit before our families the spirit and practice of the gospel.* Nothing will give a more utter distaste to religion, than direct contradiction between our profession and lives. Proud followers of an humble Saviour ! passionate, covetous, unjust, want of truth and fidelity. Our example must lead the way ; we must take them with us, &c.

4. *We must present for our families earnest and affectionate prayer.* Seek God's blessing to succeed our labors. Surely we shall feel it both a duty and delight to pray fervently for our households. If we are called to pray for all men, how much more for our own families !

5. *We must provide for our own families the means of religious instruction and public worship.* We must lead them to the house of God ; instil into them habits of reverence for divine things ; ascertain that they know the essentials ; converse with them ; place religious books within their reach, &c. Let us notice,

II. SOME THINGS ESSENTIAL TO THE DISCHARGE OF THESE DUTIES.

1. *There must be unanimity in the heads of families.* Not two heads ; not one correcting, and the other indulging. Father and mother must act in unison, both having

the same object. Children must not be trained to fear one and love the other. How many have been ruined thus!

2. *We must possess much wisdom and self-control.* Time, place, and circumstances, all to be considered. Provoke not your children. Masters must not be overbearing, &c. If we are violent and unreasonable, our families will dread and dislike us.

3. *We must seek the assistance of God's grace.* Our work is difficult and arduous, and we are short-sighted, feeble, &c. God alone, the head of all families, can well direct and qualify. Observe,

III. SEVERAL MOTIVES BY WHICH THIS COURSE MAY BE ENFORCED.

1. *We appeal to human affection.* Surely this should include the mind and soul; the intellectual and deathless spirit; their moral and their eternal condition.

2. *We appeal to our responsibility.* This is our duty. Who shall do it, if we do not? What will be our reply at the last day?

3. *We appeal to our own mercies.* God, our heavenly Father, how he instructs, counsels, and blesses us. So many of us owe much to our earthly parents.

4. *We argue from the advantages which may result.* To see our children wise, respectable, and pious; ornaments to the world; members of the church, &c. If it fails, our conscience will not upbraid us; we may boldly face them at the last day.

APPLICATION.

1. *What say you, Christian parents?* What plea do you present? Do you object for,

(1.) Want of time.
(2.) Want of ability.
(3.) Want of hope. We reply,

2. *Can time be better spent?* God will give you ability. Duty is yours.

3. *We shall meet our families at the last day.*

DAVID'S ADDRESS TO SOLOMON.

A SKETCH FOR THE YOUNG.

" And thou, Solomon, my son, know thou the God of thy fathers," &c.—1 CHRONICLES xxviii. 9.

THIS was David's advice to Solomon. A monarch's advice to his successor; a parent's advice to his son; and a godly man's advice to his posterity. Who can

read it, and not admire the sentiments it contains? who can meditate on it, and not feel its supreme importance? It inculcates religion, that one thing needful; it urges it on the attention of youth, when it is so eminently beautiful and useful; it enforces the advice by a promise the most interesting, that God will be found of those who seek him; and it concludes the lesson by an admonition the most solemn, if we forsake God he will cast us off forever. Consider, my young friends,

I. THE ADVICE AND COUNSEL THE TEXT IMPARTS. This advice refers to two things:—

1. *To the knowledge of God.* "Know thou." Now, in a knowledge of God,

(1.) *There must be the admission of his being.* "He that cometh," &c. The existence of the supreme Creator and Ruler of the universe is a sentiment almost universally entertained by civilized men; only a very few who say "There is no God," and they rather speak the sentiments of their hearts, than the conclusions of their minds. If you have doubts here, just think of the great difficulties which these doubts create. A universe originally from nothing; a world without a maker; order, beauty, arrangement, all the offspring of chance. I will not dwell on this, satisfied that you heartily and fully admit the existence of one great and blessed Deity. In the knowledge of God,

(2.) *There must be a right apprehension of his character.* What is he? A Spirit— an eternal, unchangeable Spirit; a Spirit filling all things, knowing all things, governing all things; a Being glorious, almighty, infinitely wise, unboundedly good, yet righteous and pure; in reference to our world, a God of mercy; full of compassion, &c.

(3.) *There must be a clear conception of his will.* What does he hate? Sin. What does he love? Holiness. Go through the list of sins, and it extends to all sin; go over the whole of the graces and virtues, and his love extends to each and all. But that we may not err, we have his mind revealed. He has written his statutes, and hear what a giant spirit says of it: " All scripture," &c. 2 Tim. iii. 16. An attentive regard to this book is indispensable to a true knowledge of God. In this sublime mirror we behold him in all his glory. The true knowledge of God includes,

(4.) An experimental consciousness of his favor. To know how we stand in reference to God, and God in reference to us; to seek the assurance of his love to us. If we have not repented and sought mercy, nor believed in Christ Jesus, then our state is that of enemies—carnal—under his displeasure—exposed to his wrath; his face is set against such, &c. "He is angry with the wicked every day." But to know that we have seen and felt the evil of sin; loathed, forsaken, and repented of it; prayed for, and found pardon; to have a good conscience, one made so by the blood of sprinkling; to enjoy the Holy Spirit, &c. Observe, this knowledge of God is connected in the text,

2. *With obedience to him.* "And serve him." Take his yoke upon us; engage ourselves to him, by the consecration of all we are and have; give ourselves to God; to obey him, and hearken to his voice in all things. This service,

(1.) *Must be sincere.* "With a perfect heart." That is, with a whole heart; not divided, not feignedly, nor formally, but in uprightness, and truth, and in reality. Neither must our obedience be circumscribed by our opinions, or feelings, but have respect to all his commandments and statutes. This service,

(2.) *Must be free and voluntary.* "With a willing mind." Cheerfully; with readiness and delight. The renewed man can say, "I delight to do thy will, O God!" The good man delighteth in the law of the Lord. That which is not done willingly has no real virtue in it; nor will God accept the service of terror or superstition. I add, that this knowledge or service of God must be followed by,

3. *A constant seeking of God.* "If thou seek him," &c. A good man has often occasion to seek God.

(1.) He seeks his grace in the exercise of believing devotion.

(2.) He seeks his guidance through all the perplexities of life.

(3.) He seeks his preserving protection from his numerous adversaries.

(4.) He seeks his counsel in all his engagements; acknowledges him in all his ways, &c. And,

(5.) He seeks fellowship with God. Enoch, it is said, "walked with God," &c. David said, "I will walk before the Lord," &c. Observe,

II. THE MOTIVES BY WHICH THIS COURSE IS ENFORCED. The

1st. *Is addressed to our hope.* "He will be found of us." Now, this is a great scriptural truth. God will be found of all who seek him as he has directed; he will reject none; but to the young there is an especial promise, "They that seek me early shall find me." Youthful piety is peculiarly acceptable; and in finding God, we find all the soul's chief good and portion, light, joy, and salvation; peace, rest, and consolation; providential direction and safety; the blessings of time, and glories of eternity. In God is dignity, enjoyment, riches, blessedness. "All other things shall be added," &c. "Godliness is profitable," &c. The other motive,

2. *Is addressed to our fears.* "But if thou forsake him," &c. Live without him; neglect his words and ordinances, &c.; he will cast us off.

(1.) He casts men off from his gracious restraints; and how fearful they become! given up to all sin; run headlong into vice, &c.; given up to a rebellious mind.

(2.) He casts men off from his providential solicitudes; withdraws his paternal regards; allows them to reap as they have sown; then want, rage, shame, reproach, disease, and often premature death, is the result.

(3.) He casts the incorrigible into hell. "The wicked shall be turned into hell," &c. "The wicked are driven away," &c. Now, such are the motives. In applying this subject,

1. *Let me suggest a few things to those young persons who have obeyed the voice of the text.*

(1.) Entertain lowly views of yourselves.

(2.) Cherish the fear of God daily.

(3.) Remember that personal, practical godliness must be always sought. Cherish a spirit of intense devotion.

(4.) Cleave to your Bible, "Whereby shall a young man cleanse," &c.

(5.) Be watchful in an eminent degree.

2. *To those who are resolving to act upon the spirit of the text.*

(1.) Then carry out your resolutions this very night. Go to your chambers, and prostrate yourselves before God.

(2.) Avoid your evil companions, though they may not be profligates, &c., yet if they are neglecters of religion.

(3.) Seek the society of the pious, &c.

"He that walks with wise men," &c. "I will be the companion of them that fear God," &c.

3. *To those who care for none of these things.* You have been instructed, admonished, warned, invited. Now, the responsibility is your own ; to God you must give an account.

JEHOVAH DWELLING ON EARTH.

(A CHAPEL-OPENING SKETCH.)

"But will God indeed dwell on the earth ?"—1 KINGS viii. 27.

THE text is connected with the dedication of Solomon's temple. The whole description is solemn, impressive, and magnificent. A moveable tabernacle was now superseded by one of the most splendid erections on which the sun of heaven ever shone. In the vastness of its dimensions, in the costliness of its materials, and in the resplendent appearance of the whole, it so far exceeded all previous erections, as to be worthy of its great design—a temple for the living and eternal God. Three circumstances worthy of notice were connected with its history : God himself was its artificer ; it was erected according to the plan which Infinite Wisdom directed ; it was the result of the voluntary free-will offerings of the Jewish nation, from Solomon on the throne to the peasantry of the people ; it was dedicated to God by the fervent prayers and thanksgivings of the people, through Solomon, their king. How truly grand and affecting was that dedication ! The king takes the lead in the services. Then Solomon assembled the elders of the people—the priests and Levites in their sacerdotal vestments, in connection with the chief of the men of Israel, form the august and memorable convocation. Solomon then, standing before the altar, stretches forth his hands, and lifting his eyes towards heaven, thus addresses the infinite Majesty of heaven and earth, verse 23. The text is a kind of parenthetical exclamation ; a solemn pause in the midst of his supplications, "But will God ?" &c.

I. LET US EXAMINE THE VARIOUS TERMS WHICH THE TEXT CONTAINS.

II. GIVE A SCRIPTURAL SOLUTION OF THE QUESTION PROPOSED.

I. LET US EXAMINE THE VARIOUS TERMS OF WHICH THE TEXT IS COMPOSED. The text refers to the divine Being dwelling on the earth.

1. *Let the earth be the first subject of our consideration.* The earth is represented as the footstool of Deity. It was originally given to the children of men ; it forms a beautiful part of the divine dominions, and is full of the goodness of the Lord ; it bears evident marks of the footsteps of Deity ; worthy of its great Artificer ; the scene of the divine wonders and glory. But through the entrance of sin, it has been spoiled and cursed. Eden has been converted into a desert ; paradise into a howling wilderness ; now the seat of Satan ; the usurper has seized upon it, as though it was his rightful dominion. It is the Egypt of the hellish despot—the place of his cruel oppression—the scene of crime, and darkness, and wo ; so that the earth is like one vast aceldama, or scene of horror and blood. It is the site of avowed enmity and rebellion against the Most High, and is in treasonable league with the powers of darkness. Well may we ask in reference to it, "Will God indeed dwell on the earth ?" in a world so guilty, so polluted, so vile ? Let us now consider,

2. *The glorious and blessed Being referred to in the text.* "Will God ?" Think of his magnificent celestial dwelling ; his imperial exalted palace ; his sublime throne, exalted infinitely above seraphim and cherubim. It is well also to think of the extent of his dominions. Has he not worlds upon worlds, beyond number or calculation ? Lift up your eyes on high. Behold the vastness and grandeur even of the solar system, compared with which our world is a mere speck, an atom ! But reflect upon the starry worlds beyond the influence and attraction of our sun, which are most probably the suns and centres of other systems, scattered in the immensity of space, unexplored, and inexplicable to the inhabitants of our world. Well may we ask, "Will God ?" &c.

3. *Now consider the word "dwell."* Will he "dwell ?" We know he will observe ; his omniscience beholds the whole of it at one glance, &c. Heaven, and earth, and hell are all open before him, &c. He will govern the earth, for he ruleth over all ; his dominion is a universal dominion ; he doeth according to his will, &c. ; his presence will, and must pervade all space. "Whither shall we flee," &c. "But will he

well ?" &c. Make it his residence, his abode. Now lay the emphasis of the text,

4. *On the word "indeed."* Really, manifestly ; in some certain, peculiar, especial sense. Shall its inhabitants know and discern his dwelling in their midst ? Such are the terms of which the text is composed. Well may we pause, and linger, and adore. Well ought we to pray that the Eternal Spirit would guide our minds in pursuing the solemn and momentous investigation ! Where shall our appeal be made ? To the ancient oracles of paganism ? They ask, " What God ?" &c. In the range of paganism there are innumerable deities, greater and minor : gods of the winds and of the waters ; of the tempest and the calm ; of the mountains and the valleys ; but of the great, living, and eternal God, they are utterly ignorant. We appeal to the massive tomes of ancient philosophy, and there are profound research, subtle disquisitions, &c., innumerable conjectures ; but we close these huge collections, satisfied that the world by wisdom knew not God. We ask the Deist—the votary of modern rationalism —and, instead of meeting the question with due seriousness, he treats the subject as visionary, and in place of a reply worthy of an intellectual being, you have the curled lip of scorn, the sneering look, and the vapid declaration that the great God is too much absorbed with his own perfections to care at all for this earth, or its puerile inhabitants. Let us, then,

II. GIVE A SCRIPTURAL SOLUTION OF THE QUESTION PROPOSED. Our subject convinces us of the necessity of a divine revelation ; and to that revelation, then, our appeal must be made.

1. *God did dwell in the midst of his ancient Israel.* Not only had they occasional august manifestations of the divine glory, but he appeared for them in their redemption from the Egyptian yoke ; guided and guarded, &c. ; " In the pillar," &c. ; but especially see this, Exod. xxix. 43, xl. 4. So also, when the temple was dedicated, 1 Kings viii. 10, 11 ; so also the Lord said, " Now have I chosen and sanctified this house, that my name may be there forever, and mine eyes and my heart shall be there continually."

2. *God dwelt on the earth, in the glorious incarnation of his beloved Son.* It was to this the apostle referred, " We beheld his glory, the glory," &c. Jesus thus taught

his disciples, " Whoso hath seen," &c. To this the apostle refers, " In Christ dwelt all the fulness," &c. This is the great mystery of godliness, " God manifest in the flesh," &c. This was evidenced in his teaching, miracles, death, and resurrection. " He spake with the power and majesty of God." Diseases — sorrows — winds — the dead, obeyed. The devils, too, confessed and fled before him. No wonder, when the elements of nature obeyed him, that the people exclaimed, " What manner of man," &c.

3. *God dwells in his church, by the presence of his Spirit.* Deity, enrobed in flesh, hath ascended on high, even to the right hand, &c. But according to his promise, he sent down the Divine Spirit to dwell with his people, to the end of the world, John xiv. 16. Thus he dwelt miraculously on the apostles and first disciples, and thus he now dwells in his own spiritual church as the guide, the sanctifier, and the comforter of the saints. He it is who constitutes the vitality of the kingdom of Christ ; he perfectly builds it up ; he succeeds the efforts of his servants, giving testimony to the word of his grace, and enabling the devoutly pious to worship God in spirit and in truth.

4. *God graciously dwells in the heart of every believer.* How overwhelming that stupendous passage in Isaiah lxvi. 1, 2. How delightful the saying of Christ, " If a man love me, he will keep my words, and my Father will love him, and we will come unto him, and make our abode with him," &c. " Hereby," says John, " we know that we dwell in him, and he in us, because he hath given us his Spirit." " Know ye not that ye are the temple of God, if so be God dwell in you ?"

5. *God will dwell on the earth, in the universal dominion which he has engaged to set up.* The earth is redeemed, and God has sworn that truth and righteousness shall again adorn it, so that it shall be one garden to the Lord. " That his knowledge shall cover the earth," &c. That his tabernacle shall be among men, and that he will dwell among them ; that one song of triumph shall be heard from the rising to the setting of the sun, " Hallelujah ! the Lord God omnipotent reigneth ! Hallelujah ! for the kingdoms of this world," &c. Well may we exclaim, " Blessed be the Lord God, the God of Israel, who only doeth wondrous things," &c.

APPLICATION.

1. *What an exhibition of the condescension and grace of God!* That he should hate, punish, destroy, &c., would be no marvel ; but he loves, pities, descends ; makes the earth the scene of mercy, long-suffering, and grace.

2. *How desirable that the presence of God should be secured and enjoyed in this church and congregation.* This will be its beauty, its exaltation, its establishment, its prosperity, and security. To secure this, the cross of Christ must be exalted. If Christ be honored, God will honor you. Let Christ be preached, and God will bless and succeed. To secure this, the Spirit must be constantly and fervently sought. House of prayer. He will give the plenitude of spiritual influence ; like the copious rain or the early dews. He will cause showers of blessings to descend on his chosen hill. But to secure this, a peaceful atmosphere must be maintained. He is not the God of confusion, but of peace. This is his own element. Here the Dove will hover round you, and over you, &c.

3. *I ask another question.* Will men dwell with God in heaven ? The place—heaven ; God's palace, &c. Men, worthless, &c. Oh ! yes ; they shall come from the east, and the west, &c. Who ? The believer ; the faithful servants of Christ. Then forget not, but seek this better country.

A RECOGNITION OF PIOUS VOWS

" Thy vows are upon me, O God ! I will render praises unto thee ; for thou hast delivered my soul from death ; wilt not thou deliver my feet from falling, that I may walk before God in the light of the living ?"—Psalm lvi. 12, 13.

Much is said in the scriptures of the Old Testament on the subject of vows. The earliest vow recorded, is that of Jacob in connection with the vision of Jehovah at Bethel. " If God be with me, and will keep me," &c., Gen. xxviii. 20. Hannah also vowed unto the Lord in reference to Samuel, resolving to dedicate the child to the Lord forever, 1 Samuel i. 21, 22. All of you remember the rash vow of Jephthah, and its sequel of unhappy results in reference to his daughter. It is said that the sailors of the vessel in which Jonah was

endeavoring to escape, after they had thrown him into the sea, " offered a sacrifice, and made vows," Jonah i. 16. In several portions of the Psalms, the inspired and holy man of God refers to vows ; thus he openeth one of his beautiful and sacred odes, " Praise waiteth for thee, oh God, in Zion, and unto thee shall the vow be performed," Psalm lxv. 1. Again he says, " So will I sing praise unto thy name forever, that I may daily perform my vows," Psalm lxi. 8 ; but I confine the subject at the present to those who have vowed allegiance to the Lord, and are this evening intending to ratify that vow by commemorating the love of Jesus at his sacramental table ; to you then who are now uniting yourselves to the people of God, our subject will be especially directed. We ask,

I. What the vows of the believing penitent should comprise. Their vows should include,

1. *A resolution to forsake the service of Satan and sin.* To abandon and utterly forsake the way of transgression and death. To this we are often invited, exhorted, &c. Great promises made to such. The apostle refers to the believing Romans as having done so, Romans vi. 16, 17.

2. *A resolution to yield body, soul, and spirit to God.* The apostle says, " Yield yourselves to God"—" I beseech you, brethren," &c., Romans xii. 1. This is a reasonable service—a dignified service—a happy service ; one which appeals to us from the cross. " Ye are not your own," &c. Christ must have heart, tongue, and life.

3. *To present constant homage, reverence, and supreme love to God.* God demands this, and it is our highest interest and felicity to yield it to him. The loftiest angels do this—his greatness, and glory, and power, claim our homage and reverence—his goodness and love, our supreme affection. God must have the heart—occupy the throne—sway the sceptre.

4. *To identify Christ's cause with our dearest interests.* Christ's cause must be sacred to those who love him. Apostles and confessors valued it more than worldly honor, riches, ease, liberty, or life. They toiled, and suffered, and died for it ; now it ought to be as precious to us ; and the resolve of the Christian convert should be, " If I forget thee, Jerusalem," &c. This must be continuous, daily, &c.

5. *Unfeigned attachment to God's church and people.* "Peace be within thy walls," &c. "For my brethren and companions' sake, I will now say," &c. Consecration to God must be followed by close and constant union to the followers of Christ. "They that believed were together," &c. Now, these feelings of attachment must be visible, distinct, and manifest; we are to do good unto all men, but "especially to the household of faith." Now, these vows are to be taken, and sustained and honored by the exemplification of the principles they involve. Notice,

II. THE SPIRIT IN WHICH THESE VOWS SHOULD BE MADE. In the joyful spirit of praise. "I will render praise unto thee," &c. Now here he affirms,

1. *What God had done for him.* "Delivered my soul from death." The soul in its unrenewed state is dead, "dead in trespasses and sins"—dead to God—dead to holiness, &c.—dead also judicially under the righteous sentence of eternal death; exposed to the wrath to come. Now from this death the soul is delivered—delivered meritoriously by the sacrifice of Jesus Christ—he came to deliver from the wrath to come—delivered really by the gracious and merciful influences of the Spirit of God. When the sense of guilt and condemnation is taken away—when the Spirit testifies with our spirits that we are the children of God, &c. What a great and blessed deliverance this is. Now for this deliverance, .

2. *He will cherish a thankful spirit.* "I will render praises," &c. Thus the prophet breaks forth, "O Lord, I will praise thee," &c. Now these praises are to include thanksgivings at all times, places, and occasions. "Praises" in the plural, so that the vows of God are to be honored by a spirit of holy, delightful praise—a spirit of cheerfulness and joy. We cannot be too ardent, intent, and frequent in the praises we render to the Lord; so to praise God, as never to allow the least feeling of self-righteous complacency to attach to ourselves. Notice,

III. THE PIOUS APPEAL HE MAKES TO GOD IN REFERENCE TO THE FUTURE. "Wilt not thou deliver my feet," &c. He recognises,

1. *Perils in his way.* Satan lays his snares in the pathway of the Christian. There are many worldly allurements, &c. Now we must remember this—not be forgetful, or careless, or presumptuous; not lean on our own strength; many have fallen—Noah, Lot, David, Solomon, Peter, &c.

2. *He trusts to God for security.* "Wilt not thou deliver," &c. Now in perplexity, seek counsel of your Christian friends, especially of your minister. Go to your Bible, and frequently to the closet of secret devotion; but after all trust only in God's delivering arm. "Hold thou me up," &c. Cherish a constant sense of this.

3. *He exhibits the prevailing desire of his soul.* "To walk before God," &c. Always to recognise God, to set the Lord before us—to act in all things, to please and glorify his name; and in this holy course to "walk," to make constant advances, to go "from strength to strength," &c. "One thing I do, forgetting the things that are behind," &c.

APPLICATION.

1. *Perhaps most persons here have been vow-makers.* At one time or another you have resolved to give yourselves to God; perhaps in affliction—in severe trouble—in peril—in bereavements; but in general, how evanescent they have been! "Oh, Judah! what shall I do unto thee?" "Oh, Ephraim!" &c. "Unstable as water," &c.

2. *There are some here who have vowed, and kept their vows.* What a mercy! Let God be exalted. Render praises, &c. Especially you who are for the first time to be recognised as the followers of Christ. Oh, study the text, pray over it, &c.

3. *Who will now avow his resolve to give himself entirely to God?* Let this be the great crisis—the eventful turning point—the time when it shall be said, "Behold, he prayeth," &c.

HISTORY OF HEZEKIAH.

NO. I.—HIS MORAL CHARACTER.

"For he clave to the Lord, and departed not from following him, but kept his commandments, which the Lord commanded Moses. And the Lord was with him; and he prospered whithersoever he went forth."—2 KINGS xviii. 6, 7.

HEZEKIAH was one of the most pious kings of Judah. He lived in the fear of the Lord, and was jealous for Jehovah's glory. Pre vious to his reign the people had greatly departed from the true God, and sunk into gross and wicked idolatries. See former chapter, v. ix. 11. Now, Hezekiah immediately set on foot an entire reformation. It is said of him, that " he did that which was right in the sight of the Lord," viii. 38 ; and then follows our text, " For he clave to the Lord," &c.

I. THE PIOUS COURSE HEZEKIAH PURSUED. Now, this is expressed in the following particulars:

1. *His adherence to God.* "He clave unto the Lord." This implies union with the Lord. Oneness with him ; attachment, preference, and decision. When Barnabas visited the disciples at Antioch, " he exhorted them to cleave unto the Lord," &c. It includes,

(1.) The judgment cleaving to the truth of God.

(2.) The will cleaving to the ways of God.

(3.) The affections fervently going out after God ; loving and delighting in him.

(4.) The soul's trust and confidence implicitly resting upon him. Many things are opposed to this cleaving to the Lord. Satan tries to beguile us ; world to fascinate our hearts ; unbelief would be constantly turning aside from him ; cleaving to the Lord requires the resolute determination of the soul to adhere to God under all these circumstances.

2. *He kept his commandments.* No acceptable religion without this. Knowledge, profession, attendance upon ordinances, all worthless without this. This is the evidence of our sincerity. Love to God will make his commandments pleasant and delightful. " This is the love of God," &c.

3. *He persevered in the way of holy obedience.* " And departed not," &c. Some ran well but were hindered. Impulse and excitement often prompt to a certain line of action, and then, when the novelty is over, they turn aside. Many are drawn aside by the pomps and vanities of the world ; many by sordid love of gain ; many by fear of man, or of suffering ; Hezekiah held on his way and departed not, &c. This preservation is necessary—essential. The end must crown the whole. " He that endureth to the end," &c.

II. THE DISTINGUISHED BLESSINGS WHICH HE ENJOYED. He was favored,

1. *With the divine presence.* " And the Lord was with him." This is a very comprehensive form of expression ; it includes every desirable good ; it is what God promised to Jacob, Gen. xxviii. 15. What Moses so earnestly prayed for. " If thy presence go not with us," &c. It is that which formed the great desire of David for his son Solomon, 1 Chron. xxviii. 9. The presence of the Lord is the good man's safety. " In the Lord Jehovah is everlasting strength." " A very present help," &c. The presence of the Lord is the good man's guide. He led Israel, and also all who trust in him by a right way, &c. It is his comfort. His presence makes our paradise, &c. He was favored,

2. *With continued prosperity.* " And he prospered," &c. It is said of another, " So long as he sought the Lord," &c. Now that is prosperity, when all things are tending to one great and glorious consummation ; not because a man is getting rich, or elevated in the world ; what are these, if they are in the way of sin and death ? When the mind and heart are in a state of cultivation and improvement for another world, yet " godliness is profitable unto all things," &c. A pious man enjoys what he has, much or little. " Godliness with contentment is great gain," still greater with a brightening hope of immortality and unending life. Real prosperity is of God. His favor and smile are essential to it.

APPLICATION.

1. *How many are imitating the good Hezekiah?* cleaving, following, obeying God.

2. *What encouragement for all to do so!*

3. *Will not some commence to-day?*

HISTORY OF HEZEKIAH.

NO. II.—HIS SICKNESS.

" In those days was Hezekiah sick unto death. And the prophet Isaiah, the son of Amoz, came unto him, and said unto him, Thus saith the Lord, Set thine house in order, for thou shalt die, and not live. Then he turned his face to the wall, and prayed unto the Lord, saying," &c. &c.—2 KINGS xx. 1-6.

WE previously referred you to the piety and persevering decision of Hezekiah. He effected a great national reformation ; and he personally clave unto the Lord, and departed not from following the Lord, &c. It is said of him, that God prospered him whithersoever he went forth. This world, however, is a state of mutability ; here we ought not to calculate upon our temporal blessings as abiding. Like the agitated ocean is the sea of human life : there is nothing changeless, fixed, and certain. One of the sources of trouble to man, is the affliction of body to which he is liable. Sin has sown the seeds of disease and death in our mortal system, and pain and sickness are the necessary consequences. Our subject relates to the affliction of Hezekiah, and his gracious recovery from it. Observe,

I. THE SICKNESS WHICH HE ENDURED.

1. *The sickness itself.* The nature of Hezekiah's affliction is not stated, (supposed to be the plague,) it was evidently, however, severe and dangerous, ver. 1. He was confined to his bed. Now, in his visitation, observe,

(1.) Hezekiah was not exempted, although in the prime of life, in the very midst of his days, (he was now between thirty and forty years of age.) We do not wonder at helpless children and the infirm aged ; but every period of life is alike vulnerable, &c.

(2.) His worldly elevation did not exempt him ; he was a monarch, had his crown, sceptre, throne of state, retinue, &c. ; all these are worthless as to the prevention or the removal of pain.

(3.) His eminent godliness did not exempt him. Afflictions come alike to all ; piety enables us to bear them with patience—it sanctifies them, and obtains good out of them ; but does not exempt, &c.

(4.) His extensive usefulness did not exempt him ; he filled a most important station, and that well ; he was a blessing of real worth and importance to the kingdom ; yet he was sick even unto death. Observe,

2. *The intimation he had of its fatal termination.* The prophet Isaiah, &c., ver. 1. The message evidently meant this, Thy sickness is of a mortal kind, it must naturally prove fatal ; such was its character and tendency. Notice,

3. *The direction given him.* " Set thine house in order," &c. This direction was a favorable sign as to Hezekiah's piety. He was a godly man, as such his state was secure ; he had lived to the Lord, so was ready to die, &c. ; but it was desirable that his household affairs should be arranged

and fixed. This is of importance to all persons, especially to a king, and still more so to a king who had been extensively engaged in the service of God. Let me pause in the narrative to make a few observations.

(1.) Some persons neglect a proper settlement of their temporal concerns ; and often family broils, litigation, and strife, &c., are the result.

(2.) Others do this, but neglect personal preparation for dying. They are exact, and prompt, and minute about property, &c., but they neglect their souls, are careless about religion and eternal things ; or, perhaps, professedly leave it to the last. What folly and infatuation! surely the soul is the chief; eternity most momentous ; heaven the most precious.

(3.) Others neglect both. They neither set themselves nor their houses in order. They will not entertain the subject. By turning their backs upon it, they persuade themselves the evil day is postponed.

(4.) The godly man does both. First he seeks the kingdom of God, &c. First regards the soul, and seeks for it a title and meetness for a better world ; lays up a good foundation for the future ; then he considers how he can render his riches and influence more useful to mankind after his decease, that being dead, his spirit and holy efforts may live after him ; he will be anxious that his family, the church, and the institutions of mercy, may all flourish after his decease. As we cannot enter now on the other parts of the subject, we take four views of sickness of body to which all men are liable.

1. *The origin of all sickness is sin.* But for this our bodies would have been painless and invulnerable, the seat of abiding pleasure ; such they were when they came from the hands of the great Artificer. Sin has undermined it, weakened it, and diffused through every fibre and pore the seeds of frailty and death.

2. *Most persons are called to bear it.* Few live to any great age without experiencing it. Most now present, many this day, &c. We ought rather to calculate upon it. No marvel that we are so, but the reverse.

" Our life contains a thousand springs,
   And dies if one be gone ;
Strange that a harp of thousand strings
   Should keep in tune so long."

3. *In sickness we should recognise the hand of God.* Does not spring out of the dust. To the righteous, fatherly chastisement ; to the wicked, often warning ; admonitory to all ; yet much sickness is from the manifest disregard which persons pay to the laws of nature. Health is a gift to be preserved, &c., valued, &c. How many are sick through transgression ; many too through neglect ; but all may derive good therefrom, by reflection and prayer.

4. *There will be no sickness in heaven.* World of health. No sickness or death, &c. " Sighing and sorrow shall forever flee away," &c.

APPLICATION.

1. *Let health and life be improved, &c.*

2. *In all states, seek the favor of God.* " Glorify him with your bodies and souls," &c.

HISTORY OF HEZEKIAH.

NO. III.—HIS RECOVERY.

" In those days was Hezekiah sick unto death. And the prophet Isaiah the son of Amoz came to him, and said unto him, Thus saith the Lord," &c. —2 KINGS xx. 1-6.

WE formerly adverted to the sickness of Hezekiah and the message of Isaiah, concerning its fatal termination, " Set thine house in order," &c. We have now to observe the effects which this message produced ; it was a very momentous one. Truly the most solemn which can be addressed to an immortal being. It was particularly so to Hezekiah in the meridian of life ; in the midst of the great work in which both the glory of God and the wellbeing of the nation were concerned. The effects of this message were, " Hezekiah wept sore." He was in great trouble and distress of mind. It does not appear that this arose from immoderate love of life, or distressing fear of death, or from awful forebodings of the future. But,

(1.) There was doubtless the instinctive love of being. This is of God's own planting, worthy even of the pious. To be cherished, &c.

(2.) Love to the kingdom of Israel ; no successor ; national confusion.

(3.) Love to God's cause. The reformation scarcely finished ; the blasphemers, the enemies of God, were now conspiring to overthrow. Such it appears were the reasons of Hezekiah's distress, worthy of him as a man and as a servant of God. Notice then as the leading division of the subject,

I. THE COURSE WHICH HEZEKIAH ADOPTED. He had recourse to prayer. Prayer is the remedy of the afflicted spirit. " If any man is afflicted, let him pray."

1. *His prayer was divine in its object.* He prayed to the Lord. How vain is every other refuge !

2. *It was direct and intimate.* " He turned his face to the wall." He shut out the world ; withdrew from earth ; sought immediate audience with Jehovah. What a sight ! An afflicted mortal ascending to the throne of grace, with a petition for mercy ; what a privilege to be allowed to do so. To be made welcome.

3. *It was fervent and earnest.* " I beseech thee," &c. His heart was poured out ; his soul's earnest longings were presented. With tears he supplicated, &c.

4. *It was connected with reference to his own integrity.* Now this was not self-righteous. Not boasting. He did not plead it as a merit ; he referred to his sincerity as a truth, &c. Not divided in his attachments, &c. He had enjoyed tokens of God's approbation ; now this was all true—he could appeal to God, &c. We find Job referred to his previous life. Paul also, who felt himself less than the least of all saints, had to refer to his sufferings and labors in the cause of God ; this is the privilege of the righteous, that they have constantly the rejoicing of a good conscience, &c.

5. *Yet it was evidently submissive to God's will.* His prayer is remarkable in this respect. He does not mention his life or recovery ; he thought it best to pray in general terms, and left particulars with the Lord ; no doubt his petition included restoration, yet it is clear he left it to the Lord. How wise and safe is this ! Not our will, &c. Observe,

II. THE RECOVERY WHICH HE EXPERIENCED. The decree of mortality was reversed ; his life was prolonged. In saving his life God referred,

1. *To the success of Hezekiah's prayer.* " I have heard thy prayer, I have seen thy tears," &c. God is the hearer and answerer of prayer. How potent, how almost almighty is prayer, &c. When prayer

has been fervently presented, it has stayed divine wrath. God exclaimed to Moses, " Let me alone," &c. It is right and desirable at all times. No case too extreme. Even when God said, " Thou shalt die," Hezekiah's prayer was successful. " Is any afflicted, let him pray." Hezekiah's recovery was connected,

2. *With the use of means*, verse 7. We cannot doubt the perilousness of the case without God's interposition. The disease was a fatal one, only God could stay it; but God is the author of means. In the use of wise and proper means we may expect God's blessing. Many of Christ's miracles were connected with means. Clay and spittle, &c.

3. *It was attested by a miraculous event.* Hezekiah seemed exceedingly anxious; death probably appeared at hand; hope had expired, and he sought of God a sign. Many cases of a similar kind, Gideon and the fleece, &c. This is always the sign of weak faith ; nothing can be stronger than God's word. Deity might be justly offended ; but he remembers our frame, &c. He does not break the bruised reed, &c. The sign is specified, verses 9, 10.

4. *His recovery was connected with other blessings.* God gave more than was asked, verse 6. Probably Hezekiah desired to live chiefly for these things. God anticipates and gives liberally, &c.

5. *His lengthened life was definitely stated.* " Fifteen years." To a man on the borders of death, fifteen years is a considerable period ; but what in itself? look back upon the last fifteen you have spent. To know the precise time of death is not desirable ; it is not best generally, but it was with Hezekiah. God's ways are not our ways, &c.

APPLICATION.

1. *Let the subject teach us the mutability of earthly affairs.* We know not what a day, &c. Do not expect to live without sorrow and crosses; this is indeed a valley of tears.

2. *Let it teach how important an interest in God's favor is.* God is all-sufficient.

3. *How important to redeem our time.* " So teach us to number our days," &c. " Be ye therefore ready," &c.

HISTORY OF HEZEKIAH.

NO. IV.—HIS UNGRATEFULNESS.

" But Hezekiah rendered not again according to the benefit done unto him."—2 CHRONICLES xxxii 25.

WE should not have been surprised if the text had been recorded of Cain, who with haughty self-complacency offered his sacrifice to God, but whose offering evidently had no respect to his own sinfulness or the provision of a Saviour ; or if the text had been spoken of the murmuring Israelites, who were filled with discontent and murmuring despite of all the miracles which God wrought for them in the desert ; but the text is spoken of Hezekiah, the good king Hezekiah, whose prayer obtained a long respite when the sentence of death had gone forth.

I. CONSIDER THE TEXT IN REFERENCE TO HEZEKIAH. Two inquiries will elucidate the first part of our subject.

1. *The benefits he had received.* We speak not now of the regular bounties of the divine providence and goodness ; nor yet of the especial favors of God's grace. Two events had recently transpired ; he had been sick, nigh unto death ; the solemn mandate had been addressed to him, " Set thine house," &c. But God had heard his prayer, and, moved with compassion, had healed him, and added fifteen years to his life. What an interposition of mercy, &c. The powerful Assyrian monarch, with an army so numerous and powerful as to fill the Israelites with the utmost dismay, was at his gates. God sent his angel, and in one night 145,000 of the Assyrian army were slain. Without battle, without the aid of Hezekiah's army, &c. Now these were extraordinary acts of God's goodness and mercy. Surely they would elicit the most fervent gratitude and praise ; yet it is said after all this that Hezekiah did not render, &c. We inquire then,

2. *In what way he did not render again.* We must see this as described, 2 Kings xx. 12. Hearing and witnessing the miracle which had been wrought, they came to visit the honored and distinguished monarch. In this he allowed his heart to be lifted up. With ostentation he showed them his riches, &c. He gave not God the glory of his great goodness, as he might have done, and ought to have done. Hezekiah, who removed the altars from the high

places, &c., yet allowed self for a time to reign. What reason the best have to fear their own hearts! The prophet is sent to proclaim his sin and the punishment it should produce, 2 Kings xx. 16. Hezekiah humbled himself and acknowledged the righteousness and goodness of God's administrations, 2 Kings xx. 19; 2 Chron. xxxii. 27. God's conduct towards Hezekiah in this matter is specified, verse 31. Hezekiah's heart was not perfect; lifted up, and God allowed him to lean upon it, that he might be conscious of it, and be delivered from it; like the nurse and the wayward child. Let us now consider the text,

II. IN REFERENCE TO OURSELVES. Three questions.

1. *What benefits have we received from the Lord?* How shall we describe or number them? Where shall we begin? With our temporal bounties; the good things of this life; food, raiment, dwellings, reason, health, mental enjoyments, religious privileges, sabbaths, sanctuaries, Bibles, ordinances. To the friends of Jesus, I just dwell on two points, for a few moments.

1. *Converting grace.* He has saved you from your natural lost estate. From sin and the power of Satan; from the wrath to come. Brought you into his kingdom, &c. Made you heirs of eternal life.

2. *Preserving mercy.* How great is his mercy towards them, &c. How often forgiven, sustained, blessed, &c. Kept you from the roaring lion; delivered you from innumerable perils, &c. We ask,

2. *What he has expected you to render unto him.*

(1.) Gratitude. Deep, hearty, constantly expressed and exemplified.

(2.) Supreme homage and glory. He did not design you to be lifted up, but rather humbled; he did not wish the glory to be given to his gifts, but to himself; he did not wish you to parade his blessings, but to enjoy them and use them to his glory.

(3.) Imitation of his mercy and goodness. " Be ye followers of God as dear children ;" feel as God feels; " Be merciful as your Father," &c. Do good, &c. He has filled your cup to overflowing, but not to be hoarded, nor wasted, but to run in streams of benevolence among the poor and miserable of your fellow-creatures. God puts down all this as done to himself. " I was hungry, and ye fed me," &c. We ask,

3. *Who has not fallen into the sin of Hezekiah?* Not rendered according, &c. "Examine yourselves; prove your own selves," &c. Who is not guilty? He who is clear let him stand up and reproach Hezekiah. Have we not been deficient in gratitude, in humility, in doing good? Then let Hezekiah's repentance be ours. If we feel our guilt, let us confess it. Deplore and seek mercy; trust our hearts less, and seek God's grace more and more. But one word to the unconverted, who never feel grateful, but who have been eagerly sinning against God, against his mercy, his Son, his Spirit, his forbearance. Oh! think how wicked, how base, how ruinous it must be. " There is forgiveness," &c. Seek it now, and through Christ's merits alone.

THE CHAFF AND WHEAT CONTRASTED.

"What is the chaff to the wheat? saith the Lord."—JEREMIAH xxiii. 28.

FIDELITY in any office is of the utmost importance. It is so in the confidential servant, or steward; it is so in the watchman; it is so in the physician; it is so most of all in the minister, or servant of God. He is a steward of Christ—a watchman on the walls of Zion. He is to direct the sin-sick to the great remedy; he stands forth to show unto men the way of salvation. In every age there have been faithless men who have usurped this office; men who have ministered for hire; who have sought their own profit; have taught for a morsel of bread. Such prophets existed in the time of Jeremiah. Men prophesied whom God had not sent; see verse 21. God affirms his omnipresence, verse 23; he describes the course they adopted, verse 25; then he shows how the true prophets ought to act, verse 28; and then follows the text.

I. WE SHALL APPLY THE TEXT TO THE VALUE AND IMPORTANCE OF THE DIVINE WORD, AS OUR INFALLIBLE DIRECTORY IN MATTERS OF RELIGION. The word of God is indeed the wheat—the grain of life. It is that which he has given to be the food of the soul. As such, it is adapted to our state, sufficient for our necessities; able to save the soul. It never failed when received with reverence, faith, and obedience. Now, every thing else presented to us for this purpose is chaff.

1. *What is reason in the place of the scriptures ?* A telescope in the dark ! With the light of truth, it is incalculably precious ; without it, nothing at all. Go to the rude savage tribes, and they have it ; to the cannibal hordes, and they have it.

2. *What is learning, or science, or philosophy, without the Bible ?* Go to the learned, philosophic Egyptians, who worshipped 3000 animals and plants ; go to the philosophical and scientific Grecians ; see their works of art and science. Their painters and sculptors were chiefly employed in contributing to their idolatrous temples. Go now to the eastern world, where literature both of a metaphysical and poetical character has flourished for ages, and yet the people are without God and hope in the world. If reason or learning would lead men to God and his services, then piety would flourish in the higher classes of our land, &c. ; but the reverse is the case. Beloved, there is one book of light, of legislation, of mercy ; one book to guide you to a better world—it is, *the word of the Lord.*

II. WE SHALL APPLY THE TEXT TO THE ORDINANCES OF GOD AS CONTRASTED WITH THE INSTITUTIONS OF MEN. *God's ordinances* are all founded in his own infinite skill and wisdom ; they never can be improper and unmeaning, because they are God's. *God's ordinances* are clothed with authority ; therefore they are obligatory and binding. *God's ordinances* are ever adapted to edify and do us real good ; not merely ceremonial, but means of profit. A right observance will be productive of spiritual good to every servant of God. *God's ordinances* are all clearly revealed in this book. Nothing is so, if God has not spoken. A divine ordinance must have God's express command. All *human institutions* are chaff; light, profitless, &c. You may know all such by bringing them to the balances of the sanctuary—to the divine word. They may resemble the true, but they are chaff; may appear resplendent and attractive, yet chaff; be very popular, yet chaff; have the sanction of the learned, still chaff; regarded by many good men, after all only chaff. Wheat needs no garnishing, no painting, no addition. It is the staff of life, just as God sends it.

III. WE APPLY THE TEXT TO EVERY THING WHICH MEN MAY SUBSTITUTE FOR REAL RELIGION. By real religion, we mean a conversion, a renewed heart, an obedient life, the love of God, &c. ; having the spirit and mind of Christ. How many things persons try to substitute for these :—

1. *Self-righteousness.* A regard to our own supposed excellencies ; a self-complacent trusting to ourselves. Now this, indeed, is chaff; a covering of filthy rags. The Pharisees boasted of this. Christ said, "Except your righteousness," &c.

2. *Religious profession.* Assuming the name, form, and the speech ; saying, "Lord ! Lord !" regular in attendance on the means, &c. Now, all this is right in itself, but it is not religion. "The kingdom of God is within," &c. "Ye must be born again." This in the place of piety is chaff, mere chaff.

3. *An exact regard to all the Lord's institutions.* We cannot urge this too forcibly ; yet this is only the evidence, and not piety itself. We may depend on these, and look to these, instead of to Christ and his cross ; we may be merely *ceremonial* Christians, without the life and spirit of Christ.

APPLICATION.

1. *We urge your attention to the spirit and practice which the divine word exhibits.* Study this as to information, experience, &c.

2. *Urge sinners to obtain the benefits of saving piety.* What are your pleasures ? Chaff; nothing else. Thousands have proved them so in adversity, sickness, and death. Have not you ? Then give your hearts to God ; set your hearts and souls to seek the Lord, &c.

RESPONSIBILITY.

"For unto whomsoever much is given, of him shall much be required."—LUKE xii. 48.

OUR subject is that of responsibility, a subject worthy of our very serious consideration. A right apprehension of this is very desirable ; and a feeling sense of it pervading our minds would tend greatly to preserve us from the evils to which we are exposed. To the doctrine of responsibility there are no exceptions but those of idiocy and childhood. Every man of sane mind is responsible, and the consequences involved are solemn and momentous. We ask,

I. For what are we responsible?

1. *For our existence.* The means of life are given to us, and we are bound to preserve our lives; not to expose them to unnecessary peril; not to neglect the use of those means by which the providence of God continues our being.

2. *For our natural faculties, and bodily health and vigor.* Every power of the mind was designed for some specific use and wise end: the understanding—the judgment—the memory—the affections, &c. Now, we are responsible for the right use and employment of these. So, also, bodily health is to be cherished, and all lawful solicitude to be exercised respecting it. "Do thyself no harm," is the voice of reason as well as revelation. Hence all persons who injure their bodies, impair their health, and affect their minds by gluttony and intemperance, will not be held guiltless before the Lord.

3. *For our natural and acquired talents.* One has a bright or penetrating genius; another, a discerning judgment; a third, an eloquent tongue; a fourth, a flaming intellect; a fifth, a vivid, fertile imagination. One has acquired extensive knowledge; others are familiar with tongues; while many are intimate with the wonders of nature, or the discoveries of art. For all these we are responsible.

4. *For our wealth.* Riches are only intrusted to men as talents to be laid out for the comfort of themselves, the good of society, and the glory of God. We are responsible as to the way of obtaining it; as to the love we have to it; and as to the manner in which we expend it.

5. *For our influence.* That is, power to affect others; and this is possessed more or less by every human being; the richest and the poorest; the most learned and the most illiterate; the monarch and the peasant; the youth and the sire. All possess the power of doing others good or evil.

6. *For our privileges.* How numerous are these! There is the light of revelation; the preaching of the gospel; the ordinances of religion; the throne of grace; the Christian sabbath; the communion of saints, &c.

7. *For our time.* Next to the blood of Jesus, the most precious blessing we pos-

sess. Our seed time; our period of probation; our only day of preparation for the scenes of a solemn eternity. Oh! when we think that on this short span hang everlasting results!

8. *For the activity of life, and all the good or evil we have crowded into it.* We ask,

II. To whom we are responsible? In some respects we are responsible to conscience, for the voice within demands attention; to an improvement of all our means and blessings; in some sense, also, to one another, according to our stations in life. Magistrates, and civil rulers, are responsible to the public for exercising righteous authority and rule; parents, for an affectionate and faithful discharge of their parental obligations; ministers to their people, for a full and faithful discharge of their ministerial and pastoral duties to their flocks; and thus, too, subjects are responsible to their rulers, children to their masters, and members to those who have the rule over them in the Lord. But we are responsible more especially to God as our Maker; as the bestower of all our blessings; as the Lord of conscience; and as our final judge. Every one must give an account of himself to God. We ask,

III. As to the extent of our responsibility. This the text affirms will be proportionate. "Where much is given," &c., Now, this accords,

1. *With the eternal principles of equity and righteousness.* Where there is no talent, there is no responsibility; where there are few, the responsibility is according. "Where much is given," &c. From the intellectual more will be demanded than from the illiterate; from the rich more beneficence than from the poor; from professors, more than from the profane; from spiritual persons, more than from the world; from the aged, more than the young. This accords,

2. *With the unvarying testimony of the Holy Scriptures.* This is very clearly presented to us in the history of Cain and Abel; Gen. iv. 7; Ezek. xxxiii. 17; Rom. ii. 11, &c.

3. *With the representations of the judgment-day.* Christ is called the righteous judge, who will judge every man according to his works.

4. *Does not this accord with your conscientious impressions of what is right?* All

earthly legislators act on this principle ; so all masters and parents ; and every man feels that it is right and fitting, that " where much is given," &c.

APPLICATION.

We learn,

1. *That each man is accountable to God for himself, &c.* That is, our state and character. We cannot evade it or relinquish it.

2. *That the responsibility of some is much greater than that of others.* What a weight of responsibility rests upon some present!

3. *We should seek to know how much God expects from us.*

4. *Faith in Christ will alone give us the ability necessary to a faithful discharge of the duties, &c., of life, and enable us to stand accepted in the last day.* We must win Christ, and be found in him, &c. " The just shall live by faith," &c.

5. *Unfaithfulness will involve in eternal sorrows.*

OBEDIENCE TO GOD.

" Then Peter and the other apostles answered and said, We must obey God rather than men."— ACTS v. 29.

THE apostles had been thrust into prison for obedience to their Lord and Master, Jesus Christ. God, however, had sent an angel and delivered them from prison, and had directed them to go forth into the temple, and speak the words of life to the people. In the morning, when they should have appeared before the council, it was discovered, that instead of being in confinement, they were again publishing in the temple the gospel of Jesus Christ. From thence they were brought to answer for their conduct, when the high priest said, " Did not ye straitly ?" &c. Then Peter and the other apostles answered and said, " We must obey God," &c. The subject is clearly the obligation of supreme obedience to God. Consider,

I. THE NATURE OF TRUE OBEDIENCE TO GOD. Now, it is obvious that true obedience must,

1. *Be divine in its rule.* Obedience supposes laws—laws published, recognised, and enforced with due authority. Now, there must be a rule for Christian obedi-

ence. It is not a vague thing—a matter left to fancy or feeling. This rule is the word of God. The Holy Scriptures contain the mind of God ; they are full, clear, and sufficient. It comprises all that is necessary for present godliness, and for our eternal salvation. True obedience,

2. *Must be universal in its regards.* It must respect all that the Lord hath spoken. If we select a part, so may others, &c. ; thus every commandment of God would be made null and void. All the requirements of God are the emanations of infinite wisdom, holiness, and love. Take the statute-book of any kingdom : a man is not a loyal and good subject, who obeys a few of the laws, and violates the rest. Apply it to forgery, theft, murder ; see James ii. 10. Now, the laws of God are of two kinds— *moral requirements* and *positive institutions.* The moral requirements are found in the ten commandments, and illustrated in Christ's sermon on the mount; positive institutions were numerous under the law, they are few and simple under the gospel. Now of these, the Lord's supper and baptism are the chief. Both of these are expressly enjoined ; they stand prominently in the statute-book of Zion. You would have to erase the gospels, the Acts, and the epistles, before you could erase them. Now, it is often clear that persons who would shudder to violate the moral, yet with the greatest indifference neglect the positive institutions. We ask, in both cases is not the authority the same ? Has not God manifested his severest wrath against those who have violated or neglected his positive institutions ? This was the sin of our *first parents ;* this was the sin of *Lot's wife ;* this was the sin of Uzziah, who invaded the priest's office, and was smitten with leprosy, &c. 2 Chron. xxvi. 16, &c. Unquestionably obedience is the duty of all who profess to be the loyal servants of God.

3. *It must be affectionate and sincere.* Obedience of the affections ; from love and not terror ; to please God more than escape his wrath. " This is the love of God," &c. Sincere in opposition to formal ; obedience of the heart with the body. Both must be united; both make it an acceptable sacrifice.

4. *It must be open and uncompromising* Not secret ; not with policy, &c. This is mean and dishonorable to the **sacred**

cause. The apostles and martyrs were put to death for "open" obedience. They might have thought and felt as they pleased without persecution; but the love of Christ constrained them, &c. God is to be first; his honor and laws must ever have the pre-eminence; see it in the three Hebrews; in Daniel; in the apostles on this occasion. "Whoso is ashamed of me," &c. We are to testify, to witness, &c.; "living epistles," &c.

5. *It must be constant and persevering.* Not occasional acts, but the habit of the life; the general, the persevering course, even unto death. "He that endureth," &c. "Be faithful," &c.

6. *It must be humble and evangelical.* Our obedience is necessarily that of imperfect beings. After all, unprofitable servants; no room for self-complacency, &c. All must be accepted through Christ; my person, repentance, faith, prayers, and every thing. Consider,

II. OUR OBLIGATION TO TRUE OBEDIENCE. We ought,

1. *From the authority of God.* He has the right to legislate. You do not dispute this. It is our imperative duty, then, to obey. He is the greatest of all beings, infinitely glorious, &c. Disobedience is treason, rebellion, &c.

2. *From grateful feelings to God.* Disobedience is ingratitude. Is it not so in the child? in the servant? in the subject? Think of God, his goodness, love, and mercy. Behold nature, providence, grace. Look at earth, air, sky; especially look at the cross, the scenes of Calvary, &c.

3. *From the present and eternal advantages of obedience.* "His commandments are not grievous." "In keeping of them there is great reward." "Godliness is profitable." Was it not the advantage of the Israelites to look to the brazen serpent? of Naaman, to go and dip in Jordan? of the blind man, to go and wash in Siloam? of the 3000, to repent, believe, and be baptized? It is for our interest, present and eternal, to obey God.

APPLICATION.

1. *We ought to obey God rather than men.* However great, learned, pious, or distinguished.

2. *Let our obedience be prompt and immediate.* We should obey him now. Now we can, &c.

3. *Call upon all to repent and believe the gospel.*

EZEKIEL'S VISION OF THE VALLEY OF DRY BONES.

"The hand of the Lord was upon me, and carried me out in the Spirit of the Lord, and set me down in the midst of the valley which was full of bones," &c.—EZEKIEL xxxvii. 1–10.

EZEKIEL, the writer of the prophecies of this book, was the son of Buzi, and was carried away captive to Babylon by Nebuchadnezzar, in the year of the world 3405, or 598 years before the advent of Christ. He began to prophesy in the fifth year of his captivity, and continued his sacred office for about twenty or twenty-one years. His prophecies are distinguished for their dark parabolical representations, and their highly figurative style. His descriptions are exceedingly bold, and often are wrought up with vehement energy, so as to possess a daring grandeur beyond any other portions of the sacred volume. Not so simple or perspicuous as the other prophets; but in majestic splendor he far excels them, and has no compeer, except in some of the resplendent visions of Isaiah, or the awfully grand predictions of the exiled John in Patmos. The vision we have selected for our present meditation manifestly relates to the restoration of the Jews, and is supposed to include both their return from Babylon, and also their restoration in the latter days to their own land. The former view was realized, when God turned back their captivity, and brought them back to their beloved land; their general restoration is yet to come. They appear at present scattered over the whole region of the valley of our world, without political existence or distinction; having residence everywhere, but citizenship nowhere. Their restoration, however, is matter of glorious certainty. The same hand that scattered will gather them; the same power that dispersed will collect them; and the Jewish stream of existence, which has never commingled with the waters of the common family of man, will return to fertilize and bless the land of Judea. That will be a glorious day, not only for themselves, but for the world. Hear what the apostle says, Rom. xi. 15, xxv. 6. But the vision of the prophet is beautifully applicable to the moral state of our world, and in this respect we shall now consider it. Let us accompany the prophet, and take a survey,

I. OF THE DREARY VALLEY.
II. HEAR THE INSTRUCTIONS GIVEN TO HIM. And,
III. WITNESS THE MARVELLOUS EFFECTS WHICH FOLLOWED. Let us take a survey,

I. OF THE VALLEY OF DRY BONES.

1. *The valley is a fit emblem of our world.* Originally earth was closely allied to heaven. Our world was once the abode of purity, light, and felicity; now it is fallen, debased; the region of night, misery, and death. Once the garden of the Lord—the dwelling of the holy—favored by the communications of Jehovah—the presence of angels; now a waste howling wilderness, the residence of the unbelieving, and the seat of Satan. What mists of darkness encircle it; what sorrow, and misery, and wo distract it! it is the region of night, and the shadow of death. And this is the aspect of the whole valley, in all its length and breadth; in all its extent and circumference. The whole world lieth in the wicked one.

2. *See the condition of its inhabitants.* "A valley of dry bones." One vast graveyard; one extensive charnel-house. Not covered with the recently deceased remains of humanity, but with dry bones, the scattered fragments of past generations; heap upon heap, blanched and withered by every wind of heaven. But the question arises, what has produced this scene of desolation? Has some pestilence wasted? has famine dried up the reservoirs of existence? These are the slain of sin; these are the blighted remains of the pestilence of moral evil; these have perished in the want and famine which their rebellion and departure from God had produced. Now, in reference to these bones, observe,

(1.) *Their number.* "Many, very many," verse 2. Such is the moral state of the hundreds of myriads of our race. There is no exception to this. All have sinned; all are dead in trespasses, &c.; not one righteous, &c.

(2.) *Their peculiar appearance.* "Very dry." Doubtless, there is much difference in the condition of our race. Civilization makes a great difference; hence contrast the roaming savage and the intellectual Hindoo. The light of the gospel makes a great difference; hence contrast the Hindoo and European. But yet, as to the want of moral resemblance to God, and a life of holiness, all men are in one state of condemnation and death. Observe,

(3.) *Their hopelessness.* "Can these dry bones live?" &c., verse 3. Ask the philosopher, and he will confess he has no remedy for such moral dreariness; ask the naturalist; he will say there is hope of a tree, &c.; but here the bones are disembodied; no flesh, no sinews, and therefore no hope. The prophet in humility referred the subject back to God, "O Lord, thou knowest." Notice,

II. THE INSTRUCTIONS GIVEN TO THE PROPHET. "Prophesy," &c., verse 4. That is, preach. The subject is given, "O ye dry bones, hear the word of the Lord." Now, objectors might say,

(1.) *How unphilosophical!* They cannot hear; to preach is foolish—out of the question. So might the prophet have replied. Or,

(2.) *It is unnecessary.* If they are raised, God must do it by miracle. Why, therefore, prophesy? If he will do it, he will do it. He must do all, or none. So say some very sapient persons in reference to preaching the gospel. It is no use, they say, to preach to dead sinners. When God intends to convert them, he will do it, and our calling them is in vain. Shall the wisdom of God or man stand? The prophet obeyed, and prophesied. Christ sent the apostles to preach the gospel to every creature, and they obeyed. The authority of Christ still extends to the Christian ministry; and wo, wo, wo to that man who preaches not the gospel of Christ. The prophet, no doubt, cried loudly, earnestly, "Oh! ye dry bones," &c. Now mark,

III. THE MARVELLOUS EFFECTS WHICH FOLLOWED.

1. *The dry bones heard.* The word of God can open the ears of the deaf, and can awaken the dead. The prophet might have lectured on philosophy, science, civilization, and morality, but they would not have heard. God's word is a hammer and fire; it is spirit and life. The latent caloric heard it, when he said, "Let there be light." The sea heard it; the dry land, &c.; and now the dry bones hear it.

2. *They were excited.* The stillness was disturbed, "There was a shaking," &c., verse 7. How often this has been the case,

when the gospel has exerted its power on the soul! The three thousand on the day of pentecost; the jailer, &c. Fears excited; anxiety produced; prayer offered.

3. *They were brought together.* By the word, men are brought out of the world, and thus to associate together. Thus assemblies are convened, congregations collected. Now they are seen in the sanctuary.

4. *They were clothed with sinews and flesh.* No longer mere bones, dry, &c.; no longer apparently hopeless. Appearances now favorable; begin to look like men; to act, and think, and speak as rational beings; conduct now changed, &c.; habits given up; sins relinquished, &c.; but yet the vitality of religion—spiritual life—is wanting. So the prophet is now to call on the winds, verse 9. And then,

5. *They lived.* By the wind is intended God's Holy Spirit. So often thus likened, "The wind bloweth," &c. Now, the Spirit of God resuscitates; gives newness of life; raises from the dead, &c. "It is the Spirit that quickens."

6. *They appear as an exceeding great army.* Become the soldiers of Christ; fight the battles of the Lord—the good fight; and finally, receive the victorious everlasting crown and reward.

APPLICATION.

1. Learn the morally dead state of sinners.

2. The efficacy of the divine word.

3. The importance of gospel prophesying.

4. The ability of sinners to hear and obey.

5. The Spirit's influence in regeneration.

6. The conflicts of the spiritual life.

THE SAVIOUR'S VISIT TO OUR WORLD.

A CHRISTMAS SKETCH.

"Blessed be the Lord God of Israel, for he hath visited and redeemed his people."—LUKE i. 68, 69.

Of all events, that of the advent of the Saviour was the most glorious and interesting; all things connected with it are calculated to excite our wonder and command our praise. The glorious person appearing the world from which he came, and the errand which brought him to our earth, are all subjects sublimely important and deserving our studious contemplation. It had been predicted that a herald or harbinger should prepare the way of the Lord. Now the tidings of John's conception were announced to Zechariah, but in consequence of his unbelief he was struck dumb, and it was only when John was to be circumcised according to the law that his mouth was opened, and he spake and blessed God, &c. Notice,

I. THE DECLARATION CONCERNING THE GOD OF ISRAEL. "He hath visited us."

II. THE FIGURATIVE REPRESENTATION OF THE MESSIAH. "Hath raised up a horn."

III. THE PRAISE WHICH WE ARE BOUND TO OFFER IN COMMEMORATING THIS EVENT. "Blessed," &c.

I. THE DECLARATION CONCERNING THE GOD OF ISRAEL. No term so endearing to pious Jews as that of the God of Israel; it reminded them of the covenant he had made, the deliverance he had wrought, and the blessings he had conferred. God had often visited and often redeemed them in a temporal sense; from Egypt and Babylon. Many of these visits had been of a most striking character, as when he appeared to Moses in the bush—on Sinai—in the temple; but chiefly he visited them through the medium of the prophets. God "spake unto the fathers by the prophets;" but there was one visit above all the rest and to crown the whole, that in the person of his Son. Now of this visit of Jesus observe,

1. *It had been long promised and expected.* It was the essence of the first promise, and Eve looked for it and exclaimed, "I have gotten a man from the Lord." Abel had the eye of his faith fixed upon it. So Abraham, he desired to see and did see Christ's day and was glad. To him all the prophets gave witness, and hence a general expectation had been kept up among the pious, to the time of his incarnation. In hope of Israel's Messiah thousands had fallen into the arms of the sleep of death.

(2.) It was a visit which had been *minutely* predicted. As to the miraculous nature of his advent, the place, and the time; at the time that the sceptre departed from Judah, &c.; when Daniel's seventy weeks were accomplished, then did the illustrious visitant appear.

(3.) It was a visit distinguished for a condition of *voluntary abasement.* The Godhead descending to be veiled in flesh, leaving heaven for earth, a throne for a manger, &c.

(4.) It was still a visit of *magnificence* and *glory.* The heavens were illuminated by the star; the skies resounded with the anthem of praise. Angels descended and proclaimed his birth. " Unto you is born," &c.

(5.) It was a visit of *stupendous love.* " God so loved," &c. " Herein is love," &c., " He sent his Son not to condemn," &c. " He came into the world to save," &c. Hence it was a visit of redeeming power and mercy. " And redeemed." To buy back—to deliver—emancipate.

II. THE FIGURATIVE REPRESENTATION OF THE MESSIAH. " Horn of salvation."

(1.) A horn is a symbol of power and strength, see 1 Sam. ii. 1; 2 Sam. xxii. 3.

(2.) Or it may refer to the horns of the altar to which criminals fled when in imminent peril, and where, except in case of murder, they found a sanctuary. See the case of Adonijah, 1 Kings i. 50. Now Christ is the horn of salvation to the penitent sinner who is fleeing for mercy. None can be saved elsewhere, and none can perish there.

III. THE PRAISE WE SHOULD OFFER TO GOD IN COMMEMORATING THIS EVENT. " Blessed," &c. " Thanks be to God," &c. Praise may be uttered,

1. By *the lips.* And this is right and proper. Christ must be our song.

2. By the *feelings of the heart.* By thinking, meditating, loving, and delighting in Christ.

3. By the conduct of the *life.* " We are to show forth," &c. Live to Christ, extol him in our conduct, &c. Do his will, carry out his designs.

APPLICATION.

1. *This subject condemns those who make these commemorative seasons opportunities of folly and sin.* What would heathens think?

2. *Let Christians display a spirit and conduct worthy of their profession.*

3. *Receive Christ Jesus into your hearts by personal, living faith.*

AN EPITOME OF THE GOSPEL.

" This is a faithful saying, and worthy of all acceptation, that Christ Jesus came into the world to save sinners."—1 TIMOTHY i 15.

OUR text contains an epitome of the gospel. It is one of those exceedingly rich and comprehensive passages with which the epistles of Paul abound, and yet it may be allowed the pre-eminence of what even that distinguished apostle has penned or left on record for the consolation of the church and the hope of the world. Every word in the text is precious and momentous, and the whole is so comprehensive, that we might with propriety take the text as the basis of a series of discourses on the evidences and blessings of the Christian religion. The apostle had been referring to his own history, and the text is full of the emotion of his heart, see verse 12, &c. Notice,

I. THE PERSON TO WHOM THE TEXT REFERS. " Christ Jesus." Now in contemplating the blessed person of the Saviour, we notice,

1. *His deity.* The world's Redeemer is the blessed God. Jehovah of hosts is ever represented in the Old Testament scriptures as the Redeemer of mankind. This divine character Christ also assumed. " He who hath seen me hath seen the Father." " I and the Father are one." " He thought it not robbery," &c.

2. *His humanity.* His existence is clearly intimated before he came into the world. As Deity he existed from everlasting; when he came into the world he did not appear in the overwhelming *brightness* of his divine *glory;* he came wrapped in *mortal flesh;* he tabernacled in human nature; formerly in the cloud; now in our nature. He was made of a woman, &c. " God manifest in the flesh," &c. A child born—a son given.

3. *In the union of the two natures.* Godman. Immanuel. Real man—true God. On one occasion the disciples beheld his glory; saw him ascend the mount as a man; beheld him transfigured and worshipped as the God of Moses and Elijah; this is a great mystery; it is the mystery of godliness.

II. HIS VISIT TO OUR WORLD. He came into the world; this had been long predicted and promised, long believed and expected; at length the period arrived; " the fulness of the times." Then he made his advent and paid the visit of his redeeming love, &c. Lived in it for about thirty-three years. Three things connected with the visit.

1. *His holy life.* He exhibited every holy virtue, every grace, every excellency, entire spotlessness. His life, a day without the least cloud of imperfection.

2. *His divine teaching.* He taught men the way to eternal life; he made known the way of salvation; he revealed the will of his heavenly Father.

3. *His marvellous sufferings.* Poverty, contempt, hatred, persecution, death, connected with sufferings of soul the most intense; death the most ignominious and cruel; death followed by a resurrection the most marvellous.

III. THE GREAT END OF CHRIST'S ADVENT. " To save sinners." Violators of God's law, polluted, wretched, worthless sinners; sinners without plea or merit; sinners justly perishing by reason of their own guilt. Now observe,

1. *He came to save from sin and its consequences.* Look at sin. A disease; death its consequence. Treason; hell its punishment. Crime; remorse its punishment. Now his coming did not alter the fact of men being sinners, or render their sins less deserving punishment, or bribe the justice of God so as not to punish; but he paid the exaction; he died for the sinner—in his stead—took his place, so that through Christ the sinner may be pardoned. Now God can be just, &c. Now the penalty is withdrawn; the rebel may live; no necessity for his eternal death. " God so loved," &c.

2. *Into a state of holiness and its blessed results.* A sinner merely pardoned would immediately sin again, and thus would never be meet for the holy services of a holy world. Christ came into the world to exhibit real purity, and to enforce it; but more, to obtain it for us; this he has done by procuring the Holy Spirit, who renews the heart, changes the entire man, and gives power to love and serve God. This is the essence of salvation—to restore the lost image of God; and this will ensure the bestowment of eternal glory; made pure in heart, we shall see and enjoy God forever and ever.

IV. THE APOSTLE'S REMARKS CONCERNING THIS GREAT GOSPEL SAYING. He says that it is,

1. *Faithful.* That is, it is true; it is a verity, not a fable, not an imposition; that Christ lived, wrought miracles and was crucified, is attested by heathen and Jewish writers as well as Christians. The testimonies of Christians for 300 years, who were put to death by thousands for believing it and professing it. The power and influence of this truth, wherever it has been promulgated by preaching or diffusing the gospel, prove it.

2. *It is worthy of all acceptation.* Worthy of being accepted; that is, being believed and trusted in; to accept it, is to give full credit to it, and treat it as true; to believe it with all our hearts. Now, it is worthy of *all* acceptation, that is, a cordial, decided, and grateful acceptation. With joy and thanksgiving, &c. It is worthy of being accepted *by all.* All classes—learned and illiterate—rich and poor; all grades, profane and moral; all ages, young and old.

APPLICATION.

1. *But one saying in the world that meets the sinner's case, and it is this concerning Christ.* His cross and gospel, the only ground of hope.

2. *This saying every sinner is heir to.* Gospel has sent it to every creature, even the chief; the vilest man on earth is but a sinner; the best man is a sinner too.

3. *Accept it, or it will not, cannot save you.* Do it now. Prove it, &c.

JOHN THE BAPTIST.

" Verily, I say unto you, Among them that are born of women," &c.—MATTHEW xi. 11.

JOHN the Baptist had sent two disciples to inquire into the character of Jesus, and his profession of the Messiahship. It could not be that he thus sent for his own sake, for he had seen and heard the attestation of Christ even at his baptism; but, doubtless, he did this for the sake of his own disciples, that they might receive him, and cleave to him as the sent of God. The Saviour's account of John is peculiarly forcible and striking. He refers to the plain and powerful characteristics of John's manner, in verses 7 and 8; then to his exalted office, verses 9 and 10; and thus concludes the description. Our text may refer to his peculiarly holy character—to his powerful and effective ministry; but we rather think, to the particular office of John as the herald and harbinger of Christ. In this, he was greater than any of the prophets, &c.; yet in respect of the glory of the gospel dispensation, the least of the apostles of Christ would be greater and more dignified than John. Before we enter on the life of the Baptist, let us just glance at the prophecies which had respect to him; Isaiah xl. 3, &c.; Malachi iii. 1. The concluding prophecy, which referred to Christ, also noticed his illustrious harbinger. Observe, then, in reference to the Baptist,

I. His PARENTAGE AND BIRTH. His father, Zacharias, was,

(1.) Priest of the Lord. His mother was a holy woman; the cousin of the virgin mother of Jesus. Read the description of this godly pair, Luke i. 6.

(2.) He was of the course of Abia. David divided the priests into twenty-four classes, or courses, who performed their duty in the temple week by week. The priests generally resided in cities a little distance from Jerusalem. From these they came to the temple service, and then returned to their dwellings.

(3.) Zacharias was now engaged in his priestly service of offering incense to the Lord. In offering incense, three persons were engaged: one was to remove the ashes of the previous service; another to bring the pan of burning coals from the altar of burnt sacrifice, and then retire; the third was to pour the incense on the coals, and while the smoke filled the place, to intercede with Jehovah on behalf of the people. This Zacharias was doing, when he beheld on the right side of the altar, the angel of the Lord. The fears of Zacharias were aroused. Fear is the attendant of sin. The best men feel their sinfulness, and therefore fear.

(4.) The celestial messenger, however, now reveals his errand; see Luke i. 13, &c. He also reveals his own name—"Gabriel," one of the chief and exalted attendants of God; he had six hundred years before visited Daniel.

(5.) Observe Zacharias's difficulty of belief, verse 18. Here was the struggle between doubt and faith, "Lord, I believe," &c. God's word enough; nothing can be really stronger; he evidently desired a sign. **Observe,**

(6.) The token given, verse 20. A very painful one; yet, in the midst of deserved wrath, God remembered mercy. Nothing more grievous than unbelief; it is an insult offered to the veracity of God. He was now the subject of solicitude, as he did not appear at the usual period, &c., verse 21. At length he came forth, but his appearance and manner indicated that something extraordinary had occurred, &c., verse 22. Zacharias, notwithstanding all the events which had taken place, continued his service in the temple, and when his period of ministration was ended, he returned to his own house.

(7.) At length the birth of John took place, amidst the joy and thanksgiving of his friends, verse 58; and on the day of his circumcision, they proposed to call him after the name of his father, Zacharias; but his mother said, "Nay, let him be named John." Zacharias was then appealed to, and he asked for a writing-table, and he wrote his name, "*John,*" and immediately his tongue was loosed, and he spake and praised God, verse 64–66. Let us just glance,

II. AT THE PERSONAL CHARACTER OF JOHN. Now observe,

1. *He was sanctified to the Lord from the womb.* God raised him up for his own special work and glory. The same is also recorded of Jeremiah, i. 5; and it was equally so with Samuel.

2. *He was to be a Nazarite in his course of life;* verse 15. Thus he was not to drink either wine or strong drink. God designed him for an especial work, and demanded great austerity of life. He was to be an example of self-denial and self-government to the people. One inference can be drawn from this: God has connected especial honor with those who avoid intoxicating fluids.

3. *He was to be filled with the Holy Ghost.* Thus in heart and mind, in lip and life, in knowledge, and unction, and power, he was to be a burning and shining light, and a faithful herald of his blessed Lord, &c. Learn,

1. That heads of families should study the graphic exhibition of domestic piety as given in the account of the parents of John, verse 6.

2. While we consider Zacharias and Elizabeth as highly favored of the Lord, yet think on our superior privileges and

mercies. "To us a child is born," &c.; the child Jesus; the Lord, the Saviour.

3. To testify of him messengers of mercy have been sent to us. Have we heard, believed, and been brought to a saving knowledge of Jesus?

JOHN THE BAPTIST.

SKETCH II.

"Verily I say unto you, Among them that are born of women there hath not risen a greater than John the Baptist."—MATTHEW xi. 11.

HAVING previously directed your attention to several leading features in the person of this distinguished servant of God, we now have to contemplate his ministry and public character. A word or two, however, first, respecting his personal appearance and mode of life.

(1.) *His appearance was peculiarly plain.* His garment was made of the coarse camel's hair, bound round him with a leathern girdle—a dress which had often been worn by the Jewish prophets. How great the contrast between his costume and that of some modern preachers of the gospel, who study elegance and finery; whose fingers and persons are often arrayed with rings and jewels; a sad example to the auditories they address.

(2.) *His mode of life was peculiarly austere.* "And his meat was locusts and wild honey." Locusts were only eaten by the poorest of the people; and in this description we are reminded of the humble class of persons with whom he chiefly mixed, and the abstemiousness he observed with regard to his food. Many persons live only to eat and attend to the appetites of the animal man. John only ate to live. He was indifferent to the luxuries of life, and existed to execute his high office and glorify God. In referring to John's public labors, observe,

I. THE SPHERE WHICH HE PRINCIPALLY OCCUPIED. The district called the "wilderness of Judea," was not a dreary, uninhabited part of the land, but one less populated than other regions. It would have been out of character for John to have retired from mankind, when he came expressly to teach them. In this wilderness there were several villages, of which Bethabara was one and the chief. Here, at some distance

from the noisy, busy cities, did he publish the nature of his message, and the truths of his great commission. To the standard of truth John elevated, great numbers resorted; so much so, that in hyperbolical language, "there went out to him Jerusalem, and all Judea;" that is, great numbers of the people. Notice,

II. THE SPIRIT OF JOHN'S MINISTRY. The spirit of John's ministry had been typified in the life and labors of Elijah the prophet, verse 14; Mal. iv. 5. The period when both were called, was one of general declension. In the plainness of their attire they resembled each other; in their holy daring, and lofty, courageous spirit; in their zeal for the glory of God; in faithfully reproving iniquity in exalted places; and as Elijah just went before the prophetical dispensation, and introduced it, so John came to prepare the way for the great Prophet, the heavenly teacher, and the gospel dispensation. Observe,

III. THE NATURE OF HIS MINISTRY. This embraced four things:—

1. *To convince the people of their sins.* There was a spiritual apathy on the people generally; among the Pharisees, a spirit of self-righteousness, and among the Sadducees, a spirit of skepticism and unbelief. He labored to awaken the careless, to strip the Pharisees of their hypocrisy, and to arouse all classes to a sense of religion.

2. *Repentance.* This was John's great doctrine. "Repent." Change your course of life; think differently, feel differently, act differently; he demanded, too, *fruits* of repentance; see Matt. iii. 8, &c.

3. *Baptism.* He was emphatically styled the "Baptist." In the Dutch version he is called the "dipper." He baptized the people in Jordan. On the repentance of the people, he baptized them for the remission of sins. Thus he said, "Forsake your evil doings, confess your faults, be baptized, and expect the Messiah, whose herald I am, and ye shall obtain forgiveness of sin."

4. *Thus his ministry was to prepare a people for the Lord.* Having gone forth for some period doing so, he was then honored by being called to baptize Jesus, his Lord, and introduce the Saviour to the Jewish nation. This he did, his humility being overruled by Christ; for when Jesus had come ninety miles to John, John confessed his unworthiness for the office; but the Re-

deemer said, "Suffer it to be so now, for thus it becometh," &c. It was now that John truly said to his disciples respecting his own ministry, "I must decrease, but he (i. e. Jesus) must increase."

(1.) John's ministry was to a great extent *successful.* Many heard, and feared, and turned to the Lord. His known sanctity, and his holy fidelity, gave him great influence over the people, and his name and virtues were greatly venerated by the Jews.

(2.) His ministry was, however, but of *short duration.* It is probable that John did not begin his work more than a year before Christ's baptism, and considerably before Christ's death it terminated. This will lead us to consider,

IV. THE TRAGICAL DEATH OF THE BAPTIST; Matt. xiv. 1. Herod, the tetrarch, had married his brother Philip's wife, although his brother was still living. This wicked exhibition of adultery and incest, John had faithfully reproved, and had said to Herod, "It is not lawful for thee to have her," &c., verse 4. In this the Baptist exposed his life, for Herod was urged by Herodias to kill him, and would have put him to death but for fear of the people. An occasion, however, is soon found for the removal of this preacher of righteousness, Matt. xiv. 6. Herod's birthday is kept; here was music, and feasting, and dancing; the daughter of Herodias so pleased Herod and the guests, that he said, "Ask of me," &c. Here was a rash and foolish engagement, made under the influence of sensual excitement, and made to a girl on account of her skill and grace in dancing, &c. The daughter consults with the mother, and the mother instructed her as to the nature of her request. Who could have supposed the horrid request, which the sequel of the history presents, would have been made! She asks not for an estate, riches, or glory, but for a head—the head of a living human being; the head of a servant of the living God; the head of John the Baptist!

The king is sorry. Exceedingly so, &c.; yet for his oath's sake, and for his honor with the guests, he consents. Here a wicked vow is still more wickedly kept; the principle the same as the false honor of the duellist and the gambler of our own time; the honor of fiendish spirits; of proud human demons.

The decree is given, for the request is instant. "Give me," says a young, attractive damsel, "*here,*" now at this feast, at this time, give me the head of the Baptist in a platter or dish."

The executioner is dispatched. The holy man is secretly beheaded; his head is placed in the horrid dish, and brought to the banquet of wine and revelling; the damsel receives it with the awful distortions of death in the muscles of the countenance, and she gives it to her mother. Here the affecting narrative terminates. History records that the vengeance of God rested upon each of the perpetrators of this atrocious deed. Herod's overthrow soon followed, and he was banished to Lyons, in Gaul. It is said of the impious daughter of Herodias, that as she was crossing a frozen river the ice separated, and she sank to the neck, when two pieces severed her head from the body.

APPLICATION.

1. *Learn the mysteriousness of divine providence.* The enemies of God often in purple, in pomp, &c.; John in prison; beheaded. A glance at the judgment, and the eternal state, will reconcile us to the dispensation: "Blessed are the dead who die in the Lord," and especially " for the Lord." Sooner home, sooner glorified.

2. *The snares of unlawful pleasures.* How ruinous has been the banquet! more so than war, or pestilence, or famine. How hardening, &c. Wine is not only a mocker, but often a blood-thirsty demon.

3. *Have we received the Messiah, and the kingdom he came to establish?* This is the great question; personal—individual—universal.

THE POOR, &c. OF THE STREETS AND LANES OF THE CITY INVITED.

"Then the master of the house being angry said to his servant, Go out quickly into the streets and lanes of the city, and bring in hither the poor, and the maimed, and the halt, and the blind."— LUKE xiv. 21.

OUR text is part of the parable of the marriage supper, which is designed to exhibit the abundant provision of the gospel, and the sinful rejection of it by unbelieving sinners. Man, by reason of transgression, had involved himself in wretchedness and misery. As a sinful rebel, he had forfeited all claim to the divine goodness and bounty; here we see then the grace of God in freely providing the means of happiness for his ruined creatures. The blessings of the gospel are likened to a feast, a great supper; here we have suitable provision; the richest and most costly provision; here is an overflowing provision; an abundance, enough for all; the invitation issued was of the most free and generous kind, verses 16, 17.

The conduct of the bidden guests was most ungrateful and wicked. "And they all with one consent," &c. It was then that the servants showed these things, &c.; and he said, "Go out quickly," &c. Notice,

I. THE SPHERE OF MINISTERIAL LABOR. "Streets and lanes of the city." In other passages it is said, "the highways and hedges," &c. Originally God was worshipped in the temple, and in the synagogues about Judea. When John the Baptist, however, came, he went ,abroad into the public places, and cried, "Repent ye," &c. Now Jesus acted upon the same principle. He addressed the people on the sea-shore, on the mountain top, in the highways, &c. The apostles acted in like manner, they went forth preaching the kingdom of the grace of God in the streets of Jerusalem, &c. Our missionaries have to act upon the same plan; if they were to wait until the heathen came to them, few would hear the word of life; it is desirable in our own country that this also should be done. Many never think of God or his house; but if entreated they might be induced to hear: how can this be done? both by preaching in the streets, &c., and by visiting the families in our benighted neighborhoods, and persuading them to visit the house of God.

II. OBSERVE THE OBJECTS OF MINISTERIAL EFFORT. "The poor, the maimed, the halt, and the blind." If we consider these words literally, then we may consider that the wretched, in general, are to be specially invited, &c. The gospel is emphatically sent to the poor; it is of the greatest importance to them in this life; their souls are of incalculable value—of eternal worth; but do we not see that the text is applicable in a spiritual sense to all men?

1. *All sinners are truly poor.* Poor as it respects the soul and eternity; as poor as the starving prodigal.

2. *All sinners are maimed and halt* Sin has destroyed the energies of the soul; they have not the power our holy parents in Paradise had. They are the slaves of the enemy, &c.

3. *All sinners are blind.* In the darkness of moral ignorance—in the darkness of unbelief—in the darkness of condemnation. They see not their own condition—they see not the beauty of religion—they see not the excellency of Christ—they see not the preciousness of the gospel, or the importance of salvation. A poor, maimed, blind creature, in the street, is only a faint type of the true misery of the sinner. To be blind on the verge of eternity! on the margin of the fathomless lake of fire!

II. THE DIRECTION GIVEN RESPECTING MINISTERIAL EFFORT. It is personal effort. They are to go out. Many duties connected with the ministerial work; reading, study, &c.; but all these must be in reference to the work of preaching—of inviting sinners. Now, in going out, three things are important:—

1. *We must go out in Christ's name.* We are his servants; he commissions us; all our authority is derived from him.

2. *With his message.* What he has enjoined. Many subjects might amuse, might interest, &c. Wonders of nature—of providence. The earth—the heavens, &c. No, it must be the gospel—the good news of the kingdom; publishing Christ as the only Saviour. "This is a faithful saying," &c. "The supper is ready," &c. There must be,

3. *Promptitude of action.* "Quickly." Now there are three reasons for this:—

(1.) The work is divine and spiritual: this is the chief thing. Soul and eternity first—God and his glory first.

(2.) Our time of labor is limited. What the minister does, he must do quickly. "I must work," &c. Soon we must give an account.

(3.) Sinners are perishing; every day —every hour—every moment, they are hurrying into eternity; every soul thus lost is of eternal value; then it must be done quickly; the person enveloped with flames, must be saved quickly; the ship-wrecked mariner must have the life-boat quickly; the dying sinner must have the balm of life quickly. When the soul and heaven are concerned, every thing must be done quickly.

THE WEDDING GARMENT.

APPLICATION.

1. *You have often been addressed.* Have you obeyed the gospel? Have you been brought into the favor and family of God?
2. *Urge it upon all to-night.* We exhort —we entreat—we invite all.

THE WEDDING GARMENT.

" And when the king came in to see the guests, he saw there a man which had not on a wedding garment; and he saith unto him, Friend, how camest thou in hither not having a wedding garment? And he was speechless. Then said the king to the servants, Bind him hand and foot, and take him away, and cast him into outer darkness; there shall be weeping and gnashing of teeth."— MATTHEW xxii. 11–13.

THE gospel minister must declare the whole counsel of God. We must exhibit both the promises and the threatenings; we must invite by all the greatness and preciousness of the provision, but we must also alarm by exhibiting the terrific consequences of refusing the overtures of life. In the parable of which the text is the conclusion, the embassy of love and mercy had first of all been rejected; but afterwards, a number had been prevailed upon to comply with the invitation, and the table was furnished with guests; but there is presented to us the fearful condition of one of the guests. " And when the king came in to see the guests," &c. To realize the force of the picture, imagine the splendid guest-chamber of an eastern monarch, arrayed in all the magnificence of oriental grandeur. The wedding ceremonies of the heir to the throne are to be sumptuously celebrated. The provision is costly and abundant. To add to the effect, and to exhibit the riches and glory of the feast, costly vestments are prepared for all the guests, and in these it is expected they will all appear at the royal banquet. The room is splendidly illuminated; the guests are all assembled, when the king in majestic state is announced. In looking around, an individual is perceived without the appointed garment; he is interrogated by the monarch, and it is found that he is an intruder, or one who has treated his king with contempt. He is immediately seized by the servants and borne into the gloomy prison at the base of the palace, where is darkness, and weeping and gnashing of teeth. Such might be considered the literal illustration of the text. Let us reflect on the spiritual import and design of the passage. We must consider what we are to understand,

I. BY THE WEDDING GARMENT. Now it is clear that it is the costume, or spiritual dress, necessary for the enjoyment of heaven. We need not then be in doubt on this subject. The garment is " holiness, without which no man shall see the Lord." It is the complete renewal of the soul in the likeness of the divine image, which consists of knowledge, righteousness, and true holiness. Now this holiness of heart and life is often described as a garment. " I put on righteousness, and it clothed me; my judgment was as a robe and a diadem," Job xxix. 14. Hence Isaiah says, " He hath clothed me with the garments of salvation, he hath covered me with the robe of righteousness, as a bridegroom decketh himself with ornaments, and as a bride adorneth herself with her jewels," lxi. 10. Hence the church is thus described by the psalmist, " The king's daughter is all glorious within, her clothing is of wrought gold," &c., Psalm xlv. 13. Hence too when the prodigal returned, he was adorned with the best robe. The Laodiceans were exhorted to buy gold, &c. " I counsel thee to buy of me gold tried in the fire, that thou mayest be rich; and white raiment that thou mayest be clothed," &c. Rev. iii. 18; and this agrees with the description of the heavenly company : " And lo ! a great multitude, which no man could number, of all nations, and kindreds, and people, and tongues, stood before the Lamb, clothed with white robes, and palms in their hands," Rev. vii. 9. Mark,

II. THE SOLEMN SCRUTINY. " The king came in," &c. This scrutiny,

1. *Was divine.* The survey was made by that omniscient Being whose eyes are as a flame of fire. Nothing is more dangerous than for mortals to judge one another, " Judge not," &c. It is not likely that even in a future state we shall possess the power of discerning the heart; but the king immortal, invisible, " whose eyes," &c. He seeth the thoughts afar off. Before him all things are naked, &c. At once he beheld the man without the wedding garment.

2. *This scrutiny was personal.* The guests were not surveyed in masses—not

in nations, sects, or churches, or families; but in their individual character; never was a nation all holy and sacred; nor yet a sect—nor church—nor perhaps an entire family. Religion is a personal concern; it is so from first to last; it will be so in its great and momentous consequences to all eternity.

III. THE AWFUL DETECTION. "He saw there a man," &c. We may form three conjectures as to this robeless character.

1. *It might have resulted from carelessness.* He did not attend to the requirements of the king; he never duly thought and reflected; was never deeply impressed with the dignity and glory for which a sacred preparation was necessary. How many such are now in the presence of God; no deep impression as to the necessity of vital religion, of holiness of heart.

2. *It might have resulted from procrastination.* He had perhaps been aware of the requisite costume, but had deferred the matter until it was too late. How many of such are here this evening? You believe in the doctrine of regeneration, &c.; but you remain the children of nature; spiritual piety is put off; it has been so for years; it may be so until it is too late.

3. *It might have resulted from proud and wicked preference.* Perhaps thought it not essential; had other views; would trust to the mercy of the king, or to his own beautiful habiliments. Are there not some of this class present? You do not like spiritual, internal, evangelical godliness; satisfied without this. Moral, benevolent, nominally Christians. Observe,

IV. THE AWFUL INVESTIGATION. "Friend, how camest thou," &c.

1. *This investigation was public.* Before all the guests. The enemies of Christ will be publicly confounded at the last day; clothed with shame and contempt.

2. *This investigation was reasonable.* It gave an opportunity for the exhibition of righteousness. "How," &c. Give a reason, &c. God will allow the sinner to plead. This investigation,

3. *Was overwhelming.* "He was speechless." He was surprised, detected, ashamed; he had no reason to assign, hence he was confounded. Mark,

V. THE DREADFUL PUNISHMENT. Notice,

1. *The removal.* "Take him away." From a palace to a prison—from a feast to

wretchedness—from angels to devils—from heaven to hell.

2. *The sentence.* "Cast him into outer darkness." Regions of darkness—chains of darkness—the blackness of darkness.

3. *The misery.* "There shall be weeping and gnashing," &c. The retrospect shall cause this; a life of folly, of gross infatuation, &c. The present, covered with shame, the gnawing of conscience; the gloomy prospect, no hope of release, or even alleviation. Lost, irreparably lost; lost forever.

APPLICATION.

1. *Now all that is necessary for heaven may be obtained, and that by all.*

2. *Let professors examine themselves, &c.* Are you in Christ? Have you put him on? &c.

3. *Let sinners be entreated.* Listen to the voice of the gospel and live.

THE WOMAN WITH THE BLOODY ISSUE.

"And a certain woman, which had an issue of blood twelve years, and had suffered many things of many physicians," &c.—MARK v. 25, &c.

OUR subject is one of the cures effected by the miraculous power of the Lord Jesus Christ. Numerous and astonishing were the miracles of mercy which he performed; and it is worthy of note, that the diseases he cured were such as were counted hopeless by the ordinary modes of healing. Such was the leper, yet he had but to say, "Be thou clean," &c.; such was natural blindness, yet he opened the eyes of the man born blind; such was established paralysis; but to the most inveterate instance of palsied misery he said, "Arise, take up thy bed," &c. An issue of blood, of twelve years' standing, was a disease evidently of this kind. Let us see in this diseased woman,

I. AN EMBLEM OF THE SINNER'S SPIRITUAL STATE.

II. IN HER MODE OF APPLICATION, AN EXAMPLE WORTHY OF THE SINNER'S IMITATION.

III. IN HER CURE, A PLEDGE OF THE SINNER'S ACCEPTANCE AND SALVATION. In this woman we see,

I. AN EMBLEM OF THE SINNER'S SPIRITUAL CONDITION. Four points: a distressing disease; of long continuance; growing worse and worse ; and incurable by human agency. Observe in this woman,

1. *A distressing disease.* " An issue of blood." The disease was one of Levitical uncleanness ; no doubt a cause of great suffering, and which, according to the Mosaic ritual, excluded her from the society of others. Now, sin is often thus represented. It is the plague of the heart ; it is internal and universal spiritual defilement ; see Isaiah i. 4. This moral pollution excludes the soul from the fellowship of a holy God, and the enjoyment of holy services. With this every sinner is afflicted. This woman's affliction,

2. *Was of long continuance.* " Twelve years." Thus, it was deeply seated and established in the system. The disease of sin is of still longer continuance. Look back to your youth—to your childhood ; the very first actions, thoughts, and words evince that the heart is corrupt, and the soul under the influence of moral disease. Thus for years it has been more and more deeply rooted in the system, and establishing its evil dominion and habits in the inmost recesses of the soul. The affliction of this woman,

3. *Grew worse and worse.* Sin never consumes itself ; never expires of itself ; never heals of itself ; neither is it ever stationary. Like the stream ever flowing ; tree ever growing ; waxing worse and worse ; spreading and extending its power over the whole man.

4. *It was incurable by human instrumentality.* She had felt it, and deplored it, and sought its removal. She had suffered many things, verse 26 ; she had spent all that she had ; she had applied to many physicians. How often do sinners exactly copy her example ; go to a variety of sources for happiness and peace, and find none. Sometimes to the works of the law ; sometimes to nominal religion ; sometimes to penances, fasts, &c. ; sometimes to almsgiving, &c. But all our time, all our energies, are thus employed in vain. None of these can heal or save ; all physicians of no value. Happy for this daughter of affliction that Jesus, the great healer, passed by where she dwelt ; that she heard of him ; and that she presented herself to his compassionate nature.

II. In her mode of application ; an example worthy of the sinner's imitation. Having heard of Jesus, she,

1. *Exercised faith in his healing power* For she said, " If I may," &c., verse 28. Now this was strong faith, marvellous faith, of which there had been no previous instance. He had spoken and cured diseases ; but she believed that contact with his garment was enough. Thus the sinner must believe. Observe,

2. *Her faith overcame the obstacles in her way to the Saviour.* There was a crowd of persons ; many persons intervened between her and the Messiah ; it required activity, energy, and resolution ; had she waited, or neglected the opportunity, her disease would have remained. There will ever be a crowd of obstacles in the way to the Saviour. Every penitent has so found it ; so that decision and striving are ever necessary.

3. *Her faith brought her to the saving extraction of the Redeemer's virtue.* As she desired, and believed, and hoped, so it was to her. She touched the hem of his garment, and the virtue was drawn out, " and straightway," &c., verse 29. The exercise of faith in Christ is always followed by like results. But this leads us to consider her cure,

III. As a pledge of the sinner's acceptance and salvation. The Saviour knew the effect produced by the going out of the virtue of his healing power. He interrogated her, that the case might be evident, and that he might honor the faith, and confirm the cure. In her case we have a pledge,

1. *He can save and heal the soul, as well as the body.* He came expressly to do this ; the instances are innumerable.

2. *He will save every believing, trusting sinner.* He has engaged to do it ; he loves to do it ; he longs to do it ; it is his reward and joy.

3. *He will save in the same way, and by the same means, and on the same terms.* By his inherent virtue and merits—the efficacy of his atoning blood ; by the same means— the faith of the applicant ; and on the same terms—" without money," &c. Freely, fully, and forever.

APPLICATION.

1. *How many are still afflicted with the plague of sin ?* Apply to Jesus all of you, and now. He is the only physician ; he alone can save.

2. *How many are anxious to obtain it ?*

Do not let the press keep you back; be resolved; be in earnest. Imitate the spirit and conduct of this woman.

3. *How many are healed?* Oh! exhibit much love and gratitude to Christ, and much compassion for souls. Proclaim this Saviour everywhere, &c.

MARTHA'S INORDINATE CAREFUL-NESS.

"But Martha was cumbered about much serving, and came to him, and said, Lord, dost thou not care that my sister hath left me to serve alone? bid her, therefore, that she help me. And Jesus answered and said unto her, Martha, Martha, thou art careful and troubled about many things."— LUKE x. 40, 41.

ALL circumstances and conditions of life have their respective snares and dangers. There are temptations and evils to which all persons are liable; often in danger even from lawful things. Prudence is an important virtue, but often degenerates into selfishness and distrust. Generosity and hospitality have a prominent place in religion; but here we have an instance of their excess being pernicious. Martha and Mary were two Christian sisters, who, with their brother Lazarus, resided at Bethany. They were the object of the Saviour's especial love, and were favored with his gracious visits. Here Jesus was probably often entertained by these beloved female worthies. The text refers to one instance, and shows how, with all her excellencies, Martha evinced a spirit of over-carefulness, so as to call forth the gentle yet pointed admonition of the Redeemer, "Martha, Martha, thou art careful," &c. Observe,

I. THE EVIDENCE OF MARTHA'S CAREFUL-NESS. Now, three terms are employed in reference to it. Her mind was distracted by,

1. *Multiplicity of objects.* "Was cumbered," &c. The mind is so formed that it cannot actively pursue more than one object at the same time. Our real necessities are few, our imaginary ones numberless. "Much serving" was injurious to Martha, and less serving would have been more acceptable to Christ.

2. *Her mind was tortured with over-solicitude.* "Thou art careful." Carefulness and solicitude are highly proper. Neither reason nor religion requires an improvident recklessness, or thoughtless indif-ference. A man must employ his reflective powers in providing for his household. There is a becoming care highly proper both as it respects body, soul, reputation, &c. The term often so rendered in our translation, had been better translated, "anxious;" see Matt. vi. 25–34. "Be careful," &c. This anxiety is felt when the mind is tortured and torn by care; when care throws her dark shadows across the mind, and makes it gloomy and fretful. Now, Martha was quite anxious, &c.

3. *She was distracted even to trouble.* "And troubled." Now, this is the necessary result of anxiety. Mind becomes troubled; agitated between hope and fear; perplexed; no calm, no quiet, no enjoyment; the opposite of a placid, peaceful, happy state. We have thus seen the evidences of Martha's carefulness. Consider,

II. THE EVIL OF IT. Jesus evidently designed his remark to be considered in the way of admonition. "Martha, Martha," &c. You will see,

1. *It prevented attention to better things.* Here was the Son of the most high God, the world's Messiah; yet, instead of being an intense listener to his words, she was losing this great opportunity, and distinguished privilege. Is it not so often with you? Does not over-carefulness produce neglect of the Bible? prayer? ordinances? &c.

2. *It led her into censoriousness of spirit,* "My sister hath left me," &c. This was unkind, and an evidence of bitterness of spirit, which ought not to have existed, much less appeared in presence of such an illustrious visitor. Martha is a specimen of all anxious persons; fretful and peevish tempers are often the result.

3. *It caused her to treat the Saviour with apparent disrespect.* No doubt she loved him, and intensely; but Martha ought not to have said, "Lord, dost thou not care?" Had she forgotten the dignity of her guest? Did she not know what it was his meat and drink to do? Now, anxious worldly care is ever in danger of reflecting upon the divine Redeemer, his providence, plans, &c.

4. *It subjected her to the reproof of her divine Lord.* "Martha," &c. Why so anxious? Thou blamest Mary; but I must tell thee "one thing," &c., "and Mary hath," &c. Now, worldly anxiety

ᴎ ᴇver displeasing to Christ, and ever injurious to the soul. Let us consider,

III. THE REMEDIES BY WHICH IT MAY BE AVOIDED.

1. *By allowing spiritual things to have the ascendency.* Spiritual food, raiment, health, riches, &c. "Seek ye first," &c.

2. *By cultivating a spirit of moderation in reference to temporal things.* "Let your moderation," &c. Only a little is necessary; only a little can be enjoyed; only wanted for a short time.

3. *By considering the utter inefficiency of worldly care to attain its end.* Your anxiety will produce no beneficial results; nay, it will prevent the enjoyment of what you have. "Who by anxious thought can make one hair?" &c.; see Matt. vi. 24, &c.

4. *By seriously considering the eternity into which we are hastening.* Soon we shall leave all behind—houses, riches, possessions; soon we shall have done with poverty and affliction. Oh! think of heaven and eternity! Why should pilgrims be anxious? citizens of glory!

APPLICATION.

1. *Address the moral, and those who admire religion, and are yet strangers to its power.* What is it keeps you back? Are you not careful? &c.

2. *Urge upon all, supreme attention to the salvation of the soul.*

3. *We cannot be too deeply concerned for the riches of glory.* Let us seek to "lay up treasure in heaven," &c.

MARY'S HAPPY CHOICE.

"But one thing is needful; and Mary hath chosen that good part, which shall not be taken away from her."—LUKE x. 42.

WE have previously directed your attention to the spirit Martha evinced, and the reproof which Jesus administered on her anxiety about many things. We have now to contemplate the character and spirit of Mary.

(1.) You will observe, that Mary displayed intense attention to the words of Jesus; she heard with eagerness, and with delight, the discourse of the Saviour.

(2.) The humility and reverence of Mary are also stated. "She sat at his feet." The proper place for the pupil, for the disciple. Religion ever commences in this way; attention to the truths of the gospel, and humbleness and docility of mind in the reception of its sacred contents. Our text contains the approbation of the Saviour as to Mary's conduct. "But one thing," &c. Need I say that it is clear Jesus referred to her attention to the soul; giving the preference to spiritual matters—the reception of the words of Christ; in one word, true religion is the "one thing," &c. Observe, the subject directs us,

I. To THE UNITY OF TRUE RELIGION. "One thing." It consists in the possession of the grace and Spirit of God, and this is its essential identity. There are not many true religions; never was but one true and acceptable religion. In all ages it has been one; in all climes it is one. The means of religion have varied; dispensations changed; the laws, &c., have been altered; but religion itself has ever been "one thing." True religion is connected with various blessings and privileges, yet is one in character and essence, and one word may express the whole—Love! Love to God, and love to man. Observe,

II. RELIGION IS A VOLUNTARY THING. "Mary hath chosen." Reason and revelation establish this:—

(1.) Reason despises force and coercion in all matters of mind. Force may make slaves and hypocrites, but cannot give to the soul the feelings of love and delight.

(2.) Revelation from first to last goes upon this principle. Remember what God said to Cain, "If thou doest well," &c. Joshua to the Israelites, "Behold I have set," &c. God solemnly affirms this by Ezekiel, xxxiii. 10, 11. Paul, although arrested by the supernatural appearance of the Saviour, yet was not coerced, for he says, "I was not disobedient," &c. Jesus, too, when speaking of Mary, says, "She hath chosen," &c. Let no man say he is wicked of necessity; depraved of necessity. Every man may believe and obey the gospel who hears it. "For faith cometh by," &c. "And whosoever calleth," &c. Christ laid the blame upon the will, "Ye will not," &c. Notice,

III. RELIGION IS EMPHATICALLY A GOOD THING. "That good part." It is good,

1. *In its author and origin.* Every work of God is good. It is his own creation; has his own signet; elevates men to his likeness; tested and tried by the highest standard it is good.

2. *It is good in its adaptation to the soul.*
The soul's good. It is the food of the soul;
dress, health, and life of the soul.

3. *Good in all its influences.* Breathes
good-will to all men ; in every circle and
sphere. It makes man a blessing to his
species, and an ornament to the world.

4. *Good without any admixture.* No evil
in it. Like its Author, it is light, and in it
is no darkness at all.

IV. RELIGION IS A SURE AND CERTAIN
THING. "Shall not be taken away." Here
is stability—permanent stability. You cannot say so of any thing else. Who would
dare to say it of riches ? of honor ? of
health ? of friends ? or of life ? No ; all
these are evanescent. We are never sure,
&c.; but this is sure. "Shall not ?" &c.
"God will not," &c. His gifts are without repentance. Satan cannot ; the world
cannot ; the world can neither give it nor
take it away. If lost, we must freely abandon it ; draw back, &c. It is ever sure
and certain. "He who hath begun," &c.
"I give unto my sheep," &c.

APPLICATION.

1. *What is engaging your chief attention?*
Do not trifle away time, opportunities,
means, &c.

2. *Now accept the offer of eternal life.*
Let this be the turning point. Now bow ;
now yield yourselves to God.

3. *Believers, thank God, and take courage.*
Yours is the approbation of Christ. This
is the soul's highest honor, and its sweetest
bliss.

THE ONE THING NEEDFUL.

"One thing is needful "—LUKE x. 42.

WE design on this occasion to press true
religion upon you, from its being emphatically the "one thing needful." It is indispensable to the present and eternal well-
being of man. Let us ask and answer a
few questions, so as to illustrate the sentiment of the text.

I. FROM WHENCE DOES THE NECESSITY OF
RELIGION ARISE ?

1. *From the constitution of the soul of man.*
The soul was formed and designed for religion. True religion implies knowledge—
faith—love—righteousness. The faculties
of man are capable of these, designed for
these. There is light for the understanding, truth for the judgment, motives to influence the will, love for the affections, and
peace for the conscience.

2. *From the fallen and wretched state of
man.* He is not now in a perfect, happy,
and holy state. What can disenthral him ?
what exalt ? what purify ? what console ?
Nothing but religion. Learning and education cannot.

3. *From man's responsible state and character.* Man is accountable to God. Who
does not feel this ? Every man must give
an account to God ; be judged, and rewarded or punished in the eternal state. For
this in our natural estate we are wholly unfit ; cannot shake off our accountability.
Religion invests us with a blessed meetness
for the judgment-day. It erases the stains
of past guilt ; it enters our names in the
Lamb's book of life ; gives a meetness for
eternal glory.

II. FOR WHOM IS IT NEEDFUL ? One
word might answer this ; but we must par-
ticularize.

1. *It is needful for the young.* "Wherewith shall a young man," &c. It is the
unerring pilot of the young ; it is the guardian ; it is the ornament ; it has to do with
all their concerns ; with health, reputation,
subsistence, long life. "Godliness is profitable," &c. ; see Prov. iii. 11–26.

2. *It is needful for parents and heads of
families.* Most parents are truly anxious
to feed, clothe, and educate their children ;
but if children have souls, they require
much more than this. Do they not require
a religious training ? a consistent example ?
and fervent prayer with them and for them ?
What parent can do these things without
religion ? What a fearful account will
prayerless parents have to give at the last
day !

3. *It is needful for the aged.* A man
never can outlive his evil nature and his
sins. The sinner, though he lives a hundred years, yet he shall die accursed.
How dreadful for life to be ending, and the
great work of life not begun ; for spring,
for summer, and for harvest to be over, &c.
Nothing can make the dim eye bright but
this.

4. *It is needful for the rich.*
(1.) Prevents riches from being a curse.
(2.) Does what riches cannot do—gives
peace, &c.

(3.) Makes riches a double blessing.

5. *It is needful for the poor.* Bible—the poor man's book ; Christ—the poor man's Saviour ; the gospel—the poor man's portion in life ; the crown of glory—the poor man's reward in heaven. It sanctifies and sweetens poverty, &c.

III. WHEN IS IT NEEDFUL ?

1. *In health and strength.* Even these cannot make the mind really happy without it. Religion is the true health and vigor of the soul.

2. *In times of peril and sickness.* What anxiety is connected with these ! Now, the dissipating scenes of life out of reach. How precious to know that the affliction is administered by our Friend and Father ; that he is the refiner ; that the end is our good ; to be patient, resigned, happy.

3. *In the hour of death.* To illumine ; to sustain ; to save.

APPLICATION.

1. *Let me urge all classes to choose religion.*

2. *Do it now.* This day ; this hour.—It will be important,

3. *Through all eternity.*—It is that alone which will produce everlasting felicity in the world to come.

———

THE CALL OF MATTHEW.

" And as Jesus passed forth from thence, he saw a man named Matthew, sitting at the receipt of custom ; and he said unto him, Follow me ; and he arose and followed him."—MATTHEW ix. 9.

THE blessed Redeemer was never out of the way of benevolence and mercy ; wherever he went he always found fit objects for the exercise of his grace and compassion. You will perceive in the eighth chapter, that he had been healing a man of that dreadful disease, the leprosy. Restoring the centurion's servant ; then he went out into the coast of the Gadarenes. On the voyage, by his word he stilled the tempest ; when he arrived there he restored two who had been possessed of devils ; and caused the herd of swine to receive the dispossessed spirits, which made them run violently into the sea, where they were drowned. The Gadarenes loved their swine more than the world's Redeemer, so " they besought him to depart out of their coasts." Christ then entered into a ship, and came into his own city, by which we understand Capernaum ; hence it was an ancient saying, " Bethlehem brought him forth, Nazareth brought him up, and Capernaum was his principal dwelling-place." As Jesus was passing forth, " he saw a man named Matthew." Observe,

I. THE PERSON REFERRED TO. " Matthew," &c. Let us notice,

1. *His personal history.* He is generally supposed to have been the son of a sister or cousin of the mother of Jesus, and thus was a distant relative of the Messiah. It seems after his conversion that he was also called Levi. Observe,

2. *His occupation.* He was a publican, or collector of the taxes and customs ; these taxes were levied by the Romans upon the Jews, and were exceedingly grievous to them, as being a visible mark of their subjection to the Roman yoke ; besides, these taxes were sold to the highest bidder, and the collectors of them were noted for their covetousness and rapacity ; in fact they were justly held in abhorrence by the people. You will perceive that for a Jew thus to be employed was degrading in the highest degree, as it was giving countenance to the galling tyranny of the Romans over the Jews. It will be seen then that the occupation of Matthew,

(1.) Was dishonorable to him as a Jew.

(2.) It was associated with great temptations.

(3.) And it was unfavorable to religion and humanity. Let me ask you before I pass on, what is your occupation ? What is your temporal calling ? Is it a righteous one ? Is it such a one as does not injure society ? Can you seek God's blessing upon it ? If so, do you follow it lawfully ? Do not let it engross your chief affections. Do not let it occupy your sabbaths. Do not let it ruin your souls. Notice,

II. THE ADDRESS OF THE SAVIOUR. " And Jesus said unto him, Follow me." Now you will observe,

1. *The conciseness of this address.* Two words embody it. The true nature of religion often may be expressed in a single sentence. Repent and believe the gospel. Give yourselves to God. Be ye reconciled to God. " Turn ye, turn ye," &c.

2. *Its comprehensive meaning.* " Follow me." It implies,

(1.) Renunciation of the world and sin.

We cannot pursue two opposite courses—cannot serve two masters; we cannot be of the world and of Christ; when he says, "Follow me," he says, Leave the world; forsake sin; keep afar off no longer; it implies,

(2.) Deciding for Christ. So soon as the prodigal came to himself, and stood still, he then said, "I will arise," &c. There may be many changes, yet none of them may be effective. We must resolve to be the Lord's. Decide that we will be Christ's, and he shall be ours.

(3.) Practical obedience to Christ. "Follow me." Listening to his words; sitting at his feet; embracing his truth; imbibing his spirit; imitating his conversation; treading in his steps: in one word, becoming Christians; resembling the Saviour; being humble, self-denying, as Christ was; observing all his precepts and ordinances to do them; being benevolent, and merciful, and pitiful as Christ. Notice then,

III. THE CONDUCT OF MATTHEW. "And he arose," &c.

1. *Contrast it with the conduct of many.* Many hear, but hear only; many resolve, but resolve only; many are deeply affected, but are affected only.

2. *Observe the difficulties in the way.*

(1.) He must have been totally indisposed to spiritual things. His habits, pursuits, &c.

(2.) A lucrative employment. He was getting riches; a good business; self-interest at stake.

(3.) The call involved not only the greatest sacrifices, but exposed him to persecution and reproach—to follow Christ into poverty and the hatred of the Jews—to be a disciple of one whom all reviled—to join in his cross and shame—to risk reputation, ease, and life.

3. *Observe how he acted.* "He arose," &c. He resolved, and acted decidedly, and promptly. At once he became a disciple; he conferred not with friends—nor with flesh and blood. He delayed not; he arose, and Matthew the publican became Levi the apostle of Jesus.

4. *See what followed.* He became a disciple of Jesus; a preacher of the gospel; an apostle of the cross; a martyr for the truth. It is supposed he suffered death for his religion, by being pierced with a halbert in Ethiopia, where he had long preached the gospel. In addition, he wrote the gospel which bears his name. We have thus referred you to Matthew who obeyed the call of Jesus, and arose, and followed him.

APPLICATION.

1. *Now Christ is passing by.* He is just saying what he said to Matthew. What do you reply? What is it keeps you back? Why delay?

2. *Now arise and follow Christ.* Cannot be too precipitate in this. Why reason? Why study the matter? Christ says, "Follow me." Who will obey? You, young man? &c. You, old man? &c. Shall it be said of any here, "They arose?" &c.

THE SYRO-PHENICIAN WOMAN.

"Then Jesus went thence, and departed into the coasts of Tyre and Sidon. And, behold, a woman of Canaan came out of the same coasts, and cried unto him, saying, Have mercy on me, O Lord, thou Son of David," &c.—MATTHEW xv. 21–28.

OF the blessed Saviour it is written, that he "went about doing good." He came to bless the world, and wherever he went he realized the truth of this declaration. He was eyes to the blind—ears to the deaf—speech to the dumb—health to the sick—joy to the disconsolate—mercy to the guilty—salvation to the lost—and life to the dead. At the time of the Messiah's sojourn upon earth, Satan seemed to have assumed an immense amount of power, and exercised great and despotical control over the bodies as well as the souls of mankind. Hence Jesus was often called to dispossess those who were under the direct and fearful power of the prince of darkness. One of these cases introduces us to the subject of our present discourse. Let us contemplate,

I. THE DISTRESSED SUFFERER.
II. THE MIGHTY SAVIOUR.
III. THE EFFECTUAL INTERCESSOR.
IV. THE DELIGHTFUL CURE.

I. THE DISTRESSED SUFFERER. "Daughter grievously vexed," &c. Several similar cases are revealed to us. There is the case of a youth, whose father came to Christ; the demoniac; Mary Magdalene. So the daughter in the text; under the direct agency of Satan; impelled by his evil spirit, mind, and body, &c. A young person thus tortured and afflicted; beyond human skill or power to relieve. Let us turn from the sufferer,

II. To THE MIGHTY SAVIOUR. He was sent to destroy the works of the devil; to bruise the head of the serpent; to overthrow the fell usurper; to rescue the world from his iron grasp. He had been typified by Moses, Joshua, Samson, David, &c. Three things favorable to the sufferer:—

1. *That this Saviour was then in the flesh.* She might have lived before Christ's incarnation; before the Shiloh—the Deliverer had come; but the angels had announced, &c.; the Baptist had heralded; the Holy Ghost had descended on him. He had entered on the great work; he had gone forth in all his divine energy, &c.; "mighty to save."

2. *The fame of his power had gone forth.* "Even into the coasts," &c. Four very wondrous cases had been published; the son, who was so torn and cast into the fire, &c.; Mary Magdalene, now a disciple; the restored man, out of whom the legion, &c.; a dumb and blind spirit. Many had come, and by his word the evil spirit had been conquered and dispossessed. The other favorable circumstance was,

3. *That the Saviour was near at hand.* Accessible, verse 21. Entered the coasts of Tyre and Sidon. The promise of the Saviour now ratified; his power and ability tested, and to be near at hand. Oh! happy crisis; important period; golden opportunity; accepted time; "day of salvation."

III. THE EFFECTUAL INTERCESSOR. Here was the afflicted daughter, and the Almighty Saviour. How were they brought together? The mother became the intercessor. Who so suitable? so admirably adapted? What love, what eloquence, what perseverance, and what success, &c. Notice,

1. *The reverence of her address.* She admits him to be the true Messiah; her language involved both his divinity and humanity: "O Lord! thou Son of David."

2. *The petition presented.* "Have mercy upon me." She considered her daughter as herself—her affliction as her own. Who has not felt relative troubles to be more distressing than personal ones? What father? what mother? what friend? &c. "Pity a distressed mother; an afflicted,

almost broken-hearted woman." She cried fervently. Mark! her suit is apparently neglected, verse 23. The disciples unite with her; Jesus now apparently excludes her from hope, "I am not sent," &c., verse 24. "He came to his own," &c.

3. *Her prayer is repeated.* She came, and worshipped, and said, "Lord, help me!" One of another nation—one miserable woman. "Lord, help me!" She gave him divine homage. How interesting the scene—how affecting! He then replied, as if to repulse her altogether, "It is not meet to give the children's bread unto the dogs." The Gentiles were so considered by the Jews. He assumes now the distinction of a Jew.

4. *Her plea is reiterated.* "Truth, Lord." "I know, I feel, I admit my inferiority. I am not one of the highly-favored; not a descendant of the illustrious Abraham; not a daughter of Israel. I claim not equality; I contend not for their dignity and privileges; I am willing even to be considered as a dog; let me have the privilege, and it sufficeth." "Yet the dogs," &c. The kind master does not repulse his dog, but allows it to have the crumbs and pieces that would otherwise be wasted. "Have mercy upon me," and spurn not this poor Gentile dog from thy presence. How amazing must all this have been to his disciples! Here is a poor Gentile—a woman: after silence; after an evident refusal; after being reckoned as only a dog, yet she holds fast; she perseveres; she converts an apparent refusal into an argument; and by humility, vehement earnestness, and faith, she retains the attention of the Saviour. But how and wherefore did Christ seem thus to reject her suit? He knew the state of her heart, and he knew his own purpose and intention of granting her what she sought. In this he might design to try her patience; or to excite her desires still more; or to bring forth brighter evidences of her wondrous faith; or that she might be an example to his own disciples, and to all applicants to the end of the world; or to sweeten and add to the preciousness of the boon bestowed. It was not coldness, neglect, or indifference on the part of Christ. Her heart moved not with more earnest desire towards him, than his compassion moved towards her. At length, he allows her to conquer, and to secure her point. Here notice,

IV. THE CURE OBTAINED. " Oh, woman! great is thy faith; be it unto thee," &c. Observe,

1. *He extols the successful pleader.* " Great is thy faith." It does not first appear that this was the reigning, triumphant grace. Might he not have said, Marvellous is thy self-abasement, thy humility, thy fervency, thy firmness and perseverance, thy love to thy child, thy resolve not to depart without the blessing? But in all this faith was the root, the main-spring, the active vital power of her soul. This brought her to Christ; this caused her to honor and worship Christ; to plead—to parry the thrusts—to put up with the silence—to argue the whole matter. " Faith, mighty faith, the promise sees," &c.

2. *He grants all that she sought.* " Be it unto thee as thou wilt." Faith takes hold of Christ's strength; faith restrains the wrath of God. Thus he cried to Moses, " Let me alone." It holds him fast, so that he cannot go till the blessing is given. Faith brings virtue out of Christ, though it touches but the hem of his garment. " All things are possible," &c. Her daughter was healed—the devil was ejected—and she was perfectly restored. Oh, happy child! Oh, wonderful mother! Oh, almighty and gracious Saviour! This subject addresses,

(1.) Parents and heads of families—on the duty they owe to the children under their charge.

(2.) The Christian church—on the solicitude they should evince for the religious instruction and welfare of the rising generation.

(3.) Sabbath school teachers—on the importance of leading those whom they instruct to a knowledge of the Lord Jesus Christ, the only source of spiritual health and salvation.

BETHESDA.

(A CHAPEL-OPENING SKETCH.)

" Now there is at Jerusalem by the sheep market a pool, which is called in the Hebrew tongue Bethesda, having five porches."—JOHN v. 2.

OUR text contains the name of a very interesting place in Jerusalem; a place of very great celebrity and importance to the afflicted inhabitants of that city; a place which would live in the associations and recollections of the multitude who had there found healing and temporal happiness; and a place of much anxiety to the infirm and afflicted. Every particular is given by the evangelist in the brief paragraph of which the text forms a part; read verses 2 to 4. Then there is given the history of an afflicted person, who had long been waiting to enjoy its marvellous influences; see verses 5 to 7. On him Christ had compassion, verse 8; an instantaneous cure was wrought, verse 9. We desire at this time to call your attention to a three-fold view of Bethesda:—

I. AS EXHIBITING A STRIKING REPRESENTATION OF THE LEVITICAL ECONOMY.

II. AS BEING TOTALLY SUPERSEDED BY THE GLORIOUS DISPENSATION OF THE GOSPEL.

III. AS BEING PECULIARLY APPROPRIATE TO THE PRESENT OCCASION.

I. AS EXHIBITING A STRIKING REPRESENTATION OF THE LEVITICAL ECONOMY. Observe, Bethesda was really worthy of the title it possessed. It was, indeed, a house of mercy; the removal of the infirmities of the body. The features of resemblance between Bethesda and the Levitical economy are chiefly these:—

1. *It was local.* The Levitical economy was the religion of Judea; it was associated especially with Palestine, and more immediately still with Jerusalem. Its worship, its priesthood, and its rites were designed for one circumscribed locality. This Bethesda—the house of mercy—was one small pool, limited to one locality in Jerusalem.

2. *It was limited as well as local.* At Bethesda only the first of the multitudes waiting was healed; so the benefits of Judaism were limited to one nation, including a few proselytes of other countries. The wide world was without the range; myriads of mankind strangers to its light and blessings.

3. *Its privileges and blessings were only occasional.* " At certain seasons." Numerous and long intervals between; just so that dispensation. Its ordinances were numerous, but its great rites and chief festivals were very occasional. Its great feasts three times a year; grand jubilee only every fifty years; a minor one, or sabbatical year, every seven; only one day of national expiation; one annual sacrifice.

4. *It was connected with waiting and expectation.* Here numbers were collected, and they had to look forward to, and wait for, the troubling of the waters, &c. Just such was the Levitical economy. It was one of waiting and expectation. Prophecies were given, but they had to wait for their realization; promises made, but their fulfilment was future. They had many offerings, and ceremonial institutions, but their sacrifices could not wash away sin.

> " Not all the blood of beasts
> On Jewish altars slain,
> Could give the guilty conscience peace,
> Or wash away the stain."

Thus the patriarchs and prophets looked and longed for the gospel day, but died in faith, and without the actual sight.

5. *It was not distinguished for pre-eminent benevolence.* Here was a helpless, friendless person; but no one felt sufficient interest to give him a place during the troubling of the waters. We do not say that goodness and mercy had no place in the old economy; assuredly they had, but they were not the chief and prominent glories of that dispensation. It was more an economy of law and justice than of compassion and mercy. Such are the features of resemblance. Notice, then,

II. THE JEWISH BETHESDA, AS BEING TOTALLY SUPERSEDED BY THE GLORIOUS DISPENSATION OF THE GOSPEL. Christ appeared, and dispensed with the pool. The Church of Christ may well and appositely be styled the House of Mercy. It is so in the truest and most exalted sense of the term. It is associated with a *fountain* which has been opened for sin, &c. Now, the healing fountain of divine grace totally eclipses the glory of the ancient Levitical economy, as well as supersedes the Jerusalem Bethesda. Observe, this is,

1. *Universal, not local.* Not confined to Jerusalem, or Palestine, or the Jews. It exists everywhere, where the gospel is preached. It is acceptable to the whole world, and to every creature.

> " Its streams the whole creation reach,
> So plenteous is the store;
> Enough for all, enough for each,
> Enough for evermore."

2. *Its blessings are ever accessible, and not occasional.* Every year a jubilee; every day a sabbath; every moment one of expiation; every instant one of mercy.

3. *Its blessings are present, and not in* prospect. There are, indeed, blessings in prospect; but pardon,—remission of sin,—justification,—holiness,—peace,—adoption, are all now presented. " This is the acceptable time,"&c. " The word is nigh thee," &c.

4. *It is emphatically a dispensation of love and mercy.* Grace and truth, love and embodied goodness, came by Jesus Christ, fully, gloriously, universally; and these it teaches. The disciples of Christ are constrained by this love to love the souls of those around. Such then, brethren, are some of the glories of the gospel dispensation, which entirely supersedes the Mosaical economy, and the Bethesda at Jerusalem. But there is,

III. ANOTHER APPLICATION OF THE TEXT PECULIARLY APPROPRIATE TO THE PRESENT OCCASION. May not every house erected for the preaching of the gospel, and the celebration of the ordinances of Christ, be styled " Bethesda," the House of Mercy? We ask,

1. *For whom, and to whom, is this house erected and consecrated?* To the God of mercy; to him who delighteth in mercy. Here you record his name—celebrate his praise—proclaim his glory—and here he will surely come and bless you. Here his glory shall be seen. Hearken! " The Lord loveth the gates of Zion better than all," &c.

2. *For what great purpose is this house to be devoted?* The proclamation of mercy; the rich, universal mercy of God, as flowing in the streams of the gospel; mercy to the guilty, wretched outcasts of mankind; mercy to all who need it; mercy to all who will receive it.

3. *May we not hopefully anticipate that here effusions of mercy will be enjoyed?* Who can tell how many sinners shall enjoy that promise, " Let the wicked," &c. How many penitents shall here meet the mercy promised to their fathers? How many backsliders shall here feel the application of restoring mercy? When the Lord shall say, " I will heal your backslidings; I will love you freely; for my anger is turned away." How many of the people of God shall come here, that with boldness they may approach the throne of grace?

4. *Shall not the monuments of mercy here celebrate the riches of mercy from time to time?* Oh! how delightful to contemplate brands plucked from the fire; rebels soft-

ened by divine love; prodigals accepted of their father; all meeting, and all uniting. "O Lord! we will praise thee; for, though thou wast angry," &c.

5. *I ask, finally, shall not a spirit of mercy distinguish the friends of Jesus who dwell within these walls?* As the elect of God, will not they possess bowels of mercy? Will they not exhibit the mercifulness of Jesus in their spirit, and conversation, and conduct? Will they not manifest the fruits of mercy in their lives, and thus "show forth the praises of him," &c. How desirable that at the opening services,

1. That divine mercy might be experienced by some soul as a token for good—as a kind of first-fruit. Who will be the person? Who feels his need? Who will seek, and ask, and believe?

2. Let the mercy of the Lord be the song of his redeemed people. "Oh! magnify the Lord," &c.

3. Let your generosity evince that you are deeply sensible of your obligations to the mercy of God, and that you long for his mercy to be enjoyed by others.

THE RESTORED DEMONIAC

"Now the man out of whom the devils were departed besought him that he might be with him: but Jesus sent him away, saying, Return to thine own house, and show how great things God hath done unto thee. And he went his way, and published throughout the whole city how great things Jesus had done unto him."—LUKE viii. 38, 39.

OUR text relates to the man who had been rescued from the legion of devils. His condition was now totally reversed; restored to reason and happiness, we are called to see him at the feet of the Saviour, &c. After this we are referred to two prayers offered up to Jesus; the one by the Gadarenes, a most awful instance of ignorance, selfishness, and infatuation, "that Christ would depart from them," &c. This prayer Christ answered by immediately retiring from their coast; then there is the prayer of the recovered demoniac, a prayer exceedingly proper and interesting, &c. How different to the other, "Now the man out of whom," &c. In the text we have,

I. AN INTERESTING PRAYER, WHICH NOTWITHSTANDING WAS REJECTED. Now look,

1. *At the prayer itself.* "To be with Christ." Was not this the end of Christ's mission, that he might collect souls to himself? Gather them out of the world, &c. Had he not taught, "If any man will be my disciple," &c. It seems evidently a wise and proper prayer; a pious prayer, the sign of a gracious state of soul. Consider,

2. *The probable reasons by which this prayer was dictated.* It might be the result,

(1.) Of holy cautiousness and fear. He had just been dispossessed of a legion of spirits. "A stronger than they," &c. But might they not again overcome him? &c. How natural and proper then to fear; how proper to desire to be near the deliverer, &c.

(2.) It might arise also from grateful love to Jesus; his position how interesting, at Christ's feet; he would cling to that spot; his heart was entwined around that of the Saviour; he knew not how to express his love and gratitude to Jesus.

(3.) It might arise from a desire to know more of Christ; he could not be satisfied with a few minutes, he wished to be his pupil, his personal adherent, his disciple and follower. Notice,

3. *The refusal of this request.* "But Christ sent him away." However wise, and proper, and pious the man's petition appears, Jesus determined and directed otherwise; his suit could not be granted. Now, here let us pause, and learn,

(1.) How necessary to be taught rightly to pray. We know not what we should pray for; Peter prayed on the mountain of transfiguration, that they might build tabernacles, &c. James and John that they might sit, one on the right hand and the other on the left. Paul prayed thrice that the thorn in the flesh, &c. Lord, teach us how to pray! When we have not express direction and promise we must refer all to the will of God.

(2.) We should learn to be satisfied with the Lord's good pleasure, whether he grants our requests or not. "He is too wise to err, too good to be unkind." He loves us too well to neglect our best interests, our real welfare. Observe,

II. AN IMPORTANT COMMAND WHICH WAS PIOUSLY OBEYED. "Jesus sent him," &c.

1. *Let us look at the nature of the command.* To return to his own house and show, &c. He was to be a personal witness for Christ; a monument of Christ's power and Christ's compassion. He could testify,

(1.) To the enthronement of reason. He had been beside himself, irrational; now he was intelligent, cool, reflecting.

(2.) To emancipation from the thraldom of evil spirits; released from the power of the devil.

(3.) To restoration to happiness. No longer cutting himself, a wretched outcast, but clothed and happy, &c. Then, in testifying he would have to refer,

(4.) To the author of his deliverance. "Jesus." The compassion and power of Christ. Now, let the happy saved believer apply the remarks to himself; you can testify in like manner, and to the same things. Observe,

2. *The obedience which was rendered.* "And he went his way," &c.

(1.) It was prompt and immediate. He did not cavil, nor reason, nor refuse.

(2.) It was decided and public. "Wherever he went," &c. "How great things," &c. Not afraid, nor ashamed.

APPLICATION.

1. *The end of our conversion is more than our own salvation.*

(1.) We must testify to and for the benefit of others.

(2.) We must glorify Christ. Show forth his praises, his compassion and power.

2. *The converted should not consult merely their own comfort.* But deny themselves for Christ's sake; not to be indifferent to ourselves, yet to take up our cross, &c.

3. *Christian obedience is unquestioning and exact.* To do as the Lord enjoins; just in the Lord's way. Soul entirely submissive to God.

4. *The heart's desires of the saints shall be granted in a future state.* Be with Jesus forever, &c.

THE RECOVERED LEPER.

"And, behold, there came a leper and worshipped him, saying, Lord, if thou wilt, thou canst make me clean. And Jesus put forth his hand, and touched him, saying, I will, be thou clean. And immediately his leprosy was cleansed. And Jesus saith unto him, See thou tell no man; but go thy way, show thyself to the priest, and offer the gift that Moses commanded, for a testimony unto them."—Matthew viii. 2–4.

One of the results of sin is the fearful catalogue of bodily diseases which it has introduced. Man was formed free from affliction, sorrow, and pain; neither was he liable to death; but sin has filled the world with sickness and misery. Hence,

"Fierce diseases wait around,
To hurry mortals home."

Every part of the body is alike vulnerable, alike in danger, alike susceptible of affliction and agony; some are tedious in their progress, and men groan beneath them for years; others are rapid in their course, and speedily cast their victims into the gloomy grave; some are curable, while others defy the physician's art, and medicine's power. During Christ's mission on earth he employed his benevolent power in healing the diseases both of body and mind. Our text refers to one delightful instance, to which we invite your attention on the present occasion. Consider,

I. THE INDIVIDUAL REFERRED TO. "A leper." Perhaps no condition was more truly awful and distressing; leprosy was common in Palestine, and is so still in various parts of the east; at present we shall consider it as exhibiting a striking representation of sin, the leprosy of the soul. Now leprosy,

1. *Was generally hereditary.* Thus from Adam and Eve, sin has spread into every country, and down through every generation. Men are not only born under the effects of the guilt of sin, but under its depraving and defiling power.

2. *It was small in its first appearance.* A small spot on the countenance of an inflamed red character was the first sign; those unacquainted with it might suspect no danger. Now sin is little in its beginning; look at children in their tempers, &c.; look at individuals who at one period were amiable, and have become thoroughly vile.

3. *It was deep-seated and inveterate in its nature.* The heart and blood are under its influence: so with sin, the heart is the seat, the soul is the spring and root of all the evil.

4. *It was universal in its prevalence.* All the man affected. From the head through all the extremities. No part of a leper clean; so with sin and the sinner, "the whole head," &c. All the faculties of the soul; all the senses of the body, &c.

5. *It was very loathsome in its appearance.* The eyes and countenance assumed a horrid and disgusting appearance, painful, and it rendered the person a burden to

himself, and life itself a curse : such also is sin ; it renders man abominable to God and holy angels, and fills him with anguish and misery.

6. *It excluded from society, and rendered them objects of terror to all around.* However united by the ties of kindredness, their breath was dreaded, it was the breath of disease, to touch them was to receive their malady ; not allowed to mix with the healthy, or to go into the congregation of the Lord. Travellers feared to meet them, &c. : so sin infests and excludes from the family and presence of God.

7. *It was incurable by human power, and generally produced a most awful death.* It raged until the whole person became one mass of foulness and pollution ; then the vital organs being powerfully attacked, death terminated the career of suffering : such also is the leprosy of the soul ; no man can recover himself from it ; no created power can restore ; it never cures itself. "Sin when it is finished bringeth forth death." Such was the condition of the man who applied to Christ. Notice,

II. HIS ADDRESS TO THE REDEEMER. "Lord, if thou wilt," &c.

1. *It was an address of humble respect.* "Lord." He acknowledged him as a dignified person ; received him as the Messiah, worshipped, &c.

2. *It was associated with faith.* "Thou canst." Not ordinary faith. He would not have said so to any other person on earth. Christ had the power, and this was the power of God.

3. *It contained an affecting reference to his own misery and Christ's goodness.* "If thou wilt thou canst make me clean." Nothing so important to him as this ; this was his heart's desire ; he appealed to Christ's disposition. "If thou wilt," &c.

III. THE CONDUCT OF THE SAVIOUR.

1. *Christ responded to his appeal.* And said, "I will." "His love is as great as his power," &c. Christ's willingness is established on the most immoveable truths and facts.

2. *His word was omnipotent, and conveyed the healing power.* He might have willed it, and effected it silently, but he spake, &c. ; so he did in creation, so in all his miracles. At the grave of Lazarus—to the devils who possessed the demoniac—to the raging sea, &c.

3. *He put forth his hand to testify to his*

cleanness. A touch would infect, and in any case ceremonially defile ; but Jesus now touched him to show that the foul disease was gone. What a cure ! How complete ! How instantaneous ! How free ! How precious !

4. *He sent him to the priest that his recovery might be duly attested.* The priest was appointed of God to testify when a person was cleansed and fit for society. Now this case might have been disputed, &c. He was to go at once for fear the priest might hear, and through prejudice refuse to attest, &c.

5. *He was to present a gift unto the Lord.* See Levit. xiv. 10, and if poor, verse 21. Now Christ enforced this to show that he came to fulfil all the law, &c. ; and to elicit a grateful spirit from the leper. Now let me turn to the leprous sinner.

1. *See how you are to obtain healing and purity.* From Christ ; by personal, humble, and believing application to him.

2. *See the way in which Christ will receive you.* He will freely and graciously deliver ; he desires to do this, &c. He can do it now, &c.

3. *See what Christ expects from those he has healed.* Dedication of yourselves and all you have to the Lord.

APPLICATION.

1. Bless God for health of body.

2. Especially be anxious for health of soul.

3. Praise God for the Almighty Saviour and the means of spiritual health and felicity.

4. We now invite all to be healed.

FAITH THE ANTIDOTE TO FEAR.

"Be not afraid, only believe."—MARK v. 36.

OUR text is connected with one of the Saviour's most resplendent miracles. The ruler's daughter was sick ; her father, full of anguish, applies to Jesus. His application was reverential, " for he fell at Christ's feet," &c., verse 22 ; his application was most importunate, "And besought him greatly," verse 23 ; his application evinced great parental tenderness, "My little daughter lieth at the point of death ;" his application was connected with strong faith, "Come and lay thy hands, &c., and she shall live," verse 23. Before Jesus arrived, word came from the ruler's house saying his daughter was dead, verse 35. It was then that Christ addressed to him the words of our text; the sequel is well known. He exerted his mighty power, and brought her back into the land of the living. A more difficult case could not be well conceived of; yet living faith and the power of Christ were adequate to it—and to every possible exigency they are equally adapted. Let us look at some cases wherein the text may be appropriately applied. Observe its applicability to the anxious inquirer; to the conflicting believer; to tried Christians; to the spiritual laborer; to the dying saint. We apply the text,

I. To THE ANXIOUS INQUIRER. To the individual convinced of sin—alarmed with apprehensions of wrath—trembling for fear of the devouring wrath of Deity. It may be that the sins of the convicted penitent have been enormous; aggravated; of long continuance; red as scarlet; or deeply stained as crimson. Such may see how ordinary transgressors may be saved; but they view their own state as extreme, desperate, and perhaps hopeless. Now, what shall I say to such a one? what instance present? what direction afford? Shall we refer to some preparatory work? shall we keep them back for a time from the grand remedy? shall we urge a series of external reformations? Oh! no; the deeper the guilt and misery, and the more necessitous the case, the more eager we should be to bring it at once to the great remedy. The fears of such may be most terrific; but we exclaim with all possible earnestness, "Be not afraid, only believe." Believe the incomprehensible vastness of the divine love and mercy, "As the heavens are higher," &c. Believe the readiness of God to save the greatest of transgressors, "As I live," &c. "Come, and let us reason," &c. Believe the infinite efficacy of the sacrifice of Christ, "The blood of Jesus Christ," &c. "This is a faithful saying," &c. Believe that your salvation is to be a matter of entire grace, the free gift of God, "Not by works of righteousness," &c. "By grace are ye saved," &c. Believe that God is waiting, &c., solicitous to save you, "For whosoever will come," &c. "Him that cometh," &c. " O that thou, even thou, hadst known,"

&c. Believe, and all the gracious promises of God become your own; believe, and all the virtue of Christ's merit and power will be exerted for your benefit:

" Believe, and all your sin's forgiven;
Only believe, and yours is heaven."

We apply the text,

II. To THE CONFLICTING BELIEVER. The life of the believer is a state of conflict; it is a course of moral wrestling, "We wrestle not," &c.; it is a course of contention, "Contend earnestly," &c.; a warfare, "War a good warfare," &c. Now, in this conflicting state, our enemies are very numerous, malevolent, and persevering in their assaults. We read of the "fiery darts of the devil." To be harassed with these foes incessantly, may damp the ardor and chill the enjoyments of the believer. He may be discouraged on account of the way, &c. Now, what is our advice to the conflicting believer? Philosophize—reason— be resolute—rely on the goodness of your cause? &c. No; it is, "only believe." Faith is your shield; by it you will quench all the fiery darts, &c. Faith will enable you to wield the sword of the Spirit, &c.; faith kept in lively exercise, and devils will fear and tremble; a believing application of God's word, and we successfully overcome the army of the aliens. We apply the text,

III. To THE TRIED CHRISTIAN. This is a state of probationary trial; sorrows and troubles form a great portion of our inventory; in the world, we shall, we must have tribulation. Now, what shall we do in these trials? Murmur, repine, become dispirited; or sink into inactivity and gloom? Oh! no; our text is the antidote, "Only believe." Hear David—"I had fainted unless I had believed," &c. Hearken to Jesus—"Let not your hearts be troubled," &c. Paul—"I know whom," &c. Believe these troubles are under divine direction or control; believe they are not tokens of wrath, but of love; believe that they are really light and transitory; believe they will conform to Christ, and enhance future blessedness; only believe, and then you may truly sing, "In darkest shades, if he appear," &c. We apply the text,

IV. To THE SPIRITUAL LABORER. You are anxious to please and serve God, by the practical dedication of your power and talents to his glory. In the school, training up the young, you are discouraged; but believe what God has spoken, and obey his word. "In the morning sow thy seed." In laboring to save your neighbors, &c., but so thoughtless, &c. Believe that your labor cannot be in vain; how many have succeeded. Let faith nerve you afresh. Believe in the wisdom and goodness of these efforts, "He that winneth souls," &c. "He that converteth a sinner," &c. In training up your families: perhaps some of your children "sons of Belial;" all dark and gloomy; no signs of grace. Let faith lead you to enforce scriptural tuition and discipline, and rest on that word, "Train up a child," &c. In working in the church you do not see any good arise; nor your ability to increase it; feel as cumberers of the ground, &c. Have you fervently prayed? have you pleaded with God? are you deeply anxious for the revival of religion? You cannot tell but God's blessing may have rested on the minister—on his word, &c., through your faith. Be not dispirited, use the means, and "only believe." We apply the text,

V. To THE DYING SAINT. That solemn crisis of death must be personally known by every one. To a dying saint, we would not say, "Remember your past excellent life, your long profession of religion, your rich and mellowed experience." Oh! no; we say even now, as at first, your salvation is of faith. To die safely, happily, triumphantly, you must die in faith. "Only believe." Believe in the fidelity of your God; believe in the presence of your Saviour; believe that sin is atoned for; that death is subdued; that the grave has been hallowed; that the gates of paradise have been flung wide open; that Christ has prepared mansions of blessedness for you; waits to receive you to himself, &c. Believe, and pass confidently through the valley, &c.; believe, and plunge into the swellings of Jordan; believe, and grapple with your last enemy. Hark! the conflict is over; the saint is victorious. He exclaims, "O death! where is thy sting?" &c.

OBSERVATIONS.

1. *See the reason why we are counselled only to believe.*

(1.) Faith is the first great exercise of the soul; that which unites us to God; that which builds on the good foundation.

(2.) Faith is ever accompanied by the other graces of the Spirit. It works by love; it inspires hope; it produces Christian diligence. "The work of faith."

(3.) Faith makes all that is in God ours—the Father, Son, and Spirit. It appropriates the whole Deity; it interests us in the entire Godhead; and honors all his persons and attributes.

2. *Observe the general and perpetual appropriation of the text.* To all states and circumstances in life. It is never out of place; never unseasonable; ever proper, right, necessary, and efficacious.

3. *Ascertain if this faith is exemplified in your experience.*

THE CENTURION AND HIS SERVANT

"And when Jesus was entered into Capernaum, there came unto him a centurion, beseeching him," &c.—MATTHEW viii. 5–10.

HERE we are presented with an account of one of Christ's illustrious and gracious miracles; one of those signs of goodness and power, which compelled Nicodemus to exclaim, "Rabbi, we know," &c. One astounding miracle he had just wrought, in cleansing the poor miserable leper, and then he entered into Capernaum, when he was addressed by a centurion, who came, and beseeching him, said, "Lord, my servant," &c. Notice,

I. THE APPLICANT. He was a centurion; that is, an officer having the command of one hundred soldiers. In many respects, we may be justly astonished that such an individual should be found drawing near to the Saviour. Let us glance at some of these particulars.

1. *He was a Gentile, and not of the house of Israel.* In this respect, he had not possessed the national privileges of the Jews; he had originally been involved in the darkness of paganism; his first impressions had been unfavorable to religion. Our education, the national and family privileges are of the greatest worth, and deserve our gratitude; we are also responsible for them.

2. *His profession was unfavorable to piety.* He was a military man. Few positions in life are more unfriendly to godliness. It is eminently a worldly profession; it is based on ambition and worldly glory; it is opposed to humanity and goodness;

there is little time for reflection. Now, it appears that this centurion had become attached to the Jewish religion, and most likely was a proselyte to their faith; for it is said, Luke vii. 5, "that he loved their nation, and had built for them a synagogue." Such was the applicant. Notice,

II. THE SUIT HE PRESENTED. Several things in this deserve our attention.

1. *The object of his suit.* "His servant." Many had applied to Christ on their own account; some on behalf of their relatives; as the ruler's daughter; father for his son; Peter's wife's mother, &c.; but here is a master seeking the restoration of his servant. Piety renders every station in life a blessing. It makes good parents, good children, good masters, good servants. It is highly probable that his servant had been a faithful, devoted one; thus he had secured the esteem and affection of his master. We read of several distinguished servants in the word of God. There was the excellent servant of Abraham, and the servants of Naaman, &c. What an example to masters and mistresses; what a contrast to the condition of many! How benevolent, and tender, and solicitous!

2. *The way in which he presented it.*

(1.) There was personal exertion. He came to Jesus; he employed his time and personal influence.

(2.) He was earnest in his application. "Beseeching him." Not cold and formal, but with anxious earnestness and ardor.

(3.) He displayed great reverence and humility, "Lord," &c. He assumed nothing on account of his station. When Christ complied, he answered, "I am not worthy," &c. What self-abasement! What exalted views of Christ! What a pattern!

(4.) He manifested extraordinary faith. He said, "Thy journey is not necessary," "but speak the word," &c. Thy mandate is enough; thou art Lord of all; a word will answer the mighty end, &c. He illustrated it himself by referring to his authority, verse 9. Notice,

III. THE SUCCESS HE EXPERIENCED.

1. *He was honored by the Saviour.* "When Jesus heard it, he marvelled," &c. What a contrast to the conduct of the scribes and Pharisees; to the Jews in general. Even to his own disciples, Christ pronounced this honorable distinction, "I say unto you," &c. Here confession was praised, humility exalted, and faith applauded, by the Son of God.

2. *His servant was healed;* Luke vii. 10. Here we see the result of pious, benevolent influence. The master a blessing to the servant, &c.; one the channel of good to the other, "I will bless thee and make thee a blessing."

APPLICATION.

1. *Admire this example of human excellency.* Christ did so, and honored it. Let us do so, and imitate it.

2. *See the grace and power of the Saviour.* How all-sufficient and infinitely merciful. His word is enough.

3. *Let all believers exert their influence for the good of others.* You have influence as well as the centurion. Prayer—faith—access to Christ; exert it. Have you not relatives? servants? neighbors? It is your duty, and your real advantage to do so. Do it in the closet; do it in the family; do it in the congregation of the saints. Let us all admire and feel as the centurion did, and go and do likewise.

THE PRODIGAL SON.

SKETCH I.

"And he said, A certain man had two sons; and the younger of them said to his father, Father, give me the portion of goods that falleth to me. And he divided unto them his living," &c. —LUKE xv. 11, &c.

THIS is one of the Saviour's beautiful and interesting parables. It is impossible to read it without being struck with the true picture it draws, the graphic imagery with which it abounds, and the nervous, yet simple language in which it is written. The occasion of the parable is found in the first and second verses of the chapter. Two minor parables precede and appropriately introduce it—the lost sheep, and the piece of money. It is not the design of the Spirit that the filling up of the parable should, of necessity, be spiritualized, and made to support the great end the parable was to answer. Three great lessons are evidently taught;—the depravity of the sinner and its results; the hardening and lamentable consequences of a sinful life; and the nature of true repentance, with its happy effects. At present we shall dwell on the first of these, and by a series of propositions grounded on the text endeavor to present the subject clearly to your minds.

I. ONE OF THE EVIDENCES OF A DEPRAVED AND SINFUL STATE, IS TO THROW OFF THE DIVINE AUTHORITY AND RESTRAINT. Sin thus commenced in our world. Our first parents desired to be as gods, and broke through the restrictions in reference to the tree of the knowledge of good and evil. Thus the prodigal is described as impatient —restless and anxious to escape his father's cognizance—to leave the paternal roof; to think, and choose, and act as he pleased. Thus to feel and act is the essence of sin. A loyal subject does not desire to conduct himself without respect to the constitution and laws of the land. A good child does not despise parental authority. A faithful servant desires not to act according to his own pleasure. Holy spirits do the will of God, and they are perfectly happy to be regulated by Deity. But sin rejects God's authority, bursts through his restraints, and sets up the rebel desires of the soul against God and his word.

II. GOD GIVES A PORTION OF HIS BOUNTIES EVEN TO THE WICKED AND UNGODLY. " Give me the portion," &c. Every created thing has its portion from God. Men, as the creatures of God, enjoy many blessings from the Most High. There is life with all its privileges; health, and physical comfort; reason and mental endowments; natural gifts, and talents; to some riches and influence; many privileges and opportunities of improvement, &c. A portion full of goodness and mercy.

III. A STATE OF SIN IS ONE OF DEPARTURE FROM GOD. He took his journey. Sin is forsaking God, departing from his ways. Sin creates moral distance between the soul and Jehovah. It does so as it respects his *favor*. He cannot approve, &c. His face is against the wicked. Angry, &c. His *image*,—it effaces it, &c. Every faculty suffers, — understanding, — judgment, — conscience,—affections,—desires, &c. His *family*. It excludes—drives out—separates from his holy dwelling. Sin is travelling from, not towards heaven. Wandering towards the blackness, &c., of hell. It is the way of death. By a course of sin, this state of distance is constantly increasing, widening, &c. The Christian is daily journeying nearer and nearer towards heaven : the sinner, &c., towards the abodes of eternal despair.

IV. THE PRACTICE OF SIN IS ONE OF PERVERSION AND WASTE OF THE BLESSINGS OF HEAVEN. "Wasted," &c. Sin seeketh the sacrifice of all. Health and strength, &c. The sinner wastes—wealth, and influence. The one sin of drunkenness costs this country fifty million pounds sterling of our national means. Faculties—talents, &c.—life itself, and the solemn capabilities of the soul. Sin often destroys all ; ruins the whole.

V. SIN IS PECULIARLY DEBASING TO ITS VICTIMS. The son now a slave. The rich son now poor. The son of a noble family now a swineherd. How it degrades ! how it sinks its possessors! It casts the crown of excellency from the head. It takes the robe of beauty, &c. It often affects the countenance—the face divine, and stamps the features with infamy and degradation. How many has it shut up in prison—the penal settlements. The great majority of criminals are the dissipated; abandoned, young.

VI. SIN IS OFTEN PRODUCTIVE OF UTTER WRETCHEDNESS TO BOTH BODY AND MIND. Hear the prodigal—his exclamation, " I perish with hunger." He fain would have filled himself with the husks, " the fruit of the carib tree," in shape resembling the large scarlet bean. His remuneration was not sufficient to satisfy his hunger, &c. And the swine were better fed than he. How truly is this often experienced in the circumstances that sin produces ! The evils of its effects are truly legion, for they are many—temporal—domestic—mental—and those of the conscience and spirit.

VII. SINNERS IN THEIR MISERY ARE SELDOM BEFRIENDED BY THOSE AROUND THEM. No man gave the prodigal "husks." Where are his companions who assisted him to spend his portion ? See the gambler, the pleasure-taker, the drunkard. How they all become friendless in their adversity, sickness, &c. Self seeks its own, and fawns and flatters in prosperity, but frowns and forsakes in adversity.

APPLICATION.

1. Many can read their own experience in the text.

2. Let the young ponder it well.

3. It may instruct and admonish all.

The condition described is wretched, indeed, but not hopeless. Light will break forth on our next subject.

THE PRODIGAL SON.

SKETCH II.

" And he said, A certain man had two sons: and the younger of them said to his father, Father, give me," &c.—LUKE xv. 11, &c.

IN our last discourse we contemplated the prodigal throwing off the paternal authority and restraint, claiming his share of the family portion, leaving his home and departing into a far country, spending all he had in profligacy and riotous living, reduced to a situation the most degrading and wretched, forsaken by all, and ready to die of want. Our present subject leads us to consider,

I. THAT A SINFUL CONDITION IS ONE OF INFATUATION AND MADNESS. " When he came to himself." That is, when he paused, considered, reflected, acted as a rational creature. One chief cause of continued sin, is inconsideration. Men will not know—do not consider. Passion reigns and rules. Would a man exchange home for exile—plenty for famine—a robe for rags—dignity for servile degradation—comfort for wretchedness? Yet all sinners act thus. They give gold for tinsel—bread for husks—gratifying the body at the expense of the soul. The moment of pleasure is preferred to the realities of eternity. Madness is want of judgment; and is not sin? Madness is rashness; and is not sin? Madness is acting without regard to reason, and not consulting the proper end of existence, &c. Look at the superiority of the mere animal creatures as answering the end of their existence, Isa. i. 3; Jer. viii. 6, 7.

II. THAT AFFLICTION IS SOMETIMES THE MEANS OF PRODUCING SERIOUSNESS AND REFLECTION. Just perishing! The exclamation showed his state. " I perish with hunger." We say affliction *sometimes* is the means of conversion, not always. Many leave the furnace harder and more reprobate. Many curse God and die. But there are instances of the reverse—similar to that of the prodigal. There was the wicked, blood-thirsty Manasseh, 2 Chron. xxxiii. 12. The proud, imperious Nebuchadnezzar, Dan. iv. 33, 34. Happy is it when adversity and affliction lead to consideration and repentance. No doubt there are some instances of this kind here. Some have lost a child—a parent—a friend—have been brought to the verge of the tomb, &c., and thus led to humiliation, and penitency, and prayer.

III. GENUINE REPENTANCE IS RETRACING OUR STEPS TO THE GOD WHOM WE HAVE FORSAKEN. Repentance signifies change of mind. " I think differently, I feel differently, I will act differently. I thought it best to be without restraint; not so now. I thought it best to leave my home, &c., to be the companion of profligates, to give myself to rioting. My mind is entirely altered —changed. My course shall now be the reverse. I will go back—cease to do evil, learn to do well." This is repentance, and nothing else. It always changes the conduct—changes the life. " Let the wicked man forsake his wickedness," &c. It will ever be accompanied with shame. " What fruit had ye," &c. Sorrow, keen regret, a sense of self-condemnation. The repenting sinner needs none to condemn him. He writes by far the most bitter things against himself. Overwhelmed with a sense of his ingratitude, he feels sin has injured himself—society—and offended his God. He beholds what he has forfeited, verse 17.

IV. THAT DETERMINATE RESOLUTION IS NECESSARY TO GENUINE REPENTANCE. He considers, reflects, perceives the only alternative, and then he resolves; " I will arise and go," &c. Many desire, many purpose, but yet do not *resolve*. There must be decision, determination;—this is indispensable. But it is not every resolution that is effectual.

1. *It must arise as much from a sense of the evil of sin as a fear of its punishment.* The one feeling is entirely selfish and carnal. I dread the death, but do not hate the crime, &c. But the prodigal felt that he had " sinned," that he was unworthy, &c.

2. *It must be made with a full conviction of our own weakness, and relying on God's aid.* Many have resolved presumptuously, self-righteously, and have failed. These must fail. To know our helplessness is essential;—that we can do nothing, and then God will be trusted, relied on: we must rest all *here*, " Thy grace is sufficient," &c. The Lord's help, &c.

3. *Hence it must be accompanied by earnest prayer.* God's aid must be implored, and that fervently; with all the intensity of a person in deep distress.

" Beware of Peter's word,
Nor confidently say,
I never will deny thee, Lord,
But grant I never may."

4. *The best resolutions must be promptly acted upon.* Carried out; and immediately. If we delay, the impression will vanish; if we delay, the ardor will subside, the enemy gain strength. It must be brought to the present tense; now, this day, this season, this evening, this moment.

> "I must this instant now begin
> Out of my sin t'awake;
> And turn to God, and every sin
> Continually forsake."

Thus acted the prodigal, and thus must we act, to enjoy God's favor, and obtain salvation. Now, by how many reasons may this be enforced on all unconverted sinners present! We shall confine ourselves to the following.

(1.) Have we not sufficiently felt the misery of our present state to desire deliverance? Is not a sinful state wretched, degrading, perilous? We cannot doubt the necessity of immediate extrication.

(2.) Is there not ample provision, even for prodigals, in their Father's house, if they repent? The least and the lowliest in Christ's family is infinitely better off than we are. "Better be a door-keeper," &c. "Hired servants," &c. Better be a dog to have the falling crumbs, &c.

(3.) There is but one way of access to that home. By repentance; by going and casting ourselves on his mercy; by venturing on his goodness and compassion.

(4.) No time so suitable or so sure as the present. Who then will arise? who will take the first step to-night? Is there not some young person? some head of a family or aged person? We entreat you to weigh, ponder, and now resolve. The prodigal is now on his way back. His reception and restoration we must postpone until our next discourse.

THE PRODIGAL SON.

SKETCH III.

"A certain man had two sons: and the younger of them said to his father, Father, give me," &c. —LUKE xv. 11, &c.

WE have previously contemplated the prodigal leaving his father's house; spending his portion in riotous living; reduced to want, degradation, and misery. We have also witnessed the happy change which took place in his mind; the impor-

tant pause; the noble resolve; the feelings of repentance and genuine sorrow which he experienced; and the prompt manner in which he began to retrace his steps. At this part of the parable, we must recommence our observations, "And he arose," &c.

I. OBSERVE THE ASPECT OF THE REPENTING SINNER. He is now moving towards his father's house. How different his appearance,

1. *To what it was when he abandoned his home.* Then, invested with the riches of his portion; clothed in the costume belonging to his rank; a retinue of servants; a host of professed friends. Now poor—in rags—alone—ready to perish. Yet how different,

2. *To that part of his history, when he was wasting his substance.* Look at his recklessness, profligacy; look at his company; hear the mad mirth; witness the scenes of dissipation. But, alas! it was the way of ruin—the carnival of death; the victim was fitting for the slaughter. But now he is alone—thoughtful—reflecting—serious—journeying homeward; and, notwithstanding his wretched condition, he is in the way of life and salvation. We observe, that such a difference will always be seen where genuine repentance is experienced. No conversion without such an entire change. We remark,

II. GOD SEES REPENTING SINNERS IN THE FIRST MOVEMENTS OF THEIR HEARTS AND LIVES TOWARDS HIM; verse 20. "When he was a great way off," &c. Yes; as if he had been looking out for his return. He beheld him at a great distance, and knew him. The first gracious motions of the heart are known by the Lord. That serious thought; that keen pang of regret; that contrite groan; that resolution of amendment; that sigh for happiness. He is in a merciful position, seeking the return of the sinful, wandering soul.

III. GOD HASTENS TO MEET THE CONTRITE PENITENT. He saw, had compassion, and "ran," &c. Observe these three points:—

1. *He beheld our misery*—our return from the way of rebellion, and did not feel the spirit of stern, inflexible righteousness, but the movings of love and pity.

2. *His compassion prevailed.* "Had compassion." Nothing else would serve the sinner, for he had no claim—no merit—nothing to deserve—every thing to con-

demn; but God felt the movings of compassion.

3. *Compassion brought him speedily towards his returning child.* The prodigal moves slowly; his sins are heavy; his grief oppressive; his fears numerous; but the father " runs"—hastens to meet him.

IV. GOD DISPLAYS THE UTMOST MERCY, AND THE SOFTEST TENDERNESS TOWARDS HIS PENITENT CHILDREN. " He fell on his neck, and kissed him," &c. How beautiful this scene ! The father who had been disobeyed—offended; yet he exhibits the greatest love, the most intense affection. He passes by the sin—there is no upbraiding; he passes by the pollution of the sinner, and even embraces him; he prevents his self-reproaches—his confessions, &c.; gives him the most tender token of his forgiving love; " kisses him ;" is at once reconciled, &c. How surprising ! Yet thus does God receive sinners, yea, the vilest of them; yea, thus he will receive you—every one of you, "Come, and let us reason," &c. He receives them graciously; forgives them freely.

V. THE RICHNESS OF THE DIVINE MERCY WILL NOT PREVENT THE HUMBLED CONFESSIONS OF THE TRUE PENITENT. This conduct of the father does not cause the son to think less of his sins—his wanderings. Oh ! no, but more. This makes him feel his guilt the more deeply. He must unbosom his soul by confession. His own heart requires this; his peace; especially his father's compassion. Oh ! how the tears flowed; how difficult was utterance ! his soul melted within him, and he said, "Father, I have sinned," &c., verse 21. Every word would bear emphasis.

VI. THE STATE OF THE SINNER IS COMPLETELY TRANSFORMED IN THE DAY OF CONVERSION. What is the reply of the father ? He turns from the son, and addresses the servants. The misery and wretchedness of the son must be relieved.

1. " *Bring hither the best robe.*" The rags are cast aside forever. The best— the choicest—the most expensive—the most ornamental—the most dignified is brought. What is this but the garment of salvation ; the robe of righteousness; that in which God clothes the contrite sinner; the garment of praise instead of the sackcloth of mourning.

2. *The ring is put on his finger.* The token of the father's reconciliation ; the

sign of the son's elevation to his former rank ; that which ratifies the gracious reception. This is the Holy Spirit. " Because ye are sons," &c. " The Spirit itself beareth witness," &c. " Ye have not received the spirit of fear, but adoption," &c.

3. *Shoes on his feet.* The shoes of the preparation of the gospel of peace, so that he shall now walk in the ways of peace and holiness, having the spirit of a holy, affectionate child. " He shall run in the way of his commandments to do them."

4. *The feast is provided.* " The fatted calf" is killed, and made ready, &c. He was dying of hunger—now abundance is prepared for him. Not only hunger alleviated, but a sumptuous repast, worthy of the father's riches, and of his still richer love. This is that supper revealed and tendered in the gospel ; the provision of mercy—the feast of fat things—the banquet of love, wherein all things are ready. Christ's flesh is the food of the believer. He is the Lamb slain for the life of his people. We live by faith in the Son of God.

VII. JOY AND FESTIVITY CELEBRATE THE SINNER'S RETURN AND ACCEPTANCE OF GOD. " They began to be merry." Others entered into the father's joy, and rejoiced with him ; sadness and sorrow were put away ; music, and songs, and gladness were heard. What overflowing, rich, unspeakable mercy ! Yet this is all true on the sinner's conversion to God. " I say unto you, there is joy in the presence of the angels of God," &c. What an association of joy ! The father—the servants—the son—God—angels—glorified spirits—the saints on earth —the accepted sinner. " I will praise thee," &c.

VIII. NONE BUT THE ENVIOUS AND WICKED WILL MURMUR WHEN THE VILEST ARE RECEIVED INTO THE DIVINE FAMILY. As the elder brother, &c. ; the Pharisees of old. " This man receiveth sinners," &c. Surely he came for this purpose. But is not the joy reasonable and proper, yea, indispensable ? Is it not meet ? &c.

APPLICATION.

1. *What a subject for grateful retrospection to the Christian !* How all this is familiar and delightful !

2. *What encouragement for the penitent !*

3. *What hope for all !*

CHRIST EXALTED BY THE MULTI-TUDE.

" And when he was come nigh, even now at the descent of the Mount of Olives, the whole multitude of the disciples began to rejoice and praise God with a loud voice, for all the mighty works that they had seen ; saying, Blessed be the King that cometh in the name of the Lord ; peace in heaven and glory in the highest. And some of the Pharisees from among the multitude said unto him, Master, rebuke thy disciples. And he answered and said unto them, I tell you that, if these should hold their peace, the stones would immediately cry out."—LUKE xix. 37–40.

THE passage we have selected for our present meditation is one of those striking fulfilments of prophecy in which the New Testament so amply abounds. Read the 9th verse of the 9th chapter of Zechariah. A similar prediction had been uttered by Isaiah, lxii. 11. One of these prophecies had been uttered nearly 700, and the other nearly 600 years before ; here they are literally accomplished. Every sentence is adapted to elevate the true Christian, and excite in his soul more ardent praise to the blessed Saviour. Observe from the text,

I. THAT JESUS THE SAVIOUR IS WORTHY OF THE LOFTIEST PRAISE.

II. THAT THE GODLY OF ALL AGES HAVE SUNG HIS PRAISES.

III. THAT MANY WOULD SUPPRESS THE PRAISES OF CHRIST.

IV. THAT GOD WILL EVER SECURE THE LAUDATORY EXALTATION OF HIS SON.

I. THAT JESUS THE SAVIOUR IS WORTHY OF THE LOFTIEST PRAISE. Praise is awarded to men on earth on many and varied accounts : lofty genius ; literary attainments ; distinguished heroism ; expansive benevolence ; mighty achievements. The divine Saviour should be praised,

1. For his personal excellencies. " He is fairer," &c. The desire of all nations. In Christ dwells infinite knowledge—spotless purity—unrivalled dignity—unlimited goodness—and every feature of humanity, tenderness, and grace ; a body without sinful weakness ; a mind without error or obscuration ; a soul reflecting all the moral glories of the Father.

2. For his unsearchable grace. The favor of his heart, which he manifested to a lost world ; favor that surmounted every obstacle in the way of our recovery ; favor that paid the severest price for our ransom. " Ye know the grace of our Lord Jesus Christ." " Greater love," &c. No wonder this is part of heaven's anthem, " Worthy is the Lamb that was slain."

3. For his wonderful achievements. To note all these, we must give you the history of redemption. What has he achieved ? The emancipation of the world from Satanic ignorance and vassalage ; the bestowment of divine love through the channel of his own sufferings ; the opening of the kingdom of heaven to all believers ; the sure and certain exaltation both of the bodies and souls of his people to his eternal kingdom and glory, " Father, I will that those whom thou hast given," &c. Observe,

II. THE GODLY IN ALL AGES HAVE SUNG HIS PRAISES. Abraham, the representative of the patriarchal age, looked forward to his day, and saw it, and was glad ; his heart praised the promised seed. Jacob, in his dying predictions, sang of the Shiloh, and ended his life exulting, " I have waited for thy salvation," &c. Moses chose as the subject of his eulogy, the prophet like unto himself, unto whom the people should hearken. David referred, in exalted strains, both to his character and work—his sufferings and triumph—his kingdom and glory ; he died exulting, " Blessed be the Lord God of Israel," &c. Think of the songs of all the prophets ; how they exult in Zion's delivery, and Judah's glorious king. At his birth, angels, and shepherds, and sages, all exulted in his advent. Wherever he went the mourners were made happy, the sick healed, and the lame danced for joy. On the occasion to which the text refers, the praise was public and loud, and expressive of the highest joy and exultation. The early Christians in all their assemblies sang a hymn of praise to Christ ; so now, whenever Christian assemblies meet, one great design is to bless and laud the Saviour's name. It is delightful to contemplate, that the sun never sets on those who sing the hosannas of Christ— east and west, north and south. In the torrid and frigid zones ; on eastern sultry sands, and mid polar snows, the glories of Christ are celebrated in strains of highest praise. He is praised in the happy musings of the Christian's retirement ; he is praised at the family altar ; he is praised by the rising generation of the sabbath school ; in the social prayer-meeting, and in the great congregations of his people. We notice,

III. That many would suppress the praises of Christ. In the text the Pharisees labored to do so.

1. *The skeptical and unbelieving would confine our praises to the works of nature.* They refer us to the landscape, the ocean, the firmament, &c. Or they would have us extol reason, and science, and philosophy, &c. ; but would not give one line to Jesus.

2. *The profligate would have us sing of wine, and feasting, and sensuality.*

3. *The sanguinary would have us sing of war, and victories, and warriors, and conquests.*

4. *The self-righteous would have all praise to elevate their own goodness and superiority.*

5. *The formal and supine think it unnecessary or superfluous.* Now, all and each of these subjects are opposed to the praise of Christ, as much so as the odes which exalt Mohammed, or the songs sung to the honor of the idols of the heathen. The heart cannot give its highest emotions to these and to Christ. It must be Christ and not these, or these and not Christ. We observe,

IV. That God will ever secure the laudatory exaltation of the Saviour. He secured this at the birth of Christ, by giving the mandate, " Let all the angels of God," &c. Also at his ascension, " He went up with a shout," &c. He secures this in all saints by his Holy Spirit that dwells in them. It is a spirit full of love to him, and of praise and hosanna to Christ ; it is his declared will, that Christ is to have equal honor and glory with himself. This is one of the characteristics of the Christian, he rejoices in Christ Jesus. He will secure this in heaven by the universal acclamations of angels and redeemed spirits, Rev. v. 11, &c.

APPLICATION.

1. *Are you amongst those who praise the Saviour?* Do you exult, boast, glory, extol, celebrate the praises of Christ ?

> " When he's the subject of the song,
> Who can refuse to sing ?"

I tell you who should not : those he has not compassionated—those whose nature he has not assumed—those for whom he has not died—those against whom his heart is closed—those he cannot or will not save ; but of such there is not one in this congregation, nor yet in the wide world itself.

2. *Neglect of this duty by the Christian would be criminal indeed.* " The very stones," &c. The gay, the licentious, the frivolous, all would condemn you. Let your hosanna be the hosanna of the heart, of the profession, of the life. " In all things show forth," &c.

3. *The advantages of praising Christ.* Elevates the mind, refreshes the spirit, assimilates to the beatified. It dispels clouds, banishes night, brings day. What endless matter of praise in Christ !

THE TEN VIRGINS.

SKETCH I.

" Then shall the kingdom of heaven be likened unto ten virgins, which took their lamps, and went forth to meet the bridegroom," &c.—Matt. xxv. 1, &c.

This is one of Christ's most striking and impressive parables. It has to do with events of the most momentous character. It refers to the glory of the Saviour, the necessity of vital piety, the second advent of the Messiah, the glorification of believers, and the rejection, the everlasting rejection, of those not prepared for the heavenly state. It may be necessary, and, perhaps, most edifying, that we should,

I. Review the parable in its literal signification. The event described is that of an eastern marriage procession. The bride is brought to the house of the bridegroom with great pomp and splendor. The friends of the bridegroom and bride are invited to join in the procession, and to partake of the banquet with which it would be followed. The procession was generally delayed till evening, sometimes till midnight. Those who were to grace the train must have lighted torches, or flambeaux ; and to keep these burning, they provided vessels of oil, into which they were dipped, or which they poured upon them. In the present instance the bridegroom delayed his appearance until midnight, and in the interval the virgins all slumbered and slept. At length the cry is heard, " Behold, the bridegroom cometh," &c. Then they all arise to get their torches ready, that they may go forth to meet him. Part, however, of the company had neglected a provision of oil for the future, and they exclaimed, "Our lamps are gone out." They sought assistance from the other persons in attendance, but their stock was only adequate to their own necessity. And while they labor to supply the deficiency, the bridegroom appears, and they who are ready, go forth to the honors and enjoyments of the marriage feast. The others now try to gain admission, but they are rejected, with the solemn announcement, " Verily I say unto you, I know you not." Let us now consider,

II. ITS SPIRITUAL APPLICATION.

1. *The Bridegroom is Jesus.* This is one of the general scriptural representations of the Saviour, and there is one passage in the Psalms which is almost identified in spirit with this parable, Ps. xlv. 10, &c. The prophet Isaiah, xliv. 5, also. The Saviour gave the same representation of himself in his parable of the marriage feast, Matt. xxii. 1, 2. So also when asked wherefore his disciples did not fast, as those of John, Jesus replied, " Can the children of the bridechamber mourn, as long as the bridegroom is with them," &c., Matt. ix. 15. So John the Baptist testified of Christ, John iv. 29, "He that hath the bride is the bridegroom," &c.

III. THE OBJECT OF THE BRIDEGROOM'S AFFECTION IS THE CHURCH. Thus the apostle writes to the Corinthian church. " For I am jealous over you," &c., 2 Cor. xi. 2, &c. See also Eph. v. 25. Now to render a union possible between Christ and mankind,

1. *They must have one nature.* Hence Christ took our nature upon himself, he dwelt in our flesh, became a man, made of a woman, &c. And he provided the means for restoring the sinner to the divine nature. For the renewal of his heart and life. See Titus ii. 14, and iii. 4.

2. *They must have one mind.* In our natural state, we are alienated, at enmity, &c. Now Christ, by the exhibition of his love in the gospel, overcomes this. By the power of his truth he melts the soul. By the exhibition of his own bleeding side he allures to himself, draws the soul to him ; the rebel throws down his weapons, and exclaims, " I yield, I yield," &c.

3. *In conversion the soul is espoused to Christ.* Thus the apostle said, " I have espoused you to Christ," a promise and en-

gagement of marriage. Jehovah very affectionately reminded Israel of his espousal to that people, Jer. ii. 2.

4. *The marriage celebration is reserved for his second advent.* To this John refers us in one of his visions. " Let us be glad and rejoice, for the marriage of the Lamb is come, and his wife hath made herself ready," Rev. xix. 7. With that event will conclude all the arrangements of grace, and will begin all the dignity and bliss of perfected glory to his church. The whole church of Jesus will stand thus related to Christ forever and ever. So John thus again describes the splendors of this glorious consummation, Rev. xxi. 2, &c. Now let us conclude by placing Jesus as the dignified bridegroom before you. We remind you that,

(1.) *His glory is supreme.*

(2.) *His riches are infinite.*

(3.) *His beauty unrivalled.*

(4.) *His love unspeakable, and passing understanding.*

(5.) *Are not his claims, then, irresistible ?* Notice also as to the character of true Christians ; represented as virgins in this parable. As such they are,

(1.) To be separated from the world.

(2.) To be distinguished for their purity of heart and life.

(3.) To live in the enjoyment of love to Christ, and hope of union with him forever and ever. We offer Jesus to you all. Reject him not, &c. We congratulate believers on their choice and portion. We expostulate with those who have forsaken him. Oh return, &c.

THE TEN VIRGINS.

SKETCH II.

"Then shall the kingdom of heaven be likened unto ten virgins, which took their lamps, and went forth to meet the bridegroom," &c.—MATT. xxv. 1, &c.

WE previously considered the former part of this parable, and also the general spirit of the whole, as applied to an eastern marriage ceremony. We noticed the character of Christ as a bridegroom ; believers as virgins, &c. We now have to consider the virgins,

I. IN THEIR PROFESSIONAL PROBATIONARY CONDITION. " Who took their lamps."

Now in this, the profession of Christianity is exhibited. The people of God are not in darkness, but they are light in the Lord; and they are to shine as lights in the world. Religion is to be seen, to be manifest. "City set on a hill," &c. Now the virgins are described as "taking their lamps, and going forth," &c. This profession of discipleship and friendship to Christ,

1. *Should arise from love to Christ.* In the early ages of Christianity, no fear of any other motive. Now, it is respectable; in some cases profitable. The love of Christ is the only right constraining principle. "I am crucified with Christ," &c.

2. *Must be public and open before men.* "Follow me," &c. "Let your light, &c., *before* men." "Went forth."

3. *Must be constant and continued.* Every day, place, and circumstance. In good report, and evil report, &c. Must be maintained, held fast, &c.

4. *It must be sustained by divine grace.* Grace is the "oil." This will give the profession the right tone. Beautify us; make us to be firm and persevering. Now a profession without the grace of God in the soul, will,

(1.) Be joyless; no real bliss; no real peace; no solid hope. Mechanical; no experience; no feeling in it.

(2.) It is promiseless. The promises are given to the true Christian; to the sincere follower of Christ.

(3.) It is often transitory. No root; soon given up; soon cast off. How necessary, then, the oil of divine grace! Doing all in Christ's name, and in the sufficiency of his grace. We now proceed to notice,

II. THE DELAY OF THE BRIDEGROOM, AND THE VIRGINS IN THEIR SLEEPING STATE. "The bridegroom tarried." The early Christians expected his second advent in their time. So in many ages since. But as to that period it is not revealed, except that it will be in the end of the world. Now, in the interval, one generation after another passeth away. Of the virgins it is said, "They all slumbered and slept." This evidently refers to death. Death to the godly, is falling asleep; sleeping in Jesus. Now let it be observed, that up to this period, there are no obvious distinctions between the two classes of virgins. They all have the same title; all have lamps; all are burning for a time, and they all fall asleep, waiting for the bridegroom. But

this is the grand and awful difference : the wise have prepared for the future; "the prudent man foreseeth the evil," &c. The others have been satisfied with the present; have no supply for the coming exigency. See 1 Tim. vi. 19. We notice,

III. THE SOLEMN ANNOUNCEMENT. "Behold the bridegroom cometh," &c.

1. *The period of this announcement is midnight.* At the end of our world's day. Not literal : it cannot be so to all the world.

2. *The pomp and magnificence of his coming.* The event is most momentous, and the scene truly sublime. All beings in all worlds will be interested in it. The Father now sees the end of his gracious administration to a world of sinners. Jesus now has the full crown of his joy, his promised reward. Believers now hail the day of their full and eternal redemption, the coronation of the saints. Angels now grace the train of the descending Judge, the glorified Messiah. Devils and lost spirits now tremble, as they wait for the passing of their final sentence and their irrevocable doom. The dead, small and great, hear the trumpet's loud, shrill blast; and the graves, and the sea, and death, and hades, give up their dead. "Behold the bridegroom cometh," is heard by each and every human being. "Then all those virgins," &c. And now we notice,

IV. THE AWFUL DEFICIENCY OF THE FOOLISH VIRGINS IS DISCOVERED. And the foolish said, "Give us," &c. What a discovery! Lamps gone out! and gone out when most needed. What shall they do? They apply to the wise virgins. "Give us of your oil;" but the wise reply, "Not so," &c., verse 9. In this life we cannot give grace to each other. How much less then! Let me suppose a few cases which this passage suggests. Parents and children;—and the former have only had the provision of oil, and for the son to say to his father, Give me of your oil; the daughter to her mother, &c. Wives and husbands;—and the latter have not had the store of oil, and shall say, "Give me," &c. The pastor and people, and they shall say to him, "O give us," &c. Not a saint will have more than his own state will require. Will any in this assembly put the request? or will any have to give the refusal? Notice,

V. THE CONCLUSION OF THE CEREMONY, AND THE CONSUMMATION OF THE FEAST. The wise join in the train and are acknowledged

as the friends of the bridegroom, and they go into the marriage. Their hopes are now realized; their desires now fulfilled; their joys now complete; their salvation now perfected, and that forever. The bliss, the glory, are unutterable. But the foolish virgins labor to supply the deficiency in seeking oil. But " the door is shut." What a solemn sentence!

(1.) The door of opportunities and means now shut. Not a messenger, not a sanctuary, not a sermon; the season of means all passed forever.

(2.) The door of mercy, which had been open to all for thousands of years, now shut. The king has laid aside the golden sceptre.

(3.) The door of hope;—only one in the universe, and that closed : everywhere else black despair.

(4.) The door of heaven which Christ opened, as our sacrifice and priest. But now he has retired from the intercessory, and has given the keys of authority to the Father, that God may be all and in all. And the exclusion is absolute;—urgent entreaty avails not. They knock, and cry " Lord, Lord," &c. But the solemn sentence concludes the fearful scene. " Verily, I say unto you," &c.

APPLICATION.

1. Let the subject lead to solemn examination. Are we Christ's real disciples? Have we the oil of grace in our hearts— laid up? Do we wait for Christ's coming? Is this the end of our lives? the one grand object ever in view?

2. Exhortation to earnestness and diligence. This is the one thing needful, &c. Be steadfast and immoveable. Be diligent, that ye may be found, &c.

3. It inculcates vigilance on all. "Watch," &c.· In one sense Christ comes at death. At least our probationary opportunities then end. Oh then, let us live, and pray, and watch. " Hold fast that which thou hast," &c.

THE GOOD SAMARITAN.

" Which now of these three, thinkest thou, was neighbor unto him that fell among the thieves," &c.—LUKE x. 36, 37.

IT is somewhat doubtful whether this is a parable or a narrative of facts which had come under the notice of the Redeemer; yet we admit that some of the chief instructions of Jesus were delivered in parables. When he wished to set forth the readiness of God to receive humble, repenting sinners, he delivered the series of parables connected with the lost sheep, lost piece of silver, and the prodigal son; when he wished to exhibit the importance of humility and the abominableness of pride and self-righteousness, he delivered the parable of the Pharisee and the publican. When he wished to show the various results arising from hearing the gospel, he delivered the parable of the sower and the seed. When he wished to show the eternal advantages of righteous poverty over worldly pomp and splendor, he discoursed on the rich man and Lazarus. When he desires to show the extent of the benevolent law of God, which says, " Thou shalt love thy neighbor as thyself," he presents before them the scene connected with the text. We are called to contemplate,

I. A FELLOW-BEING IN IMMINENT PERIL AND DISTRESS, verse 30. " A certain man," &c. Part of the way from Jerusalem to Jericho lay through a desert, which was so infested with robbers as to be termed the bloody way; for greater safety, persons generally travelled in company; but here is a poor lonely traveller who falls into the hands of the robbers, who is stripped of his garments, wounded, and left half dead. The miseries of our world seem chiefly to be reducible to three kinds.

1. *Self-procured.* There is an inseparable connection between certain courses of conduct and suffering; some of the ways of men lead to penury, disease, and death. " The way of transgressors is hard." Even in this life it is often ill with the wicked. The way of sin, shame, and ruin.

2. *Some of the miseries of life are clearly sent from God.* How often the wise, and good, and prudent, suffer. Behold the patriarch Jacob; look at Job; "Shall we receive good at the hand of the Lord," &c. But observe,

3. *A great amount of our suffering is from our fellow-men.* Behold those children covered with shame and misery! whence is it? From their wicked parents. See those parents heart-broken! how is it? Their children are vile, irreverent, without natural affection. See that man ruined in his reputation and property. How is it? He has

been swindled out of his property, &c. Sin ripens men for every crime ; hence, daily the possessions and lives of men are taken by beasts of prey, in the shape and form of men. Here is a poor man! They have taken his money and his clothes, and wounded him ; left him weltering in his gore, "half dead." "The tender mercies of the wicked are cruel." We are called to witness,

II. Two OFFICIAL RELIGIONISTS EXHIBITING A TOTAL WANT OF HUMANITY. One of them is a priest, the other a Levite, individuals closely connected with the rites of a divine religion. No doubt the hopes of the man would be revived as he saw two travellers, especially when he beheld their priestly apparel ; the priest, however, went at once on the other side, as if he had not seen him, or were intent on some more important business. The other stood opposite and looked, and then he too, whatever he might feel, passed by, &c. Perhaps he pitied, but he helped not. Observe, they trampled upon the principles of humanity, patriotism, and religion ; that religion is hypocritical and totally false, which does not produce works of goodness and mercy. What avails religious knowledge ? What avails religious profession ? What avails assumed sanctity of life ? "God is love." "Jesus went about," &c. "Pure religion," &c. "To do good," &c. We are called to witness,

III. A MANIFESTATION OF MERCY WHERE IT MIGHT HAVE BEEN LEAST EXPECTED, verse 33. "But a certain Samaritan," &c.

(1.) He was arrested in his course. "Came where he was." Easy to have evaded, &c.

(2.) He examined into his condition.

(3.) He had compassion ; his heart melted, and it was not merely sentimental.

(4.) He entered on a course of kindness, &c. "Bound up his wounds," lest he should bleed to death ; poured in wine as an astringent to cleanse, &c.; oil as an emollient to heal ; did not leave him to his fate ; set him on his beast, &c. ; took him to the inn, gave him two denarii, and engaged to pay the remainder. Here was *generous, practical,* and *continued goodness.* Think of the excuses he might have made, "I am a Samaritan, I hate him, and if he had seen me thus he would not have helped me. Let his own people help. I am on a journey," &c. Consider,

IV. CHRIST'S PRACTICAL APPLICATION OF THIS PARABLE. "Go and do likewise." When you see human misery do not neglect it. According to your means and opportunity do good.

(1.) Such a course will be exceedingly pleasing to God.

(2.) Have a happy influence on your own hearts.

(3.) Will secure you an interest in the benign providence of God, Psalm xli. 1, &c.

(4.) Will not go unrewarded at the last day, Matthew xxv. 35, &c.

APPLICATION.

1. *The subject has been considered by some as representing the character and work of Christ.*

(1.) Man's condition, &c.

(2.) The inefficiency of the law and sacrifices to help.

(3.) The gracious visitation of Christ to our world.

(4.) His provision ; wine and oil ; his precious blood, and divine Spirit.

(5.) His taking him to the banqueting house of his church, &c. Christ is now passing. We learn,

2. *True mercy embraces both the bodies and souls of men.* Christian benevolence is universal ; it extends to all objects; not a mere relative or domestic feeling ; not local—not national. Wherever there is a human being in misery, whether of body or soul, we are bound to show compassion and help.

THE PHARISEE AND PUBLICAN.

"Two men went up into the temple to pray the one a Pharisee and the other a publican," &c.— LUKE xviii. 10–14.

PRAYER forms a leading exercise in every system of religion under heaven; it was one of the evidences of patriarchal piety ; it was one of the frequent services of the tabernacle, and afterwards of the temple. Mohammedanism is distinguished for its numerous prayers. Pagans of every grade and age have performed their devotional services to their imaginary deities. The worshippers of Baal cried from morning to evening to their senseless idol. How important then that Christians should not allow ignorant pagans to rise in condemnation against them at the last day ; but it is no every thing which men present, that God will regard or acknowledge as prayer; to this end is the scope and design of the parable before us. Let us,

I. CONSIDER THE CHARACTER AND PRAYER OF THE PHARISEE, AND HIS REJECTION OF THE LORD.

1. *The person.* A Pharisee, of the strictest sect of the Jews.. Persons who made pretences to very superior piety, but who generally were filled with the spirit of self-righteousness and spiritual pride. Men who sought their own glory rather than the glory of God.

2. *The place to which he repaired.* "The temple." Building erected for God's worship and glory. Here the sacrifices were presented, the law read, and prayer offered to God; it was emphatically to be a house of prayer for all nations. One of the leading designs of worship is, to make prayer and supplication to God.

3. *The service he offered.* I cannot call it prayer, for not one word of petition, or supplication, or intercession is found in it. There was, however, apparent *thanksgiving*, and that is part of prayer, but even that, while it professed to honor God, was a mere exaltation of self. What he said was in commendation of himself under the mask of thanking God. He thanked God because he was,

(1.) *Not as other men.* Not so vile as the vilest; but probably he might owe much of this to his education, to parental restraints, and the more favorable circumstances in which the providence of God had placed him. What would you think of a man, even in the presence of his fellow-mortals, praising himself because he was not a savage, or an assassin, because some of his fellow-men were such!

(2.) But he refers to his *good deeds.* "I fast," &c. These he thinks render God under obligations to him, or at any rate, give him a right to God's peculiar regards.

(3.) *But he contrasts himself with his fellow-worshipper.* How odious! "Or even as this publican." Instead of feeling pity or compassion for him, instead of giving him a place in his prayers, he tries to exalt himself by abasing his fellow. Yet how often are we thus guilty! How often do we hear for others! How often institute invidious comparisons! This was his service, but where was the prayer? Where the confession of sin—the contrition —the supplication? He asks no favor, seeks no pardon, entreats no grace. Self possessed the throne, and he was totally ignorant of his own heart, of the purity of God's character and law.

(4.) Let us notice the *result.* God was not honored nor pleased. God beheld him afar off; his only reward was the delusion of his own heart, the infatuated self-complacency of his own soul. Observe,

II. THE CHARACTER AND PRAYER OF THE PUBLICAN WITH HIS ACCEPTANCE OF GOD.

1. *He worships in the same place, but feels unworthy of the privilege.* Stands afar off, considers it holy ground, fears to draw near: how slow his approach, how reverent!

2. *He would not look towards God's holy place.* "Would not lift," &c. Why would he not look up? He thought of its purity, and felt his vileness; he thought of its goodness and his ingratitude; he thought of its holiness and his guilt with its desert, and therefore lifted not his eyes, &c.

3. *He smote upon his breast.* He was inwardly smitten—his conscience condemned; he felt his guilt, his worthlessness, and smote upon his breast. Ah! that treacherous heart—that ungrateful, wicked heart.

4. *He prayed fervently for mercy.* In this prayer,

(1.) *The object was right.* "God" the only object of prayer. Who hears and answers prayer.

(2.) *The confession was appropriate.* God demands confession. There are promises given to it. Is it not proper? If God would dispense with it, the ingenuous penitent could not. "A sinner." He extenuates not—he mentions not one righteous act. A sinner—nothing else, nothing better.

(3.) *His request was suitable.* He asks for mercy, not justice, but mercy, compassion, to the unworthy; kindness to the miserable. Every sinner needs this; nothing else will save.

(4.) *His suit was granted.* He went down "justified." "Rather," is in italics. God was glorified, God's justice and mercy; God heard, approved, and accepted the suppliant, and granted his request. God was propitious, and he received mercy. From the whole we learn,

1. *How liable are we to be deceived as to our true state!* Do not err in this; be not the victims of infatuation, especially as to self-righteousness.

2. *How necessary is self-abasement!* Grace always humbles, always prostrates. If we are not abased we are strangers to God's grace; no exception to this; nothing will supply its place.

3. *What encouragement to the contrite!* "To that man will I look," &c. "A broken and contrite heart," &c. How many of you have felt thus? Prayed thus, &c. If not, do so now. God is seated on a throne of grace; draw near and look to the sacrifice God has provided; utter this fervently, and you shall not, you cannot pray in vain, &c.

THE PENITENT MALEFACTOR.

"And he said unto Jesus, Lord, remember me when thou comest into thy kingdom," &c.— LUKE xxiii. 42, 43.

THE circumstances attending the death of Jesus were of the most wonderful kind. The blessed Messiah had for three years been traversing the land of Judea, illumining the benighted, healing the sick, and making the miserable and desponding happy. No teacher had ever delivered such discourses; no one had ever wrought such miracles; no one had ever exhibited such piety, benignity, and love; yet, by the malice of his own countrymen, he is persecuted even to death, and we are called to witness him enduring all the painful agonies attending crucifixion. He is now dying the ignominious death of the cross; but his death, like every other part of his wonderful history, is distinguished by scenes of the most wonderful character. The rocks rend —the earth quakes—the sun is darkened —and the veil of the temple is rent in twain. During these amazing phenomena, we are called to witness the conduct of those robbers who were suffering with Christ. One of them joined in the unbelieving railing of the surrounding mob, and said, "If thou be the Christ," verse 39. "But the other," verse 40, and text. There are two leading divisions.

I. THE PRAYER HE PRESENTED.
II. THE ANSWER HE RECEIVED.

I. THE PRAYER HE PRESENTED. Two things must be noticed before we enter upon his prayer.

(1.) *The character of the suppliant.* He is denominated a thief and malefactor. It is probable that he had been a public rob-ber—a daring outlaw; and not improbable that they had been confederates in crime; doubtless one of the most debased and abandoned of criminals, for only such were condemned to crucifixion.

(2.) *The situation in which he was placed.* Suffering the extreme sentence of the law; enduring the horrible death of crucifixion; a situation of extreme debasement and agony. Life was just ebbing out; on the verge of the eternal state; the world and time receding; his day of probation just expiring. Observe, then, his prayer.

1. *Short, yet comprehensive.* A few words embody all his requests; but in those words what an immensity of meaning!

2. *It was spiritual in its object.* It referred not to the body; not to ease or mitigation; or to his life. It all had respect to the soul and a future world.

3. *It was a prayer of mighty faith.* Faith in the *soul's immortality;* faith in a future state, &c., of rewards; it was faith in Jesus Christ. Observe, he addresses him as *Lord;* but where were the signs of his dignity and power? Yet he honored him as the Messiah—as having an invisible kingdom. "Thy kingdom;" and herein he recognised the Godhead of Christ, as the Lord of the invisible world. He acknowledged his *prerogative* to dispense future rewards, "Remember me," &c.; but it was also *mighty, wondrous* faith. Consider his character; his condition in life; his unfavorable position as to means. Contrast his state with the worthies of the Old Testament, or the disciples of the New. Moses believed; but then God addressed him, and showed him the symbol of his presence in the burning bush. Abraham believed; but then he had many precious promises. Isaiah believed; but he saw his glory. John the Baptist believed; but he saw the heavens opened, &c. The disciples believed; but they beheld his mighty works, &c.; they saw his miracles, &c.; transfiguration, &c.; even Saul of Tarsus was surrounded by his resplendent glory; but the dying malefactor beheld Christ in the depths of his sorrows; in the period of his abasement; reviled and crucified as an enemy to God and man; and yet through the whole his faith penetrated, and he recognised in that sufferer the Lord of the universe, and the only Saviour of the world; yet he so believed in Christ as to rest his

soul upon him, and depended upon his mercy for eternal life. He saw no sceptre—beheld no crown—had no prospect of a kingdom—that is, to the eye of sense, yet he recognised all these as rightly belonging to Jesus the Messiah, and as such he prayed, " Lord, remember," &c.

4. *This prayer was associated with the genuine fruits of repentance.* Saving faith and repentance are ever joined together. We do not add repentance as if it followed faith; generally it goes before; but in all cases it is connected with it. He confesses his own guilt, " We indeed suffer justly," &c., verse 41 ; he rebukes the impiety of his suffering fellow-malefactor, " Dost thou not fear God ?" &c., verse 40 ; he affirms the innocency and the holiness of Christ, " But this man hath done nothing amiss," verse 41. Thus, his last moments were spent in confession of sin, in reproof of wickedness, and in vindicating the Redeemer.

5. *His prayer was effectual.* He did not pray in vain ; and who ever did ? Jesus was not so much absorbed in his own agonies as to neglect the suppliant by his side. He listened to his petition ; he entertained his request ; and richly exhibited towards him the fulness of his grace. Christ came into the world to save sinners, and his last act was to deliver one of the chief of them from guilt and eternal death. Notice,

II. The answer he received. " And Jesus said, Verily, I say," &c. Now, let us look at the various features this answer exhibited.

1. *It was immediate.* He did not defer, or put off his suit. On some occasions Christ tried the faith of the applicants, as the Syro-Phenician woman ; but this was a desperate matter. Here life was expiring; and therefore at once Jesus mercifully replied to his petition.

2. *It was compassionate and merciful.* He had no claim ; no right. Natural death was a penalty of his crimes against man, and eternal death the penalty for his sins against God. But the compassion of Jesus was affected. He saw him ready to perish, and therefore beheld a fit object on whom to bestow the last blessing of his mission to our world. He came unto Christ, and Christ opened his heart to receive him ; he believed in him, and Jesus gave him the desire of his trembling spirit.

3. *The answer was peculiarly strong and positive.* Christ might have said, " I will

not forget thy prayer, but will show thee mercy." But Jesus resolved to fill him with ecstasy and joy, by the most solemn assurance that his prayer was successful, " Verily," &c. " I pledge my name, and honor, and truth, and faithfulness, that this petition shall be granted."

4. *It was superabundant.* He prayed to be remembered, but Christ treats with him richly, most munificently. He gave unto him a splendid promise—a blissful assurance of a place and portion with him in glory, " To-day thou shalt," &c. Here are three things :

(1.) The place—*Paradise.* This word is of Persian origin, and signifies a garden of pleasure—a figurative description of heaven. It is used in reference to the garden of Eden ; but Paul in his holy vision when caught up to heaven, calls it paradise, 2 Cor. xii. 4. John, also, in Revelation ii. 7, says, " To him that overcometh will I give to eat of the tree of life, which is in the midst of the paradise of God."

(2.) In paradise he was to be *with Christ.* It is Christ's presence that constitutes the light and bliss of glory. The richest assurance he ever gave was this, " Where I am, there ye shall be also."

> " There we shall see his face,
> And never, never sin," &c.

(3.) He was to be with Christ in paradise *that day.* " To-day." " Before the sun sets thou shalt enjoy the light and glory of heaven. As a trophy of my grace, I will present thee this day to my Father, ' before angels, and the spirits of just men made perfect.' "

APPLICATION.

1. *Learn the richness and freeness of the grace of Christ.* The dying malefactor stands out on the page of the gospel that no sinner may despair. Here we see what grace can do—forgive, and cleanse, and glorify in a few hours.

2. *No encouragement for the presumptuous.* Only this case. Only one to prevent the abuse of God's long-suffering. A peculiar case altogether.

3. *The way of salvation.* Application to Christ.

4. *Death at once conveys to glory.* To die in Christ is instant, inexpressible, and eternal gain.

SATAN'S PALACE, &c.

" When a strong man armed keepeth his palace,
his goods are in peace," &c.—LUKE xi. 21, 22.

NOTHING so completely blinds the mind
and hardens the heart as envy. It is one
of those evil principles which completely
poison the soul, render it totally callous,
and prepare it for every evil work. It was
this that led Cain to become a fratricide,
and slay his own brother; this that led the
sons of Jacob to devise the death of Joseph;
this that caused Haman to attempt the destruction of all the Jews in the kingdom of
Persia; it was this that led the Pharisees
to treat Jesus with such scorn and unbelief.
As often as possible they denied his miracles; and when they could not do that,
they wickedly said that he cast out devils
by the power of the prince of devils. To
this the Saviour thus replies, verse 17. He
then illustrates his power in casting out
devils by the figurative language of the
text. Notice,

I. THE STRIKING REPRESENTATION OF
SATAN.

II. THE TRUE DESCRIPTION OF HIS PALACE.

III. THE MANNER IN WHICH HE KEEPETH
POSSESSION. And,

IV. HOW IT IS BESIEGED, AND SATAN
DISPOSSESSED. Observe,

I. A STRIKING REPRESENTATION OF SA-
TAN. He is described in verses 18 and 19
as Beelzebub; that is, the prince of the
devils. He is the head and leader of
the fallen angels, Rev. ix. 11. He is called Apollyon; i. e. a destroyer. He is also
styled the old dragon; the serpent; the
adversary; the deceiver; Lucifer, the
fallen bright one; Belial; accuser; and
devil, or diabolus, signifying the slanderer.
Now, the reality of such a being,

1. Is fully established by the sacred scriptures. By some who profess to believe the
Bible it is said that the name simply refers
to the principle of evil, and not to any living spirit. But the word of God as clearly
teaches the existence of a Devil as the existence of God, and employs such terms as
cannot apply to a mere principle. As a
real spirit, he conversed with Eve; persuaded her to believe his lies rather than
God's truth; and hence he is called the
father of lies. As such, he accused Job,
and thirsted for his destruction; as such,
he tempted Jesus; as such, he is said to

go up and down as a roaring lion; as such,
Christ said he desired to have Peter, &c.
We are exhorted to be vigilant, and resist
the devil. It is said, too, that the devil and
his fallen compeers are reserved for the
judgment of the great day; see Jude 6;
Rev. xx. 10.

2. The text refers to his power. He is
described as a " strong man." Angels are
said to excel in strength. We do not imagine this was impaired by their apostacy.
His power may denote,

(1.) His authority. And he is a prince;
the god of this world; the ruler of the
powers of disobedience. It may denote,

(2.) His dominions. How vast and extensive! He usurped God's earth, and here
he has his kingdom of darkness. In it are
countless myriads of subjects—of men and
women prostrate beneath his hellish and
cruel yoke.

(3.) See the effects of his control. In
Christ's day many human bodies were possessed. Look at the demoniac; look at
the child possessed; look at the mental
and moral effects of his influence on the
souls of mankind.

(4.) Consider how he has maintained
his possessions. For thousands of years.
Learning, science, philosophy, and a thousand systems for effecting human happiness,
have been vain and fruitless, and he has
even resisted the reign of God extensively
to this hour. Notice,

II. THE TRUE DESCRIPTION OF HIS PALACE.
That is, the human heart; the soul of man.
As his palace,

1. Here he dwells. This is his residence.
As the Spirit of God dwells in the Christian,
so the spirit of Satan dwells in the unrenewed soul. The various faculties and
powers of the soul are the apartments of
this palace, and these are all occupied by
the prince of darkness. He surrounds the
understanding with the curtains of delusion;
he debases the judgment with diabolical
perverseness; he decorates the imagination
with pictures of uncleanness; he fills the
affections with earthly things. Worldliness,
vanity, or pride, furnishes the residence of
the god of this world. As his palace,

2. Here he has his throne. God is not
the Lord of the unrenewed heart. Here
Satan is exalted and served; here he receives the homage of the intellect, and the
willing service of the heart and life. Over
the mind, and heart, and life, he sways his

sceptre, and has unlimited and incessant obedience. He says to one, ' Go! and he goes ;' and to another, ' Come ! he comes.' Observe,

III. THE MANNER IN WHICH HE KEEPETH POSSESSION. It is said he keepeth his palace, and thus his goods are in peace. Now, he keepeth his palace by his wiles and stratagems ; by the subtlety and deceit he exercises. He does this,

1. *By keeping it in darkness.* Darkness is the element suited to his designs. He labors to keep men in ignorance of themselves, of God, of their responsibility, &c.; see 2 Cor. iv. 4.

2. *He keepeth it, under the influence of sense.* Sense has only to do with the palpable things of the present, " What shall I eat," &c. The body absorbs all the anxieties. Time present is every thing, &c. He urges men to seek present wealth, pleasures, &c. ; he keeps this world first and uppermost, &c.

3. *He keepeth it, by the influence of procrastination.* He says there is plenty of time ; ample means ; lengthened opportunities ; no need for present reflection ; death is a great way off; and thus to invitations and warnings the soul replies, " When I have a convenient season," &c.

4. *He keepeth it, by producing lethargy and torpor of spirit.* Hardens the heart ; petrifies the feeling ; stupifies the conscience ; gives an opiate to the powers of reflection, &c.; so that insensibility is produced, and consideration and anxiety annihilated. Such persons are like a man sleeping on the top of a mast ; or a person walking heedlessly on the very verge of a burning crater ; or blindfolded, rushing onward on the margin of a fearful chasm. He sometimes keeps it,

5. *By clothing the spirit in the habiliments of despair.* What a fearful sight is this ! Hope extinguished ; the fell mists of despair surrounding the mind. He then says, " Means are useless ; the distance from heaven is too great ; guilt too heavy ; disease incurable." He fills the soul with the affecting language, " The harvest is past," &c.

IV. HOW IT IS BESIEGED, AND SATAN DISPOSSESSED.

1. *The glorious personage by whom this is effected.* " Stronger." Almighty ; allpowerful. His word effected wonders.

2. *The means employed are the gospel, and* the *Spirit of Christ.* The gospel is the power of God, &c. The truth makes free. It proclaims liberty, &c.; opens the eyes ; awakens, excites, and draws the victims from the way of death.

3. *The change effected is wondrous and delightful.* Satan's power destroyed, and himself expelled. The soul becomes the palace of Christ. " Christ in you the hope of glory."

APPLICATION.

1. Believers, bless your deliverer.
2. Sinners, call on Christ to save you.
3. The victims of Satan's power must share his final doom.

VESSELS OF WRATH

" The vessels of wrath fitted to destruction."—ROMANS ix. 22.

" How readest thou ?" is an important and necessary question to every diligent student of the divine word. If persons could read without having their views affected by preconceived opinions, then, generally, they would arrive at the meaning of the Holy Spirit. But it is too common to read the Bible, that we may establish our own opinions from its divine pages. It should be our desire that our opinions and judgment should be guided entirely by its hallowed truths. Men in law have to read with exactness, to know the spirit of the statute they are consulting. Chemists and apothecaries have to read carefully, that they may compound the medicines with accuracy and precision. Men of science have to exercise great attention, to understand the various laws of mechanism. Surely much more care is necessary to understand the truths of revelation,—truths which relate to immortality and eternal life. Negligent Bible reading, and reading with a mind under a sectarian bias, have been productive of the most awful mistakes and perversions of the divine word. This is especially true of this epistle, and more especially as to this chapter. The scope and tendency of the seventh, eighth, ninth, tenth, and eleventh chapters, are evident ; —the sovereign right of God to cast off the Jews, and elect the Gentiles to the privileges of the gospel ;—and to establish and illustrate this, is the one great design of the apostle. The doctrines usually deduced, are the unconditional election of some persons, and the unconditional reprobation or rejection of others, as an act of divine sovereignty. Let us at this time consider the immediate language of the text. We ask,

I. Who are the characters?

II. What are the evidences of that character? And,

III. Their final end. We ask,

I. Who are the characters? We might expatiate on the diversity of character specified in God's word. We might refer to the skeptic, the scoffer, the blasphemer, the sensualist, the proud, the worldly, the trifler, &c. There is one scriptural expression including the whole, "He that believeth not," &c. John iii. 36. All despisers and rejecters of the gospel of Christ, however profane, or however externally moral, are included. It is a fearfully wide range. How many are within it! Now, it may be noted that such fit themselves for destruction. God does not. He is the fountain of holiness and goodness. Satan alone cannot; he aids. It is his work to allure and deceive, but the sinner must co-operate,—be his willing slave. Men cannot make others such, except in the same sense in which Satan does so. It is the sinner's personal act. "O Israel, thou hast destroyed thyself,"—self-destroyed. Sin destroys, as disease destroys the body. As rust destroys the iron; or the moth, the garment; or poison, life; or crime brings to an ignominious end. Unbelief destroys, as it neglects the remedy, puts away the Saviour, and rejects the intervention of God's mercy. Every sinner, therefore, fits himself as a vessel of wrath.

II. What are the evidences of that character? Two kinds of evidence.

1. *Internal.* Known only to the individual and God. Without any love to God, any delight in holiness, any internal trust and reliance on Jesus Christ; where the heart is indisposed to spiritual things.

2. *External.*

(1.) Indifference to God's holy word. A man must love and delight in it if he would be saved.

(2.) Neglect of the means of grace, especially prayer and hearing the gospel. These are essential to salvation.

(3.) Worldliness of spirit. "If any man love the world," &c.

(4.) Disregard of God's authority; living in sin; doing the work of the evil one. We need not add more signs of those who are vessels fitted for destruction. Consider then,

III. Their fearful end. "Destruction." This does not mean annihilation. It is evident that the wicked, as well as the righteous, will exist forever. But it signifies the infliction of that wrath which their sin deserved. The psalmist has in view the metaphor of the text, Ps. ii. 10, 12. "Upon the wicked God will rain fire," &c. "The wicked shall be turned," &c. "These," it affirms, "shall go away into everlasting punishment," &c. Now this may be called destruction,

1. *As it will be the annihilation of all hope.* An indefinite kind of hope sustains men here;—a vague, uncertain idea that they will not eventually perish. This is sometimes based on God's mercy; on his indifference to the actions of mankind; on the certainty of all men being saved at last, through Christ; or on the exercise of repentance at the last hour. But now the candle of the wicked will be put out, and not one ray of hope irradiate the horizon of their prison forever.

2. *The utter cessation of all enjoyment.* What is existence without enjoyment? Destruction involves this, that they shall have no peace, no pleasure, no bliss, forever. The ordinary enjoyments of time are passed away; the sinful enjoyments of sense, &c. Not one stream of enjoyment left. The rich man requested a *drop of water*, but in vain.

3. *The righteous infliction of God's displeasure.* Imprisoned in hell; shut up in utter darkness; cast into the fiery lake; the companion of the devil and his angels. The preying of the worm of conscience; probably in sight of heaven, within hearing of its melody; yet excluded, and totally unfit for the felicity of glory.

APPLICATION.

Learn,

1. *It is the wickedness of sinners that ruins their souls.* Charge it not on some eternal decree; it is the inward resolving of the soul to live in iniquity. Charge not the unmercifulness of God; it is the want of compassion in your own souls. Say not

it is necessity ; it is the necessity of your own will. God says, " As I live," &c. ; Jesus says, " Ye will not," &c. ; the Holy Spirit says, " If ye will hear my voice," &c.

2. *Vessels of destruction may be changed into vessels of mercy.* " If the wicked will turn from his wickedness," &c. " Hear, and your souls shall live," &c. " Unto you is the word of this salvation sent," &c. " He that believeth shall be saved," &c. Do you want instances ? There is Manasseh ; there is the woman that was a sinner ; the extortionate Zaccheus ; the dying thief ; Saul of Tarsus ; many in this congregation. May you be enrolled in the same record of salvation and mercy.

VESSELS OF MERCY.

" Vessels of mercy, which he had afore prepared unto glory."—ROM. ix. 23.

THERE are two great cardinal truths of our holy religion : that the misery and ruin of the sinner is of himself, and that the happiness and salvation of the Christian is of God. These truths are equally true and important. To lay the sinner's ruin at the door of God, is an attack upon his goodness and mercy, and giving falsity to his own asseveration, that he has no pleasure in the death of him that dieth. To ascribe the salvation of the righteous to themselves, would be to rob God of his glory, and destroy the gospel system of grace altogether. There are three important questions which arise from the text.

I. WHO ARE THE VESSELS OF MERCY ?
II. HOW DO THEY BECOME SUCH ?
III. WHAT IS THEIR FINAL DESTINATION ?

I. WHO ARE THE VESSELS OF MERCY ? Now the scriptures affirm all men to be *objects* of mercy. " God is good to all, and his tender mercies," &c. But an object and a vessel are very different. A vessel of mercy, is one receiving and containing within it the saving mercy of God. Observe the vessels of mercy,

1. *Heard the gospel of mercy.* " This is a faithful saying," &c. Heard of the mercy promised to the guilty ; had the overtures of mercy made to them ; were urged to receive it—to accept it.

2. *Such have received the revelation of mercy made to them.* Paul did so, and was not disobedient to the heavenly vision. The three thousand on the day of Pentecost did so, and received the gift of the Holy Ghost. The jailer did so, and confessed his faith in the Lord Jesus. So also have the saints afar off ; they heard the invitation, and drew nigh. Enemies, they accepted the terms of amnesty ; guilty, received the pardon through the blood of Christ, in which they had redemption, &c.

3. *Such give evidence of their changed and saved condition.* Delight in the God of mercy ; rejoice in the merciful Saviour ; glory in his cross ; exhibit the spirit of mercy, by living in peace, and exercising compassion to those around them. They live as those redeemed and raised from sin, and misery, and death.

II. HOW DO THEY BECOME SUCH ? Not by lineage, as the children of Abraham ; or of pious ancestry. Not by education, or the power of religious example. Not by acts of self-righteousness, &c.

1. *By the exercise of free grace on the part of God.* The grace of God bringeth salvation, &c. Salvation is traceable to this source, and no other. " Not by works of righteousness," &c. He has mercy because he will ; because he delights in mercy ; because it is rich, free, boundless, everlasting.

2. *Through the merits of the Lord Jesus Christ.* Gift of God, &c., through Christ. His obedience ; his spotless purity ; his sacrificial death. " He loved us, and gave himself," &c. " Though he was rich," &c. " He suffered, the just," &c. " Himself bare," &c. " With his stripes," &c.

" 'Tis all our hope, and all our plea,
For us the Saviour died."

3. *By simple and meritless faith on the part of the sinner.* Pardon is presented, the sinner receives it, and it becomes his own. He hears by faith, and lives. He looks, and is saved. He runs into the refuge, and is delivered. He opens his mouth in prayer, and God fills his soul with the saving influences of the Holy Spirit. In this there is no merit, unless accepting a pardon by a culprit is such. I would just add, that all the saints are vessels of mercy, and become such, by this one simple, saving process.

III. WHAT IS THIER FINAL DESTINATION ? " Afore prepared unto glory." I doubt if these words literally refer to the Christian's eternal destination; see Rom. viii. 30. There is a glory which pertains to all saints here. "All we with open face beholding," &c. There are glorious titles, glorious privileges, glorious promises, here. But let us look to the final destiny of the vessels of mercy. They are destined,

1. *To a world of glory.* Called to God's eternal kingdom of glory, they shall dwell forever in the blissful regions of immortality. Born again, to an inheritance, &c. To be the associates of angels, and to dwell with Abraham and Isaac, &c., in the kingdom of their Father forever.

2. *To a glorious condition of both soul and body.* The *soul* made intellectual, and perfect in holiness; invested with power to enjoy the blaze of eternal light, emanating from the face of God and the Lamb. The *body* to be raised in the likeness of Christ's glorious body; to be free from all the weakness, frailties, and pollutions of the flesh, and made holy in their degree, as God himself is holy.

3. *To a glorious reward.* To sit on a throne of dominion and power; to wear a crown of glory; to enjoy all the love of God, and all the bliss of the divine presence; to drink of the streams of pleasure; to partake of the fruit of the tree of life; in one word, to be "forever with the Lord." "In thy presence is fulness of joy," &c.

APPLICATION.

1. *Learn the true title of every Christian.* A vessel of mercy, not of merit, or excellency. Of mercy, first and last, and always.

"I the chief of sinners am,
But Jesus died for me."

2. *The Christian's present state.* One of preparation; of spiritual growth; of increasing grace; spiritual advancement. Let us not forget this. Be this our one great concern, to "work out our own salvation," &c.

3. *God waits to be gracious to every sinner.* You may all become vessels of mercy, and *now.* "For, behold, now is the accepted time," &c.

THE CONQUERING REDEEMER.

"And I saw, and behold a white horse: and he that sat on him had a bow; and a crown was given unto him: and he went forth conquering, and to conquer."—REVELATION vi. 2.

THE prophecies of Ezekiel and the visions of John contain figurative representations of the most sublime description; this kind of writing is common to all oriental authors, especially to the poets. It must necessarily follow that such portions of the holy scriptures are difficult of interpretation. Commentators have been exceedingly divided on the meaning of many of the prophecies of the apocalyptic vision. Some writers of critical eminence have applied the text to the victories of Titus and Vespasian, who came from the east and obtained complete dominion over Judea, destroyed Jerusalem, and carried the Jews captive into all lands. Others have referred the passage to the reign of Constantine. I think the very reading of the text impresses the mind, that however celebrated Titus and Vespasian might be, a greater than they were is here; neither should we be warranted in applying it to Constantine, seeing that the reign of Constantine began the era of the corruption of Christianity, and did more mischief to the interests of true religion than all the fires which persecution ever kindled. Scripture is often the safest interpreter of scripture. For an explanation of this passage of this book, I refer you then to the 19th chapter and 11th verse. Our text, doubtless, refers to the glorious achievements of the Lord Jesus Christ. Let us notice,

I. THE SUBLIME REPRESENTATION GIVEN OF THE REDEEMER. And,

II. THE CHARACTER OF HIS GLORIOUS ACHIEVEMENTS. Notice,

I. THE SUBLIME REPRESENTATION GIVEN OF THE REDEEMER. Observe,

1. *His martial appearance.* Seated on a horse of war. Here we interpret the symbol as expressive of the *power* of Christ. "All power is given," &c. Bozrah's conqueror, &c., "mighty to save," &c. Of the *dignity* of Christ, see Psalm ii. 1. Of the *courage* of Jesus. He united meekness with the most undaunted intrepidity and courage; he appeared single-handed; he thirsted for the conflict; he trod the winepress, &c. See the description of the war horse, Job xxxix. 19. Notice,

2. *The description of the horse on which the Redeemer goes forth.* "White," not

black, or pale, or red. Though Zechariah saw him upon a *red* horse, and though Isaiah speaks of his being red in his appearance, they referred to his personal conflicts in obtaining our redemption. "White horses," were reserved for generals, captains, and commanders. *Joshua* had a conversation with Jesus, as captain, when he stood over against Jericho. *Paul* represents Jesus as the captain of our salvation, &c. Now, the "white horse" seems symbolical,

(1.) Of the purity of Christ's person. Warriors were often the very basest of mankind; avaricious, proud, cruel, desperate. Jesus, essential holiness, purity embodied, heart of love, a life of truth and benevolence.

(2.) Of the righteousness of his claims. The spoiler and oppressor may ride upon horses of a crimson hue, as characteristic of their injustice and their oppressions. War is generally based on unrighteousness; often on no other principle but power; no object but ambition; no end but gain. Christ's warfare is one of eternal righteousness, equity, &c. He designs to regain his revolted dominions. Satan has usurped the dominion of this world, though made by Christ, and for Christ; filled it with terror and misery. Jesus contemplates its restoration to its original allegiance, purity, and glory. He is heir of the world, &c.; heir of all things; he has a right to reign, &c.

(3.) Of the felicity of his administration. Desolation and wo attend the footsteps of earthly warriors—countries ravaged, cities burned, families ruined, streams of blood flowing; often followed by famine and pestilence; how delightful the contrast! Jesus's conquests obliterate wo and misery. The desert rejoices, and the wilderness blossoms as the rose; justice and benevolence ever accompany his steps. One song is heard, "Glory to God," &c.

> " Blessings abound where'er he reigns;
>   The prisoner leaps to lose his chains:
>   The weary find eternal rest,
>   And all the sons of want are blest."

Observe,

3. *The warlike instrument which Jesus bears.* "He had given him a bow," one of the most ancient and universally used instruments; now this bow is, *The truth of his blessed gospel.* All Christ's victories

are to be obtained by this; this in the hands of the Holy Spirit is to evangelize the world, see John xvi. 7–14. He gained the personal victory over Satan by this— he sent out his servants with this—he frees men, he regenerates, he sanctifies by this. His word is likened to the hammer, fire, &c. "Our gospel," &c. "I am not ashamed," &c. "We preach Christ crucified," &c. See Psalm xlv. 5. Notice,

4. *His regal dignity.* "Crown." Not the essential crown of his Godhead, but his mediatorial one. Given him as king of Zion—the Head of his church. Now of this crown we notice it is,

(1.) A crown for which he covenanted and suffered, Isaiah liii. 6 ; Phil. ii. 6.

(2.) A crown which as our exalted king he now wears in heaven, Acts v. 30 ; Heb. ii. 9; Rev. v. 6. Observe,

II. THE CHARACTER OF HIS GLORIOUS ACHIEVEMENTS. "He went forth," &c. Now here we must glance,

1. *At the enemies he had to encounter.* Powers of earth and hell. Satan and the world allied. Judaism, Paganism, Mohammedanism, papacy, infidelity, and sin of every class. Observe,

2. *The conquests he gained.* He went forth "conquering." He conquered by his personal prowess in the *desert*, by miracles, on the cross, in the grave, from thence by his gospel. When John saw him he had obtained the great first general victory in the city of his death. Where was Pilate, the Jewish Sanhedrim, Calvary ? &c. A victory over 3000 souls, and soon increased to 5000; from thence he went from conquering to conquer in Samaria, Athens, Corinth, Rome, &c. In the first ages he went forth, till Paul thus writes, Col. i. 16.

3. *He is still going forth, and there are immense triumphs for Jesus to gain.* Hence he goes forth from conquering to conquer. The world yet lieth in the arms of the wicked one. Six hundred millions yet in battle array against God, and against his Anointed. He is going forth now, in the east and west, north and south. " And this gospel," &c. "The stone cut out," &c. "Christ's conquering car," &c. Isaiah lx. 1–5, 21, 22. O yes! he must reign, and he must conquer, until the song of the world's jubilee is heard from every hill and vale, "Hallelujah! Hallelujah! for the Lord God Omnipotent reigneth!"

APPLICATION.

1. *Let the subject be applied personally.* Are you numbered among the conquests of Christ? Have you ceased to rebel and fight? Have you sued for peace? Have his arrows stuck fast? Are you enrolled among his friends? Are you the soldiers of the cross? If so, rejoice! Happy are ye, &c. If not, reflect upon your state; it is one of wretchedness, one of hopelessness, and one of certain ruin. Christ will break his enemies in pieces as a potter's vessel. " Wo unto him," &c. " Kiss the son, lest he be angry with thee, and thou perish from the way, when his anger is kindled but a little." " Agree with thine adversary whilst thou art in the way with him," &c.

2. *Remember you cannot aid Jesus unless you are enlisted under his banner.* Your gold, &c., he will scorn, if your heart be with his enemies. He demands first yourselves, then what you have.

3. *The friends of Jesus are deeply interested in the triumphs of the cross.* You are on one side of the mighty contest; your prayers must be there then; your personal efforts must be there; your pecuniary aid must be there also. Think of the territories yet unoccupied; think of the sin which yet abounds; think of the myriads and millions who are still perishing for lack of knowledge; think of the claims of humanity; think of Christ; and oh! think of the day of the Lord, when the Saviour shall be revealed in flaming fire, &c.

ALL THINGS FOR THE CHRISTIAN'S GOOD.

" And we know that all things work together for good to them that love God, to them who are the called according to his purpose."—ROMANS viii. 28.

ALL scripture was given by inspiration, and all scripture is profitable, &c.; but there is infinite variety in the portions of the divine word. The word of God may resemble the heavenly firmament, but some portions are more radiant and bright than others. Some passages of the word resemble the milky way in the heavens; some texts shine forth with unusual brightness and celestial lustre. The chapter in which our text is found is like the brightest portion of the heavens, and our text is the most resplendent star of that radiant galaxy. I doubt if any passage of the holy word has been more generally useful to the Christian church, or more especially consoling to the believer in trouble. Let us, then, examine it, and see what counsel and consolation may be deduced from it. Let us,

I. EXPLAIN THE CHARACTER PRESENTED TO US. " Them that love God," &c. Now, here are three things:—

1. *The divine purpose.* Now, by this purpose we understand God's pre-determination to offer to mankind the blessings of salvation in Christ Jesus; and it was God's purpose that the Jews first of all should receive this offer, Romans i. 16; Luke xxiv. 46, 47. Now, the gospel was first published to the Jews, and then, according to God's purpose, afterwards to the Gentiles, Ephesians i. 7–11. Observe,

2. *The divine calling.* To call, is to invite, to entreat, &c. Now, it was God's purpose that in this order—the Jew first, and then the Gentile—should be called by the messages of truth to participate in all the blessings of the gospel. Thus the provision of the gospel is likened to a feast, and men are to be called to come in and enjoy the banquet. Jesus Christ called in the days of his ministry sinners to repentance; the apostles and disciples thus called men to repent and believe the gospel. Thus the believers at Rome had been called according to God's gracious purpose.

3. *The divine principle.* " Love God." Those who had thus been called, and who had obeyed the call, became the subjects of God's mercy and favor. Such had been chosen of God to be his people, his sons and daughters, and the love of God had been shed abroad in their hearts by the Holy Ghost given unto them. Now, this divine principle imparted to them is evinced in loving God, " We love him because he first loved us." All who have believingly obeyed the call of the gospel, love God. They love him as their creator, preserver, but especially as their redeemer. They love his name, his word, his people, his ordinances; they love God truly and fervently in spirit; they love to meditate on God—to commune with God—to hold converse with him; and they earnestly desire to love him more, and to serve him better. Let us,

II. ILLUSTRATE THE TRUTH AFFIRMED. " All things work together for good." Now, a few preliminary things must be noticed. The term, "all things," must in one thing be limited; sin must not be included, for sin is evil in its nature, influence, and tendency; and if sin could be included, then with propriety we might say, " Let us sin that grace may abound." But the apostle says to this, "God forbid." Then when it is said, " all things work together for good," we must take the word " good" in its highest acceptation; not present enjoyment, but final well-being. The soul in its moral advantages, and eternity in its final decisions, must both be taken into consideration. Limit your views to the present, and think only of immediate happiness, and the text would be inexplicable. Notice then, with this prefatory explanation,

1. *The extent of the thing specified.* " All things." All things in heaven; the blessed God, the Father, Son, and Spirit, angels, &c., spirits of the just made perfect. All on earth; all men; good men, by their prayers and love; and bad men, by their hatred and opposition. All events; prosperous and adverse—joyous and grievous —health and sickness—prosperity and adversity—life and death. All things in hell; Satan and his agents, by their frowns and temptations, though not joyous but grievous, yet afterwards is yielded the peaceable fruits, &c. All things in nature, providence, and grace.

2. *The operation stated.* " All things *work.*" There is nothing in the mental or moral department of the universe entirely quiescent. " All things work;" thoughts, desires, imaginations, all work and produce their kind. All events and occurrences tend to some end. As in nature, so in the mental kingdom; as wind, light, rain, dew, calms, and tempests, all operate to some end; so all things in providence and grace work, and have a tendency to produce some effect. Notice,

3. *The universal harmony declared.* "All things work *together.*" There is diversity of element, but the operation and the end are harmonious. Look at that musical instrument; all the notes and sounds are different, yet they all produce harmonious melody. Look at that most beautiful creature, light: there are seven prismatic colors, quite distinct and dissimilar; through a prism you perceive them separately, but they all unite together, and form that soft and radiant emblem of the Creator. Look

at that scene in nature: there is the mountain with its craggy summit; the verdant valley, the flowing stream, and the roaring cataract; how diverse are the various parts, yet how harmoniously they unite to form the landscape and please the eye. Look at that piece of mechanism: see the various parts, in their action how opposite; wheels within wheels are moving in one direction, and a second in another, yet they all work together, and accomplish the design of the inventor. Look at the human body: what variety of parts and operations; some parts receiving nutrition, others throwing various elements out of the system; inspiring the air to supply the lungs, and respiring air again from the lungs, as it were, living and dying by rotation; and yet all these work together to sustain life and prolong our existence.

4. *The final end affirmed.* " All things work together for good." Separately, some things appear to work for good, and others for evil; but conjointly, they all tend to one blessed end, the real and eternal good of them that love God, &c. Now, let us establish this, for the apostle says, " We know," &c.

(1.) I appeal to scripture declarations. And in reference to positive and manifest blessings proof is unnecessary; so we will confine our attention to afflictions, sorrows, &c. Hebrews xii. 11; Romans v. 5, &c.; James i. 2, &c., " For our light afflictions," &c.

(2.) I appeal to scripture facts. There was Jacob and his final good in the time of famine, &c. See how " all things work:" even the envy of his sons is overruled, &c.; Joseph sold, &c.; Simeon, &c.; Benjamin demanded, &c. "All these things are against me," &c. Oh! no; they are all working together, &c. There was Moses, his final good, and the good of Israel; but see the events of his career: edict; exposed in the fragile ark—yet how all things worked. There was the blessed Jesus; his final exaltation; and the salvation of myriads, &c. But behold his birth, life, sufferings, and death; but they all worked, &c., Acts ii. 23.

(3.) I appeal to scripture, as exemplified in your experience. Have you not proved the truth of the text in many cases? You thought that severe loss would have ruined you—that bereavement crushed, that sickness destroyed you; but now you observe how necessary they were; that they all worked together, &c.

1. *Are you the characters described?*
2. *Rejoice in God's good providence.* In his universal, benignant reign.
3. *Cultivate the grace of contentment.* Be not murmurers; or anxious; or in haste.
4. *Look to the termination.* The soldier —the traveller—the mariner does this. Oh! cherish the spirit of the text, &c.

THE DEATH OF THE RIGHTEOUS.

" Let me die the death of the righteous, and let my last end be like his!"—NUMBERS xxiii. 10.

OUR text contains the expressed desire of the wicked Balaam, and it has doubtless been the desire of thousands equally estranged from holiness and God. Even the wicked know that they must die, and it is well that they should think and reflect upon it. But, like innumerable other vanities of the imagination, this wish will be fruitless in its results, to all who continue alienated from purity and God. The end of Balaam was what may reasonably be expected to be that of all who live a life like his. The text refers to a character that we must define, an event that we must illustrate, and a desire that must be regulated.

I. A CHARACTER THAT WE MUST DEFINE. " The righteous." None are such by nature; none are such by mere education or parental discipline; none are such by self-exertion. This character is divine, and therefore of God. It includes,

1. *Justification.* By which, through faith in the Lord Jesus, we are constituted righteous, and dealt with as such. Isa. xlv. 25; Rom. iii. 16.

2. *Regeneration.* Born from above; born of God; partakers of the divine nature. This is the new man; the holy nature which the children of God possess. John iii. 3, &c.; Col. iii. 10.

3. *Sanctification.* Or the progress of the new man in holiness; the spiritual growth, and advancement in the divine life. This includes also the consecration of the heart to the service and glory of God. An increasing conformity to the holy image of the blessed God, 2 Cor. iii. 18.

4. *Practical obedience;* or righteousness of life. This is the great evidence of righteousness of heart. The fruit testifies that the tree is made good; that the fountain has become pure. He only is righteous who doeth righteousness. Those who have received Christ Jesus the Lord, walk in him; following his example, treading in his imitable steps. " Being made free from sin," &c. Rom. vi. 22.

II. AN EVENT THAT WE MUST ILLUSTRATE. " The death of the righteous." Even the righteous must die. The righteous of all ages, except Enoch and Elijah, have died. The righteous patriarchs, prophets, apostles, and fathers, have all died. " It is appointed unto men once to die," &c. But the righteous die,

1. *Under the immediate direction of God.* The wicked often die prematurely. By their own hands; by the hands of the executioner; by the power of sin producing disease; by the judgments of God. But the righteous, in life, in sickness, and in old age, are the especial objects of the divine care. They are in his hand, " and precious in his sight is the death of his saints." When their work is done he calls them home. When they are meet for glory, he receives them to himself. The righteous die,

2. *In a state of gracious security.* They die in covenant with God; with an interest in Christ; the subjects of the indwelling Spirit; heirs of glory. " Die in the Lord." " Death is theirs." Not an enemy to destroy, but a messenger to conduct them to their better home. Death cannot separate the saint from Jesus. The righteous often die,

3. *In ecstasy and triumph.* " Have an abundant entrance ministered unto them," &c. Thus died Stephen, with the vision of glory before his eyes. Hearken to the apostle, " I have fought the good fight," &c. So thousands and myriads. Death has been victory. " O death, where is thy sting!" &c. Thus Payson: " The battle is fought, and the victory is won." The righteous always at death,

4. *Enter upon a life of immortality.* They are intimately present with the Lord. Ascend to the Saviour's God, and to their God, &c. To die is gain, immediate, consummate, eternal gain. " Blessed are the dead who die in the Lord," &c. Then it is that Christ receives them to himself, &c.

Death is the gate of life—the vestibule of glory. Our text contains,

III. A DESIRE THAT MUST BE REGULATED. " Let me," &c. It is a very proper desire. Should be the desire of every human being. But it will be fruitless unless it is regulated,

1. *By a personal regard to the character of the righteous.* The character and the death are united ; they cannot be separated. We cannot die their death if we are wicked, impenitent, or merely moral, or only professors of righteousness. We must attain the spirit and principle of the righteous. It must be regulated,

2. *By a preparation for dying.* This, by the righteous, cannot be forgotten. He, therefore, acts, and prays, and believes, in reference to this solemn event. He is anxious to be ready for the coming of the Son of Man ; to have the robe and the Spirit ; the lamp and the oil ; the title and the meetness. This is the only desire of any value. It must be regulated,

3. *By a constant deference to the divine will.* The righteous cannot suggest any thing as to the mode, the place, or the circumstances of dying. They say, " My times are in thy hand." They regard present duties and privileges, and leave all that concerns the act of dying in the Lord's hands. " I will wait all the days," &c. With God are the issues both of death and life.

APPLICATION.

1. *The subject of the text is solemn.* Dying is always an awful, momentous thing ; the great crisis in man's history ; the point on which hang the everlasting destinies of the soul. And, remember, all must die Oh yes ! there will be no discharge from this war.

2. *What is your prospect respecting death ?* I ask not what you wish or imagine ; but what is the well-grounded prospect ? Oh, appeal to your heart, conscience, life, and see if they refer to a safe and happy death-bed.

3. *How different is the death of the wicked from that of the righteous !* Dark, dreary, hopeless ; the beginning of sorrows ; the prelude to everlasting woes. Oh ! avoid this. Deprecate this.

INDEX TO THE TEXTS

OF

SKETCHES AND SKELETONS OF SERMONS,

IN THE

PULPIT CYCLOPÆDIA.

INDEX TO THE TEXTS.

THE END.

Date Due

		MAY 20 '64	
3-25-55	OCT 9 '58		
4-16-55	NOV 22 '58	NOV 18 '64	
5-12-55	JAN 8 '60	DEC 3 '64	JAN 8 '77
	FEB 11 '60	JAN 5 '65	JAN 29 '74
9-28	MAY 27 '60	JAN 21 '66	OCT 7 '75
N-10		MAR 4	F
JAN 13 '56	DEC 3 '60		F
JAN 27 '56	APR 4 '61	MAR 29 '66	DEC 3 '80
APR 28 '66	APR 12 '61	JAN 3 '67	
		JUN 1 '67	DEC 4 '85
MAY 26 '56	APR 19 '61		
JUL 13 '56	OCT 20 '61	Aug 30	AUG 30 '89
SEP 18 '56	NOV 30 '61	OCT 10 '67	
OCT 19 '56	JAN 10 '82	MAR 2 '68	
DEC 14 '56	Jan 18	MAR 13 '68	
DEC 21	NOV 13 '69	DEC 9 '68	
MAR 18 '57	Nov 20	APR 29 '70	
APR 3 '57	FEB 1 '64	MAY 26 '70	
MAR 11 '58	4.3.64	9-7	
JAN 27 '58			

LINCOLN BIBLE INSTITUTE
PRINTED IN U. S. A.